ROUTLEDGE HANDBOOK OF SPORT EXPERTISE

Understanding and developing expertise is an important concern for any researcher or practitioner working in elite or high-performance sport. Whether it's identifying talented young athletes or developing methods for integrating cutting-edge sport science into daily coaching practice, scientists, coaches, and researchers all need to understand the skills, characteristics, and knowledge that distinguish the expert performer in sport.

The *Routledge Handbook of Sport Expertise* is the first book to offer a comprehensive overview of current research and practice in the emerging field of sport expertise. Adopting a multidisciplinary, multifaceted approach, the book offers in-depth discussion of methodological and philosophical issues in sport expertise, as well as the characteristics that describe sporting "experts" and how they can be facilitated and developed. Exploring research, theory, and practice, the book also examines how scientists and practitioners can work together to improve the delivery of applied sport science.

With contributions from many of the world's leading researchers in expertise and skill acquisition in sport, the *Routledge Handbook of Sport Expertise* is important reading for any advanced student, researcher, coach, or sport science support officer looking to better understand this cutting-edge topic.

Joseph Baker is Associate Professor and Head of the Lifespan Health and Performance Laboratory in the School of Kinesiology and Health Science at York University, Canada. He has also held visiting researcher/professor positions in the Carnegie Research Institute at Leeds Metropolitan University in the United Kingdom, Victoria University and the Australian Institute of Sport in Australia, and the Institute of Sport Science at Westfälische Wilhelms-Universität Münster in Germany. His research considers the varying influences on optimal human development, ranging from issues affecting athlete development and skill acquisition to barriers and facilitators of successful aging. Joe is Past President of the Canadian Society for Psychomotor Learning and Sport Psychology and the author/editor of five books, two journal special issues, and more than 100 peer-reviewed articles and book chapters.

Damian Farrow holds a joint appointment in Australia with Victoria University and the Australian Institute of Sport (AIS) as Professor of Skill Acquisition. Appointed as the inaugural AIS Skill Acquisition Specialist and Discipline Head of Psychology and Skill Acquisition, he was responsible for the research and support of coaches seeking to develop the skills of Australian athletes, and he works with a wide range of national sporting organisation high-performance programmes. Damian's research interests centre on understanding the factors critical to developing talent/sport expertise, with a specific focus on perceptual and decision-making skills and practice methodology. Damian has written over 80 peer-reviewed articles and book chapters, six books, and made over 150 presentations at inter/national coaching and scientific conferences. He is an editorial board member of the *Journal of Science and Medicine in Sport* and the *International Journal of Sports Science and Coaching* and a member of sports science advisory panels for the Australian Football League, Cricket Australia, Tennis Australia, and Surfing Australia.

ROUTLEDGE HANDBOOK OF SPORT EXPERTISE

Edited by Joseph Baker and Damian Farrow

LONDON AND NEW YORK

First published 2015
by Routledge
2 Park Square, Milton Park, Abingdon, Oxon OX14 4RN

and by Routledge
711 Third Avenue, New York, NY 10017

Routledge is an imprint of the Taylor & Francis Group, an informa business

© 2015 J. Baker & D. Farrow

The right of the editors to be identified as the author of the editorial material, and
of the authors for their individual chapters, has been asserted in accordance with
sections 77 and 78 of the Copyright, Designs and Patents Act 1988.

All rights reserved. No part of this book may be reprinted or reproduced or utilised
in any form or by any electronic, mechanical, or other means, now known or
hereafter invented, including photocopying and recording, or in any information
storage or retrieval system, without permission in writing from the publishers.

Trademark notice: Product or corporate names may be trademarks or registered
trademarks, and are used only for identification and explanation without intent
to infringe.

British Library Cataloguing-in-Publication Data
A catalogue record for this book is available from the British Library

Library of Congress Cataloging-in-Publication Data
A catalog record for this book has been requested

ISBN: 978-0-415-83980-8 (hbk)
ISBN: 978-1-315-77667-5 (ebk)

Typeset in Bembo
by Apex CoVantage, LLC

Printed and bound in the United States of America by Publishers Graphics,
LLC on sustainably sourced paper.

CONTENTS

List of figures	*ix*
List of tables	*xiii*
About the contributors	*xv*

1 A [very brief] review of the historical foundations of sport expertise: an introduction to the Handbook — 1
Joseph Baker and Damian Farrow

2 Expert anticipation and pattern perception — 9
Damian Farrow and Bruce Abernethy

3 Aiming for excellence: the quiet eye as a characteristic of expertise — 22
Mark R. Wilson, Joe Causer, and Joan N. Vickers

4 On attentional control: a dimensional framework for attention in expert performance — 38
Keith R. Lohse

5 Information-movement coupling as a hallmark of sport expertise — 50
John van der Kamp and Ian Renshaw

6 How experts make decisions in dynamic, time-constrained sporting environments — 64
Markus Raab and Werner Helsen

7 Movement automaticity in sport — 74
Rob Gray

Contents

8 Expertise in the performance of multi-articular sports actions — 84
Paul S. Glazier, Machar M. Reid, and Kevin A. Ball

9 Breadth and depth of knowledge in expert versus novice athletes — 95
John Sutton and Doris J. F. McIlwain

10 Psychological characteristics of expert performers — 106
Geir Jordet

11 Physical qualities of experts — 121
Tim J. Gabbett

12 Expert performance in sport: an ecological dynamics perspective — 130
Keith Davids, Duarte Araújo, Ludovic Seifert, and Dominic Orth

13 Defining expertise: a taxonomy for researchers in skill
acquisition and expertise — 145
Joseph Baker, Nick Wattie, and Jörg Schorer

14 Issues in the collection of athlete training histories — 156
Melissa J. Hopwood

15 Issues in the measurement of anticipation — 166
David L. Mann and Geert J. P. Savelsbergh

16 Eye tracking methods in sport expertise — 176
Derek Panchuk, Samuel Vine, and Joan N. Vickers

17 New methods for studying perception and action coupling — 188
Cathy M. Craig and Alan Cummins

18 Methods for measuring pattern recall and recognition
in sport experts — 198
Adam D. Gorman

19 Capturing group tactical behaviors in expert team players — 209
Duarte Araújo, Pedro Silva, and Keith Davids

20 Methods for measuring breadth and depth of knowledge — 221
Doris J. F. McIlwain and John Sutton

21 Measuring psychological determinants of expertise: dispositional factors — 232
Bradley Fawver, Garrett F. Beatty, and Christopher M. Janelle

Contents

22 Psychological determinants of expertise: emotional reactivity, psychological skills, and efficacy 245
Garrett F. Beatty, Bradley Fawver, and Christopher M. Janelle

23 Issues in the measurement of physiological and anthropometric factors 259
David Pyne and Naroa Etxebarria

24 Issues and challenges in developing representative tasks in sport 269
Ross A. Pinder, Jonathon Headrick, and Raôul R. D. Oudejans

25 Challenges to capturing expertise in field settings 282
Ian Renshaw and Adam D. Gorman

26 Genomics of elite sporting performance 295
Yannis P. Pitsiladis and Guan Wang

27 Diversification and deliberate play during the sampling years 305
Jean Côté and Karl Erickson

28 Psychological characteristics and the developing athlete: the importance of self-regulation 317
Laura Jonker, Marije T. Elferink-Gemser, E.J. Yvonne Tromp, Joseph Baker, and Chris Visscher

29 Family and peer influences in the development of sport expertise 329
Jessica Fraser-Thomas and Theresa Beesley

30 Deliberate practice in sport 347
Paul R. Ford, Edward K. Coughlan, Nicola J. Hodges, and A. Mark Williams

31 Development of tactical creativity in sports 363
Daniel Memmert

32 Birthdate and birthplace effects on expertise attainment 373
Nick Wattie, Dany J. MacDonald, and Stephen Cobley

33 Career length, aging, and expertise 383
Sean Horton, Joseph Baker, and Patricia Weir

34 Changing role of coaches across development 394
Clifford J. Mallett and Steven Rynne

Contents

35 The use of observation as a method to develop expertise in coaching and officiating   404
Diane M. Ste-Marie and David J. Hancock

36 Five evidence-based principles of effective practice and instruction   414
David T. Hendry, Paul R. Ford, A. Mark Williams, and Nicola J. Hodges

37 Efficacy of training interventions for acquiring perceptual–cognitive skill   430
Jörg Schorer, Florian Loffing, Rebecca Rienhoff, and Norbert Hagemann

38 The future of sport expertise research: barriers and facilitators in theory and practice   439
Damian Farrow and Joseph Baker

Index   *445*

FIGURES

2.1	An example of a volleyball digger being temporally occluded with Plato™ occlusion goggles when receiving a serve.	13
2.2	Example of a pattern recall task being completed for Australian football.	17
3.1	A representation of the proposed links between attentional networks, the quiet eye (QE), and movement control.	24
4.1	A schematic representation of two major dimensions of attentional control: the associative-dissociative dimension and the external-internal dimension.	42
4.2	Schematics illustrating how different dimensions of attention may have different effects.	44
5.1	Visual representation of mean bound, back foot, and front foot landing positions in the umpire and no umpire conditions.	53
5.2	The optics for a ball that approaches head-on.	55
5.3	The optics of a ball passing to the left of the observer.	58
6.1	A visual information-processing model of skilled performance.	68
6.2	Number of scientific publications on football refereeing in the physical and perceptual-cognitive field.	70
7.1	Mean distance the putter head travelled after a signal was presented that indicated the stroke should be stopped as quickly as possible.	79
8.1	A graphical representation of proximal-to-distal sequencing of segmental motion, using the golf swing as an exemplar multi-articular action.	86
8.2	Comparisons of body segment and club motions between golfers of different skill levels.	87
8.3	Both inter- and intra-individual movement variability, which is usually considered to be a reflection of "noise," are commonly thought to reduce to a minimum with expertise.	88
11.1	Influence of fatigue on tackling technique in rugby league players.	127
12.1	An example of how practice constraints act as information to influence behavior during performance, shaping the regulation of action.	132

Figures

12.2 Exemplifies both how performance emerges from constraints on performer-environment relationships, and how performance environments might evolve over time relative to the skills of the individual. — 134

12.3 Example of the basic principles of a metastable performance region as detailed in Pinder *et al.* (2012). — 140

13.1 Taxonomy categories. — 147

13.2 Performance change over time in Olympic athletic (A) and aquatic (B) events with at least 10 consecutive occurrences. — 151

13.3 A hypothetical, expanded taxonomy of expertise using accumulated experience. — 153

15.1 Demonstration of a participant wearing occlusion goggles and attempting to (a) verbally predict the direction of a ball, and (b) hit a ball bowled by a cricket bowler in the study by Mann *et al.* (2010a). — 171

16.1 The Applied Sciences Laboratories (ASL) Mobile Eye (a) and the EyeVision software (b) user interface. — 180

16.2 The SensoMotoric Instruments (SMI) Eye Tracking Glasses (a) and the BeGaze user interface (b). — 181

16.3 A screen grab of the Quiet Eye Solutions software analysis environment used by Vine and Wilson (2011) showing the external video of the participant, the view from the scene camera of the eye tracker, and the coding entry fields. — 183

17.1 Perception of an opening gap in a defensive rugby line that is used in a decision-making task. — 191

17.2 Avatars were created in a virtual environment based on real motion capture data of elite Australian cricketers bowling. — 194

17.3 Participant wearing head-mounted display and control unit, taking part in a deceptive movement task. — 195

17.4 An expert goalkeeper immersed in a virtual interactive environment where realistic curved free kicks were presented. — 195

19.1 Upper panels depict the centroids' coupled oscillations of two teams during six-a-side, small-sided games in: A) X-direction, and B), Y-direction. — 211

19.2 Stretch indices, team spreads, and surface areas time series of two competing teams during five-a-side games. — 213

19.3 A) Examples of triangles interception. B) Effective surface area with offensive and defensive triangles. — 214

19.4 Exemplar spatial distribution maps of two players during a four-a-side game; A) regional player; B) national player. — 215

19.5 Exemplar players' Voronoi cells in two small-sided games (five versus five and five versus three) in single frames (goalkeepers excluded). — 216

19.6 Playing patterns of one English Premier League team according to the goalkeepers' actions. — 217

23.1 Systematic approach to design and implementation of a special project in support of expert athletes. — 260

26.1 Genome-wide association signals for elucidation of four models related to common and complex traits (Gibson, 2012). — 298

26.2 Feasibility of identifying genetic variants by risk allele frequency and strength of genetic effect (Manolio *et al.*, 2009). — 299

Figures

26.3 Power vs. effect size for 100 cases and 100 controls under the multiplicative, additive, dominant, and recessive models, assuming a low prevalence of the trait at 0.1 for MAF varied from 0.05 to 0.5.   300

26.4 DNA test (sport gene) being offered at Tallinn Airport, Estonia.   301

28.1 Talent development model, including personal, task-related, general characteristics and environment-related characteristics.   318

28.2 The self-regulatory process in phases.   320

30.1 Hours accumulated in solitary deliberate practice by 18 years of age for violinists who are middle-aged professionals, best in academy, good in academy, and music teachers.   348

30.2 Mean (SD) outcome scores (out of 30 points) for the (a) weaker and (b) stronger kicks of the expert, intermediate, and expert control groups for the pre-test, post-test, and retention test.   357

31.1 The evaluation of the individual eight actions in front of the goal concerning their tactical creativity (from 0 to 10, 0 = not creative, 10 = highly creative).   364

31.2 Overview of the central cognitive performance factors that underlie all actions in team and racket sports.   365

31.3 The development processes of the tactical creativity (z-value) for children and adolescents at the age of seven, 10, and 13 years.   366

31.4 The six Ds fostering tactical creativity in team and racket sports.   368

33.1 Performance of elite PGA golfers from 25 to 50 years of age relative to peak performance.   389

36.1 Percentage of time in a practice session spent in playing form (i.e., play- or game-type activities), training form (i.e., drill-type activities), and transitions between these across 36 coaching sessions in English youth cricket.   415

36.2 Summary schematic highlighting the key principles of effective practice organization and instruction and how these are moderated by motivational influences.   425

TABLES

3.1	A summary of the studies that have examined expertise differences in quiet eye in targeting tasks.	26
3.2	A summary of the studies that have examined expertise differences in quiet eye in interceptive tasks.	28
3.3	A summary of the studies that have examined the effect of increased anxiety on quiet eye and performance.	30
3.4	A summary of the studies that have examined the utility of quiet eye training with novice and experienced performers.	33
7.1	Steps involved in execution of a golf putt.	75
13.1	Proportion of professional athletes who make the hall of fame.	149
23.1	Forty metre sprint data for expert male Australian super rugby players.	264
26.1	Major study cohorts in genetics of elite performance.	296
28.1	Means and standard deviations for number of training hours per week, reflection and effort, n and % for academic level and repeating class for the number of measurements per age group subdivided by competitive level.	322
30.1	Four different types of practice activities that potentially comprise sport training but that differ with respect to the intention of the activity.	354
32.1	Summary of city sizes that are over- and under-represented, across the studies that investigated the birthplace effect.	377

ABOUT THE CONTRIBUTORS

Bruce Abernethy is with the University of Queensland, Australia (UQ), where he is Executive Dean of the Faculty of Health and Behavioural Sciences. He also holds a substantive appointment as Professor of Skill Acquisition and Motor Control within the School of Human Movement Studies at UQ and a Visiting Professor appointment at the University of Hong Kong where he was the inaugural Chair Professor of the Institute of Human Performance from 2004-2011. A first-class honours graduate and university medallist from the University of Queensland and a PhD graduate from the University of Otago, New Zealand, Prof. Abernethy is an International Fellow of the US National Academy of Kinesiology, a Fellow of the Australian Sports Medicine Federation, and a Fellow of Exercise & Sports Science Australia. He is the author of a large number of original research papers on skill acquisition and co-author of the texts The Biophysical Foundations of Human Movement and The Creative Side of Experimentation. Along with his students and collaborators, Prof. Abernethy has conducted a number of research projects on the characteristics of expertise and on the development of expert performance in sport, including projects funded by the by the Australian Research Council (ARC), the Australian Sports Commission, the Research Grants Council of Hong Kong, the Australian Football League, and Cricket Australia.

Duarte Araújo is Associate Professor at the Faculty of Human Kinetics at University of Lisbon in Portugal. He is the director of the Laboratory of Expertise in Sport. He is the president of the Portuguese Society of Sport Psychology and a member of the National Council of Sports. His research on expertise and decision-making has been funded by the Fundação para a Ciência e Tecnologia, Portugal.

Joseph Baker is Associate Professor and Head of the Lifespan Health and Performance Laboratory in the School of Kinesiology and Health Science at York University, Canada. He has also held visiting researcher/professor positions in the United Kingdom, Australia, and Germany. His research considers the varying influences on optimal human development, ranging from issues affecting athlete development and skill acquisition to barriers and facilitators of successful aging. Joe is author/editor of seven books and more than 150 peer-reviewed articles and book chapters.

Kevin A. Ball is a sports biomechanics researcher at ISEAL, Victoria University, Australia. Kevin's main research focus is concerned with kicking expertise, and examines the area across a number

About the contributors

of disciplines including biomechanics, skill acquisition, and physiology. This is combined with Kevin's applied work as specialist kicking coach for elite teams. Prior to this, Kevin spent seven years working at the Australian Institute of Sport Biomechanics unit and has published over 100 scientific articles on a number of sports, including kicking sports and golf.

Garrett F. Beatty is a Ph.D. student in the Performance Psychology Laboratory in the Department of Applied Physiology and Kinesiology at the University of Florida, USA. Garrett has published and presented his research extensively. His research interests lie in understanding the strategies individuals employ to regulate their emotional experiences and maximise performance.

Theresa Beesley is a Ph.D. candidate in the School of Kinesiology and Health Science at York University, Canada. Her research focuses on exploring the process of positive youth development within various youth sport contexts, and is supported by the Social Sciences and Humanities Research Council of Canada (SSHRC) and Sport Canada's Research Initiative (SCRI).

Joe Causer is Senior Lecturer in Applied Sport Psychology at the Research Institute for Sport and Exercise Sciences, Liverpool John Moores University, UK. Joe's main research interest is expert performance, with a particular emphasis on anxiety, implementing training interventions to overcome the potentially negative affects of anxiety on performance, and identifying how experts mediate these affects. Joe is also interested in the mechanisms underpinning performance in elite sport and how factors such as fatigue and attentional demands affect these mechanisms. Other areas of interest are skill acquisition, action observation, perceptual-cognitive skills, visuomotor control, and motor learning.

Stephen Cobley, Ph.D., is Senior Lecturer in Skill Acquisition & Motor Control and Sport & Exercise Psychology in the Faculty of Health Sciences at the University of Sydney (Australia). Steve recently coedited "Talent identification and development: International perspectives" (Routledge, 2012), and his research interests examine developmental factors that constrain learning and performance.

Jean Côté is Professor and Director in the School of Kinesiology and Health Studies at Queen's University at Kingston, Canada. His research interests are in the areas of sport expertise, children in sport, coaching, and positive youth development. Dr. Côté is regularly invited to present his work to both sport-governing organisations and academic conferences throughout the world.

Edward K. Coughlan is a postgraduate researcher at the Research Institute for Sport and Exercise Sciences, Liverpool John Moores University, UK. His research focuses on the study of expert performance and skill acquisition in applied domains. He currently works with elite athletes developing robust skill acquisition strategies for optimal performance.

Cathy M. Craig completed a Ph.D. in perception and action psychology in 1997 under the supervision of Professor Dave Lee. She then moved to the University of Aix-Marseille, France, where she lectured at the Sports Science Faculty before taking up a post at Queen's University Belfast, UK. She has published a large body of work looking at how the timing of movement is affected by the dynamics of the sensory information presented to an observer. By using innovative methods such as immersive, interactive virtual reality, her research focuses on understanding how patterns of sensory information can be used to improve motor performance in both sporting (decision-making in rugby or stopping curved free kicks in soccer) and health-related contexts (e.g., balance training in older adults or

About the contributors

people with Parkinson's). She is currently the head of the School of Psychology at Queen's University Belfast, UK, and director of the Movement Innovation Lab.

Alan Cummins has been working as part of the Movement Innovation Lab, Queen's University Belfast (QUB), UK, for the last five years. He completed his Ph.D. in the School of Nursing and Midwifery, QUB, which investigated the use of movement-based gaming with traumatised young people. With dual qualifications in psychology and computer science he has designed, developed, and delivered a number of exciting research projects in sports (rugby, soccer, and cricket) and health (trauma, autism, Parkinson's disease, and stroke), accounting for both technological and psychological components of the research. He specialises in understanding the appropriate use of graphics, sound, and interactive technology to provide studies and interventions, both in the lab and out in the field.

Keith Davids is Professor of Motor Learning at the Centre for Sports Engineering Research, Sheffield Hallam University, UK, and FiDiPro at the Faculty of Sport and Health Sciences, University of Jyväskylä, Finland. He graduated from the University of London, UK, and gained a Ph.D. at the University of Leeds, UK. His research programme in ecological dynamics investigates constraints on coordination tendencies in athletes and sports teams classed as nonlinear dynamical systems. Ideas from ecological psychology and nonlinear dynamics have been integrated into a nonlinear pedagogy. In this programme he currently supervises doctoral students from UK, France, Finland, Australia, and New Zealand.

Marije T. Elferink-Gemser works at the Center for Human Movement Sciences, UMCG, University of Groningen, the Netherlands. Her main research topic is "talent in sports", applying a multidimensional and longitudinal approach. In addition, she is associate professor at HAN University of Applied Sciences, Arnhem-Nijmegen, the Netherlands, to translate theory into practice.

Karl Erickson is a postdoctoral scholar in the Institute for Applied Research in Youth Development at Tufts University (Boston), USA. His research interests focus on athlete expertise and personal development in youth sport, particularly the influence of coaching and other interpersonal interactions in different sport contexts.

Naroa Etxebarria is a teaching fellow and course convenor in sport studies at the University of Canberra. She has a Ph.D. thesis titled *Physiology and Performance of Cycling and Running during Olympic Distance Triathlon*. Etxebarria has held positions in elite athlete support at both the Australian Institute of Sport and English Institute of Sport. Etxebarria's research focuses on the development, evaluation, and application of endurance training to inform coaching practice and maximise sport performance. Her specific research interests are characterising sport demands and devising training strategies to improve endurance performance.

Damian Farrow holds a joint appointment in Australia with Victoria University and the Australian Institute of Sport (AIS) as Professor of Skill Acquisition. Appointed as the inaugural AIS Skill Acquisition Specialist and Discipline Head of Psychology and Skill Acquisition, he was responsible for the research and support of coaches seeking to develop the skills of Australian athletes, and he works with a wide range of national sporting organisation high-performance programmes. Damian's research interests centre on understanding the factors critical to developing talent/sport expertise, with a specific focus on perceptual and decision-making skills and practice methodology.

About the contributors

Bradley Fawver is a Ph.D. student in the Performance Psychology Laboratory in the Department of Applied Physiology and Kinesiology at the University of Florida, USA. Brad's primary research interest is the impact of emotional states on approach-avoidance behaviour, including the attentional and regulatory mechanisms that modify motoric outcomes. He has published and presented widely in these areas.

Paul R. Ford is Senior Lecturer in the School of Sport and Exercise Sciences, Liverpool John Moores University, UK. His research examines expert performance, its attributes, and its acquisition. He is a member of the European College of Sport Science (ECSS), the Expertise and Skill Acquisition Network (ESAN), and the British Association of Sport and Exercise Sciences (BASES HPSA).

Jessica Fraser-Thomas is Assistant Professor in the School of Kinesiology and Health Science at York University in Toronto, Canada. Her research focuses on children and youths' development through sport, with a particular interest in positive youth development, psychosocial influences (i.e., coaches, family, peers), and withdrawal. Currently she is working on projects exploring children's earliest introductions to organised sport, characteristics of sport programmes that facilitate optimal youth development, and how youth sport models may inform master athletes' development. Jessica is a former elite athlete. She now parents five young sport participants and occasionally competes in triathlons.

Tim J. Gabbett has 20 years of experience working as an applied sport scientist for a wide range of sports. He holds two Ph.D.s – the first in human physiology, and the second in the "Applied Science of Professional Rugby League". He has published over 150 peer-reviewed articles and has presented at over 100 national and international conferences.

Paul S. Glazier is a research fellow at the Institute of Sport, Exercise and Active Living at Victoria University in Melbourne, Australia. He has expertise in sports biomechanics, motor control, skill acquisition, and performance analysis of sport, and has authored or coauthored over 40 peer-reviewed journal articles, invited book chapters, and published conference papers in these areas. His current research interests include: the biomechanics-motor control interface, the application of dynamical systems theory to movement coordination and control, and the functional role of movement variability. Paul has also provided sport science services to a wide range of athletes and teams, from regional juniors to Olympic and world champions, in a variety of sports.

Adam D. Gorman is Lecturer in Motor Control and Learning at the University of the Sunshine Coast, Australia. He was previously employed at the Australian Institute of Sport (AIS) for 10 years as a Skill Acquisition Specialist where he worked in an applied, high-performance environment with athletes and coaches from a range of different sports, including basketball, volleyball, water polo, and swimming. Adam's main research interest is broadly centred around the area of perceptual expertise, specifically focusing upon factors such as decision-making, pattern perception, and anticipation. His other research interests are related to factors that maximise skill acquisition, including the use of a constraints-led approach and the application of representative designs.

Rob Gray received a BA degree in psychology from Queen's University, Canada, in 1993, and MS and Ph.D. degrees in psychology from York University, Canada, in 1995 and 1998, respectively. He was a research scientist with Nissan Cambridge Basic Research from 1998 to 2001 before joining the Department of Applied Psychology at Arizona State University, USA. From 2006 until 2010

About the contributors

he served as the head of the Department of Applied Psychology and as a research psychologist for the United States Air Force. He is currently a reader in perception and action in the School of Sport, Exercise & Rehabilitation Sciences at the University of Birmingham (UK). He is the author of more than 80 published refereed journal articles and chapters. He serves as an associate editor for the *Journal of Experimental Psychology: Human Perception and Performance* and is an editorial board member for *Human Factors* and *Journal of Experimental Psychology: Applied*. In 2007, he was awarded the Distinguished Scientific Award for Early Career Contribution to Psychology from the American Psychological Association and the Earl Alluisi Award for Early Career Achievement in the Field of Applied Experimental & Engineering Psychology.

Norbert Hagemann is Full Professor of Sport Psychology at the University of Kassel, Germany. He received his Ph.D. from the University of Münster for his thesis, *Heuristic Problem Solving Strategies of Team Coaches*. Professor Hagemann studies the cognitive processes underlying how athletes perform in training and competitive situations.

David J. Hancock completed his education and postdoctoral fellowship in Canada, and is now an assistant professor in the Division of Allied Health Sciences at Indiana University Kokomo, USA, tasked with creating a new exercise and sport science degree. David's main research areas include sports officiating, perceptual expertise, and contextual influences on talent development. David teaches several courses at Indiana University Kokomo including sport psychology, motor development, motor learning, and philosophy of coaching.

Jonathon Headrick is a Ph.D. scholar in the School of Exercise and Nutrition Sciences at Queensland University of Technology, Brisbane, Australia. His research interests include the application of an ecological dynamics approach for studying the role of emotion in learning and skill acquisition in sport.

Werner Helsen is Full Professor in Motor Learning and Control at the Faculty of Kinesiology and Rehabilitation Sciences of the KU Leuven, Belgium. He is programme director and head of the Perception and Performance Laboratory. His research interests focus on the visual control of voluntary movement, as well as on the development and acquisition of expert perception and performance.

David T. Hendry is a doctoral candidate working in the Motor Skills Laboratory at the University of British Columbia in Vancouver, Canada. His main research interests lie in the development of sport expertise, skill acquisition, and sports coaching. He completed his undergraduate degree in sport science from Edinburgh Napier University and his MSc in Kinesiology from the University of British Columbia. David has also operated as an elite-level soccer coach with Glasgow Rangers F.C. and the Scottish F.A.

Nicola J. Hodges is Professor in Motor Behaviour (Kinesiology) at the University of British Columbia, Canada. She studies the mechanisms of motor learning, with a focus on instructions and demonstrations. She studies both new learners and more skilled individuals, predominantly using sports-based tasks and athletes to inform her research.

Melissa J. Hopwood is the National Pathway Manager with Australian Canoeing. Her doctoral research involved the construction and validation of the Developmental History of Athletes Questionnaire (DHAQ), and a large-scale examination of the development of sport expertise.

About the contributors

This research was completed through Victoria University, Australia, in conjunction with the Australian Institute of Sport and York University, Canada. Melissa's research interests include skill acquisition, athlete development, and coach development. Having held various positions at the Australian Institute of Sport and the Canadian Sport Centre Ontario, Melissa is particularly interested in conducting applied research and implementing evidence-based practices in high-performance sporting environments.

Sean Horton, Ph.D., resides in the Kinesiology Department at the University of Windsor, Canada. His research interests lie primarily in the area of skill acquisition and expert performance, both in young and aging athletes. His most recent work has focused on older adults and the extent to which high levels of performance can be maintained into the later stages of life.

Christopher M. Janelle is Professor and Director of the Performance Psychology Laboratory in the Department of Applied Physiology and Kinesiology at the University of Florida, USA. His research interests focus on the interaction of emotion, attention, and movement. He has published over 80 refereed journal articles and book chapters, and he coauthored the *Handbook of Sport Psychology*. Chris serves on the editorial board of five journals, including the *Journal of Sport & Exercise Psychology,* and is a fellow of the American Psychological Association (Division 47).

Laura Jonker is Research Manager at the Royal Dutch Football Association. Her main focus is research on football development. In 2011 she finished her Ph.D. on the role of self-regulation for sport expertise at the Center for Human Movement Sciences, UMCG, University of Groningen, the Netherlands, where she still works part-time.

Geir Jordet is Professor at the Norwegian School of Sport Sciences, Norway, where he conducts research on psychology and elite performance. He is also director of psychology at the Norwegian Centre of Football Excellence, owned by the Norwegian Professional Soccer League, and he regularly advises leading European professional soccer organisations.

Florian Loffing is a postdoctoral fellow at the Institute of Sports and Sports Sciences of the University of Kassel, Germany. He obtained his Ph.D. from the University of Muenster, Germany, for a thesis on handedness in tennis. Florian's research interests focus upon the perceptual-cognitive processes that underlie skilled performance in sports.

Keith R. Lohse is the principal investigator of the Motor Learning Lab at Auburn University, USA. He received a joint Ph.D. in psychology, cognitive science, and neuroscience in 2012 from the University of Colorado, USA and worked as a postdoctoral research associate at the University of British Columbia, Canada from 2012 until 2014. His research focuses on understanding the psychological and physiological changes that underlie the (re)acquisition of motor skills. When not in the lab, Keith is an avid rock climber, trail runner, and cartoonist.

Dany J. MacDonald, Ph.D., is Assistant Professor in the Department of Applied Human Sciences at the University of Prince Edward Island, Canada. His main research interests are in identifying characteristics of youth sport that are most effective for fostering positive personal development through sport. He is also interested in measurement issues and has developed an instrument to measure positive development in sport. Finally, he conducts research on athlete development and coaching to further understand the mechanisms that contribute to elite athlete development and expertise.

About the contributors

Clifford J. Mallett is Associate Professor of Sport Psychology in the School of Human Movement Studies at the University of Queensland, Australia. He is a former Olympic track coach, whose research is focused on the coaches' behaviours in creating an adaptive motivational climate, mental toughness, high-performance learning, and development.

David L. Mann is a faculty member in the Faculty of Human Movement Sciences at Vrije University Amsterdam in the Netherlands. His area of research interest is the acquisition of visual-motor expertise. He is a clinical optometrist, having previously been the clinic director at the School of Optometry and Vision Science at the University of New South Wales in Sydney, Australia. He did his Ph.D. on vision and expertise in sport while at the skill acquisition section of Sports Science & Sports Medicine at the Australian Institute of Sport in Canberra, Australia. He is currently the director of the International Paralympic Committee's Research and Development Centre for the classification of athletes with vision impairment in Paralympic competition. His work has been funded by organisations such as the Netherlands Organisation for Scientific Research (NWO), the International Paralympic Committee (IPC), the International Blind Sport Federation (IBSA), the Netherlands Olympic Committee (NOC★NSF), and Cricket Australia.

Doris J. F. McIlwain is Associate Professor in the Department of Psychology at Macquarie University, Sydney, Australia. She studies personality, emotion, memory, and movement, employing mixed-method designs. Her recent papers appear in *Personality and Individual Differences, Educational Philosophy and Theory, Discourse Processes, Music Perception*, and *British Journal of Health Psychology*.

Daniel Memmert is Professor and Head of the Institute of Cognitive and Team/Racket Sport Research, German Sport University Cologne, Germany, with a guest professorship (2014) at the University of Vienna (Austria). He received his Ph.D. and habilitation in sport science from the Elite University of Heidelberg, Germany. His research areas of interests are cognitive science, human movement science, computer science, and sport psychology. He has 16 years of teaching and coaching experience and has (co)authored more than 100 publications, 30 books and book chapters, and he is an ad hoc reviewer for international journals. He has trainer licences in soccer, tennis, snowboard, and skiing.

Dominic Orth is a Ph.D. student at the University of Rouen, France, and Queensland University of Technology (QUT), Australia. He completed his Masters degree by research at the School of Exercise and Nutrition Science at QUT. His research programme examines the role of adaptive movement variability in skilled climbers.

Raôul R. D. Oudejans is Associate Professor at the MOVE Research Institute Amsterdam, Faculty of Human Movement Sciences, VU University, the Netherlands. His main research and teaching areas are perception and movement in sports and other high-pressure contexts. For the last 15 years, Raôul has specialised in the visual control of the basketball shot, as well as in training and performing under pressure.

Derek Panchuk was recently appointed as National Lead in Skill Acquisition at the Australian Institute of Sport. He has been in Australia for six years since completing his MSc and Ph.D. at the University of Calgary on the quiet eye in ice hockey goaltenders with Joan N. Vickers. Derek's research interests include examining how vision, attention control, and motor performance interact in the acquisition of skilled performance, and how perceptual-motor skills can be trained in high-performance and developing athletes. His current research seeks to identify how attention control and decision-making are affected by fatigue, to develop strategies to maintain

About the contributors

performance under physical stress, and how exercise can alter attention control and cognitive performance across the life span.

Ross A. Pinder is a skill acquisition specialist with the Australian Paralympic Committee. His research interests include ecological dynamics approaches to perception and action in sport, and he is primarily interested in maximising skill learning in sport through the design of representative experimental and practice environments.

Yannis P. Pitsiladis, MMEDSci., FACSM. Following 15 years at the University of Glasgow, UK, where he created the largest known DNA biobank from world-class athletes, Yannis was appointed professor of sport and exercise science at the University of Brighton.

David Pyne is a sports scientist in the Department of Physiology at the Australian Institute of Sport (AIS). Pyne has 25 years of experience at the AIS and has been involved with every Australian Olympic Swimming Team from Seoul, 1988 to London, 2012. He has extensive experience with expert performers in basketball, rugby union, rugby league, Australian Football, cricket, and swimming. His work in the areas of exercise and the immune system, the applied physiology of swimming, and fitness and conditioning for team sports is recognised internationally. Pyne has published over 200 peer-reviewed papers and holds adjunct professor appointments at the University of Canberra, Australia, James Cook University, Australia, and Griffith University, Australia. He was foundation editor of the *International Journal of Sports Physiology and Performance* from 2004 to 2009. Pyne is a member of Sports Medicine Australia and a fellow of the American College of Sports Medicine, USA.

Markus Raab is Head of the Institute of Psychology at the German Sport University and Head of the Department of Performance Psychology. Additionally he is research professor at London South Bank University, UK. The main focus of the research programme in performance psychology is on motor learning and motor control, and judgment and decision-making in sports and beyond. He favors a simple, heuristic approach and an embodied cognition approach to understand the interaction of sensorimotor and cognitive behaviour from a psychological perspective.

Machar M. Reid has been the High-Performance Manager at Tennis Australia since 2008. Prior to that time, Machar worked with the International Tennis Federation and a variety of top 100 professional and junior tennis players. He received a Ph.D. from the University of Western Australia in biomechanics in 2007 and has collaborated on over 100 popular and scientific publications.

Ian Renshaw is Senior Lecturer in the School of Human Movement Studies at Queensland University of Technology, Australia. Ian's main research interests lie in understanding perception and action in sport, with particular emphasis on developing effective learning environments. To that end, Ian is particularly interested in the development of a nonlinear pedagogy for talent development, teaching, and coaching of sport. Current research projects include psychology and metastability in nonlinear pedagogy, the implementation of nonlinear pedagogy in schools, emergent decision-making in football referees, and representative learning design in sporting run-ups.

Rebecca Rienhoff finished her Ph.D. at the University of Muenster, Germany, in the Institute of Sport and Exercise Sciences. Her specific research interests during the Ph.D. focused on the field of expertise, especially perceptual expertise, attention, and motor learning.

About the contributors

Steven Rynne is Lecturer in Sport Coaching in the School of Human Movement Studies at the University of Queensland, Australia. Dr. Rynne is a cycling coach and has a range of research interests related to the learning of high-performance sport coaches, as well as domestic and international sport-for-development settings.

Geert J. P. Savelsbergh is Professor for Youth and Sport and Head of the Motor Control Group at MOVE, the Netherlands. In the period from 1991 until 1996, he was a research fellow of the Royal Netherland Academy of Arts and Sciences, and in 2008 he received an honorary doctorate of the Faculty of Medicine and Health Sciences, University of Ghent, Belgium. His research interest is the visual regulation of movement in sport, motor control, and learning. He has published over 170 papers in international, peer-reviewed scientific journals and is the editor of *Infant Behavior and Development* and associate editor of *International Journal of Sport Psychology*. He (co)supervised 25 Ph.D. projects and currently supervises 11 Ph.D. projects in the Netherlands, Australia, Brazil, Belgium, the UK, and South Africa. He has a special interest in ball sports such as football, tennis, cricket, and golf. He has recently published two books: *Athletic Skills Model for Optimal Talent Development* with staff from Ajax Amsterdam and the Dutch National Football team, and *Dual in the Sixteen* on football penalties with Dr. John van der Kamp.

Jörg Schorer (Ph.D.) is Professor and Director of the Institute of Sport Science, University of Oldenburg, Germany. His research interests concern life-span development and maintenance of elite performance and include general questions regarding factors that affect skill acquisition and development.

Ludovic Seifert is Associate Professor at the Faculty of Sport Sciences at University of Rouen in France. He conducts his research in the field of motor learning and motor control regarding expertise in sport, movement variability, and dynamics of learning. He gained a Ph.D. about expertise and coordination dynamics in swimming at University of Rouen, France, in 2003, then a certification to supervise research in 2010. He is also mountain guide certified by the International Federation of Mountain Guides Associations (IFMGA) and now investigates expertise and motor learning in climbing.

Pedro Silva is Assistant Professor at the Faculty of Sports of Porto University, Portugal, and a member of the Centre for Research, Education, Innovation and Intervention in Sport. His research is funded by the Fundação para a Ciência e Tecnologia and focuses on the influence of practice task constraints on team and individual tactical behaviours.

Diane M. Ste-Marie is Professor and Director/Associate Dean of the School of Human Kinetics at the University of Ottawa, Canada. Her current research involves optimising motor learning and performance through the use of observation, with a specific interest in observation of the self. Diane also explores the functions of observational learning used by athletes, coaches, and sport officials. She has been president for the North American Society for the Psychology of Sport and Physical Activity and the Canadian Society for Psychomotor Learning and Sport Psychology. She is an editorial board member of *Psychology of Sport and Exercise*.

John Sutton is Professor of Cognitive Science at Macquarie University, Sydney, Australia, where he was previously in the Department of Philosophy. His recent research on autobiographical and social memory and on skilled movement has been published in *Phenomenology and the Cognitive Sciences, Journal of Experimental Psychology: Learning, Memory, and Cognition, Biological Theory, Journal of Mental Imagery*, and *Sport in Society*.

About the contributors

E. J. Yvonne Tromp, MSc is a Ph.D. student at the Center for Human Movement Sciences, UMCG, University of Groningen, the Netherlands. Her main research focuses on the exploration of "beliefs in self and others" and how these beliefs may affect decisions and team interaction within youth ice hockey and talented basketball players.

John van der Kamp is Assistant Professor at the Faculty of Human Movement Sciences at the VU University Amsterdam in the Netherlands. He is also a visiting assistant professor at the Institute of Human Performance of the University of Hong Kong in Hong Kong. John's main topic of interest is (visual) perception in action. In this context, he published several studies on interceptive action that address anticipation and movement control. This includes work on learning and development in ball catching and on expertise in goal keeping and penalty taking skills in soccer.

Joan N. Vickers is Professor in the Faculty of Kinesiology, University of Calgary, Alberta, Canada. She received her doctorate from the University of British Columbia, Canada, in the areas of cognition, eye movements, and motor behaviour. Joan is the director of the Neuro-Motor Psychology Laboratory, where she maintains a research programme in gaze control, visual attention, and motor behaviour. Her main discovery is the "quiet eye", which is a characteristic of elite performers in many sport, medical, and law enforcement tasks. The "quiet eye" has been featured in Golf Digest, on Scientific American Frontiers with Alan Alda, and has also been featured on CNN and the Discovery Channel, in The Wall Street Journal, The New York Times, and many other outlets.

Samuel Vine is Lecturer in Performance Psychology in the Department of Sport and Health Sciences at the University of Exeter, UK. Sam completed his Ph.D. at Exeter in 2010, worked as an associate teaching fellow for one year, before being appointed as a lecturer in August 2011. Sam's research is interested in the acquisition, refinement, and resilient performance of skills. He examines the visual, attentional, and physiological processes that underpin learning and expertise. He is particularly interested in the quiet eye phenomenon, and theories of motor learning (e.g., implicit learning) and anxiety (e.g., attentional control theory). Sam's research is applicable to a range of different domains (e.g., sport, surgery, military, and aviation) and populations (e.g., children, elite performers, and patients).

Chris Visscher is Professor and Director of the Center for Human Movement Sciences, UMCG, University of Groningen, the Netherlands. His main research focuses on youth sports, sports and cognition, and talent development.

Guan Wang obtained her Ph.D. in integrated biology at the University of Glasgow, UK, in 2013. She is now involved in the application of omics technologies in athletes at the University of Brighton, UK.

Nick Wattie, Ph.D., is Assistant Professor of Kinesiology in the Faculty of Health Sciences at the University of Ontario Institute of Technology, Canada. His research focuses on psychosocial and environmental constraints on sport participation and sport expertise, as well as the psychosocial and physical health outcomes associated with sport participation.

Patricia Weir, Ph.D., is Professor in the Department of Kinesiology at the University of Windsor, Canada. Her research interests lie in the area of the maintenance of motor performance with

About the contributors

age. She is interested in the role that physical activity and sport play in contributing to successful aging, the psychosocial factors influencing participation, and the impact of sport across the life span.

A. Mark Williams is Professor and Head of Sport Sciences at Brunel University, London, UK. He has published extensively in areas related to expertise, skill acquisition, and talent identification and development. He is fellow of the BPS, BASES, and ECSS and is accredited as a practitioner to work in High Performance Sport. He is currently a special advisor to the English Institute of Sport and several professional sports.

Mark R. Wilson is Associate Professor in Psychology and Human Movement Science at the University of Exeter, UK. His research examines cognitive processes underlying the learning and skilled performance of visually guided skills across domains (e.g., sport, surgery, military, driving, aviation), ability levels (e.g., from expert performers to patient groups), and the life span (from children to elderly patients). A major focus of this work has been the study of objective measures of visual attention (primarily using gaze tracking technology) and the influence of anxiety on attention and subsequent performance.

1

A [VERY BRIEF] REVIEW OF THE HISTORICAL FOUNDATIONS OF SPORT EXPERTISE

An introduction to the Handbook

Joseph Baker and Damian Farrow

Discussions of the varying factors affecting human attainment can be traced back at least as far as the days of Plato. However, Francis Galton's first use of the phrase "nature and nurture" to describe the sources of individual differences in 1874 marked an important milestone in modern conceptualizations of this debate. Since then, arguments over the role of environmental influences versus innate characteristics have become more heated and taken on important social and political implications (see Herrnstein & Murray, 1994; Pinker, 2002). Over the past 150 years, these issues have come to dominate scientific (as well as non-scientific) discussions.

Increased interest in this area during the mid-1800s was undoubtedly driven by the publication of Darwin's *Origin of Species* in 1859, which informed Galton's (1869, 1883) contributions most notably, but also those of William James (1890) and Lewis Terman (1925). Much of this work was based on the conclusion that biology was the chief constraint to expertise and achievement. Indeed, Terman's appropriately titled *Genetic Studies of Genius* (Terman, 1925; Terman & Oden, 1947, 1959), one of the longest and most ambitious longitudinal studies in history, was based primarily around this notion. Similarly, in 1918 Fisher introduced the statistic of "heritability," which can be defined as "the proportion of the total phenotypic variance that is associated with genetic variance in a specific sample with a specific genetic composition and environmental context" (Vitzmuth, 2003, p. 541). This heritability statistic, describing individual variation as the influence of individual alleles, dominant alleles, and environmental variance, emphasized the role of nature in human development and accomplishment.

Conversely, work from the environmentalist camp during the same period also reinforced this dualist "all or nothing" approach – the idea that individuals start as a "tabula rasa" (blank slate) with no innate traits or characteristics and that all forms of learning and behavior result from interactions with our environment. This social deterministic viewpoint is best demonstrated by Watson's famous boast:

> Give me a dozen healthy infants and my own specified world to bring them up in, and I'll guarantee to take anyone at random and train him to become any kind of specialist

I might select – doctor, lawyer, artist . . . regardless of his talents, penchants, tendencies, abilities, vocations and race of his ancestors.

(1924, p. 104)

Over the past 150 years, this debate has been marked by radical shifts in opinion, usually driven by social/cultural factors (Pinker, 2002). For instance, many of the atrocities of the Second World War were strongly rooted in biological determinism and after 1945, political and intellectual thought changed to endorse positions based on the notion that differences between individuals were the result of opportunities and experience. With work beginning on the Human Genome Project in 1990 and publication of the genome in 2001, discussions shifted once again, as epitomized by James Watson's quote: "we used to think our fate was in the stars. Now we know, in large measure, our fate is in our genes" (Jaroff, 1989).

The field of sport science has shown a similar pendulum swing with social zeitgeist informing the "theories of the day." Below, we review the dominant movements in this field as they relate to skill acquisition and expertise, before describing the book sections and chapters in the Handbook that follows.

Some of the earliest empirical studies of skill acquisition and expertise come from Bryan and Harter (1897, 1899), who considered the time course of learning in Morse code operators. Although not specifically aiming to inform over 100 years of research that followed, they were pioneers in work on automaticity, variability, and improvements in performance over time (Lee & Swinnen, 1993). Similarly, early studies such as Book (1925), Snoddy (1926), and Crossman (1959) focused on relatively simple motor tasks (typing, mirror tracing, and cigar rolling skills, respectively) and likely did not foresee the lasting impact their studies would have on the field of skill acquisition and motor learning. Nonetheless, these early studies established an important foundation for the field (see Newell & Rosenbloom, 1981).

The search for a global motor ability

With the emergence of Spearman's G, proposed to represent a general quality of intelligence (Spearman, 1904), in the early part of the 20th century researchers began to explore whether a similar function might explain the dominance of certain people in athletic tasks. The *generalized motor ability* concept is built on the notion that a) individual motor skills are related to one another, b) a single global ability underpins each individual ability, and c) people are capable of performing all motor skills at similar levels. A related concept considers *motor educability*, referring to a general ability to learn motor skills (i.e., those with a high motor educability would more easily learn any motor task; see, for example, Gire & Espenschade, 1942; Gross *et al.*, 1956; McCloy, 1937). During the 1950s and 1960s there was considerable research attention invested in building support for the notion of a global motor ability that might explain the "all-around athlete." However, contrary to the notion of a generalized motor ability, correlational studies (see, for example, Drowatzky & Zuccato, 1967) found very little association even between different forms of the same motor ability (e.g., balance). Similarly, there is very little support for the notion of a general motor educability. Generally speaking, the overwhelming evidence supports the notion that motor (and perceptual, cognitive, as well as some physiological) capabilities are largely independent and highly specific to the types of experiences and training individuals have – although it should be noted that the search for general tests of motor coordination to inform talent detection, and to a lesser extent talent identification, has seen renewed interest in the last few years (see Faber *et al.*, 2014; Vandorpe *et al.*, 2012).

A [very brief] review

Emergence of "expertise" as a field of study

With the lack of evidence to support general abilities to underpinning skilled performance, researchers began to focus on specific skills and characteristics that might vary between groups at different skill levels. Incredibly important in this area were the chess studies of Adriaan de Groot (1965) and Herbert Simon and William Chase (1973; Chase & Simon, 1973), which tried to explain the performance of elite chess players using paradigms from the rapidly developing field of cognitive psychology. In particular, Simon was fundamentally important in contributing early work to what would become the field of artificial intelligence and used computer models as analogies for human decision-making and cognitive processing.

Similarly, the emergence of the field of "cognitive psychology" during this time did much to influence (and possibly constrain) much of the work that followed. In a very general sense, cognitive psychology focuses on the influence of mental processes (e.g., attention, memory, perception) on behavior. Understanding how cognitive processes differed between experts and non-experts became fundamental research questions in early expertise research. In a series of pioneering studies in the 1980s, Janet Starkes and her colleagues examined the cognitive advantage in sports like basketball and volleyball (see Allard & Starkes, 1980; Starkes, 1987), at around the same time Bruce Abernethy (drawing from Jones & Miles, 1978 and Salmela & Fiorito, 1979; see Abernethy & Russell, 1984, 1987) was examining the qualities underpinning expert anticipation in racquet sports like squash and badminton. Collectively, these independent programs of research highlighted that differences between experts and their less-skilled counterparts were not related to innate physical or cognitive abilities (termed "hardware" by Starkes & Deakin, 1984), but rather seemed to be learned capacities resulting from their considerable experience playing their sport (termed "software").

Concurrent with the work in sport by Starkes, Abernethy, and others (e.g., Hubert Ripoll, Fran Allard, Claude Allain, Dennis Glencross, and Harold Whiting, to name a few), Anders Ericsson was developing a research program examining the role of practice and training in explaining the performance of experts in domains such as music and memory. Ericsson, Chase, and Faloon (1980), for example, were able to train an average undergraduate participant (SF) to be able to recall up to 80 individual digits in a row, recited at one-second intervals. Perhaps the most significant of Ericsson's contributions, at least in terms of the present volume, was his 1993 study of musicians. This work became the basis for his concept of "deliberate practice" (Ericsson *et al.*, 1993), which proposed that it was not simply training of any type, but a prolonged engagement in deliberate practice (i.e., activities that require effort, do not lead to immediate rewards, and are done with the purpose of improving performance) that was necessary for expertise. Although the concept of deliberate practice was initially explored in musicians, it was rapidly applied to other domains (see Ericsson, 1996), with perhaps no domain embracing it to the extent that sport has (see Baker & Young, 2014 for a review).

Over the past four decades, sport researchers have done much to develop the burgeoning field of human expertise to the point where it has become a legitimate field of specialization. Early texts such as Ericsson and Smith's (1991) *Toward a General Theory of Expertise,* Starkes and Allard's (1993) *Cognitive Issues in Motor Expertise*, and Bloom's (1985) *Developing Talent in Young People* were important foundational texts in the field of expertise in general and sport expertise in particular. Since then, several other influential texts have been published, including Ericsson's (1996) *The Path to Expertise* and Starkes and Ericsson's (2003) *Expert Performance in Sports*. More recently, scholars have considered issues ranging from the process of talent identification and athlete development (e.g., Baker *et al.*, 2012; Hodges & Williams, 2012) to more appropriate ways of integrating current sport science into daily coaching practice (Farrow *et al.*, 2013; Vickers, 2007). However, until now there has not been a comprehensive resource for scientists, practitioners, and students working in this area.

Routledge Handbook of Sport Expertise

In the Handbook that follows, leading researchers from around the globe provide "state of the science" reviews of their areas of specialization. Chapters 2–11 focus on the diverse characteristics of expert performers. As is evident from these chapters, the field of sport expertise has been dominated by research focusing on perceptual-cognitive and psychological qualities.

- Damian Farrow and Bruce Abernethy (Chapter 2) summarize current understanding of expert anticipatory and pattern perception skill.
- Chapter 3, by Mark Wilson, Joe Causer, and Joan Vickers, examines gaze behaviors of expert performers, offering an unparalleled overview of this area of sport expertise.
- In Chapter 4, Keith Lohse summarizes current understanding of attentional control in expert sport performance, providing some new perspectives on how it can be defined.
- Chapter 5, by John van der Kamp and Ian Renshaw, considers perception-action coupling in understanding the movement quality of experts, highlighting the importance of considering movement control when investigating anticipatory skill.
- Chapter 6, by Markus Raab and Werner Helsen, considers expert decision-making in both players and officials, particularly as it relates to team sport athletes.
- Rob Gray's chapter on movement automaticity provides a systematic review of the nature of automatic performance as related to skill level (Chapter 7).
- Paul Glazier, Machar Reid, and Kevin Ball's chapter reviews the nature of expertise in sports that require speed and/or accuracy of multi-articular actions (e.g., throwing, kicking, and hitting actions), as well as highlighting several methodological issues (Chapter 8).
- John Sutton and Doris McIlwain provide an illuminating overview of how experts use their knowledge representation in Chapter 9.
- Sport psychologists have always been interested in understanding how psychological factors affect the acquisition and manifestation of superior performance. In Chapter 10, Geir Jordet summarizes current knowledge on the psychological characteristics of expert performance.
- In Chapter 11, Tim Gabbett summarizes research on physical and anthropometric factors of sports experts and how these variables interact to produce expert performance.

In Chapters 12–25, methodological and theoretical issues in sport expertise research are examined. The goal of this section is to provide the interested reader with a summary of important details about current methods in sport expertise research. The topics are very diverse, reflecting the range of research questions being considered in this field.

- In the first chapter in this section (Chapter 12), Keith Davids *et al.* review sport expertise from the perspective of ecological dynamics. From this perspective, expert performance reflects an athlete's capacity to adapt his/her movements to the dynamics of the sport environment.
- In Chapter 13, Joseph Baker, Nick Wattie, and Jörg Schorer present a taxonomic scheme for categorizing skill in expertise research and highlight the problems that have been persistent in prior work without this type of categorization system.

A [very brief] review

- Melissa Hopwood (Chapter 14) discusses the methodological concerns with the collection of athlete training history data using retrospective methods and proposes several areas where the collection of these data could be improved.
- In Chapter 15, David Mann and Geert Savelsbergh discuss how expert anticipation is typically measured, and address some contemporary concerns in using these techniques.
- Derek Panchuk, Sam Vine, and Joan Vickers explore methodological issues researchers face when using eye movement recordings in their examination of expert sport performance in Chapter 16.
- Chapter 17, by Cathy Craig and Alan Cummins, describes "immersive interactive virtual reality" (i2VR), a relatively new methodology (and perhaps the future) for studying how perception can influence action choices.
- In Chapter 18, Adam Gorman provides an overview of recall and recognition paradigms used in sport research, and discusses considerations surrounding their application and interpretation of the data collected.
- Duarte Araújo, Pedro Silva, and Keith Davids examine approaches to capture group-based characteristics of expert teams in Chapter 19.
- In Chapter 20, Doris McIlwain and John Sutton discuss methods of collecting data pertaining to expert knowledge. They take a broader approach to this issue than has been considered in the past and highlight several intriguing areas of future work.
- In two chapters (Chapters 21 and 22) Bradley Fawver, Garrett Beatty, and Christopher Janelle examine the myriad issues that affect the acquisition of valid and reliable data about the psychological processes associated with elite performance. In the first chapter, the authors consider "dispositional factors" such as motivation, personality, mood, and attentional style, while in the second chapter, "emotional reactivity, psychological skills, and efficacy" are the foci.
- Chapter 23, by David Pyne and Naroa Etxebarria, examines methods to collect physiologic and anthropometric data on expert performers, an area under-represented in "traditional" sport expertise work.
- Ross Pinder, Jonathon Headrick, and Raôul Oudejans (Chapter 24) discuss the importance of developing representative tasks in sports research and practice. In addition, the authors provide several practical guidelines that can be used by researchers to ensure greater representative design in their research designs.
- Acquisition of data from actual fields of competition has becoming increasingly important. In the final chapter of this section, Ian Renshaw and Adam Gorman summarize the challenges to capturing expertise in field settings, providing some wonderful real world examples (Chapter 25).

Chapters 26–37 focus on the process of expertise development. From the role of practice and genetics to family members and coaches, this section reviews the incredibly diverse range of factors influencing the acquisition of sport skill.

- In Chapter 26, Yannis Pitsiladis and Guan Wang summarize their research program examining the role of genetic and genomic factors in explaining expert performance in sport.
- Jean Côté and Karl Erickson review the value of different types of developmental experiences in youth sport on the development of sport expertise in adulthood (Chapter 27).
- Self-regulatory skills are emerging as important factors in athlete development. In Chapter 28, Laura Jonker, Marije Elferink-Gemser, Yvonne Tromp, Joseph Baker, and Chris Visscher examine how these skills develop over time and how they relate to athlete outcomes during development.

- In the first of several chapters examining the role of social agents on developing expertise, Jessica Fraser-Thomas and Theresa Beesley (Chapter 29) summarize what is known about the influence of family members and peers on expertise development.
- In Chapter 30, Paul Ford, Edward Coughlan, Nicola Hodges, and Mark Williams examine the concept of deliberate practice as both an activity in sport and a scientific theory. The authors evaluate research in sport regarding the amount of deliberate practice required, when it should begin, and what it should comprise for developing and professional athletes.
- Often the difference between winners and losers in high-performance sport contexts relates to performers' use of creative approaches to a situation. In Chapter 31, Daniel Memmert examines the role of sport-related creativity and how this quality is developed.
- Does place or date of birth have lasting effects on athlete development? Nick Wattie, Dany MacDonald, and Stephen Cobley examine these issues in Chapter 32.
- Expert athletes seem to be able to maintain high levels of performance to a greater extent than ever before. In Chapter 33, Sean Horton, Joseph Baker, and Patricia Weir examine issues of career length and the influence of age on expertise.
- Cliff Mallett and Steven Rynne examine the role of the coach in the acquisition of sport expertise, with a particular emphasis on how this role changes across development (Chapter 34).
- Sporting expertise is not solely the domain of athletes. In Chapter 35, Diane Ste-Marie and Dave Hancock consider how the specific instructional method of observational learning can be used to develop expertise in coaches and officials.
- David Hendry, Paul Ford, Mark Williams, and Nicola Hodges explore research on effective practice and instruction (Chapter 36). Subsequently, they provide five evidence-based principles to create efficient, challenging, and engaging practice sessions.
- As the importance of perceptual skill became more obvious to expertise researchers, the question of whether these skills could be more easily and rapidly trained became increasingly important. In Chapter 37, Jörg Schorer, Florian Loffing, Rebecca Rienhoff, and Norbert Hagemann summarize the impressive literature examining training interventions for the acquisition of perceptual-cognitive skill.

In the final chapter of this Handbook, we take a look at the critical research developments of the past and the exceptional work that is happening currently, to try to provide an (albeit brief) overview of what the future looks like in this exciting field of science.

Without exception, the chapters are outstanding, which was not a surprise to us given the quality of the researchers who provided contributions to this volume. However, what we did not predict was that the contributors would write reviews that are particularly insightful for highlighting areas where our understanding is particularly limited. This information will be invaluable for the next generation of sport expertise researchers as they build on the foundations developed by many of the contributors to this text.

References

Abernethy, B., & Russell, D.G. (1984) 'Advanced cue utilisation by skilled cricket batsmen', *Australian Journal of Science and Medicine in Sport*, 16: 2–10.

Abernethy, B., & Russell, D.G. (1987) 'The relationship between expertise and visual search strategy in a racquet sport', *Human Movement Science*, 6: 283–319.

Allard F., & Starkes L.L. (1980) Perception in sport: volleyball. *Journal of Sport Psychology*, 2, 22–33.

A [very brief] review

Baker, J., Cobley, S., & Schorer, J. (2012). *Talent identification and development in sport: International perspectives*, Oxford, UK: Routledge.

Baker, J., & Young, B. (2014) '20 years later: Deliberate practice and the development of expertise in sport', *International Review of Sport and Exercise Psychology*, 7: 135–57.

Bloom, B. S. (1985) *Developing talent in young people*, New York: Ballantine Publishing Group.

Book, W. F. (1925) *The psychology of skill*, New York: Gregg.

Bryan, W. L., & Harter, N. (1897) 'Studies in the physiology and psychology of the telegraphic language', *Psychological Review*, 4: 27–53.

Bryan, W. L., & Harter, N. (1899) 'Studies on the telegraphic language: The acquisition of a hierarchy of habits', *Psychological Review*, 6: 345–75.

Chase, W. G., & Simon, H. A. (1973) 'Perception in chess', *Cognitive Psychology*, 4: 55–81.

Crossman, E.R.F.W. (1959) 'A theory of the acquisition of speed-skill', *Ergonomics*, 2: 153–66.

de Groot, A. D. (1965) *Thought and choice in chess*, The Hague: Mouton.

Drowatzky, J. N., & Zuccato, F. C. (1967) 'Interrelationships between selected measures of static and dynamic balance', *Research Quarterly*, 38: 509–10.

Ericsson, K. A. (1996) *The road to excellence: The acquisition of expert performance in the arts and sciences, sports, and games*, Hillsdale, NJ: Erlbaum.

Ericsson, K. A., Chase, W. G., & Faloon, S. (1980) 'Acquisition of a memory skill', *Science*, 208: 1181–2.

Ericsson, K. A., Krampe, R. Th., & Tesch-Römer, C. (1993) 'The role of deliberate practice in the acquisition of expert performance', *Psychological Review*, 100: 363–406.

Ericsson, K. A., & Smith, J. (1991) *Toward a general theory of expertise: Prospects and limits*, Cambridge: Cambridge University Press.

Faber, I. R., Oosterveld, F.G.J., & Hijhuis-Van der Sanden, M.W.G. (2014) 'Does an eye-hand coordination test have added value as part of talent identification in table tennis? A validity and reproducibility study', *PLOS ONE*, 9(1): e85657. doi:10.1371/journal.pone.0085657

Farrow, D., Baker, J., & MacMahon, C. (2013) *Developing sports expertise: Researchers and coaches put theory into practice*, Oxford, UK: Routledge.

Fisher, R. A. (1918) 'The correlation between relatives on the supposition of Mendelian inheritance', *Philosophical Transactions of the Royal Society*, 52: 399–433.

Galton, F. (1869) *Hereditary genius*, London: Macmillan.

Galton, F. (1874) 'On men of science: Their nature and their nurture', *Nature*, 9: 344–5.

Galton, F. (1883) *Inquiries into human faculty and its development*, London: Macmillan.

Gire, E., & Espenschade, A. (1942) 'The relationship between measures of motor educability and learning specific motor skills', *Research Quarterly*, 13: 43–56.

Gross, E., Griessel, D. C., & Stull, G. A. (1956) 'Relationship between two motor educability tests, a strength test, and wrestling ability after eight weeks of instruction', *Research Quarterly*, 27: 395–402.

Herrnstein, R., & Murray, C. A. (1994) *The bell curve: Intelligence and class structure in American life*, New York: Free Press.

Hodges, N. J., & Williams, A. M. (2012) *Skill acquisition in sport: Research, theory and practice*, Oxford, UK: Routledge.

James, W. (1890) *Principles of psychology*, New York: Holt.

Jaroff, L. (1989, March) 'The gene hunt', *Time*, 133: 62–7.

Jones, C. M., & Miles, T. R. (1978) 'Use of advanced cues in predicting the flight of a lawn tennis ball', *Journal of Human Movement Studies*, 4: 231–5.

Lee, T. D., & Swinnen, S. P. (1993) 'Three legacies of Bryan and Harter: Automaticity, variability, and change in skilled performance', in J. L. Starkes & F. Allard (eds) *Cognitive issues in motor expertise*, Amsterdam: North Holland, 295–316.

McCloy, C. H. (1937) 'An analytic study of the stunt type tests as a measure of motor educability', *Research Quarterly*, 8: 46–55.

Newell, A., & Rosenbloom, P. S. (1981) 'Mechanisms of skill acquisition and the law of practice', in J. R. Anderson (ed) *Cognitive skills and their acquisition*, Hillsdale, NJ: Erlbaum, 1–55.

Pinker, S. (2002) *The blank slate: The modern denial of human nature*, New York: Viking.

Salmela, J. H., & Fiorito, P. (1979) 'Visual cues in ice-hockey goaltending', *Canadian Journal of Applied Sport Sciences*, 4: 56–9.

Simon, H. A., & Chase, W. G. (1973) 'Skill in chess', *American Scientist*, 61: 394–403.

Snoddy, G. S. (1926) 'Learning and stability', *Journal of Applied Psychology*, 10: 1–36.

Spearman, C. (1904) '"General intelligence," Objectively determined and measured', *The American Journal of Psychology*, 15: 201–92.

Starkes, J. L. (1987) 'Skill in field hockey: The nature of the cognitive advantage', *Journal of Sport Psychology*, 9: 146–60.

Starkes, J. L., & Allard, F. (1993) *Cognitive issues in motor expertise*, Amsterdam: North Holland.

Starkes, J. L., & Deakin, J. (1984) 'Perception in sport: A cognitive approach to skilled performance', in W. F. Straub & J. M. Williams (eds) *Cognitive sport psychology*, Lansing, NY: Sport Science Associates, 115–28.

Starkes, J. L., & Ericsson, K. A. (2003). *Expert performance in sports: Advances in sport expertise*, Champaign, IL: Human Kinetics.

Terman, L. (1925) *Genetic studies of genius*, Stanford: Stanford University Press.

Terman, L. M., & Oden M. H. (1947) *The gifted child grows up*, Stanford: Stanford University Press.

Terman, L. M., & Oden, M. H. (1959) *The gifted group at mid-life*, Stanford: Stanford University Press.

Vandorpe, B., Vandendriessche, J. B., Vaeyens, R., Pion, J., Lefevre, J., Philippaerts, R. M., & Lenoir, M. (2012) 'The value of a non-sport-specific motor test battery in predicting performance in young female gymnasts', *Journal of Sports Sciences*, 30(5): 497–505.

Vickers, J. (2007) *Perception, cognition and decision-training: The quiet eye in action*, Champaign, IL: Human Kinetics.

Vitzthum, V. J. (2003) 'A number no greater than the sum of its parts: the use and abuse of heritability', *Human Biology*, 75: 539–88.

Watson, J. B. (1924) *Behaviorism*, New York: Norton.

2

EXPERT ANTICIPATION AND PATTERN PERCEPTION

Damian Farrow and Bruce Abernethy

Mention of expert athletes such as tennis player Roger Federer, footballer Cristiano Ronaldo, or basketball All-Star Dwayne Wade usually conjures images of exquisite skills based on the impression that they have more time and/or space in which to act than their competitors. Expert athletes competing in interceptive sports such as tennis or cricket, or in invasion games (team sports) such as football or basketball, must process an array of perceptual information from their environment in short periods of time in order to successfully execute an appropriate action. For example, a basketball player needs to consider the position of teammates and opponents, his/her own court position, and that of the ball to elicit a successful action. The outcome of this perceptual-cognitive process is often referred to as *anticipatory skill*, or the capability that enables an athlete to commence his/her response to an opponent's action or pattern of play in advance. Colloquially, team sport coaches often describe the player with anticipatory skill as a "good driver in heavy traffic" – the basketball player who seemingly knows what is going to happen two passes before the ball is passed, the racquet sports player already moving into position before his/her opponent has hit the ball. While these players may not always appear to be the fastest movers around the court, their ability to accurately forecast a game's future ensures they have time on their side.

The aim of this chapter is to delve into the sport expertise literature and detail the underpinning perceptual-cognitive processes responsible for the expert athlete's anticipatory skill or appearance of "having all the time in the world." In the first section we detail the importance of recognizing that anticipatory sport expertise is task specific and does not emerge on generalized measures. We then focus on sport-specific, perceptual-cognitive differences and specifically, what information sources expert athletes use to inform their anticipatory responses. This section will focus on interceptive sports such as tennis or cricket and distinguish between current and prior (probabilistic) information sources. The final section of the chapter will then review the extant literature on the pattern perception skills of expert athletes in invasion games (team sports) such as football and basketball. While there are numerous methodological considerations associated with the work to be reviewed in this chapter, these will not be covered as greater treatment can be found in the companion methodological section (see Chapters 15, 25).

Anticipatory expertise is task specific

A story was strongly circulated that my ability to make runs was because of exceptional eye-sight which enabled me to see the ball earlier . . . Tests revealed my reaction was minutely slower than that of the average university student.

(Bradman, 1958)

As illustrated in the above quotation from Australian cricket batting legend Sir Donald Bradman,[1] one of the more robust findings of the sport expertise literature is that the measurement of expert performance needs to be task or sport specific and does not emerge on generalized measures (Helsen & Starkes, 1999; Williams & Ericsson, 2005). In the context of anticipatory skill, this caveat of sport expertise has been explored by some who have suggested that generic optometric parameters (e.g., visual acuity, depth perception) and neural processing abilities (e.g., visual reaction time, fast information processing) contribute to expert performance (e.g., Banister & Blackburn, 1931; Blundell, 1985). An underlying assumption of this body of research is that the physical capability of the visual system to receive information is a characteristic that may differentiate expert from novice athletes. Yet the supporting evidence for this assumption is less compelling. Hughes, Blundell, and Walters (1993) reported that although elite table tennis players had significantly better dynamic visual acuity, a wider visual field, and superior recognition of peripheral targets compared to less-skilled players, the differences only accounted for less than 5 per cent of the population variance. Applegate and Applegate (1992) investigated the relationship between degraded visual acuity and basketball set shot shooting performance and found no decline in shooting performance despite decreased visual acuity. More recently, Mann, Abernethy, and Farrow (2010) demonstrated that refractive visual blur did not significantly degrade cricket batting skill until the visual conditions approximated legal blindness. Such a finding reinforces that substantial degradation of visual clarity is possible before acuity is a limiting factor for interceptive performance.

Multifactorial measurement approaches have also produced evidence discounting the importance of basic visual processing contributing to perceptual-cognitive expertise. Starkes (1987) investigated the relative importance of generic visual attributes compared to sport-specific, cognitive attributes when explaining expertise differences within the sport of field hockey. Results demonstrated that none of the generic capacities (simple reaction time, dynamic visual acuity, and coincident anticipation) significantly contributed to the prediction of expertise. In perhaps the most comprehensive examination of this issue, Helsen and Starkes (1999) adopted a multidimensional approach to predict performance between expert, intermediate, and novice soccer and field hockey players and found that 84 per cent of variance was accounted for by sport-specific capacities and the only generic, visual component to even contribute slightly (3 per cent) was peripheral visual range in the horizontal dimension.

As posited by Abernethy and Wood, "increasingly the consensus is that expert and novice athletes are not characterized by differences in basic visual function" (2001, p. 204). One possible reason for this is that the variety of factors that contribute to sport performance limits the likelihood of vision alone correlating strongly with expert perceptual-motor performance. Any visual deficiency may be compensated for by superior performance in other aspects of performance, such as psychological or physical strength. However, the most likely reason is that generalized (not sport-specific) tests only measure the visual reception of information rather than the sport-specific, perceptual interpretation of visual information – it is the latter that appears to be the critical feature in distinguishing the visual-perceptual skill of expert and novice performers

(Abernethy & Wood, 2001). In summary, the findings of studies exploring generic visual attributes have been equivocal and have generally been unable to demonstrate a systematic, reproducible link between the visual parameter tested and sport performance, particularly as it pertains to the manifestation of expertise (see Helsen & Starkes, 1999; Starkes, 1987 for reviews).

Sport-specific, perceptual-cognitive differences

In contrast to the minimal contribution generic visual components make to expert sport performance, sport-specific, visual-perceptual capacities have been found to contribute significantly to sport expertise. Specifically, expert sport performers demonstrate a superior capacity to interpret different types of sport-specific visual information for the production of action. This perceptual advantage expresses itself, most notably, in sport-specific tests of anticipatory skill and pattern perception.

Anticipatory skill in interceptive actions

The best evaluation I can make of a player is to look in his eyes . . .

(Michael Jordan)

The capability to anticipate is particularly valuable in time-stressed interceptive sports for a number of reasons. First, in a situation like the tennis return of a serve, it may be necessary to begin moving before an opponent has even struck the ball in order to successfully intercept it (Glencross & Cibich, 1977; but also see Triolet *et al.*, 2013). Second, it provides a player with more time to prepare a response, which may increase the likelihood of successful response execution. Finally, anticipation may also effectively reduce the expert's information-processing load.

In many sport tasks, especially fastball interceptive sports, there are two distinct sources of information potentially available to the performer and there is some evidence of expertise-related differences in attunement to these different sources of information. There is skill execution information available during the *current* skill event arising directly from the opponent's movement pattern; plus there is contextual information available to a performer *before* the opponent commences the skill execution emanating from a priori knowledge of both players' strengths, weaknesses and preferences, court or field position, expectancies, and event probability information (see Buckolz *et al.*, 1988).

Current information sources

The biomechanical properties of most sport skills ensure that performers must adhere to a relatively predetermined sequence of skill execution if they are to produce a biomechanically efficient action. For example, to hit a powerful tennis serve whilst maintaining an acceptable level of accuracy, a player must produce hip to shoulder rotation that leads to a ballistic, sequential, over-arm action of the shoulder, arm, and wrist in order to serve the ball (e.g., Elliott *et al.*, 1986).

This constraint on a server guarantees that at some point prior to racquet-ball contact a receiving player will be provided with invariant movement pattern information that is reliably predictive of the forthcoming service direction and spin. The fact that this battle of deception and perception is readily quantifiable has provided sport expertise researchers with an opportunity to understand what phases of a movement pattern provide anticipatory information for expert athletes.

A primary information source demonstrated to facilitate anticipation is the opponent's pre-contact movement pattern. In sports as diverse as tennis (Farrow & Abernethy, 2003; Goulet *et al.*, 1989), squash (Abernethy, 1990), badminton (Abernethy & Russell, 1987; Abernethy & Zawi, 2007), ice hockey (Panchuk & Vickers, 2009; Salmela & Fiorito, 1979), soccer (Savelsbergh *et al.*, 2002; Williams & Burwitz, 1993), volleyball (Wright *et al.*, 1990), cricket (Abernethy & Russell, 1984; Müller *et al.*, 2006), and handball (Cañal-Bruland *et al.*, 2010; Loffing & Hagemann, 2014), research has consistently demonstrated earlier pickup of anticipatory information by expert players relative to novices. A variety of experimental approaches have been used to examine this expertise effect, with the most prominent methodology having been the *temporal occlusion approach*. This approach relies on the selective presentation of differing amounts of advance and ball-flight information of a direct opponent completing a sport-specific action. For example a tennis receiver is provided visual snapshots of different phases of the service action of an opponent (e.g., from serve commencement until peak ball toss, or from peak ball toss to racquet-ball contact). Traditionally, film or video footage was edited to produce these action sequences, whereas in the last 20 years the use of occlusion goggles have also been prevalent (see Figure 2.1). Within this approach, participants are typically required to predict the opponent's action (e.g., stroke direction in tennis) from the information available to them under the different temporal occlusion conditions. A significant change in the prediction accuracy from one occlusion condition to the next is assumed to be indicative of information pickup from within the additional viewing period. Prediction accuracies superior to chance levels provide confirmatory evidence for significant information pickup. In one of the first applications of this approach, Abernethy and Russell (1987) demonstrated that expert badminton players were able to pickup information to improve their prediction accuracy during an early time window (the period from 167 to 83 milliseconds prior to the ball being struck) from which novices could not extract information. By examining the key kinematic changes in the opponent's action during this time period (primary motion of the opponent's dominant arm) inference could be made as to differential information usage by the different skill groups (see Chapters 5 and 15 for greater comment on this methodological approach).

A more frequent approach in recent times has also been the use of spatial occlusion, which seeks to identify from *where*, rather than from *when*, in a dynamic display is information extracted. Spatial occlusion approaches typically have a common temporal occlusion point (e.g., all trials occluded at the point of racquet-ball contact in the tennis example), but visibility of different display features (e.g., racquet of the server, server's head, racquet and arm, lower body) are selectively masked (nowadays using advanced video editing). The logic behind the spatial occlusion methodology is that prediction performance will suffer in direct proportion to the importance of the information source being masked. For example, application of spatial occlusion techniques in the Abernethy and Russell (1987) study provided results that complemented those from the temporal occlusion manipulation in suggesting that the motion of the racquet and the arm holding the racquet contained information that could be used by expert performers, whereas novices were reliant solely on the motion of the racquet as a source of anticipatory information. Consistent with the temporal occlusion approach findings, results from the application of the spatial occlusion technique across a variety of sports have repeatedly shown the expert performers' extraction of earlier kinematic information to guide their anticipation relative to novice or less-skilled counterparts (e.g., Abernethy, 1990; Loffing & Hagemann, 2014; Müller *et al.*, 2006; Panchuk & Vickers, 2009; Williams & Davids, 1998).

Further, skilled performers are seemingly attuned to the coordinative structures inherent in strongly sequenced biomechanical sports actions. For example, Müller *et al.* (2006) demonstrated cricket batsmen extracted advance information from a bowler's hand position relative to the

Figure 2.1 An example of a volleyball digger being temporally occluded with Plato™ occlusion goggles when receiving a serve.

position of the forearm rather than simply the wrist or the forearm alone. This information pickup strategy has been termed a "global" process rather than a "local" process, where in the latter there is an overreliance on one kinematic information source (see Loffing & Hagemann, 2014; Williams *et al.*, 2009). While obviously the information sources differ between sports, the expert performer's pickup of predictive movement pattern information from earlier, more proximal information in the kinematic chain of an action remains a robust finding relative to less-skilled performers who are reliant on later-occurring, locally presented information.

While the temporal and spatial occlusion paradigms provide a useful means of identifying the key time windows where information pickup is likely to occur, it does not readily provide information to substantiate a direct relationship between perceptual expertise and the kinematics of the action being viewed. However, the use of a point-light display offers a means of extracting such evidence and a more direct indication of the key motion centers providing anticipatory information to the performer. The point-light technique involves presenting the motion of the joint centers of a performer in the absence of all other normal display features (such as pictorial cues for form, size, and orientation). Each joint center is represented by a single, disconnected light point that, when static, is completely ambiguous. However, as Johansson (1973) famously demonstrated, only brief visual exposure to the motion of these joint centers was necessary for the action being viewed to be identified. Abernethy and colleagues (Abernethy *et al.*, 2001; Abernethy & Zawi, 2007) have applied a similar methodology via a temporal occlusion approach to the racquet sports of squash and badminton in an attempt to isolate the key informational (kinematic) sources used by expert and novice players to predict the direction and depth of strokes. Findings revealed that the same time windows for information pickup and expertise differences occurred within the degraded point-light displays as the normal video display, supporting the existence of a direct link between perceptual expertise and the kinematics of the action being viewed. Further, selective manipulation of these key joint centers provides an opportunity for a more focused future investigation of the relative importance of different body segments as information sources for the perception and prediction of whole body movement patterns (see also Huys *et al.*, 2009; Pollick *et al.*, 2001; Ward *et al.*, 2002).

Another approach frequently used to assess, albeit indirectly, information pickup in sport settings has been to record players' eye movements as they view, and ideally respond to, a perceptual display identical, or at least very similar, to that they would encounter in the natural setting (see Chapters 3 and 16 for more information on gaze tracking). It has been hypothesized that players' visual search patterns may provide a good indication of the location of the most informative features of an opponent's action that may be used for anticipatory purposes. In some instances, studies measuring visual search patterns have supported the occlusion-based research findings relating to the identification of what kinematic information sources experts are using in their preparation of a response to an opponent's action (e.g., McRobert *et al.*, 2009; Savelsbergh *et al.*, 2002; Singer *et al.*, 1996; Williams *et al.*, 1994a, 1994b). However, while many of these studies show some visual search differences between experts and less-skilled performers, the differences are sometimes small and quite variable, suggesting that visual search differences cannot alone explain information-processing differences and performance differences between experts and others (Abernethy, 1990). Consequently, research attention has focused on examining the specific task constraints, such as number of players in a contest, that influence the visual search patterns adopted by performers (e.g., Roca *et al.*, 2013; Vaeyens *et al.*, 2007a, 2007b; Williams & Davids, 1998). Further, as the measurement technology has evolved, researchers have also begun to compare the visual search behaviors of performers using traditional video-based tasks with in situ tasks in an effort to better understand the processes underlying anticipatory behavior. The results of such work have demonstrated that the magnitude of the expertise differences found are larger in more representative tasks, and in some cases the visual search behaviors are different (Alfonso *et al.*, 2012; Bruce *et al.*, 2012; Dicks *et al.*, 2010) (see Chapters 5 and 15).

One very specific task constraint that has been of interest to sport expertise researchers in recent times is the actual battle between perception and deception of action (e.g., Cañal-Bruland *et al.*, 2010; Jackson *et al.*, 2006; Pollick *et al.*, 2001). While some interceptive actions may not require the need for deception of an opponent, deceptive movements are commonplace in many tasks, such as penalty situations in football or water polo, combat sports, and the one-on-one tackle/evasion situation in football codes. Typical of the pattern of findings in this area were those of Jackson *et al.* (2006), who demonstrated that skilled rugby players were not susceptible to deceptive information presented in a one-on-one tackle situation, whereas less-skilled players were. Such a result suggests that the attunement to advance visual information predictive of the opponent's action extends to both genuine and deceptive movements. Williams *et al.* (2009) suggested that due to skilled players' usage of global information sources they may be harder to deceive than less-skilled players, as an opponent would need to make significant changes in his/her movements across a greater number of kinematic locations in order to successfully deceive a skilled opponent. In other words, the "global" perceptual approach may inoculate the skilled perceiver against "local" perturbations (Williams *et al.*, 2009; however, also see Rowe *et al.*, 2009, highlighting the importance of specific task constraints).

Prior (contextual) information sources

> In the past he was too dependent on his serve up the T on the Ad side, yesterday he kept one of the best returners off balance by mixing up his spots which allowed him to use his favourite serve up the T on the AD – when he needed it – for free points.
>
> *(Justin Gimelstob, professional tennis player, describing how*
> *Andy Roddick defeated Andy Murray)*

The above quote provides a nice example of the second important source of information available when performing skills requiring anticipation. That is, the knowledge performers bring with them to the performance setting and their subsequent attunement to contextual probability information as the match unfolds. The study of the mechanisms through which expert and novice performers utilize *prior information sources* is relatively underdeveloped compared to our understanding of the processes utilized in attending to *current* information sources.

A key reason for this disparity in understanding pertains to the methodological difficulties associated with the manipulation of event probability. Within the laboratory-based research on *current information* usage, event probability (or the likelihood of each particular stimulus-response option occurring) is artificially controlled to be equal (but see Paull & Glencross, 1997 for an exception). However, the performance setting is seldom characterized by such equality; rather, the probability or expectancy of a particular response is affected by factors such as the respective court or field positions of players, relative stroke frequencies, and an opponent's strengths and weaknesses (Alain & Proteau, 1980; Buckolz *et al.*, 1988). While it is difficult to simulate accurately in a laboratory setting the natural knowledge of event probabilities that accrues with years of experience, studies that have attempted to undertake such simulations have indicated that subjective probabilities, at least when critical threshold levels are reached, drive anticipatory movements.

Expert and novice performers vary in the extent to which they are attuned to variances in the probability of other key events, such as court positioning and relative stroke frequencies. It is reasoned that experts may have greater understanding of probability information than novices (i.e., they may understand better the possibilities opponents have available to them and what their likely choice may be). Paull and Glencross (1997) demonstrated that baseball batters improved their anticipatory response when count information (ball and strike information that contextualizes the options available to a pitcher) was added to a simulated batting task. It was argued that such event probability information reduced the uncertainty of pitch type and provided batters with a degree of preparation equivalent to an additional 2.2 meters of ball flight time. Abernethy *et al.* (2001) used liquid crystal occluding spectacles during simulated squash play to demonstrate that expert players have a greater capacity to move to the correct quadrant of the court to hit a return stroke in the complete absence of advance information from the hitting action of the opposing player. Novices were not attuned to these same information sources (or, at least, not attuned as well as experts) and tended to be more reliant on relatively late-occurring current information such as ball flight.

More recently, Farrow and Reid (2012) manipulated the event probabilities of a simulated tennis serve-and-return scenario such that the first serve of each game was hit to the same location. After eight occurrences of this invariant probability information, highly skilled players' response times were indicative of their capacity to utilize this information in addition to the more typical pre-contact kinematic information available from the service action. In contrast, the less-skilled players were unaware of the probability information available and were reliant on the appearance of ball flight information to determine their response.

Pattern perception

> People talk about skating, puck handling and shooting, but the whole sport is angles . . . forgetting the straight direction the puck is going, calculating where it will be diverted, factoring in all the interruptions.
>
> *(NHL legend, Wayne Gretzky)*

As nicely described by hockey great Wayne Gretzky, pattern perception is the ability to recall and recognize patterns and structures inherent in the perceptual display. Expert advantages in this capacity were initially demonstrated in domains such as chess (Chase & Simon, 1973; de Groot, 1965) and bridge playing (Charness, 1979), and are now equally prevalent in sport expertise literature. The experimental method utilized in the original studies of pattern recognition in sport involved a performer being presented with a brief slide (approximately five seconds of exposure) of a structured or unstructured piece of game play. For example, within the game of basketball, a structured pattern would usually contain attacking or defensive patterns of play, whereas an unstructured pattern may relate to a timeout or turnover of possession. Importantly, both slide types would contain similar numbers of individual elements (or players) to recall. In the structured slides, the elements conformed to a pattern meaningful to expert performers, whereas in the unstructured slides the elements (player positions) are completely random. Having viewed the slide, participants are then required to either (a) *recall* the final locations of all the players when the slide is occluded, or (b) *recognize* those slides that have been previously presented relative to those that have not. The former task is by far the most prevalent in studies of sport expertise (see Chapter 18 for a methodological review). Typically, expert performers have been found to both recognize and recall more information from structured patterns commonly encountered within their sport. However, this advantage is typically lost when an unstructured pattern is displayed, rendering the performance of experts and novices as indistinguishable. While progression from slide displays to video presentation of the stimuli have occurred (see Figure 2.2), the results have remained robust

Figure 2.2 Example of a pattern recall task being completed for Australian football.

across a wide variety of sporting patterns, including basketball, hockey, football, volleyball, and rugby (Allard *et al.*, 1980; Borgeaud & Abernethy, 1987; Gorman *et al.*, 2012; Helsen & Starkes, 1999; North *et al.*, 2011; Starkes, 1987; Williams *et al.*, 1993; Williams & Davids, 1995; although, see North *et al.*, 2009 for an exception).

It has been reasoned that the pattern recognition procedure probes a player's ability to recognize rapidly what is developing in terms of an offensive or defensive pattern of play, and thus take advantage of this awareness of what a teammate or opponent is likely to do next (Starkes *et al.*, 1994). The expert's superior perceptual performance compared to that of a novice on the structured pieces of play has only been linked to the expert's ability to view large amounts of structured information, and reorganize it into fewer, larger chunks of information that are more easily remembered and accessed to produce the required pattern. The process of perceiving sport-specific patterns as chunks rather than individual items, such as individual players, allows an expert to process the relevant patterns at a faster rate and facilitates a deeper level of processing (Helsen & Starkes, 1999; Williams *et al.*, 1993). Further, it has been suggested that skilled participants initially extract motion information and temporal relationships between features, such as the players (relational information), before matching this stimulus representation with a template or complex representation (North *et al.*, 2009; Williams *et al.*, 2006). In contrast, less-skilled participants, due primarily to a lack of experience encoding structured patterns of play from within their sport domain, possess a less-developed encoding process.

As previously suggested by Starkes *et al.* (1994), pattern perception is thought to facilitate anticipatory performance. That is, in order to make a fast and accurate decision, a player must first recognize the pattern of play unfolding (North *et al.*, 2009). Alternatively, it has also been suggested that pattern recall is not task related, as it taps processes not explicitly used in a performance setting and, hence, adds little to our understanding of anticipatory pattern perception in the real world (e.g., Ward *et al.*, 2006). A range of studies has investigated this relationship between pattern perception and anticipation as measured by pattern recognition or recall and anticipatory skill. The results have been relatively consistent in demonstrating that pattern recall is a relatively strong predictor of anticipatory performance, explaining between 20 and 40 per cent of variance (Farrow *et al.*, 2010; Starkes, 1987; Williams & Davids, 1995).

However, these findings are likely to be heavily context dependent and subject to unique task constraints (Farrow *et al.*, 2010; Mann *et al.*, 2007; Ward & Williams, 2003; Williams & Ericsson, 2005). The influence of task constraints on the relationship between pattern perception and anticipation has been nicely captured in recent work by Roca *et al.* (2013), who demonstrated that the perceptual-cognitive processes underpinning anticipatory skill and decision-making differ, depending on whether the critical information is near or far away from the performer. In this study, the "far" condition represented the ball being down the other end of the football pitch and hence players were found to search the pattern as a whole (indicating use of relational information between players), whereas when the ball and players were "near" the performer, the visual search pattern focused on the player in possession of the ball (indicating a use of postural cue information).

A twist to the traditional pattern recognition paradigm has also been used to examine the degree to which pattern perception has an anticipatory element. First introduced by Didierjean and Marmèche (2005), participants were presented with a pair of schematic basketball patterns (as static slides) and were asked to determine whether the second slide was the next likely progression in play. When the patterns were presented in the normal progression of a game the experienced basketball players tended to be less accurate than when the patterns were not presented in a chronological order. The authors suggested that the experienced players were anticipating the movements of the players within the patterns and thus encoding the first presented image as a possible subsequent play state, rather than encoding the image in its original form. This work was extended by Gorman and colleagues (Gorman *et al.*, 2011; Gorman *et al.*, 2012; Gorman *et al.*, 2013), using a more representative task that continued to support the notion that pattern perception is anticipatory in nature for expert performers (see Chapter 18 for more detail).

Concluding remarks

This chapter has provided a necessarily brief overview of more than 30 years of sport expertise research dedicated to understanding how sport experts in time-stressed interceptive sports or invasion sports utilize the perceptual information available to them to make anticipatory responses. In sum, expert athletes have been found to selectively attend to sport-specific advance and invariant information from an opponent's movement kinematics, situational probability information present prior to and during a match, as well as commonly occurring structural patterns of play. The net result of this earlier, more effective information extraction by expert athletes is that they are able to create the appearance of "having all the time in the world" with which to prepare and execute a response in time-stressed situations. While the extant literature reviewed has been successful in uncovering a great deal about expert anticipatory performance, a contemporary challenge for sport expertise researchers is to contextualize this work as closely as possible within the performance setting in an effort to better understand the interaction between these perceptual-cognitive and motor processes and the variety of information sources available to a performer.

Note

1 Donald Bradman possessed a batting average of 99.94 runs from 52 international test matches. This is a feat unparalleled by any other cricket batsman. Graeme Pollock holds the second best all-time average of 60.97 runs.

References

Abernethy, B. (1990) 'Anticipation in squash: Differences in advance cue utilization between expert and novice players', *Journal of Sports Sciences*, 8: 17–34.

Abernethy, B., Gill, D., Parks, S.L., & Packer, S.T. (2001) 'Expertise and the perception of kinematic and situational probability information', *Perception*, 30: 233–52.

Abernethy, B., & Russell, D.G. (1984) 'Advance cue utilisation by skilled cricket batsmen', *The Australian Journal of Science and Medicine in Sport*, 16: 2–10.

Abernethy, B., & Russell, D.G. (1987) 'Expert-novice differences in an applied selective attention task', *Journal of Sport Psychology*, 9: 326–45.

Abernethy, B., & Wood, J. (2001) 'Do generalized visual training programs for sport really work? An experimental investigation', *Journal of Sport Sciences*, 19: 203–22.

Abernethy, B., & Zawi, K. (2007) 'Pickup of essential kinematics underpins expert perception of movement patterns', *Journal of Motor Behavior*, 39(5): 353–67.

Afonso, J., Garganta, J., McRobert, A., Williams, A.M., & Mesquita, I. (2012) 'Visual search behaviours and verbal reports during film-based and in situ representative tasks in volleyball', *European Journal of Sport Science*. doi:10.1080/17461391.2012.730064

Alain, C., & Proteau, L. (1980) 'Decision making in sport', in C.H. Nadeau, W.R. Halliwell, K.M. Newell, & G.C. Roberts (eds) *NASPSPA proceedings, psychology of motor behavior and sport (1979)*, Champaign, IL: Human Kinetics, 465–77.

Allard, F., Graham, S., & Paarsalu, M.E. (1980) 'Perception in sport: Basketball', *Journal of Sport Psychology*, 2: 14–21.

Applegate, R.A., & Applegate, R.A. (1992) 'Set shot shooting performance and visual acuity in basketball', *Optometry and Vision Science*, 69: 765–8.

Banister, H., & Blackburn, J.M. (1931) 'An eye factor affecting proficiency at ball games', *British Journal of Psychology*, 21: 382–4.

Blundell, N. (1985) 'The contribution of vision to the learning and performance of sports skills: Part 1: The role of selected visual parameters', *The Australian Journal of Science and Medicine in Sport*, 17(3): 3–11.

Borgeaud, P., & Abernethy, B. (1987) 'Skilled perception in volleyball defense', *Journal of Sport Psychology*, 9: 400–6.

Bradman, D. (1958) *The art of cricket*, Sydney: ETT Imprint.

Bruce, L., Farrow, D., Raynor, A., & Mann, D.L. (2012) 'But I can't pass that far! The influence of motor skill on decision making', *Psychology of Sport and Exercise*, 13(2): 152–61.

Buckolz, E., Prapavesis, H., & Fairs, J. (1988) 'Advance cues and their use in predicting tennis passing shots', *Canadian Journal of Sports Science*, 13(1): 20–30.

Cañal-Bruland, R., van der Kamp, J., & van Kesteren, J. (2010) 'An examination of motor and perceptual contributions to the recognition of deception from others' actions', *Human Movement Science*, 29: 94–102.

Charness, N. (1979) 'Components of skill in bridge', *Canadian Journal of Psychology*, 31: 1–16.

Chase, W.G., & Simon, H.A. (1973) 'Perception in chess', *Cognitive Psychology*, 4: 55–81.

de Groot, A.D. (1965) *Thought and choice in chess*, The Hague: Mouton.

Dicks, M., Button, C., & Davids, K. (2010) 'Examination of gaze behaviors under in situ and video simulation task constraints reveals differences in information pickup for perception and action', *Attention, Perception, Psychophysics*, 72: 706–20.

Didierjean, A., & Marmèche, E. (2005) 'Anticipatory representation of visual basketball scenes by novice and expert players', *Visual Cognition*, 12: 265–83.

Elliott, B., Marsh, T., & Blanksby, B. (1986) 'A three-dimensional cinematographic analysis of the tennis serve', *International Journal of Sport Biomechanics*, 2: 260–71.

Farrow, D., & Abernethy, B. (2003) 'Do expertise and the degree of perception-action coupling affect natural anticipatory performance?', *Perception*, 32: 1127–39.

Farrow, D., McCrae, J., Gross, J., & Abernethy, B. (2010) 'Revisiting the relationship between pattern recall and anticipatory skill', *International Journal of Sport Psychology*, 41: 91–106.

Farrow, D., & Reid, M. (2012) 'The contribution of situational probability information to anticipatory skill', *Journal of Science and Medicine in Sport*, 15(4): 368–73.

Glencross, D. J., & Cibich, B. J. (1977) 'A decision analysis of game skills', *Australian Journal of Sports Medicine*, 9: 72–5.

Gorman, A. D., Abernethy, B., & Farrow, D. (2011) 'Investigating the anticipatory nature of pattern perception in sport', *Memory & Cognition*, 39: 894–901.

Gorman, A. D., Abernethy, B., & Farrow, D. (2012) 'Classical pattern recall tests and the prospective nature of expert performance', *The Quarterly Journal of Experimental Psychology*, 65: 1151–60.

Gorman, A. D., Abernethy, B., & Farrow, D. (2013) 'Is the relationship between pattern recall and decision-making influenced by anticipatory recall?', *The Quarterly Journal of Experimental Psychology*. doi: 10.1080/17470218.2013.777083

Goulet, C., Bard, C., & Fleury, M. (1989) 'Expertise differences in preparing to return a tennis serve: A visual information processing approach', *Journal of Sport & Exercise Psychology*, 11: 382–98.

Helsen, W. F., & Starkes, J. L. (1999) A multidimensional approach to skilled perception and performance in sport', *Applied Cognitive Psychology*, 13: 1–27.

Hughes, P., Blundell, N., & Walters, J. (1993) 'Visual and psychomotor performance of elite, intermediate and novice table tennis competitors', *Clinical and Experimental Optometry*, 76(2): 51–60.

Huys, R., Cañal-Bruland, R., Hagemann, N., Beek, P. J., Smeeton, N. J., & Williams, A. M. (2009) 'Global information pickup underpins anticipation of tennis shot direction', *Journal of Motor Behavior*, 41: 158–70.

Jackson, R. C., Warren, S., & Abernethy, B. (2006) 'Anticipation skill and susceptibility to deceptive movements', *Acta Psychologica*, 123: 355–71.

Johansson, G. (1973) 'Visual perception of biological motion and a model for its analysis', *Perceptual Psychophysics*, 14: 201–11.

Loffing, F., & Hagemann, N. (2014) 'Skill differences in visual anticipation of type of throw in team-handball penalties', *Psychology of Sport and Exercise*, 15: 260–7.

Mann, D. L., Abernethy, B., & Farrow, D. (2010) 'The resilience of natural interceptive actions to refractive blur', *Human Movement Science*, 29(3): 386–400.

Mann, D. T., Williams, A. M., Ward, P., & Janelle, C. M. (2007) 'Perceptual-cognitive expertise in sport: A meta-analysis', *Journal of Sport & Exercise Psychology*, 29: 457–78.

McRobert, A. P., Williams, A. M., Ward, P., & Eccles, D. W. (2009) 'Tracing the process of expertise in a simulated anticipation task', *Ergonomics*, 52(4): 474–83.

Müller, S., Abernethy, B., & Farrow, D. (2006) 'How do world-class cricket batsmen anticipate a bowler's intention?', *The Quarterly Journal of Experimental Psychology*, 59(12): 2162–86.

North, J. S., Ward, P., Ericsson, A., & Williams, A. M. (2011) 'Mechanisms underlying skilled anticipation and recognition in a dynamic and temporally constrained domain', *Memory*, 19: 155–68.

North, J. S., Williams, A. M., Hodges, N., Ward, P., & Ericsson, K. A. (2009) 'Perceiving patterns in dynamic action sequences: Investigating the processes underpinning stimulus recognition and anticipation skill', *Applied Cognitive Psychology*, 23: 878–94.

Panchuk, D., & Vickers, J. N. (2009) 'Using spatial occlusion to explore the control strategies used in rapid interceptive actions: Predictive or prospective control?', *Journal of Sports Sciences*, 27(12): 1249–60.

Paull, G., & Glencross, D. (1997) 'Expert perception and decision making in baseball', *International Journal of Sport Psychology*, 28: 35–56.

Pollick, F. E., Fidopiastis, C., & Braden, V. (2001) 'Recognising the style of spatially exaggerated tennis serves', *Perception*, 30: 323–38.

Roca, A., Ford, P. R., McRobert, A. P., & Williams, A. M. (2013) 'Perceptual-cognitive skills and their interaction as a function of task constraints in soccer', *Journal of Sport & Exercise Psychology*, 35: 144–55.

Rowe, R., Horswill, M. S., Kronvall-Parkinson, M., Poulter, D., & McKenna, F. (2009) 'The effect of disguise on novice and expert tennis players' anticipation ability', *Journal of Applied Sport Psychology*, 21: 178–85.

Salmela, J. H., & Fiorito, P. (1979) 'Visual cues in ice hockey goaltending', *Canadian Journal of Applied Sports Sciences*, 4: 56–9.

Savelsbergh, G. J. P., Williams, A. M., van der Kamp, J., & Ward, P. (2002) 'Visual search, anticipation and expertise in soccer goalkeepers', *Journal of Sports Sciences*, 20: 279–87.

Singer, R. N., Cauraugh, J. H., Chen, D., Steinberg, G. M., & Frehlich, S. G. (1996) 'Visual search, anticipation, and reactive comparisons between highly-skilled and beginning tennis players', *Journal of Applied Sports Psychology*, 8: 9–26.

Starkes, J., Allard, F., Lindley, S., & O'Reilly, K. (1994) 'Abilities and skill in basketball', *International Journal of Sport Psychology*, 25: 249–65.

Starkes, J. L. (1987) 'Skill in field hockey: The nature of the cognitive advantage', *Journal of Sport Psychology*, 9: 146–60.

Triolet, C., Benguigui, N., Le Runigo, C., & Williams, A. M. (2013) 'Quantifying the nature of anticipation in professional tennis', *Journal of Sports Sciences*, 31: 820–30.

Vaeyens, R., Lenoir, M., Williams, A. M., Mazyn, L., & Philippaerts, R. M. (2007a) 'The effects of task constraints on visual search behavior and decision-making skill in youth soccer players', *Journal of Sport & Exercise Psychology*, 29: 147–69.

Vaeyens, R., Lenoir, M., Williams, A. M., Mazyn, L., & Philippaerts, R. M. (2007b) 'Visual search behavior and decision-making skill in soccer', *Journal of Motor Behavior*, 39: 395–408.

Ward, P., & Williams, A. M. (2003) 'Perceptual and cognitive skill development in soccer: The multidimensional nature of expert performance', *Journal of Sport & Exercise Psychology*, 25: 93–111.

Ward, P., Williams, A. M., & Bennett, S. (2002) 'Visual search and biological motion perception in tennis', *Research Quarterly for Exercise and Sport*, 73: 107–12.

Ward, P., & Williams, A. M., & Hancock, P. A. (2006) 'Simulation for performance and training', in K. A. Ericsson, N. Charness, P. J. Feltovich, & R. R. Hoffman (eds) *The Cambridge handbook of expertise and expert performance*, Cambridge: Cambridge University Press, 243–62.

Williams, A. M., & Burwitz, L. (1993) 'Advance cue utilization in soccer', in T. Reilly, J. Clarys, & A. Stibbe (eds) *Science and football*, vol. 2, London: E. & F. N. Spon, 239–44.

Williams, A. M., & Davids, K. (1998) 'Visual search strategy, selective attention, and expertise in soccer', *Research Quarterly for Exercise and Sport*, 69(2): 111–28.

Williams, A. M., Davids, K., & Burwitz, L. (1994a) 'Ecological validity and visual search research in sport', *Journal of Sport & Exercise Psychology*, S16: 22.

Williams, A. M., Davids, K., Burwitz, L., & Williams, J. G. (1994b) 'Visual search strategies in experienced and inexperienced soccer players', *Research Quarterly for Exercise and Sport*, 65(2): 127–35.

Williams, A. M., & Ericsson, K. A. (2005) 'Perceptual-cognitive expertise in sport: Some considerations when applying the expert performance approach', *Human Movement Science*, 24: 283–307.

Williams, A. M., Hodges, N. J., North, J. S., & Barton, G. (2006) 'Perceiving patterns of play in dynamic sport tasks: Investigating the essential information underlying skilled performance', *Perception*, 35: 317–32.

Williams, A. M., Huys, R., Cañal-Bruland, R., & Hagemann, N. (2009) 'The dynamical information underpinning anticipation skill', *Human Movement Science*, 28: 362–70.

Williams, M., & Davids, K. (1995) 'Declarative knowledge in sport: A by-product of experience or a characteristic of expertise?', *Journal of Sport & Exercise Psychology*, 17: 259–75.

Williams, M., Davids, K., Burwitz, L., & Williams, J. (1993) 'Cognitive knowledge and soccer performance', *Perceptual and Motor Skills*, 76: 579–93.

Wright, D. L., Pleasants, F., Gomez-Meza, M. (1990) 'Use of advanced visual cue sources in volleyball', *Journal of Sport and Exercise Psychology*, 12: 406–14.

3

AIMING FOR EXCELLENCE

The quiet eye as a characteristic of expertise

Mark R. Wilson, Joe Causer, and Joan N. Vickers

Talent hits a target no one else can hit; genius hits a target no one else can see.

(Arthur Shopenhauer, 1788–1860)

While the above quotation may simply be using the concepts of perception and action as a metaphor for genius, research has revealed that expert sport performers actually do attend to "to-be-acted-upon" targets differently than their less-skilled counterparts. Indeed, a consistent body of research has revealed significant differences between the gaze behaviors of experts and non-experts when performing sport skills. With experience and through training, experts learn to conserve limited cognitive resources and strategically direct their gaze control system to maximize information acquisition and guide accurate, goal-directed movement (Land, 2009). There has been increasing interest in understanding the perceptual-cognitive advantage of expert performers, with experts differing from non-experts on sport-specific measures of attention allocation and information pickup (Causer & Williams, 2013; Mann *et al.*, 2007).

This chapter discusses research that points to a role for effective gaze behavior in supporting expert-like planning and control of visually guided skills. Specifically, the role of a particular gaze strategy – the quiet eye (QE; Vickers, 1996) – in underpinning expert performance will be discussed in four main sections:

1 *What is the QE?* Defining the QE and reviewing the literature that has identified the QE as a discriminating characteristic of expertise.
2 *QE and competitive pressure.* A key characteristic of expertise is being able to execute skills when it matters most. We discuss the role of the QE in maintaining performance under pressure.
3 *QE training.* Discussing interventions that can help even experienced performers extend their QE and improve performance.
4 *Future directions.* Discussing how researchers should further our understanding of how the QE "works" to support skilled performance.

What is the quiet eye (QE)?

The QE is the final fixation to a target during the preparation phase of a goal-directed movement. Specifically, the QE is defined for a given motor task as the final fixation or tracking gaze directed to a single location or object in the visuomotor workspace within three degrees of visual angle (or less) for a minimum of 100 milliseconds (ms) (Vickers, 1996, 2007). The onset of the QE occurs before a critical phase of the motor task and the offset occurs when this final fixation deviates off the target by more than three degrees of visual angle for more than 100 ms. The QE represents a critical period of cognitive processing during which the parameters of the movement such as force, direction, and velocity are fine-tuned and programmed (Vickers, 1996). It is during this period when sensory information is synthesized with the mechanisms necessary to both plan (preprogram) and control (online) the appropriate motor response.

The key processes underpinning the QE period – setting parameters for movement, processing appropriate environmental cues, synchronizing motor strategies (Mann et al., 2007) – are related to functions of attentional control. Over the last decade we have learned a good deal about the basic mechanisms of visual-attentional control at both functional and neural levels. For example, fMRI data indicate the role of a large-scale fronto-parietal network, which is involved in both top-down control of attention and in attentional orienting to strong stimulus cues (Corbetta & Shulman, 2002). This network is involved both in excitatory guidance of attention to behaviorally relevant targets and in the suppression of irrelevant distraction (Medendrop et al., 2011; Mevorach et al., 2006, 2010).

The quiet eye and attention

Corbetta et al.'s model of attention reflects the delicate balance between a goal-directed, top-down (dorsal) and stimulus-driven, bottom-up (ventral) system (Corbetta & Shulman, 2002; Corbetta et al., 2008). First, a top-down, goal directed, attentional system (dorsal attention network), which is centered on the dorsal posterior parietal and frontal cortex, is important for response or action selection and is involved in linking relevant stimuli to appropriate motor responses. Second, a stimulus-driven, attentional system (ventral attention network), centered on the temporoparietal and ventral frontal cortex, is recruited during the detection of salient and unattended stimuli (Corbetta et al., 2008).

Both the dorsal and ventral systems interact dynamically during normal perception to determine where and what we attend to. However, when attention is focused, the ventral system is suppressed to prevent reorienting to distracting/irrelevant cues (Corbetta et al., 2008). Therefore, Vickers' (1996) suggestion that longer QE periods may allow performers an extended duration of response programming, while minimizing distraction from other cues, can be explained using the model of Corbetta and colleagues; the QE helps maintain effective, goal-directed attentional control, while reducing the impact of the stimulus-driven, attentional system (see Figure 3.1).

Kinematic correlates

Longer QE durations provide a period to efficiently pass visually acquired goal position information to the motor control systems, which should therefore result in movement kinematics and patterns of muscle activation that are more effective for successful skill performance (Vickers, 2009; Figure 3.1). For example, Causer et al. (2010) revealed that not only did elite shotgun shooters have significantly longer QE durations than their sub-elite counterparts, but they also had more efficient gun barrel kinematics. Stronger evidence of a role of QE in supporting efficient

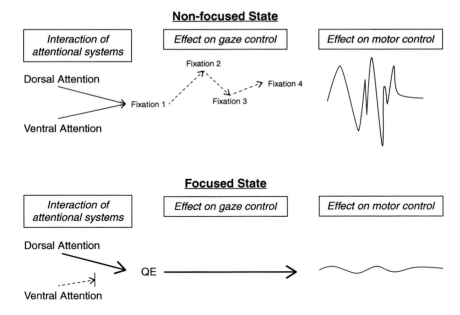

Figure 3.1 A representation of the proposed links between attentional networks, the quiet eye (QE), and movement control.

kinematics is provided by QE training studies (e.g., Causer *et al.*, 2011a; Moore *et al.*, 2012). Causer *et al.* (2011a) reported that a QE-trained group of elite shotgun shooters displayed significantly reduced gun barrel displacement and absolute peak velocity (over and above improvements revealed by a control group), despite neither of these variables being explicitly trained. Similarly, Moore *et al.* (2012), in a golf putting task, found that, following training, a QE-trained group of novices displayed more efficient club head acceleration and electromyography (EMG) activity in the extensor carpi radialis muscle of the left arm than their control group counterparts.

Neural correlates

The use of event-related potentials (ERP) has been reported in various psychophysiological investigations that have examined attentional processes involved prior to task execution. The ERP is derived from the average of multiple responses and represents the temporal relationship of cortical activation to a specific event, thereby providing a time-locked index of the psychological correlates of performance (Fabiani *et al.*, 2000). The Bereitschaftspotential (BP) is a class of ERP that is of particular interest when studying the preparatory period preceding task execution. The BP is a negative potential that precedes an actual, intended, or imagined event by one to 1.5 seconds (s) and indexes anticipatory attention and movement preparation (Simonton, 2004). Mann *et al.* (2011) explored the association of the BP and QE period in high and low handicap golfers during execution of a golf putt. The low handicap golfers were more accurate and less variable in their performance than the high handicap golfers. Systematic differences in QE duration and BP were observed, with experts exhibiting a prolonged QE period and greater cortical activation in the right-central region compared to non-experts. A significant association between cortical activation and QE duration was noted, longer QE being positively correlated with the magnitude (negativity) of the BP.

Aiming for excellence

Quiet eye research evidence

Since Vickers' (1996) seminal study in basketball free-throw shooting, evidence has been growing supporting the QE as an objective measure of attentional control predicting motor performance. In Mann *et al.*'s (2007) meta-analysis of perceptual-cognitive expertise in sport, the QE was reported as one of three gaze behaviors that differentiated experts from their non-expert counterparts. A moderate to large effect size was uncovered ($r = 0.62, p < .001$). On average, experts maintained a QE duration that was approximately 62 per cent longer than non-experts. These findings were consistent over tasks that were as diverse as rifle shooting (Janelle *et al.*, 2000) and volleyball service return (Vickers & Adolphe, 1997). The following section outlines the two types of discrete sport skills where expertise differences in QE have most frequently been examined: targeting and interceptive tasks.

Targeting tasks

Targeting tasks are self-paced and generally require a great deal of accuracy as an object is propelled towards a distal target. In sports such as golf, archery, and shooting, the ability to accurately select the correct parameters for movement is crucial for successful performance. Access to pertinent visual stimuli and the effective processing of information are essential in these sports (Causer *et al.*, 2010). For example, successful performance in golf putting requires the golfer to attend to cues related to distance, direction, and force, which are in turn influenced by environmental conditions (e.g., slope, grain direction). Accordingly, the visual system must orient to and process the most salient perceptual cues necessary to ascertain both distance and direction information, while working memory is called upon for matching stroke tempo with the requisite stroke force (Mann *et al.*, 2011). Vickers (2012) postulates that experts are better able to maintain the longer duration QE that helps to organize and sustain the underlying organization and control of this information (via dorsal networks, while suppressing ventral attention). Table 3.1 below outlines studies that have examined proficiency differences in QE in targeting skills.

While there are differences in the actual QE values reported, depending on specific task demands, it is evident that experts' QE durations are generally longer than their non-expert counterparts. From a basic perspective of reward-based learning, it is likely that experts have found that adopting a task-optimal QE increased the expected probability of success of the subsequent action (see Gottlieb, 2012). Current research suggests that a longer QE helps to ensure both the efficient preplanning of the movement response (e.g., Klostermann *et al.*, 2013; Mann *et al.*, 2011) and its subsequent online control under visual guidance (Oudejans *et al.*, 2002; Vine *et al.*, 2013). The relative weighting of preplanning and online control functions for the QE will depend on task-specific demands. For example, in rifle shooting, where the movement time (trigger pull) is short, the QE duration likely reflects a purely preprogramming function (Janelle *et al.*, 2000). In golf putting, the QE appears to provide both a preprogramming (Mann *et al.*, 2011) and online control (Vine *et al.*, 2013) function.

The QE literature may seem counterintuitive in that experts generally "do more with less" visual information than non-experts. For example, experts can anticipate more accurately than novices even when visual information is limited or occluded (see Chapter 2 of this volume). Why should experts need more information via a longer QE in order to be accurate than less expert performers in targeting skills? We suggest that a single, long, final fixation to a relevant target is actually *more* efficient than a series of fixations around the target. The longer QE durations found for experts in the studies outlined in Table 3.1 are typically measured within a similar preparation period as non-expert performers. Therefore, experts do not necessarily extend the absolute processing period, but are more efficient at executing relatively longer QE durations within the time available.

Table 3.1 A summary of the studies that have examined expertise differences in quiet eye in targeting tasks.

Authors	Year	Sport/Task	Participants	Findings
Vickers	1992	Golf putting	5 low handicap (0–8) and 7 high handicap (10–16) golfers	QE duration was significantly longer for low handicap (2 s) than high handicap golfers (1.5 s).
Vickers	1996	Basketball free-throw shooting	8 elite shooters (M = 75% accuracy) and 8 near-elite shooters (M = 42% accuracy)	QE duration was significantly longer for elite (~900 ms) than near-elite (~350 ms) performers.
Williams, Singer, & Frehlich	2002	Billiards potting	12 highly skilled and 12 less-skilled players	Experts had significantly longer QE durations on successful shots (~600 ms) than non-experts (~300 ms).
Janelle, Hillman, Apparies, Murray, Meili, Fallon, & Hatfield	2000	Rifle shooting	12 elite and 13 non-elite marksmen	QE was significantly longer (11 s) for elite shooters than non-elite shooters (7 s).
Nagano, Kato, & Fukuda	2006	Football penalty	3 better performers and 3 poorer performers	The top scorers had significantly longer QE durations than their less successful counterparts.
Wilson, McGrath, Vine, Brewer, Defriend, & Masters	2011	Laparoscopic surgery	10 experienced surgeons (> 60 procedures) and 15 novice surgeons (< 10 procedures)	Experienced operators used a significantly longer QE period than novices (1120 ms versus 600 ms) to guide precision grasping movements and hence needed fewer grasp attempts (2.5 versus 3.3).
Mann, Coombes, Mousseau, & Janelle	2011	Golf putting	10 low handicap (< 2) and 10 mid-handicap (10–12) golfers	Experts had significantly longer QE durations (> 2 s) than non-experts (< 2 s).
Panchuk & Vickers	2011	Line walking	11 professional ballet dancers; 9 control adults	QE duration prior to stepping on the line was significantly longer for ballet dancers (2,350 ms) than the controls (1,330 ms), and significantly further ahead (55% of fixations were straight ahead, cf. 26% for controls).

Author	Year	Task	Participants	Findings
Vickers & Lewinski	2012	Officer-involved shooting; live simulation	11 elite Emergency Response Team officers and 13 rookies	Elite accuracy 75% and rookie 54%. Elite officers kept their QE on assailant for ~350 ms before pulling trigger; rookies employed saccadic gestures back to sights of their own gun and often fired without fixating assailant. On catch trials, when a phone was drawn instead of a gun, the rookies shot the assailant on 62% of trials, compared to 19% for the elite.
Rienhoff, Baker, Fischer, Strauss, & Schorer	2012	Dart throwing	13 skilled (competitive) darts players; 16 novices (physical education students)	QE duration differences between skilled and less-skilled players were not statistically significant ($p = 0.08$; ES = 0.52).
Rienhoff, Hopwood, Fischer, Strauss, Baker, & Schorer	2013	Basketball free throw& darts	13 elite basketball players	Throwing accuracy and quiet eye duration for skilled and less-skilled basketball players were examined in basketball free-throw shooting and the transfer task of dart throwing. Skilled basketball players showed significantly higher throwing accuracy and longer quiet eye duration in the basketball free-throw task compared to their less-skilled counterparts.
Wilson, Miles, Vine, & Vickers	2013	Throwing and Catching	57, 8–10-year-old children were divided into high (HMC: n = 16), median (MMC: n = 25) and low (LMC: n = 16) coordination abilities.	The HMC group was more successful in the catching task than both other groups (catching percentage: HMC = 92%, MMC = 62%, LMC = 35%) and had longer targeting QE fixations before the release of the ball (HMC = 500 ms, MMC = 410 ms, LMC = 260 ms) and longer tracking QE durations before catching (HMC = 260 ms, MMC = 200 ms, LMC = 150 ms).
Harvey, Vickers, Snelgrove, Scott, & Morrison	2014b	Thyroidesctomy: identification and dissection of the recurrent laryngealnerve (RLN) in a human cadaver model	3 highly experienced (HE) surgeons and 7 low experienced (LE)	HE surgeons rated higher than LE through blind review of gaze videos; groups did not differ in operating time or hand MT. HE had a longer QE duration on the RLN prior to dissections (2.4s) compared to 844 ms for the LE.

Mark R. Wilson et al.

Interceptive tasks

Interceptive timing tasks require coordination of the athlete's body, or a held implement, and an object, or target area, in the environment. Whereas targeting tasks generally have a fixed and consistent target, interceptive tasks are often moving in a predictable or unpredictable way towards or away from the athlete. For interceptive tasks, athletes have to develop strategies to fixate and track the target object, as well as process and anticipate the speed and direction of the object and consistently update that information based on environmental perturbations. Alongside this, athletes also have to program the forces, distances, and direction of their limbs in order to coincide their action with the moving target (see Table 3.2).

Table 3.2 A summary of the studies that have examined expertise differences in quiet eye in interceptive tasks.

Authors	Year	Sport/Task	Participants	Findings
Vickers & Adolphe	1997	Volleyball service return	12 Team Canada Men's Team – elite receivers versus near-elite	Elite receivers fixated on ball earlier and tracked for ~400 ms before ball reached the net, compared to 0 ms for near-elite.
Panchuk & Vickers	2006	Ice hockey goal tending	8 elite goaltenders at college and semi-pro level	On saves, QE duration was significantly longer before puck left stick (~900 ms) than goals for all goaltenders.
Rodrigues, Vickers & Williams	2002	Table tennis return	Elite table tennis players and non-elite recreational players	No significant QE difference in groups due to QE being measured only during flight of the ball.
Causer, Bennett, Holmes, Janelle, & Williams	2010	Shotgun shooting	24 elite and 24 sub-elite shotgun shooters in trap, double trap, and skeet	Elite shooters demonstrated both an earlier onset and a longer relative duration of QE than their sub-elite counterparts. Also, in all three disciplines, QE duration was longer and onset earlier during successful compared with unsuccessful trials for elite and sub-elite shooters.
Piras & Vickers	2011	Soccer goaltending	Male college and club level	Saves occurred during kick when duration QE was longer (~900 ms) on a "visual pivot" location between the ball and kicking leg.
Millslagle, Hines, & Smith	2013	Softball umpires	4 expert; 4 near expert	Experts fixated earlier and for a longer period of time on the area where the ball would be released, and were able to track the ball earlier and for a longer period of time.

Aiming for excellence

Vickers (2007) identified three gaze control phases for interceptive actions: object recognition, object tracking, and object control. During the object recognition phase, fixations and pursuit tracking are used to determine the trajectory and movement parameters of the target. The object tracking phase involves smooth pursuit tracking to keep the target in the fovea (the center of the retina where there is close pairing of ganglion cells to photoreceptors, thereby permitting greatest visual acuity) to ensure any changes in trajectory are detected. Finally, in the object control phase, fixations and tracking behaviors are used to stabilize the eyes as the target is successfully intercepted.

The most effective method of determining object flight varies depending on the task. For predictable object flight, fixations or pursuit tracking early in the flight should enable an athlete to successfully intercept the object (Vickers, 2007). For more unpredictable object flights, such as baseball pitching or cricket bowling, a continuous tracking strategy will be more effective to enable the athlete to make online adjustments based on late deviations to the object flight (Causer *et al.*, 2010). Predictions of object flight can be made in certain tasks before the object has started moving, such as penalty kicks, based on early postural cues of the opponent (Causer & Williams, 2013), which can then be corroborated by early ball flight information. However, in most interceptive tasks, early detection of the target followed by a continuous tracking of the target seems to be the most effective strategy. For example, in a series of studies, Causer *et al.* (2010, 2011a, 2011b) examined the gaze strategies of expert and less-skilled shotgun shooters. Analysis of eye movement data showed that expert shooters demonstrated an earlier target pickup (QE onset) and a longer target tracking (QE duration) when compared to their less-skilled counterparts. Successful shots were characterized by the trend in both skill levels compared to unsuccessful shots, demonstrating that this gaze strategy is the most effective.

Researchers have shown similar findings in other interceptive tasks, such as in ice hockey goaltending (Panchuk & Vickers, 2006) and table tennis or volleyball returns (Rodrigues *et al.*, 2002; Vickers & Adolphe, 1997). Panchuck and Vickers (2006) found that QE duration was longer for saves, compared to goals, with the fixations on the moving puck critical to successful interception. Vickers and Adolphe found early detection of the ball and longer QE duration on the ball led to more successful serve returns. It is clear from the data presented above and in Table 3.2 that an early onset of QE and longer QE duration is critical for the successful interception of objects: the early QE onset maximizes the tracking time and enables early flight information to be processed, while a longer QE duration provides sufficient time for flight trajectory information to be accurately calculated.

QE and competitive pressure

An important characteristic of expert performers is their ability to perform at their limits just when it matters most – usually under intense competitive pressure. The ability to control attention and remain focused under elevated anxiety has frequently been discussed as a key component of success in sport, and there is considerable research evidence suggesting that anxiety-induced disruptions to attentional control lead to degradation in task performance (see Janelle, 2002; Wilson, 2012 for reviews). Several studies have revealed that the QE may be a useful index of optimal attentional control, and sensitive to the influence of increased anxiety (e.g., Behan & Wilson, 2008; Causer *et al.*, 2011b; Vickers & Williams, 2007; Wilson *et al.*, 2009; see Table 3.3).

For example, Wilson *et al.* (2009), in a basketball free-throw task, found that under conditions of elevated cognitive anxiety, QE durations were reduced, as participants took more fixations

Table 3.3 A summary of the studies that have examined the effect of increased anxiety on quiet eye and performance.

Authors	Year	Sport/Task	Participants	Findings
Vickers & Williams	2007	Biathlon/rifle shooting during 5 power output levels: Pre, 55%, 70%, 85%, 100% of individual capacity	10 Elite (international) biathletes	Athletes who choked (performed worse under high pressure compared to a practice condition) had shorter QE duration than practice condition. Those who did not choke maintained a longer QE duration after 100% power output during the high-pressure situation.
Behan & Wilson	2008	Simulated archery	20 trained students	QE durations (as a percentage of the alignment phase) reduced significantly from 62% in low-pressure to 50% in high-pressure session.
Wilson, Vine, & Wood	2009	Basketball free throw	10 university basketball players	There were significant reductions in both the QE duration (by 34%) and performance (by 26%) in the high-threat compared with control condition.
Wood & Wilson	2010	Football penalty	18 university footballers	Players fixated the goalkeeper for longer during the aiming phase and hit the ball more centrally when under pressure and with a moving goalkeeper.
Causer, Holmes, Smith & Williams	2011	Shotgun shooting	16 elite shotgun shooters	Shooters demonstrated shorter QE durations, and less efficient gun motion, along with a decreased performance outcome (fewer successful trials) under high compared with low-anxiety conditions.
Nibbeling, Oudejans, & Daanen	2012	Dart throwing	11 experts; 9 novices	Novices' QE durations reduced significantly when they were anxious, whereas experts' didn't.
Vine, Lee, Moore, & Wilson	2013	Golf putting	50 expert golfers (mean handicap of 3.6)	QE duration was significantly shorter on the missed putt in a shootout than other putts.
Causer, Harvey, Snelgrove, Arsenault & Vickers	2014	Surgical knot-tying	20 first year medical students divided into quiet eye (QE) or technical (TT) training groups	Both QE and TT groups significantly improved knot-tying performance post-intervention, with QE group improving significantly more than the TT. More efficient eye movements and movement times were reported for the QE group. The QE group transferred their performance improvements into a high anxiety condition; the TT group reverted to pre-test scores.

around the vicinity of the target compared with a low-anxiety condition. These findings are consistent with other research by Behan and Wilson (2008) in simulated archery and Nibbeling *et al.* (2012) in a dart-throwing task. Furthermore, Causer *et al.*, (2011b) found that in a shotgun-shooting task, anxiety shortened QE durations by delaying the onset of QE under conditions of elevated anxiety. In all four of these studies, these reductions in the efficiency of attentional control (QE) were also associated with poorer performance.

The theoretical support for this impairment in attentional control comes from a recent theory developed by Michael Eysenck and colleagues to explain how trait anxiety might influence cognitive performance – attentional control theory (ACT; Eysenck *et al.*, 2007). Eysenck *et al.* (2007) suggest that anxiety is likely to cause a diversion of processing resources from task-relevant stimuli toward task-irrelevant (and particularly threatening) stimuli. This impairment in attentional control is proposed to occur irrespective of whether these stimuli are external (e.g., environmental distractors) or internal (e.g., worrying thoughts). The authors explicitly relate this impairment of attentional control to a disruption in the balance of the two attentional systems outlined by Corbetta and colleagues.

According to ACT, anxiety alters the strength of output from the pre-attentive threat evaluation system, so that threat-related stimuli are more likely to capture attention. In this way, anxiety increases the sensitivity of the stimulus-driven system (ventral attention), making individuals more distractible, at the expense of goal-directed control (dorsal attention). In terms of QE, this increased sensitivity of ventral attention is likely to disrupt efficient QE processing, and subsequent visuomotor performance. A long QE duration prior to and during task performance may therefore be needed to suppress competing stimuli/emotions and allow the dorsal network to carry out the action as planned (Wilson, 2012). Indeed, Vickers and Williams (2007) found that elite biathletes who increased their QE duration during simulated competition compared with practice were less susceptible to the adverse effects of anxiety. As such, the authors suggested that the act of allocating attention externally to critical task information (via the QE) may insulate athletes from the debilitating effects of anxiety.

Quiet eye training

Several researchers have examined the potential of training perceptual-cognitive skills such as QE in sport and other domains (see Causer *et al.*, 2012; Vine *et al.*, 2014 for recent reviews). QE training is typically carried out in six steps:

1 Expertise research is carried out to determine the four QE characteristics of experts as they perform the task: the specific location, an early onset prior to a critical movement, an offset that is task specific, a longer duration.
2 Videos of expert QE are coupled with instruction and/or routines.
3 Trainees are tested on the same task while wearing a mobile eye tracker.
4 The trainees are taught how to mirror the QE focus of the experts through a process of video modeling, video feedback, and questioning, thus allowing them to witness the task performed through the eyes of an expert.
5 The trainees are shown their own QE as collected in step 3. Questions are asked in relation to the difference between the four QE characteristics of the expert compared to their own.
6 The trainee selects one of the QE characteristics to adopt and practice over a number of trials. Steps 4–6 are repeated as needed.

Vine and colleagues have recently demonstrated that novice performers can expedite the acquisition of sporting skills and be more resilient to pressure via QE training, compared to via traditional, technical instructions (see Moore *et al.*, 2012; Vine & Wilson, 2010, 2011). For example, Vine and Wilson (2011) examined the efficacy of a training intervention designed to improve QE characteristics in basketball free throws. The authors examined whether such training would protect participants against disruptions in attention when anxious. Novice participants were allocated to either a control or QE training group, with the latter receiving a 360-trial training period. The training group performed more accurately than a control group across retention tests, under "normal" conditions. Under increased anxiety, the control group performed worse than in the pre-test, whereas the QE training group maintained their levels of performance (see also Vine & Wilson, 2010).

While elite athletes might have developed longer QE durations than their novice counterparts, this does not mean that they cannot improve further and be more resilient to the effects of competitive pressure. In fact, expert performers can also benefit from similar QE training programs. For example, Causer *et al.* (2011b) developed a training program designed to improve QE characteristics in elite, international skeet shooters. The participants in the training group underwent an eight-week intervention consisting of eight training sessions and three video feedback sessions. Participants in the training group improved the efficiency of their gaze behaviors, as indexed by earlier QE onset and longer QE duration, from the pre- to post-test. However, the control group showed no changes in gaze characteristics. Furthermore, the training group increased shooting accuracy from 63 per cent in the pre-test to 77 per cent in the post-test; there were no differences in the control group. The improved accuracy scores transferred into competition, with the training group scoring higher in competitions post- compared to pre-intervention. Also, the intervention group demonstrated more efficient kinematic behaviors post- compared to pre-test, as indexed by decreased gun barrel displacement and absolute peak velocity. These results highlight the potential of training key skills to enhance performance at any skill level.

QE training can be a useful practical intervention for dealing with pressure, especially as it can fit extremely well within a performer's existing pre-performance routine. Singer's five-step strategy, a particular example of a pre-performance routine, has been shown to facilitate learning and performance in a number of laboratory and field studies (see Singer, 2000). It focuses on creating the conditions for a "just do it" performance state and emphasizes that optimally focused attention is best achieved by selecting one appropriate, external cue. The QE may be seen as part of such a pre-performance routine, helping the performer focus on what he or she can control (an external, process-related cue) rather than on non-productive (internal) thoughts and emotions (see Mann *et al.*, 2011; Wilson & Richards, 2011). The purpose of such a routine is to help the performer 'focus with a quiet eye and execute with a quiet mind.'

One of the important strengths inherent in the QE literature is that the studies have adopted meaningful tasks where eye-hand coordination can be examined in situ. The concept has also proved robust enough to apply outside of the sporting environment. Indeed, research has identified expert-novice differences in QE in tasks as varied as firearm scenarios in law enforcement (Vickers & Lewinski, 2012), surgery (Harvey *et al.*, 2014a; Wilson *et al.*, 2011), and children's motor coordination ability (Wilson *et al.*, 2013) (see Table 3.4). Recent research has also suggested that QE training might be effective in these domains (Wilson *et al.*, 2011; Miles *et al.*, 2014).

Table 3.4 A summary of the studies that have examined the utility of quiet eye training with novice and experienced performers.

Authors	Year	Sport/Task	Participants	Findings
Adolphe, Vickers & Laplante	1997	Volleyball service return	9 Men Team Canada	Longer QE duration early on the ball after QE training. Three year follow-up – high 72% reception versus 68% for top receivers in World Cup League.
Harle & Vickers	2001	Basketball free throw	Three teams playing Collegiate basketball	The QE trained team improved free-throw percentage by 23% over two seasons. One control team reduced performance by 1% and the other increased by 13%.
Oudejans, Koedijker, Bleijendaal, & Bakker	2005	Basketball jump shot	10 elite players (best shooters on their team)	The attention-trained group improved performance in games from 46% to 61%, after training, whereas a control group did not improve (remaining at 42%).
Vickers	2007	Golf putting	14 elite university team and club players divided by handicap (range 0–29, average 11.5) into QE-trained and gaze-trained groups	QE group significantly increased QE duration and QE dwell time more than gaze-trained. QE-trained were more accurate than gaze-trained, but not significantly.
Vine & Wilson	2010	Golf putting	14 novice golfers	The QE-trained group maintained more effective attentional control (QE = 2800 ms) and performed significantly better in the pressure test compared to the control group (QE = 900 ms). Furthermore, longer QE periods were associated with better performance across all test putts.
Vine & Wilson	2011	Basketball free throw	16 novice basketball players	The QE-trained group maintained more effective visual-attentional control (QE = 550 ms) and performed significantly better in the pressure test compared to the control group (QE = 300 ms).
Vine, Moore, & Wilson	2011	Golf putting	22 elite golfers (mean handicap of 3) divided into QE-trained and control groups who were given no awareness of their gaze control	The QE-trained group maintained their optimal QE under pressure conditions, whereas the control group experienced reductions in QE when anxious, with subsequent effects on performance. These advantages transferred to the golf course, where QE-trained golfers made 1.9 fewer putts per round, compared to pre-training, whereas the control group showed no change in their putting statistics.

(Continued)

Table 3.4 (Continued)

Authors	Year	Sport/Task	Participants	Findings
Causer, Holmes, & Williams	2011	Shotgun shooting	20 elite shotgun shooters divided into a QE-trained and control groups	The QE group significantly increased their mean QE duration, used an earlier onset of QE, and recorded higher shooting accuracy scores from pre-test to post-test. The QE group significantly reduced gun barrel displacement and absolute peak velocity in the post-test compared with the pre-test. A transfer test based on performance during competition indicated that QE group significantly improved shooting accuracy from pre- to post-intervention. No pre-test to post-test differences were observed for the control group on the measures reported.
Wood & Wilson	2011	Football penalty	10 university players following QE training and 10 in a control group	Results from a retention test indicated that the QE-trained group had more effective visual-attentional control, were significantly more accurate, and had 50% fewer shots saved by the goalkeeper than the control group.
Moore, Vine, Cooke, Ring, & Wilson	2012	Golf putting	40 novice golfers	The quiet eye group performed more accurately and displayed more effective gaze control, lower club head acceleration, greater heart rate deceleration, and reduced muscle activity than the technical-trained group during retention and pressure tests.
Wood & Wilson	2012	Football penalty	10 university players following QE training and 10 in a control group	QE participants significantly reduced their perceptions of outcome uncertainty (contingency) and increased their perceptions of shooting ability (competence) and ability to cope with the pressure (control), compared to control participants, when taking part in a penalty shootout task.
Causer, Harvey, Snelgrove, Arsenault & Vickers	2014	Surgical knot-tying	20 first-year medical students divided into quiet eye (QE) or technical (TT) training groups	Both QE and TT groups significantly improved knot-tying performance post-intervention, with QE group improving significantly more than the TT. More efficient eye movements and movement times were reported for the QE group. The QE group transferred their performance improvements into a more complex transfer test; the TT group reverted to pre-test scores.
Miles, Vine, Wood, Vickers, & Wilson	2014	Catching	16, 10-year-old children	Significant interaction effects for performance and quiet eye durations revealed that only the QET group significantly lengthened QE durations, which contributed to significant improvements in catching from pre- to post-test (23% cf. 4%).

Future directions and conclusions

While recent research has started to improve our understanding of the processes underpinning the QE performance relationship (e.g., Klostermann *et al.*, 2013), future research needs to further this understanding of *how* the QE works. Important questions include:

- To what extent are task differences important in understanding how the QE underpins performance?
- How exactly does maintaining a longer QE help performance under pressure?
- To what extent is the timing of the QE more important than duration?
- Is the QE crucial in sport skills that require decision-making?
- What are the underlying neurological events that occur during the QE period?

To conclude, the body of literature reviewed in this chapter suggests that a longer QE helps to ensure both the efficient preplanning of a movement and its subsequent online control, irrespective of whether the task is a self-paced targeting task or an interceptive timing task. While elite performers will have learned to adopt effective QE durations via experience, these can still break down under pressure and therefore it may be important to implement QE training programs to ensure systematic gaze behaviors to maintain focus on critical cues.

References

Adolphe, R., Vickers, J. N., & Laplante, G. (1997) 'The effects of training visual attention on gaze behaviour and accuracy: A pilot study', *International Journal Of Sports Vision*, 4: 28–33.

Behan, M., & Wilson, M. (2008) 'State anxiety and visual attention: The role of the quiet eye period in aiming to a far target', *Journal Of Sport Sciences*, 26: 207–15.

Causer, J., Bennett, S. J., Holmes, P. S., Janelle, C. M., & Williams, A. M. (2010) 'Quiet eye duration and gun motion in elite shotgun shooting', *Medicine & Science In Sports & Exercise*, 42: 1599–1608.

Causer, J., Harvey, A., Snelgrove, R., Arsenault, G., & Vickers, J. N. (2014) 'Quiet eye training expedites surgical knot tying: A randomized controlled study', *The American Journal of Surgery*, 208: 171–7.

Causer, J., Holmes, P. S., Smith, N. C., & Williams, A. M. (2011b) 'Anxiety, movement kinematics, and visual attention in elite-level performers', *Emotion*, 11: 595–602.

Causer, J., Holmes, P. S., & Williams, A. M. (2011a) 'Quiet eye training in a visuomotor control task', *Medicine & Science In Sports And Exercise*, 43: 1042–49.

Causer, J., Janelle, C. M., Vickers, J. N., & Williams, A. M. (2012) 'Perceptual training: What can be trained?', in N. J. Hodges & A. M. Williams (eds) *Skill acquisition in sport: Research, theory and practice*, London: Routledge, 306–24.

Causer, J., & Williams, A. M. (2013) 'Improving anticipation and decision making in sport', in P. O'donoghue, J. Sampaio, & T. Mcgarry (eds) *The Routledge handbook of sports performance analysis*, London: Routledge, 21–31.

Corbetta, M., Patel, G., & Shulman, G. L. (2008) 'The reorienting system of the human brain: From environment to theory of mind', *Neuron*, 58: 306–24.

Corbetta, M., & Shulman, G. L. (2002) 'Control of goal-directed and stimulus driven attention in the brain', *Nature Reviews Neuroscience*, 3: 201–15.

Eysenck, M. W., Derakshan, N., Santos, R., & Calvo, M. G. (2007) 'Anxiety and cognitive performance: Attentional control theory', *Emotion*, 7: 336–53.

Fabiani, M., Gratton, G., & Coles, M.G.H. (2000) 'Event related brain potentials: Methods, theory, and applications', in J. T. Cacioppo, L. G. Tassinary, & G. G. Berntson (eds) *Handbook of psychophysiology*, Cambridge: Cambridge University Press, 53–84.

Gottlieb, J. (2012) 'Attention, learning and the value of information', *Neuron*, 76: 281–95.

Harle, S., & Vickers, J. N. (2001) 'Training quiet eye improves accuracy in the basketball free throw', *The Sport Psychologist*, 15: 289–305.

Harvey, A., Vickers, J. N., Snelgrove, R., Scott, M. F., & Morrison, S. (2014a) 'Expertise differences in performance and quiet eye duration during identification and dissection of the recurrent laryngeal nerve', *American Journal Surgery*. doi: 10.1016/J.Amjsurg.2013.07.033

Harvey, A., Vickers, J. N., Snelgrove, R., Scott, M. F., & Morrison, S. (2014b). 'Expert surgeon's quiet eye and slowing down: expertise differences in performance and quiet eye duration during identification and dissection of the recurrent laryngeal nerve', *American Journal of Surgery*, 207: 187–93.

Janelle, C. M. (2002) 'Anxiety, arousal and visual attention: A mechanistic account of performance variability', *Journal of Sports Sciences*, 20: 237–51.

Janelle, C. M., Hillman, C. H., Apparies, R. J., Murray, N. P., Meili, L., Fallon, E. A., & Hatfield, B. D. (2000) 'Expertise differences in cortical activation and gaze behavior during rifle shooting', *Journal of Sport & Exercise Psychology*, 22: 167–82.

Klostermann, A., Kredel, R., & Hossner, E. J. (2013) 'The "quiet eye" and motor performance: Task demands matter!', *Journal of Experimental Psychology. Human Perception and Performance*, 39: 1270–8.

Land, M. F. (2009) 'Vision, eye movements, and natural behaviour', *Visual Neuroscience*, 26: 51–62.

Mann, D.T.Y., Coombes, S. A., Mousseau, M. B., & Janelle, C. M. (2011) 'Quiet eye and the bereitschaftspotential: Visuomotor mechanisms of expert motor performance', *Cognitive Processing*, 12(3): 223–34.

Mann, D.T.Y., Williams, A. M., Ward, P., & Janelle, C. M. (2007) 'Perceptual-cognitive expertise in sport: A meta-analysis', *Journal of Sport & Exercise Psychology*, 29: 457–78.

Medendrop, W. P., Buchholz, V. N., Van Der Werf, J., & Leone, F. (2011) 'Parietofrontal circuits in goal-oriented behaviour', *European Journal of Neuroscience*, 33: 2017–27.

Mevorach, C., Hodsoll, J., Allen, H. A., Shalev, L., & Humphreys, G. W. (2010) 'Ignoring the elephant in the room: A neural circuit to down-regulate salience', *Journal of Neuroscience*, 30: 6072–9.

Mevorach, C., Humphreys, G. W., & Shalev, L. (2006) 'Opposite biases in salience-based selection for the left and right posterior parietal cortex', *Nature Neuroscience*, 9: 740–2.

Miles, C.A.L., Vine, S. J., Wood, G., Vickers, J. N., & Wilson, M. R. (2014) 'Quiet eye training improves throw and catch performance in children', *Psychology Of Sport & Exercise*, 15: 511–15.

Millslagle, D. G., Hines, B. B., & Smith, M. S. (2013) 'Quiet eye gaze behavior of expert, and near-expert, baseball plate umpires', *Perceptual & Motor Skills*, 116: 69–77.

Moore, L. J., Vine, S. J., Cooke, A., Ring, C., & Wilson, M. R. (2012) 'Quiet eye training expedites motor learning and aids performance under pressure: The roles of response programming and external attention', *Psychophysiology*, 49: 1005–15.

Nagano, T., Kato, T., & Fukuda, T. (2006) 'Visual behaviors of soccer players while kicking with the inside of the foot', *Perceptual & Motor Skills*, 102: 147–56.

Nibbeling, N., Oudejans, R.R.D., & Daanen, H.A.M. (2012) 'Effects of anxiety, a cognitive secondary task, and expertise on gaze behaviour and performance in a far aiming task', *Psychology Of Sport & Exercise*, 13: 427–35.

Oudejans, R.R.D., Koedijker, J. M., Bleijendaal, I., & Bakker, F. C. (2005). 'The education of attention in aiming at a far target: Training visual control in basketball jump shooting', *International Journal of Sport and Exercise Psychology*, 3: 197–221.

Oudejans, R.R.D., Van De Langernberg, R. W., & Hutter, R. I. (2002) 'Aiming at a far target under different viewing conditions: Visual control in basketball jump shooting', *Human Movement Science*, 21: 457–80.

Panchuk, D., & Vickers, J.N. (2006) 'Gaze behaviors of goaltenders under spatial–temporal constraints', *Human Movement Science*, 25: 733–52.

Panchuk, D., & Vickers, J.N. (2011) 'Effect of narrowing the base of support on the gait, gaze and quiet eye of elite ballet dancers and controls', *Cognitive Processing*, 12: 267–76.

Piras, A., & Vickers, J. N. (2011) 'The effect of fixation transitions on quiet eye duration and performance in the soccer penalty kick: Instep versus inside kicks', *Cognitive Processing*, 12: 245–55.

Rienhoff, R., Baker, J., Fischer, L., Strauss, B., & Schorer, J. (2012) 'Field of vision influences sensory-motor control of skilled and less-skilled dart players', *Journal of Sports Science & Medicine*, 11: 542–50.

Rienhoff, R., Hopwood, M. J., Fischer, L., Strauss, B., Baker, J., & Schorer, J. (2013) 'Transfer of motor and perceptual skills from basketball to darts', *Frontiers in Psychology*, 4: 593. doi: 10.3389/Fpsyg. 2013.00593

Rodrigues, S. T., Vickers, J.N., & Williams, A. M. (2002) 'Head, eye and arm co-ordination in table tennis: An exploratory study', *Journal of Sport Sciences*, 20: 171–86.

Simonton, D. K. (2004) *Creativity in science: Chance, logic, genius, and zeitgeist*, Cambridge: Cambridge University Press.

Singer, R. N. (2000) 'Performance and human factors: Considerations about cognition and attention for self-paced and externally-paced events', *Ergonomics*, 43: 1661–80.

Vickers, J. N. (1992) 'Gaze control in putting', *Perception*, 21: 117–32

Vickers, J.N. (1996) 'Visual control when aiming at a far target', *Journal of Experimental Psychology. Human Perception and Performance*, 22: 342–54.

Vickers, J. N. (2007) *Perception, cognition and decision training: The quiet eye in action*, Champaign, IL: Human Kinetics Publishers.

Vickers, J. N. (2009) 'Advances in coupling perception and action: The quiet eye as a bidirectional link between gaze, attention and action', in M. Raab, J. Johnson, & H. Heekeren (eds) *Progress in brain research*, vol. 174. The Netherlands: Elsevier, 279–88.

Vickers, J. N. (2012) 'Neuroscience of the quiet eye in golf putting', *International Journal of Golf Science*, 1: 2–9.

Vickers, J. N., & Adolphe, R. (1997) 'Gaze behaviour while tracking an object and aiming at a far target', *International Journal of Sports Vision*, 4: 17–25.

Vickers, J. N., & Lewinski, W. (2012) 'Performing under pressure: Gaze control, decision making and shooting performance of elite and rookie police officers', *Human Movement Science*, 31: 101–17.

Vickers, J. N., & Williams, A. M. (2007) 'Performing under pressure: The interactive effects of physiological arousal, cognitive anxiety and gaze control in elite biathlon shooters', *Journal of Motor Behavior*, 39: 381–94.

Vine, S. J., Lee, D., Moore, L. J., & Wilson, M. R. (2013) 'Quiet eye and choking: Online control breaks down at the point of performance failure', *Medicine & Science in Sports & Exercise*, 45: 1988–94.

Vine, S. J., Moore, L. J., & Wilson, M. (2011) 'Quiet eye training facilitates competitive putting performance in elite golfers', *Frontiers in Psychology*, 2: 8. doi: 10.3389/Fpsyg. 2011.00008

Vine, S. J., Moore, L. J., & Wilson, M. R. (2014) 'Quiet eye training: The acquisition, refinement and resilient performance of targeting skills', *European Journal of Sports Sciences*, 14(S1): S235–S242.

Vine, S. J., & Wilson, M. R. (2010) 'Quiet eye training: Effects on learning and performance under pressure', *Journal Of Applied Sport Psychology*, 22: 361–76.

Vine, S. J., & Wilson, M. R. (2011) 'The influence of quiet eye training and pressure on attention and visuomotor control', *Acta Psychologica*, 136: 340–6.

Williams, A. M., Singer, R. N., & Frehlich, S. G. (2002) 'Quiet eye duration, expertise, and task complexity in near and far aiming tasks', *Journal of Motor Behavior*, 34: 197–207.

Wilson, M. R. (2012) 'Anxiety: Attention, the brain, the body and performance', in S. Murphy (ed) *Handbook on sport and performance psychology*, New York: Oxford University Press, 173–90.

Wilson, M. R., McGrath, J., Vine, S. J., Brewer, J., Defriend, D., & Masters, R.S.W. (2011) 'Perceptual impairment and visuomotor control in virtual laparoscopic surgery', *Surgical Endoscopy*, 25: 2268–74.

Wilson, M. R., Miles, C. A., Vine, S. J., & Vickers, J. N. (2013) 'Quiet eye distinguishes children of high and low motor coordination abilities', *Medicine & Science in Sports & Exercise*, 45: 1144–51.

Wilson, M. R., & Richards, H. (2011) 'Putting it together: Skills for pressure performance', in D. Collins, A. Button, & H. Richards (eds) *Performance psychology*, Edinburgh, UK: Elsevier, 337–60.

Wilson, M. R., Vine, S. J., & Wood, G. (2009) 'The influence of anxiety on visual attentional control in basketball free-throw shooting', *Journal of Sport & Exercise Psychology*, 31: 152–68.

Wood, G., & Wilson, M. R. (2010) 'A moving goalkeeper distracts penalty takers and impairs shooting accuracy', *Journal of Sports Sciences*, 28: 937–46.

Wood, G., & Wilson, M. R. (2011) 'Quiet-eye training for soccer penalty kicks', *Cognitive Processing*, 12: 257–66.

Wood, G., & Wilson, M. R. (2012) 'Quiet-eye training, perceived control and performing under pressure', *Psychology of Sport and Exercise*, 13: 721–8.

4

ON ATTENTIONAL CONTROL

A dimensional framework for attention in expert performance

Keith R. Lohse

Introduction

A good mantra when discussing attention is to say, "it's a bit more complicated than that." This short and unsatisfying phrase is usually not wrong, but begs the question of what complexity we add and how that improves our understanding. This is a major issue when it comes to attentional control and expert performance. In this chapter, I present a framework for exploring the multidimensional nature of attention in sport expertise. The major goal of this framework is to integrate binary distinctions that are often discussed in the literature to view attention as a multifaceted construct where the "optimal" focus of attention is dynamic and context dependent. This framework is useful for understanding the different ways in which attention can be deployed before, during, and after the execution of complex skills and the differential effects that attention might have on learning versus performance. A few major principles can still be drawn (e.g., expert performance is impaired when attention is internally focused on the execution of a skill) and I review evidence for how attention might be affecting the motor system to ultimately shape behavior but, of course, it is going to be a bit more complicated than that.

To begin, human movement is composed of intentional and non-intentional processes. Neurophysiologically, the motor system is a complex interplay between implicit and explicit processes, from monosynaptic reflexes in the spinal cord at one level all the way up to complex volitional movements that unfold over time at another level (for a detailed review, see Kandel *et al.*, 1991). Furthermore, there are aspects of motor control that we are aware of, aspects that we are not aware of, and aspects we may gain awareness of after perceiving their effects (for a neuropsychological model, see Frith *et al.*, 2000). Human beings are normally quite unaware of many details of our own movements (Fourneret & Jeannerod, 1998). However, even when we are not explicitly aware of the errors or changes in our movements, we can implicitly modify these movements in order to maintain accurate performance (Goodale *et al.*, 1994). Although we may subsequently become aware of these implicitly guided corrections, humans often show signs of adjusting to perturbations well before explicit awareness of the perturbation (Castelio *et al.*, 1991; Knoblich & Kircher, 2004). Thus, many aspects of motor control normally lie outside of explicit awareness, and the nervous system seems quite able to detect errors, plan corrections, and adjust movements without top-down guidance in many situations. This level of implicit control is even more developed in experts, who have automatized complex skills through years of practice.

Implicit control has important implications when discussing attention for several reasons. First, we need to clearly delineate when we are talking about "overt" attention that is directly observable (e.g., gaze, head orientation) or "covert" attention, which is an inferred mental state (e.g., concentration, focus). Second, a major dimension within covert attention is whether attention should be associative (i.e., focusing on the execution of a skill) or dissociative (i.e., focusing on an irrelevant stimulus separate from execution). Overall, novices benefit from associative attention, but this skill-focused attention becomes a hindrance to experts, who have proceduralized these complex motor skills (Beilock & Carr, 2001; Gray, 2004). Third, covert attention can also be external (i.e., directed to the effects of a movement on the environment) or internal (i.e., directed to the motion of the body itself). Along this dimension, an external focus of attention is generally beneficial to expert and novice performance (see Marchant, 2010; Wulf, 2013). Both of these dimensions – associative/dissociative and external/internal – suggest that optimal performance depends on what is being attended to and the skill level of the performer. Thus, these theories suggest an interplay between implicit and explicit processing in motor control (see Hikosaka *et al.*, 2002; Willingham, 1998).

This review presents a multidimensional model of attention that will help researchers and practitioners explore the relationship between explicit and implicit motor control to improve learning and performance. I review four different dimensions that are often presented as dichotomies in research and studied independently: overt versus covert attention, associative versus dissociative attention, external versus internal attention, and the effects of attention on learning versus performance. These dimensions are often studied in isolation because it is important to keep other dimensions constant to truly understand the effects of manipulating any single dimension. However, when scaling research back to applied problems, it is important to consider how these different dimensions might interact with each other. There are relatively few experiments that have studied multiple dimensions simultaneously (see Castaneda & Gray, 2007; Neumann & Brown, 2013), and more research integrating these different dimensions with different skill levels and tasks is needed.

Overt versus covert attention

A major distinction in research on attention is between *overt attention*, which is directly observable by a researcher (such as gaze direction and dwell times in eye tracking; see Chapters 3 and 16), and *covert attention*, which is a psychological process inferred through experimental methods (such as the addition of secondary tasks to induce distraction, or specifically worded instructions to bias concentration to a particular aspect of the skill). Although this chapter deals primarily with covert attention, the importance of overt attention to performance should not be underestimated (see Land, 2009; Vine *et al.*, 2012). For instance, training skilled basketball players how to direct their visual attention during free-throw shooting not only improved performance in laboratory assessments, but led to lasting improvements in in-game performance compared to control groups (Harle & Vickers, 2001).

It is also important to note that overt and covert attention may not be completely independent. For instance, training to maintain overt attention can increase resilience to high-pressure transfer tests (Vine & Wilson, 2011), which may in part be due to how maintenance of overt attention prevents covert attention from being inwardly directed to skill execution (i.e., focusing on controlling your gaze prevents you from focusing on explicitly controlling your movements). Thus, manipulations of overt attention can have direct and indirect effects on performance; that is, ensuring the performer is focused on more goal-relevant information for a longer period of time could directly influence performance by allowing more useful or better quality sensory information to guide the action (see Land, 2009). Manipulations of overt attention could also have indirect effects on performance through covert attention. For instance, instructing learners to control their gaze rather than their mechanics may induce a more external focus of attention (for discussion, see Vine *et al.*, 2012; see also Chapter 3 in this volume).

In contrast, some researchers have controlled for overt attention during execution while manipulating covert attention. For instance, even when vision is occluded, an external focus of attention facilitates performance in a manual tracking task (Schlesinger *et al.*, 2012) and dart throwing (Sherwood *et al.*, 2014). Participants in those experiments perform better with vision than without vision, but the relative benefit of an external focus over an internal focus remains, regardless of vision. These results provide strong evidence that the benefits of an external focus of attention are not completely explained by vision. However, these data do not preclude the possibility that attentional focus instructions may have an indirect effect on vision in a normal setting when subjects have vision of the target and their own actions during execution. Thus, external focus instructions are still beneficial in the absence of vision, but when vision is present it is not clear how covert attentional states may indirectly affect overt attention.

Associative versus dissociative foci

Another dimension of attentional control has to do with *what* a performer is focusing on and, specifically, is that focus something about the execution of the skill or something unrelated to the skill? For the purposes of this chapter, we will talk about an ***associative focus***, which is a focus on something related to the execution of the skill, and a ***dissociative focus***, which is a focus on something unrelated to the execution of the skill. These labels, associative and dissociative, roughly correspond to two different areas of research. The first area of research deals with how these attentional foci affect skilled motor performance (e.g., Beilock & Carr, 2001; Beilock & Gray, 2012). The second area of research deals with how the attentional foci affect perceptions of fatigue or physiological responses to exercise (e.g., Baden *et al.*, 2005; Russell & Weeks, 1994; Tenenbaum & Connolly, 2008). Although this second area of research is definitely related to attentional control and human performance, reviewing these data are beyond the scope of this chapter. Rather than discussing these affective data (see Ekkekakis, 2003; Lind *et al.*, 2009), my review will deal with the effects of attention on experts' control of movements.

The question of whether attention should be associative or dissociative relates to implicit and explicit levels of motor control. Directing attention to the execution of the task itself can be beneficial for learning a new task, and many models of motor learning posit that novices need to progress from a stage of highly controlled processing to a stage in which complex motor skills can be executed with little explicit attention (Fitts & Posner, 1967; Willingham, 1998). At the expert stage, an associative focus of attention can actually be detrimental to performance (Beilock & Carr, 2001). It is strange to think that "paying attention" to what you are doing can actually make you worse, but across a range of athletic tasks, novice performance suffers under a dissociative focus (Jackson *et al.*, 2006; Leavitt, 1979; Smith & Chamberlin, 1992), whereas expert performance suffers under an associative focus (Beilock *et al.*, 2004; Beilock *et al.*, 2002; Gray, 2004).

Although novices benefit from an associative focus on the step-by-step execution of motor skills, experts have a very different level of control and can execute a more complex skill as a continuous "unit" or motor program. An expert volleyball player, for example, might have a well-developed motor program for "hitting a powerful serve." The expert can focus on hitting the serve at this relatively abstract level during movement execution without explicitly attending to the details of the movement. For a novice, "hitting a powerful serve" is computationally meaningless because he/she cannot represent the motor skill at that level of cognition (Schack, 2004;

Schack & Mechsner, 2006). As a result, when experts adopt an associative focus on the step-by-step execution of a skill, they may "deproceduralize" that skill by invoking a more explicit mode of control that leads to worse performance.

For instance, Gray (2004; see also Chapter 7) used a baseball simulation to study the relationship between performance and explicit awareness of movement quality in skilled baseball players. Batting performance was defined by the number of successful hits in the simulator and explicit awareness was measured by having participants make judgments about the direction of the bat when a tone was presented during the swing (associative focus) or make judgments about the frequency of the tone itself (dissociative focus). For the dissociative condition, novices' performance was negatively affected by the secondary task of judging the tone, whereas experts were not significantly affected. For the associative condition, however, experts performed worse and showed increased movement variability when judging the motion of the bat during the swing. Movement variability in this case was a measurement of swing duration ratios (i.e., time spent in the wind up, pre-swing, swing phase, and follow through), suggesting that when experts were directing their attention to the swing itself, there was a breakdown in the temporal coupling of this highly practiced skill. In a follow-up experiment using expert batters (Gray, 2004; Experiment 2) there was also a significant positive relationship between errors in batting performance and accuracy in the associative task, suggesting that when experts were more aware of the details of their motions, their batting performance was worse compared to when they were less aware.

Similarly, Beilock and colleagues (2002) used a dual-task paradigm to explore the effects of associative and dissociative attention in golf putting (Experiment 1) and in dribbling a football with the dominant and non-dominant foot (Experiment 2). In both cases, skilled athletes performed better with a dissociative secondary task than with an associative secondary task. Interestingly, in Experiment 2, there was a change in the pattern of results when athletes were required to use their non-dominant leg. For the dominant leg, the typical result was replicated such that novices benefited from an associative secondary task, whereas experts benefited from a dissociative secondary task. For the non-dominant leg, however, both novices and experts performed better with an associative secondary task than with a dissociative secondary task. Both groups performed better with an associative focus for the non-dominant leg because, presumably, experts have less detailed motor representation for that leg (more akin to the representations of novices).

More recently, Beilock and Gray (2012) looked at the effects of associative and dissociative secondary tasks in a golf putting study and measured how the different foci affected accuracy and kinematics in novice and expert golfers. For experts, accuracy was poorest under the associative secondary task (compared to the dissociative secondary task) and when probes were presented during the backswing (compared to the downswing). Interestingly, this shift in attention also affected amplitude of the downswing. Normally, the amplitude of the downswing scales to the distance of the putt, and this positive relationship was found for experts in the dissociative condition. In the associative condition, however, the magnitude of this relationship was significantly reduced. It is important to note that experts typically have better regulation of downswing amplitude than do novices (Delay *et al.*, 1997); thus, inducing an associative focus reduced experts to a more "novice-like" movement and level of performance.

This experimental work is consistent with research showing that experts and novices have very different mental representations of complex skills (Schack & Mechsner, 2006) and skilled performance at later stages of learning relies on different neural networks than performance in the early stages of learning (Willingham, 1998). In sum, these data suggest that the highly integrated knowledge structures of experts allow them to control skilled movements at a relatively high level of representation, and when attention is directed to a lower level of control than what experts normally operate under, this can have detrimental effects on performance.

External versus internal foci

Another dimension of attentional control is not what a performer is focusing on, but *how* a performer is focusing. Along this dimension, attention can roughly be categorized as ***external***, on the effects of a movement on the environment, or ***internal***, on the motion of the body itself. I argue that the internal-external dimension is orthogonal to the associative-dissociative dimension (see Figure 4.1). As such, attentional focus could be external and associative (e.g., focusing on the trajectory of the ball during a football free kick) or external and dissociative (e.g., focusing on the sound of the crowd during a free kick). Similarly, attentional focus could be internal and associative (e.g., focusing on the position of the plant leg during a free kick) or internal and dissociative (e.g., focusing on your breathing during a free kick). I begin by reviewing recent studies of internally versus externally focused attention and then discuss the few studies that have experimentally crossed internal-external and associative-dissociative conditions.

A large number of studies have explored different types of internally and externally focused attention compared to each other or to a control condition across a wide range of participant populations (for a detailed review, see Wulf, 2013). Many of these studies have explored internal-external focus effects in novices and generally found that novices benefit from an external focus of attention. A number of studies have recently explored internal-external focus effects in skilled performers and these studies are reviewed below. In general, there is experimental evidence to suggest that experts and novices benefit from an external focus (see Wulf, 2013), but experts benefit from a more distal focus than novices (Bell & Hardy, 2009; Perkins-Ceccato et al., 2003; Wulf et al., 2000; Wulf & Su, 2007).

With respect to sport performance, a number of recent studies have explored the effects of externally focused attention in skilled or expert athletes. Expert and novice sprinters, for instance, had faster response times out of the blocks and faster run times overall when focused externally, compared to internal focus and control conditions (Ille et al., 2013). Similarly, Stoate and Wulf (2011) found that swim times in the front crawl for elite swimmers were faster in the external and control conditions than in an internal focus condition. This result suggests that elite athletes might be more inclined to endogenously adopt an external focus of attention, but questionnaire results also showed swimmers who adopted an internal focus in the control condition were significantly slower than swimmers who adopted an external focus. Thus, whether focus was imposed

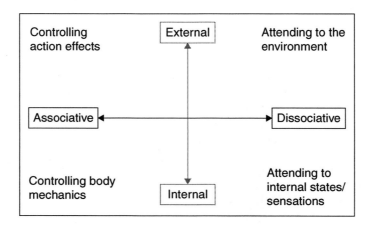

Figure 4.1 A schematic representation of two major dimensions of attentional control: the associative-dissociative dimension and the external-internal dimension.

externally through instructions (as in the external and internal focus conditions) or endogenously (as in external/internal focus in the control condition), an external focus of attention was associated with faster swimming speeds.

An external focus improves performance in complex tasks such as sprinting or swimming, and there are data to suggest that an external focus enhances the efficiency of sustained performance as well. Schücker, Hagemann, Strauss, and Völker (2009) instructed trained runners to focus their attention on three different aspects of a task while running on a treadmill at 75 per cent of VO_{2max} intensity for 10 minutes. Runners concentrated on their form (internal-associative), on their breathing (internal-dissociative), and on the virtual environment (arguably external-dissociative). Results showed an increased running economy in the external focus condition. This effect was replicated in a recent study (Schücker *et al.*, 2013) that measured oxygen consumption (VO_2), heart rate, blood lactate, and Ratings of Perceived Exertion (RPE) while running at 85 per cent of VO_{2max} intensity. A dissociative-external focus of attention led to the lowest VO_2 while sustaining this high pace.

The benefits of externally focused attention have also been shown for rapid, powerful movements in addition to prolonged, sustained efforts. Skilled shot putters, for instance, have been shown to throw greater distances when adopting an external-associative focus compared to an internal-associative focus or a neutral control condition (Makaruk *et al.*, 2013). Other results suggest that externally focused instructions are an effective means for improving performance in explosive tasks that require rapid force production such as the vertical jump (Wulf *et al.*, 2010), the standing long jump (Porter *et al.*, 2010), or the sprint start (Ille *et al.*, 2013).

A partial explanation for improved performance in these rapid movements that require high levels of force production comes from a separate body of research showing that inter-muscular coordination appears to be disrupted by an internal focus. During isokinetic elbow flexion, for example, an external focus of attention led to reduced EMG activity in the biceps brachii (Greig & Marchant, 2014). In isometric plantar flexion, an internal focus of attention led to greater coactivation of the soleus (agonist) and tibialis anterior (antagonist) at 30 per cent, 60 per cent, and 100 per cent of maximum voluntary contraction that had to be maintained for four seconds (Lohse & Sherwood, 2012). In the dynamic task of the vertical jump, Wulf, Dufek, Lozano, and Pettigrew (2010) found that surface EMG activity was generally lower in the external focus condition for numerous lower extremity muscles even as jump height increased, suggesting more efficient vertical jump mechanics.

Neumann and Brown (2013) conducted a similar experiment using surface EMG to study muscle activation during a sit-up. Participants performed sit-ups in four conditions: an external-associative condition, an external-dissociative condition, an internal-associative condition, and an internal-dissociative condition. Internal-associative (on the abdominal muscles) and external-associative instructions (on "smooth" movement) were provided by a prerecorded script in an audio-visual recording. The external-dissociative condition required participants to watch part of a netball match, whereas the internal-dissociative condition required participants to do mental arithmetic, guided by the audio-visual stimuli. The external-associative condition led to the lowest EMG activity in the rectus abdominus, the lowest heart rate, and the greatest range of motion (the pace of the sit-ups was set to a metronome).

Another study that has crossed associative-dissociative and internal-external conditions is a study by Castaneda and Gray (2007). In that study, using a baseball batting simulation, batting performance was examined as a function of an internal-associative focus (on the movement of the hands), an external-associative focus (on the movement of the bat), and two dissociative foci – on irrelevant auditory tones and on the ball leaving the bat. Although irrelevant auditory tones are unequivocally an external-dissociative focus, the ball leaving the bat is arguably an external-associative focus (similar to the movement of the bat during the pitch). Skilled batters performed best when focusing on the ball leaving the bat and worst when focused on the movement of their hands during the swing. (Less-skilled batters generally benefited from associative compared to dissociative foci.) A similar pattern of results was found for skilled and unskilled footballers dribbling with their dominant and non-dominant foot (Ford, Hodges, & Williams, 2005). In that experiment, an internal focus on a relevant effector (foot; internal-associative) or irrelevant effector (arm; internal-dissociative) disrupted expert performance with the dominant foot compared to a control condition and an external-dissociative task, but no significant differences were found when skilled players used their non-dominant foot.

Learning versus performance and the time course of attention

Previous discussions of attentional control have debated the appropriate focus of attention for learning a skill versus performing a skill. Novices benefit from associative attentional foci rather than dissociative, which makes sense because novices lack robust procedural representations of a motor skill and must rely on more cognitive, working memory-based control. Within associative foci, there is considerable evidence suggesting novices' performance and learning benefit from external focus instructions (see Wulf, 2013). However, Lohse, Sherwood, and Healy (2014) trained participants for three days under internal-associative or external-associative instructions in a dart-throwing task. On subsequent retention and transfer tests, subjects received either the same instructions or the opposite instructions, creating four groups: external-external (EE), external-internal (EI), internal-external (IE), and internal-internal (II). There was some evidence that the focus of attention during training had a significant effect at test, but the largest benefits of an external focus of attention were for performance. Thus, attentional focus instructions during training had almost no effect on testing performance compared to instructions received during testing. Thus, EE and IE groups were generally more accurate than II and EI groups, suggesting that although attentional focus may affect learning, it has its largest effects on performance.

This study raises questions about the temporal/dynamic nature of the optimal focus of attention, shown abstractly in Figure 4.2. In the discussion below, we want to consider different types of attentional foci for learning versus performance (Figure 4.2A) and consider the time course of executing a motor skill (preparation, execution, and evaluation; Figure 4.2B) for expert athletes. Most experimental work on attention, whether it explores learning or performance, has

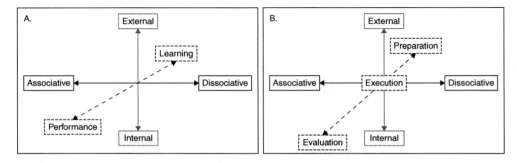

Figure 4.2 Schematics illustrating how different dimensions of attention may have different effects, depending on the goal of the task (e.g., optimizing learning or optimizing immediate performance; A) or the time course of the action (e.g., preparation for the action, execution of the action, or evaluation of the action after the fact; B).

been based on attentional focus manipulations that affect execution. Comparatively little work has been done on the preparatory or evaluative phases that are also part of expert performance.

This learning-performance distinction is important for experts because, although there is a surfeit of experimental studies examining expert performance, very few studies have experimentally explored how experts continue to learn/refine skills after they have reached a high level of performance. (Experimental learning studies are usually conducted with novel tasks and novice participants for the sake of experimental control; see Williams & Ericsson, 2008.) There are exceptions (Hodges & Franks, 2002; Zanone & Kelso, 1997), but most experimental work has studied the acquisition of new skills in novices, not the refinement of existing skills in experts, and it is not clear if these principles generalize. However, recent translational work (Button & Farrow, 2012; Williams *et al.*, 2012) does provide evidence (through case studies) about how motor learning interventions might be designed to refine/change motor skills in experts.

Williams *et al.* (2012) presented two case studies that were conducted in the United Kingdom: one with elite archers and one with Olympic shooters (from various shooting disciplines). The archery intervention required these well-trained athletes to adopt a new, more efficient pattern of drawing a bow that would lead to more precise results. In order to break the archers' entrenched movement patterns, coaches and skill acquisition specialists designed an intervention that would take advantage of several different motor learning principles: (1) fading the use of video feedback to reduce dependence on feedback (Winstein & Schmidt, 1990), (2) manipulating difficulty to create challenge points during learning (Guadagnoli & Lee, 2004), and (3) reducing verbal instruction with the use of task constraints to prevent athletes from focusing internally on their own mechanics during execution (Masters & Maxwell, 2008; Wulf, 2013).

At first, the use of video feedback after early trials to adjust one's mechanics seems to contradict the final point about preventing athletes from focusing on their mechanics (i.e., watching and evaluating your own movement patterns seems inescapably "internal"). However, if we adopt a dynamic and dimensional view of attention this contradiction is resolved. Video feedback after a trial promotes an internal-associative focus during movement evaluation, but critically it also allows experts to compare internal feedback about their form to a visual reference. Reduced verbal instruction and the use of task constraints during execution then promotes an external-associative focus, which allows for greater implicit control of the movement.

A similar issue is raised in the case study with Olympic shooters. The goal of that intervention was to expedite the onset of a quiet eye period and increase the quiet eye duration. In order to change gaze behavior in these experts, video feedback was used to allow the athletes to see their gaze patterns on successful versus unsuccessful shots. A four stage pre-shot routine was also developed, instructing athletes to (1) stand at attention with detailed instructions about rifle placement, head angle, and starting gaze position; (2) call for the targets when fully prepared; (3) direct focus to the first target, continually track the target, and make sure the target is in visual focus before shooting; and (4) use a stable and consistent gun motion, keeping a constant velocity.

As with the archery example, there seem to be contradictions in how attention should be directed while shooting, but these contradictions are resolved by adopting a dynamic view of attention. In the preparation stage, attention is first directed internally to aspects of stance and head position to make sure the starting position is reliable. As the shooter moves into the execution stage, attention is directed externally to visually tracking the target and the smooth motion of the gun. Finally, in the post-trial evaluation phase, attention is directed internally to how the shooters' eyes were moving during execution, but the use of this post-trial feedback decreases with practice.

These initial data are informative, but must be treated with caution, as there was no random assignment or appropriate control groups. Future experimental research with experts is needed in order to understand the dynamic nature of attention with any certainty. That said, case studies with experts and experimental work with both experts and novices suggest that adopting an external-associative focus of attention during execution is important for achieving optimal performance. (In both of the presented case studies, these interventions led to large enough improvements to be meaningful in competition.) Skill acquisition specialists and coaches should minimize internal cues and manipulate task constraints (when possible) to promote an external focus during execution. Conversely, the use of post-trial video feedback and an internal-associative focus in the evaluation stage might be beneficial for refining the movements of experts, but this feedback should be used in early trials and the use of feedback should decrease with practice to prevent athletes from becoming dependent on the presence of feedback.

Conclusions

Attention is a difficult concept to grapple with. A lot of high-quality experimental studies have given us insights, but also left us with a lot of questions. I think that it is useful to adopt a multidimensional approach to thinking about attention in sport expertise. We can look at slices of this multidimensional space to try and understand how different attentional variables might interact with each other to improve performance or to improve learning. Considerable experimental work needs to be done, but a few major findings seem well supported:

1 Experts are negatively affected by an associative-internal focus. Thus, coaches should use external cues to promote the appropriate attentional focus during practice, which will then be reinvested under pressure in competition (see Gray, 2011 for more on attention and arousal).
2 Across a range of tasks, an external focus of attention leads to more *effective* movements (e.g., increased accuracy, greater displacements, greater velocities), but also to more *efficient* movements (e.g., reduced oxygen consumption, reduced muscle activation during movement).
3 Studies on performance show experts are impaired by an internal-associative focus during movement execution. It is less clear how attention should be directed during preparation and evaluation stages to optimize learning. More research needs to be done in these areas.

Execution might be particularly sensitive to an associative-internal focus because explicitly monitoring the details of movement interferes with control processes that are normally implicit (Snyder & Logan, 2012), thus disrupting the coordination of complex movements (Kal *et al.*, 2013; Lohse *et al.*, 2014). In order to understand the dynamic nature of attentional control in experts, we need more experimental work that explores long-term learning. Such work will also need to be specific to when and how attention is directed during practice (e.g., the preparation, execution, or evaluation stages I suggest here). Ultimately, I think that this multidimensional framework is helpful for studying and understanding attention, but (I would readily concede) the reality is probably more complicated than that.

References

Baden, D. A., McLean, T. L., Tucker, R., Noakes, T. D., & St. Clair Gibson, A. (2005) 'Effect of anticipation during unknown or unexpected exercise duration on rating of perceived exertion, affect, and physiological function', *British Journal of Sports Medicine*, 39: 742–6.

Beilock, S. L., Bertenthal, B. I., McCoy, A. M., & Carr, T. H. (2004) 'Haste does not always make waste: Expertise, direction of attention, and speed versus accuracy in performing sensorimotor skills', *Psychonomic Bulletin & Review*, 11: 373–9.

On attentional control

Beilock, S. L., & Carr, T. H. (2001) 'On the fragility of skilled performance: What governs choking under pressure?', *Journal of Experimental Psychology: General*, 130: 701–25.

Beilock, S. L., Carr, T. H., MacMahon, C., & Starkes, J. L. (2002) 'When paying attention becomes counter-productive: Impact of divided versus skill-focused attention on novice and experienced performance of sensorimotor skills', *Journal of Experimental Psychology: Applied*, 8: 6–16.

Beilock, S. L., & Gray, R. (2012) 'From attentional control to attentional spillover: A skill-level investigation of attention movement, and performance outcomes', *Human Movement Science*, 31: 1473–99.

Bell, J. J., & Hardy, J. (2009) 'Effects of attentional focus on skilled performance in golf', *Journal of Applied Sport Psychology*, 21: 163–77.

Button, C., & Farrow, D. (2012) 'Working in the field (Southern Hemisphere)', in N. J. Hodges and A. M. Williams (eds) *Skill acquisition in sport: Research, theory, and practice*, New York: Routledge, 367–80.

Castaneda, B., & Gray, R. (2007) 'Effects of focus of attention on baseball batting performance in players of differing skill levels', *Journal of Sport & Exercise Psychology*, 29: 60–77.

Castelio, U., Paulignan, Y., & Jeannerod, M. (1991) 'Temporal dissociation of motor responses and subjective awareness: A study in normal subjects', *Brain*, 114: 2639–55.

Delay, D., Nougier, V., Orliaguet, J. P., & Coello, Y. (1997) 'Guiding the swing in golf putting', *Nature*, 405: 295–6.

Ekkekakis, P. (2003) 'Pleasure and displeasure from the body: Perspectives from exercise', *Cognition and Emotion*, 17: 213–39.

Fitts, P. M., & Posner, M. I. (1967) *Human Performance*, Belmont, CA: Brooks/Cole.

Ford, P., Hodges, N. J., & Williams, A. M. (2005) 'Online attentional-focus manipulations in a soccer-dribbling task: Implications for the proceduralization of motor skills', *Journal of Motor Behaviour*, 37: 386–94.

Fourneret, P., & Jeannerod, M. (1998) 'Limited conscious monitoring of motor performance in normal subjects', *Neuropsychologia*, 36: 1133–40.

Frith, C. D., Blakemore, S. J., & Wolpert, D. M. (2000) 'Abnormalities in the awareness and control of action', *Philosophical Transactions of the Royal Society B*, 355: 1771–88.

Goodale, M. A., Jakobson, L. S., Milner, A. D., Perrett, D. I., Benson, P. J., & Hietanen, J. K. (1994) 'The nature and limits of orientation and pattern processing visuomotor control in a visual form agnosic', *Journal of Cognitive Neuroscience*, 6: 46–56.

Gray, R. (2004) 'Attending to the execution of a complex sensorimotor skill: Expertise differences, choking, and slumps', *Journal of Experimental Psychology: Applied*, 10: 42–54.

Gray, R. (2011) 'Links between attention, performance pressure, and movement in skilled motor action', *Current Directions in Psychological Science*, 20: 301–6.

Greig, M., & Marchant, D. (2014). Speed dependant influence of attentional focusing instructions on force production and muscular activity during isokinetic elbow flexions. *Human Movement Science*, 33: 135–148. doi:10.1016/j.humov.2013.08.008.

Guadagnoli, M. A., & Lee, T. D. (2004) 'Challenge point: A framework for conceptualizing the effects of various practice conditions in motor learning', *Journal of Motor Behavior*, 36: 212–24.

Harle, S., & Vickers, J. N. (2001) 'Training quiet eye improves accuracy in the basketball free throw', *The Sport Psychologist*, 15: 289–305.

Hikosaka, O., Nakamura, K., Sakai, K., & Nakahara, H. (2002) 'Central mechanisms of motor skill learning', *Current Opinion Neurobiology*, 12: 217–22.

Hodges, N. J., & Franks, I. M. (2002) 'Learning as a function of coordination bias: Building upon pre-practice behaviours', *Human Movement Science*, 21: 231–58.

Ille, A., Selin, I., Do, M. C., & Thon, B. (2013) 'Attentional focus effects on sprint start performance as a function of skill level', *Journal of Sports Sciences*, 31: 1705–12.

Jackson, R. C., Ashford, K., & Norsworthy, G. (2006) 'Attentional focus, dispositional reinvestment, and skilled motor performance under pressure', *Journal of Sport & Exercise Psychology*, 28: 49–68.

Kal, E. C., van der Kamp, J., & Houdijk, H. (2013) 'External attentional focus enhances movement automatization: A comprehensive test of the constrained action hypothesis', *Human Movement Science*, 32: 527–39.

Kandel, E. R., Schwartz, J. H., & Jessell, T. (1991) *Principles of neural science*, East Norwalk, CT: Appleton & Lange.

Knoblich, G., & Kircher, T. T. J. (2004) 'Deceiving oneself about being in control: Conscious detection of changes in visuomotor coupling', *Journal of Experimental Psychology: Human Perception and Performance*, 30: 657–66.

Land, M. F. (2009) 'Vision, eye movements, and natural behavior', *Visual Neuroscience*, 26: 51–62.

Leavitt, J. L. (1979) 'Cognitive demands of skating and stickhandling in ice hockey', *Canadian Journal of Applied Sport Science*, 4: 46–55.

Lind, E., Welch, A. S., & Ekkekakis, P. (2009) 'Do "mind over muscle" strategies work?', *Sports Medicine*, 39: 743–64.

Lohse, K. R., Jones, M. C., Healy, A. F., & Sherwood, D. E. (2013) 'The role of attention in motor control', *Journal of Experimental Psychology: General*. doi: 10.1037/a0032817.

Lohse, K. R., & Sherwood, D. E. (2012) 'Thinking about muscles: The neuromuscular effects of internally focused attention in accuracy and fatigue', *Acta Psychologica*, 140: 236–45.

Lohse, K.R., Jones, M.C., Healy, A.F. & Sherwood, D.E. (2014). The role of attention in motor control. *Journal of Experimental Psychology: General, 143*, 930–948. doi: 10.1037/a0032817.

Makaruk, H., Porter, J. M., & Makaruk, B. (2013) 'Acute effects of attentional focus on shot put performance in elite athletes', *Kinesiology*, 45: 55–62.

Marchant, D. C. (2010) 'Attentional focus instructions and force production', *Frontiers in Psychology*, 1: 210.

Masters, R., & Maxwell, J. (2008) 'The theory of reinvestment', *International Review of Sport and Exercise Psychology*, 1: 160–83.

Neumann, D. L., & Brown, J. (2013) 'The effect of attentional focus strategy on physiological and motor performance during a sit-up exercise', *Journal of Psychophysiology*, 27: 7–15.

Perkins-Ceccato, N., Passmore, S. R., & Lee, T. D. (2003) 'Effects of focus of attention depend on golfer's skills', *Journal of Sports Sciences*, 21: 593–600.

Porter, J. M., Ostrowski, E. J., Nolan, R. P., & Wu, W.F.W. (2010) 'Standing-long jump performance is enhanced when using an external focus of attention', *Journal of Strength and Conditioning Research*, 24: 1746–50.

Russell, W. D., & Weeks, D. L. (1994) 'Attentional style in ratings of perceived exertion during physiological exercise', *Perceptual Motor Skills*, 78: 779–83.

Schack, T. (2004) 'The cognitive architecture of complex movement', *International Journal of Sport and Exercise Psychology*, 2: 403–38.

Schack, T., & Mechsner, F. (2006) 'Representation of motor skills in human long-term memory', *Neuroscience Letters*, 391: 77–81.

Schlesinger, M., Porter, J.M., & Russell, R. (2012) 'An external focus of attention enhances manual tracking of occluded and visible targets', *Frontiers in Psychology*, 3: 591.

Schücker, L., Anheier, W., Hagemann, N., Strauss, B., & Völker, K. (2013) 'On the optimal focus of attention for efficient running at high intensity', *Sport, Exercise, and Performance Psychology*, 2: 207–19.

Schücker, L., Hagemann, N., Strauss, B., & Völker, K. (2009) 'The effect of attentional focus on running economy', *Journal of Sports Sciences*, 27: 1241–8.

Sherwood, D.E., Lohse, K.R., & Healy, A.F. (2014). Judging joint angles and movement outcome: Shifting the focus of attention in dart-throwing. Journal of Experimental Psychology: *Human Perception and Performance, 40*, 1903–1914. doi: 10.1037/a0037189.

Smith, M. D., & Chamberlin, C. J. (1992) 'The effects of adding cognitively demanding tasks on soccer skill performance', *Perceptual and Motor Skills*, 75: 955–61.

Snyder, K. M., & Logan, G. D. (2012) 'Monitoring-induced disruption in skilled typewriting', *Journal of Experimental Psychology: Human Perception and Performance*, 39: 1409–20.

Stoate, I., & Wulf, G. (2011) 'Does the attentional focus adopted by swimmers affect their performance?', *International Journal of Sports Science and Coaching*, 6: 99–108.

Tenenbaum, G., & Connolly, C. T. (2008) 'Attention allocation under varied workload and effort perception in rowers', *Psychology of Sport and Exercise*, 9: 704–17.

Vine, S. J., Moore, L. J., & Wilson, M. R. (2012) 'Quiet eye-training: The acquisition, refinement and resilient performance of targeting skills', *European Journal of Sport Science*, iFirst Article: 1–8.

Vine, S. J., & Wilson, M. R. (2011) 'The influence of quiet eye training and pressure on attention and visuo-motor control', *Acta Psychologica*, 136: 340–6.

Williams, A. M., & Ericsson, A. K. (2008) 'From the guest editors: How do experts learn?', *Journal of Sport & Exercise Psychology*, 30: 653–62.

Williams, A. M., Ford, P., Causer, J., Logan, O., & Murray, S. (2012) 'Working at the "coal face" in the UK', in N. J. Hodges & A. M. Williams (eds) *Skill acquisition in sport: Research, theory, and practice*, New York: Routledge, 367–80.

Willingham, D. B. (1998) 'A neuropsychological theory of motor skill learning', *Psychological Review*, 105: 558–84.

Winstein, C. J., & Schmidt, R. A. (1990) 'Reduced frequency of knowledge of results enhances motor skill learning', *Journal of Experimental Psychology: Learning, Memory, and Cognition*, 16: 677–91.

Wulf, G. (2013) 'Attentional focus and motor learning: A review of 15 years', *International Review of Sport and Exercise Psychology*, 6: 77–104.

Wulf, G., Dufek, J. S., Lozano, L., & Pettigrew, C. (2010) 'Increased jump height and reduced EMG activity with an external focus', *Human Movement Science*, 29: 440–8.

Wulf, G., McNevin, N. H., Fuchs, T., Ritter, F., & Toole, T. (2000) 'Attentional focus in complex skill learning', *Research Quarterly for Exercise and Sport*, 71: 229–39.

Wulf, G., & Su, J. (2007) 'External focus of attention enhances golf shot accuracy in beginners and experts', *Research Quarterly for Exercise and Sport*, 78: 384–9.

Zanone, P. G., & Kelso, J. A.S. (1997) 'Coordination dynamics of learning and transfer: Collective and component levels', *Journal of Experimental Psychology: Human Perception and Performance*, 23: 1454–80.

5

INFORMATION-MOVEMENT COUPLING AS A HALLMARK OF SPORT EXPERTISE

John van der Kamp and Ian Renshaw

Introduction

Dexterity in interceptive actions is a necessary factor for achieving success in many sports; think of soccer and handball goalkeeping, returning balls in tennis, badminton and squash, or baseball and cricket batting. Here, excelling requires sport players to coordinate their action with the oncoming ball with an extraordinary degree of accuracy; only then are they able to intercept the ball at the right place and time. Perhaps remarkably, most research efforts have been directed at anticipating the outcomes of future events based upon information generated by an opponent's action before the ball gets underway (see Abernethy *et al.*, 2012) (see also Chapter 4). That is, researchers have presumed that waiting for information that arises from ball flight leaves insufficient time to execute the return action, even though ball flight provides the most reliable and accurate information for interception. Accordingly, many researchers have shown that expert sport players have superior anticipatory skills; that is, they are capable of using the comparatively less reliable and accurate information that arises prior to ball flight.

However, much of the evidence stems from laboratory paradigms that tend to overlook the role of movement control in anticipation. This research mainly focused on perceptual judgments regarding the general direction to which the player would have to move. For example, investigations using the occlusion paradigm, in which sport players are presented with video displays of the opponent's action that are terminated at various times during the unfolding of those actions, ask sport players to respond by making verbal or pen and paper judgments of the ball's landing location. Participants do not actually move to try to intercept a ball. Van der Kamp, Rivas, van Doorn, and Savelsbergh (2008) have argued that such laboratory studies are inherently limited in that they do not allow the expert sport players to take full advantage of the fast, online movement control supported by the dorsal vision for action system (see Milner & Goodale, 1995, 2008). Consequently, it is likely that participants' explicit judgments in the laboratory only involve the ventral vision for perception system, whereas in competitive situations on the court or on the pitch, interceptive actions are grounded in both perceptual judgment and movement control, commensurate with an interactive involvement of the two vision systems. Van der Kamp *et al.* (2008) therefore pleaded for the use of more representative experimental designs that necessitate participants to actually intercept balls. In fact, a recent meta-analysis confirms that experts' superiority is more evident in research when they actually perform sporting actions that include interceptions (Travassos *et al.*, 2013), once again indicating that movement control is a hallmark of expertise in interceptive actions. Additionally, performance analysis suggests that for some sports, movement control skills may be far more pertinent than anticipatory skills – and much more so than previously presumed. For example, Triolet, Benguigui, Le Runigo, and Williams (2013) counted the frequency of anticipatory behaviors in professional tennis. Anticipatory behaviors were defined as actions that were started before the opponent had contacted the ball. Surprisingly perhaps, at least relative to the volume of research addressing anticipatory skills, only a mere five to 15 per cent of the actions were anticipatory. The great majority of actions were initiated after the ball was hit, indicating that to get to the right place at the right time experts players can actually use information from ball flight – or at least the first part of its trajectory (see also Shim *et al.*, 2005). This emphasizes that researchers need to scrutinize the role of control (as it arguably capitalizes directly on information from ball flight) when they aim to understand expertise in interceptive actions. The current chapter provides an overview of this literature from the perspective of the ecological approach (Gibson, 1966, 1979). After introducing the ecological approach, we move onto discussing key research studies that have enhanced our understanding of perceptual learning, before concluding by discussing some of the practical implications and the need for future research using real world sporting tasks (see Chapter 15 for a consideration of methodological issues).

The ecological approach

The emergence of ecological psychology (Gibson, 1966, 1979) has provided movement scientists with opportunities to develop further understanding of the way that expertise in action, and movement control in particular, is developed (Davids *et al.*, 2012: Warren, 2006) (see also Chapter 12 for a theoretical overview). In the following sections we describe the concepts that underpin an ecological approach to movement control and learning.

Information and movement control

The developing focus of enhancing understanding of perception and action via natural tasks and activities owes much to the theoretical concepts of ecological psychology (Gibson, 1979; Chemero, 2009). Ecological psychologists see perception as being *direct* and emphasize the "organism-environment system" in perceiving and acting. In particular, ecological psychologists address the problem of how information acts to guide or constrain actions in certain environments. Biological movement systems are surrounded by huge arrays of energy (e.g., the optic array) that are lawfully structured by objects, events, and places of the environment. Consequently, the structured patterns of energy are specific to these objects, events, and places. The structured patterns inform about the environment. Accordingly, perceiving the environment is conceived as the pickup of this information and because the structured patterns are specific to the environment, there is no need for further processing of the information for perception to be truthful. It is in this sense that perception is direct. In order to pick up this information, Gibson (1979) attributed a significant role to the observer's movements. These movements co-structure the arrays of energy. Hence, the observer's orientation and displacements in the environment are specified in the structured patterns of energy, enabling the information-based control of movement. In essence, "perceiving and acting is a circularly casual process involving (a) forces giving rise to flows/forms/times, and (b) flows/forms/times constraining or giving rise to forces" (Turvey & Carello, 1986, p. 134). Acting within the environment causes changes to the patterns of energy that provide information about the dynamics of the "organism-environment" system. This is an important idea because it implies lawful relations between the kinematics of a movement and the structured patterns of energy. The structured patterns of energy (also known as *invariants*) can act as information for guiding a performer's actions (i.e., movement control). Ecological psychologists formalize this in a so-called law of control (see Warren, 1984):

$$M(t) = a + b * O(t),$$ (Eq. 1)

In this equation *M(t)* and *O(t)* stand for the controlled movement variables and the optic variable,[1] respectively. The constants *a* and *b* are parameters that reflect how movement and information variables are coupled. Let us explain this in a little more detail.

Many sports require athletes to adjust gait to achieve nested task constraints within the regulations of the game. In cricket, for example, the laws of the game stipulate that the bowler must have some part of his foot behind the front line, known as the popping crease, when delivering the ball. Coaches and bowlers have taken this to mean that the ideal, final front foot placement is one where the foot cuts the front line, enabling the ball to be delivered as close as possible to the batter, reducing the batter's response time. Failure to land with the heel behind the popping crease results in the delivery being declared illegal, or a "no-ball." Similarly, in long jumping, the athlete must position the foot on the board, while keeping maximum possible running speed. Many cricket coaches believe that bowlers' run-ups are stereotyped. This view is clearly seen when we observe bowlers measuring the run-up with tape measures, and moving their marker after bowling a no-ball. Athletes do something similar in preparation for their jump. However, extensive analyses of the gait adjustments and the information to regulate these adjustments in the run-up phase in long jumping and cricket bowling would put a question mark against these practices. For example, a behavioral study of the long jump run-up by Montagne, Cornus, Glize, Quaine, and Laurent (2000) (see also Lee *et al.*, 1982) found that stride length was continuously adjusted depending on the total amount of adjustment needed – particularly in the last few strides before takeoff. Warren, Young, and Lee (1986) showed how this can be done. Stride length can be increased by increasing step time. Warren *et al.* showed that two skilled runners increased step time by applying a larger vertical component of the impulse to the ground. By kicking off harder, the body is launched higher in the air, and step time increases. According to the authors, the change in vertical impulse is regulated by the optic variable called tau (i.e., $\tau(\varphi)$, Lee, 1976). Tau is the relative rate of change of the optical angle φ subtended by the target on the ground in the point of observation (i.e., the eye). When running with constant speed, tau specifies the time-to-contact with the target. The difference between the two time-to-contacts (i.e., $\Delta\tau(\varphi)$, or delta tau) for the next landing position of the foot and the ensuing landing position (e.g., the board) informs about the required stride time to step between the two targets. Warren *et al.* (1986) express this direct mapping of movement and optic variables in a law of control, which is equivalent to Eq. (1):

$$I_v = mg * \Delta\tau(\phi),$$ (Eq. 2)

Consequently, adjustments in the vertical impulse I_v (i.e., the regulated movement variable) are a function of the changes in the optic variable $\Delta\tau(\varphi)$ scaled by body mass *mg* (note that step time T is a function of vertical impulse I_v, body mass *m*, and the gravity constant *g*: $T = I_v / mg$).

Renshaw and Davids (2004) confirmed the continuous movement control for bowlers' run-ups in professional cricketers. Almost all of the run-ups were regulated, and these regulations were spread over the whole length of the run-ups, whereas in the long jump they were more restricted to the final steps before takeoff (de Rugy *et al.*, 2002). This demonstrates that stride

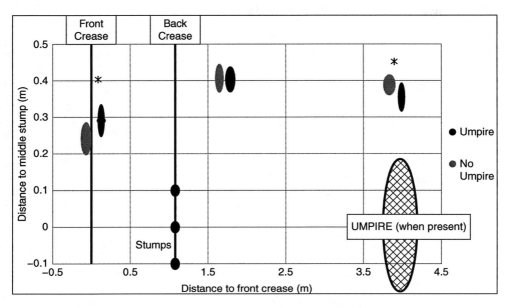

Figure 5.1 Visual representation of mean bound, back foot, and front foot landing positions in the umpire and no umpire conditions (*denotes significant differences at p < 0.01). When there was no umpire present, bound and front foot footfalls were relatively nearer to the batsman and resulted in more no-balls being bowled.

length adjustments are controlled by information in relation to the popping crease. In effect, our own work (Greenwood, 2014; Renshaw et al., 2003; Renshaw & Davids, 2007) showed that the presence of the umpire and stumps act as important information sources for bowlers to regulate their run-ups. Renshaw et al. (2003) had a professional fast bowler bowl under three different visual conditions: normal match conditions with the umpire present, stumps only, and crease markings only. While the bowler was able to achieve similar levels of variability at front-foot contact across conditions, the manipulation of information sources resulted in different patterns of footfall during the run-up and different mean distances of final footfall from the crease line. In essence, the landing position for the bound footfall was relatively nearer the crease line as information was removed. Hence, the umpire and/or stumps constitute necessary information sources for accurate footfall placement during the run-up. Further support for this was found in a study of the run-up in four elite developmental cricket fast bowlers (Greenwood, 2014). With these athletes, the umpire condition resulted in lower variability throughout the run-up, less need for visual regulation to adjust steps near the bowling crease, an increase in maximal running velocity, and fewer no-balls bowled (see Figure 5.1).

Learning: education of attention and calibration

Where does this leave us with learning? With respect to the law of control, ecological psychologists hold that learning either entails a change in the exploited movement or informational variables or a change in how they relate to each other. To start with the former, rather than regulating vertical impulse (i.e., I_V) to adjust step length and time, a less-skilled long jumper may modify running speed (i.e., change the distance the body travels within the same step time) by regulating horizontal impulse (i.e., I_H). Although this may be successful, it requires, as Warren et al. (1986) have argued, that the long jumper leans forward to avoid imbalances, resulting in an inefficient running pattern. To ameliorate, the long jumper should shift towards controlling or regulating vertical impulse (I_V) instead of the horizontal impulse (I_H). Accordingly, learning entails a change in the controlled movement variable. Analogously, more skilled movement control can also be achieved through a change in the information that is linked to movement. For example, a less-skilled long jumper may exploit an optic variable called looming (i.e., $\dot{\varphi}$ or the absolute rate of change of the optical angle φ), which co-varies with time but does not specify it. To advance, the long jumper must use a time-specifying variable, such as delta tau (i.e., $\Delta\tau(\varphi)$). Accordingly, learning is typified by a shift from using non-specifying to specifying information variables, a process which Gibson described as *education of attention* (Gibson, 1966; Michaels & Beek, 1995; van der Kamp *et al.*, 2003). Put differently, some informational variables are more useful for movement control than others. In this regard, specifying variables may be considered perfect variables, because they allow movement control to be robust (or adaptive) in many, or even all, situations. However, initially, when faced with a novel situation an athlete may rely on non-specifying variables to regulate the movement (Beek *et al.*, 2003). Non-specifying variables are less useful, because the movements can only be controlled satisfactorily in a restricted set of situations, if any (Withagen, 2004, Jacobs *et al.*, 2001). This goes together with action not always being accurate or sometimes going wrong. Hence, when learning, a player searches for the more useful informational variables (e.g., the umpire in cricket bowling), and expertise entails the convergence on the most useful, specifying variable for the task at hand. In the next section, we review the literature for the empirical support of these ideas for learning and expertise in interceptive actions. First, we elaborate a second process that underlies learning – *calibration*. Calibration refers to the scaling of the relation between the controlled movement variable and the informational variable that the player attends to (e.g., Cabe & Wagman, 2010; Withagen & Michaels, 2002, 2004; see also van der Kamp *et al.*, 2003). It establishes *how* (changes in) information impact the execution of movement (rather than *what* information impacts movement, as in the education of attention). In the law of control, calibration is represented by change in the constants (*a* and *b* in Eq. 1). In regulating stride length, calibration involves optimizing how changes in delta tau ($\Delta\tau(\varphi)$) impact on vertical impulse (I_V); that is, the athlete must learn how hard to kick off for a given required step time. In fact, calibration is continuous because the dynamics of the actor and the environment are never constant (Fajen, 2008a). For instance, the athlete's mass can vary from day to day and the rigidity of the ground differs from place to place. Hence, expert sport players must not only be capable of forming appropriate couplings between movement and information variables, but also continually recalibrate them to the ever-changing dynamics (see Chapter 8 for further discussion on movement control).

Current research findings

In this section, we review the evidence that learning and expertise in movement control of interceptive actions indeed encompasses changes in the information that players attend to (i.e., education of attention) and/or changes in the way the information affects movement (i.e., calibration). In fact, scrutinizing the literature shows that surprisingly little is known about how sport players do acquire mappings between movement and information variables, and how they are refined with experience. Consequently, one of the main conclusions – and admittedly, not the most exciting one – is that it is essential to initiate much more research with (expert) sports players. Having said this, however, there are a good number of studies that do address education of attention and calibration during (short-term) learning of interceptive actions. This work includes learning in university students as well as in infants within a year after birth. We start with the latter.

The development of catching in infants

Typically, infants reach for moving toys from three to four months after they are born (von Hofsten, 1983). More often than not, they bring the toy to the mouth if they succeed in grasping it. What does this imply for the development of movement control? Among other things, an infant trying to get a moving toy must learn to control when to start moving the arms. In its simplest form this can be understood by presuming that the infant initiates the arm movement when the toy is at some critical distance or time from the (future) interception point. This entails the mapping of a movement variable (e.g., arm acceleration) to an informational variable that relates to distance (e.g., the optical angle φ subtended by the toy) or time (e.g., τ(φ) or tau). Van Hof, van der Kamp, and Savelsbergh (2006) investigated whether improved catching during early development goes together with a change in using optical variables. Three- to nine-month-old infants were seated in a baby chair while balls of different size approached the infant from the front with constant velocity. Using an eye patch, infants watched the ball either with one eye (i.e., monocular viewing) or two eyes (i.e., binocular viewing). Until six months of age, arm movement onset toward the ball was influenced by ball size; they started to reach earlier (i.e., longer before the ball arrives at the interception point) for larger balls than smaller balls. They did so both under monocular and binocular viewing. Hence, infants use an optic variable that co-varies with ball size, such as the optic angle φ, which results in more misses for the smallest ball: infants were somewhat late. For more successful interception, the use of a variable that specifies time would be more suitable, because it provides the infants with the same amount of time to complete the catching action irrespective of ball diameter. This occurred after six months of age, but only under binocular viewing. Under monocular viewing, ball size still affected the timing of the catch. In fact, adults demonstrate similar timing patterns under monocular and binocular viewing as a function of object size (van der Kamp *et al.*, 1997). Older infants have learnt to attend to optic variables that – apparently – specify or strongly co-vary with the time until the ball arrives at the interception point. In all likelihood, this variable is the binocular equivalent for τ(φ), the relative rate of change of angle of target vergence, δ (Laurent *et al.*, 1996). The neuro-anatomical substrates involved in detecting binocular information only develop postnatally after three to four months. The younger infants therefore are more reliant on monocular variables. In sum, young infants learning to intercept moving objects shift from using monocular to binocular variables. In fact, additional longitudinal observations confirm that the convergence to binocular variables is a key process in infants developing adaptive control of interceptive actions.

In a second study, van Hof (van Hof, 2005; van Hof *et al.*, 2008) assessed the change in variable use in the development of catching more directly by determining the critical values of different optical variables for the moment the catch was initiated. The examined variables were optical angle (i.e., φ), looming or the rate of change of the optical angle (i.e., $\dot{\varphi}$), and tau (i.e., τ(φ)) (Figure 5.2).[2] Infants were presented with toys that approached with different (constant) velocities. It was reasoned that when the value of an optical variable at the moment of onset

$$\tau(\varphi) = \frac{\varphi}{\dot{\varphi}} \approx \frac{Z}{\dot{Z}} = TTC$$

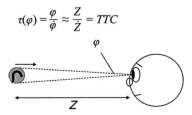

Figure 5.2 The optics for a ball that approaches head-on.

is the same across velocities, then the control of movement onset is consistent with the use of this variable. Between three and five months of age, infants made many attempts but were often unsuccessful. By contrast, six- to seven-month-olds were more advanced catchers, but still less proficient than eight- to nine-month-old infants who consistently caught most of the balls they tried to intercept. In addition, most of the youngest infants initiated the catch when the optical angle φ reached a constant value, irrespective of ball speed. They started moving when the ball was at a constant distance from the interception point. Consequently, catching performance was very much influenced by object speed: the faster the ball moved, the less time to produce the catch. In fact, these types of error may have forced six- to seven-month-olds to shift attention to better specifying optical variables, such as looming and tau, which are closely related to the time remaining before the ball reaches the point of interception. And indeed, the majority of infants between six and nine months of age initiated their catch at either a constant value of looming or tau. In sum, the development of catching involves a change in optical variables infants attend to, as is anticipated by the conjecture that learning entails the education of attention.

Learning to avoid head-on collisions

The control law proposed for infant catching is not very refined. Information merely serves as a trigger, while control laws can also account for the continuous regulation of movement. Imagine a racing cyclist who sees a dog dashing across the road, or a Formula 1 driver who approaches a crashed car. Should they slam on the brakes, or should they brake more gradually and slowly increase deceleration? When should they start braking? Fajen addressed these issues in a neat series of experiments (Fajen & Devaney, 2006, Fajen, 2007, 2008a, 2008b) by investigating the information that drivers use to stop for an obstacle. He focused particularly on whether performance improvements can be understood in terms of attunement to (better) specifying variables. To brake safely drivers must keep the required deceleration below the highest deceleration they can generate; otherwise, a collision is imminent. Deceleration equals $v^2/2z$, where v is current speed and z the distance to the stopping location (i.e., in front of the obstacle), and can be continuously adjusted by changing the position of the brake pedal. Consequently, Fajen proposes a law of control that relates pedal displacement, the controlled movement variable, to information that specifies deceleration:

$$p = k \star (GOFR \star \dot{\phi}/\phi), \qquad\qquad \text{(Eq. 3)}$$

Here p is pedal displacement (equivalent to the rate of deceleration), which is expressed in percentage of its maximum, GOFR is the global optic flow of the textured ground surface, which is proportional to v, $\dot{\phi}/\phi$ is the ratio of the optic angle of the approached obstacle and its rate of change, which equals v/z or the inverse of the time-to-contact with the obstacle, and finally, k is a calibration constant. An experienced driver who exploits GOFR $\star$ $\dot{\phi}/\phi$ to regulate pedal displacement consistently stops at the intended stopping location. However, a less-experienced driver, who uses less-reliable optical variables, which co-vary with but do not specify the required deceleration, will show systematic errors. For instance, drivers who are not attuned to GOFR would find that they sometimes err dependent on their speed, while drivers that are not attuned to $\dot{\phi}/\phi$ may err if the obstacle's size varies. Fajen tested this with a simple driving simulator. Initially, a participant's pedal displacement was clearly affected by vehicle speed and obstacle size. Participants tended to brake early with low speeds and large obstacles. However, with practice these effects quickly reduced or completely vanished, with the adjustments in required deceleration becoming similar across variations in speed and size (Fajen & Devaney, 2006; Fajen, 2008a).

This shows that participants shift from using non-specifying to specifying variables. Perhaps the most interesting finding is that the shift occurred under some practice conditions but not others, suggesting that the education of attention is not simply a consequence of practice. For instance, the speed effects only disappeared when ground texture was simulated. This makes obvious sense because information about vehicle speed is carried in the global optic flow (i.e., GOFR), whereas in the absence of ground texture only local flow from the obstacle is available. More intriguingly, the biases in deceleration (or pedal displacement) from vehicle speed and obstacle size only disappeared if, during practice, both factors were varied. Practicing with variations in speed did reduce the speed effect but did not completely dissolve it, and size effect did not disappear when only obstacle size was varied (Fajen & Devaney, 2006). Apparently, with a narrow range of variations (i.e., either in vehicle speed or obstacle size) attunement does occur, but quickly stabilizes on using non-specifying variables (e.g., GOFR or $\dot{\varphi}/\varphi$). We agree with Fajen and Devaney (2006) that this is not due to a lack of motivation on the part of the participants – they do converge on specifying variables if the variation during practice is larger! Probably, the non-specifying variables to which they converged resulted in small systematic errors that made it hard to find information that promotes further attunement to specifying variables (Fajen & Devaney, 2006, p. 312; see also Jacobs & Michaels, 2007). Accordingly, the participants' performance was often "good enough," but not perfect. For sport players this implies that the degree to which they will (or perhaps can) learn to attend to specifying information may depend on the amount of variability under which they practice. We will return to this issue in the concluding section.

It is important to emphasize that pedal displacement p (i.e., required deceleration) in the control law for braking refers to the percentage of maximum displacement that the driver can produce. This means that the driver must know the dynamics of the braking system. It is quite clear that drivers do indeed know, although they may only become aware when the dynamics of the braking system are different (e.g., immediately after a service to replace old brakes). The car's maximum deceleration also varies with load, the slope of the road, etc. Initially, the changed dynamics may result in minor hiccups, such as late braking, but drivers typically adjust rapidly. Adapting to changed dynamics involves calibration. For instance, if the gain of the braking system decreases (e.g., from 12 m/s² to 9 m/s²), then the driver must brake harder; that is, push the pedal further for the same amount of change in the value of the optic variable. Fajen (2007) demonstrated that this change in gain led to a systematic overshoot that participants rapidly overcame. Instead of a change in optic variable, Fajen (2007, 2008b) argues that this relearning involved recalibration. However, a more rigorous demonstration of calibration is provided by the work of Jacobs and Michaels (2006), to which we turn next.

Catching on

Ever since the pioneering by H.T.A. Whiting, catching has been a favorite task to study how much and what information is needed to perform accurately. In this section, we discuss the work of Jacobs and Michaels, who used catching to demonstrate that "the sophistication of expert performance derives from the improved fit of experts to their environments" (2006, p. 322). They proposed that as expertise develops, individuals attune to more useful optical variables (i.e., education of attention), and, in addition, they scale their actions towards the optic variables (i.e., calibration). To shed greater light on these processes, Jacobs and Michaels (2006) had seated participants catch swinging balls that passed next to them (Figure 5.3). To understand how participants controlled interception they modified the *required velocity model* (Bootsma, Fayt, Zaal, & Laurent, 1997). The model holds that acceleration of the hand (i.e., A_{hand}) is a function of the current lateral hand velocity (V_{hand}) and the hand velocity that is required to reach the interception

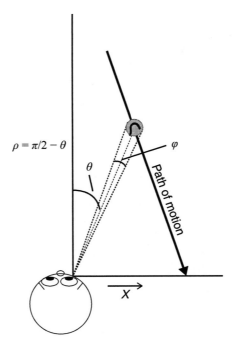

Figure 5.3 The optics of a ball passing to the left of the observer.

point in time. This required hand velocity, in turn, is a function of the current lateral positions of the hand (X_{hand}) and the ball and the time it takes for the ball to reach the interception point. Jacobs and Michaels (2006) describe this with the following law of control:

$$A_{hand} = c_1 \left(\frac{c_2 O - X_{hand}}{(\dot{\phi}/\phi - (\dot{\rho})/\rho) - 1} - V_{hand} \right), \quad \text{(Eq. 4)}$$

The optic variable O in the nominator refers to candidate optic variables[3] that specify or co-vary with the current lateral distance between the hand and the ball, and the denominator is a compound optical variable that specifies the ball's time to arrival. The nominator and denominator combine into the required hand velocity. During learning, a change of optic variable O implies education of attention, and a change in constants c_1 and c_2 indicates calibration. A change in c_1 can be interpreted as how change in the value of information impacts acceleration, whereas a change in c_2 can be conceived as how a change in the optic variable O scales to a change in value for kinaesthetic information about hand position (i.e., presuming that hand position is felt). The experimental strategy of Jacobs and Michaels was to plug candidate optical variables O as inputs into the mathematical model derived from Eq. 4 to see which best fits the observed hand movement kinematics. In addition, the two calibration constants c_1 and c_2 are free to vary to find the best fit. Having introduced the basic maths, we can now turn to the experimental observations. Jacobs and Michaels found that the precision of catching improved over a block of 60 practice trials. Participants, however, adopted individual strategies to achieve this improvement. They exploited different optic variables and to some extent changed their use of optic variables available to guide hand movements with practice; that is, they demonstrated some degree of education of attention. However, convergence was relatively minor. Calibration appeared much more important in explaining the improved performance. In particular, the same difference between required and current hand velocities led to larger increases in hand acceleration (i.e., c_i increased with practice). It thus appears that when individuals have some level of expertise in a task (such as in the current ball catching task, where participants were over 75 per cent successful in contacting the ball to start with), they show less change in the optic variable of choice, as they are often able to exploit specifying variables already. A change in variable use is less of a requirement. Further improvements are then achieved by calibrating the way information affects movement. This is of significance for practitioners interested in developing expertise in interceptive tasks. We will discuss the implications below.

Research and practical implications

To recap so far, we have shown that there has been an overemphasis on attempting to show that anticipation is the key to expert performance in interceptive sports. We believe, however, that the superior performance of experts can *also* be attributed to more effectively exploiting optical variables for guiding movements. As such, we have demonstrated that developing expertise is predicated on learning to attune to and calibrate specifying information. These findings have important implications for practitioners interested in designing effective learning programs, a point we consider next.

Applying what we have found

Research challenges sport practitioners in terms of how they should educate the attention of developing experts. Use of non-specifying information in the initial stages of learning can be somewhat problematic (although, as we mentioned earlier, we have little empirical evidence from sporting tasks to back up this claim), but does not necessarily need to be so. As Withagen (2004, p. 242) highlights, "a human being who intercepts 70 per cent of the balls thrown at him or her because she exploits a non-specifying, moderately informative variable will not die because of it." While this is not a problem for novices or recreational sport players, for those aiming for expertise, survival is important and is often matched with a desire for perfection. Any athlete who reaches higher levels of competition and continues to rely on non-specifying variables will eventually metaphorically "die." This is an important point. These players must learn to attend to specifying variables. However, for players that perform "good enough," but do not yet excel, reliance on non-specifying, moderately informative variables may be fairly resistant to further attunement (Beek *et al.*, 2003). Instead, they may be inclined to only calibrate the variable to which they are attuned. If the exploited non-specifying variable results in only small errors, then performers may find it difficult to find information to guide further attunement. Consequently, they will stick to non-specifying variables.

Following this, an important question is what practitioners can do to ensure that athletes do not get "stuck" on non-specifying variables. As we have seen, key to this may be a broadening of the range of variability during practice (Fajen & Devenay, 2006). Indeed, recent evidence from perceptual learning studies indicates that variable practice is most effective in enhancing perceptual skills (Dicks *et al.*, in press). Rather than specificity of practice, practitioners need to provide high levels of variability to allow performers to search for the more useful information to control their actions. In tennis, for example, coaches would ensure that a performer faces opponents with different styles (left handers and right handers, baseline players and serve and volleyers, topspinners or backspinners) and on different surfaces, as tennis experts have to play on grass, hard courts, and clay surfaces. In sports such as long jumping, variability could be added to practice by requiring athletes to run up from different distances as well as in different conditions, such as running to jump into a head wind, not just with a tail wind, because this is what normally happens in elite competition (the London Olympic final of 2012 was run with jumpers running into the wind). Notice the difference with more traditional attempts to learn to standardize the run-up. In summary, by enhancing variable practice in training (and ensuring it is encountered in performance) learners are more likely to make sizeable errors when using moderately inform-ative variables. The key point is that this provides the opportunity to explore their environments and learn to converge to information that is most useful for them. Finally, in this approach the most useful information is not decided for the performer in advance (nor is it the same for each performer), and therefore puts them in control and at the center of the learning process. This fits well in a nonlinear pedagogical approach to the development of expertise (Renshaw *et al.*, 2009).

We need to make a couple more general points on this issue. First, because information for action is tightly coupled to a performer's action capabilities, it is to be expected that (different) individuals would potentially exploit different information even in the same situation. This requires coaches to carefully consider the design of practice and also to understand interceptive skill at the level of the individual and refrain from making assumptions that all players will be able to exploit available information for movement control or affordance perception. For exam-ple, Dicks, Davids, and Button (2010) highlighted that goalkeepers who were slower at diving initiated their dives earlier when facing a penalty kick than those who had faster movement times, meaning they relied on non-specifying information available in the early part of the pen-alty taker's run-up, in contrast to faster movers who could wait longer and use more specifying information. As such, it is important that coaches provide opportunities to re-educate attention (or potentially recalibrate) when changes in action capabilities such as improved speed, strength, or hitting ability, for example, have improved as a result of practice.

These examples have considered how practitioners can facilitate the education of attention; for calibration, however, specificity relative to such circumstances is important as well.

The significance of preparing for action

In line with Jacobs and Michaels (2006), it is important that once sport performers have settled on a variable they see as useful (be it non-specifying or specifying) they are then provided with opportunities to calibrate it so that it is adjusted to the current requirements of the environment; for example, when warming up or in the very early stages when performing in a competition. Expert sport players must be capable of continually calibrating and recalibrating these variables to the ever-changing, dynamic, performance landscapes, with changes in interacting constraints often occurring on very short time frames. Calibration is therefore crucial for expert sport perfor-mance, and there is some anecdotal evidence in the sporting literature that suggests that expertise is founded on calibrating one's actions to new constraints as quickly as possible to optimize per-formance. For example, going back to our earlier example from long jumping, when jumping at a new venue, the expert jumper will use the warm-up to adapt to the different rebound properties of new runways, with different atmospheric conditions and often moment-to-moment changes in wind velocity even within one run-up. Add to this the changes in individual constraints (e.g., fatigue) and task constraints (e.g., current field position as a competition unfolds) and it is clear that expert jumpers need to be able to very quickly learn how hard to kick off for a given required step time at any moment in time. And of course, such calibration is equally important for elite athletes in other sports (e.g., for new balls in a tennis match, a change of bat in cricket or racquet in squash, the speed of the ball on a wet surface after a rain shower in soccer, etc.).

Future research

Our discussion highlights that there is a need for dedicated research studies that consider what optical variables expert sport players attune to and how differences in the intrinsic dynamics of individuals impact on variable selection. For example, when designing learning tasks to develop sporting expertise – such as catching a ball or moving towards a target to jump, throw, or vault – the understanding of which optic variables, say, beginners might first attune to and what other optic variables might be available is important to identify. An interesting question that has not yet been answered is whether or not experts still achieve expert levels of performance if they are attuned to non-specifying variables to which they can expertly calibrate their movements. At present we simply do not know if attunement and subsequent calibration of non-specifying variables acts to limit the level of expertise that an individual can achieve. As such, there is a need for more longitudinal studies that chart individual pathways to expertise in terms of first identifying the optic variables upon which they come to rely on and then categorizing changes in developing perception and action couplings. The identification of specifying optic variables in sporting tasks is not a trivial issue. Once identified, they then allow practice interventions to be set up in a principled manner. Finally, it is critical to deepen understanding of how a learner is informed to either search for different information or to (re)calibrate the mapping between information and action. In this regard, Withagen and Michaels (2005) have argued that some patterns of error are more likely to induce education of attention, whereas other patterns more often result in calibration. For practitioners, this may turn out to be pertinent for tailor-made structuring of practice sessions.

Notes

1 We refer to optic variables as a way of example. Information can also be carried by auditory, haptic, and proprioceptive variables, to name a few.
2 These are all monocular variables, but the infants may or may not use their binocular equivalents. However, van Hof (2005, van Hof *et al.*, 2008) did not address this issue.
3 Descriptions of all the candidate optic variables go beyond the aims of the paper. The interested reader is referred to Jacobs and Michaels (2006).

References

Abernethy, B., Farrow, D., Gorman, A., & Mann, D. (2012) 'Anticipatory behavior and expert performance', in A. M. Williams & N. J. Hodges (eds) *Skill acquisition in sport: Research, theory and practice*, New York: Routledge, 287–305.
Beek, P. J., Jacobs, D. M., Daffertshofer, A., & Huys, R. (2003) 'Expert performance in sport: Views from the joint perspectives of ecological psychology and dynamical systems', in J. Startkes & A. Ericsson (eds) *Expert performance in sport*, Champaign, IL: Human Kinetics, 321–44.
Bootsma, R. J., Fayt, V., Zaal, F.T.J., & Laurent, M. (1997) 'On the information-based regulation of movement: What Wann (1996) may want to consider', *Journal of Experimental Psychology Human Perception & Performance*, 23: 1282–9.
Cabe, P. A., & Wagman, J. B. (2010) 'Characterizing perceptual learning using regression statistics: Development of a perceptual calibration index', *American Journal of Psychology*, 123: 253–67.
Chemero, A. (2009) *Radical embodied cognitive science*, Cambridge, MA: MIT Press.
Davids, K., Renshaw, I., Pinder, R. A., Araújo, D., & Vilar, L. (2012) 'Principles of motor learning in ecological dynamics: A comment on functions of learning and the acquisition of motor skills (with reference to sport)', *The Open Sports Sciences Journal*, 5: 113–7.
de Rugy, A., Taga, G., Montagne, G., Buekers, M. J., & Laurent, M. (2002) 'Perception-action coupling model for human locomotor pointing', *Biological Cybernetics*, 87(2): 141–50.
Dicks, M., Davids, K., & Button, C. (2010) 'Individual differences in the visual control of intercepting a penalty kick in association football', *Human Movement Science*, 29: 401–11.

Dicks, M., van der Kamp, J., Withagen, R., & Koedijker, J. (in press) '"Can we hasten the expertise by video simulations?" Considerations from an ecological psychology perspective', *International Journal of Sport Psychology*.

Fajen, B. R. (2007) 'Rapid recalibration based on optic flow in visually guided action', *Experimental Brain Research*, 183: 61–74.

Fajen, B. R. (2008a) 'Perceptual learning and the visual control of braking', *Attention, Perception & Psychophysics*, 70: 1131–8.

Fajen, B. R. (2008b) 'Learning novel mappings from optic flow to the control of action', *Journal of Vision*, 8: 1–12.

Fajen, B. R., & Devaney, M. C. (2006) 'Learning to control collisions: The role of perceptual attunement and action boundaries', *Journal of Experimental Psychology: Human Perception and Performance*, 32(3): 300–13.

Gibson, J. J. (1966) *The senses considered as perceptual systems*, Boston: Houghton Mifflin.

Gibson, J. J. (1979) *The ecological approach to visual perception*, Hillsdale, NJ: Erlbaum.

Greenwood, D. (2014) 'Informational constraints on performance of dynamic interceptive actions', unpublished thesis, Brisbane: Queensland University of Technology.

Jacobs, D. M., & Michaels, C. F. (2006) 'Lateral interception I: Operative optical variables, attunment, and calibration', *Journal of Experimental Psychology: Human Perception and Performance*, 32: 443–58.

Jacobs, D. M., & Michaels, C. F. (2007) 'Direct learning', *Ecological Psychology*, 19: 321–49.

Jacobs, D. M., Runeson, S., & Michaels, C. F. (2001) 'Learning to visually perceive the relative mass of colliding balls in globally and locally constrained task eologies', *Journal of Experimental Psychology: Human Perception and Performance*, 27: 1019–38.

Laurent, M., Montagne, G., & Durey, A. (1996) 'Binocular invariants in interceptive tasks: A directed perception approach', *Perception*, 25: 1437–50.

Lee, D. N. (1976) 'A theory of visual control of braking based on information about time to collision', *Perception*, 5: 437–59.

Lee, D. N., Lishman, J. R., & Thomson, J. A. (1982) 'Regulation of gait in long jumping', *Journal of Experimental Psychology: Human Perception and Performance*, 12: 259–66.

Michaels, C. F., & Beek, P. J. (1995). 'The state of ecological psychology', *Ecological Psychology*, 7: 259–78.

Milner, A. D., & Goodale, M. A. (1995) *The visual brain in action*, Oxford: Oxford University Press.

Milner, A. D., & Goodale, M. A. (2008) 'Two visual systems re-viewed', *Neurospsychologica*, 12(46): 774–85.

Montagne, G., Cornus, S., Glize, D., Quaine, F., & Laurent, M. (2000) 'A perception-action coupling type of control in long jumping', *Journal of Motor Behavior*, 32: 37–43.

Renshaw, I., & Davids, K. (2004) 'Nested task constraints shape continuous perception-action coupling control during human locomotor pointing', *Neuroscience Letters*, 369: 93–8.

Renshaw, I., & Davids, K. (2007) 'Why do fast bowlers bowl no-balls: "It's bloody laziness lad" and other explanations!', paper presented at the Cricket Australia Sports Science & Sports Medicine Conference.

Renshaw, I., Davids, K., Chow, J., & Shuttleworth, R. (2009) 'Insights from ecological psychology and dynamical systems theory can underpin a philosophy of coaching', *International Journal of Sport Psychology*, 40: 580–602.

Renshaw, I., Rotheram, M., Kemshall, S., Wilkinson, R., & Davids, K. (2003) 'Manipulating perceptual information and cricket bowling: A case study', *Proceedings of the International Australasian Winter Conference on Brain Research*, 21: 1.5. Retrieved from https://web.psy.otago.ac.nz/awcbr/Abstracts/Abstracts2003.htm#Renshaw.

Shim, J., Carlton, L. G., Chow, J. W., & Chae, W. K. (2005) 'The use of anticipatory visual cues by highly skilled tennis players', *Journal of Motor Behavior*, 37: 164–75.

Travassos, B., Davids, K., Araújo, D., & Esteves, P. T. (2013) 'Performance analysis in team sports: Advances from an ecological dynamics approach', *International Journal of Performance Analysis in Sport*, 13: 83–95.

Triolet, C. , Benguigui, N., Le Runigo, C., & Williams, A. M. (2013) 'Quantifying the nature of anticipation in professional tennis', *Journal of Sport Sciences*, 31: 820–30.

Turvey, M. T., & Carello, C. (1986) 'The ecological approach to perceiving-acting: A pictorial essay', *Acta Psychologica*, 63: 133–5.

van der, Kamp, J., Oudejans, R.R.D., & Savelsbergh, G.J.P. (2003) 'The development and learning of the visual control of movement: An ecological perspective', *Infant Behavior and Development*, 26: 495–515.

van der Kamp, J., Rivas, F., van Doorn, H., & Savelsbergh, G. (2008) 'Ventral and dorsal system contributions to visual anticipation in fast ball sports', *International Journal of Sport Psychology*, 39: 100–30.

van der Kamp, J., Savelsbergh, G.J.P., & Smeets, J. (1997) 'Multiple information sources in interceptive actions', *Human Movement Science*, 16: 787–822.

van Hof, P. (2005) *Perception-action couplings in early infancy*, Enschede, NL: Febodruk.

van Hof, P., van der Kamp, J., & Savelsbergh, G.J.P. (2006) 'Three- to eight-month-old infants' catching under monocular and binocular vision', *Human Movement Science*, 25: 18–36.

van Hof, P., van der Kamp, J., & Savelsbergh, G.J.P. (2008) 'The relation between infants' perception of catchableness and the control of catching', *Developmental Psychology*, 44: 182–94.

von Hofsten, C. (1983) 'Catching skills in infancy', *Journal of Experimental Psychology: Human Perception & Performance*, 9: 75–85.

Warren, W. H. (1984) 'Perceiving affordances: Visual guidance of stair climbing', *Journal of Experimental Psychology: Human Perception and Performance*, 10: 683–903.

Warren, W.H. (2006) 'The dynamics of perception and action', *Psychological Review*, 113: 358–89.

Warren, W. H., Young, D. S., & Lee, D. N. (1986) 'Visual control of step length during running over irregular terrain', *Journal of Experimental Psychology: Human Perception and Performance*, 12: 259–66.

Withagen, R. (2004) 'The pickup of non-specifying variables does not entail indirect perception', *Ecological Psychology*, 16: 237–53.

Withagen, R., & Michaels, C. F. (2002) 'The calibration of walking transfers to crawling: Are action systems calibrated?', *Ecological Psychology*, 14: 223–34.

Withagen, R., & Michaels, C. F. (2004) 'Transfer of calibration in length perception by dynamic touch', *Perception & Psychophysics*, 66: 1282–92.

Withagen, R., & Michaels, C. F. (2005) 'The role of feedback information for calibration and attunement in perceiving length by dynamic touch', *Journal of Experimental Psychology: Human Perception and Performance*, 31: 1379–90.

6

HOW EXPERTS MAKE DECISIONS IN DYNAMIC, TIME-CONSTRAINED SPORTING ENVIRONMENTS

Markus Raab and Werner Helsen

Michael Jordan, elected sportsman of the century and member of the Memorial Basketball Hall of Fame, achieved in 1,072 games 32,292 points (roughly 30.1 points per game). This record holds as the highest scoring career average in basketball. Each of the individual decisions to pass or shoot to achieve such impressive records is based on multiple factors. In this chapter we are mainly interested in the decision-making part of the process. Other psychological factors (see Chapters 5–9) and non-psychological factors, such as physical or anthropometric aspects of expert performance, are discussed elsewhere in this book (see Chapter 15). Within the decision-making and judgment literature, choices have been discussed for many tasks, sports, and people. Here we will scope our review on two groups of people (athletes and referees) and short-term choices that relate to direct sensorimotor interaction with the environment (or in the lab). For a larger overview of choices beyond referees and athletes, such as spectators, coaches, and managers, or of choices on long-term dimensions such as career transitions, we refer to overviews (e.g., Bar-Eli *et al.*, 2011). Further, we refrain from reporting on methodological and training aspects of decision-making, but rather focus on decision-making as an important characteristic of expert performance. So how do experts make decisions or choices between options?

What is the content of decision-making in sports?

Choices in general are often related to two concepts: judgment and decision-making. Whereas sometimes these concepts are used interchangeably or refer to definitions such that decisions are viewed as judgments that describe the choice between alternatives (e.g. Drucker, 1966), in the following we will differentiate these concepts. Judgments refer to a "set of evaluative and inferential processes that people have at their disposal and can draw on in the process of making decisions" (Koehler & Harvey, 2004, p. xv). Decision-making refers to "the process of making a choice from a set of options, with the consequences of that choice being crucial" (Bar-Eli *et al.*, 2011, p. 6).

To illustrate, judgments made by soccer referees use cues to decide whether a foul of a defender against an attacker is present or not. The set of evaluative and inferential processes involved in such a judgment may, for instance, involve inferences based on the physical contact between the players (Morris & Lewis, 2010). In contrast, other social inferential processes hinder good judgments, such as stereotype processes related to the height of a player (Van Quaquebeke & Giessner, 2010), the player's reputation (Rainey *et al.*, 1989), or gender (Souchon *et al.*, 2004). To illustrate further, the decision-making of Michael Jordan may involve search processes for information to generate options, such as "pass to a teammate" or "shoot," select between those based on selection processes and execute the what and how decision in a dynamic and accurate way. Again, a set of these processes may foster good decision-making such as fixating gaze to information-rich areas (Magill, 1993), whereas other factors, such as considering too many low-valid cues or low-valid options, can hinder good choices (Raab, 2012).

Certainly the described judgments and decision-making do involve processes and factors not presented here, such as the ones discussed above in other sections of this text about anticipation, pattern perception, gaze behavior, attentional control, and the interactions in the sensorimotor and cognitive systems as a whole. Whereas we acknowledge the complexity of such interactions we will focus only on some of them below, providing a coherent and selective chapter on how experts make choices. Current trends on the multidimensional aspect of such choices (Raab, 2012), the effects of sensorimotor processes of such cognitive characteristics as described in theories of embodiment (Pizzera, 2012) are beyond what we can review here.

Current taxonomies used to classify decision-making vary across a wide range of dimensions. For instance, one set of taxonomies separates different types of decisions, such as inference (the best/true outcome is known) versus preference (best/true outcome is unknown) decisions (Koehler & Harvey, 2004). Others compare risk decisions (probabilities of each outcome are known) from uncertainty decisions (probabilities are unknown or not reliable). Another set of taxonomies refers to competences of decision-making often as an umbrella term to list a set of abilities and skills that an expert decision maker has brought with him or has adapted to in development (Gagne, 2004). The list of chapters in the text on characteristics of expert performers reflects such thinking and could be used to differentiate recall from recognition processes (e.g., Chapter 2), different types of knowledge (McPherson, 1999) or convergent (rule-based) and divergent (creative) processes (Memmert, 2011 and Chapter 31). In the same vein but temporally ordered, different processes that are involved in decision-making can be listed. A well-known structure refers to sequential information processing, such that first the problem presents itself, followed by identification and generation of options, then the assessment, selection, and initiation of choices is established and after which the executed choice is evaluated (e.g., Orasanu & Connolly, 1993).

In summary, all of the above taxonomies may serve as a starting point to describe expert decision makers in sports. However, it seems obvious that some taxonomies are not well suited for the type of judgments and decisions we focus on here, as most of them are not easy to be aligned to inference/preference or risk/uncertainty choices. The described set of competences or a sequential set of processes depends on the theoretical frameworks that spurred such taxonomies and is the focus of the next section.

How are decisions made in sport?

An answer to the question of how decisions are made depends on the scientist you ask. In a recent overview, up to 300 theories in judgment and decision-making were reported (Bar-Eli *et al.*, 2011, p. 30, Figure 3.1), from which only about a dozen have been applied to the sporting domain. From the dozen applied to sport we will select three of them to illustrate how theories describe and explain how decisions in sport are made, what empirical findings support their explanations, and extend the findings to specific components of decision-making processes and summarize consequences for expert decision-making in sports.

Markus Raab and Werner Helsen

Theories

We will focus on an ecological dynamics approach based on Brunswik (see Chapter 12) and applied to sports from Araújo *et al.* (2006) (see also Chapter 19), the decision field theory (DFT) of Townsend and Busemeyer (1993) and applied to sports from Raab and Johnson (2004), and on a simple heuristics approach from Gigerenzer, Todd, and the ABC Research Group (1999) applied to sports from Raab (2012). A more detailed comparison and application to sports can be found in Bar-Eli *et al.* (2011) and Raab (2012), from which the following is used for a reduced description. In short, the ecological dynamics approach describes a choice as "relaxing the performer-environment system to the most attractive state in the potential landscape" (Araújo *et al.*, 2006, p. 662). For example, in a decision to start either on the left or the right side (two attractor states) of a starting line of a sailing regatta, the parameter "wind direction" is used in a function to explain or predict the probability of a sailor choosing the left or right side (Araújo *et al.*, 2006). In a computational approach such as the decision field theory (Busemeyer & Townsend, 1993, for parameters and equations), a decision is a result of a deliberate "sequential sampling process." In this case, "wind direction" and other parameters (parameter importance defined by attention shifts) are sampled over time until a threshold of preference for one option is met that triggers the execution of the preferred option. In the simple heuristics approach (Raab, 2012) a choice is based on a sequence of search, stopping, and decision rules. Cues are searched for in order. If "wind direction" is the most valid information and the cue differentiates between the two options (left or right side of the starting line), the search is stopped and the option with the higher or positive cue value is selected (cf. Raab, 2012, p. 112).

Box 1   Example of theory application (adapted from Bar-Eli, Plessner, & Raab, 2011, p. 38)

Theory Application

Example: Imagine a playmaker in basketball who needs to decide whether to pass to the center player or to the left wing player. How would different theories describe this choice process?

Ecological dynamic approach: In an ecological dynamic approach the pass options are attractors on an attractor landscape with various depths (validities in terms of simple heuristics). In such a familiar task the valid options are chosen because affordances turn options into valid and first-generated options. This theory can describe choices of players based on affordances without intermediated memory processes of options. The theory can explain different choices of the same individual in different situations by assuming noise or transitions from one option to another option in the system. It cannot describe how long a decision will take, or the phenomenon of preference reversal.

Decision field theory: Calculate utilities for different options, but as attention shifts from one option to another, option valences shift over time until one meets a threshold, resulting in a choice. Can explain probability and dynamic choices under time pressure. Can explain differences between and within individuals. Can predict decision time. Cannot explain how thresholds are learned or set.

Take-the-best (simple heuristic): Use the most valid cue first (e.g., base rate of success of center and wing player); if the base rate is not equal, stop search for further cues and pass to the player with the higher base rate. Take-the-best can explain how people cope with a number of choices and cues under limited time. It can explain preference reversals under time pressure and how people represent structured information and options. It cannot explain how long a choice will take, and it cannot easily explain how cue validities are learned or how individual differences in the same situation develop.

Empirical evidence

Most of the theoretical descriptions above refer to preferences in the theoretical framework that cannot be empirically tested and cannot be validated by focusing only on the outcome of a choice, as in the simple example presented – all theories would predict that sailors consider the "starting line position" based on the cue "wind direction." However, if the situation is more complex the different theories may differ in predicting the type of choice, the decision time or "what" and "how" information used. To illustrate, in the decision field theory all cues can be used to choose one option over another. In the ecological dynamics approach the change to an attractor state that stands for a decision in favor of one choice could also be achieved by using all the information available. Different to these two predictions, the simple heuristic approach limits the use of information by starting at the most valid one and stopping as soon as the first cue differentiates between the two options at hand. Further, before option selection, different predictions can be formulated for option generation. As option generation has been studied in the simple heuristics approach and less so in the other two approaches it will be compared to specific alternative models. The recognition-primed model (Klein, 1997) assumes a pure recognition-primed decision that requires coming up with only one option (perception-action), in contrast to generating a few options until a satisfying option is found (simple heuristics, Johnson & Raab, 2003), and in contrast to prediction that all appropriate options based on a long-term working-memory model (LTWM; computational approach, North *et al.*, 2011) are considered. Whereas take-the-first predicts a negative relationship between the number of options generated and choice quality, a LTWM predicts the inverse relationship. There is empirical evidence for all the models, and future research should evaluate what role personal, task-specific, or situation-specific factors play in these differences.

Empirical findings to specific processes

Another line of comparison is whether a new theory can explain previous findings or is able to produce new hypotheses. For illustration, consider the empirical evidence that experts, compared to novices, have longer fixation durations and a lower number of fixations in a sport choice task (Helsen & Starkes, 1999a), whereas in other experiments in the same sport the opposite has been found (Williams & Ward, 2007). From the simple heuristics perspective, we would predict that search is based on the importance of the cues and their relationships. If one cue is more important than the sum of the other cues, experts can use this knowledge – which they gain from experience – and stop their search after considering one cue. However, if choosing between options requires more cues, then experts should focus on different cues, and more of them, than novices. Thus empirical evidence that seems contradictory can be integrated in one explanation.

In summary, the theoretical explanations provided so far explain how decisions are made in general. The examples given show that the predictions of the theories can be used to explain sport choices and generalize expert decision-making, as will be discussed in the next sections.

Expert perception and decision-making

Research on expert perception and decision-making in sport has expanded substantially in the last few decades (for an overview, see Starkes & Ericsson, 2003). As expert performers show consistently superior athletic performance over an extended period of time (Starkes, 1993), they must excel in the physiological, technical, cognitive (tactical/strategic, perceptual/decision-making), and psychological (regulation/coping, emotional) domain (Janelle & Hillman, 2003). In this part, we will focus on the perceptual-cognitive aspects of expert performance in dynamic, time-constrained sporting environments. Perceptual skills include pattern recall and recognition, the use and extraction of anticipatory cues, visual search strategies, and signal detection. Cognitive or decision-making skills are based on the interpretation of information acquired through perceptual skills and its suitability for effective response selection (Janelle & Hillman, 2003).

Skilled perception, predominantly visual, precedes and determines appropriate action in sport (Williams & Ward, 2003). In early research on perceptual skill in sport (Banister & Blackburn, 1931), experts were thought to have superior vision over novices. Vision scientists and optometrists, who are interested in characteristics at the level of the visual receptors, consider the "hardware" components of the visual information-processing system to discriminate experts from novices. Hardware components refer to those aspects that are likely to be innate, perhaps genetically limited, and assumed to be a fixed commodity (for an overview, see Starkes et al., 2001). No empirical evidence for systematic differences between novice and expert athletes, however, has emerged on these visual parameters (Helsen & Starkes, 1999a). Although visual hardware does not seem to differentiate between expertise levels, a deficiency in visual hardware can impair performance. Corrections of these deficits are necessary and might enhance performance (Abernethy, 1986; Abernethy & Wood, 2001).

Subsequently, it has been suggested that experts and novices can be distinguished by their ability to organize, interpret, and utilize the available visual information ("software"), rather than by physical characteristics and capabilities of the visual sensory system ("hardware"), provided vision is adequate (Abernethy, 1986). Consequently, the visual information-processing system plays a crucial part in sport performances. It consists of three sequential steps shown in Figure 6.1 (Abernethy, 1986, 1996). After the reception of visual stimuli by the retina (i.e., fovea, parafovea, and visual periphery), the first step is the perception process by which the performer detects and selects the appropriate input that is indispensable for future action. The perceptual mechanism reorganizes and interprets only the most relevant information for further processing. Step two, the cognition or decision-making phase, involves response selection, the process by which a decision is taken about the most appropriate action. The decision mechanism selects an appropriate motor response and passes this information on to the effector mechanism. The effector mechanism, or the third step, organizes the hierarchical, sequential, and temporal aspects

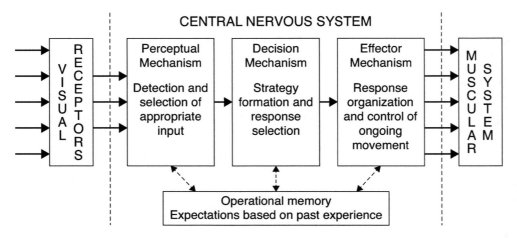

Figure 6.1 A visual information-processing model of skilled performance, adapted from Abernethy (1986).

of the planned action. This involves organization, initiation, and control of the movement. The commands are then passed on to the muscle groups for the actual execution of the movement. All three steps in the central nervous system are influenced by the performer's expectations based on past experience.

As Starkes and Deakin (1984) originally proposed, it is indeed the visual "software" that sets the limits to sport performance and discriminates between different skill levels. In this respect, the visual information-processing system is influenced by the performer's past experience and, consequently, susceptible to domain-specific practice and learning (Starkes *et al.*, 2001). As a result of training, expert performers make adaptations to facilitate effective anticipation and decision-making in sport (for an overview, see Williams & Ward, 2003). An ever-expanding volume of research has been conducted on changes in perceptual-cognitive skills with the expert-novice approach, a generally acknowledged approach to study performance differences liable to achieving expertise (for an overview, see Starkes *et al.*, 2001). The most commonly used techniques are error detection (e.g., McMorris & Graydon, 1997), eye movement registration (e.g., Helsen & Starkes, 1999b), film occlusion (e.g., Williams & Burwitz, 1993), mental chronometry (e.g., Helsen & Pauwels, 1988), recall (e.g., Williams & Davids, 1995), recognition (e.g., Williams *et al.*, 1994), signal detection (e.g., Tenenbaum *et al.*, 1999), and verbal reports (e.g., McPherson, 1999).

Expert decision-making in referees

Within team sports, different roles are involved in the skill development and skill execution of athletes and players. Still, research on sport expertise focuses mainly on the athletes or players. Relatively little research is conducted on other roles in sports. Besides trainers and coaches, who can have a tremendous impact on skill development (bearing in mind the importance of deliberate practice), the role of the judge or referee is crucial to make competitions and matches possible. In sports such as gymnastics, figure skating, and diving, judges determine the winner. In team sports such as basketball, football, handball, and volleyball or racquet sports such as tennis and squash, they ensure that players properly follow the rules of play. Although their main responsibility is to fulfill a rather guiding role, they too can have a significant impact on the outcome of a match. Taking this into consideration, expert athletes and players deserve expert judges and referees (see Chapter 35).

Although similarities can be assumed among several roles (e.g., declarative knowledge), differences are apparent (MacMahon *et al.*, 2007). From a perceptual-cognitive perspective, athletes and players make an appropriate action based on perception, while judges and referees make appropriate decisions without a real need for a skilled action (Ste-Marie, 1999). From a physical perspective, the physical fitness of the referee is not the most important factor in expertise. Nevertheless, referees in open sports have to be in excellent physical shape to keep up with play, certainly in fast-moving ball games like association football. In contrast, players have to get the best out of their physical capacities to perform at top level. These examples suggest that research findings on athletes and players cannot automatically be extrapolated to judges and referees.

In association football, research on refereeing is dominated by studies on the physical aspects. Since 2004, research on perceptual-cognitive aspects has started to rise (see Figure 6.2). If other sports were also considered (e.g., rugby) then the trend for more perceptual-cognitive papers would be even clearer.

From a perceptual-cognitive perspective, the role of the judge or referee can be quite interesting as a subject of research. In open sports, it is very difficult to evaluate the quality of players' decisions or actions. Trainers, coaches, or researchers can propose the best possible decision or

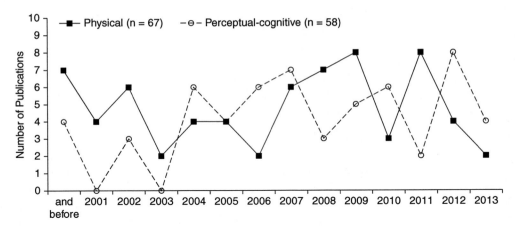

Figure 6.2 Number of scientific publications on football refereeing in the physical and perceptual-cognitive field.

action in game situations, but the player can make a totally different decision or action, nevertheless scoring a point or a goal. In contrast to decisions of players, decisions of referees can be balanced against a correct decision or a consensus decision. In tennis, for example, the accuracy of decisions of line judges can rather easily be calculated with the Hawk Eye ball-tracking system (Mather, 2008). Not every decision, however, can be taken objectively or compared as easily in refereeing. In some game situations, the referee has to interpret an action (e.g., a tackle incident in football: should the referee show a yellow or a red card?).

More recently, objectively measurable decisions of referees and assistant referees in association football were used to study the human visual information-processing system (Catteeuw et al., 2009a). For referees, primarily the decisions that could be verified with a consensus decision of the referee's committee of FIFA (Fédération Internationale de Football Association) were investigated (cf. Gilis et al., 2006; MacMahon et al., 2007). For assistant referees, mainly offside decision-making, the primary job of the assistant referee, was taken into consideration. Offside decisions can be verified very accurately with video and software tools (Gilis et al., 2008; Gilis et al., 2009; Helsen et al., 2006).

Even at the highest standards like the FIFA World Cup, the UEFA Champion's League, or the English Premier League, no assistant referee is, or will ever be, infallible, because of the difficulty of offside decision-making and the unpredictability of the game (Catteeuw et al., 2010a, 2010b). However, expert assistant referees can be distinguished from less successful expert assistant referees, not so much on the perceptual level but rather on the cognitive or decision-making level. No differences were found for visual scan patterns of different levels of expert assistant referees. Additionally, an offside decision-making program showed no changes in the visual scan patterns of international-standard assistant referees (Catteeuw et al., 2009b). These observations suggest that expert assistant referees are better able to give meaning to the available input. The limiting factor to offside decision-making expertise seems to be the subsequent step – i.e., the response selection or decision-making – and this issue has been addressed just recently by Put et al. (2013).

Another interesting aspect of studying referees is the absence of a clear culture of practice. This leaves scope for investigation of the exposure, experience, and practice necessary to develop role-specific decision-making skills. Similar to medicine and the military, simulations of performance are often not feasible. A match, an operation, or a humanitarian intervention is the moment to perform for a referee, a surgeon, or a general, respectively. The stage to perform is at the same time the best moment for training role-specific skills ("learning on the job"), and experience is built on repetition of actual performances (MacMahon *et al.*, 2007). This questionable strategy will not necessarily lead to expertise as immediate (external) feedback is often absent (Williams & Davids, 1995). Researchers should, therefore, investigate the possibilities to create and develop training programs with clear feedback mechanisms.

A third aspect is the extent to which refereeing skills are domain specific. Research on transfer of skills between domains or between different roles within one domain is limited. Studies by Abernethy, Baker, and Côté (2005) and Smeeton, Ward, and Williams (2004) reported transfer of pattern recall of game-related stimuli between sports with similar structures, such as football and field hockey. However, studies on transfer between different roles in one domain revealed role specificity (Allard *et al.*, 1993; Gilis *et al.*, 2006; MacMahon *et al.*, 2007; Williams & Davids, 1995). These findings have implications for comparisons of roles across similar domains or different roles in one domain. In this respect, it is interesting to find out how domain-specific refereeing skills are, or if they are transferable to other domains.

Professional team sports represent physically and perceptual-cognitively demanding environments, with incorrect refereeing decisions having a great impact on the financial interests of several actors. This leads to high demands for all teams involved, including referees and assistant referees that are expected to lead and control matches in an appropriate way. They need highly developed perceptual-cognitive skills, because their decisions can be crucial for the outcome of the match. Obviously, referees and assistant referees deserve professional support from coaches, doctors, instructors, physiotherapists, psychologists, and scientists to prepare themselves optimally for the match. In this respect, the last part of this chapter considered the different mechanisms mediating decision-making performance. Even relatively small amounts of decision-making training enhance decision-making performance (see Chapter 37). Therefore, referees and assistant referees should be provided with additional perceptual-cognitive skill training to reduce decision-making errors as much as humanly possible. In addition to being of benefit to match officials in general and assistant referees in particular, our observations may have a broader impact on society by exploring the validity and generalizability of existing conceptual models, as well as methods for developing perceptual-cognitive skill. In particular, our findings may have implications for those attempting to improve decision-making in other performance domains (e.g., airplane piloting, air traffic control, (micro)surgery, police decision-making, the military), as well as to motor learning and skill acquisition in many daily life activities and professional settings (e.g., traffic).

In conclusion, this chapter defines choices in sports, differentiating judgments and decision-making, providing three prototypical theories on how decision-making in sport can be explained, and providing ample evidence on current studies of expert decision-making in this field. A conclusion is reached that a multidimensional approach is needed to describe and understand expert decision-making, and thus this chapter relates to many specific perceptual, motor, and cognitive components discussed elsewhere in this book. Given the omnipresence of decision-making in expert behavior, the research and practice of expert decision-making will inevitably involve a love/hate relationship when explaining success and failure.

References

Abernethy, B. (1986) 'Enhancing sports performance through clinical and experimental optometry', *Clinical and Experimental Optometry*, 69: 189–96.

Abernethy, B. (1996) 'Training the visual-perceptual skills of athletes: Insights from the study of motor expertise', *American Journal of Sports Medicine*, 24: 89–92.

Abernethy, B., Baker, J., & Côté, J. (2005) 'Transfer of pattern recall skills as a contributor to the development of sport expertise', *Applied Cognitive Psychology*, 19: 705–18.

Abernethy, B., & Wood, J. M. (2001) 'Do generalized visual training programmes for sport really work? An experimental investigation', *Journal of Sport Sciences*, 19(3): 313–18.

Allard, F., Deakin, J., Parker, S., & Rodgers, W. (1993) 'Declarative knowledge in skilled motor performance: Byproduct or constituent?', in J. L. Starkes & F. Allard (eds) *Cognitive issues in motor expertise*, Amsterdam: Elsevier Science Publishers B.V., 95–107.

Araújo, D., Davids, K., & Hristovski, R. (2006) 'The ecological dynamics of decision making in sport', *Psychology of Sport and Exercise*, 7: 653–76.

Banister, H., & Blackburn, J. M. (1931) 'An eye factor affecting proficiency at ball games', *British Journal of Psychology*, General Section, 21(4): 382–4.

Bar-Eli, M., Plessner, H., & Raab, M. (2011) *Judgment, decision-making, and success in sport*, Oxford, UK: Wiley.

Busemeyer, J. R., & Townsend, J. T. (1993) 'Decision field theory: A dynamic-cognitive approach of decision making in an uncertain environment', *Psychological Review*, 100: 432–59.

Catteeuw, P., Gilis, B., Garçia-Aranda, J. M., Tresaco, F., Wagemans, J., & Helsen, W. F. (2010a) 'Offside decision making in the 2002 and 2006 FIFA World Cups', *Journal of Sports Sciences*, 28: 1027–32.

Catteeuw, P., Gilis, B., Wagemans, J., & Helsen, W. F. (2010b) 'Offside decision making of assistant referees in the English Premier League: Impact of physical and perceptual cognitive factors on match performance', *Journal of Sports Sciences*, 28: 471–81.

Catteeuw, P., Helsen, W. F., Gilis, B., Van Roie, E., & Wagemans, J. (2009b) 'Visual scan patterns and decision-making skills of association football assistant referees in offside situations', *Journal of Sport & Exercise Psychology*, 31: 786–97.

Catteeuw, P., Helsen, W. F., Gilis, B., & Wagemans, J. (2009a) 'Decision-making skills, specificity, and deliberate practice in association football refereeing', *Journal of Sports Sciences*, 27: 1125–36.

Drucker, P. (1996) *The effective executive*, New York: Harper and Row.

Gagne, F. (2004) 'Transforming gifts into talents: The DMGT as a developmental theory', *High Ability Studies*, 15: 119–47.

Gigerenzer, G., Todd, P. M., & the ABC Research Group (1999) *Simple heuristics that make us smart*, New York: Oxford University Press.

Gilis, B., Helsen, W., Catteeuw, P., van Roie, E., & Wagemans, J. (2009) 'Interpretation and application of the offside law by expert assistant referees: Perception of spatial positions in complex dynamic events on and off the field', *Journal of Sport Sciences*, 27(6): 551–63.

Gilis, B., Helsen, W., Catteeuw, P., & Wagemans, J. (2008) 'Offside decisions by expert assistant referees in association football: Perception and recall of spatial positions in complex dynamic events', *Journal of Experimental Psychology, Applied*, 14(1): 21–35.

Gilis, B., Weston, M., Helsen, W., Junge, A., & Dvorak, J. (2006). 'Interpretation and application of the laws of the game in football incidents leading to player injuries', *International Journal of Sport Psychology*, 37: 121–38.

Helsen, W. F., Gilis, B., & Weston, M. (2006) 'Errors in judging "offside" in association football: Test of the optical error versus the perceptual flash-lag hypothesis', *Journal of Sports Sciences*, 24(5): 521–8.

Helsen, W. F., & Pauwels, J. M. (1988) 'The use of a simulator in evaluation and training of tactical skill in football', in T. Reilly, A. Lees, K. Davids, & W. J. Murphy (eds) *Science and football*, London: E. & F. N. Spon, 493–497.

Helsen, W. F., & Starkes, J. L. (1999a) 'A multidimensional approach to skilled perception and performance in sport', *Applied Cognitive Psychology*, 13: 1–27.

Helsen, W. F., & Starkes, J. L. (1999b) 'A new training approach to complex decision making for police officers in potentially dangerous interventions', *Journal of Criminal Justice*, 27: 395–410.

Janelle, C. M., & Hillman, C. H. (2003) 'Expert performance in sport: Current perspectives and critical issues', in J. L. Starkes & K. A. Ericsson (eds) *Expert performance in sports: Advances in research on sport expertise*, Champaign, IL: Human Kinetics: 19–48.

Johnson, J., & Raab, M. (2003) 'Take the first: Option-generation and resulting choices', *Organizational Behavior and Human Decision Processes*, 91: 215–29.

Klein, G. (1997) 'The recognition-primed decision model: Looking back, looking forward', in C. E. Zsambok & G. Klein (eds) *Naturalistic decision making*, Mahwah, NJ: Erlbaum, 285–92.

Koehler, D. J., & Harvey, N. (2004) *Blackwell handbook of judgment and decision making*, Oxford, UK: Blackwell.

MacMahon, C., Helsen, W., Starkes, J. L., & Weston, M. (2007) 'Decision-making skills and deliberate practice in elite association football referees', *Journal of Sports Sciences*, 25(1): 65–78.

Magill, R. (1993) *Motor learning: Concepts and applications*, 3rd ed., Madison: WCB Brown & Benchmark.

Mather, G. (2008) 'Perceptual uncertainty and line-call challenges in professional tennis', *Proceedings of the Royal Society*, Series B, 275: 1645–51.

McMorris, T., & Graydon, J. (1997) 'The effect of exercise on cognitive performance in soccer-specific tests,' *Journal of Sports Sciences*, 15(5): 459–68.

McPherson, S. L. (1999) 'Tactical differences in problem representations and solutions in collegiate varsity and beginner female tennis players', *Research Quarterly for Exercise and Sport*, 70: 369–84.

Memmert, D. (2011) 'Creativity, expertise, and attention: Exploring their development and their relationships', *Journal of Sports Sciences*, 29: 93–102.

Morris, P. H., & Lewis, D. (2010) 'Tackling diving: The perception of deceptive intentions in association football (soccer)', *Journal of Nonverbal Behavior*, 34: 1–13.

North, J., Ward, P., Ericsson, K. A., & Williams, A. M. (2011) 'Mechanisms underlying skilled anticipation and recognition in a dynamic and temporally constrained domain', *Memory*, 19(2): 155–68.

Orasanu, J., & Connolly, T. (1993) 'The reinvention of decision-making', in G. Klein, R. Orasanu, R. Calderwood, & C. Zsambok (eds) *Decision-making in action: Models and methods*, Norwood, NJ: Ablex, 3–20.

Pizzera, A. (2012) 'Gymnastic judges benefit from their own motor experience as gymnasts', *Research Quarterly for Exercise and Sport*, 83(4): 603–7.

Put, K., Wagemans, J., Jaspers, A., & Helsen, W.F. (2013) 'Web-based training improves on-field offside decision -making performance', *Psychology of Sport and Exercise,* 14(4): 577–585.

Raab, M. (2012) 'Simple heuristics in sports', *International Review of Sport and Exercise Psychology*, 1–17.

Raab, M., & Johnson, J. G. (2004) 'Individual differences of action orientation for risk-taking in sports', *Research Quarterly for Exercise and Sport*, 75(3): 326–36.

Rainey, D. W., Larsen, J. D., & Stephenson, A. (1989) 'The effects of a pitcher's reputation on umpires' calls of balls and strikes', *Journal of Sport Behavior*, 12(3): 139–50.

Smeeton, N. J., Ward, P., & Williams, A. M. (2004) 'Do pattern recognition skills transfer across sports? A preliminary analysis', *Journal of Sports Sciences*, 22: 205–13.

Souchon, N., Coulomb-Cabagno, G., Traclet, A., & Rascle, O. (2004) 'Referees' decision making in handball and transgressive behaviors: Influence of stereotypes about gender of players', *Sex Roles*, 51: 445–53.

Starkes, J. L. (1993) 'Motor experts: Open thoughts', in J. L. Starkes & F. Allard (eds) *Cognitive issues in motor expertise*, Amsterdam: Elsevier Science Publishers B.V., 3–16.

Starkes, J. L., & Deakin, J. (1984) 'Perception in sport: A cognitive approach to skilled performance', in W. F. Straub & J. M. Williams (eds) *Cognitive sport psychology*, Lansing, NY: Sport Science Associates, 115–28.

Starkes, J. L., & Ericsson, K. A., eds (2003) *Expert performance in sport*, Champaign, IL: Human Kinetics.

Starkes, J. L., Helsen, W. F., & Jack, R. (2001) 'Expert performance in sport and dance', in R. N. Singer, H. A. Hausenblas, & C. M. Janelle (eds) *Handbook of sport psychology*, London: Routledge, 174–201.

Ste-Marie, D. M. (1999) 'Expert-novice differences in gymnastic judging: An information-processing perspective', *Applied Cognitive Psychology*, 13(3): 269–81.

Tenenbaum, G., Stewart, E. & Sheath, P. (1999) 'Detection of targets and attentional flexibility: Can computerised simulation account for developmental and skill-level differences?', *International Journal of Sport Psychology*, 30: 261–82.

Van Quaquebeke, N., & Giessner, S. R. (2010) 'How embodied cognitions affect judgments: Height-related attribution bias in football foul calls', *Journal of Sport & Exercise Psychology*, 32: 3–22.

Williams, A. M., & Burwitz, L. (1993) 'Advance cue utilization in soccer', in T. Rielly, J. Clarys, & A. Stibbe (eds) *Science and football II*, London: E. & F.N. Spon, 239–44.

Williams, A. M., & Davids, K. (1995) 'Declarative knowledge in sport: A by-product of experience or a characteristic of expertise?', *Journal of Sport & Exercise Psychology*, 17: 259–78.

Williams, A. M., Davids, K., Burwitz, L., & Williams, J. G. (1994) 'Visual strategies in experienced and inexperienced soccer players', *Research Quarterly for Exercise and Sport*. 65(2): 127–35.

Williams, A. M., & Ward, P. (2003) 'Perceptual expertise in sport: Development', in A. Ericsson & J. L. Starkes (eds) *Expert performance in sports: Advances in research on sport expertise*, Champaign, IL: Human Kinetics, 220–49.

Williams, A. M. & Ward, P. (2007) 'Anticipation skill in sport: Exploring new horizons', in G. Tenenbaum & R. Eklund (eds) *Handbook of sport psychology*, New York: Wiley, 203–23.

7

MOVEMENT AUTOMATICITY IN SPORT

Rob Gray

Legendary UCLA basketball coach John Wooden once said, "the importance of repetition until automaticity cannot be overstated" (Wooden 1997, p. 52). Indeed, reaching a stage where some skills can be performed "automatically" is thought to be one of the main goals of sport training and one of the defining characteristics of being an expert (e.g., Gibson, 1969; Abernethy, 1993). But what exactly does it mean for a sport skill to be "automatic" and how exactly is this desired state achieved through training? The goals of this chapter are threefold: (i) define the concept of automaticity in the context of sport, (ii) examine theories of how automaticity is achieved, and (iii) review sport science research, which has tested the combined predictions of skill acquisition and automaticity theories.

What is automaticity in sport?

Although there are multiple definitions (e.g., Moors & De Houwer, 2006), the term "automaticity" in sport is typically used to refer to the ability to execute a skill using no (or very few) information-processing resources (i.e., attention and working memory). Automatic processes are thought to be ones that, once initiated, run to completion without further conscious guidance by the performer (Shiffrin & Schneider, 1977). When a skill can be executed in this fashion, the performer has resources available to process other sources of information not directly required for the task. In order to understand the definition further we need to consider the different ways in which skill execution can occur.

When we perform a skill there are different modes of control that can be used. At one extreme, commonly called *controlled processing mode*, a performer executes an action by following a series of explicit steps, which are held in working memory, and by focusing his/her attention on each part of the action (Shiffrin & Schneider, 1977). Each stage in skill execution is consciously controlled and monitored. For example, when executing a complex movement in sports, the performer must remember where he/she has been instructed to position his/her different body parts and focus attention on his/her body to determine if positioning is correct. In this performance mode, the information-processing demands of the skill are very high and there are few, if any, leftover resources available for processing task-irrelevant information.

At the other extreme, commonly called *automatic processing mode*, skill execution relies on motor programs or procedures, which, once initiated, run without the use of attentional or working-memory

Movement automaticity in sport

resources. The skill is executed unconsciously as it is thought to involve "muscle memory" or motor programs (i.e., well-developed internal commands for how the different body parts should be moved) rather than high-level cognitive control. In this mode, the performer has information-processing resources available for handling task-irrelevant information.

How is automaticity achieved?

As first proposed by Paul Fitts (e.g., see Fitts & Posner, 1967; see also Anderson, 1983), these controlled and automatic processing modes are thought to be characteristics of the early and late stages of skill acquisition, respectively. For novice performers, it has been proposed that skill execution requires that attention be paid to each component stage of the motor act – i.e., controlled processing. For example, a novice golfer must actively process (i.e., actively remember and focus his/her attention on) all of the steps listed in Table 7.1 when executing a putt. At this level of performance (referred to as the "cognitive" or "declarative" stage) it is assumed that skill execution depends on a set of un-integrated control structures that must be held in working memory and attended to in a step-by-step fashion. These attentional and memory requirements result in the slow, non-fluent, and error-prone movement execution that is the hallmark of a novice performer.

As expertise develops through practice, and the performer reaches the highest stage of skill execution (the "autonomous" or "procedural" stage), it has been proposed that the role of attention and working memory in performance changes dramatically. At this stage the conscious step-by-step control of execution is no longer required. Instead skill execution is assumed to operate by fast, efficient control "procedures" that function largely without the assistance of working memory or attention (Logan, 1988). At this final stage it is proposed that skill

Table 7.1 Steps involved in execution of a golf putt.

1. Judge the line of the ball.	12. Weight – distribute weight evenly, about 50:50, or with a little more weight on the left foot.
2. Judge the grain of the turf.	
3. Judge the distance and angle to the hole.	13. Backswing – swing the club straight back. The distance back that the club goes must equal the through stroke distance.
4. Image the ball going into the hole.	
5. Position the ball somewhere between the center of your feet. You should be able to look straight down on top of the ball.	14. Stroke – the club must accelerate through the ball. Finish with the "face" of the club head pointing directly at the target.
6. Align shoulders, hips, knees, and feet parallel and to the left of the target (e.g., imagine railroad tracks from the ball to the cup – feet outside the tracks, the ball in the middle).	15. Length of the stroke – it is better to err to a shorter more compact stroke rather than a longer stroke.
	16. Stroke direction – straight back and straight through.
7. Grip – thumbs should be pointed straight down, palms facing each other, a light grip.	17. Stroke rhythm – not too fast and not too slow.
8. Posture – stand tall enough so that if you were to practice putting for 30 minutes you would not experience a stiff or sore back.	18. Keep head and lower body stationary throughout stroke and swing with the arms.
	19. Wrists – should not break during the stroke.
9. Arms – should hang naturally and be relaxed.	20. Arms and shoulders – should do most of the work.
10. Hands – should be relative to ball position. Hands should be slightly in front of the ball.	21. Head/trunk/hips/legs – should remain still during the stroke.
11. Head position – eyes should be positioned directly over the ball.	22. Watch the ball go into the hole.

Reproduced with permission from Beilock and Carr (2001).

automaticity has been achieved. It is also frequently proposed that automatic skills are "encapsulated" such that, once they are initiated, it is difficult for the performer to inhibit or alter them (McLeod *et al.*, 1985).

A key advantage that automaticity is thought to give an athlete is the available attentional and working-memory resources to process information in the environment not directly related to movement control. First, the performer is more likely to detect situational/contextual information that is not required for movement control but may serve to improve performance success. For example, if an expert footballer does not need to actively monitor the position of his/her body when dribbling, he/she will have processing capacity available to attend to the movements of opponents and teammates. Second, the performer is less likely to be affected by the introduction of stimuli irrelevant to the sporting task (e.g., a fan yelling an insult or waving his hands in the background).

How does an athlete progress from the novice/declarative stage to the expert/procedural stage of skilled performance? It has been proposed that through repetition of the skill during an intermediate "associative" stage of skill acquisition, motor procedures are developed as different subcomponents of the action and are grouped or "chunked" (Anderson, 1983). For example, steps 5–12 in Table 7.1 may be combined to form an integrated motor procedure for "addressing the ball" in golf putting. When this chunking of steps is achieved, the performer need only initiate the procedure rather than actively process each step. This can also be conceptualized as a transition from multi-step to single-step memory retrieval (Logan, 1988).

The theory of skill acquisition described above is the traditional view that has dominated most of the research in this area and been the basis for most coaching methods (Masters, 1992). More recently it has been proposed that automaticity in skilled performance can be achieved without the need to progress through a controlled processing stage (involving declarative, explicit knowledge about the action). In theories of *implicit learning*, it is proposed that motor procedures (or "action-outcome contingencies") can be developed passively and unconsciously without: (i) giving the performer an explicit set of instructions about how to perform the action and (ii) the performer actively (i.e., through the use of attentional and memory resources) testing and identifying the steps involved in successful execution of the action (Masters, 1992). In this type of learning, the goal is to keep performance "automatic" throughout the entire skill acquisition process as deliberate efforts are made to limit controlled processing during execution; e.g., by reducing the availability of information-processing resources through the use of secondary task loading.

Research on automaticity in sport

If we combine traditional skill acquisition (i.e., those involving a controlled processing state) and automaticity theories there are several predictions that can be made about the nature of performance (and the supporting attentional mechanisms and memory structures) as a function of skill level. For example, if it involves the automatic processing mode, expert performance should be: (i) relatively unaffected by the introduction of an irrelevant secondary task which requires attentional and/or working-memory resources, (ii) associated with a poorer ability to verbalize the stages involving skill execution (i.e., "expertise-induced amnesia") since these stages are not attended or held actively in memory, and (iii) relatively "encapsulated" (difficult to alter or suppress the action once it has been initiated).

Another important prediction of skill acquisition and automaticity theories concerns pressure-induced failures of performance (i.e., "choking under pressure"). It has been proposed that high-pressure situations prompt skilled performers to shift their attention inwards so that the focus is on movement execution; e.g., the constrained action hypothesis proposed by Wulf and colleagues (reviewed in Wulf & Prinz, 2001) and the reinvestment theory proposed by Masters

(1992). This inward attentional shift is thought to harm performance because actions that were formerly controlled by highly efficient and automatic motor programs are now controlled by explicit (conscious) attentional processes that are known to be slow and error prone; i.e., pressure causes a "de-automatization" of skill execution. Therefore, a fourth prediction is that, when under pressure, some expert performers will exhibit behaviors consistent with controlled (rather than automatic) processing. I next review experimental evidence for each of these predictions in detail.

Prediction 1: experts should be relatively unaffected by the introduction of a secondary task that requires attentional and/or working-memory resources

Using a secondary task of visual shape identification, Leavitt (1979) was the first to demonstrate that the introduction of a secondary task hinders sensorimotor skill execution for novices, but not expert performers. In this study, skating speed while stick handling through pylons was significantly slower under dual-task conditions for novice hockey players as compared with experts. Similar results have been found for soccer ball dribbling (Smith & Chamberlin, 1992) and ball catching (Parker, 1981). However, despite the large effects found in these studies, the manipulations used do not permit clear inferences about the attentional processes involved in skill execution. As discussed in detail by Beilock, Carr, MacMahon, and Starkes (2002), the use of a visual discrimination task is likely to have caused considerable structural interference; i.e., it may have interfered with detection of the sensory information required for the primary sport task (Wickens, 1980). Because novice performers are more reliant on visual feedback (Williams et al., 1992), differences in performance could be explained at the level of visual processing.

Beilock, Wierenga, and Carr (2002) conducted a series of experiments that more clearly elucidated how processing of secondary tasks varies as a function of expertise. In this study, novice and experienced golfers executed a primary task of putting while simultaneously performing a secondary task of monitoring a stream of auditory signals (either words or tones of different frequencies) for a particular target signal. They found that the mean putting error was not significantly different in single-task and dual-task conditions for expert golfers whereas the mean error was 4 cm greater in the dual-task than in the single-task conditions for novices. Auditory target detection failures were similar in the single-task and dual-task conditions for both groups. These findings suggest that the difference in putting performance between novice and expert golfers was due to the fact that experts have sufficient attentional resources available to perform the auditory monitoring without hindering putting performance, whereas novices do not. In a separate study, Beilock et al. (2002) found that this secondary auditory monitoring task had similar effects on the ability of expert and novice soccer players to dribble through a series of pylons. This effect has also been demonstrated in a variety of other perceptual-motor skills, including returning a tennis serve (Goulet et al., 1992), baseball batting (Gray 2004), and dance (Kuczynski et al., 2011).

As described above, it has been proposed that the additional attentional resources available to expert performers may convey an advantage beyond being able to handle irrelevant distractions, namely a superior ability to process information in the external environment that can be used to improve performance (e.g., the position of opponents and/or the outcomes of one's actions). To test this prediction, Castaneda and Gray (2007) compared two different secondary tasks in a batting simulation: an *irrelevant/external condition* in which batters were required to judge the frequency of an auditory signal and a *relevant/external condition* in which batters were required to judge the direction the ball was travelling as it left their bat (see Chapter 4). Consistent with the first prediction of this chapter, both of these secondary tasks were associated with poorer performance in novices relative to single-task conditions. These two conditions were not equivalent for expert batters, however. When attention was directed to the simulated ball leaving the bat, performance was significantly better as compared to when attention was directed to information in the environment that was irrelevant to hitting (tone frequency). It was proposed that this occurred because attending to the ball leaving the bat allows the connection between the action and its perceivable effects to be strengthened (Prinz, 1990; Gray & Beilock, 2011); i.e., because the batter is attending to the movement effect instead of an irrelevant stimulus. So, in this instance, having more processing resources available to perform the secondary task had a direct benefit on performance because it allowed for more effective detection of task-relevant information. See also Land *et al.* (2013) for a similar effect in golf putting.

Prediction 2: expert performers should have less access to information about movement execution

It has been proposed that expert performers should have poorer ability to verbalize the stages involved in skill execution – an effect often called "expertise-induced amnesia" (Beilock & Carr, 2001) – for two primary reasons. First, the procedural knowledge underlying expert-level performance is by definition less accessible to verbal recall than the declarative knowledge structures used by novices. Second, because less attention is devoted to skill execution, memory of its components should be worse for expert players. It has been demonstrated in many studies that memory is enhanced for targets that are attended, relative to ones that are not (e.g., Craik *et al.*, 1996).

Beilock, Wierenga, and Carr (2002) tested this prediction by comparing novice and expert golfers in the dual-task putting paradigm described above. After each block of 30 putts, participants completed a questionnaire designed to assess their episodic recollection for the last putt they had executed (i.e., all of the steps they went through during the putt). The main finding was that the mean number of steps listed in the questionnaire was significantly lower for expert golfers than for novice golfers. In other words, episodic memories for the step-by-step execution of the action were impoverished in experts relative to novices.

The effect described above refers to episodic memory (i.e., memory about a specific recent event). A very different pattern of results is seen for generic, explicit memory for skill execution (i.e., memory about how a skill is typically performed without reference to a specific performance). Given that it has been proposed that the initial stage of skill acquisition involves extensive processing of declarative knowledge about skill execution, expert performers (who have already presumably completed this stage) should have more extensive generic, explicit knowledge as compared to novices. Indeed, this pattern of results is exactly what was found in a second condition tested in the study by Beilock, Wierenga, and Carr (2002) described above: the number of generic steps for how to execute a golf putt was significantly greater for expert golfers as compared to novices.

A final piece of evidence relevant to this prediction comes from studies examining training methods designed to induce implicit learning such as dual-task procedures (Masters, 1992) and errorless learning (Maxwell *et al.*, 2001). A consistent finding in these lines of research is that these training methods result in impoverished generic, explicit knowledge at the end of training relative to traditional training methods that involve giving the performer explicit instructions at the beginning of training.

Prediction 3: expert performance should be "encapsulated"

A common element of most theories of automaticity is the idea that once an action is initiated in automatic processing mode it runs without any need for monitoring or guidance from the performer (e.g., Bargh, 1992). This has often led to the corollary assumptions that automatic processing involves actions that are "open loop" (i.e., actions that, once initiated, cannot be altered by the performer on the basis of perceptual feedback) and are therefore informationally encapsulated (McLeod et al., 1985). More specifically, these assumptions suggest that once an action has been initiated (e.g., a golfer starts moving the club or a basketball player begins moving his/her hands to take a shot) an expert performer should have a lesser ability to stop or adjust the movement in response to an external signal/cue presented after movement has been initiated as compared to a less-skilled performer; i.e., expert skill execution should be relatively impenetrable.

These assumptions are problematic, however, because they confound perceptual control and attentional control. Just because an action is continuously regulated on the basis of perceptual information neither necessarily means that attention to the action is required nor that it is easier to consciously access the perceptual-motor processes during execution; for example, to make an explicit judgment about movement. Perceptual-control modes (i.e., open versus closed loop) and cognitive-controlled modes (i.e., controlled versus automatic processes) are independent aspects of motor skill.

This was recently demonstrated in a study of golf putting by Beilock and Gray (2012). In this study, novice and expert golfers were asked to stop their putting stroke as quickly as possible in response to an auditory signal presented in different phases of the action (e.g., backswing versus downswing). Because it has been proposed that the different phases of a golf putt for expert golfers involves different perceptual-control modes (Coello et al., 2000; Craig et al., 2000), it was predicted that the ability of expert golfers to inhibit their putting stroke (relative to novices) would depend on the phase in which the stop signal was presented. As shown in Figure 7.1,

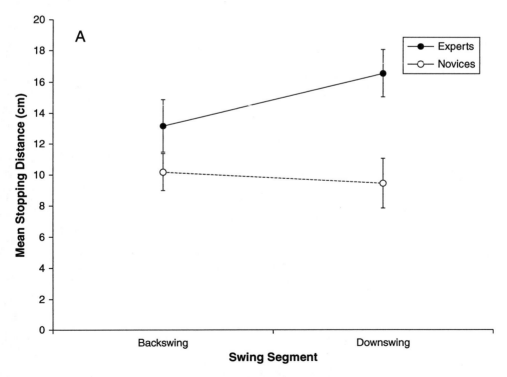

Figure 7.1 Mean distance the putter head travelled after a signal was presented that indicated the stroke should be stopped as quickly as possible. Reproduced with permission from Beilock and Gray (2012).

there was no significant effect of skill level on stopping ability (as quantified by the distance the putter head travelled after the signal was presented) when the stop signal was presented in the backswing, whereas novices were significantly better at stopping their swings when the signal was presented in the downswing. Therefore, it does not seem to be the case that expert performance is generally more encapsulated or impenetrable relative to novice performance, but instead it depends on the nature of the perceptual mode used.

Prediction 4: pressure can lead to an increase in controlled processing in experts

Explicit monitoring theories suggest that pressure situations raise self-consciousness and anxiety about performing correctly (Baumeister, 1984). This focus on the self is thought to prompt individuals to turn their attention inward on the specific processes of performance in an attempt to exert more explicit monitoring and control than would be applied in a non-pressure situation. Explicit, internal attention to step-by-step skill processes and procedures is thought to disrupt well-learned or proceduralized performance processes that normally run largely outside of conscious awareness (e.g., Wulf *et al.*, 2010).

Gray (2004) directly investigated the relationship between attentional control and pressure in baseball batting. In the study, two different dual tasks were employed: an extraneous task (discrimination of the frequency of an auditory tone) and a skill-focused task (judging the direction of bat movement at the instant the tone was presented). Consistent with traditional skill acquisition theories, experts were significantly more accurate in the former task whereas novices were significantly more accurate in the latter. In a separate experiment, it was further shown that when expert baseball batters were placed under pressure, performance in the skill-focused secondary task was significantly improved (see also Gray & Allsop, 2013). This finding is consistent with the idea that pressure can increase the amount of attentional resources devoted to skill execution; i.e., performance became more controlled and less automatic.

Further evidence in support of this idea can be seen when the effects of pressure on the movement kinematics of expert performers are analyzed. In the Gray (2004) study described above, it was found that the increase in skill-focused attention under pressure was also associated with increased variability in the sequencing and timing of the different motor responses involved in swinging (Welch *et al.*, 1995). As described above, higher variability in movement is expected when performance is based on un-integrated, step-by-step control. Similarly, Gray, Allsop, and Williams (2013) recently reported that putting kinematics of expert golfers who "choked" under pressure showed patterns typical of those associated with novices – i.e., smaller downswing amplitudes, more symmetrical putting stroke. These findings again suggest that pressure can cause a regression to an earlier, more controlled stage of skill execution.

It should be noted, however, that it has also been proposed that "choking under pressure" may not involve skill de-automatization resulting from an inward shift of attentional focus. Distraction theories propose that performance failures in experts are caused by resources being taken away from the processing of task-relevant information (e.g., a perceptual cue used to initiate a particular motor procedure) and devoted to worries about the situation (Wine, 1971) and/or threatening stimuli (i.e., attentional control theory; Eysenck & Calvo, 1992). Given that this theoretical approach has also been strongly supported by empirical evidence (e.g., Wilson *et al.*, 2007; Oudejans *et al.*, 2011), an important goal for future research is to understand the relative importance of these two different mechanisms of performance failure and how they might be integrated (e.g., Nieuwenhuys & Oudejans, 2012).

Summary and conclusions

Reaching a state where a sport skill involves automatic processing of movement is one of the primary goals of athletic training. When this state is attained there are several proposed benefits for skilled performance, which have largely been supported from empirical data. First, movements become faster and more consistent because they are less reliant on slow and inefficient attentional and working-memory resources. Second, the athlete is less susceptible to the negative effects of distraction from task-irrelevant information (e.g., a spectator's voice) because he/she has processing resources available to handle such an event. Finally, the athlete will have a greater capacity for processing task-relevant information that is not directly required for movement execution, such as the position of opponents and/or the outcome of their actions.

Along with these positive aspects, it has also been proposed that automaticity comes at a cost, as it has associated negative effects. First, due to the reduced role of attention and working memory, automatic processing can lead to "expertise-induced amnesia" – an effect supported by empirical evidence from studies of episodic memory and implicit learning. While such memory impoverishments might have little negative consequence for the immediate performance of an athlete they may limit her/his ability to correct flaws in technique – an effect that should be explored in future research.

A second proposed negative effect associated with movement automaticity is related to the concept of information encapsulation; namely, automatic processing should be associated with a lesser ability to alter or inhibit a sport skill once it has been initiated. This could be problematic, given that in some sports it can be advantageous to be able to make such changes to a movement effectively; e.g., a goaltender saving a deflected shot in ice hockey or a baseball batter "checking"/stopping his/her swing (Gray, 2009). However, this prediction does not seem to be supported by empirical evidence (e.g., Beilock & Gray, 2012) and confounds perceptual with attentional control.

A final, more controversial, negative aspect of automaticity is the potential for skill de-automatization resulting from shifts of attentional focus associated with performance pressure. Once a skill reaches automatic processing mode not only does it not require conscious attentional and working-memory process, but it also appears to be the case that such processes must "keep out of the way" for successful skill execution to occur. For example, when attention is focused on movement execution via a dual task it can have disastrous consequences on expert performance, effectively reducing performance outcome success to that of a novice (e.g., Beilock *et al.*, 2002; Gray, 2004). As discussed above, the extent to which pressure also causes controlled processes to interfere with automaticity, as proposed by explicit monitoring and associated theories, is an issue that is currently being hotly debated.

Given the importance of reaching a level of automaticity in sport, one critical aspect of this area of research is to understand how to reach this stage as quickly and effectively as possible. Although there are general theories of how this might be achieved (e.g., Fitts & Posner, 1967; Anderson, 1983), one of the major limitations of research on movement automaticity is the relative dearth of research investigating the transition between the different processing modes. As can be seen in the literature reviewed in this chapter, the vast majority of studies in this area have involved comparisons between end states; i.e., comparing the information processing associated with expert versus novice performance. There are very few studies that have investigated the intermediate "associative stage" in which it is proposed the transition between processing modes occurs. Understanding this stage is, of course, crucial for designing effective training programs in sports.

Finally, recent research investigating implicit learning challenges whether the concepts of automatic and controlled processes hold any value in understanding skilled performance in sport

References

Abernethy, B. (1993) 'Attention', in R. N. Singer, M. Murphey, & L. K. Tennant (eds) *Handbook of research on sport psychology*, New York: Macmillan.

Anderson, J. R. (1983) *The architecture of cognition*, Cambridge, MA: Harvard University Press.

Bargh, J. A. (1992) 'The ecology of automaticity: Toward establishing the conditions needed to produce automatic processing effects', *American Journal of Psychology*, 105: 181–99.

Baumeister, R. F. (1984) 'Choking under pressure—Self-consciousness and paradoxical effects of incentives on skillful performance', *Journal of Personality and Social Psychology*, 46: 610–20.

Beilock, S. L., & Carr, T. H. (2001) 'On the fragility of skilled performance: What governs choking under pressure?', *Journal of Experimental Psychology: General*, 130: 701–25.

Beilock, S. L., Carr, T. H., MacMahon, C., & Starkes, J. L. (2002) 'When paying attention becomes counter-productive: Impact of divided versus skill-focused attention on novice and experienced performance of sensorimotor skills', *Journal of Experimental Psychology: Applied*, 8: 6–16.

Beilock, S. L., & Gray, R. (2012) 'From attentional control to attentional spillover: A skill-level investigation of attention, movement, and performance outcome relations', *Human Movement Science*, 31: 1473–99.

Beilock, S. L., Wierenga, S. A., & Carr, T. H. (2002) 'Expertise, attention, and memory in sensorimotor skill execution: Impact of novel task constraints on dual-task performance and episodic memory', *The Quarterly Journal of Experimental Psychology: Human Experimental Psychology*, 55: 1211–40.

Castaneda, B., & Gray, R. (2007) 'Effects of focus of attention on baseball batting performance in players of different skill level', *Journal of Sport & Exercise Psychology*, 29: 59–76.

Coello, Y., Delay, D., Nougier, V., & Orliaguet, J. P. (2000) 'Temporal control of impact movement: The time from departure control hypothesis in golf putting', *International Journal of Sport Psychology*, 31: 24–46.

Craig, C. M., Delay, D., Grealy, M. A., & Lee, D. N. (2000) 'Guiding the swing in golf putting', *Nature*, 405: 295–6.

Craik, F.I.M., Govoni, R., Naveh-Benjamin, M., & Anderson, N. D. (1996) 'The effects of divided attention on encoding and retrieval processes in human memory', *Journal of Experimental Psychology: General*, 125: 159–80.

Eysenck, M. W., & Calvo, M. G. (1992) 'Anxiety and performance: The processing efficiency theory', *Cognition and Emotion*, 6: 409–34.

Fitts, P. M. & Posner, M. I. (1967) *Human performance*, Belmont, CA: Brooks/Cole.

Gibson, E. J. (1969) *Principles of perceptual learning and development*, New York: Appleton-Century-Crofts.

Goulet, C., Bard, C., & Fleury, M. (1992) 'Attentional demands in the identification and return of a tennis serve', *Canadian Journal of Sport Sciences*, 17: 98–103.

Gray, R. (2004) 'Attending to the execution of a complex sensorimotor skill: Expertise differences, choking and slumps', *Journal of Experimental Psychology: Applied*, 10: 42–54.

Gray, R. (2009) 'A model of motor inhibition for a complex skill: Baseball batting', *Journal of Experimental Psychology: Applied*, 15(2): 91–105.

Gray, R. & Allsop, J. (2013) 'Interactions between performance pressure, performance streaks and attentional focus', *Journal of Sport & Exercise Psychology*, 35: 368–86.

Gray, R., Allsop, J., & Williams, S. (2013) 'Changes in putting kinematics associated with choking and excelling under pressure', *International Journal of Sport Psychology (Performance under Pressure Special Issue)*, 44: 387–407.

Gray, R., & Beilock, S. L. (2011) 'Hitting is contagious: Experience and action induction', *Journal of Experimental Psychology: Applied*, 71: 49–59.

Kuczynski, M., Szymanska, M., & Biec, E. (2011) 'Dual-task effect on postural control in high-level competitive dancers', *Journal of Sport Sciences*, 29: 539–45.

Land, W. M., Tenebaum, G., Ward, P., & Marquardt, C. (2013) 'Examination of visual information as the mediator of external focus of attention benefits', *Journal of Sport & Exercise Psychology*, 35: 250–9.

Leavitt, J. L. (1979) 'Cognitive demands of skating and stickhandling in ice hockey', *Canadian Journal of Applied Sport Sciences*, 4: 46–55.

Movement automaticity in sport

Logan, G. D. (1988) 'Toward an instance theory of automatization', *Psychological Review*, 95: 492–527.

Masters, R.S.W. (1992) 'Knowledge, knerves and know-how—The role of explicit versus implicit knowledge in the breakdown of a complex motor skill under pressure', *British Journal of Psychology*, 83: 343–58.

Maxwell, J. P., Masters, R.S.W., Kerr, E., & Weedon, E. (2001) 'The implicit benefit of learning without errors', *The Quarterly Journal of Experimental Psychology*, 54A: 1049–68.

McLeod, P., McLaughlin, C., & Nimmo-Smith, I. (1985) 'Information encapsulation and automaticity: Evidence from the visual control of finely timed actions', in M. I. Posner & O.S.M. Marin (eds) *Attention and performance, XI*, Hillsdale, NJ: Erlbaum, 391–406.

Moors, A., & De Houwer, J. (2006) 'Automaticity: A theoretical and conceptual analysis', *Psychological Bulletin*, 132: 297–326.

Nieuwenhuys, A., & Oudejans, R.R.D. (2012) 'Anxiety and perceptual-motor performance: Toward an integrated model of concepts, mechanisms, and processes', *Psychological Research*, 76: 747–59.

Oudejans, R.R.D., Kuijpers, W., Kooiman, C. C., & Bakker, F. C. (2011) 'Thoughts and attention of athletes under pressure: Skill-focus or performance worries?', *Anxiety, Stress, and Coping*, 24: 59–73.

Parker, H. (1981) 'Visual detection and perception in netball', in M. Cockerill & W. W. MacGillivary (eds) *Vision and sport*, Cheltenham, UK: Stanley Thornes.

Prinz, W. (1990) 'A common coding approach to perception and action', in O. Neumann & W. Prinz (eds) *Relationships between perception and action*, Berlin: Springer-Verlag, 167–201.

Shiffrin, R. M., & Schneider, W. (1977) 'Controlled and automatic human information processing: II perceptual learning, automatic attending, and a general theory', *Psychological Reviews*, 56: 465–501.

Smith, M. D., & Chamberlin, C. J. (1992) 'Effect of adding cognitively demanding tasks on soccer skill performance', *Perceptual and Motor Skills*, 75: 955–61.

Welch, C. M., Banks, S. A., Cook, F. F., & Draovitch, P. (1995) 'Hitting a baseball: A biomechanical description', *Journal of Orthopaedic and Sports Physical Therapy*, 22: 193–201.

Wickens, C. D. (1980) 'The structure of attentional resources', in R. S. Nickerson (ed) *Attention and performance*, vol. 8, Hillsdale, NJ: Lawrence Erlbaum Associates, 239–54.

Williams, A. M., Davids, K., Burwitz, L., & Williams, J. G. (1992) 'Perception and action in sport', *Journal of Human Movement Studies*, 22: 147–204.

Wilson, M., Smith, N. C., & Holmes, P.S. (2007) 'The role of effort in influencing the effect of anxiety on performance: Testing the conflicting predictions of processing efficiency theory and the conscious processing hypothesis', *British Journal of Psychology*, 98: 411–28.

Wine, J. (1971) 'Test anxiety and direction of attention', *Psychological Bulletin*, 76: 92–104.

Wooden, J. (1997) *Wooden: A lifetime of observations and reflections on and off the court*, New York: McGraw Hill.

Wulf, G., Chiviacowsky, S., Schiller, E., & Ávila, L.T.G. (2010) 'Frequent external-focus feedback enhances motor learning', *Frontiers in Psychology*, 1: 190. doi: 10.3389/fpsyg.2010.00190

Wulf, G., & Prinz, W. (2001) 'Directing attention to movement effects enhances learning: A review', *Psychonomic Bulletin & Review*, 8: 648–60.

8

EXPERTISE IN THE PERFORMANCE OF MULTI-ARTICULAR SPORTS ACTIONS

Paul S. Glazier, Machar M. Reid, and Kevin A. Ball

Introduction

Multi-articular, or multi-joint, actions are integral to all sports. The purpose of this chapter is to critically evaluate the literature and provide a summary of the technical features that distinguish experts from non-experts performing multi-articular sport actions, specifically throwing, kicking, and hitting actions. The biomechanics of these sport techniques, and the theoretical principles governing them, have been well documented in the scientific literature (see Atwater, 1979; Putnam, 1993; Fleisig *et al.*, 1996; Bartlett, 2000; Elliott, 2000; Kellis & Katis, 2007; Bartlett & Robins, 2008; Elliott *et al.*, 2008 for comprehensive reviews) and we draw upon this body of knowledge to focus our analysis on particular aspects of technique that are known to be linked to fast, accurate, and consistent performance outcomes. Although we limit our summary to the biomechanical aspects of expertise in throwing, kicking, and hitting actions, we recognize the important role that perception plays in the successful execution of these multi-articular actions, and that perception and movement cannot, and should not, be considered independently of one another (see Savelsbergh & Bootsma, 1994; Williams *et al.*, 1999; Davids *et al.*, 2002; Warren, 2006; Fajen *et al.*, 2008; Zelaznik, 2014). Accordingly, we recommend that this chapter be read in conjunction with others in this book, specifically Chapter 5 by van der Kamp and Renshaw and Chapter 12 by Davids, Araújo, Seifer, and Orth.

Biomechanical characteristics distinguishing experts from non-experts during the performance of multi-articular sport actions

It is somewhat self-evident that expert and non-expert throwers, kickers, and hitters differ, not only in terms of the speed, accuracy, and consistency of performance outcomes, but also the techniques they use to produce those outcomes. However, most biomechanical studies examining these multi-articular sport actions have generally not focused on establishing differences in "technique"—defined by Lees as ". . . the *relative* position and orientation of body segments as they *change* during the performance of a sport task" (2002, p. 814, our emphasis)—between performers of various skill levels. Rather, these investigations have typically attempted to identify relationships between technical characteristics and performance outcomes within groups of performers who are relatively homogenous in terms of expertise or experience (e.g., De Witt &

Expertise in multi-articular sport actions

Hinrichs, 2012; Worthington *et al.*, 2013). Typically, these technical characteristics have been presented as time-discrete kinematic variables describing segmental motions at key moments—as prescribed, for example, by deterministic or hierarchical performance models (see Lees, 1999, for a review)—but this approach, at best, provides only snapshots of isolated aspects of "technique." Some biomechanical analyses of multi-articular sport actions have compared kinematics, kinetics, and muscle activation characteristics across experimental conditions, such as dominant versus non-dominant limb (e.g., Sachlikidis & Salter, 2007), fatigued versus unfatigued states (e.g., Rota *et al.*, 2014), successful versus unsuccessful trials (e.g., Göktepe *et al.*, 2009), and maximal versus submaximal effort (e.g., Zhang *et al.*, 2011), and across groups, such as males versus females (e.g., Barfield *et al.*, 2002) and seniors versus juniors (e.g., Delextrat & Goss-Sampson, 2010) but skill level has rarely been included as an additional independent variable.

In the following subsections, we identify specific aspects of throwing, kicking, and hitting techniques that have either been empirically associated with, or have been theoretically linked to, the production of fast, accurate, and consistent performance outcomes, and we examine how these technical features differ between experts and non-experts. Given the remit of this book and the nature of the research area it covers, we primarily consider studies that have directly examined biomechanical differences among performers of different skill levels. We neither compare and contrast studies that have considered experts and non-experts separately, nor do we attempt to extrapolate findings from correlation studies on expert performers to non-expert performers, although it could be argued that these types of studies could legitimately fall under the "expertise" rubric.

Sequencing and timing of body segment motions

A key feature of all throwing, kicking, and hitting techniques is the sequencing and timing of body segment motions (e.g., Atwater, 1979; Putnam, 1993; Bartlett, 2000; Elliott, 2000). Although the underpinning biomechanical mechanisms and the ubiquity of this particular sequence of segmental motions are still subject to much debate (e.g., Marshall & Elliott, 2000; Fradet *et al.*, 2004), it is generally accepted that, during the performance of these multi-articular actions, energy and momentum are initially generated in the larger, heavier, more proximal body segments before being transferred sequentially to the smaller, lighter, more distal body segments through a precisely timed series of segmental accelerations and decelerations (see Figure 8.1). This proximal-to-distal transfer of energy and momentum along the upper extremity-linked segment system for throwing and hitting, and lower extremity-linked segment system for kicking, has been termed variously as the "summation of speed" (Bunn, 1955), "acceleration-deceleration" (Plagenhoef, 1971), "kinetic linking" (Kreighbaum & Barthels, 1996), "proximal-to-distal sequencing" (Putnam, 1991), and the "kinematic chain" (Bartlett, 1999), and has been demonstrated in a range of multi-articular sport actions, including batting (e.g., Stretch *et al.*, 1998) and bowling (e.g., Glazier *et al.*, 2000) in cricket, the serve (e.g., Elliott *et al.*, 1986) and forehand groundstrokes (e.g., Elliott & Marsh, 1989) in tennis, batting (e.g., Welch *et al.*, 1995) and pitching (e.g., Pappas *et al.*, 1985) in baseball, full and partial golf swings (e.g., Tinmark *et al.*, 2010), instep kicking in soccer (e.g., Nunome *et al.*, 2006) and rugby (e.g., Zhang *et al.*, 2012), javelin (e.g., Mero *et al.*, 1994) and handball throwing (e.g., Jöris *et al.*, 1985), and water polo shooting (e.g., Elliott & Armour, 1988).

According to the limited number of studies that have compared experts and non-experts performing throwing, kicking, and hitting actions, most appear to suggest that all performers, regardless of skill level, exhibit a proximal-to-distal sequence of segmental motion, but the magnitudes of segmental linear and angular velocities are greater in experts (e.g., Burden & Bartlett,

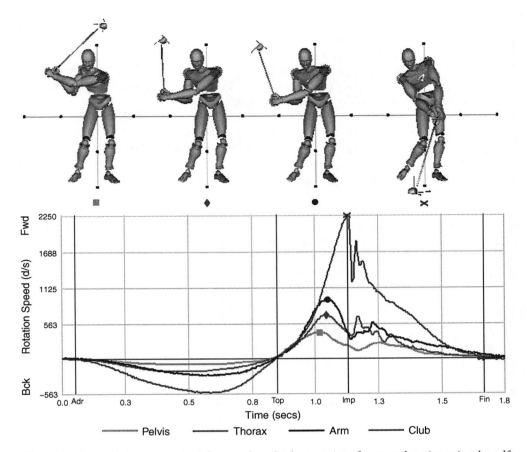

Figure 8.1 A graphical representation of proximal-to-distal sequencing of segmental motion, using the golf swing as an exemplar multi-articular action. Owing to the need to reduce time series measurements to single data points for statistical analysis purposes during group-based comparisons of experts and non-experts, it is common for proximal-to-distal sequencing to be expressed as the peak linear or angular velocities of key body segments. Here, however, entire angular velocity time series measurements for each body segment in the upper extremity-linked segment system and the golf club are presented for a professional golfer. As shown, energy and momentum generation commences with the rotation of the pelvis and is transferred sequentially to the thorax, lead arm, and club through a series of angular accelerations and decelerations. Each successive segment peaks faster and later than the preceding segment. The smooth shape and orderly nature of the curves representing each body segment are hallmark features of an efficient, fluid and well-coordinated golf swing. Used with permission from Phil Cheetham.

1990; Bartlett et al., 1996). For example, in their comparison of novice, club-level, and elite javelin throwers, Bartlett et al. (1996) reported that all throwers produced the same temporal order of peak horizontal velocities of the shoulder, elbow, and hand of the throwing arm, but the magnitudes of these peak horizontal velocities were significantly greater in the elite group compared to the novice and club-level groups. Similar findings have also been reported by Burden and Bartlett (1990) for cricket fast bowling—a multi-articular action that has been considered biomechanically comparable to javelin throwing (Bartlett, 2000). They compared the upper extremity kinematic chain of international fast bowlers and collegiate fast-medium bowlers and found that the former not only had higher joint center velocities than the latter, but also the differences in velocities between the two groups became more pronounced in progressively more distal joint centers. In baseball batting, Inkster, Murphy, Bower, and Watsford (2011) reported that highly skilled hitters exhibited significantly greater angular velocities of the pelvis and lead elbow compared to less-skilled hitters, which apparently contributed to the significantly higher linear bat speeds generated by the former. However, curiously, no other upper extremity segment or joint peak angular velocities or their timings were reported.

The analysis procedures and research designs used in many of the above studies have, in some respects, limited the insights that can be drawn from these investigations and potentially provided misleading information about characteristics distinguishing experts from non-experts in the performance of multi-articular sport actions. In particular, the emphasis on time-discrete kinematic variables has generally precluded insights from being made into interactions of body segments comprising the kinematic chain, and group-based research designs have tended to mask key differences among individuals within their respective skill group. A good example of these anomalies can be found in the study of Cheetham, Rose, Hinrichs, Neal, Mottram, Hurrion, and Vint (2008), which examined differences in segmental sequencing between amateur (n = 19) and professional (n = 19) golfers. Of the 15 time-discrete kinematic variables used to describe the motion of the pelvis, thorax, arm, and club during the golf swing, 14 were shown to be significantly greater in magnitude for professionals compared to amateurs. However, no significant mean differences between the two groups in the timing of peak rotational speeds of body segments and club relative to impact existed, although amateurs were more variable in their timing. When multiple angular velocity time series measurements were examined for selected golfers, individual differences became apparent in terms of the sequencing, timing, and interaction of body segments (see Figure 8.2). Other studies have also demonstrated how group- and

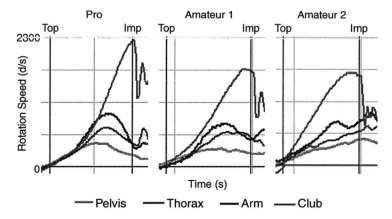

Figure 8.2 Comparisons of body segment and club motions between golfers of different skill levels. These graphs indicate differences between a professional ("Pro") and two amateurs ("Amateur 1" and "Amateur 2") in the sequencing, timing, and interaction of body segment and club rotations during the downswing phase of the golf swing. The "Pro" exhibited comparatively smooth accelerations and decelerations with the rotational speed of each segment peaking higher and later than the preceding segment in the kinematic chain. In contrast, "Amateur 1" exhibited lower peak rotational speeds, which are out of sequence (lead arm peaks before thorax), and poorer accelerations and decelerations. "Amateur 2" exhibited no deceleration of the pelvis and thorax before impact, and the rotational speed of the lead arm peaks well before impact before decelerating and accelerating again, leading up to, and through, impact. These graphs indicate that some of the results derived from the group-based analysis for this study (i.e., no significant difference in the order and timing of peak rotational speeds of segments between amateurs and professionals) are not demonstrable in individual golfers. Used with permission from Phil Cheetham.

individual-based analyses can produce equivocal, and often conflicting, results (e.g., Dufek *et al.*, 1995; Ball *et al.*, 2003; Ball & Best, 2012). Accordingly, caution should be applied when making generalized, "on average" statements based on the findings of group-based analyses in expertise research, especially if applying them in a talent identification context, since ". . . propositions about people cannot necessarily be derived from propositions about the mean of people because the patterns found by aggregating data across people do not necessarily apply to individuals" (Bouffard 1993, p. 371).

Inter- and intra-individual movement variability

The amount of variability in the movement patterns of throwing, kicking, and hitting actions is usually considered, often intuitively, to be a good indicator of level of expertise. Since experts generally produce more consistent performance outcomes than non-experts, it is often assumed that the movement patterns used by experts to produce those outcomes are more consistent (i.e., less variable) over repeated performance trials than those used by non-experts (e.g., Phillips, 1985). Furthermore, as the pathway to expertise in these multi-articular actions is often considered to be a progression towards a perceived "ideal" technique (e.g., Sherman *et al.*, 2001), it is typically assumed that there is less variability among the throwing, kicking, and hitting actions of experts than non-experts. A schematic describing the putative relationship between inter- and intra-individual movement variability and expertise in the performance of multi-articular sports actions is provided in Figure 8.3.

Owing to the research designs and methods habitually used by sport biomechanists, and because it has often been deemed to have negligible practical significance due to its association with unwanted system "noise" (see Glazier *et al.*, 2006), only a limited number of studies have investigated movement variability in throwing, kicking, and hitting actions, and even fewer have compared differences between experts and non-experts. Bradshaw, Keogh, Hume, Maulder, Nortje, and Marnewick (2009) and Fleisig, Chu, Weber, and Andrews (2009) confirmed that expert golfers and baseball pitchers, respectively, were less variable than non-experts, but both operationalized movement variability as simply the coefficient of variation and standard deviation of various, isolated, time-discrete variables over repeated performance

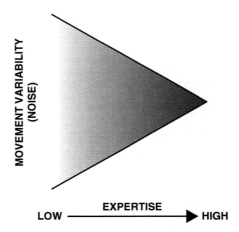

Figure 8.3 Both inter- and intra-individual movement variability, which is usually considered to be a reflection of "noise," are commonly thought to reduce to a minimum with expertise.

Expertise in multi-articular sport actions

trials. These analytical approaches, however, are inherently limited because, amongst other issues identified by Newell and Corcos (1993), they provide little information about variability of the underlying coordination patterns.

The problem with focusing essentially on outcome measures was nicely demonstrated in the often-cited study of Arutyunyan, Gurfinkel, and Mirskii (1968), which compared expert and novice marksmen in a simulated pistol shooting task—another type of multi-articular sport action. As could be anticipated, skilled marksmen were found to exhibit less variability in the performance outcome (radial scatter of "shots") than unskilled marksmen. However, skilled marksmen were shown to exhibit more variability in the coupling relationships between joints of the shooting arm than unskilled marksmen. It was concluded that, whereas unskilled marksmen attempted to rigidly fix their shoulder, elbow, and wrist joints, skilled marksmen allowed them to co-vary, thus minimizing any errors in the position and orientation of the gun barrel and, therefore, reducing the radial scatter of "shots." This study indicates the need to examine outcome variability in relation to coordination variability in throwing, kicking, and hitting actions across performers of different skill levels, particularly in light of recent research showing that stable performance outcomes are often a product of variable coordination patterns (see Newell & James, 2008 for a recent review). Indeed, preliminary insights from Button, MacLeod, Sanders, and Coleman (2003) on free throwing in basketball and Schorer, Baker, Fath, and Jaitner (2007) on penalty shooting in handball have indicated that the functionality of intra-individual movement variability may differ between experts and non-experts; i.e., skilled throwers tend to exhibit functional variability in that it enables task goals to be accomplished, whereas less-skilled throwers tend to exhibit dysfunctional variability in that it jeopardizes the successful attainment of task goals.

Although, to date, it has received only very limited coverage in the literature, the commonly held assumption that there is less inter-individual variability among the throwing, kicking and hitting actions of experts than non-experts has not been well supported in biomechanical studies. Schöllhorn and Bauer (1998) investigated differences in throwing technique among male and female national and international javelin specialists and heptathletes. They reported highly individual movement patterns, especially among the elite male specialists, who exhibited more inter-individual variability than the female throwers. It was speculated that this greater variability may be attributable to the greater variety of nationalities of the male throwers and the different sociocultural constraints (e.g., coaching ideologies, etc.) of those nations. They also found greater movement variability among the international-standard female specialists compared to the national-standard female specialists, thus contradicting the often-held view that increased expertise involves the gradual refinement of technique towards a common optimal, or template, movement pattern (see Brisson & Alain, 1996). This study is noteworthy because it represents one of the first attempts to move beyond conventional reductionist paradigms in biomechanics to truly analyze differences in "technique" between performers of various skill levels (see Schöllhorn *et al.*, 2014 for a review).

Range of motion and utilization of stored elastic energy

Two further, somewhat interrelated, technical characteristics that may distinguish experts from non-experts performing multi-articular sport actions are range of motion at key joints and the utilization of elastic energy stored in muscles crossing those joints. In principle, an increased range of motion will increase the distance over which the throwing, kicking, or hitting limb can be accelerated, resulting in greater speed of the end-effector, hitting implement or projectile at the moment of impact or release. As experts are generally able to produce more speed in more distal body segments than non-experts, it follows that the former may use a greater range of motion at key joints than the latter. This proposal, however, has only received limited support in the literature. For example, in the aforementioned study of Bartlett *et al.* (1996), elite javelin throwers were shown to exhibit a longer acceleration path or range of motion of the throwing arm than club-level and novice javelin throwers, which the authors argued was a potentially important contributory factor in the observed differences in release speed and throwing distance among the groups. In contrast, both McTeigue, Lamb, Mottram, and Pirozzolo (1994) and Egret, Dujardin, Weber, and Chollet (2004) reported no significant differences in the pelvis-thorax separation angle at the top of the backswing (the "X-factor") between expert and non-expert golfers, despite the magnitude of the X-factor being significantly associated with golf driving performance (Myers *et al.*, 2008). Further contributing to the ambiguity of the relationship between range of motion and expertise is that, when chip kicking in soccer, the hip and knee joints of the kicking leg have been shown to move through a smaller and larger range of motion, respectively, in more skilled kickers compared to novices (Chow *et al.*, 2007). The equivocal nature of the aforementioned findings indicates that the hypothesized unidirectional relationship between range of motion and expertise is not universal and is somewhat dependent on the prevailing task constraints.

If an increased range of motion is also accompanied by eccentric loading (pre-stretch) of the active muscle(s) spanning the joint(s)—for example, through counter-rotating the preceding proximal body segment in the linked segment system—transient elastic energy can, in principle, be used to produce a more forceful concentric contraction, leading to a greater increase in the speed of more distal body segments. This feature may be a distinguishing factor between experts and non-experts performing multi-articular sport actions since, again, the former tend to generate more speed in distal body segments than the latter. Cheetham, Martin, Mottram and St. Laurent (2001) demonstrated how both low and high handicap golfers were able to make use of stored elastic energy during the golf swing by increasing the X-factor during the early downswing. This move—termed the "X-factor stretch"—involves the rotation of the pelvis back towards the target whilst the thorax is still either completing the backswing or is stationary at the top of the backswing. Both low and high handicap golfers increased the X-factor, on average, by 19 per cent and 13 per cent, respectively, and this difference was reported to be statistically significant. Interestingly, no significant difference in the mean X-factor at the top of the backswing was reported between the two groups, thus corroborating the results of McTeigue *et al.* (1994) and Egret *et al.* (2004). In skilled soccer kickers, Shan and Westerhoff (2005) suggested that increased trunk rotation and contralateral arm extension and abduction during the preparatory phase produced a "tension arc" that provided greater muscle pre-stretching across the trunk flexors, hip flexors, and quadriceps of the kicking leg, leading to increased force production during the action phase. The pre-stretching of limb and trunk muscle groups, however, was less evident in novice soccer kickers. More effective use of stored elastic energy has also been suggested as a reason why expert tennis players performing the power serve are able to produce faster ball speeds than non-experts (Girard *et al.*, 2005).

Concluding remarks and recommendations for future research

The purpose of this chapter was to critically evaluate the literature and provide a summary of the technical features that distinguish experts from non-experts performing multi-articular sport actions. Of the comparatively few studies that have examined skill level differences in throwing, kicking, and hitting actions, most have adopted a product- rather than a process-oriented focus, which has tended to yield limited, and oftentimes trivial, findings (e.g., experts generate larger peak body segment angular velocities and produce greater release speeds and more accurate

Expertise in multi-articular sport actions

outcomes than non-experts). Furthermore, the somewhat arbitrary and inconsistent selection of time-discrete performance parameters across studies has made making conclusive statements about skill level differences challenging, and the almost exclusive use of group-based research designs has tended to mask individual differences within groups, thus permitting only probabilistic statements to be made about technical differences between experts and non-experts. In future studies, it is recommended that greater recognition is given to the biomechanical principles of movement (see Lees, 2002) and that the selection of performance parameters be based on more rational grounds, such as a theoretical model of performance (see Lees, 1999). Although deterministic or hierarchical models do have inherent limitations (see Glazier & Robins, 2012), they at least provide sound justification for the inclusion and analysis of specific variables and could help increase coherence between studies. It is also recommended that future research on expertise in the performance multi-articular sport actions explores, and makes use of, more individual-based research designs and associated methodologies, such as coordination profiling (Button *et al.*, 2006), which can provide further insights into the consistency and variability of "technique" and how it relates to variations in speed, accuracy, and consistency of performance outcomes within and between different skill levels.

Acknowledgments

We thank Phil Cheetham for permitting the reproduction of Figures 8.1 and 8.2.

References

Arutyunyan, G. A., Gurfinkel, V. S., & Mirskii, M. L. (1968) 'Investigation of aiming at a target', *Biophysics*, 13: 536–8.

Atwater, A. E. (1979) 'Biomechanics of overarm throwing movements and of throwing injuries', in R. S. Hutton & D. I. Miller (eds) *Exercise and sport sciences reviews—Volume 7*, New York: Franklin Institute, 43–85.

Ball, K., & Best, R. (2012) 'Centre of pressure patterns in the golf swing: Individual-based analysis', *Sports Biomechanics*, 11: 175–89.

Ball, K. A., Best, R. J., & Wrigley, T. V. (2003) 'Body sway, aim point fluctuation and performance in rifle shooters: Inter- and intra-individual analysis', *Journal of Sports Sciences*, 21: 559–66.

Barfield, W. R., Kirkendall, D. T., & Yu, B. (2002) 'Kinematic instep kicking differences between elite female and male soccer players', *Journal of Sports Science and Medicine*, 1: 72–9.

Bartlett, R. (1999) *Sports biomechanics: Reducing injury and improving performance*, London: E. & F. N. Spon.

Bartlett, R. (2000) 'Principles of throwing', in V. M. Zatsiorsky (ed) *Biomechanics in sport: Performance enhancement and injury prevention*, Oxford: Blackwell Science, 365–80.

Bartlett, R., Müller, E., Lindinger, S., Brunner, F., & Morriss, C. (1996) 'Three-dimensional evaluation of the kinematic release parameters for javelin throwers of different skill levels', *Journal of Applied Biomechanics*, 12: 58–71.

Bartlett, R., & Robins, M. (2008) 'Biomechanics of throwing', in Y. Hong & R. Bartlett (eds) *Routledge handbook of biomechanics and human movement science*, London: Routledge, 285–96.

Bouffard, M. (1993) 'The perils of averaging data in adapted physical activity research', *Adapted Physical Activity Quarterly*, 10: 371–91.

Bradshaw, E. J., Keogh, J. W. L., Hume, P. A., Maulder, P. S., Nortje, J., & Marnewick, M. (2009) 'The effect of biological movement variability on the performance of the golf swing in high- and low-handicapped players', *Research Quarterly for Exercise and Sport*, 60: 185–96.

Brisson, T. A., & Alain, C. (1996) 'Should common optimal movement patterns be identified as the criterion to be achieved?', *Journal of Motor Behavior*, 28: 211–23.

Bunn, J. W. (1955) *Scientific principles of coaching*, Englewood Cliffs, NJ: Prentice-Hall.

Burden, A. M., & Bartlett, R. M. (1990) 'A kinematic comparison between elite fast bowlers and college fast-medium bowlers', in *Proceedings of the sports biomechanics section of the British Association of Sports Sciences*, no. 15, Leeds: British Association of Sports Sciences.

Paul S. Glazier et al.

Button, C., Davids, K., & Schöllhorn, W. (2006) 'Coordination profiling of movement systems', in K. Davids, S. Bennett, & K. Newell (eds) *Movement system variability*, Champaign, IL: Human Kinetics, 133–52.

Button, C., MacLeod, M., Sanders, R., & Coleman, S. (2003) 'Examining movement variability in the basketball free-throw action at different skill levels', *Research Quarterly for Exercise and Sport*, 74: 257–69.

Cheetham, P. J., Martin, P. E., Mottram, R. E., & St. Laurent, B. F. (2001) 'The importance of stretching the "X-factor" in the downswing of golf: The "X-factor stretch"', in P. R. Thomas (ed) *Optimising performance in golf*, Brisbane: Australian Academic Press, 192–9.

Cheetham, P. J., Rose, G. A., Hinrichs, R. N., Neal, R. J., Mottram, R. E., Hurrion, P. D., & Vint, P. F. (2008) 'Comparison of kinematic sequence parameters between amateur and professional golfers', in D. Crews & R. Lutz (eds) *Science and golf V: Proceedings of the World Scientific Congress of Golf*, Mesa, AZ: Energy in Motion Inc., 30–6.

Chow, J. Y., Davids, K., Button, C., & Koh, M. (2007) 'Variation in coordination of a discrete multiarticular action as a function of skill level', *Journal of Motor Behavior*, 39: 463–79.

Davids, K., Savelsbergh, G., Bennett, S. J., & van der Kamp, J. (2002) *Interceptive actions in sport: Information and movement*, London: Routledge.

Delextrat, A., & Goss-Sampson, M. (2010) 'Kinematic analysis of netball goal shooting: A comparison of junior and senior players', *Journal of Sports Sciences*, 28: 1299–1307.

De Witt, J. K., & Hinrichs, R. N. (2012) 'Mechanical factors associated with the development of high ball velocity during an instep soccer kick', *Sports Biomechanics*, 11: 382–90.

Dufek, J. S., Bates, B. T., Stergiou, N., & James, C. R. (1995) 'Interactive effects between group and single-subject response patterns', *Human Movement Science*, 14: 301–23.

Egret, C. I., Dujardin, F. H., Weber, J., & Chollet, D. (2004) '3-D kinematic analysis of the golf swings of expert and experienced golfers', *Journal of Human Movement Studies*, 47: 193–204.

Elliott, B., Alderson, J., & Reid, M. (2008) 'Biomechanics of striking and kicking', in Y. Hong & R. Bartlett (eds) *Routledge handbook of biomechanics and human movement science*, London: Routledge, 311–22.

Elliott, B., & Marsh, T. (1989) 'A biomechanical comparison of the topspin and backspin forehand approach shots in tennis', *Journal of Sports Sciences*, 7: 215–27.

Elliott, B., Marsh, T., & Blanksby, B. (1986) 'A three-dimensional cinematographic analysis of the tennis serve', *International Journal of Sport Biomechanics*, 2: 260–71.

Elliott, B. C. (2000) 'Hitting and kicking', in V. M. Zatsiorsky (ed) *Biomechanics in sport: Performance enhancement and injury prevention*, Oxford: Blackwell Science, 487–504.

Elliott, B. C., & Armour, J. (1988) 'The penalty throw in water polo: A cinematographic analysis', *Journal of Sports Sciences*, 6: 103–14.

Fajen, B. R., Riley, M. A., & Turvey, M. T. (2008) 'Information, affordances, and the control of action in sport', *International Journal of Sport Psychology*, 40: 79–107.

Fleisig, G., Chu, Y., Weber, A., & Andrews, J. (2009) 'Variability in baseball pitching biomechanics among various levels of competition', *Sports Biomechanics*, 8: 10–21.

Fleisig, G. S., Barrentine, S. W., Escamilla, R. F., & Andrews, J. R. (1996) 'Biomechanics of overhand throwing with implications for injuries', *Sports Medicine*, 21: 421–37.

Fradet, L., Botcazou, M., Durocher, C., Cretual, A., Multon, F., Prioux, J., & Delamarche, P. (2004) 'Do handball throws always exhibit a proximal-to-distal segmental sequence?', *Journal of Sports Sciences*, 22: 439–47.

Girard, O., Micallef, J. P., & Millet, G. P. (2005) 'Lower-limb activity during the power serve in tennis: Effects of performance level', *Medicine & Science in Sports & Exercise*, 37: 1021–29.

Glazier, P. S., Paradisis, G. P., & Cooper, S. M. (2000) 'Anthropometric and kinematic influences on release speed in men's fast-medium bowling', *Journal of Sports Sciences*, 18: 1013–21.

Glazier, P. S., & Robins, M. T. (2012) 'Comment on "Use of deterministic models in sports and exercise biomechanics research" by Chow and Knudson (2011)', *Sports Biomechanics*, 11: 120–2.

Glazier, P. S., Wheat, J. S., Pease, D. L., & Bartlett, R. M. (2006) 'The interface of biomechanics and motor control: Dynamic systems theory and the functional role of movement variability', in K. Davids, S. Bennett, & K. Newell (eds) *Movement system variability*, Champaign, IL: Human Kinetics, 49–69.

Göktepe, A., Ak, E., Söğüt, M., Karabörk, H., & Korkusuz, F. (2009) 'Joint angles during successful and unsuccessful tennis serves kinematics of tennis serve', *Joint Diseases and Related Surgery*, 20: 156–60.

Inkster, B., Murphy, A., Bower, R., & Watsford, M. (2011) 'Differences in the kinematics of the baseball swing between hitters of varying skill', *Medicine & Science in Sports & Exercise*, 43: 1050–4.

Jöris, H. J. J., Edwards van Muyen, A. J., van Ingen Schenau, G. J., & Kemper, H. C. G. (1985) 'Force, velocity and energy flow during the overarm throw in female handball players', *Journal of Biomechanics*, 18: 409–14.

Kellis, E., & Katis, A. (2007) 'Biomechanical characteristics and determinants of instep soccer kick', *Journal of Sports Science and Medicine*, 6: 154–65.

Kreighbaum, E., & Barthels, K. M. (1996) *Biomechanics: A qualitative approach for studying human movement*, 4th ed., Boston, MA: Allyn and Bacon.

Lees, A. (1999) 'Biomechanical assessment of individual sports for improved performance', *Sports Medicine*, 28: 299–305.

Lees, A. (2002) 'Technique analysis in sport: A critical review', *Journal of Sports Sciences*, 20: 813–28.

Marshall, R. N., & Elliott, B. C. (2000) 'Long-axis rotation: The missing link in proximal-to-distal segmental sequencing', *Journal of Sports Sciences*, 18: 247–54.

McTeigue, M., Lamb, S. R., Mottram, R., & Pirozzolo, F. (1994) 'Spine and hip motion analysis during the golf swing', in A. J. Cochran & M. R. Farrally (eds) *Science and golf II: Proceedings of the World Scientific Congress of Golf*, London: E. & F.N. Spon, 50–8.

Mero, A., Komi, P. V., Korjus, T., Navarro, E., & Gregor, R. J. (1994) 'Body segment contributions to javelin throwing during the final thrust phases', *Journal of Applied Biomechanics*, 10: 166–77.

Myers, J., Lephart, S., Tsai, Y. S., Sell, T., Smoliga, J., & Jolly, J. (2008) 'The role of upper torso and pelvis rotation in driving performance during the golf swing', *Journal of Sports Sciences*, 26: 181–8.

Newell, K. M., & Corcos, D. M. (1993) 'Issues in variability and motor control', in K. M. Newell & D. M. Corcos (eds) *Variability and motor control*, Champaign, IL: Human Kinetics, 1–12.

Newell, K. M., & James, E. G. (2008) 'The amount and structure of human movement variability', in Y. Hong & R. Bartlett (eds) *Routledge handbook of biomechanics and human movement science*, London: Routledge, 93–104.

Nunome, H., Ikegami, Y., Kozakai, R., Apriantono, T., & Sano, S. (2006). 'Segmental dynamics of soccer instep kicking with the preferred and non-preferred leg', *Journal of Sports Sciences*, 24, 529–41.

Pappas, A. M., Zawacki, R. M., & Sullivan, T. J. (1985) 'Biomechanics of baseball pitching: A preliminary report', *American Journal of Sports Medicine*, 13: 216–22.

Phillips, S. J. (1985) 'Invariance of elite kicking performance', in D. A. Winter, R. W. Norman, R. P. Wells, K. C. Hayes, & A. E. Patla (eds) *Biomechanics IX-B*, Champaign, IL: Human Kinetics, 539–42.

Plagenhoef, S. (1971) *Patterns of human motion: A cinematographic analysis*, Englewood Cliffs, NJ: Prentice-Hall.

Putnam, C. A. (1991) 'A segment interaction analysis of proximal-to-distal sequential segment motion patterns', *Medicine and Science in Sports and Exercise*, 23: 130–44.

Putnam, C. A. (1993) 'Sequential motions of body segments in striking and throwing skills: Descriptions and explanations', *Journal of Biomechanics*, 26 (suppl. 1): 125–35.

Rota, S., Morel, B., Saboul, D., Rogowski, I., & Hautier, C. (2014) 'Influence of fatigue on upper limb muscle activity and performance in tennis', *Journal of Electromyography and Kinesiology*, 24: 90–7.

Sachlikidis, A., & Salter, C. (2007) 'A biomechanical comparison of dominant and non-dominant arm throws for speed and accuracy', *Sports Biomechanics*, 6: 334–44.

Savelsbergh, G. J.P., & Bootsma, R. J. (1994) 'Perception-action coupling in hitting and catching', *International Journal of Sport Psychology*, 25: 331–43.

Schöllhorn, W. I., & Bauer, H. U. (1998) 'Identifying individual movement styles in high performance sports by means of self-organizing Kohonen maps', in H. J. Riehle & M. Vieten (eds) *XVI international symposium on biomechanics in sports*, Konstanz: Konstanz University Press, 574–7.

Schöllhorn, W., Chow, J. Y., Glazier, P., & Button, C. (2014) 'Self-Organising Maps and cluster analysis in elite and sub-elite athletic performance', in K. Davids, R. Hristovski, D. Araújo, N. Balagué Serre, C. Button, & P. Passos (eds) *Complex systems in sport*, London: Routledge, 145–59.

Schorer, J., Baker, J., Fath, F., & Jaitner, T. (2007) 'Identification of interindividual and intraindividual movement patterns in handball players of varying expertise levels', *Journal of Motor Behavior*, 39: 409–21.

Shan, G., & Westerhoff, P. (2005) 'Full-body kinematic characteristics of the maximal instep soccer kick by male soccer players and parameters related to kick quality', *Sports Biomechanics*, 4: 59–72.

Sherman, C. A., Sparrow, W. A., Jolley, D., & Eldering, J. (2001) 'Coaches' perceptions of golf swing kinematics', *International Journal of Sport Psychology*, 31: 257–70.

Stretch, R., Buys, F., Du Toit, E., & Viljoen, G. (1998) 'Kinematics and kinetics of the drive off the front foot in cricket batting', *Journal of Sports Sciences*, 16: 711–20.

Tinmark, F., Hellström, J., Halvorsen, K., & Thorstensson, A. (2010) 'Elite golfers' kinematic sequence in full-swing and partial-swing shots', *Sports Biomechanics*, 9: 236–44.

Warren, W. H. (2006) 'The dynamics of perception and action', *Psychological Review*, 113: 358–89.

Welch, C. M., Banks, S. A., Cook, F. F., & Draovitch, P. (1995) 'Hitting a baseball: A biomechanical description', *Journal of Orthopaedic & Sports Physical Therapy*, 22: 193–201.

Williams, A. M., Davids, K., & Williams, J. G. (1999) *Visual perception and action in sport*, London: Routledge.

Worthington, P. J., King, M. A., & Ranson, C. A. (2013) 'Relationships between fast bowling technique and ball release speed in cricket', *Journal of Applied Biomechanics*, 29: 78–84.

Zelaznik, H. N. (2014) 'The past and future of motor learning and control: What is the proper level of description and analysis?', *Kinesiology Review*, 3: 38–43.

Zhang, Y., Liu, G., & Xie, S. (2012) 'Movement sequences during instep rugby kick: A 3D biomechanical analysis', *International Journal of Sports Science and Engineering*, 6, 89–95.

Zhang, Y., Unka, J., & Liu, G. (2011) 'Contributions of joint rotations to ball release speed during cricket bowling: A three-dimensional kinematic analysis', *Journal of Sports Sciences*, 29: 1293–1300.

9

BREADTH AND DEPTH OF KNOWLEDGE IN EXPERT VERSUS NOVICE ATHLETES

John Sutton and Doris J. F. McIlwain

Knowledge and sport expertise

Questions about knowledge in expert sport are not only of applied significance: they also take us to the heart of foundational and heavily disputed issues in the cognitive sciences. To a first (rough and far from uncontroversial) approximation, we can think of expert "knowledge" as whatever it is that grounds or is applied in (more or less) effective decision-making, especially when in a competitive situation a performer follows one course of action out of a range of possibilities. In these research areas, studies of motor expertise have for many years actively contributed to broader debates in philosophy and psychology (Abernethy *et al.*, 1994; Williams *et al.*, 1999). When we navigate the world flexibly and more or less successfully, how much is this due to a capacity to *represent* it? In considering alternative options, or planning future actions, we seem to transcend our present environment in some way: what is the balance or relation here between highly tuned bodily dispositions and background *knowledge* of the world and its patterns? What changes in these regards as we gain experience and adapt to more complex and challenging environments? Is know-how fundamentally different in kind from ordinary factual knowledge of the world, or knowledge-that? And if expertise in a domain does involve or depend on a knowledge base that is somehow more organized or deeper than that of novices, how is this knowledge selectively and appropriately deployed, often under severe time constraints?

The complex, highly structured, culturally embedded worlds of elite sport afford extraordinary opportunities for cognitive scientists to study the mind in action. Experts voluntarily dedicate years to arduous self-transformation, integrating their perceptual, cognitive, and motor capacities with respect to their chosen domain in ways that may be entirely different from most participants in psychological or cognitive neuroscientific experiments. At this stage of science, at least for the kind of questions we listed above, we suspect that sport still has more to offer cognitive theory than vice versa. There is as yet no general theory of the varieties of human knowledge and the roles they may play in skillful actions of any kind that can simply be applied to the sport domain. However, such theories must be tested against the unique features of expert performance in the natural ecologies of sport.

The tasks posed in professional sport are extremely diverse, and both the role and the application of expert knowledge will likely vary widely. This is true, first, across individuals: within the same sport, and even at similar levels, significant variability across performers is often due as much, if not more, to differences in cognitive style – in players' characteristic patterns of options taken and tactical decisions made – as to distinct physical or technical skills. Second, the situational constraints of different sport scenarios shape what knowledge may be relevant and how it may be used. So researchers should not rush to find a single general theory of expert knowledge in sport, for there may be genuine differences across settings in what experts know and how they deploy that knowledge. In this chapter we have in mind, for the most part, more open sporting environments in which the situation and demands can change rapidly, and the expert must respond to more or less unpredictable events in either team or individual contexts. While the distinction is not absolute, the contrast is with more closed sports in which the performer initiates movement herself, more independently of the task environment, and – in some cases – aims primarily to reproduce a sequence of actions, rather than having to adapt on the fly to dynamic events around her. Think of soccer, with its more or less continuous motion, as opposed to many forms of gymnastic routine, or the rapidly changing passages of play in a long tennis rally, in which the players' movements and decisions sometimes seem to be interactively, dynamically coupled, as opposed to competitive diving. Expert knowledge in more closed sporting contexts may take different forms.

In complex open sports, reliance on knowledge is often treated with some suspicion by elite athletes and coaches, and ambivalent attitudes to expert knowledge are also apparent in the theories we discuss in this chapter. The concept of "knowledge" is seen by some as overly static, as referring to internal psychological structures that seem too rigid to explain fast decision-making and action in sport. In some contexts, expert practitioners' lore privileges heavily practiced, embodied movement skills over any residual cognitive representation, and intuitive decision-making on the basis of vast experience over any deliberate or thoughtful use of background knowledge. As we will see, some leading psychological theories in sport science take a similar view. In the next section, we discuss existing taxonomies of kinds of knowledge. But in practice too the terms "knowledge" and "thinking" arguably have a range of distinct meanings. We can illustrate this with an anecdote. At the 2010 Cricket Australia conference on science, medicine, and coaching in cricket, two successful and reflective elite coaches, who were also close collaborators, spoke in succeeding sessions. In a panel on the increasing need for cricket batters to adapt both to new forms of the game and to more rapidly changing situations on the field, one ex-elite player and coach noted, "as we all know, the best batters are the best thinkers." Within minutes, in the following session, his colleague was saying, "as soon as a batter starts *thinking*, you know he's in trouble." As we will suggest, both perspectives make sense once we clarify the terms. *Over*thinking your game is widely demonized in elite sport: it may be seen as anxious worrying, or as excessive focus on aspects of the mechanics of performance which may be useful in practice, but in competition should be left to grooved, embodied routines. There are clear bases for these beliefs: in some circumstances, monitoring the components of one's actions, or trying to impose cognitive control over lower level movement steps, disrupts an effectively chunked, smoothly unfolding, practiced skill. But we can also make sense of the alternative conception of thinking, by which leading athletes do sometimes draw *directly* on a rich, organized, and sophisticated knowledge base in order to respond appropriately to highly dynamic environmental and performance demands.

Before working through a range of theories about the nature and use of knowledge in expert sport, we underline certain general features of skilled performance at the highest levels. Elite athletes commonly face new challenges and unexpected forms of pressure. There are no simple repetitions in sport. Even when an expert faces familiar opposition in the same location on a different occasion, much of relevance may have shifted: confidence, fitness, rankings, recent technical issues, competition stage, mood, weather, motivation, and other contextual factors are rarely identical. So performers must constantly take themselves further, going beyond their particular past experience. Their repertoires of embodied skill are flexible, so they can adapt effectively to new opponents or teammates, unpredictable or unfriendly environments, and the constantly monitored state of their body. They value the ability to *generalize* skills to increasingly challenging conditions, and often structure training regimes around preparing to cope outside their "comfort zone." Such variability is to be expected: challenging, more or less unfamiliar conditions are just part of the deal at elite levels of performance. For sure, not every athlete is equally adaptable, equally able to reorient online, on-the-fly performance by "thinking on her feet." In most sports, there are many routes to, and styles of, excellence. But those with exceptional tactical skills who can extend themselves, who rapidly pick up and respond to new circumstances may receive different levels of recognition, perhaps as "students of the game" (McPherson, 2008, p. 155). The basis of such adaptability is uncertain, and nothing we have said so far suggests that it must involve unusual forms of knowledge. But sport science has to respect these phenomena of expert performance, and in particular offer clear accounts of how empirical results gained in more controlled settings might link to or explain such features of the competitive environment. In this chapter we first discuss the distinct kinds of knowledge which might be important for expert performance, before examining particular attempts to tap sophisticated sport-specific knowledge.

Kinds of knowledge in expert sport

In his excellent sport psychology textbook, Aidan Moran begins a discussion of expert-novice differences by stating, "experts have a more extensive knowledge-base of sport-specific information . . . [they] *know more* about their specialist domains than do relative novices" (2004, p. 178). We observe experts performing better than novices across a range of scenarios: their perceptual systems are exquisitely attuned to subtle cues, and as they effectively anticipate what is coming next their actions are already taking shape. Researchers who focus on expert knowledge argue that it drives this rich integration of perception and action. Experts' perceptual skills are informed by what they know, as certain combinations of sensory stimuli, and not others, appear salient. A vast and unique body of experience shapes each elite performer's knowledge base, which helps her to filter and select relevant, current input and ignore everything irrelevant, and which is in turn constantly updated as new events transpire. Studies of perceptual anticipation and skill in sport are often described as addressing "perceptual-cognitive" expertise (MacMahon & McPherson, 2009; Roca *et al.*, 2013), as researchers acknowledge the *intelligence* built into expert perception.

Terminology in this area can be confusing, and the utility of the term "knowledge" in this context is not secure: a richer vocabulary would be welcome. Most theorists refer to a standard taxonomy in cognitive science by which "declarative knowledge" is distinguished from "procedural knowledge." Roughly, declarative knowledge is knowledge of facts, whereas procedural knowledge is knowledge of how to act. The uses of these terms, however, are far from consistent, and these concepts should not be presented as if there is a clear scientific consensus. Before we discuss each in turn, we note the direct relevance of parallel debates about knowing-how and knowing-that. Gilbert Ryle argued powerfully in *The Concept of Mind* (1949) that knowing how to do something is prior to, and independent of, knowledge of any set of facts, attacking what he called the "intellectualist" view that knowing how to do something simply consists in knowledge of certain facts. This is a live and controversial issue in contemporary philosophy (Fantl, 2012; Gascoigne & Thornton, 2013; Stanley & Krakauer, 2013). Although this literature has potentially rich connections to the study of knowledge in sport expertise, the mere existence of a distinction in cognitive science between declarative and procedural knowledge does not confirm that Ryle was right (Devitt, 2011). Neither the nature of procedural knowledge nor the relation between the two is settled in such a way as to decide this issue, and perhaps the terms are still best thought of as broadly descriptive labels rather than well-defined explanatory or natural kind terms.

To a first approximation, then, declarative knowledge of facts is explicit and can in principle be consciously accessed. The category includes not only semantic knowledge of both general and specific information (about the typical nature of a sporting venue, for example, or about an opponent's recent results), but also episodic memory, such as an expert's recall of her last game against the opponent (Sutton, 2007; Sutton & Williamson, 2014). Two connected preliminary points are needed here. First, this use of "knowledge" does not entail that experts' "knowledge" is *all* true or accurate. In philosophy and in many ordinary contexts it would be more natural to say that they have certain *beliefs* about the world, or *model* the world in such and such a way: people may – and often do – *believe* things that are not true, but in ordinary language we cannot *know* something that is not true. As Moran's term "knowledge base" suggests, the relevant notion here is more liberal and inclusive: the sport expert's "knowledge" is a complex, heterogeneous, dynamic body of information, which may fit more or less neatly with reality. Second, someone knows many things he is not currently thinking about: e.g., John knew the result of the Melbourne Ashes test of 1982–83 before he thought about it again just now, and indeed he has known it for years. So knowledge, like belief, can take a dispositional form, when someone is disposed to act appropriately on the basis of knowledge if prompted, as well as an occurrent form, when she exercises that knowledge now.

Talking of declarative knowledge as explicit knowledge of facts, in the standard way we have so far, can easily be taken to suggest either that declarative knowledge is itself linguistic in form, or at least that it is essentially verbalizable. Although verbal reports are a vital source of evidence, as we discuss further below and in the associated chapter on methods for studying expert knowledge (see Chapter 20), declarative knowledge should not be *defined* as reportable. The representational media of declarative knowledge may be entirely non-linguistic in form. As well as the possibility of sensory, imagistic, or kinesthetic forms of representation, cognitive psychologists use terms like "schemas" and "situation models" to describe dynamically updated ways in which experts richly map their domain, and there is no reason to assume that the content of such mental models can be easily or accurately translated into verbal form. Not everything that is consciously accessible is thereby also verbally articulable: an expert can know or accurately map certain features of the world, as revealed for example in successful action, without necessarily being able to *explain* what she knows.

In the case of sport, of course, what the expert "knows" may be not only inarticulable, but also not accessible at all. On many views, at least parts of the knowledge base may operate at a subpersonal level: experts need not be aware, for example, of the knowledge which guides their eye movements so as to pick up information from only the relevant parts of the perceptual scene. This is then, on most views, part of procedural rather than declarative knowledge. Given this very rough sense of the distinction, and smoothing over finer-grained theoretical issues, we can characterize three broad approaches to knowledge in sport expertise. The strongest views are those on which the expert makes significant use of declarative as well as procedural knowledge in action, where the interaction between the two can take a range of distinctive forms: we discuss approaches of this kind in the following section. Here, first, we briefly look at the other two general options. Some argue that procedural knowledge is the core of the expert advantage, with declarative knowledge being either irrelevant or an actively disruptive force, while others suggest that experts are not drawing substantially on *knowledge* at all.

First, in approaches based on general theories of expertise like that of Anderson (1982), procedural knowledge is seen as a system of "if-then" production rules or recipes for motor

Breadth and depth of knowledge

performance: for McPherson and Thomas, this aspect of sport knowledge includes "patterns or rules for generating patterns of actions to produce goal related changes in the context of a game situation" (1989, p. 192), thus linking conditions to actions. On such views, procedural knowledge is not profoundly different in *kind* from declarative knowledge, but merely has different contents and – most importantly – different modes of application. Indeed, on most such views, deriving originally from Fitts and Posner (1967) as well as Anderson (1982), knowledge of a relevant domain is first declarative in form, but then with experience becomes "proceduralized" such that its deployment in experts is automatic and unconscious. In the transition to expertise, items of knowledge that were originally distinct are linked or compiled, so that the number of individual variables to be retrieved is reduced: likewise, actions that tend to follow each other are composed into linked or chunked sequences.

On these views, once the expert's knowledge is thoroughly proceduralized, action production becomes automated and independent of cognitive control. Neither explicit knowledge nor explicit memory is required in driving expert performance, and in turn on this view no rich episodic memories of performance will be encoded and retained. Effective responses to perceptual input are both faster and more effortless for experts because their actions are "controlled in real time by procedural knowledge that requires little attention, operates largely outside of working memory, and is substantially closed to introspection" (Beilock & Carr, 2001, p. 702). Experts may well also have more "extensive and systematic" explicit general knowledge about their domain than do novices, but this is not the essence of their skill advantage. Such declarative knowledge, indeed, should, if these views are correct, operate only "offline" rather than during performance. For experts, the *online* control of action by declarative rather than procedural knowledge is detrimental to performance, breaking up the uninterrupted units of the proceduralized control structures, leading to an unwanted focus on the component parts of the motor process: Masters and Maxwell (2008), for example, argue that when experts consciously reinvest declarative knowledge from an earlier stage of their training, performance will regress. Many current theories of choking in elite sport explain severe breakdown under pressure on this basis, as resulting from inappropriate self-monitoring or attention to motor execution when experts suffer "paralysis by analysis" (Baumeister, 1984; Masters, 1992; Beilock & Gray, 2007; see also Christensen *et al.*, in press).

Whereas on these accounts procedural knowledge drives expert sport performance in real time in smooth and effortless ways that declarative knowledge cannot, more radical are claims that knowledge is not directly involved at all. For Araújo and colleagues, "the distinction between declarative and procedural knowledge is elusive, since both types of knowledge are verbal formulations" (2010, p. 1088). This may not be quite the right way to put the worry, since the representational resources in question are not meant to be linguistic in form or exhausted by verbal output. But the alternative claim is that expert performance is best characterized as the ability or skill to perform certain actions: it is to be explained *simply* on the basis of such embodied capacities or dispositions, such that the element of "knowledge," understood as a representational system or model independent of the current environment, drops out of consideration. There are both constructive and critical strands to these lines of thought. An extensive body of theory and empirical research in ecological dynamics has, as described elsewhere in this handbook (see Chapter 12 for example), shown how specific regularities in the environment richly shape and constrain the opportunities for action. When there are organisms in that environment which are appropriately attuned in that they have developed "the functional capacity to pick up relevant information to guide actions" (Araújo & Davids, 2011, p. 14), the environment "is perceived directly in terms of what an organism can do . . . not dependent on a perceiver's expectations, nor mental representations linked to specific performance solutions, stored in memory" (Silva *et al.*, 2013, p. 767). Following J. J. Gibson, ecological sport psychologists deny that *knowledge about* the task domain, in the form of representational schemas or organized expert memory structures, is the core of expert skill. Instead, the expert does have *knowledge of* the environment, but this is simply "the ability to complete an action by detecting the surrounding informational constraints in order to regulate behaviors" (Silva *et al.*, 2013, p. 767).

So for these theorists, no specialist knowledge or expert memory is *acquired* in skill acquisition: the idea that expert advantages must be due to enriched or better organized information in a knowledge base is seen as a residue of classical cognitivist theory which does not apply in the domain of sport and movement (compare Dreyfus, 2002). Perception and action are coupled without mediation, so there is no central role for knowledge or cognition (Chemero, 2009). Part of the point here is that the moving, embodied organism is active in an information-rich environment, so that perception and action are fundamentally situated (Clark, 1997; Robbins & Aydede, 2009): "the skilled regulation of action is actually distributed over the organism-environment system" (Araújo & Davids, 2011, p. 14). But ecological theorists add that the increasing attunement or calibration of the expert performer to the available environmental information is a primitive biological or dynamical consequence of task experience which must not be cashed out in terms of "increasing amounts of knowledge in memory or more sophisticated movement representations" (Araújo & Davids, 2011, p. 10).

Again, this debate about sport expertise mirrors and runs alongside long-standing and difficult controversies in the cognitive sciences at large. If densely interconnected natural and cognitive ecologies heavily constrain action opportunities, are the unique and context-sensitive options taken by skilled performers on particular occasions fully explained in terms of attunement, embodied disposition, and intuitive response? Is there a middle-ground position between these knowledge-free theories and the more classical information-processing models, which have often seemed too rigid and slow to account for dynamic expert performance? This is the challenge for sport researchers who retain a role for knowledge in their accounts of expertise. Is there a kind of knowledge that is less like a clunky set of internalized propositions, and that could explain the dynamics of interactive movement in high-speed, expert sport? Versions of the classical frame problem for artificial intelligence threaten here (Wheeler, 2008). If the knowledge base is as rich and full as seems necessary to explain the range of expert skill, how can it be searched effectively at speed? How do the lessons of new experience generalize rapidly, without explicit attention to each possible context? How can certain recipes be updated on the fly during performance while others are untouched? In the following section, we show how some theorists of expert knowledge seek to address the paradox that experts must have much more knowledge to search through than novices, but seem to be able to retrieve and act on it faster and with less effort than novices (Moran, 2004).

Approaches to expert knowledge in sport

The two approaches we discuss in this section draw in different ways on the same theoretical framework to suggest how experts meet this challenge and access distinctive memory systems in performance. Experts work around the usual capacity limits of long-term memory by chunking specialist knowledge in rich and organized forms, and by developing fine-grained retrieval structures that permit rapid, controlled access to knowledge, which can then play a dynamic role in the control of ongoing action (Ericsson & Kintsch, 1995). This long-term working memory theory (LTWM) has been applied in many domains of expertise research. It is not the only relevant theory, and there remain many questions about the theoretical details and commitments, but it has proved productive in driving work on sport expertise (Ward *et al.*, 2013).

In a sustained research program, Sue McPherson and colleagues have sought to tap expert knowledge by asking players across a range of sports to report their thoughts during competition,

Breadth and depth of knowledge

with reference to what has just occurred or to their immediate plans. Elite tennis players, for example, are asked between points what they were thinking about while playing the last point, or simply what they are thinking about now. The use of verbal report data raises methodological issues (see Chapter 20), but such "think-aloud" protocols, involving immediate retrospective reporting, are the most promising way to explore the breadth, depth, and diversity of the knowledge base (Ericsson, 2006; Eccles, 2012). The idea is not that reported thoughts are themselves "blueprints for motor performance," but that they "play an integral role in determining players' response selections" (French & McPherson, 1999, p. 180). Consistent patterns of difference in expert and novice knowledge have been found across sports including tennis, baseball, volleyball, and basketball.

First, McPherson and colleagues find microlevel differences in what experts attend to during competition. While novices and less-experienced players often attend "to irrelevant conditions in the current environment" (French & McPherson, 1999, p. 185), experts are thinking in more thorough, more varied, and more fine-grained terms about current conditions – such as their opponent's strengths or weaknesses – and about specific actions and responses (McPherson, 1994, 1999, 2000). Where novices tend to think in terms of a general goal of winning, experts generate more detailed planning concepts. In a landmark study of baseball players' thoughts as they prepare to bat against a particular pitcher, for example, McPherson and MacMahon (2008) found that stronger players quickly develop an extensive profile of the pitcher's strengths and preferences, which allows them to generate detailed predictions about a specific upcoming pitch.

Next, McPherson identifies two key, larger-scale memory structures. Experts develop action plan profiles, which link conditions to possible responses. In contrast, while less experienced baseball players may have some general baseball knowledge, they find it harder to connect to the actual circumstances of a game situation: several younger players, in another study, "continuously rehearsed the same plan prior to every pitch" (French & McPherson, 2004, p. 417). Further, experts have elaborate current event profiles that keep track of active relevant information: these tactical scripts include updates on a current opponent, conditions, and other contextual factors, and can guide adjustments to performance during competition. Expectations can be both highly specific and constantly modified. Crucially, experts can use these current event profiles to monitor and interpret shot selections and tactics, guiding the modification of performance in real time. Verbal labels or maxims attach to knowledge structures with a definite history, so that the expert can use them to interpret specific movement problems. This capacity to use information derived from particular prior experience is striking: whereas an expert monitored how the present situation relates to his own past performance and that of his opponent, novices "did not access past events or information from previous competitions" (French & McPherson, 2004, p. 418).

McPherson's studies have both applied and theoretical implications. In contrast to the idea that any explicit thinking may disrupt embodied performance, these results lead her to "advocate that players periodically record their thoughts during competition" (McPherson & Kernodle, 2003, p. 162). The knowledge structures identified in this research are, as McPherson and colleagues see it, the key means by which experts precisely identify the immediate problems facing them. Of course, a range of other factors underlies response selection, including those responsible for perceptual anticipation and action execution. But, as MacMahon and McPherson state forthrightly, the knowledge base is the "driving mechanism which influences component behavior:" this is, as they acknowledge, "a more hierarchical view . . . with knowledge base as the driver" (2009, p. 571–2). Reports of thought processes can thus be integrated with other process tracing measures such as eye movements.

This is exactly the approach taken in another line of mixed-method research by Ward, McRobert, and colleagues. The well-established expert advantages in perceptual anticipation, such that experts attend to relevant advance cues and can predict the time course of events earlier and more accurately, are not isolated from cognition, but spring from and, in turn, test and update the experts' elaborated knowledge. Their underlying representations of the specialist domain in long-term working memory "provide a dual function: they provide memory support for performance, in the form of planning, monitoring and evaluations, while simultaneously enabling retrieval structures to be built and updated 'on the fly' that promote direct access to task pertinent options" (McRobert *et al.*, 2009, p. 475). In a series of experiments using simulated, video-based task environments, in sports including cricket and football, these researchers integrate study of expert eye movement with analysis of verbal report data gathered immediately after specific responses.

Employing a related scheme for coding experts' verbal reports of their thought processes, four major types of cognitive statement categories are distinguished: *monitoring* of current actions and descriptions of current events, *evaluations* and assessments or appraisals of relevant events, *predictions* which anticipate what might occur next or in future, and *planning* statements identifying possible decisions or looking for alternatives beyond the next response (Roca *et al.*, 2011, 2013). Across a series of studies, experts are found to discuss more task-relevant options whereas novices think about more irrelevant options (Ward *et al.*, 2013); experts engage in more prediction and more planning than less-skilled performers, and in some settings also deploy more evaluative statements (McRobert *et al.*, 2011). In football, for example, Ward and colleagues (2013) conclude that experts are "dynamically encoding and integrating the evolving pattern of play on the fly, apprehending and representing each possible threat posed by the opposing team hierarchically, while excluding from their situation model the opposing players who did not pose a threat" (2013, p. 250). Likewise, in a cricket batting task, expertise involved "the development and constant update of elaborate knowledge representations that guide input and retrieval of pertinent information from the visual scene and from long-term memory in an integrated manner" (McRobert *et al.*, 2011, p. 532).

By manipulating the amount of relevant contextual information available, McRobert and colleagues could also assess the way experts integrate recent history into their ongoing knowledge and assessment of a situation so as to better predict the likely sequence of events. They presented the same test stimuli – video of balls bowled by the same cricket bowlers – either in actual sequence as performed, replicating match conditions, or embedded in a random sequence of deliveries from six different bowlers. In the former, high-context condition, expert batters' eye movements differed in that their fixations were of reduced duration, as a result of the cumulative information available about the particular bowler. Further, in this high-context condition batters' verbal reports included more evaluation and planning statements than in the low-context condition (McRobert *et al.*, 2011). Such experimental study of the way that recent context interacts with longer-term knowledge is a particularly promising avenue for assessing what is likely a central contributing factor in experts' performance advantage in competitive settings.

Further challenges for the study of breadth and depth of knowledge

We conclude with three brief suggestions about natural extensions of the lines of enquiry described so far, in turn addressing methods, knowledge in relation to other aspects of expert psychology, and knowledge in teams. As we gain increasingly sophisticated and realistic methods for the experimental study of expertise, we can also afford to extend the ways we seek to tap expert knowledge in the wild, in the complex and culturally embedded settings where experts actually train, swap notes, and perform. This means in part the wider range of qualitative methods for analyzing expert talk and thought, as discussed in our companion chapter on methods (see Chapter 20). However, because the kind of tacit knowledge which characterizes expert performance

Breadth and depth of knowledge

is not easily achieved and not easily communicated, it also suggests integrating empirical sport science more with ethnographic research. We can learn to listen better to what elite athletes say to each other and to their coaches and support staff. These are obviously not direct lines into the springs of action, but equally the terms which experts have developed for communicating and renegotiating aspects of skilled performance are not likely to be wholly confabulatory. Talk about embodied skills can be analogical and indirect, with groups of experts often evolving local responses to the challenges of languaging experience, often "beyond the easy flow of everyday speech" (Sheets-Johnstone, 2009, p. 336). Ethnographic work in these fields often takes the form of participant involvement, as the researcher becomes enculturated into a cultural and physical setting which transforms their bodies, perceptual-cognitive systems, and understanding of the world: examples include work on boxing (Wacquant, 2003), capoeira (Downey, 2005), martial arts (Samudra, 2008), mountain bike racing (Bicknell, 2010), and yoga (McIlwain & Sutton, 2014). Sport psychologists could potentially benefit from attempting the kind of longer-term immersion in the specific culture of expert practitioners at which anthropologists have excelled.

Second, to counter the concern that invocations of "knowledge" isolate or reify an inner realm of mental representations cut off from the rest of the expert's embodied psychology, the rich links between cognition and emotion should be further highlighted in research on expert knowledge. In some cases, emotional knowledge relating to one's own states is itself likely to be better organized in experienced athletes; in other cases, styles of emotion-regulation and emotion-management in performance will partly depend on a sophisticated understanding of the task domain. McPherson's studies again include suggestive results on these topics. Concurrent and immediate retrospective verbal data from less-skilled players include more general emotional reactions to events during play, whereas discussion among experts tended to direct such thoughts into either tactical plans or motivational comments, often linked to potential cues for concentration (French & McPherson, 1999). In some contexts, experts will likely be able to learn more from their own emotional processes, so our methods need to be able to examine the relations between knowledge and emotion.

Finally, alongside and in conjunction with the study of knowledge in individual sport experts, we would like to better understand the roles of knowledge in expert team performance. Some information-processing perspectives on shared knowledge focus on the coordination of explicit knowledge across team members (Reimer *et al.*, 2006), whereas in contrast dynamical and ecological approaches reject talk of shared knowledge in favor of shared affordances (Silva *et al.*, 2013). But emergent knowledge in successful and experienced teams must be more than the mere aggregation of explicit knowledge across the individual members. In many team sports, individuals have dramatically distinct roles and are unlikely to share much or all unique, first-order knowledge that is specific to a particular role. Yet in an effective team, a higher order, transactive memory system is in place such that team members more or less share an understanding of how that knowledge and expertise is distributed within the group. The mechanisms of communication within the group must be highly diverse. More implicit forms of alignment and interpersonal interaction, including various practiced means of non-verbal communication, complement more explicit modes of collaboration in expert teams (Eccles & Tenenbaum, 2004; Williamson & Cox, 2014; Williamson & Sutton, 2014). The study of knowledge in expert teams is one of a range of fascinating areas for research on breadth and depth of knowledge.

Acknowledgments

Our special thanks to the editors. We are also grateful to Kath Bicknell, Clare MacMahon, and David Mann for assistance. Our thinking on these topics owes much to our long-term collaborators Wayne Christensen and Andrew Geeves.

References

Abernethy, B., Burgess-Limerick, R., & Parks, S. (1994) 'Contrasting approaches to the study of motor expertise', *Quest*, 46: 186–98.

Anderson, J. (1982) 'Acquisition of cognitive skill', *Psychological Review*, 89: 369–406.

Araújo, D., & Davids, K. (2011) 'What exactly is *acquired* during skill acquisition?', *Journal of Consciousness Studies*, 18: 7–23.

Araújo, D., Travassos, B., & Vilar, L. (2010) 'Tactical skills are not verbal skills: A comment on Kannekens and colleagues', *Perceptual and Motor Skills*, 110: 1086–8.

Baumeister, R. F. (1984) 'Choking under pressure: Self-consciousness and paradoxical effects of incentives on skillful performance', *Journal of Personality and Social Psychology*, 46(3): 610–20.

Beilock, S. L., & Carr, T. H. (2001) 'On the fragility of skilled performance: What governs choking under pressure?', *Journal of Experimental Psychology: General*, 130: 701–25.

Beilock, S. L., & Gray, R. (2007) 'Why do athletes choke under pressure?', in G. Tenenbaum & R. C. Eklund (eds) *Handbook of sport psychology*, Hoboken, NJ: John Wiley & Sons, 425–44.

Bicknell, K. (2010) 'Feeling them ride: Corporeal exchange in cross-country mountain bike racing', *About Performance*, 10: 81–91.

Chemero, A. (2009) *Radical embodied cognitive science*, Cambridge, MA: MIT Press.

Christensen, W., Sutton, J., & McIlwain, D. J.F. (in press) 'Putting pressure on theories of choking: Towards an expanded perspective on breakdown in skilled performance', *Phenomenology and the Cognitive Sciences*. DOI 10.1007/s11097-014-9395-6, published online 17 October 2014.

Clark, A. (1997) *Being there: Putting brain, body, and world together again*, Cambridge, MA: MIT Press.

Devitt, M. (2011) 'Methodology and the nature of knowing how', *Journal of Philosophy*, 108: 205–18.

Downey, G. (2005) *Learning capoeira*, Oxford: Oxford University Press.

Dreyfus, H. L. (2002) 'Intelligence without representation: Merleau-Ponty's critique of mental representation', *Phenomenology and the Cognitive Sciences*, 1: 367–83.

Eccles, D. W. (2012) 'Verbal reports of cognitive processes', in G. Tenenbaum, R. Eklund, & A. Kamata (eds) *Measurement in sport and exercise psychology*, Champaign, IL: Human Kinetics, 103–17.

Eccles, D. W., & Tenenbaum, G. (2004) 'Why an expert team is more than a team of experts: A socio-cognitive conceptualization of team coordination and communication in sport', *Journal of Sport & Exercise Psychology*, 26: 542–60.

Ericsson, K. A. (2006) 'Protocol analysis and expert thought: Concurrent verbalizations of thinking during experts' performance on representative tasks', in K. A. Ericsson, N. Charness, P. J. Feltovich, & R. R. Hoffman (eds) *The Cambridge handbook of expertise and expert performance*, Cambridge: Cambridge University Press, 223–41.

Ericsson, K. A., & Kintsch, W. (1995) 'Long-term working memory', *Psychological Review*, 102: 211–45.

Fantl, J. (2012) 'Knowledge how', *Stanford Encyclopedia of Philosophy*. Online. Retrieved from http://plato.stanford.edu/archives/spr2014/entries/knowledge-how/ (accessed 22 July, 2014).

Fitts, P. M., & Posner, M. I. (1967) *Human performance*, Belmont, CA: Wadsworth.

French, K. E., & McPherson, S. L. (1999) 'Adaptations in response selection processes used during sport competition with increasing age and expertise', *International Journal of Sport Psychology*, 30: 173–93.

French, K. E., & McPherson, S. L. (2004) 'Development of expertise in sport', in M. R. Weiss (ed) *Developmental sport and exercise psychology: A lifespan perspective*, Morgantown, WV: Fitness Information Technology, 403–23.

Gascoigne, N., & Thornton, T. (2013) *Tacit knowledge*, Durham, UK: Acumen.

MacMahon, C., & McPherson, S. L. (2009) 'Knowledge base as a mechanism for perceptual-cognitive tasks: Skill is in the details!', *International Journal of Sport Psychology*, 40: 565–79.

Masters, R., & Maxwell, J. (2008) 'The theory of reinvestment', *International Review of Sport and Exercise Psychology*, 1: 160–83.

Masters, R.S.W. (1992) 'Knowledge, knerves and know-how: The role of explicit versus implicit knowledge in the breakdown of a complex motor skill under pressure', *British Journal of Psychology*, 83: 343–58.

McIlwain, D. J.F., & Sutton, J. (2014) 'Yoga from the mat up: How words alight on bodies', *Educational Philosophy and Theory*, 46: 655–73.

McPherson, S. L. (1994) 'The development of sport expertise: Mapping the tactical domain', *Quest*, 46: 223–40.

McPherson, S. L. (1999) 'Tactical differences in problem representations and solutions in collegiate varsity and beginner female tennis players', *Research Quarterly for Exercise and Sport*, 70: 369–84.

McPherson, S. L. (2000) 'Expert-novice differences in planning strategies during collegiate singles tennis competition', *Journal of Sport & Exercise Psychology*, 22: 39–62.

McPherson, S. L. (2008) 'Tactics: Using knowledge to enhance sport performance', in D. Farrow, J. Baker, & C. MacMahon (eds) *Developing sport expertise*, London: Routledge, 155–71.

McPherson, S. L., & Kernodle, M. W. (2003) 'Tactics, the neglected attribute of expertise: Problem representations and performance skills in tennis', in J. A. Starkes & K. A. Ericsson (eds) *Expert performance in sports*, Champaign, IL: Human Kinetics, 137–67.

McPherson, S. L., & MacMahon, C. (2008) 'How baseball players prepare to bat: Tactical knowledge as a mediator of expert performance in baseball', *Journal of Sport & Exercise Psychology*, 30: 755–78.

McPherson, S. L., & Thomas, J. R. (1989) 'Relations of knowledge and performance in boys' tennis: Age and expertise', *Journal of Experimental Child Psychology*, 48: 190–211.

McRobert, A. P., Ward, P., Eccles, D. W., & Williams, A. M. (2011) 'The effect of manipulating context-specific information on perceptual-cognitive processes during a simulated anticipation task', *British Journal of Psychology*, 102: 519–34.

McRobert, A. P., Williams, A. M., Ward, P., & Eccles, D. W. (2009) 'Tracing the process of expertise in a simulated anticipation task', *Ergonomics*, 52: 474–83.

Moran, A. P. (2004) *Sport and exercise psychology: A critical introduction*, London: Routledge.

Reimer, T. R., Park, E. S., & Hinsz, V. B. (2006) 'Shared and coordinated cognition in competitive and dynamic task environments: An information-processing perspective for team sports', *International Journal of Sport and Exercise Psychology*, 4: 376–400.

Robbins, P., & Aydede, M. (2009) *The Cambridge handbook of situated cognition*, Cambridge: Cambridge University Press.

Roca, A., Ford, P. R., McRobert, A. P., & Williams, A. M. (2011) 'Identifying the processes underlying anticipation and decision-making in a dynamic time-constrained task', *Cognitive Processing*, 12: 301–10.

Roca, A., Ford, P. R., McRobert, A. P., & Williams, A. M. (2013) 'Perceptual-cognitive skills and their interaction as a function of task constraints in soccer', *Journal of Sport & Exercise Psychology*, 35: 144–55.

Ryle, G. (1949) *The concept of mind*, Chicago: University of Chicago Press.

Samudra, J. K. (2008) 'Memory in our body: Thick participation and the translation of kinesthetic experience', *American Ethnologist*, 35: 665–81.

Sheets-Johnstone, M. (2009) *The corporeal turn*, Exeter, UK: Imprint Academic.

Silva, P., Garganta, J., Araújo, D., Davids, K., & Aguiar, P. (2013) 'Shared knowledge or shared affordances? Insights from an ecological dynamics approach to team coordination in sports', *Sports Medicine*, 43: 765–72.

Stanley, J., & Krakauer, J. W. (2013) 'Motor skill depends on knowledge of facts', *Frontiers in Human Neuroscience*, 7, article 503.

Sutton, J. (2007) 'Batting, habit, and memory: The embodied mind and the nature of skill', *Sport in Society*, 10: 763–86.

Sutton, J., & Williamson, K. (2014) 'Embodied remembering', in L. Shapiro (ed) *The Routledge handbook of embodied cognition*, London: Routledge, 315–25.

Wacquant, L. (2003) *Body and soul: Notebooks of an apprentice boxer*, Oxford: Oxford University Press.

Ward, P. R., Ericsson, K. A., & Williams, A. M. (2013) 'Complex perceptual-cognitive expertise in a simulated task environment', *Journal of Cognitive Engineering and Decision Making*, 7: 231–54.

Wheeler, M. (2008) 'Cognition in context: Phenomenology, situated robotics, and the frame problem', *International Journal of Philosophical Studies*, 16: 323–49.

Williams, A. M., Davids, K., & Williams, J. G. (1999) *Visual perception and action in sport*, London: E. & F.N.

Williamson, K., & Cox, R. (2014) 'Distributed cognition in sports teams: Explaining successful and expert performance', *Educational Philosophy and Theory*, 46: 640–54.

Williamson, K., & Sutton, J. (2014) 'Embodied collaboration in small groups', in C. T. Wolfe (ed) *Brain theory: Essays in critical neurophilosophy*, London: Palgrave, 107–33.

10

PSYCHOLOGICAL CHARACTERISTICS OF EXPERT PERFORMERS

Geir Jordet

The aim with this chapter is to discuss some of the psychological characteristics that distinguish expert or elite athletes from novices or non-elites. Based on a careful inspection of the sport psychology and expertise research literatures, an attempt is made to structure the chapter after a set of fundamental behaviors that experts are hypothesized to engage in:

Characteristic 1. Expert athletes passionately play
Characteristic 2. Expert athletes persistently pursue performance
Characteristic 3. Expert athletes self-regulate their learning
Characteristic 4. Expert athletes cope with change and adversity
Characteristic 5. Expert athletes cope with competitive pressure

The focus will be on the psychological processes or mechanisms that drive, facilitate or support experts' (or prospective experts') behaviors in a sport context. This review attempts to cover much, combining research from several different theoretical and methodological paradigms. Hence, it will not be exhaustive, but it will address selected key areas of importance. Further, the focus is on empirical results related to experts/novices or elites/non-elites and consequently, theoretical and methodological considerations will be kept to a minimum.

Expert athletes passionately play

Play is sometimes defined as voluntarily and freely being engaged in an activity with involvement in the activity as an end in itself (Huizinga, 1950; Suits, 1977). One would logically expect expert performers to experience the activity that they spend so much time doing as meaningful and enjoyable. This section will address the evidence that exists for such a claim, and the psychological processes that are associated with play.

In sport expertise research, deliberate play refers to "a form of sporting activity that involves early developmental physical activities that are intrinsically motivating, provide immediate gratification and are specifically designed to maximize enjoyment" (Côté *et al.*, 2007, p. 186). Although deliberate play can be viewed as similar to free play in that both are characterized by fun and immediate gratification, deliberate play is believed to be "loosely monitored" (versus not monitored in free play), with "no focus on immediate correction" (versus no correction) and the sources of enjoyment being "predominantly inherent" (versus inherent) (Côté *et al.*, 2003). There is much documentation that expert athletes' sport activities in their early years are characterized by fun, enjoyment, and play. For example, elite youth soccer players reported more play activities than non-elites between the ages of six and 12 (Ford *et al.*, 2009), and Olympic-level athletes reported that their sport was enjoyable, rewarding, thrilling, and engaging in their investment years (Durand-Bush & Salmela, 2002). There is also evidence that adult expert athletes engage in play and enjoy their sport; anecdotal experiences abound in some of the best performers. For example, two of the most outstanding soccer players in the world through all times express it like this: "I play in the same way now as when I was a little boy. I walk out there and have fun. If I could, I would have played a game every day" (Lionel Messi, in Balague, 2012, p. 214) and "to play soccer gave me a unique calm. And this feeling – just the same feeling that I've always had and still have: Give me a ball and I am enjoying myself" (Diego Maradona, 2005, p. 11). Researchers find the same; in a study of 328 Olympic-level athletes, the goal of "having fun" was one of the three most-cited goals (together with winning and improving performance) (Weinberg *et al.*, 2000). These descriptions can be linked to more theoretically driven research on motivational processes such as intrinsic motivation and passion.

Intrinsic motivation

Self-determination theory proposes that people have certain intrinsic needs, among them the need for autonomy (i.e., need to have control over one's actions), relatedness (i.e., need to feel connected with other people), and competence (i.e., need to have a positive effect on outcomes and surroundings) (Deci & Ryan, 2000). High levels of self-determined or autonomous motivation, where these needs are fulfilled, are associated with a series of positive outcomes, among them positive well-being, good health, and increased performance (for a review, see Ntoumanis, 2012).

Intrinsic motivation is regarded as the most self-determined or autonomous form of motivation, whereas different types of extrinsic motivation are less self-determined or more controlled (Deci & Ryan, 2008). Several studies describe intrinsic motivation in experts. For example, in a study of characteristics of expert cricket players, one emerging factor was strong intrinsic motivation in the form of fun, enjoyment, and love/passion for the game, which was thought to ensure a strong and persistent commitment to development and performance (Weissensteiner *et al.*, 2009). In another study, there was no difference between U15, U17, U19, and senior professional soccer players on intrinsic and extrinsic motivation, with intrinsic motivation remaining relatively high even for the more elite groups (i.e., the U19 and first team players) (Forzoni & Karageorghis, 2001). This suggests that intrinsic motivation can remain high as elite athletes progress through age and performance levels. Moreover, studies have identified links between self-determination and performance (Gillet *et al.*, 2009; Gillet *et al.*, 2010; Mouratidis *et al.*, 2008) and between self-determination and performance development behaviors such as goal setting, leadership, and emotional regulation (Taylor & Bruner, 2012). However, recent research suggests that athletes may have several coexisting types of motivation, and that a profile involving high intrinsic (autonomous) *and* high extrinsic (externally controlled) motivation is associated not only with high performance, but also with emotional and physical exhaustion (Gillet *et al.*, 2012). These authors concluded that high levels of extrinsic motivation could be adaptive for performance in competitive settings, if it is accompanied by high intrinsic motivation. With this said, despite the popularity of self-determination research in sport psychology, we still do not know much about self-determination at different levels of expertise/performance.

Passion

Passion has been defined as a strong inclination toward an activity that one likes (or loves) and finds important, where time and energy is invested (Vallerand, 2012). A study with two different athletic samples links higher levels of passion to deliberate practice and to better performance (Vallerand *et al.*, 2008). Thus, passion has been suggested to be a fundamental ingredient of expert performance (Vallerand, 2012). Vallerand (2012; Vallerand *et al.*, 2008) distinguishes between two forms of passion; harmonious passion (an autonomous form of regulation) tends to be positively related to performance and well-being, whereas obsessive passion (more controlled regulation) seems only related to performance, though possibly with higher risks of maladaptive consequences such as exhaustion, overtraining, and burnout. However, there is some evidence that athletes with high obsessive passion do not experience more negative affect than athletes high on harmonious passion (Sheard & Golby, 2009); a study of ice hockey players showed that those with high obsessive passion playing in competitive leagues (more elite) reported more adaptive adjustment than players with harmonious passion, whereas players with harmonious passion adjusted better in less competitive leagues (less elite) (Amiot *et al.*, 2006).

Expert athletes persistently pursue performance

A central component of Ericsson's deliberate practice framework is that the purpose of deliberate practice is to improve performance, and this activity is not enjoyable in itself (Ericsson *et al.*, 1993). In a study of elite youth soccer players, all referred to the love of the game as their primary motivation (Holt & Dunn, 2004). However, in a study by the same group of researchers, players who were about to be cut from their club (hence labeled less successful, non-elite) also referred to the love of the game as their core motive (Holt & Mitchell, 2006). This suggests that love of the game may not be the discriminatory factor. Interestingly, however, the successful players in the first study (Holt & Dunn, 2004) pointed to a motive that the unsuccessful (non-elite) players (Holt & Mitchell, 2006) did not refer to – the determination to achieve success. In this section, evidence will be reviewed related to how experts commit to and pursue performance.

Commitment to performance

In qualitative interviews, Olympic/world championship-level athletes expressed being incredibly committed to achieving their goals in sport (Orlick & Partington, 1988; Mallett & Hanrahan, 2004). In a study of seven world-class athletes in different sports, among the factors shown to be important for making it to that level were competitiveness, drive, and commitment to excel in sport (MacNamara *et al.*, 2010a). Similarly, in a longitudinal study, 65 young Dutch soccer players were measured on a series of psychological variables and then revisited after a period of 15 years to see whether they had become successful professional players (Van Yperen, 2009). The 18 players who at that time had reached professional status were distinguished by their higher levels of goal commitment as a young player (e.g., "I am strongly committed to pursuing my goals"). There were no differences in the type of goals they had (all wanted to become a professional player) or on the average number of hours per week spent on soccer.

Commitment to performance also seems to distinguish elites from non-elites in studies where commitment was not the targeted factor under investigation. In one such study elite athletes (county standard) scored higher than athletes at the university and club standard on mental toughness, but this was primarily due to differences in commitment (Crust & Azadi, 2010). The importance of mental toughness is reflected in two other studies, designed to unveil the psychological characteristics of cricket experts. In the first, a series of psychological skills (i.e., mental toughness, resilience, perfectionism, self-belief, confidence, optimism, ability to cope with adversity) were identified among 14 expert cricket players, coaches, and administrators as being critical for expert cricket batsman development (Weissensteiner *et al.*, 2009). In a subsequent study, a group of highly skilled and less-skilled batsmen filled out a set of quantitative psychological questionnaires, but only overall mental toughness score (including self-belief, motivation, commitment, and perseverance) emerged as significantly discriminating the two groups (Weissensteiner *et al.*, 2012).

A related construct that has been identified as a characteristic of high performers is perfectionism, which refers to an intense commitment to a high standard that logically should facilitate elite performers' performance development (e.g., Gould *et al.*, 2002; Hardy *et al.*, 1996; Stoeber *et al.*, 2009). However, much of the research that identifies perfectionism as a defining characteristic is atheoretical, and does not consider the multidimensional nature of this construct, which encompasses both elements of extreme achievement striving as well as neurotic commitment to flawlessness and conditional self-acceptance (Hall *et al.*, 2012). Unfortunately, despite accounts from elite athletes and research showing that certain parts of perfectionism are positively related to performance (Stoll *et al.*, 2008), there is very little empirical research on the multidimensional nature of perfectionism and elites/non-elites. Moreover, leading researchers in this field (Hall *et al.*, 2012) have argued that debilitating personal consequences come from the same psychological processes that result in high levels of performance motivation, making perfectionism a construct that may undermine rather than facilitate long-term performance, particularly when faced with challenge and difficulty.

Performance-related goals

Many researchers believe that to understand people's motivation, their goals need to be understood (Roberts, 2012). Athletes have a range of goals driving their involvement, ranging from economic advancement (Onywera *et al.*, 2006) to need for achievement (Roberts, 2012). Achievement goal theory is popular among sport motivation researchers (more than 300 published studies are reported; Roberts, 2012) and is based on the notion that motivation (i.e., behavior) is linked to the type of goal that an individual has (Maehr & Nicholls, 1980; Roberts, 2012). Task-oriented individuals use self-referenced criteria to judge success, and feel successful when they have mastered a task, learned something new, or improved their skills; on the contrary, ego-oriented individuals use other-referenced criteria and feel competent when they have outperformed others. A review of the research gives mixed results on the difference between elites and non-elites in task and ego orientation. Elite athletes have been reported as being high on both task orientation and ego orientation (i.e., Mallett & Hanrahan, 2004; Pensgaard & Roberts, 2000; Pensgaard *et al.*, 1999), higher on task orientation (Kavussanu *et al.*, 2011; Treasure *et al.*, 2000), higher on ego orientation (White & Duda, 1994), lower on ego orientation (White & Zellner, 1996), and lower on task orientation (Carpenter & Yates, 1997). Regardless of the ultimate combination that might be associated with expert performance, the combination of high ego/low task orientation seems to place athletes at increased risk of drop out, burnout, and other maladaptive motivational consequences (Lemyre *et al.*, 2007).

A related motivation theory considers an individual's motives to approach or avoid different situations (Elliot, 1999). Approach motivation is generally associated with adaptive achievement processes (i.e., high performance) and avoidance motivation with maladaptive processes (i.e., low performance) (see review by Roberts *et al.*, 2007). When these constructs are combined with achievement goal constructs, performance-approach goals (focusing on outperforming others) are hypothesized to be associated with higher performances than performance-avoidance goals (focusing on not being outperformed by others), whereas mastery-approach goals are seen to be adaptive for many achievement-related consequences, with mastery-avoidance goals having more mixed consequences (Elliot & Harackiewicz, 1996; Roberts *et al.*, 2007). While this work has generally considered motivation in general, there has been some research examining differences between performers at different levels of skill. Track and field athletes with better personal-best rankings score higher on performance-approach and mastery-approach goals, and are generally more approach-oriented than avoidance-oriented, compared to athletes with lower personal-best scores (Stoeber & Crombie, 2010). Thus, better athletes tend to be more oriented towards outperforming others than they are oriented towards not losing to others. Similarly, triathletes who are more approach-oriented than avoidance-oriented performed better in races (Stoeber *et al.*, 2009).

Making sacrifices for performance

Elite athletes seem willing to make heavy sacrifices for success in their sport (Bloom, 1985; Gould *et al.*, 2002). For example, Simpson and Wrisberg (2013) found that professional boxers sacrificed family time, social time with friends, habits, and even money to be able to dedicate more time and energy to training and preparation. The same was expressed by cricket experts, where work ethic and willingness to make sacrifices were presented as important for reaching expertise (Weissensteiner *et al.*, 2009).

Theoretically based research on making sacrifices is less developed in sport. However, some potentially relevant constructs are self-control and grit. Self-control has been defined as the capacity to alter one's responses to achieve a desired state or outcome that otherwise would not arise naturally, and involves both control of impulses and processes related to delay of gratification (e.g., Bauer & Baumeister, 2011; De Ridder *et al.*, 2012). In a recent study (Toering & Jordet, 2014), we found that dispositional self-control was significantly higher in a sample of professional soccer players ($N = 639$) than in the general population, and more elite players (i.e., those in the highest professional league level and/or with senior national team experience) had higher scores than their less-skilled counterparts. Interestingly, self-control scores were positively related to sleep, but negatively related to time on the Internet and time playing video games. This suggests that players with high self-control work on themselves to alter the desire to stay up at night and/ or engage in immediately gratifying activities (such as surfing the net or playing video games), and that they potentially get better rest than other players as a result.

A related construct is "grit," defined as a trait-based perseverance and passion for long-term goals, which entails working strenuously toward challenges, and maintaining effort and interest over a long period of time despite failure, adversity, and plateaus in progress (Duckworth *et al.*, 2007). It has been linked to elite performers and high performance in several non-sport samples (Duckworth *et al.*, 2007), but no research has yet been published on this in sport.

Expert athletes self-regulate their learning

Many elite/expert athletes refer to the importance of quality training for their development and performance (Durand-Bush & Salmela, 2002; MacNamara *et al.*, 2010a; Orlick & Partington, 1988). Moreover, we know that Ericsson's notion of deliberate practice has distinctive characteristics that are hypothesized to make it effective (e.g., purposeful practice where tasks are chosen to overcome weaknesses, balancing effort and recovery, with careful monitoring of performance; Ericsson *et al.*, 1993). In this section, evidence for expert-novice differences will be reviewed with respect to the manner in which athletes learn.

Psychological characteristics of experts

Self-regulation of learning has been defined as the extent to which individuals are metacognitively, motivationally, and behaviorally proactive participants in their own learning process (Zimmerman, 2006). Expert athletes are hypothesized to take an active, self-regulatory role in their own learning process, and hence learn more effectively than non-expert athletes. Zimmerman developed a model based on three microanalytic phases of practice: forethought (preceding practice), performance control (during practice), and self-reflection (following each practice effort). He tested it first by allowing male experts, non-experts, and novices to practice basketball free throws (Cleary & Zimmermann, 2001). Compared to the non-experts and novices, experts set significantly more specific free-throw goals, planned their practice by choosing more specific/technique-oriented strategies to achieve their goals, had higher self-efficacy, and attributed their failure to faults in specific techniques. In a follow-up study (Kitsantas & Zimmerman, 2002), generally the same results were found with female experts, non-experts, and novices practicing the volleyball overhand serve. The experts set more specific technique or process goals, exhibited more structured planning of their practice, used more specific, technical strategies, self-monitored their technique more during practice, self-evaluated after practice, thought more about their errors, and were likely to seek out social assistance by coaches and other teammates.

Extending Zimmerman's work, we found that young Dutch elite soccer players from top league clubs (belonging to the top one per cent of players in their age group in the Netherlands) consistently scored higher on self-regulation of learning (i.e., planning, reflection, self-monitoring, evaluation, effort, and self-efficacy) than less-skilled players, and significantly higher on reflection (Toering *et al.*, 2009). In addition, in a video observation study, players who scored high on self-regulation of learning also naturally engaged in more developmental activities with respect to practice, such as focusing, communicating, and coming early to practice (Toering *et al.*, 2011). These results have been replicated at the highest level of soccer, showing that world-class professional soccer players are students of "their game," engaging in active self-regulation of their learning (Horrocks, 2012). In other sports, elite athletes also scored higher on reflection than athletes at a lower level (Jonker *et al.*, 2011).

In a recent experimental study designed to test deliberate practice theory during practice itself, 45 Gaelic football players from three levels of expertise (expert, intermediate, and control) were observed practicing predefined kicks over a period of four weeks (Coughlan *et al.*, 2013). The results supported predictions from deliberate practice theory, in that experts consistently engaged in behaviors that led to more permanent improvements in performance. Specifically, compared to the intermediate group, the experts found practice more effortful, rated practice as less enjoyable, practiced a more challenging skill, and used a random-practice approach. In addition, they were more engaged in behaviors associated with self-regulation of learning, such as extensively planning and monitoring their kicks.

Expert athletes cope with change and adversity

The athletic career can be viewed as "a succession of stages and transitions that includes the athlete's initiation into and continued participation in organized competitive sport" (Alfermann & Stambulova, 2007, p. 713). The prospective expert athlete will experience a range of changes and difficulties. Recent investigations show that expert athletes' development follows complex and nonlinear pathways, with many transitions and "bumps in the road" (Abbott *et al.*, 2005; Collins & MacNamara, 2012; Gulbin *et al.*, 2013; MacNamara *et al.*, 2010b; Ollis *et al.*, 2006). The ability to cope with, and adapt to, these transitions and temporary setbacks seems pivotal.

Adversarial growth

Setbacks and adversity may help performers grow (Collins & MacNamara, 2012).

Adversarial growth refers to the positive psychosocial changes that can follow from adverse life circumstances (Linley & Joseph, 2004). For instance, a recent study of elite athletes suggests that the ability to grow from adversity may be a defining psychosocial characteristic of expert athletes. In a comparison of "super champions" (60+ national team games and five+ world championship medals) and "almosts" (high-level youth, but no more than second division as adult) (Collins *et al.*, 2014), some interesting differences were detected. Where the "almosts" tended to experience a smooth ride up to the adult level, the champions had a slow, often bumpy progression. In addition, when the "almosts" experienced challenges and setbacks, many would respond negatively – type "why me," "I'm unlucky," or "It's not fair" – while the super champions would react much more positively to similar challenges ("use it as stimulation").

Coping styles and strategies

Some studies suggest elite athletes possess a series of coping strategies to deal with obstacles and stress (Holt & Dunn, 2004), whereas unsuccessful athletes seem to lack such strategies (Holt & Mitchell, 2006). Some studies have explored the coping strategies of elite athletes. Problem-oriented coping denotes strategies that attempt to alter or manage the situation that causes the stress, whereas emotion-oriented coping refers to efforts to regulate the emotional impact of stressful events (Lazarus & Folkman, 1984) and avoidance coping refers to attempts to mentally or behaviorally disengage from the situation (Roth & Cohen, 1986). In one study, professional rugby players reported using more problem-oriented strategies than emotion-oriented or avoidance-oriented strategies (Nicholls *et al.*, 2006). Elite adolescent golf players, however, seem to use a wide selection of problem-focused, emotion-focused, and avoidance strategies (e.g., Nicholls, 2007; Nicholls *et al.*, 2005a, 2005b).

Unfortunately, comparisons of elite and non-elite coping strategies are rare (Hoar *et al.*, 2006; Gaudreau *et al.*, 2010). However, among male athletes, elites used more approach coping and non-elites more avoidance coping. In females, elites used more avoidance coping and non-elites more approach coping (Gan *et al.*, 2009). In another study, elite athletes used more avoidance coping than non-elites (Anshel & Si, 2008). Finally, from a longitudinal study of young elite soccer players who, at the adult age, either became professional players or not, there were no differences between the two groups of youth players to the extent to which they experienced stressors, but the players who later became professionals reported engaging more in problem-oriented coping and seeking out more social support (Van Yperen, 2009).

Hardiness

Hardiness is a personality characteristic hypothesized to affect one's emotional response to stress, and hence protect against the negative impact of stress (Kobasa, 1979). It has three components: commitment (deeply involved and won't give up), challenge (views change as enjoyment rather than threat), and control (influential over events in life). In several sport studies, elites outscored non-elites on hardiness. In a large sample of more than 1,500 athletes from different sports, international competitors scored significantly higher than their lesser counterparts on commitment and control, but not on challenge (Sheard & Golby, 2010). In a study of professional rugby players from three different levels, players from the top level (international level) scored higher than players from the other two levels on all subscales (Golby & Sheard, 2004). Similarly, a study of

Psychological characteristics of experts

elite motorcycle racers found that the top 10 per cent of the sample (ranked over a season) scored significantly higher on hardiness than the bottom 10 per cent, but the small sample prevented reliable subscale analyses (Thomas *et al.*, 2013).

Coping with injuries

Finally, sport injuries represent a specific type of adversity that both expert and non-expert athletes encounter. There is a substantial body of research documenting that positive psychological responses to injury are associated with a higher and faster return to sport at one's pre-injury level of performance (for recent reviews, see Ardern *et al.*, 2013; Brewer, 2010). Interestingly, there is some evidence that professional or elite athletes, compared to their less-skilled counterparts, experience higher levels of emotional disturbance at the onset of an injury (Johnston & Carroll, 2000) and higher pressure to return quickly at the risk of forcing an injury (Bianco, 2001). However, no studies have directly compared the psychological responses to injury in athletes at different levels of performance or expertise (Ardern *et al.*, 2013). With that said, several psychological processes and skills where elite athletes generally score higher than non-elites have been shown to affect the injury-coping process positively. Elite athletes' higher scores on hardiness (Wadey *et al.*, 2011), goal setting (Johnson, 1997), and self-confidence (Johnson, 1997) suggest that even though elite/expert athletes may experience higher levels of stress following an injury, they are better equipped to deal with it.

Expert athletes cope with competitive pressure

Performance pressure is referred to as a major source of stress in competitive sport (e.g., Gould *et al.*, 1993; McKay *et al.*, 2008). Hence, any athlete who reaches an elite level will necessarily encounter high levels of competitive pressure. Thus, it is reasonable to expect that expert athletes have developed ways to cope with pressure. However, it has been documented that experts occasionally experience severe levels of pressure, use maladaptive coping strategies, and choke under pressure (Hardy *et al.*, 1996; Jordet & Hartman, 2008; Jordet *et al.*, 2007; Zheng *et al.*, 2011). In this section, evidence will be presented for both experts' ability to adaptively cope with pressure and their vulnerability to choking under pressure.

Coping with success, status, and expectations

Interviews with successful athletes show that winning increases the pressure to deliver future performances (Jackson *et al.*, 1998a, b; Kreiner-Phillips & Orlick, 1993). The most frequently cited dimension describing the post-Olympic experience in 18 Australian gold medalists was "experiencing expectations and pressure from others," mentioned by 72 per cent of the athletes (Jackson *et al.*, 1998a). With this said, several studies have highlighted the ability of world-class athletes to successfully cope with pressure, maintain performance, and keep winning once they have become successful (e.g., MacNamara *et al.*, 2010a; Durand-Bush & Salmela, 2002). Many top athletes respond to the added pressure by maintaining hunger for success, retaining realistic expectations, being willing to move out of their comfort zone (MacNamara *et al.*, 2010a), and/or changing their performance environment to seek fresh ideas from coaches/teachers (MacNamara *et al.*, 2010b).

Yet there is evidence for expertise-induced failure, where status and expectations following successful performances are associated with "choking." Choking under pressure is often defined as performing worse than expected in situations with a high degree of perceived importance

(Baumeister, 1984; Beilock & Gray, 2007). In a study of performing under pressure in major tournament soccer penalty shootouts, the truly world-class players (defined as players who had received a prestigious individual award) performed significantly worse than players with lower public status (Jordet, 2009a). Similarly, players from teams with the highest status performed worse than players from teams with lower status (Jordet, 2009b). Comparable effects were found in German soccer, where top league players missed more decisive penalty shots than players from lower league teams (Kocher *et al.*, 2008). Further, in an analysis of tennis tournament finals, the favorites were clearly better than the underdogs in most instances, but not in finals that featured the combination of a) large monetary awards and b) the tournament trophy displayed in the players' sight (Bijleveld *et al.*, 2011). The researchers argued that the monetary rewards trigger choking under pressure when a subtle reward cue reminds the players of what is at stake.

Coping with competitive anxiety

Several studies have addressed psychological processes associated with competitive pressure in elites and non-elites. With respect to pre-competition anxiety, elite athletes from different sports report experiencing fewer problems with, and better management of, anxiety (e.g., Durand-Bush *et al.*, 2001 Hayslip *et al.*, 2010; Mahoney *et al.*, 1987; Meyers *et al.*, 1999). More specifically, elites and non-elites do not differ much in terms of intensity of cognitive or somatic anxiety symptoms, but elites generally interpret the direction of their symptoms as more facilitative or constructive to performance than non-elites (e.g., Jones *et al.*, 1994; Jones & Swain, 1995; Neil *et al.*, 2012).

Further, compared to non-elites, elite performers reach their peak anxiety some time before competition and have anxiety symptoms more under control when they are due to perform (Hardy *et al.*, 1996; Neil *et al.*, 2012). In a classical study, expert skydivers were shown to peak in physiological arousal well in advance of their jump, and then decline, whereas novices started with low levels of arousal, which progressively increased (Fenz & Epstein, 1967).

Only a handful of studies have experimentally examined the effects of anxiety on experts, and novices' performance. The first study was with karate experts and novices, where anxiety was manipulated by adding a competitive situation and an ego threat (heavy critique of the participants' former trials) (Williams & Elliot, 1999). Anxiety had a larger effect on the visual search of the novices than it had on the experts, producing more ineffective fixations to peripheral areas of the visual display. In another study, anxiety was manipulated by having participants perform a dart-throwing task while positioned high and low on a climbing wall (Nibbeling *et al.*, 2012). The increased anxiety resulted in a significant decrease in dart-throwing performance for the novices, accompanied by less functional gaze behavior. These effects were not observed for the experts, but both groups increased their mental effort and performance time, and reduced their performance on a secondary task, suggesting that anxiety led to a decrease in processing efficiency in both groups.

Coping mechanisms/strategies

There is generally much self-report-based evidence that elite athletes score higher than non-elites on psychological skills and strategies that protect against the aversive effects of competitive pressure. Elite athletes consistently score higher than non-elites on self-confidence (e.g., Durand-Bush *et al.*, 2001; Hayslip *et al.*, 2010; Mahoney *et al.*, 1987; Orlick & Partington, 1988; Weissensteiner *et al.*, 2009), on focus/concentration (e.g., Durand-Bush *et al.*, 2001; Mahoney *et al.*, 1987), planning for competition (Orlick & Partington, 1988), and the use of psychological skills such as goal setting, imagery, self-talk, and relaxation (Hayslip *et al.*, 2010). For example, in interviews with world-class athletes about the path to the top (MacNamara *et al.*, 2010a), all reported using, or having used, a series of psychological strategies (such as imagery, arousal control) to deal with the pressures associated with competition.

With respect to experimental evidence, we see a different pattern of results. Again, experts are vulnerable to certain types of choking. In some studies, people with the highest working-memory capacity fail under conditions of high pressure (Beilock & Carr, 2005). This follows the distraction hypothesis of choking, where pressure is believed to induce worry, which, when it is not sufficiently coped with, takes up working-memory resources, resulting in decreased performance. In other studies, experts' performance suffers when they carefully monitor step-by-step performance, whereas less-experienced performers benefit from such skill focus (Beilock *et al.*, 2002). This follows the explicit monitoring hypothesis, where pressure prompts conscious monitoring and controlling of actions that normally are conducted without conscious control, and this disrupts natural skill execution (Baumeister, 1984). Explicitly monitoring one's performance under pressure would then explain why participants in laboratory experiments take longer times under pressure than under no pressure (e.g., Masters, 1992). Further, when performers are instructed to act as quickly as possible, experts benefit and novices suffer (Beilock *et al.*, 2004).

In field studies of elite performers, somewhat different mechanisms are observed. Video analyses of soccer penalty shooters in major elite tournaments consistently show that players under high-threat conditions respond with escapist behaviors. Specifically, players who take shots in negative valence conditions (where a miss produces an instant loss; Jordet & Hartman, 2008) had high individual status (Jordet, 2009a), represented countries with high team status (Jordet, 2009b), or played for a country with a recent history of penalty shootout losses (Jordet *et al.*, 2011); all exhibited faster preparation times than the players under less threat. This might suggest that the players attempt to get their shots quickly done and over with. In some instances, high threat was also associated with diverting one's gaze away from the goal and the goalkeeper, suggesting that these elite players attempt to avoid visually taking in the stressful information (Jordet & Hartman, 2008).

Conclusions

In general, there is still relatively little research that has directly examined psychological discriminators between performers at different levels of skill. Thus, much of the research presented here comes from sport psychology studies of elites and non-elites and is based on retrospective and/ or self-report methodology, which needs to be supplemented with more controlled experimental methods for more reliable conclusions to be made. With that said, the available evidence summarized in this review does suggest a few general areas where experts can be distinguished with respect to psychological processes.

With respect to future research, it would be particularly useful to know more about a) the roles that different types of passion may have for athletes at different levels of performance; b) whether experts indeed have higher levels of perfectionism, grit, and self-control than novices; c) the exact ways that elite athletes self-regulate their learning more or better than non-elites; d) the specific traits, processes, and coping strategies that experts employ to cope with transitions, setbacks, and adversity; and e) the specific conditions under which experts are better equipped than novices to cope with pressure and when they are more likely to choke.

References

Abbott, A., Button, C., Pepping, G. J., & Collins, D. (2005) 'Unnatural selection: Talent identification and development in sport', *Nonlinear Dynamics, Psychology, and Life Sciences*, 9: 61–88.

Alfermann, D., & Stambulova, N. (2007) 'Career transitions and career termination', in G. Tenenbaum & R. Eklund (eds) *Handbook of sport psychology*, New Jersey: John Wiley & Sons, 712–33.

Amiot, C. E., Vallerand, R. J., & Blanchard, C. M. (2006) 'Passion and psychological adjustment: A test of the person-environment fit hypothesis', *Personality and Social Psychology Bulletin*, 32: 220–9.

Anshel, M. H., & Si, G. (2008) 'Coping styles following acute stress in sport among elite Chinese athletes: A test of trait and transactional coping theories', *Journal of Sport Behavior*, 31: 3–21.

Ardern, C. L., Taylor, N. T., Feller, J. A., & Webster, K. E. (2013) 'A systematic review of the psychological factors associated with returning to sport following injury', *British Journal of Sports Medicine*, 47: 1120–6.

Balague, G. (2012) *Pep Guardiola: Another way of winning: The biography*, London, UK: Orion Books.

Bauer, I. M., & Baumeister, R. F. (2011) 'Self-regulatory strength', in K. Vohs & R. Baumeister (eds) *Handbook of self-regulation*, 2nd ed., New York: Guilford Press, 64–82.

Baumeister, R. F. (1984) 'Choking under pressure: Self-consciousness and paradoxical effects of incentives on skillful performance', *Journal of Personality and Social Psychology*, 46: 610–20.

Beilock, S. L., Bertenthal, B. I., McCoy, A. M., & Carr, T. H. (2004) 'Haste does not always make waste: Expertise, direction of attention, and speed versus accuracy in performing sensorimotor skills', *Psychonomic Bulletin & Review*, 11: 373–9.

Beilock, S. L., & Carr, T. H. (2005) 'When high-powered people fail. Working memory and "choking under pressure" in math', *Psychological Science*, 16: 101–5.

Beilock, S. L., Carr, T. H., MacMahon, C., & Starkes, J. L. (2002) 'When paying attention becomes counterproductive: Impact of divided versus skill-focused attention on novice and experienced performance of sensorimotor skills', *Journal of Experimental Psychology: Applied*, 8: 6–16.

Beilock, S. L., & Gray, R. (2007) 'Why do athletes "choke" under pressure?', in G. Tenenbaum & R. Eklund (eds) *Handbook of sport psychology*, 3rd ed., New Jersey: John Wiley & Sons, 712–33.

Bianco, T. (2001) 'Social support and recovery from sport injury: Elite skiers share their experiences', *Research Quarterly for Exercise & Sports*, 72: 376–88.

Bijleveld, E., Custer, R., & Aarts, H. (2011) 'When favourites fail: Tournament trophies as reward cues in tennis finals', *Journal of Sports Sciences*, 29: 1463–70.

Bloom. B. S. (1985) *Developing talent in young people*, New York: Ballantine.

Brewer, B. W. (2010) 'The role of psychological factors in sport injury rehabilitation outcomes', *International Review of Sport & Exercise Psychology*, 3: 40–62.

Carpenter, P. J., & Yates, B. (1997) 'Relationships between achievement goals and the perceived purposes of soccer for semi-professional and amateur players', *Journal of Sport & Exercise Psychology*, 19: 302–11.

Cleary, T. J., & Zimmerman, B. J. (2001) 'Self-regulation differences during athletic practice by experts, non-experts, and novices', *Journal of Applied Sport Psychology*, 13: 185–206.

Collins, D., & MacNamara, Á. (2012) 'The rocky road to the top', *Sports Medicine*, 42: 907–14.

Collins, D., McCarthy, A., & MacNamara, Á. (2014) *Super champions, champions, and almosts*, manuscript submitted for publication.

Côté, J., Baker, J., & Abernethy, B. (2003) 'From play to practice: A developmental framework for the acquisition of expertise in team sports', in J. L. Starkes & K. A. Ericsson (eds) *Expert performance in sports: Advances in research on sport expertise*, Champaign, IL: Human Kinetics, 89–114.

Côté, J., Baker, J., & Abernethy, B. (2007) 'Practice and play in the development of sport expertise', in G. Tenenbaum & R. Eklund (eds) *Handbook of sport psychology*, 3rd ed., New Jersey: John Wiley & Sons, 184–202.

Coughlan, E. K., Williams, A. M., McRobert, A. P., & Ford, P. (2013) 'How experts practice: A novel test of deliberate practice theory', *Journal of Experimental Psychology: Learning, Memory, and Cognition*, 40(2): 449–58.

Crust, L., & Azadi, K. (2010) 'Mental toughness and athletes' use of psychological strategies', *European Journal of Sport Science*, 10: 43–51.

Deci, E. L., & Ryan, R. M. (2000) 'The "what" and "why" of goal pursuits: Human needs and the self-determination of behavior', *Psychological Inquiry*, 11: 227–68.

Deci, E. L., & Ryan, R. M. (2008) 'Facilitating optimal motivation and psychological well-being across life's domains', *Canadian Psychology*, 49: 14–23.

Psychological characteristics of experts

De Ridder, D.T.D., Lensvelt-Mulders, G., Finkenauer, C., Stok, F.M., & Baumeister, R. F. (2012) 'Taking stock of self-control: A meta-analysis of how trait self-control relates to a wide range of behaviors', *Personality and Social Psychology Review*, 16: 76–99.

Duckworth, A. L., Peterson, C., Matthews, M. D., & Kelly, D. R. (2007) 'Grit: Perseverance and passion for long-term goals', *Journal of Personality and Social Psychology*, 92(6): 1087–101.

Durand-Bush, N., & Salmela, J. H. (2002) 'The development and maintenance of expert athletic performance: Perceptions of world and Olympic champions', *Journal of Applied Sport Psychology*, 14(3): 154–71.

Durand-Bush, N., Salmela, J. H., & Green-Demers, I. (2001) 'The Ottawa mental skills assessment tool (OMSAT-3)', *The Sport Psychologist*, 15: 1–19.

Elliot, A. J. (1999) 'Approach and avoidance motivation and achievement goals', *Educational Psychologist*, 34: 169–89.

Elliot, A. J., & Harackiewicz, J. (1996) 'Approach and avoidance achievement goals and intrinsic motivation: A mediational analysis', *Journal of Personality and Social Psychology*, 70: 968–80.

Ericsson, K. A., Krampe, R. T., & Tesch-Romer, C. (1993) 'The role of deliberate practice in the acquisition of expert performance', *Psychological Review*, 100: 363–406.

Fenz, W. D., & Epstein, S. (1967) 'Gradients of physiological arousal in parachutists', *Psychosomatic Medicine*, 29: 33–51.

Ford, P. R., Ward, P., Hodges, N. J., & Williams, A. M. (2009) 'The role of deliberate practice and play in career progression in sport: The early engagement hypothesis', *High Ability Studies*, 20: 65–75.

Forzoni, R. E., & Karageorghis, C. I. (2001) 'Participation motives in elite soccer across age groups: A test of cognitive evaluation theory', in A. Papaioannou, M. Goudas, & Y. Theodorakis (eds) *Proceedings of the International Society of Sport Psychology (ISSP) 10th World Congress of Sport Psychology*, vol. 3, Christodoilidi Publications, 318–20.

Gan, Q., Anshel, M. H., & Kim, J. K. (2009) 'Sources and cognitive appraisals of acute stress as predictors of coping style among male and female Chinese athletes', *International Journal of Sport and Exercise Psychology*, 7: 68–88.

Gaudreau, P., Nicholls, A., & Levy, A. R. (2010) 'The ups and downs of coping and sport achievement: An episodic process analysis of within-person associations', *Journal of Sport & Exercise Psychology*, 32: 298–311.

Gillet, N., Berjot, S., & Gobancé, L. (2009) 'A motivational model of performance in the sport domain', *European Journal of Sport Science*, 9: 151–8.

Gillet, N., Berjot, S., Vallerand, R. J., Amoura, S., & Rosnet, E. (2012) 'Examining the motivation-performance relationship in competitive sport: A cluster-analytic approach', *International Journal of Sport Psychology*, 43: 79–102.

Gillet, N., Vallerand, R. J., Amoura, S., & Baldes, B. (2010) 'Influence of coaches' autonomy support on athletes' motivation and sport performance: A test of the hierarchical model of intrinsic and extrinsic motivation', *Psychology of Sport and Exercise*, 11: 155–61.

Golby, J., & Sheard, M. (2004) 'Mental toughness and hardiness at different levels of rugby league', *Personality and Individual Differences*, 37: 933–42.

Gould, D., Dieffenbach, K., & Moffett, A. (2002) 'Psychological characteristics and their development in Olympic champions', *Journal of Applied Sport Psychology*, 14: 172–204.

Gould, D., Jackson, S., & Finch, L. (1993) 'Sources of stress in national champion figure Skaters', *Journal of Sport & Exercise Psychology*, 15: 134–59.

Gulbin, J., Weissensteiner, J., Oldenziel, K., & Gangé, F. (2013) 'Patterns of performance development in elite athletes', *European Journal of Sport Science*, 13(6): 605–14.

Hall, H. K., Hill, A. P., & Appleton, P. R. (2012) 'Perfectionism: A foundation for sporting excellence or an uneasy pathway toward purgatory?', in G. C. Roberts & D. C. Treasure (eds) *Advances in motivation in sport and exercise*, 3rd ed., Champaign, IL: Human Kinetics, 129–68.

Hardy, L., Jones, G., & Gould, D. (1996) *Understanding psychological preparation for sport: Theory and practice of elite performers*, Chichester, UK: Jones Wiley & Sons.

Hayslip, B., Petrie, T. A., MacIntire, M., & Jones, G. (2010) 'The influences of skill level, anxiety and psychological skills use on amateur golfers' performances', *Journal of Applied Sport Psychology*, 22: 123–33.

Hoar, S. D., Kowalski, K. C., Gaudreau, P., & Crocker, P.R.E. (2006) 'A review of coping in sport', in S. Hanton & S. D. Mellalieu (eds) *Literature reviews in sport psychology*, New York: Nova Science Publishers, 47–90.

Holt, N. L., & Dunn, J.G.H. (2004) 'Toward a grounded theory of the psychosocial competencies and environmental conditions associated with soccer success', *Journal of Applied Sport Psychology*, 16: 199–219.

Holt, N. L., & Mitchell, T. (2006) 'Talent development in English professional soccer', *International Journal of Sport Psychology*, 37: 77–98.

Horrocks, D. (2012) 'Brains in their feet?', *The Psychologist*, 15: 88–9.

Huizinga, J. (1950) *Homo ludens*, London: Routledge.

Jackson, S. A., Dover, J., & Mayocchi, L. (1998a) 'Life after winning gold: I. Experiences of Australian Olympic gold medallists', *The Sport Psychologist*, 12: 119–36.

Johnson, U. (1997) 'A three-year follow-up of long-term injured competitive athletes: Influence of psychological risk factors on rehabilitation', *Journal of Sport Rehabilitation*, 6: 256–71.

Johnston, L. H., & Carroll, D. (2000) 'The psychological impact of injury: Effects of prior sport and exercise involvement', *British Journal of Sports Medicine*, 34: 436–9.

Jones, G., Hanton, S., & Swain, A. (1994) 'Intensity and interpretation of anxiety symptoms in elite and non-elite sports performers', *Personality and Individual Differences*, 17: 657–63.

Jones, G., & Swain, A. B. J. (1995) 'Predispositions to experience facilitating and debilitating anxiety in elite and non-elite performers', *The Sport Psychologist*, 9: 201–11.

Jonker, L., Elferink-Gemser, M. T., & Visscher, C. (2011) 'Differences in self-regulatory skills among talented athletes: The significance of competitive level and type of sport', *Journal of Sports Sciences*, 28: 901–8.

Jordet, G. (2009a) 'When superstars flop: Public status and "choking under pressure" in international soccer penalty shoot-outs', *Journal of Applied Sport Psychology*, 21: 125–30.

Jordet, G. (2009b) 'Why do English players fail in soccer penalty shoot-outs? A study of team status, self-regulation, and choking under pressure', *Journal of Sport Sciences*, 27: 97–106.

Jordet, G., & Hartman, E. (2008) 'Avoidance motivation and choking under pressure in soccer penalty shoot-outs', *Journal of Sport & Exercise Psychology*, 30: 452–9.

Jordet, G., Hartman, E., & Jelle-Vuijk, P. (2011) 'Team history and choking under pressure in major soccer penalty shootouts', *British Journal of Psychology*, 103(2): 268–83.

Jordet, G., Hartman, E., Visscher, C., & Lemmink, K.A.P.M. (2007) 'Kicks from the penalty mark in soccer: The roles of stress, skill, and fatigue for kick outcomes', *Journal of Sports Sciences*, 25: 121–9.

Kavussanu, M., White, S. A., Jowett, S., & England, S. (2011) 'Elite and non-elite male footballers differ in goal orientation and perceptions of parental climate', *International Journal of Sport and Exercise Psychology*, 9: 284–90.

Kitsantas, A., & Zimmerman, B. J. (2002) 'Comparing self-regulatory processes among novice, non-expert, and expert volleyball players: A microanalytic study', *Journal of Applied Sport Psychology*, 14: 91–105.

Kobasa, S. C. (1979) 'Stressful life events, personality, and health: An inquiry into hardiness', *Journal of Personality and Social Psychology*, 37: 1–11.

Kocher, M. G., Lenz, M., & Sutter, M. (2008) 'Performance under pressure: The case of penalty shootouts in football', in P. Andersson, P. Ayton, & C. Schmidt (eds) *Myths and facts about football: The economics and psychology of the world's greatest sport*, Newcastle, UK: Cambridge Scholars Publishing, 61–72.

Kreiner-Phillips, K., & Orlick, T. (1993) 'Winning after winning: The psychology of ongoing excellence', *The Sport Psychologist*, 7: 31–48.

Lazarus, R. S., & Folkman, S. (1984) *Stress, appraisal and coping*, New York: Springer.

Lemyre, P. N., Roberts, G. C., & Stray-Gundersen, J. (2007) 'Motivation, overtraining and burnout: Can self-determined motivation predict overtraining and burnout in elite athletes', *European Journal of Sports Sciences*, 7: 115–32.

Linley, P. A., & Joseph, S. (2004) 'Positive change following trauma and adversity: A review', *Journal of Traumatic Stress*, 17: 11–21.

MacNamara, A., Button, A., & Collins, D. (2010a) 'The role of psychological characteristics in facilitating the pathway to elite performance. Part 1: Identifying mental skills and behaviors', *The Sport Psychologist*, 24: 52–73.

MacNamara, Á., Button, A., & Collins, D. (2010b) 'The role of psychological characteristics in facilitating the pathway to elite performance. Part 2: Examining environmental and stage-related differences in skills and behaviors', *The Sport Psychologist*, 24: 74–96.

Maehr, M. L., & Nicholls, J. G. (1980) 'Culture and achievement motivation: A second look', in N. Warren (ed) *Studies in cross-cultural psychology*, 3rd ed., New York: Academic Press, 221–67.

Mahoney, M. J., Gabriel, T. J., & Perkins, T. S. (1987) 'Psychological skills and exceptional athletic performance', *The Sport Psychologist*, 1: 181–99.

Mallett, C. J., & Hanrahan, S. J. (2004) 'Elite athletes: What makes the "fire" burn so brightly?', *Psychology of Sport & Exercise*, 5: 183–200.

Psychological characteristics of experts

Maradona, D. A. (2005) *El Diego: The autobiography of the world's greatest footballer*, London: Yellow Jersey Press.

Masters, R.S.W. (1992) 'Knowledge, knerves and know-how: The role of explicit versus implicit knowledge in the breakdown of a complex motor skill under pressure', *British Journal of Psychology*, 83: 343–58.

McKay, J., Niven, A.G., Lavallee, D., & White, A. (2008) 'Sources of stress amongst elite UK track athletes', *The Sport Psychologist*, 22: 143–63.

Meyers, M.C., Bourgeois, A.E., LeUnes, A. D., & Murray, N.A. (1999) 'Mood and psychological skills of elite and sub-elite equestrian athletes', *Journal of Sport Behavior*, 23: 399–409.

Mouratidis, M., Vansteenkiste, M., Lens, W., & Sideridis, G. (2008) 'The motivating role of positive feedback in sport and physical education: Evidence for a motivational model', *Journal of Sport & Exercise Psychology*, 30: 240–68.

Neil, R., Wilson, K., Mellalieu, S.D., Hanton, S., & Taylor, J. (2012) 'Competitive anxiety intensity and interpretation: A two-study investigation into their relationship with performance', *International Journal of Sport & Exercise Psychology*, 10(2): 96–111.

Nibbeling, N., Oudejans, R.R.D., & Daanen, H.A.M. (2012) 'Effects of anxiety, a cognitive secondary task, and expertise on gaze behavior and performance in a far aiming task', *Psychology of Sport & Exercise*, 13: 427–35.

Nicholls, A.R. (2007) 'A longitudinal phenomenological analysis of coping effectiveness among Scottish international adolescent golfers', *European Journal of Sport Science*, 7: 169–78.

Nicholls, A.R., Holt, N.L., & Polman, R.C.J. (2005a) 'A phenomenological analysis of coping effectiveness in golf', *The Sport Psychologist*, 19: 111–30.

Nicholls, A.R., Holt, N.L., Polman, R.C.J., & Bloomfield, J. (2006) 'Stressors, coping, and coping effectiveness among professional rugby union players', *The Sport Psychologist*, 20: 314–29.

Nicholls, A.R., Holt, N.L., Polman, R.C.J., & James, D.W.G. (2005b) 'Stress and coping among international adolescent golfers', *Journal of Applied Sport Psychology*, 17: 333–40.

Ntoumanis, N. (2012) 'A self-determination theory perspective on motivation in sport and physical education: Current trends and possible future research directions', in G.C. Roberts & D. C. Treasure (eds) *Motivation in sport and exercise*, 3rd ed., Champaign, IL: Human Kinetics, 91–128.

Ollis, S., MacPherson, A., & Collins, D. (2006) 'Expertise and talent development in rugby refereeing: An ethnographic enquiry', *Journal of Sports Sciences*, 24(3): 309–22.

Onywera, V. O., Scott R. A., Boit, M.K., & Pitsiladis, Y.P. (2006) 'Demographic characteristics of elite Kenyan runners', *Journal of Sports Sciences*, 24: 415–22.

Orlick, T., & Partington, J. (1988) 'Mental links to excellence', *The Sport Psychologist*, 2: 105–30.

Pensgaard, A. M., & Roberts, G.C. (2000) 'The relationship between motivational climate, perceived ability and sources of distress among elite athletes', *Journal of Sports Sciences*, 18: 191–200.

Pensgaard, A. M., Roberts, G.C., & Ursin, H. (1999) 'Motivational factors and coping strategies of Norwegian Paralympic and Olympic winter sport athletes', *Adapted Physical Activity Quarterly*, 16: 238–50.

Roberts, G. C. (2012) 'Motivation in sport and exercise from an achievement goal theory perspective: After 30 years, where are we?', in G. C. Roberts & D. C. Treasure (eds) *Advances in motivation in sport and exercise*, 3rd ed., Champaign, IL: Human Kinetics Publishers, 5–58.

Roberts, G.C., Treasure, D. C., & Conroy, D. E. (2007) 'The dynamics of motivation in sport: The influence of achievement goals on motivation processes', in G. Tenenbaum & R. C. Eklund (eds) *Handbook of sport psychology*, 3rd ed., New York: Wiley & Sons, 3–30.

Roth, S., & Cohen, L. J. (1986) 'Approach, avoidance, and coping with stress', *American Psychologist*, 41: 813–19.

Sheard, M., & Golby, J. (2009) 'Investigating the "rigid persistence paradox" in professional rugby union football', *International Journal of Sport & Exercise Psychology*, 7: 101–14.

Sheard, M., & Golby, J. (2010) 'Personality hardiness differentiates elite-level sport performers', *International Journal of Sport and Exercise Psychology*, 8: 160–9.

Simpson, D., & Wrisberg, C. (2013) 'Fail to prepare, prepare to fail: Professional boxers' experience of training', *The Sport Psychologist*, 27: 109–19.

Stoeber, J., & Crombie, R. (2010) 'Achievement goals and championship performance: Predicting absolute performance and qualification', *Psychology of Sport & Exercise*, 11: 513–21.

Stoeber, J., Uphill, M.A., & Hotham, S. (2009) 'Predicting race performance in triathlon: The role of perfectionism, achievement goals, and personal goal setting', *Journal of Sport & Exercise Psychology*, 31: 211–45.

Stoll, O., Lau, A., & Stoeber, J. (2008) 'Perfectionism and performance in a new basketball training task: Does striving for perfection enhance or undermine performance?', *Psychology of Sport & Exercise*, 9: 620–9.

Suits, B. (1977) 'Words on play', *Journal of the Philosophy of Sport*, 4: 117–31.

Taylor, I. M., & Bruner, M. W. (2012) 'The social environment and developmental experiences in elite youth soccer', *Psychology of Sport & Exercise*, 13: 390–6.

Thomas, S., Reeves, C., Agombar, J., & Greenlees, I. (2013) 'Personality hardiness at different levels of competitive motorcycling', *Perceptual & Motor Skills: Exercise & Sport*, 116: 315–21.

Toering, T. T., Elferink-Gemser, M. T., Jordet, G., Jorna, C., Pepping, G. J., & Visscher, C. (2011) 'Self-regulation of practice behavior among elite youth soccer players: An exploratory observation study', *Journal of Applied Sport Psychology*, 23: 110–28.

Toering, T. T., Elferink-Gemser, M. T., Jordet, G., & Visscher, C. (2009) 'Self-regulation and performance level of elite and non-elite youth soccer players', *Journal of Sports Sciences*, 27: 1509–17.

Toering, T. T., & Jordet, G. (2014) 'Self-control in professional football players', manuscript submitted for publication.

Treasure, D. C., Carpenter, P. J., & Power, K.T.D. (2000) 'Relationships between achievement goal orientations and the perceived purposes of playing rugby union for professional and amateur players', *Journal of Sports Sciences*, 18: 571–7.

Vallerand, R. J. (2012) 'The dualistic model of passion in sport and exercise', in G. C. Roberts & D. C. Treasure (eds) *Advances in motivation in sport and exercise*, 3rd ed., Champaign, IL: Human Kinetics Publishers, 169–206.

Vallerand, R. J., Mageau, G. A., Elliot, A. J., Dumais, A., Demers, M., & Rousseau, F. (2008) 'Passion and performance attainment in sport', *Psychology of Sport & Exercise*, 9: 373–92.

Van Yperen, N. W. (2009) 'Why some make it and others do not: Identifying psychological factors that predict career success in professional adult soccer', *The Sport Psychologist*, 23: 317–29.

Wadey, R., Evans, L., Hanton, S., & Neil, R. (2011) 'An examination of hardiness throughout the sport injury process', *British Journal of Health Psychology*, 17: 103–28.

Weinberg, R., Burton, D., Yukelson, D., & Weigand, D. (2000) 'Perceived goal setting practices of Olympic athletes: An exploratory investigation', *The Sport Psychologist*, 14: 279–95.

Weissensteiner, J., Abernethy, B., & Farrow, D. (2009) 'Towards the development of a conceptual model of expertise in cricket batting: A grounded theory approach', *Journal of Applied Sport Psychology*, 21: 276–92.

Weissensteiner, J. R., Abernethy, B., Farrow, D., & Gross, J. (2012) 'Distinguishing psychological characteristics of expert cricket batsmen', *Journal of Science and Medicine in Sport*, 15: 74–9.

White, S. A., & Duda, J. L. (1994) 'The relationship of gender, level of sport involvement, and participation motivation to task and ego orientation', *International Journal of Sport Psychology*, 25: 4–18.

White, S. A., & Zellner, S. R. (1996) 'The relationship between goal orientation, beliefs about the causes of sport success, and trait anxiety among high school, intercollegiate, and recreational sport participants', *The Sport Psychologist*, 10: 58–72.

Williams, A. M., & Elliott, D. (1999) 'Anxiety, expertise, and visual search strategy in karate', *Journal of Sport & Exercise Psychology*, 21: 362–75.

Zheng, C., Price, J., & Stone, D. F. (2011) 'Performance under pressure in the NBA', *Journal of Sports Economics*, 12(3): 231–52.

Zimmerman, B. J. (2006) 'Development and adaptation of expertise: The role of self regulatory processes and beliefs', in K. A. Ericsson, N. Charness, P. J. Feltovich, & R. R. Hoffman (eds) *The Cambridge handbook of expertise and expert performance*, New York: Cambridge University Press, 705–22.

11

PHYSICAL QUALITIES OF EXPERTS

Tim J. Gabbett

Supporters of sporting contests marvel at the athletic achievements and prowess of their idols. If we were to follow the interactions at any weekend BBQ or over a beer at the local pub, sporting discussions will generally lead to the "expertise" of specific players, and the factors that separate him/her from the "average elite player." "*He has soft hands*" or "*he's so strong and powerful, no player can stop him*."

The debate surrounding whether sporting expertise develops as a function of physical (e.g. speed, endurance, strength, etc.) or skill (e.g. technique, decision-making ability) qualities has also extended to the research environment. In their study of elite Australian Football League (AFL) players, Berry and Abernethy (2003) divided players into those that had become successful as a result of expert perception and decision-making skill (i.e. "the footballers") and those that had become successful as a result of their physical qualities (i.e. "the athletes"). While much of this report was devoted to the factors that contribute to the development of game-specific decision-making ability, an underemphasized component of this research was that players can still become successful in the AFL with average decision-making ability – if they have well-developed physical qualities. Indeed, various expertise researchers (e.g. Starkes & Ericsson, 2003) have suggested that skillful sporting performance is constrained by physical limitations, indicating that while "experts" are likely to kick the winning goal in the final minutes of the championship match, it is often their well-developed physical qualities that put that player in the position to make the important play.

This chapter examines the physical qualities of experts, non-experts, and novices. In addition, rather than viewing physical and skill attributes as two independent qualities, the relationship between physical qualities and skill, playing performance, and match activity profiles will be discussed. Finally, a conceptual model of game-specific training, which incorporates both conditioning and skill training, is provided as a stimulus to promote transfer of physical fitness to competitive performances.

Tim J. Gabbett

Physical qualities of experts and novices

Differences between higher- and lesser-skilled players

Researchers have assessed the relative importance of physical qualities to playing success by comparing athletes who were selected to participate in a team (starters) with players from the same squad that were not selected (non-starters) (Gabbett, 2009a; Gabbett *et al.*, 2009; Young *et al.*, 2005). Young *et al.* (2005), for example, investigated the physical qualities of starters and non-starters in Australian football. They found that selected players were older, more experienced, had better leg power and sprinting speed, and covered greater distance in the Yo-Yo intermittent recovery test (level 2) than non-selected players. In junior elite (Gabbett *et al.*, 2009) and sub-elite (Gabbett, 2009a) rugby league players, starters tended to be taller, have faster change of direction speed, and greater playing experience than non-starters. Moderate to large differences were also detected between starters and non-starters for acceleration, maximum velocity, and estimated maximal aerobic power (Gabbett, 2009a; Gabbett *et al.*, 2009). More recently, the relative importance of physical, anthropometric, and skill qualities to team selection in professional rugby league has been investigated. Players selected to play in the first National Rugby League game of the season were older, more experienced, and leaner and had faster 10 m and 40 m sprint times, and superior vertical jump performances, maximal aerobic power, tackling proficiency, and dual-task draw and pass ability than non-selected players (Gabbett *et al.*, 2011b, 2011c). Collectively, these results suggest a relation between physical fitness and the playing level attained, and that selected physical, anthropometric, and skill qualities may influence selection in team sports.

Discriminant analysis

Researchers have also used the results from physiological and anthropometric testing to conduct discriminant analyses. These discriminant analyses provide regression equations that can be used to predict selection on the basis of the dependent variables. Of the studies that have been performed, results are equivocal, with physical qualities predicting selection in some sports (e.g., junior Australian football, professional rugby league) (Gabbett *et al.*, 2011c; Keogh, 1999), but not others (e.g. junior volleyball) (Gabbett *et al.*, 2007a). Gabbett *et al.* (2007a) investigated if physiological, anthropometric, and skill test results discriminated between junior volleyball players of varying playing ability. Participants underwent measurements of stature, standing reach stature, body mass, skinfold thickness, overhead medicine ball throw, vertical jump, spike jump, 5 m and 10 m speed, "T" test agility, maximal aerobic power, and passing, setting, serving, and spiking technique and accuracy. Selected skill test results (i.e., passing technique and serving technique), but not physiological and anthropometric data discriminated between successful (i.e., selected) and unsuccessful (i.e., non-selected) talent-identified junior volleyball players. The discriminant analysis correctly predicted 17 out of 19 selected players and five out of nine non-selected players, respectively, and consequently 22 out of 28 total players. The prediction equations corresponded to an overall accuracy of 78.6 per cent for all players, and an accuracy of 89.5 per cent and 55.6 per cent for the selected and non-selected players, respectively. These findings demonstrate that by using the classification functions, it is possible to discriminate with better than chance accuracy whether junior volleyball players will be correctly selected into a talent identification squad using assessments of their passing and serving technique. However, while the classification functions correctly selected 17 out of 19 players (i.e., 89.5 per cent), the accuracy of the classification functions for predicting non-selection was lower (i.e., five out of nine players, 55.6 per cent). These findings demonstrate

Physical qualities of experts

that while above average passing and serving technique may facilitate selection, factors in addition to, or other than, passing and serving technique may influence non-selection.

Keogh (1999) examined the physical and anthropometric qualities that discriminated between players selected or not selected in an under-18 Australian football team. Selected players were taller and had greater upper-body strength than non-selected players. The discriminant analysis function predicted with 80 per cent accuracy whether each player was successful or unsuccessful in gaining selection. While these results clearly demonstrate that physical qualities are important to predicting selection in junior Australian football, the prediction equations developed by Keogh (1999) may not be directly applicable to elite players, as any developed model is best suited to the population from which it is derived.

In a study of professional rugby league players, a combination of four physical and skill qualities (skinfold thickness, dual-task draw and pass proficiency, maximum velocity, and decision accuracy on the reactive agility test) contributed to the discriminant classification functions predicting selection for the first competitive match of the season (Gabbett *et al.*, 2011c). However, while the classification functions correctly selected 53 out of 68 selected players (i.e., 77.9 per cent), and 38 out of 52 starting players (i.e., 73.1 per cent), the accuracy of the classification functions for predicting non-selection (46 out of 77 players, 59.7 per cent) and non-starters (10 out of 16 players, 62.5 per cent) was lower. Given that the discriminant analysis functions were developed from teams selected to play in the first competition game, it is likely that selection in repeated matches would lead to more robust conclusions and a higher predictive accuracy for non-selected players. In addition, although well-developed lean body mass, draw and pass proficiency, speed, and perceptual skill may facilitate selection, factors in addition to, or other than, these qualities may influence non-selection. While a wide range of physiological, anthropometric, and skill qualities were included in the discriminant model, and contributed to team selection, it is possible that other unmeasured qualities (e.g. attitude, mental resilience, coordination, etc.), and the "intuitive expertise" of the expert coach's eye also contribute to team selection. However, the results are interesting from the perspective that the use of a combination of physiological, anthropometric, and skill qualities to predict selection was in approximately 70 per cent agreement with selections made by the coach.

Relationship between physical qualities and performance

Skill

Given that skillful performance may be constrained by physical limitations (Starkes & Ericsson, 2003), researchers have recently attempted to determine the relationship between tests of physical fitness and skill. We recently developed a standardized drill to assess the skill of one-on-one tackling. The following criteria were developed to assess the tackling capability of rugby league players (Gabbett, 2009b; Gabbett *et al.*, 2010; Gabbett *et al.*, 2011a):

1 Contact is made at the center of gravity
2 Initial contact is made with the shoulder
3 Body position square and aligned
4 Leg drive on contact
5 Watch the target onto the shoulder
6 Center of gravity is forward of the base of support

The physiological and anthropometric correlates of rugby league tackling capability have been previously examined (Gabbett, 2009b; Gabbett *et al.*, 2010; Gabbett *et al.*, 2011a). In a study of amateur players, it was found that better tacklers had superior acceleration over 10 meters and faster change of direction speed (Gabbett, 2009b). Tackling capability in professional and elite junior players was also closely associated with acceleration and lower-body muscular power (as estimated from a vertical jump test). No association was found between tackling capability and change of direction speed (Gabbett *et al.*, 2010; Gabbett *et al.*, 2011a). It was suggested that improvements in lower-body muscular power and acceleration might result in improvements in tackling capability.

Several studies have also examined the relationship between anthropometric characteristics and tackling capability over a range of competitive levels (Gabbett, 2009b; Gabbett *et al.*, 2010; Gabbett *et al.*, 2011a). A study examining the tackling capability of junior elite and sub-elite players found that elite players were generally taller, leaner, and heavier than sub-elite players. However, no anthropometric characteristics were associated with tackling capability. This is in contrast to a study examining amateur senior players, which reported that several anthropometric characteristics were associated with superior tackling capability (Gabbett, 2009b). It was found that players with superior tackling capability had lower skinfold thickness, lower body mass, smaller waist and gluteal measurements, and lower levels of endomorphy, leading the author to suggest that at an amateur level lean body mass may improve tackling capability due to the superior power-body mass ratio. Similarly, Gabbett *et al.* (2011a) found that at professional and semi-professional level, low skinfold thickness was significantly associated with tackling capability, whereas stature and body mass were not. The differences between studies may reflect the differing impact anthropometric characteristics have at different playing levels. Moreover, it is highly likely that the difference in stature and body mass between early and late maturers observed in junior elite and sub-elite players decreases considerably at the senior playing level.

In their review article, Young and Rath (2011) explored the role of physical qualities (specifically strength qualities) on foot velocity in football kicking. The authors suggested that the hip flexors and knee extensors were important to kicking performance. In addition, some limited evidence suggested that strength of the support leg, trunk muscles, hip adductors, and the muscles that control pelvic rotations also contributed to effective kicking performance (Young & Rath, 2011). Although biomechanical factors are likely to contribute to effective kicking performance, these findings suggest that improvements in physical qualities may also lead to improvements in sport-specific skill.

Playing performance

The superior playing performance of elite team sport athletes is often attributed to the greater physiological capacities of these athletes. Although successful performance in team sports is dependent (at least in part) on well-developed physiological capacities, players also require the ability to exhibit high levels of skill under pressure and fatigue. Indeed, the significance of high physical fitness levels is reduced if the physiological parameter does not transfer to improved playing performance. For example, in collision sports (e.g., American football, rugby union, rugby league), an increase in muscular power is irrelevant unless the enhanced physical capacity transfers to improved leg drive in tackles. In addition, the value of an increase in aerobic fitness is negated if the ability of players to defend for multiple sets is unchanged or players are unable to exhibit a high level of skill under fatigue. With this in mind, several studies have examined the link between physical qualities and playing performance (Fry & Kraemer, 1991; Gabbett *et al.*, 2007b, 2011b; Sawyer *et al.*, 2002; Young & Pryor, 2007).

Physical qualities of experts

Young and Pryor (2007) investigated the relationship between selected physical qualities (e.g. height, body mass, hand span, arm length, standing reach, vertical jump, 5 m and 20 m sprint times, agility, sit and reach flexibility, and estimated maximal aerobic power [$\dot{V}O_2$max]) and performance indicators (e.g., selection for the first game of the season, number of possessions, marks, hitouts, and "votes") in junior elite Australian football players. The match committee of each club awarded "votes" to the six players on their team considered to be the best players in each game. Shorter and lighter players, and those possessing greater acceleration and aerobic power, gained the most possessions, whereas fast acceleration was the only physical quality to discriminate between higher and lower vote winners. Players from the top four teams had a greater standing reach height and were heavier than players from the bottom four teams, but no differences were found between the top and bottom teams for any fitness measure. The authors concluded that shorter and heavier players, with greater acceleration and endurance qualities, were more likely to acquire possessions and be awarded votes, but the development of these qualities did not guarantee team success (Young & Pryor, 2007).

Sawyer *et al.* (2002) investigated the relationship between selected physiological capacities (speed, agility, muscular strength, and power) and playing ability in American football players and found a strong association between vertical jump results and most measures of playing ability. The authors concluded that lower-body muscular power was important to playing success in American football, and that improvements in vertical jump results were likely to transfer to improved playing ability. Similarly, Fry and Kraemer (1991) found that one repetition maximum (RM) bench press, one RM power clean, vertical jump, and 40-yard sprint test results successfully discriminated American football players of different playing abilities. However, while American football and rugby league players both rely on speed, agility, and muscular power, the nature of the games differs considerably. Indeed, unlike American football, rugby league players are required to have a role in both attack and defense, thereby increasing the aerobic demands on players while also requiring them to express a high level of skill under greater fatigue. Although significant relationships have been observed between physical fitness and playing ability in American football players (Fry & Kraemer, 1991; Sawyer *et al.*, 2002), the extent to which improvements in physiological capacities transfer to improved playing performance in other team sports is unclear.

Match activity profiles

Several researchers have explored the relationship between tests of physical qualities and physical match performance in high-intensity intermittent team sports (Castagna *et al.*, 2009, 2010; Krustrup *et al.*, 2003, 2005; Rampinini *et al.*, 2007). Rampinini *et al.* (2007) investigated the relationship between tests of physical qualities and match physical performance in professional soccer players. Players with better performance on a repeated-sprint test covered greater match distance at high-speed sprinting. Better performance on an incremental field test was also associated with greater total distance and high-/very high-intensity running during match play. Castagna *et al.* (2009, 2010) and Krustrup *et al.* (2003, 2005) found that elite, young male and female soccer players with better performance on the Yo-Yo intermittent recovery test performed more running and high-intensity activity during match play. These findings suggest a relationship between tests of physical qualities and physical performance during match play; better-developed physical qualities generally lead to greater physical performance in soccer competition.

Recently, we investigated the relationship between physical qualities and match activity profiles in division 1, 2, and 3 amateur Australian football players (Stein, Gabbett, Townshend, & Dawson, unpublished observations). Division 1 players possessed greater maximum velocity, Yo-Yo intermittent recovery (level 2) scores, and 2 km time trial performances than division 2 and 3 players. In addition, division 1 players covered greater relative distance, and greater relative distances at moderate and high intensities during match play, than division 2 and 3 players. Division 2 players had better 2 km time trial performances than division 3 players. Positive associations were found between 10 m acceleration, maximum velocity, Yo-Yo intermittent recovery (level 2) test, and 2 km time trial performances and relative distance, and the relative distance covered in moderate and high-intensity running. These findings demonstrate that recreational Australian football players competing at a higher level also exhibit greater physical qualities and activity profiles than less-skilled players. Acceleration and maximum velocity, 2 km time trial, and Yo-Yo intermittent recovery test performances discriminated between players of different playing levels, and were related to physical match performance in recreational Australian football, suggesting that the development of these qualities may contribute to improved match performance in recreational Australian football players.

More recently, the relationships between physical qualities and match activity profiles have been documented in semi-professional rugby league (Gabbett et $al.$, 2013; Gabbett & Seibold, in press). Significant and very large ($r = 0.96$) associations were found between lower-body strength and the frequency of repeated, high-intensity effort bouts performed; when controlling for playing position, players with better full-squat performances performed more repeated, high-intensity effort bouts in competition. These findings demonstrate the importance of lower-body muscular strength to physical match performance in semi-professional rugby league players. The very large association between lower-body strength and the number of repeated, high-intensity effort bouts performed in competition is of interest, particularly given the lack of association between measures of upper-body strength, strength endurance, and prolonged, high-intensity, intermittent running ability and repeated-effort performance. Previous studies have reported a significant, but modest association ($r = 0.38$) between measures of lower-body muscular power and tackling proficiency in rugby league players (Gabbett et $al.$, 2011a). Given the large amount of collision activity performed in repeated, high-intensity effort bouts (Gabbett, 2012), the above findings highlight the importance of lower-body strength to repeated-effort performance in rugby league. While a significant correlation does not imply cause and effect, these results suggest that improvements in lower-body strength may facilitate greater repeated, high-intensity effort work rates in semi-professional rugby league. Moreover, while important to team selection, these findings suggest that upper-body strength, strength endurance, and prolonged, high-intensity, intermittent running ability contribute minimally to repeated-effort performance in rugby league players.

While previous researchers have investigated relationships between selected running qualities (e.g., speed, repeated sprint, and prolonged, high-intensity, intermittent running) and physical match performance (Castagna et $al.$, 2009, 2010; Krustrup et $al.$, 2003, 2005; Rampinini et $al.$, 2007), to the author's knowledge, few studies have assessed the relationship between strength qualities and physical match performance in a prolonged, high-intensity, intermittent team sport. The unique collision demands of American football and rugby league match play make strength a requisite quality for competitors in order to effectively tolerate the blunt force trauma that occurs in tackles and the physical stress associated with wrestling activities. While a significant association between lower-body strength and distances covered at both low and high speeds was an unexpected finding (Gabbett & Seibold, in press), greater absolute strength is likely to have resulted in players performing these wrestling and grappling activities at a lower relative intensity than weaker players. Consequently, players were likely to have greater physical reserves to devote to the running demands of competition.

Despite the reported link between physical qualities and match activity profiles, a recent study has reported that high-caliber players (subjectively rated by coaches) performed less total and high-speed running distance per minute, yet had more involvements with the football per unit

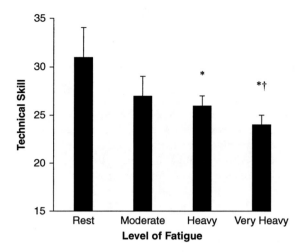

Figure 11.1 Influence of fatigue on tackling technique in rugby league players.

of distance than comparatively low-caliber players (Johnston et al., 2012). These findings suggest that tactical awareness and the ability to efficiently execute game-specific skills are important factors that should be considered when interpreting data on physical match performance.

Interaction between physical qualities and skill under fatigued conditions

Gabbett (2008) investigated the influence of fatigue on tackling ability in rugby league players and examined the relationship between selected physiological capacities and fatigue-induced decrements in tackling ability. Players performed a one-on-one tackling drill before strenuous exercise, and again following game-specific, repeated-effort exercise comprised of progressively increasing intensities (corresponding to "moderate," "heavy," and "very heavy" intensity), in order to induce fatigue that was representative of match conditions. Video footage was taken from the rear, side, and front of the defending player, and tackling technique was objectively assessed using standardized technical criteria. In addition, all players underwent measurements of standard anthropometry, speed, muscular power, agility, and estimated $\dot{V}O_2$max. Consistent with a progressive increase in fatigue, total repeated effort time, heart rate, blood lactate concentration, and ratings of perceived exertion, each increased throughout the repeated effort protocol. Fatigue resulted in progressive reductions in tackling technique (Figure 11.1). Players with the best tackling technique in a non-fatigued state demonstrated the greatest decrement in tackling technique under fatigued conditions. In addition, a significant association was found between $\dot{V}O_2$max (r = −0.62) and agility (r = 0.68) and fatigue-induced decrements in tackling technique. From a practical perspective, these findings suggest that strength and conditioning programs designed to develop endurance and change of direction speed qualities may reduce fatigue-induced decrements in tackling technique.

Young et al. (2010) investigated the effect of exercise on kicking accuracy in elite Australian football players. Players performed a kicking accuracy test by kicking at a bull's-eye on a target projected onto a screen. They then performed 2x2-minute time trials, separated by a 3-minute recovery. Immediately after the time trial, the players repeated the kicking accuracy test. Interestingly, the physiological stress imposed by exercise resulted in a 2.7 per cent (non-significant) increase in kicking accuracy. Fitter players (as estimated from performance on the time trials) and those with greater playing experience had significantly better kicking accuracy under conditions of physiological stress. The authors suggested that greater endurance and playing experience might facilitate kicking accuracy under moderate fatigue.

What happens in the "real world?"

While this chapter has predominantly focused on the physical qualities that discriminate experts and novices, it is important to recognize that (1) physical qualities are rarely expressed independently of skill and (2) (according to Starkes & Ericsson, 2003) skillful performance is dependent (at least in part) on well-developed physical qualities. In this respect, skill and physical qualities are not two isolated components of performance, but rather are closely intertwined. Consequently, the development of sporting expertise rarely occurs as either skill or fitness development in isolation, but rather involves the successful integration of skill acquisition and physical performance to further develop the specific strengths and weaknesses of athletes. While the head coach is responsible for the overall performance of the team, different staff within the team work closely with the coach and players in order to develop physical qualities and the transfer of skill. The physiologist (and strength and conditioning coach) is responsible for understanding the physical demands of the sport. His/her role includes identifying and developing the individual musculoskeletal and physiological limitations of players, in order to adequately prepare players for the most demanding passages of play. Ultimately, his/her goal is to observe these physical qualities expressed in game-specific passages of play. Equally, assistant coaches (and skill acquisition specialists) are responsible for identifying the factors (e.g., fatigue, pressure) that may influence the execution of skill and developing training scenarios that regularly expose players to these demands. The goal is to maximize transfer of learning from the training environment to the high-pressure environment of competition.

Conclusion

In summary, this chapter has highlighted the importance of well-developed physical qualities to sporting performance. The higher playing intensity at the elite level is often attributed to the greater physical capacities of these players. Given the established relationships between physical qualities, team selection, playing performance, and match activity profiles, a compelling case can be presented for the importance of physical training in the development of expertise.

References

Berry, J., & Abernethy, B. (2003) 'Expert game-based decision-making in Australian football: How is it developed and how can it be trained?', unpublished research report prepared for the Australian Football League Research Board.

Castagna, C., Impellizzeri, F., Cecchini, E., Rampinini, E., & Alvarez, J. C. (2009) 'Effects of intermittent-endurance fitness on match performance in young male soccer players', *Journal of Strength and Conditioning Research*, 23: 1954–9.

Castagna, C., Manzi, V., Impellizzeri, F., Weston, M., & Barbero Alvarez, J. C. (2010) 'Relationship between endurance field tests and match performance in young soccer players', *Journal of Strength and Conditioning Research*, 24: 3227–333.

Fry, A. C., & Kraemer, W. J. (1991) 'Physical performance characteristics of American collegiate football players', *Journal of Applied Sport Science Research*, 5: 126–38.

Gabbett, T., Georgieff, B., & Domrow, N. (2007a) 'The use of physiological, anthropometric, and skill data to predict selection in a talent-identified junior volleyball squad', *Journal of Sports Sciences*, 25: 1337–44.

Physical qualities of experts

Gabbett, T., Kelly, J., & Pezet, T. (2007b) 'Relationship between physical fitness and playing ability in rugby league players', *Journal of Strength and Conditioning Research*, 21: 1126–1133.

Gabbett, T., Kelly, J., Ralph, S., & Driscoll, D. (2009) 'Physiological and anthropometric characteristics of junior elite and sub-elite rugby league players, with special reference to starters and non-starters', *Journal of Science and Medicine in Sport*, 12: 215–22.

Gabbett, T. J. (2008) 'Influence of fatigue on tackling technique in rugby league players', *Journal of Strength and Conditioning Research*, 22: 625–32.

Gabbett, T. J. (2009a) 'Physiological and anthropometric characteristics of starters and non-starters in junior rugby league players, aged 13–17 years', *Journal of Sports Medicine and Physical Fitness*, 49: 233–9.

Gabbett, T. J. (2009b) 'Physiological and anthropometric correlates of tackling ability in rugby league players', *Journal of Strength and Conditioning Research*, 23: 540–8.

Gabbett, T. J. (2012) 'Sprinting patterns of National Rugby League competition', *Journal of Strength and Conditioning Research*, 26: 121–30.

Gabbett, T. J., Abernethy, B., & Jenkins, D. G. (2011a) 'Correlates of tackling ability in high-performance rugby league players', *Journal of Strength and Conditioning Research*, 25: 72–9.

Gabbett, T. J., Jenkins, D. G., & Abernethy, B. (2010) 'Physiological and anthropometric correlates of tackling ability in junior elite and sub-elite rugby league players', *Journal of Strength and Conditioning Research*, 24: 2989–95.

Gabbett, T. J., Jenkins, D. G., & Abernethy, B. (2011b) 'Relationships between physiological, anthropometric, and skill qualities and playing performance in professional rugby league players', *Journal of Sports Sciences*, 29: 1655–64.

Gabbett, T. J., Jenkins, D. G., & Abernethy, B. (2011c) 'Relative importance of physiological, anthropometric, and skill qualities to team selection in professional rugby league', *Journal of Sports Sciences*, 29: 1453–61.

Gabbett, T. J., & Seibold, A. (in press) 'Relationship between tests of physical qualities, team selection, and physical match performance in semi-professional rugby league players', *Journal of Strength and Conditioning Research*.

Gabbett, T. J., Stein, J. G., Kemp, J. G., & Lorenzen, C. (2013) 'Relationship between tests of physical qualities and physical match performance in elite rugby league players', *Journal of Strength and Conditioning Research*, 27: 1539–45.

Johnston, R. J., Watsford, M. L., Pine, M. J., Spurrs, R. W., Murphy, A., & Pruyn, E. C. (2012) 'Movement demands and match performance in professional Australian football', *International Journal of Sports Medicine*, 33: 89–93.

Keogh, J. (1999) 'The use of physical fitness scores and anthropometric data to predict selection in an elite under 18 Australian rules football team', *Journal of Science and Medicine in Sport*, 2: 125–33.

Krustrup, P., Mohr, M., Amstrup, T., Rysgaard, T., Johansen, J., Steensberg, A., . . . Bangsbo, J. (2003) 'The yo-yo intermittent recovery test: Physiological response, reliability, and validity', *Medicine and Science in Sports and Exercise*, 35: 697–705.

Krustrup, P., Mohr, M., Ellingsgaard, H., & Bangsbo, J. (2005) 'Physical demands during an elite female soccer game: Importance of training status', *Medicine and Science in Sports and Exercise*, 37: 1242–8.

Rampinini, E., Bishop, D., Marcora, S. M., Ferrari Bravo, D., Sassi, R., & Impellizzeri, F. M. (2007) 'Validity of simple field tests as indicators of match-related physical performance in top-level soccer players', *International Journal of Sports Medicine*, 28: 228–35.

Sawyer, D. T., Ostarello, J. Z., Suess, E. A., & Dempsey, M. (2002) 'Relationship between football playing ability and selected performance measures', *Journal of Strength and Conditioning Research*, 16: 611–16.

Starkes, J. L., & Ericsson, K. A. (2003) *Expert performance in sports: Advances in research on sport expertise*, Champaign, IL: Human Kinetics.

Young, W., Gulli, R., Rath, D., Russell, A., O'Brien, B., & Harvey, J. (2010) 'Acute effect of exercise on kicking accuracy in elite Australian football players', *Journal of Science and Medicine in Sport*, 13: 85–9.

Young, W. B., Newton, R. U., Doyle, T. L., Chapman, D., Cormack, S., Stewart, G., & Dawson, B. (2005) 'Physiological and anthropometric characteristics of starters and non-starters and playing positions in elite Australian Rules Football: A case study', *Journal of Science and Medicine in Sport*, 8: 333–45.

Young, W. B., & Pryor, L. (2007) 'Relationship between pre-season anthropometric and fitness measures and indicators of playing performance in elite junior Australian Rules football', *Journal of Science and Medicine in Sport*, 10: 110–18.

Young, W. B., & Rath, D. A. (2011) 'Enhancing foot velocity in football kicking: The role of strength training', *Journal of Strength and Conditioning Research*, 25: 561–6.

12

EXPERT PERFORMANCE IN SPORT

An ecological dynamics perspective

Keith Davids, Duarte Araújo, Ludovic Seifert,
and Dominic Orth

This chapter provides an account of how expertise in sport is acquired, from the framework of ecological dynamics. Ecological dynamics research has shown that expert performance in sport is predicated on an athlete's capacity to functionally adapt his/her movements to the dynamics of complex performance environments by continuously perceiving information to regulate goal-directed actions. Here we selectively focus on the contribution of three key theoretical ideas from ecological dynamics: perceptual attunement to affordances, harnessing neurobiological system degeneracy, and exploiting adaptive movement variability in a metastable system state. We relate these ideas to practical examples from sport performance throughout, discussing how they might inform the design of practice strategies.

The ecological dynamics perspective on expert performance in sport and the acquisition of expertise

Ecological dynamics emphasizes the study of organism–environment systems, a central theme in ecological science. Ecological science is committed to studying information-based behavioral transactions between individual organisms, and between individual organisms and relevant properties of a specific performance environment, including objects, surfaces, terrains, and niches that comprise the physical surroundings. Within an ecological dynamics approach, organisms and their performance environments form complex and dynamical systems, characterized by continuous interactions between key system components, and continuous change or activity across different timescales (Davids *et al.*, 2013; Davids *et al.*, 2014). These key ideas have important implications for considering expertise in sport since ecological dynamics is concerned with understanding the relationship between an athlete and key properties of a performance environment. Relevant properties complement physical characteristics, psychological, emotional, and social processes which continuously constrain athlete-environment interactions (Chow, 2013; Seifert *et al.*, 2013a). In addressing this complexity, ecological dynamics integrates ecological psychology and dynamical systems theory for understanding a performer's intentional actions with respect to a performance environment (Araújo *et al.*, 2006).

Expert performance in sport

Ecological psychology

Ecological dynamics emphasizes the mutually constraining relations between perceptual and action subsystems in humans for coordinating action (Gibson, 1979). To exemplify, in the sport of long jumping, light reaches the eyes of a jumper after being reflected off surrounding objects and surfaces – the takeoff board, the pit, a windsock placed near the jumping area – providing each performer with information for regulating stride adjustments during the run-up and jump preparation phases of performance (Greenwood *et al.*, 2013). The organization of functional performance behaviors is underpinned by dynamically intertwined relations between intentions, perception, and action in each individual. During performance, an individual's intended movements generate perceptual information, which, in turn, constrains the emergence of further movements. For example, information perceived by a basketball player on court is constrained by specific actions (e.g., when dribbling or defending) and by intentions (e.g., to play conservatively or to take risks) (Cordovil *et al.*, 2009). In climbing, Seifert and colleagues (2014) observed how skilled climbers perceived different properties of ice surface structure to adapt their actions with ice tools and crampons. When they perceived holes in the ice surface left by previous climbers, hooking actions emerged. Conversely, when the ice was smooth and dense, the climbers used swinging actions to create the holes needed for a safe and rapid traversal. In turn, a climber's movements continuously change his/her relationship with the performance environment and create information for new action opportunities. Seifert and coworkers (2014) reported that skilled climbers used a large range of actions, including movement coordination patterns that crossed two limbs, leading them to detect different sources of kinesthetic information, and supporting different body positions on the ice to maintain equilibrium and achieve a traversal. For instance, symmetric use of limbs with ice tools and crampons led them to adopt *X-shaped* body positions, which faced the ice surface. When they sought asymmetric anchorages on the icefall, more functional *side-to-the-icefall* body positions emerged.

These examples demonstrate Gibson's (1979) insights on the importance of maintaining relationships between key sources of information and actions through carefully structured practice strategies for developing experts. Different sources of perceptual information present opportunities for different performers to execute specific actions in sport. These actions in turn create information that supports further goal-directed behaviors in a cyclical fashion. For this reason, practice task design must simulate the ecological constraints of performance (see Withagen *et al.*, 2012). In doing so, a major aim of pedagogists – i.e., achieving behavioral correspondence between learning and performance environments – can be met and should enhance the development of expertise in sport (Pinder *et al.*, 2011a, 2011b). In the development of expertise in sport these ideas suggest that practicing athletes need to be given opportunities to search for and use information to guide their actions. This is best achieved through practice tasks that allow continuous movement interactions (not static drills), opportunities for exploration of the performance environment (not prescription of a specific movement pattern to imitate), and inclusion of key information sources that will be present during performance (e.g., other players in team games [Orth *et al.*, 2014] and relevant court/pitch markings [Headrick *et al.*, 2012], see Figure 12.1).

Dynamical systems theory

A second important constituent of ecological dynamics is dynamical systems theory, a multidisciplinary, systems-led approach encompassing mathematics and physics, and their extensions to biology and psychology. In this theory, natural phenomena can be explained, at multiple scales

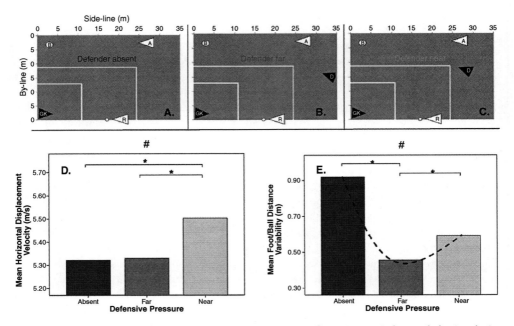

Figure 12.1 An example of how practice constraints act as information to influence behavior during performance, shaping the regulation of action. Panels A, B, and C show an experimental design detailed in Orth et al. (2014). In this experiment, eight soccer players were asked to, from a standing start, run along the sideline of a soccer field toward the byline, where a ball was positioned, and make a pass back to a receiving player at the penalty spot. They did this under three different conditions, a total of four trials each condition for each individual. **Panel A.** shows Condition 1, where there was no defender present during the performance. **Panel B.** shows Condition 2, where a defender was positioned at a relatively far distance and instructed to shut down the attacker. **Panel C.** shows Condition 3, where a defender was positioned at a relatively close distance. **Panel D.** shows the average running speed of the players. This data shows how only when the defender was near did running velocity of the attacker increase significantly. **Panel E.** shows the overall average foot-to-ball distance standard deviation of the attacking players for each condition. Importantly, regulation was induced by the mere presence of a defender, even without the need for players to run faster. The data exemplifies how movement variability is sensitive to environmental sources of information embedded within performance contexts, and in the sport performance context is not just a form of internally produced noise incurred by maximal efforts. For reasons such as these, in ecological dynamics it is the performer-environment informational relationship that is emphasized for driving pedagogical practice. Note: **A** = attacker; **B** = ball; **D** = defender; **GK** = goalkeeper; **m** = meters; **m/s** = meters per second; **R** = receiver; **#** = significant main effect; ***** = significant between condition effect.

of analysis, with the same underlying, abstract principles, regardless of a system's structure and composition (e.g., the coordination of a player's movements and a team's attacking and defensive play can be understood through analyzing system changes over space and time). These key ideas are instrumental in capturing how the continuous coupling (coadaptation) between a performer and a performance environment can be formally modeled, theoretically conceptualized, and empirically studied. Warren (2006) proposed the term *behavioral dynamics* to capture the ongoing spatial and temporal characteristics of the coordination between an individual and an environment. His ideas have been extrapolated to the study of movement coordination and control and the acquisition of expertise in sport (Davids et al., 2008; Davids et al., 2003; Handford et al., 1997). Understanding the continuous coupling, and adaptation, of information and actions has been stimulated by theoretical insights of Bernstein (1967). He drew attention to how the abundance of motor system degrees of freedom can be exploited by continual (re)organization during goal-directed performance (Bernstein, 1967). Ecological dynamics emphasizes the importance of developing experts being required to continuously reorganize and coadapt their actions, perception, and cognitions as they seek to achieve their specific task goals (in team sports these include keeping possession of the ball, attempting to score, covering teammates and space, and dribbling). The continuous reorganization of system degrees of freedom is not driven by the environment. As Whiting (1991) once succinctly captured the coordination problem in sport: action is not reaction! Coordination of movement and between individuals in a performance environment emerges from their coadaptive behaviors (Davids *et al.*, 2012).

In this systems approach, many biomechanical degrees of freedom are available for movement regulation, demonstrating the wealth of options available to the central nervous system for motor task performance (Davids *et al.*, 2006; Davids & Glazier, 2010). The abundance of system degrees of freedom is simultaneously a wonderful resource to be exploited by an athlete and an organizational challenge for a performer's central nervous system during skill acquisition (Davids & Glazier, 2010). The number of motor system degrees of freedom to be regulated by an individual changes significantly with the increasing complexity of an action to be coordinated, exemplified by the difference in performing a forward entry dive into a pool and the performance of a backward three-and-a-half somersault from a 3 m springboard (Barris *et al.*, 2013a). At a different scale of analysis, coordination between players in a team also involves the continuous (re)organization of the team's degrees of freedom (individual players) when attacking and defending together. However, the creation of synergies between the component parts of the body and between the team players provides the functional means for task goals to be achieved through coordination (Wu & Latash, 2014).

In ecological dynamics, expertise in sport is revealed by functional coordination solutions that are assembled from system components by individual athletes to satisfy the unique set of constraints interacting upon him/her (Davids *et al.*, 2008). From this perspective, the physical characteristics of the performance environment, the morphology of each individual's body, information variables, and specific task constraints all interact to constrain goal-directed activity (Araújo *et al.*, 2004; Warren, 2006). Due to these continuous interactions, explanations of expertise, based solely on either personal (e.g., genes or psychological processes) or environmental constraints (e.g., amount of practice undertaken), are fundamentally limited (Baker & Davids, 2006). Some current estimations suggest, for example, that between 22 to 36 per cent of performance variance can be explained by genetic constraints (Phillips *et al.*, 2010; Simonton, 2007). Research on physical activity, exercise, and sport performance displays little support for either biologically or environmentally deterministic perspectives (Baker & Davids, 2006).

Skill acquisition and expert performance in sport

Our research suggests that traditional theories of skill acquisition tend to overvalue the importance of repetition of an ideal movement pattern (e.g., Adams, 1971; Ericsson *et al.*, 1993; Gentile, 1972). There has been considerable criticism of the notion that a putative "common optimal movement" pattern exists (see Brisson & Alain, 1996; Schöllhorn *et al.*, 2006). The belief that expert performance can be achieved through constant rehearsal of an idealized movement pattern (e.g., a classical technique) is pervasive in many sports (Seifert *et al.*, 2013a). It is exemplified by the erroneous obsession that some coaches have with the acquisition of a specific set of mechanics for *the* golf swing, to be perfected through hours of practice under the constant conditions of a golf driving range. It is also instantiated in the perception of elite springboard divers, that preparatory movements (the hurdle step), considered less than ideal, should be terminated through "baulking," discontinuation of the aerial and water entry phases of the dive (Barris *et al.*, 2013b). Conversely, evidence shows that baulking, especially in the absence of a perceived injury risk, can be considered a maladaptive behavior by the athlete because it leads to penalty points in the competitive environment, inhibits the diver from experiencing how to adapt ongoing movements to a varied, initial hurdle step, and can lead to a loss of hundreds of practice trials each week (Barris *et al.*, 2013a; Barris *et al.*, 2014).

In ecological dynamics, the capacity to adapt movements to dynamic interacting constraints of a performance environment, to achieve specific intentions and make decisions, broadly defines expertise (Davids *et al.*, 2008; Seifert *et al.*, 2013a). From a constraints-led perspective, skill acquisition is proposed as a search for *functional coordination solutions* that emerge from individual, task-oriented, and environmental constraints (Newell, 1986). Expert performance is captured by the emergence of an *increasingly more functional athlete-environment relationship acquired over time with task experience* (Davids *et al.*, 2008). This view of skill and expertise as a *more functional relationship* is distinct from theories that emphasize the repetition of a particular movement pattern or coordination mode through constant practice. It recognizes the need for each individual learner to adapt to, and satisfy, the unique array of interaction constraints impinging on him/her at a specific stage of development and level of experience. Expert performers are able to constantly (and subtly) *reinvent themselves* as key constraints change; that is, as new opponents set unique challenges, as rules change, as equipment evolves, and as maturation and aging affects the systems of each athlete's body (see Figure 12.2 for a summary).

The role of adaptive capacities in expert sport performance is reflected in the variety of behaviors that highly skilled athletes can display during performance and their ability to vary

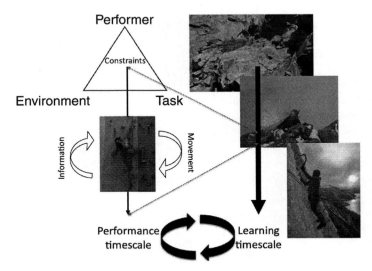

Figure 12.2 Exemplifies both how performance emerges from constraints on performer-environment relationships, and how performance environments might evolve over time relative to the skills of the individual. A characteristic of the development of expertise is that it evolves over an extended timescale, providing a basis where skills can influence the different contexts that individuals perform under. As skill evolves, individuals might experience new environmental properties (for example, rock, snow, ice) and equipment (safety equipment, icepicks). Such potential diversity in experiences leads to highly unique individual adaption, and some underpinning features of the learning process somehow allow expert performers to constantly reinvent themselves so that they may transfer their skills into highly demanding performance contexts where key constraints can change in highly unpredictable ways.

those behaviors from trial to trial to achieve similar performance outcomes (Seifert *et al.*, 2013a). Adaptive movement variability provides individuals with the capacity to maintain performance outcome stability in the face of perturbations within dynamic performance environments (e.g., successfully driving a golf ball to an intended playing area on different course layouts or in varied weather conditions). These ideas imply that an important practice strategy should be to compose a perceptual-motor workspace within which (developing) experts can search for functional coordination solutions, rather than require them to rehearse putative, "ideal" movement techniques. As we discuss next, this functional practice strategy should include the design of affordances, the enhancement of adaptive behaviors through harnessing inherent degeneracy in human movement systems, and aid to exploit system metastability.

Key aspects of expert performance in sport: attunement to affordances, harnessing neurobiological system degeneracy, and exploiting metastability during learning

Perceptual attunement to affordances

The theory of affordances was conceived by Gibson (1979) to explain how organisms detect information and perceive properties of their environment that can be used to regulate their decisions and actions. Affordances are opportunities for action that can selectively invite behaviours of an individual in a specific performance environment (Withagen & Chemero, 2012). The key relationship between the physical properties of a performance environment and an individual's action capabilities provides a veritable landscape of affordances in sport (e.g., the trajectory of a ball to catch, hit, or avoid, or a gap to dribble through). As he/she acquires expertise, the performer becomes attuned to affordances that can support achievement of performance goals in specific circumstances. The ability to perceive an affordance is predicated on an individual's ability to detect information in a performance environment relative to his/her existing action capabilities (e.g., whether a hold on a rock affords a vertical pinch hand-grasp or horizontal crimp hand-grasp action for a climber during a traversal, Phillips *et al.*, 2012).

To underline the notion that the *relations* between an individual and a performance environment constitute affordances (i.e., they are not an entity to be memorized), Gibson (1966) distinguished between *knowledge of* and *knowledge about* the environment. He proposed that *knowledge about* the environment involves perception, which is indirect or mediated by language, symbols, pictures, and verbal instructions, all of which can facilitate analogical reasoning and verbal communication of what an information source means. This is the type of knowledge used when coaches verbally instruct an athlete on how to perform a movement pattern or about a defensive formation to adopt in a team game like water polo. *Knowledge of* the environment, in contrast, describes how a biological organism can perceive the surrounding layout of its performance environment in the scale of its body and action capabilities (Turvey & Shaw, 1995, 1999). According to Gibson (1966), *knowledge of* the environment facilitates the completion of an action in a performance environment because it involves the perception of invariants used to control action directly. To exemplify, *knowledge of* the environment in water polo involves the pickup of perceptual variables that specify properties of a ball skidding on the water surface, which selectively *constrain* functional behaviors, such as gripping with wet fingers or hitting with the hand. These behaviors are functional for performance behaviors such as keeping possession of the ball or defending a shot in the pool (see also Araújo *et al.*, 2009 for applications to basketball). Seifert and colleagues (2014) showed how expert climbers tended to use subtle combinations of kinesthetic, haptic, acoustic, and visual information to regulate their actions, while beginners were dominated by one source of information. To maintain stability on an ice surface, beginners in climbing typically rely on information from *depth* of an ice tool blade entering the frozen icefall, while experts perceive haptic information from *vibration* from the ice tool, acoustic feedback from the *sound* of the blade, and *vision* of the anchorage. Beginners also showed less perceptual attunement to environmental properties than experts, displaying a global perception of environment properties, which does not specify action accurately. For instance, in ice climbing, whereas experts can distinguish information from the handle and blade of the ice tools, beginners only take into account the ice tool globally. Their global perception of their relationship with the performance environment cannot specify how information from separate parts of the ice tool can interact with the dynamics of the icefall, including ice thickness, steepness, and density, as they alter during an ascent.

Warren (2006) exemplified how affordances are relational in humans, demonstrating how they remain available over a range of spatiotemporal values of a variable. What this signifies is that the same object, event, or surface can selectively invite different behaviors of the same performer over time and, of course, different behaviours from different individuals (Withagen & Chemero, 2012). Warren (1984) proposed that, at extremes on the spatiotemporal scale that represent the limits of an affordance, there corresponds a boundary region beyond which an organism must perceive a different affordance in order to interact with the environment as intended. During learning, a number of different body-environment relationships can be facilitated to emerge in practice, and these relationships are predicated on the scalable relations between specific personal constraints (such as body dimensions [Hristovski *et al.*, 2006] and action capabilities [Orth *et al.*, 2014]) and environmental properties. To enhance expertise in sport, a suitable strategy is to modify practice tasks for different learners to help them probe the boundaries between affordances. To exemplify, on a tennis court the acquisition of skill in the backhand volley might be facilitated by designing different affordances into a practice rally between a player and coach/training partner. Different types of feeds by a coach afford the performance of different shots by a specific athlete. In some feeds a backhand or forehand drive may emerge from a tennis player and under specific task constraints (a specific ball trajectory relative to the practicing player) the backhand volley will emerge. There is rarely a need for verbal specification of the "correct" (most functional) shot to play under different competitive constraints, and a skilled coach will not specify a shot afforded to a developing expert in a specific game situation. Specific strokes emerge as a developing expert gains *knowledge of* a performance environment through perceiving an affordance of a ball in flight and acting upon it (Carvalho *et al.*, 2013). A specific affordance will selectively emerge in game situations based on the individual constraints of each athlete (differentiated by speed on the ground, anticipation, arm span and reach, and tactical intentions), exemplifying how cognitions, actions, and perceptions are intertwined to achieve performance goals.

This idea clarifies how constraint manipulation forms the basis of practice design in sport. This pedagogical approach can enhance expertise by the creation of a perceptual-motor landscape in which specific actions are more likely to emerge from individuals. In this respect, a learning environment should not be considered as a "neutral" landscape of possibilities. Rather, the design of particular opportunities for action can be potentiated by inviting actions from individual learners (Withagen *et al.*, 2012). Perceptual-motor landscape (affordance) design by coaches in sport is driven by questions such as: what performance aspects need to be strengthened? What information-movement couplings need to be emphasized in affordance design? How can a performer or team coadapt to the specific tactical strategies of opponents? Key phases in learning to pick up affordances to regulate actions include the education of intention, the education of attention, and calibration. Perceptual attunement occurs during expertise development when athletes learn to

Expert performance in sport

distinguish which sources of information to attend to in which specific performance situations, and also when to attend to these perceptual variables.

Here we can consider these theoretical ideas by considering a basic problem in ball sports: when and how long to watch a ball in flight to organize an interceptive action. With extended practice, developing players converge from sources of information that may be less useful in one specific situation to perceptual variables that are more useful under a range of different performance circumstances. For example, early in learning, many ball players keep their eyes on the ball (e.g., a batter in cricket watching ball flight to strike the ball). As expertise in a sport is enhanced, a player becomes attuned to a wider range of spatial and temporal perceptual variables and gains a greater sensitivity to the contextual consequences of his/her actions (Araújo *et al.*, 2006). Later in learning, cricketers begin to converge on more useful information from a bowler, such as body orientation, arm position, and hand adjustments prior to ball release (Pinder *et al.*, 2011b).

This process of perceptual attunement is supported by system degeneracy – the ability of elements that are structurally different to perform a similar function or yield a similar output, an essential feature of skilled behaviour (Edelman & Gally, 2001; Mason, 2010). For instance, research has established how expert players in field hockey reach the same performance outcomes (e.g., ball velocity) with different movement patterns (Brétigny *et al.*, 2011). In particular, they exhibited kinematic differences in relation to their role on the field (defenders versus midfielders and forwards): forwards used a shorter backswing duration than defenders, which is a real advantage in contexts of temporal pressure as movement preparation time is shortened and prevents any risk of ball interception (Brétigny *et al.*, 2011).

After perceptual attunement is enhanced, the developing expert undergoes calibration, or the scaling of the perceptual-motor system to information. In these individuals, body dimensions and action capabilities are not static, but often change due to development, aging, and/or training. When body dimensions and action capabilities change, actions that were once impossible may become possible (or vice versa, see Fajen *et al.*, 2008). These ideas illustrate the importance of recognizing individual differences in the way that skilled performers achieve functional task solutions. For example, as young adults, tennis players can reach passing ball trajectories to volley rather than having to wait for the ball to bounce to drive it. With aging, system reorganization in older adult players might signify that letting a ball bounce for a drive is a more functional shot than striving to volley a passing ball early. This example also highlights how athletes' effective body dimensions can be mediated by using equipment in sport such as racquets, roller blades, bats, and sticks. In acquiring expertise, constant calibration and recalibration are necessary to establish and update the mapping between the relevant properties of the world that are perceived, and the actions achieved. Calibration during extensive periods of practice makes it possible for performers to perceive the world in intrinsic units (e.g., related to their individual limb segment dimensions), even after changes in body dimensions and action capabilities due to development, training, and growth. For a calibrated performer, body-scaled and action-scaled affordances can be directly and reliably perceived by simply picking up the relevant sources of information to regulate actions (Fajen *et al.*, 2008). Although recalibration occurs quite rapidly, it is likely that continued experience leads to further refinement in calibration. Affordances that are both body and action scaled become more prevalent in sport, as expertise is enhanced. Processes like education of intention, attunement, and calibration can occur at all phases of expertise development.

Intentions selectively change as a function of experience, suggesting that attention will shift to different information sources throughout the learning process (Davids *et al.*, 2012; Jacobs & Michaels, 2007). For example, in sports like swimming and mountain biking, although a major competitive goal might be the rapid displacement across the aquatic environment or forest track, a novice's intentions are primarily to avoid sinking in a pool or falling off a bike. As skill level and expertise changes, specific intentions and performance goals are likely to change radically too, such as via a prospective control process (Montagne, 2005) or conditioned coupling (Van Geert, 1994). For instance, Seifert *et al.* (2011) showed high inter-individual variability of coordination patterns in novice swimmers that could relate to an exploratory phase with regard to environmental constraints: they experience the Archimedes's principle by dealing with constraints of gravity and buoyancy, captured by Newton's third law of producing an action to get a reaction in the opposite direction. These novice behaviors may relate to various intentions for the same task goal; in particular, the priority of novice swimmers is not only to advance in the water, but also to balance (stay in a ventral position), float (stay at the water surface), breathe (avoid bringing hands to the chest in order to keep the head above water), and perceive the layout of the aquatic environment (Newton's law and Archimedes's principle). Later in learning, expert swimmers become more attuned to information, helping them to swim quickly and economically (Seifert *et al.*, 2011). These examples show how different ways of achieving performance are featured in both the movement system and in environmental properties. Ecological dynamics conceptualizes this variability in behavior for achieving the same outcomes as a reflection of inherent system degeneracy. We now consider how degeneracy provides a functional explanation for behavioural variability shown in expert movement coordination.

Harnessing inherent degeneracy in neurobiological systems

Degeneracy exists at all levels of neurobiological systems (e.g., genetic, neuronal, perceptual, musculo-skeletal) and emerges when components differing in structure achieve a similar function in an environmental context (Edelman & Gally, 2001). Mason proposed that degeneracy exists in systems "where structurally different components perform a similar, but not necessarily identical, function with respect to context" (2010, p. 277). This conceptualization of degeneracy emphasizes the important role of movement variability in achieving performance outcomes, implying a shift away from a normative categorization of an action as, for example, a "classic technique" in sport. Degeneracy is a functional property because it provides neurobiological systems with flexibility and variability, which is adaptive, enhancing their resistance to internal and external perturbations. In human movement systems, degeneracy infers how the same function can be achieved by two different biomechanical architectures, each involving different joints (i.e., many structures-to-one function), as well as by several joints working together (i.e., one structure-to-many functions), whilst leaving some joints free for future involvement (Seifert *et al.*, 2013a; Mason, 2010).

Degeneracy signifies how an individual can vary movement behavior (structurally) without compromising function and is an important aspect of skilled sport performance. It has been investigated in a range of sport-related activities, including simulated skiing (Nourrit *et al.*, 2003), riding a pedalo (Chen *et al.*, 2005), basketball shooting (Rein *et al.*, 2010), soccer kicking (Chow *et al.*, 2008), and breaststroke swimming (Komar *et al.*, 2014). Degeneracy supports the functional robustness and adaptability of human movement systems, providing a compelling explanation why variation in perceptual-motor behaviors is needed within and across individuals during goal-directed activities. Our work has shown that it is an important characteristic to exploit in becoming expert in sport (Chow *et al.*, 2011; Chow, 2013).

Exploiting neurobiological degeneracy requires the performer to continuously seek to (re) establish coordinated relations amongst limbs, joints and environmental surfaces, objects and events in a performance environment, regulated by different perceptual variables. For example, numerous effector systems (limbs) may be (re)assembled in several distinct ways to resolve the same task outcome or adapt to variations in the task demands (such as in performance conditions when advanced information for actions are hidden by opponents or disguised for deception) (Davids & Araújo, 2010). Examples of the functionality of degeneracy in sport are endless and include: (i) in tennis, a backhand or forehand stroke in a rally can be achieved by using one hand or two hands; (ii) in football, a defensive interception can achieved by heading the ball, sliding through the ball with the left or right foot, using the body to block a shot, or "nicking" the ball with a toe end (a goalkeeper might use his/her head, hands, body, and feet in defending a shot); (iii) excellent teams use degeneracy by varying their offensive and defensive patterns to coadapt to performance conditions (small or large fields, weather conditions) and especially opposition tactical changes (strengths and weaknesses); and (iv), in judo, when rule changes in permitted gripping actions occur, the same throws are being observed during competition, but with modified grips by performers.

In seeking to become expert, athletes can exploit inherent system degeneracy to achieve their task objectives by strategically (re)stabilizing or destabilizing their coupling of movement and information. Over extended timescales system degeneracy provides a platform for individuals to discover new affordances and restabilize information-movement couplings, leading to expectations that *different* coordination solutions might selectively emerge to achieve the *same* performance outcomes through exploratory practice. The role of practice in exploiting degeneracy can be helpful for athletes to generate new coordination solutions as well as adapt existing movement patterns so that they satisfy the constraints of a particular performance context (Barris *et al.*, 2013b). If individuals were to over-practice under fixed task and environmental constraints (e.g., driving a golf ball at a driving range or baulking when preparing to dive from a springboard), the acquisition of expertise would be hindered by lack of opportunities to continuously coadapt movement patterns to changing environmental constraints. Constraint manipulation by skilled coaches can induce learning to promote exploration and adaptation in a systematic manner, enhancing the dexterity of an athlete, a most significant property of expertise in sport. Newell (1996) recognized the importance of Bernstein's insights that movement expertise is predicated on dexterity; that is, ". . . the capacity to solve a motor problem – correctly, quickly, rationally, and resourcefully. Dexterity is finding a motor solution for any situation and in any condition . . ." (1967, p. 398). In sport, expertise is not expressed by the capacity to repeat an idealized movement pattern in an identical way from trial to trial, but rather by the *achievement of functional coordination solutions* in dynamic performance environments.

This key idea in ecological dynamics provides the basis for a theoretically principled and pragmatic approach to progressive, long-term, sustained skill acquisition at all performance levels in the progression from novice to expert status (Davids *et al.*, 2012). Under the constraints-based framework, expertise development can be enhanced by identifying affordances as selective constraints on an individual's learning and managing these effectively with respect to interactions in the learning environment. Early in learning, an aspiring expert begins to explore information-movement couplings that allow patterns of coordination to remain stable under perturbation.

Exploiting system metastability

Inducing functional exploration is needed to enhance coordination and control. This aspect of expert performance can be achieved through modifying key constraints that act on the dynamic, spatiotemporal relationships that individuals form during performance. An important goal for sport pedagogists is to help learners explore system metastability. Metastability involves switching between (and stabilizing) different functional coordination tendencies to achieve performance goals. For example, in ball sports like cricket and tennis, experts can switch between equally

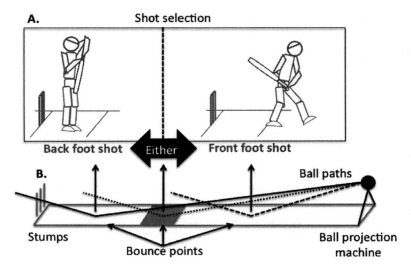

Figure 12.3 Example of the basic principles of a metastable performance region as detailed in Pinder et al. (2012). **Panel A**. shows two qualitatively different actions for intercepting a cricket ball. **Panel B**. shows that choice of which movement coordination emerges is sensitive to the position at which the ball bounces on the pitch. Closer to the stumps a back foot shot is used and closer to the ball release point a front foot shot is used. The data in Pinder et al. (2012) showed that at a certain location (around 7.5 m from the stumps) both actions were equally likely to occur, and without performance deteriorating. In ecological dynamics this region is termed the metastable performance region. Because performance can be maintained, it appears to naturally (without instruction) induce behavioral variability, which might be useful for adapting to subtle variations in constraints or exploring different ways of organizing the movement system. Importantly, this principle appears to be a generalizable phenomenon across different sports (for an example, in boxing see Hristovsky et al., 2006). The implications for learning are only just starting to be considered (Chow, 2013).

functional strokes to achieve a specific performance goal of defending against, or attacking, the opposition (for an example, see Figure 12.3 that summarizes the work in Pinder et al., 2012). In a metastable system state, multiple information-movement couplings functionally coexist under the same constraints and are expressed randomly from trial to trial. Metastability exists when, under the same constraints, there is the coexistence of segregating tendencies (for action to be performed relatively independently of the environment) and of integrating tendencies (for action to be performed relatively dependently on the environment) (Kelso, 2012). There is no constant force stemming from either the performer's personal constraints (intrinsic dynamics) or task constraints that requires performance behavior to reflect a fixed stable state. Metastable regimes in practice support the emergence of rich and variable patterns of behavior that are functional (e.g., support task success, help adaptation, and uncover new information).

Although theoretically conceptualized as a mechanism for learning, the role of metastability in learning complex, goal-directed behaviors has rarely been operationalized, or tested in sport (Chow et al., 2011). It has been operationalized in a study of striking a heavy bag in boxing and in analysis of a defensive stroke in cricket batting (Hristovski et al., 2006; Pinder et al., 2012). The notion of a metastable regime can be exemplified in the sport of climbing and operationally defined by the trial-to-trial dynamics of (i) body-wall coordination patterns and (ii) "technical" perceptual-motor actions that regulate the stability of the body-wall orientations used for surface traversal. Under a metastable regime in climbing, the individual learner should be capable of expressing coordination patterns that are intrinsically stable, as well as patterns that are relatively novel but highly functional for adapting performance to dynamic, environmental constraints (Seifert *et al.*, 2013b). An individual placed in a metastable regime has the opportunity to explore a variety of movement control strategies. Some strategies might be highly predictive (based on preplanned intentions), others responsive to ongoing dynamical constraints of a performance environment (based on external environmental information). With increasing expertise, athletes are neither too reactive in their response to environmental information sources, nor too pre-organized in their actions. For example, in competitive climbing, while there is some value in previewing climbing surfaces from the ground in order to consider potential traversal routes, ultimately climbing actions are emergent as affordances of specific surface holds are perceived during performance.

Summary: the characteristics of expertise in sport

In this chapter we provided an ecological dynamics rationale for understanding expertise in sport, discussing three key ideas for enhancing expertise. The main characteristics of expert performance from this perspective include:

1 The view that processes of cognition, perception, and action are intertwined in a complex way as expert performers switch between *dependence on* and *independence of* environmental information sources in performance (see point 5 below). Preferred coordination tendencies are harnessed during performance, but experts are not locked in to specific environmental constraints (in a reactive manner) during performance. Their actions can be guided by a combination of intentions and the perception of specific information sources to perform an activity in a particular way to achieve specific performance goals.
2 An important aspect of expert behavior is the capacity to *perceive affordances* by learning to detect key sources of environmental information that support successful task performance. Expertise can be enhanced by pedagogists' understanding of how to design affordances into learning programs.
3 *Individual differences are paramount* as personal constraints of expert performers are satisfied in achieving task performance goals in different ways (see point 6 below). The influence of personal constraints eschews the notion of a common, optimal movement pattern towards which all performers should aspire, because affordances are uniquely *body scaled* and *action scaled* for each individual expert athlete.
4 Expert performance is characterized by a subtle blend of stability and flexibility that results in *adaptive movement variability*. Variability is only functional and adaptive when an individual is able to exploit system flexibility and stability, as and when needed, to achieve successful performance outcomes. This idea signifies that either stable or flexible movement patterns can be adopted when required, so some aspects of movement coordination can remain stable while other components can exhibit greater flexibility. This capacity captures how system degeneracy is harnessed by expert individuals (again, see point 6 below).
5 Since an expert's *emergent actions* are continuously regulated by the intertwined processes of intentions, perceptions, and action, they are neither *completely dependent* on environmental information (reactive, completely information driven) nor *completely independent* of environmental information (whole movement configurations planned in advance of an unfolding situation because these prescribed action plans are weakly stable). This capacity of expertise is predicated on *system metastability*, which underpins creative and adaptive performance in sport.

Keith Davids et al.

6 The adaptability of actions harnesses the neurobiological system property of *degeneracy*, which can be exploited to allow individuals to achieve the same performance outcomes using different coordination patterns.

7 An important practical implication of the three key ideas discussed in this ecological dynamics explanation of expertise acquisition in sport is that in experimental work on expert performance or during expert practice programs, task constraints need to be *representative* of a performance environment and contain opportunities for emergent actions that are functionally adaptive, and not prescribed in advance by experimenters or coaches.

References

Adams, J. A. (1971) 'A closed-loop theory of motor learning', *Journal of Motor Behavior*, 3: 111–19.

Araújo, D., Davids, K., Bennett, S., Button, C., & Chapman, G. (2004) 'Emergence of sport skills under constraints', in A.M.W.N. J. Hodges (ed) *Skill acquisition in sport: Research, theory and practice*, London: Routledge, Taylor & Francis, 409–33.

Araújo, D., Davids, K., Cordovil, R., Ribeiro, J., & Fernandes, O. (2009) 'How does knowledge constrain sport performance? An ecological perspective', in D. Araújo, H. Ripoll, & M. Raab (eds) *Perspectives on cognition and action in sport*, New York: Nova Science Publishers, 119–31.

Araújo, D., Davids, K., & Hristovski, R. (2006) 'The ecological dynamics of decision making in sport', *Psychology of Sport and Exercise*, 7(6): 653–76.

Baker, J., & Davids, K. (2006) 'Genetic and environmental constraints on variability in sport performance', in K. Davids, S. Bennett, & K. M. Newell (eds) *Movement system variability*, Champaign, IL: Human Kinetics, 85–108.

Barris, S., Davids, K., & Farrow, D. (2013a) 'Representative learning design in springboard diving: Is dry-land training representative of a pool dive?', *European Journal of Sport Science*, ahead of print: 1–8.

Barris, S., Farrow, D., & Davids, K. (2013b) 'Do the kinematics of a baulked take-off in springboard diving differ from those of a completed dive', *Journal of Sports Sciences*, 31(3): 305–13.

Barris, S., Farrow, D., & Davids, K. (2014) 'Increasing functional variability in the preparatory phase of the takeoff improves elite springboard diving performance', *Research Quarterly for Exercise and Sport*, 85: 97–106.

Bernstein, N. (1967) *The coordination and regulation of movement*, New York: Pergamon.

Bretigny, P., Leroy, D., Button, C., Chollet, D., & Seifert, L. (2011) 'Coordination profiles of the expert field hockey drive according to field roles', *Sports Biomechanics*, 10: 339–50.

Brisson, T. A., & Alain, C. (1996) 'Should common optimal movement patterns be identified as the criterion to be achieved?', *Journal of Motor Behavior*, 28(3): 211–23.

Carvalho, J., Araújo, D., Travassos, B., Esteves, P., Pessanha, L., Pereira, F., & Davids, K. (2013) 'Dynamics of player's relative positioning during baseline rallies', *Journal of Sports Sciences*, 31(14): 1596–605.

Chen, H. H., Liu, Y. T., Mayer-Kress, G., & Newell, K. M. (2005) 'Learning the pedalo locomotion task', *Journal of Motor Behavior*, 37(3): 247–56.

Chow, J. Y. (2013) 'Nonlinear learning underpinning pedagogy: Evidence, challenges, and implications', *Quest*, 65(4): 469–84.

Chow, J. Y., Davids, K., Button, C., & Koh, M. (2008) 'Coordination changes in a discrete multi-articular action as a function of practice', *Acta Psychologica*, 127(1): 163–76.

Chow, J. Y., Davids, K., Hristovski, R., Araújo, D., & Passos, P. (2011) 'Nonlinear pedagogy: Learning design for self-organizing neurobiological systems', *New Ideas in Psychology*, 29(2), 189–200.

Cordovil, R., Araújo, D., Davids, K., Gouveia, L., Barreiros, J., Fernandes, O., & Serpa, S. (2009) 'The influence of instructions and body-scaling as constraints on decision-making processes in team sports', *European Journal of Sport Science*, 9(3): 169–79.

Davids, K., & Araújo, D. (2010) 'The concept of "organismic asymmetry" in sport science', *Journal of Science and Medicine in Sport*, 13(6): 633–40.

Davids, K., Araújo, D., Hristovski, R., Passos, P., & Chow, J. Y. (2012) 'Ecological dynamics and motor learning design in sport', in N. J. Hodge & A. M. Williams (eds) *Skill acquisition in sport: Research, theory and practice*, 2nd ed., London: Routledge, 112–30.

Davids, K., Araújo, D., Vilar, L., Renshaw, I., & Pinder, R. (2013) 'An ecological dynamics approach to skill acquisition: Implications for development of talent in sport', *Talent Development and Excellence*, 5: 21–34.

Davids, K., Bennett, S., & Newell, K. (eds) (2006) *Movement system variability*, Champaign, IL: Human Kinetics.

Davids, K., Button, C., & Bennett, S. (2008) *Dynamics of skill acquisition: A constraints-led approach*, Champaign, IL: Human Kinetics.

Davids, K., & Glazier, P. (2010) 'Deconstructing neurobiological coordination: The role of the biomechanics-motor control nexus', *Exercise and Sport Sciences Reviews*, 38(2): 86–90.

Davids, K., Glazier, P., Araújo, D., & Bartlett, R. (2003) 'Movement systems as dynamical systems: The functional role of variability and its implications for sports medicine', *Sports Medicine*, 33(4): 245–60.

Davids, K., Hristovski, R., Araújo, D., Balague-Serre, N., Button, C., & Passos, P. (eds) (2014) *Complex systems in sport*, London: Routledge.

Edelman, G. M., & Gally, J. A. (2001) 'Degeneracy and complexity in biological systems', *Proceedings of the National Academy of Sciences*, 98: 13763–8.

Ericsson, K. A., Krampe, R. T., & Tesch-Römer, C. (1993) 'The role of deliberate practice in the acquisition of expert performance', *Psychological Review*, 100: 363–406.

Fajen, B. R., Riley, M. A., & Turvey, M. T. (2008) 'Information, affordances, and the control of action in sport', *International Journal of Sport Psychology*, 40: 79–107.

Gentile, A. M. (1972) 'A working model of skill acquisition with application to teaching', *Quest*, 17: 3–23.

Gibson, J. J. (1966) *The senses considered as perceptual systems*, Boston: Houghton Mifflin.

Gibson, J. J. (1979) *The ecological approach to visual perception*, Boston: Houghton Mifflin.

Greenwood, D., Davids, K., & Renshaw, I. (2013) 'Experiential knowledge of expert coaches can help identify informational constraints on performance of dynamic interceptive actions', *Journal of Sports Sciences*. doi: 10.1080/02640414.2013.824599

Handford, C., Davids, K., Bennett, S., & Button, C. (1997) 'Skill acquisition in sport: Some applications of an evolving practice ecology', *Journal of Sports Sciences*, 15(6): 621–40.

Headrick, J., Davids, K., Renshaw, I., Araújo, D., Passos, P., & Fernandes, O. (2012) 'Proximity-to-goal as a constraint on patterns of behaviour in attacker–defender dyads in team games', *Journal of Sports Sciences*, 30(3): 247–53.

Hristovski, R., Davids, K., & Araújo, D. (2006) 'Affordance-controlled bifurcations of action patterns in martial arts', *Nonlinear Dynamics, Psychology, and Life Sciences*, 10(4): 409–44.

Jacobs, D. M., & Michaels, C. F. (2007) 'Direct learning', *Ecological Psychology*, 19(4): 321–49.

Kelso, J.A.S. (2012) 'Multistability and metastability: Understanding dynamic coordination in the brain', *Philosophical Transactions of the Royal Society of London. Series B, Biological Sciences*, 376: 906–18.

Komar, J., Chow, J. Y., Chollet, D., & Seifert, L. (2014) 'Effect of analogy instructions with an internal focus on learning a complex motor skill', *Journal of Applied Sport Psychology*, 26(1): 17–32.

Mason, P. H. (2010) 'Degeneracy at multiple levels of complexity', *Biological Theory*, 5(3): 277–88.

Montagne, G. (2005) 'Prospective control in sport', *International Journal of Sport Psychology*, 36(2): 127–50.

Newell, K. M. (1986) 'Constraints of the development of coordination', in M. G. Wade & H.T.A. Whiting (eds) *Motor development in children: Aspects of coordination and control*, Dordrecht, NL: Martinus Nijhoff Publishers, 341–60.

Newell, K. M. (1996) 'Change in movement and skill: Learning, retention, and transfer', in M. L. Latash & M. T. Turvey (eds) *Dexterity and its development*, Mahwah, NJ: Psychology Press, 393–429.

Nourrit, D., Delignières, D., Caillou, N., Deschamps, T., & Lauriot, B. (2003) 'On discontinuities in motor learning: A longitudinal study of complex skill acquisition on a ski-simulator', *Journal of Motor Behavior*, 35(2): 151–70.

Orth, D., Davids, K., Araújo, D., Passos, P. & Renshaw, I. (2014). Effects of a defender on run-up velocity and ball speed when crossing a football. *European Journal of Sports Sciences* 14(sup1):S316–S323. DOI:10.1080/17461391.2012.696712

Phillips, E., Davids, K., Renshaw, I., & Portus, M. (2010) 'Expert performance in sport and the dynamics of talent development', *Sports Medicine*, 40(4): 271–83.

Phillips, K. C., Sassaman, J. M., & Smoliga, J. M. (2012) 'Optimizing rock climbing performance through sport-specific strength and conditioning', *Strength and Conditioning Journal*, 34: 1–18.

Pinder, R. A., Davids, K., & Renshaw, I. (2012) 'Metastability and emergent performance of dynamic interceptive actions', *Journal of Science and Medicine in Sport*, 15(5): 437–43.

Pinder, R. A., Davids, K., Renshaw, I., & Araújo, D. (2011a) 'Manipulating informational constraints shapes movement reorganization in interceptive actions', *Attention, Perception, & Psychophysics*, 73(4): 1242–54.

Pinder, R. A., Davids, K., Renshaw, I., & Araújo, D. (2011b) 'Representative learning design and functionality of research and practice in sport', *Journal of Sport & Exercise Psychology*, 33(1): 146–55.

Rein, R., Davids, K., & Button, C. (2010) 'Adaptive and phase transition behavior in performance of discrete multi-articular actions by degenerate neurobiological systems', *Experimental Brain Research*, 201(2): 307–22.

Schöllhorn, W. I., Beckmann, H., Michelbrink, M., Sechelmann, M., Trockel, M., & Davids, K. (2006) 'Does noise provide a basis for the unification of motor learning theories?', *International Journal of Sport Psychology*, 37: 186–206.

Seifert, L., Button, C., & Davids, K. (2013a) 'Key properties of expert movement systems in sport: An ecological dynamics perspective', *Sports Medicine*, 43(3): 167–78.

Seifert, L., Leblanc, H., Hérault, R., Komar, J., Button, C., & Chollet, D. (2011) 'Inter-individual variability in the upper – Lower limb breaststroke coordination', *Human Movement Science*, 30(3): 550–65.

Seifert, L., Orth, D., Hérault, R., & Davids, K. (2013b) 'Affordances and grasping patterns variability during rock climbing', in T. Davis, P. Passos, M. Dicks, & J. Weast-Knapp (eds) *Studies in perception and action XII: Seventeenth international conference on perception and action*, London: Psychology Press, Taylor & Francis, 114–18.

Seifert, L., Wattebled, L., Herault, R., Poizat, G., Adé, D., Gal-Petitfaux, N., & Davids, K. (2014) 'Neurobiological degeneracy and affordances detection support functional intra-individual variability of inter-limb coordination in complex discrete task', *PLOS One*, 9(2): e89865. doi:10.1371/journal.pone.0089865

Simonton, D. K. (2007) 'Talent and expertise: The empirical evidence for genetic endowment', *High Ability Studies*, 18(1): 83–5.

Turvey, M. T., & Shaw, R. E. (1995) 'Toward an ecological physics and a physical psychology', in R. L. Solso & D. W. Massaro (eds) *The science of the mind: 2001 and beyond*, New York: Oxford University Press, 144–69.

Turvey, M. T., & Shaw, R. E. (1999) 'Ecological foundations of cognition. I: Symmetry and specificity of animal–environment systems', *Journal of Consciousness Studies*, 6(11–12): 95–110.

Van Geert, P. (1994) *Dynamic systems of development: Change between complexity and chaos*, England: Harvester Wheatsheaf.

Warren, W. H. (1984) 'Perceiving affordances: Visual guidance of stair climbing', *Journal of Exerimental Psychology: Human Perception and Performance*, 10(5): 683–703.

Warren, W. H. (2006) 'The dynamics of perception and action', *Psychological Review*, 113(2): 358–89.

Whiting, H.T.A. (1991) 'Action is not reaction! A reply to Mcleod and Jenkins', *International Journal Sport Psychology*, 22: 296–303.

Withagen, R., & Chemero, A. (2012) 'Affordances and classification', *Philosophical Psychology*, 25: 521–37.

Withagen, R., de Poel, H. J., Araújo, D., & Pepping, G. J. (2012) 'Affordances can invite behavior: Reconsidering the relationship between affordances and agency', *New Ideas in Psychology*, 30: 250–8.

Wu, Y. H., Latash, M. L. (2014) 'The effects of practice on coordination', *Exercise and Sport Sciences Reviews*, 42: 37–42.

13

DEFINING EXPERTISE

A taxonomy for researchers in skill acquisition and expertise

Joseph Baker, Nick Wattie, and Jörg Schorer

Communication is impeded by the facts that not all who use [the] language speak it fluently and that those fluent in it do not all speak the same dialect.

(Simpson, 1964)

Lack of clarity regarding definitions used in research has obvious implications for scientists working in the area. The quote above highlights the frustration of scientists over the lack of a comprehensive system for the classification of groups in the evolutionary sciences. A similar issue resonates in the domains of skill acquisition and expertise development. Over the past four decades, our understanding of how skilled performers acquire their exceptional skill has grown considerably (see Ericsson *et al.*, 2007, for a review); despite this increasing knowledge, researchers examining the acquisition and maintenance of expertise often face a problem that, if not handled properly, can undermine the overall impact of their results and the quality of their contribution to the knowledge base. The problem concerns how to classify skill levels into categories to facilitate description and analysis. The purpose of this chapter is to summarize general approaches used in the past, and to propose a taxonomy of sport skill classification that could aid researchers in this area.

Identifying expertise

On the one hand, sport performers at the high and low ends of the skill continuum are easy to identify by virtue of their accomplishments (e.g., Olympic or world championship medals), in the case of experts, or their complete lack of capability or knowledge in the case of naïvetés. On the other hand, there seems to be significant inconsistency regarding how performers are categorized. Several researchers (Charness & Schultetus, 1999; Starkes *et al.*, 2004) have noted the difficulty defining precisely what constitutes expert performance.

Generally, researchers have taken two approaches to this issue. In the first, distribution-based criteria (i.e., individual differences) are used where experts are identified based on where they fall relative to everyone else in their population (Ericsson & Charness, 1994). In these cases, experts might be identified as performers in the top 10 per cent of the population or with scores that are two standard deviations above mean performance for the population (i.e., falling in the top five per cent, such as the approach used in Baker *et al.*, 2005a). A key component of this approach is that experts are distinguishable from others in their population by virtue of their exceptionality (Ericsson, 1996; Ericsson & Smith, 1991).

However, this approach can be problematic when trying to clearly identify experts in domains where performance cannot be measured objectively or where scores are based on subjective criteria or social standards such as judging an art contest or scoring performers in a figure skating competition (Starkes *et al.*, 2004). A second issue is that this approach to expertise is exclusionary. One can only be an expert at something when he or she has distinguished him or herself from others (i.e., he or she is special). From this perspective, over-learned skills such as speech and gait would not constitute expertise since these are tasks that the majority of individuals master during their lifetime, and as a result consistently superior performance is not identifiable.

A second approach to defining expertise is to use a specific standard of performance to classify experts from other categories of skill. Instead of using individual differences between performers as the basis for classification, this approach considers whether individuals can meet a preset criterion level of performance for a given skill. By this definition, skills such as speech, gait, and reading would constitute domains of expertise. Although it has been used less frequently in expertise studies, some (e.g., Helton, 2004; Wagner & Stanovich, 1996) have argued that this approach more fully encompasses all domains of expertise. However, despite the compelling arguments associated with this position, most studies of sport expertise have used comparison-based paradigms such as expert versus novice or expert versus non-expert. The reasons for this are relatively straightforward, at least from a study design perspective. In order to create a design with the greatest likelihood of identifying differences in the outcomes under examination, comparing groups that are furthest apart in terms of skill acquisition would be more beneficial, since the amount of variance between those groups is maximal and most likely to show differences in mean-based inferential statistics.

Another concern with definitions of expertise in many sports is the range of defining characteristics, even in the same sport but across positions. For any sport measured in centimeters, seconds, or kilograms a definition for criteria is obvious. In the 100 m sprint, for example, any time faster than 10 seconds could be reasonably considered as expert performance. However, how does one set up similar objective criteria for scaling performance in sports like figure skating or rhythmic gymnastics, where outcomes are based on movement outcomes and the *quality* of the movement? Perhaps even more problematic are team sports, where performance is the end result of not just individual performance but collective performance of several athletes working to meet common goals (see Chapter 19). Similarly, how can one quantify the differences between playing positions in team sports such as basketball where each position may have different tasks to fulfill? For instance, the emphasis for a playmaker may be to provide a greater number of assists, compared to centers who may be expected to produce more rebounds than playmakers. Moreover, understanding performance in this domain becomes even more complicated as new types of players emerge. Dirk Nowitzki, star of the Dallas Mavericks in the National Basketball League (NBA), was suddenly someone big, who could win the three-point shooting contest. Although the end objective of each team may be the same (i.e., to win the game by scoring more than the opponent), at a given point in time each team is a dynamic interaction of a host of variables that certainly changes throughout and between seasons as new players are developed and integrated into the team environment (see Araújo *et al.*, Chapter 19).

Why do we need a taxonomy?

Regardless of the approach to studying expert performance (outlined above), classifying or categorizing performers for the purpose of comparison has been common practice. As such, the accuracy and appropriateness of our expertise taxonomy is a central issue in the study of

Defining expertise

expert performance, both from a theoretical and methodological perspective. Although the dominant approach to the study of expertise continues to the expert versus novice paradigm, Abernethy, Thomas, and Thomas (1993) criticized the domain's focus on this design and emphasized the need to move beyond "expert-novice" comparisons to explore intermediate stages of expertise development. Unfortunately, not much has changed in 20 years and researchers continue to use largely vague distinctions between skill groups, such as expert versus non-expert (e.g., Baker *et al.*, 2003; Kitsantas & Zimmerman, 2002) or skilled versus unskilled/less skilled (e.g., Williams *et al.*, 2009; Williams *et al.*, 2006).

Movement away from these simple comparisons would be useful for understanding the qualitative and quantitative changes that performers go through in their development from naïveté to expert. This information would also be helpful for testing and refining general models of skill acquisition such as the theory of deliberate practice (Ericsson *et al.*, 1993). Understanding the entire process of skill acquisition requires exploration of the intermediate steps between naïveté and expert (Baker *et al.*, 2012). Ideally, this would be done via longitudinal designs that examine the nuances of an athlete's development in real time; however, given the logistical and administrative difficulties of conducting longitudinal research in this area (e.g., very few people who start the process become experts), a more manageable and feasible approach is to better understand differences between the various phases of development (e.g., between naïveté and novice, or advanced and expert).

In the sections below we propose a general taxonomy that can be used for identifying various skill groups in skill acquisition and expertise research. In order for any taxonomy to work, it is important that rules constraining its use are identified up front. Therefore, in subsequent sections we highlight several issues and concerns relevant to any taxonomy before proposing a system for grouping participants in expertise-related research.

A proposed taxonomy for skill in sport

Below we delineate the various stages in skill acquisition from naïve to eminence. In creating this taxonomy (Figure 13.1), we reviewed broad approaches to grouping and categorization used

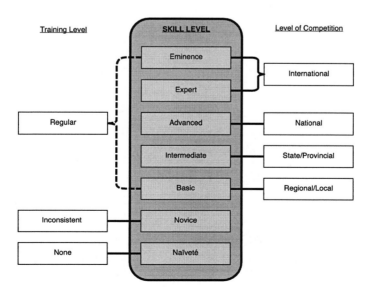

Figure 13.1 Taxonomy categories.

Joseph Baker et al.

by others to generate divisions that encompass the range of performers available to researchers in sport. In many instances these distinctions will be meaningful only in the context of sport where the determining factors of performance are relatively unique. In some cases, groups can be defined by where they fall in the normal distribution of the overall population of athletes participating in a sport (e.g., all tennis players or all gymnasts), whereas in others more general criteria are necessary. For instance, those with a clear absence of training (naïveté) are easy to define. Similarly, those who operate at the highest levels of functioning (expert and eminence) are also readily quantifiable. However, categories between these two extremes are based on more general factors (e.g., competition and participation levels).

Early stages of skill development

In the taxonomy, training frequency is an important distinguisher of athlete "type." In the next two "early" stages of skill development, training is either non-existent (in the case of the naïveté) or irregular (in the case of the novice).

Naïveté

As proposed by others (Chi, 2006; Hoffman, 1998), the naïveté is one who is completely unfamiliar with the domain of interest. Although traditional paradigms have used expert versus novice comparisons, the use of naïve performers could be very valuable in studies of expertise, particularly those exploring the role of different forms and quantities of training in skill acquisition. Arguably, the expert versus naïveté is a superior design for comparing performers at the two ends of the skill continuum compared to the more traditionally used expert versus novice paradigm.

Novice

A novice is someone newly initiated with limited knowledge of the domain. Although this level of skill is one of the most common in expertise research due to the seemingly ubiquitous expert-novice paradigm, the term "novice," at least as used in many previous investigations, has been vague and includes participants ranging from club players (e.g., McPherson, 1994) to totally inexperienced (e.g., Schorer *et al.*, 2007). In this taxonomy, we suggest that the term novice be reserved for participants with irregular involvement in a domain and a minimal amount of accumulated experience.

Transitional stages of skill development

Once training has become a regular occurrence in the life of the developing athlete, he or she moves into transitional stages of skill development. The total number of hours will vary depending on a range of factors (discussed above), but the regularity of training is a key element distinguishing athletes in these more advanced levels of skill from those at early stages.

Basic

After progressing past the novice level, when individuals have a level of skill that allows them to complete the fundamental requirements of their sport (i.e., they understand the rules of the game and are able to perform the specific motor-performance requirements of the sport), we suggest this encapsulates a "basic" level of skill. This would reflect those playing at local or regional levels of competition.

Defining expertise

Intermediate and advanced

Distinguishing performers in transitional stages of development is difficult. Ultimately, researchers are left to use available objective criteria to organize participants into categories that meaningfully represent the distinct characteristics of their current capabilities. Organized levels of competition typically have "built-in" constraints that determine the appropriate level of competition an athlete has access to; those who have the skill to play at a national or international level are not normally limited from competing at this level (provided they have the necessary resources to allow participation), whereas those who do not have this level of skill are prohibited from competing. Due to this inherent "meritocracy," we have used the terms "intermediate" to reflect athletes currently playing at state or provincial levels of competition but no higher and "advanced" to reflect those whose play is currently limited to national levels of competition (and/or high levels of intercollegiate competition such as the NCAA).

Peak levels of skill development

Expert

As noted earlier, defining expert performance can be difficult. Where it can be objectively measured, and when normally distributed within a population, expert performance is defined as performance two standard deviations from the mean performance for the population (i.e., within the top five per cent of performance). When it cannot be objectively measured, defining criteria become more vague and can include expert evaluation (e.g., the case for judging in aesthetic sports like figure skating and diving) or social recognition (e.g., receiving awards). General rules such as the 10-year rule and/or the 10,000-hour rule are usually not appropriate for establishing expertise due to the relatively weak relationship between simple experience and attainment (see Ericsson *et al.*, 1993 and Hambrick *et al.*, 2014).

Eminence

Some (Starkes *et al.*, 2004) have proposed a stage of development that distinguishes between levels of expertise. While experts would include all who meet the criteria noted above, there is some evidence that another division is necessary. For instance, in professional sports very few participants (between one per cent and four per cent of experts; see Table 13.1) would be expected to gain entrance into the hall of fame. This accomplishment would require a distinction beyond "expert," which we have called "eminence" (i.e., recognized superiority). Others have proposed

Table 13.1 Proportion of professional athletes who make the hall of fame.

Sport	Total N[a]	Hall of Fame N (%)[b]
Ice Hockey	6,562	246 (4%)
Baseball	17,498	203 (1%)
Football	23,969	260 (1%)
Basketball	3,969	90 (2%)
Total	51,998	799 (2%)

Note: Data from official archives for each professional sport (nhl.com, mlb.com, nfl.com, nba.com). [a] = total number of athletes who played in the respective sports up to the 2010 season; [b] = total number of athletes who were inducted into the respective halls of fame up to the 2010 season.

Joseph Baker et al.

similar terms; for instance, Starkes *et al.* proposed "transcendent expertise" and Chi (2006) proposed "master." However, we feel "eminence" is a more direct and appropriate term for this stage of development (see also Murray, 2003).

Issues with any taxonomy of skill

Athlete development as a stage-based process

Dividing athlete development into stages may not accurately reflect what is likely to be a continuous process of adaptation to training constraints in incredibly dynamic environments. However, while it is best to consider, at least conceptually or theoretically, athlete development as an ongoing and continuous process, doing so limits analyses and research designs to correlational approaches. Certainly when the research question and data are appropriate for this type of analysis then this approach is warranted; however, experimental designs that consider differences between skill groups (e.g., expert versus novice, non-experts, etc.) are widely used in expertise research. Therefore, group-based analysis will be necessary in many circumstances, necessitating the creation of a strong taxonomy of skill categories. A stage-based approach acknowledges the fact that some athletes proceed through the different stages/levels of sport in a non-continuous way. Indeed, while some systems have strictures in place, others allow exceptional athletes to skip stages (e.g., forego an intermediate step to move directly to a more advanced level of skill) if they have sufficient capability. Further, progression of some athletes through the sport development system may involve forward movement generally, as well as periods of regression to lower levels of skill/competition (see also Gulbin *et al.*, 2013). For example, a baseball player's tenure at the top professional level (Major League Baseball) may be interrupted during his career by a temporary return to a lower skill category (e.g., AAA baseball) in order to refine/improve the skills needed for the top skill category.

Age as a confounder of skill acquisition in sport

If we view athlete development generally as a continuous process of adaptation, then there will be a strong relationship between athlete age and skill development, particularly given the relationship between age and training hours (see Baker & Young, 2014). Furthermore, many sport systems have strictures in place that effectively limit the level athletes (particularly developing athletes) are allowed to participate in. For example, athletes must spend at least *one year* "out of high school" before being eligible to play in the National Basketball Association (NBA). When possible, participants in any investigation should be similar in age or age may confound the analyses. Individuals in one category of the taxonomy can, with sufficient time and training, move into upper levels of skill. However, this does not undermine the value of these comparisons, particularly given the arduous journey to the highest levels of performance.

Limitations of using training hours to define skill levels

Researchers seeking to organize performers of different levels of proficiency should avoid the sole use of quantitative metrics such as hours of training, or a single aggregate of hours of training for a group, since the number of hours required for a given level of skill (e.g., to become an expert) can vary significantly. Evidence suggests that experts are far from homogeneous with respect to the role of accumulated hours of training in the development of expertise. For example, research on expert Ironman triathletes observed that the accumulated hours of training ranged from approximately 8,000 to 20,000 hours (Baker *et al.*, 2005a). Furthermore, Hambrick and colleagues (Hambrick

Defining expertise

et al., 2014) observed that the average percentage of variance in chess performance that was explained by deliberate practice was approximately 34 per cent. Lastly, there is evidence that the accumulated hours of training needed to reach an expert level can change over time. For example, a German reality TV show recently challenged contestants to compete in the "wok-skeleton," which required them to race down a bobsleigh track while sitting in a wok. One of the last world champions is Georg Hackl, who used to be the world champion and Olympic gold medalist in skeleton. However, the number of people who have competed in this sport is very limited (N < 200), which represents an extreme in terms of both depth of competition and sport "maturity" when compared with global sports like soccer or volleyball. Clearly, fields that are newer and less developed would require fewer hours of training than fields that are more established (Baker & Horton, 2004). Moreover, as a field develops and evolves, the skills required for proficiency become more and more refined, and the role of direct influences increases (compare also recent work in developing expertise in the sport of skeleton; Bullock et al., 2009).

Importantly, there is evidence indicating that the "evolution" of performance in most sports is dynamic and unpredictable, which makes it difficult to predict the relationship between training and future performance. Figure 13.2 illustrates the change in Olympic record performance for

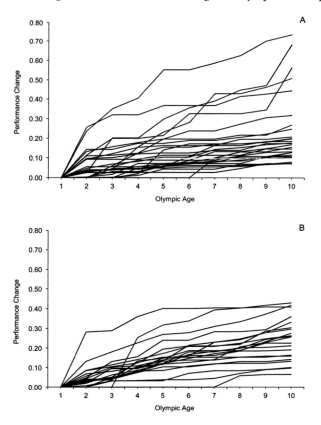

Figure 13.2 Performance change over time in Olympic athletic (A) and aquatic (B) events with at least 10 consecutive occurrences. To compare across the different sports, data were normalized using a score of zero to represent world record performance at the first occurrence of the event in the Olympics. Subsequent performance was then considered relative to that first occurrence. In the event that one particular Olympics had more than one record performance, only the winning performance was considered. Note: flat sections in the trend line indicate Olympic games without record-breaking performances.

athletic and aquatic events (i.e., sports with objective measures of performance) performed in at least 10 Olympic games (i.e., at least a 40-year span of data), and highlights the significant degree of variability in improvement across different sports over time. While the average increase over time was 24 per cent (SD = 16 per cent), improvements ranged from seven per cent in the men's 4x100 m relay event to 74 per cent in the men's discus event. It is important to note that for ease of discussion, the Olympic sports in Figure 13.2 were compared from a common origin and rates of progression were tracked from this point forward. However, performance of these Olympic events did not begin at the same point in time. For instance, the 10-Olympic-year examination of the men's marathon event began with the marathon's first occurrence in 1896, whereas the examination for the men's 100 m breaststroke began with the first occurrence in 1968. At a given point in time, (e.g., 1980) these sports will have evolved to different points on their respective developmental profiles (84 years and 12 years of advancement respectively), which may compound relationships between quantity of training and skill/performance.

Eliminating the use of "non-expert"

Although the expert versus novice paradigm has dominated much of the laboratory-based expertise research, the expert versus non-expert comparison is also common in studies comparing the training histories and environmental characteristics of top performers to those who did not make the same level of achievement. The use of non-expert groups, however, has not been operationalized in a strong way. For instance, Baker *et al.* (2003) described their non-expert group as athletes who had at least 10 years of experience but limited success (i.e., competition below national level), whereas Cleary and Zimmerman (2001) distinguished experts and non-experts based on their proficiency in a basketball free-throw task (non-experts had less than 55 per cent accuracy). On the surface, it seems that the "non-expert" descriptor would be useful for understanding differences between experts and those at lower levels of skill; however, the term "non-expert" may be too vague to be useful in scientific studies. Replacing it with the most appropriate descriptor from the categories above would provide comparisons that are more meaningful and informative.

Future work and continuing evolution of the taxonomy

As noted above, there are limitations to any taxonomy of skill. We clearly acknowledge that these categories will not encapsulate all performers (e.g., the recreational player with atypical skills for someone new to a sport), but will broadly include the majority of those at each skill level. One of the challenges inherent to any category-based comparison methodology is the possibility that considerable heterogeneity exists within a category. As with any aggregate data there is the possibility of erroneously inferring that group-level relationships exist at an individual level (Everitt, 2004). As such, to decrease the risk of making ecologically inaccurate conclusions it may be necessary to someday increase the specificity within our expertise taxonomy categories. Like Darwin's finches, which possessed remarkably different characteristics but were nonetheless all finches, expert athletes may too possess remarkably different characteristics (a similar argument was made by Schorer & Elferink-Gemser, 2013 for playing positions in sports). Individual expert performers can emerge from notably different progressions, essentially creating different "types" of experts.

There is evidence that considerable variability exists between athletes in terms of the accumulated experience required to reach an expert level of performance (see Baker *et al.*, 2005a) and that deliberate practice alone cannot account for all (or even most) of the variance in determining expertise (Baker *et al.*, 2005b; Hambrick *et al.*, in press). Therefore, as a better understanding of the different processes of expertise development is gained, a more specific taxonomy may someday emerge from our proposed general taxonomy. Hypothetically, there may be distinct clusters, or types, of experts within our proposed expert category. For example, if the distribution of accumulated practice hours could be obtained for an entire population of *expert athletes*, it would be possible to plot accumulated practice as a z-score distribution on the x-axis and taxonomy category along the y-axis (see Figure 13.3). This sort of methodology could help to identify different, and perhaps more homogenous, subgroups within our taxonomy categories. For illustrative purposes we have identified three possible subgroups within Figure 13.3: rapid experts (those who attain expertise more rapidly than normal), typical experts (those who attain expertise at the normal rate), and slow experts (those who attain expertise more slowly than normal). However, as of this writing there is not enough information on the different subgroups of expert athletes to accurately anchor such a scale on a "mean" (z-score = 0) and assign z-scores to accumulated practice values (although an argument could be made for 10,000 hours). However, with enough data, it may someday be possible to assign z-score ranges that actually help to demarcate different subgroups of experts (or subgroups of other skill level taxonomy groups for that matter). We only use this example – and accumulated practice hours – to provide an indication of what is not currently captured in our taxonomy, and to provide a hypothetical level of depth that could evolve over time. Indeed, our example could even evolve to include additional axes for factors such as age or genetic characteristics.

It is also important to note that this taxonomy is designed to provide a general system for categorizing skill across sport. More specific examinations of individual sports may be best served by the development of more sophisticated (and less generalizable) profiles of performance metrics across development. A comprehensive understanding of each sport's unique pattern of skill development (i.e., "proficiency scaling," Hoffman *et al.*, 2013) would be invaluable for those working with athletes, as it could be used to identify those who are meeting performance indicators more rapidly or slowly than normal. This knowledge has clear implications for improving talent

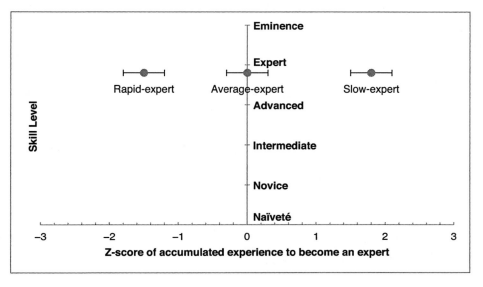

Figure 13.3 A hypothetical, expanded taxonomy of expertise using accumulated experience (represented as a z-score, with the group mean = 0) to represent the potentiality of subcategories (rapid expert, typical expert, and slow expert) within the proposed general taxonomy categories.

identification and athlete development; however, the task will not be simple. Consider, for example, the development of a performance profile for the acquisition of a single skill in basketball – the free throw. This would require an understanding of how performance of this skill changes over the skill acquisition timespan, incorporating factors such as changes in growth and maturation (e.g., how do the physics of executing the free throw change as the performer increases in height, weight, etc.?) and/or differences in the performance environment over time (e.g., how does increased performance pressure affect execution of the task?). Understanding these nuances must then be replicated for each skill in the performance domain. In some domains, where the skills necessary for performance are low in number (e.g., closed tasks such as darts or target shooting), this task will be infinitely less arduous than other domains (e.g., basketball, soccer), where the skills required are many and continually evolving.

Concluding remarks

We readily admit that the system we have proposed has limitations; however, continued attention and discussion of these issues are necessary to ensure that emerging evidence can be optimally integrated into the knowledge base regarding acquisition of sport skill. This taxonomy represents a starting point for designing superior studies and comparison groups in studies of sport expertise.

References

Abernethy, B., Thomas, K. T., & Thomas, J. R. (1993) 'Strategies of improving understanding of motor expertise', in J. L. Starkes & F. Allard (eds) *Cognitive issues in motor expertise*, Amsterdam: Elsevier, 317–56.

Baker, J., Begats, S., Busch, D., Strauss, B., & Schorer, J. (2012) 'Training differences and selection in a talent identification system', *Talent Development and Excellence*, 4: 23–32.

Baker, J., Côté, J., & Abernethy, B. (2003) 'Sport specific training, deliberate practice and the development of expertise in team ball sports', *Journal of Applied Sport Psychology*, 15: 12–25.

Baker, J., Deakin, J., & Côté, J. (2005a) 'Expertise in ultra-endurance triathletes: Early sport involvement, training structure, and the theory of deliberate practice', *Journal of Applied Sport Psychology*, 17: 64–78.

Baker, J., Deakin, J., & Côté, J. (2005b) 'On the utility of deliberate practice: Predicting performance in ultra-endurance triathletes from training indices', *International Journal of Sport Psychology*, 36: 225–40.

Baker, J., & Horton, S. (2004) 'A review of primary and secondary influences on sport expertise', *High Ability Studies*, 15: 211–28.

Baker, J., & Young, B. Y. (2014) '20 years later: Deliberate practice and the development of expertise in sport', *International Review of Sport and Exercise Psychology*, 7: 135–57.

Bullock, N., Gulbin, J. P., Martin, J. T., Ross, A., Holland, T., & Marino, F. (2009) 'Talent identification and deliberate programming in skeleton: Ice novice to winter Olympian in 14 months', *Journal of Sports Sciences*, 27: 397–404.

Charness, N., & Schultetus, R. S. (1999) 'Knowledge and expertise', in F. T. Durso, R. S. Nickerson, R. W. Schvaneveldt, S. T. Dumais, D. S. Lindsay, & M.T.H. Chi (eds) *Handbook of applied cognition*, Chichester: John Wiley & Sons, 57–81.

Chi, M.T.H. (2006) 'Two approaches to the study of experts' characteristics', in K. A. Ericsson, N. Charness, P. Feltovich, & R. Hoffman (eds) *Cambridge handbook of expertise and expert performance*, Cambridge, UK: Cambridge University Press, 121–30.

Cleary, T. J., & Zimmerman, B. J. (2001) 'Self-regulation differences during athletic practice by experts, non-experts and novices', *Journal of Applied Sport Psychology*, 13: 185–206.

Ericsson, K. A. (1996) *The road to excellence: The acquisition of expert performance in the arts and sciences, sports and games*, Mahwah, NJ: Erlbaum.

Ericsson, K. A., & Charness, N. (1994) 'Expert performance: Its structure and acquisition', *American Psychologist*, 49: 725–47.

Ericsson, K. A., Krampe, R. T., & Tesch-Römer, C. (1993) 'The role of deliberate practice in the acquisition of expert performance', *Psychological Review*, 100: 363–406.

Defining expertise

Ericsson, K. A., Roring, R. W., & Nandagopal, K. (2007) 'Giftedness and evidence for reproducibly superior performance: An account based on the expert performance framework', *High Ability Studies*, 18: 3–56.

Ericsson, K. A., & Smith, J. (1991) 'Prospects and limits in the empirical study of expertise: An introduction', in K. A. Ericsson & J. Smith (eds) *Toward a general theory of expertise: Prospects and limits*, Cambridge, UK: Cambridge University Press, 1–38.

Everitt, B. S. (2004) *The Cambridge dictionary of statistics*, London: Cambridge University Press.

Gulbin, J. P., Croser, M. J., Morley, E. J., & Weissensteiner, J. R. (2013) 'An integrated framework for the optimisation of sport and athlete development: A practitioner approach', *Journal of Sports Sciences*, 31: 1319–31.

Hambrick, D. Z., Oswald, F. L., Altmann, E. M., Meinz, E. J., Gobet, R., & Campitelli, G. (2014) 'Deliberate practice: Is that all it takes to become an expert?', *Intelligence*. 45: 34–45.

Helton, W. S. (2004) 'Expertise development: Animal models?', *Journal of General Psychology*, 131: 86–96.

Hoffman, R. R. (1998) 'How can expertise be defined? Implications of research from cognitive psychology', in R. Williams, W. Faulkner, & J. Fleck (eds) *Exploring expertise*, Edinburgh: University of Edinburgh Press, 81–100.

Hoffman, R. R., Ward, P., Feltovich, P. J., DiBello, L., Fiore, S. M., & Andrews, D. H. (2013) *Accelerated expertise: Training for high proficiency in a complex world*, New York: Psychology Press.

Kitsantas, A., & Zimmerman, B. J. (2002) 'Comparing self-regulatory processes among novice, non-expert, and expert volleyball players: A microanalytic study', *Journal of Applied Sport Psychology*, 14: 91–105.

McPherson, S. L. (1994) 'The development of sport expertise: Mapping the tactical domain', *Quest*, 46: 223–40.

Murray, C. (2003) *Human accomplishment: The pursuit of excellence in the arts and sciences, 800BC to 1950*, New York: Harper Collins.

Schorer, J., Baker, J., Fath, F., & Jaitner, T. (2007) 'Identification of inter- and intra-individual movement patterns in varying expertise levels', *Journal of Motor Behavior*, 39: 409–21.

Schorer, J & Elferink-Gemser, M.T. (2013). How good are we at predicting athletes' futures? In D. Farrow, J. Baker and C. MacMahon (Eds.). *Developing sports expertise: Researchers and coaches put theory into practice.* New York: Routledge, 30–39.

Simpson, G. (1964) 'The meaning of taxonomic statements', in S. L. Washburn (ed) *Classification and human evolution*, London: Routledge, 1–31.

Starkes, J. L., Cullen, J. D., & MacMahon, C. (2004) 'A model of the acquisition and retention of expert perceptual-motor performance', in A. M. Williams & N. J. Hodges (eds) *Skill acquisition in sport: Research, theory and practice*, London: Routledge, 259–81.

Wagner, R. K., & Stanovich, K. E. (1996) 'Expertise in reading', in A. Ericsson (ed) *The road to excellence: The acquisition of expert performance in the arts and sciences, sports and games*, Mahwah, NJ: Erlbaum, 189–225.

Williams, A. M., Hodges, N. J., North, J. S., Barton, G. (2006) 'Perceiving patterns of play in dynamic sport tasks: Investigating the essential information underlying skilled performance', *Perception*, 35: 317–32.

Williams, A. M., Huys, R., Cañal-Bruland, R., Hagemann, N. (2009) 'The dynamical information underpinning anticipation skill', *Human Movement Science*, 28: 362–70.

14

ISSUES IN THE COLLECTION OF ATHLETE TRAINING HISTORIES

Melissa J. Hopwood

As highlighted in the previous section of this text, expert sport performance is characterized by a variety of skills and abilities; however, a question asked by many athletes, coaches, parents, sports fans, and sport scientists is: how did these athletes become so great? While the process of expertise development will be explored in detail in other areas of this text, it is important to consider and acknowledge methodological issues in the collection of athlete developmental history information.

Since the proportion of the broad population who become international or professional athletes is very small and the task of predicting who will become a sporting great among a sample of young athletes is near impossible, longitudinal studies to examine the development of sport expertise are characteristically not practical. Therefore, in order to understand the processes of, and requirements for, the development of sport expertise, it is typically necessary to recruit highly skilled athletes and ask them to reflect on various factors that may have influenced their involvement and subsequent success in sport.

Retrospective approaches to the study of sport expertise have been adopted by many researchers to explore the influence of factors such as practice volume (Baker *et al.*, 2003a; Helsen *et al.*, 1998; Hodges & Starkes, 1996; Ward *et al.*, 2007), diversity of sport involvement (Baker *et al.*, 2003b; Baker *et al.*, 2005; Berry *et al.*, 2008; Ford & Williams, 2008; Soberlak & Côté, 2003; Ward *et al.*, 2007), familial support (Côté, 1999; Sloane, 1985), and psychological characteristics (Gould *et al.*, 2002; Orlick & Partington, 1988) on the development of sport expertise. The majority of these studies have required athletes to think back often 20 years or more and identify specific behaviors, characteristics, and details of involvement in various sporting activities. Inherent in these retrospective investigations is a degree of error related to how accurately details from the past can be recalled. Therefore, considerable attention must be devoted to examining reliability and validity of data collected in this manner.

This chapter will highlight common methods for the collection of retrospective athlete training and developmental history information, and will discuss a number of analytical considerations when determining reliability and validity of data. A brief summary of our current understanding of reliability and validity of retrospective recall for a range of factors believed to be associated with the development of sport expertise is also provided.

Methodological approaches for collecting athlete training histories

The two most common methods for collecting athlete training and developmental history information include the conduct of qualitative interviews and the administration of quantitative questionnaires. The most appropriate methodological approach will be determined by the nature and purpose of each investigation, so careful consideration must be given to the benefits and limitations of each design prior to the commencement of data collection.

Qualitative interviews

Qualitative retrospective recall approaches have been utilized in a large number of wide-ranging investigations pertaining to the development of sport expertise (Baker *et al.*, 2003a, 2003b; Baker *et al.*, 2005; Berry *et al.*, 2008; Bloom, 1985; Carlson, 1988; Côté, 1999; Durand-Bush & Salmela, 2002; Law *et al.*, 2007; Phillips *et al.*, 2010a; Soberlak & Côté, 2003; Weissensteiner *et al.*, 2009). These studies typically involve a series of one-on-one interviews between a researcher and an athlete, or occasionally athletes' parents and/or a coach. Interviews usually follow a semi-structured interview guide, containing a sequence of open-ended questions relating to various aspects of the athletes' development. Depending upon the participants' responses, the researcher may pose additional probing or follow-up questions to obtain as much information as possible on the topic of interest. When collecting training history information, charts and tables can be used during the interview process to facilitate recall of involvement in various practice activities throughout different stages of development (Côté *et al.*, 2005). Major advantages of adopting a qualitative approach for the study of sport expertise development are that interviews generate large amounts of detailed information, misunderstandings can be identified and overcome, ambiguous responses can be clarified, unexpected information can be followed up and recorded, and context can be provided around results. However, conducting and analyzing qualitative interviews can be particularly labor intensive and time consuming, so sample sizes for qualitative investigations tend to be relatively small.

Quantitative questionnaires

Quantitative questionnaires provide an alternative approach to qualitative interviews to overcome the limitations associated with small sample sizes (for example, statistical power and generalizability of findings). Initially, the use of questionnaires in studies of sport expertise development were confined to simple investigations of hours spent participating in various practice activities (Helsen *et al.*, 1998; Hodges & Starkes, 1996; Starkes *et al.*, 1996), and in fact, the participant samples involved in these studies were still relatively small and homogenous. More recently, several groups have administered in-depth questionnaires to large numbers of athletes, occasionally from a wide variety of sports, in order to obtain a more detailed understanding of the factors associated with sport expertise development (Gibbons *et al.*, 2002; Memmert *et al.*, 2010; Moesch *et al.*, 2011; Oldenziel *et al.*, 2003; Ward *et al.*, 2007). Quantitative questionnaires can be administered in hard-copy, pencil-and-paper format or electronically via Internet-based software packages. Respondents can complete the questionnaire in a supervised setting with the researcher present to provide instructions and assistance, or unsupervised at a time and location of the participant's choosing. While researchers generally do not have as strict control over the quality of responses when utilizing questionnaires compared to interview procedures, ease of administration and efficiency of data analysis allow for the recruitment of much larger, more diverse participant samples, often counterbalancing the limitations of this design.

Both qualitative and quantitative approaches to the collection of athlete training and developmental history information require athletes to think back and remember very specific details of their past, so a degree of forgetting and uncertainty is inevitable. Therefore, the assessment of reliability and validity of data is critical for all investigations involving retrospective recall approaches.

Methods for assessing reliability and validity of athlete training histories

In general, reliability is concerned with the repeatability of information obtained from a test/measurement instrument (Strube, 2000) and validity is concerned with the accuracy of information (Bryant, 2000). In the context of athlete training histories, reliability refers to how consistently athletes can recall details of their past involvement in sport, and validity refers to how accurate athletes' recall is. Various forms of reliability and validity exist, so when examining reliability and validity of athlete training histories, the most relevant forms are test-retest reliability, internal consistency, concurrent validity, and convergent validity.

Test-retest reliability

Test-retest reliability refers to the ability of a measurement instrument to elicit the same results when completed by the same respondent, under the same conditions, on two separate occasions (Strube, 2000). Examination of test-retest reliability is perhaps the most common and most simple approach for assessing consistency of retrospective recall for athlete training history information, particularly when utilizing quantitative questionnaire methodologies (Ford & Williams, 2008; Helsen *et al.*, 1998; Memmert *et al.*, 2010; Moesch *et al.*, 2011; Ward *et al.*, 2007). To determine test-retest reliability, participants complete the test procedures (i.e., the interview or questionnaire) on two separate occasions, ideally, several weeks apart. Responses from each test occasion are then compared and assessed for consistency.

Internal consistency

Another simple method for determining reliability of athlete recall is to assess internal consistency. Internal consistency signifies that items within a single tool that propose to measure the same general construct converge on the same conclusions (Strube, 2000). For investigations involving retrospective recall of athlete training history information, internal consistency can be assessed via the incorporation of redundant items into the measurement tool, such that participants are essentially asked the same question multiple times during the one test occasion, but in slightly different ways. Similarity of responses between redundant items indicates high internal consistency, representing high-quality, trustworthy data. Assessment of response similarity between redundant items is a technique that has been utilized for establishing reliability of recall in a number of studies related to sport expertise development (Baker *et al.*, 2003a, 2003b; Baker *et al.*, 2005; Hodges *et al.*, 2004; Moesch *et al.*, 2011; Oldenziel *et al.*, 2003).

Concurrent validity

Establishing reliability or consistency of athlete recall of training history information is important; however, determining the accuracy or validity of the information is even more critical. The most important type of validity to consider when assessing the trustworthiness of athlete training history information is concurrent validity, demonstrated when data correlate well with a criterion measure (Bryant, 2000). Common methods for examining concurrent validity of athlete training and developmental history information include comparison of retrospectively recalled data with details recorded in training diaries (Baker *et al.*, 2005; Helsen *et al.*, 1998; Hodges & Starkes, 1996; Ward *et al.*, 2007) and consultation of independent records such as news items and published results (Berry *et al.*, 2008; Durand-Bush & Salmela, 2002; Law *et al.*, 2007; Phillips *et al.*, 2010b). Data could also be cross-referenced against results reported in previous investigations of a similar nature involving participants with similar demographics. While assessment of concurrent validity is important, it is often difficult as training diaries and independent records are not usually available for all years and all aspects of athletes' involvement in their sport. Assessment of convergent validity offers an alternative approach to determining the accuracy of athlete recall for training and developmental history information.

Convergent validity

Convergent validity refers to the degree to which multiple measures of the same construct collected via different test procedures demonstrate agreement (Bryant, 2000). In studies of sport expertise, convergent validity is quite easily and most commonly measured through the conduct of semi-structured interviews with parents and/or coaches of participating athletes (Baker *et al.*, 2003a, 2003b; Berry *et al.*, 2008; Durand-Bush & Salmela, 2002; Law *et al.*, 2007; Oldenziel *et al.*, 2003; Soberlak & Côté, 2003). In this case, parents and coaches are asked similar questions to those posed to athletes, and responses are triangulated between sources.

Given the importance of confirming reliability and validity of athlete training and developmental history information for all investigations pertaining to the development of sport expertise involving retrospective recall techniques, it is essential to build appropriate protocols into the study design to allow for assessment of test-retest reliability, internal consistency, concurrent validity, and convergent validity of all data. Once data are collected, attention must then turn to conducting the appropriate statistical tests to accurately scrutinize reliability and validity before any further analyses are undertaken.

Statistical approaches for analyzing reliability and validity of athlete training histories

As evidenced by the number of references cited above for each approach to assessing reliability and validity, the vast majority of studies involving retrospective recall techniques for investigations of the development of sport expertise have incorporated one or more tests of reliability and/or validity to confirm trustworthiness of the data at hand. In most cases, researchers tend to report "acceptable" levels of agreement between sources, indicating reasonable reliability and/or validity. However, upon critical review of the literature, a number of limitations related to the statistical approaches utilized in previous investigations are apparent.

One major concern is that previous assessments of reliability and validity have typically involved Pearson product-moment correlation analyses (Baker *et al.*, 2003a, 2003b; Baker *et al.*, 2005; Berry *et al.*, 2008; Côté *et al.*, 2005; Helsen *et al.*, 1998; Hodges & Starkes, 1996; Ward *et al.*, 2007). This is problematic, as Pearson correlations are a bivariate statistic, intended for assessing the strength of the association between two different variables (Haggard, 1958). Therefore, calculation of the Pearson product-moment correlation coefficient for assessing consistency of recall between multiple measurements of the same variable is inappropriate. A more suitable statistic for assessing the strength of the relationship between multiple measurements of the same variable is the univariate intraclass correlation coefficient (ICC; Haggard, 1958). Surprisingly, very few studies assessing reliability and/or validity of athlete training histories have adopted the ICC over the Pearson correlation coefficient, despite its theoretical superiority (Ford & Williams, 2008; Hopwood, 2013).

Although the ICC may be a more appropriate statistic than the Pearson correlation coefficient, a major limitation remains with the use of correlation analyses for the purpose of assessing reliability and validity. Correlation coefficients provide valuable information regarding the strength of the relationship between two variables; however, they do not address the degree of similarity between the variables (Bland & Altman, 1986; Costa-Santos *et al.*, 2011; Kottner & Dassen, 2008; Müller & Büttner, 1994). This is a critical distinction because it is possible for two sets of data to be highly correlated, but not similar in magnitude (Bland & Altman, 1986). The ICC can, therefore, be a misleading representation of similarity between multiple measures of the same variable, so is still not the ideal statistic to apply when attempting to establish reliability and validity of retrospective recall for athlete training and developmental history information. Furthermore, correlation coefficients are only suitable for application to continuous data (Müller & Büttner, 1994), leading to the requirement for an alternative statistical approach when assessing reliability and validity of categorical variables.

Per cent agreement (PA) statistics offer a suitable solution to the limitations associated with correlation analyses. PAs are most commonly calculated when data are categorical, indicating the proportion of responses that are identical across multiple test occasions (Bahrick *et al.*, 1996; Ropponen *et al.*, 2001). However, PA and the inverse calculations of per cent error, per cent difference, and delta scores can also be applied to continuous variables, as evident within several studies of sport expertise development (Baker *et al.*, 2005; Law *et al.*, 2007; MacDonald *et al.*, 2009; Soberlak & Côté, 2003). Other alternatives recognized as robust measures of agreement between multiple measures of the same variable include kappa statistics (Cohen, 1960), standard errors of measurement and coefficients of variation (Atkinson & Neville, 1998; Hopkins, 2000), as well as limits of agreement and Bland-Altman plots (Bland & Altman, 1999). However, kappa statistics are limited in application to categorical data, whereas standard errors of measurement, coefficients of variation, limits of agreement, and Bland-Altman plots are restricted to continuous data sets. Since PA statistics can be applied to both categorical and continuous variables they could be considered a more favorable method for analyzing reliability and validity of retrospectively recalled athlete training and developmental history information.

While PA statistics are proposed to be the most appropriate indicator of reliability and validity for athlete training histories, the use of a combination of statistical methods for assessing reliability and validity has previously been recommended within the fields of nursing, medicine, and sport science (Atkinson & Neville, 1998; Kottner & Dassen, 2008). Therefore, calculation of both PA and ICCs may provide the most comprehensive assessment of reliability and validity, as this approach allows for consideration of absolute agreement and relative consistency between measurements (Atkinson & Nevill, 1998). Ford and Williams (2008) utilized a combined statistical approach involving PA and ICCs for assessing test-retest reliability of athlete training histories, and more recently, Hopwood and colleagues (Hopwood *et al.*, 2013b) proposed a rigorous methodology for assessing reliability and validity of retrospectively recalled athlete training and developmental history information also involving the calculation of both PA and ICC statistics. Given the issues highlighted with previous statistical approaches for the assessment of reliability and validity of athlete training histories, it is recommended that future studies consider adopting a combined PA and ICC methodology such as the one advocated by Hopwood *et al.* (2013b) to encourage robust, uniform analyses of reliability and validity for retrospectively recalled athlete training and developmental history information, across the sport expertise development domain.

Collecting athlete histories

Criteria for interpreting reliability and validity of athlete training histories

While a robust statistical approach to the assessment of reliability and validity of athlete training histories is critical, even more pertinent are strict criteria for interpreting the results of reliability and validity analyses. Reviewing related literature, the lack of a standard scale for interpreting reliability and validity statistics is both obvious and alarming. This is particularly true for interpretation of the recommended PA and ICC statistics, with highly variable levels of agreement interpreted as indicative of "acceptable" reliability and/or validity.

Take, for example, the following results involving interpretation of ICC statistics. An investigation assessing reliability of a medical diagnostic test considered a correlation coefficient of .65 to represent "good" reliability (Costa-Santos *et al.*, 2011), while values of .90 have been recommended as the cutoff criteria for "high" correlations in tests of physiological capacities (Lemmink *et al.*, 2004). Investigations of reliability of retrospective recall for recreational and occupational physical activity have tended to consider ICC values above .65 as representative of a "high" correlation (Ropponen *et al.*, 2001), whereas values of .35 to .55 have been considered "moderate" (Ainsworth *et al.*, 1999; Reis *et al.*, 2005). Unfortunately, since ICCs have not traditionally been calculated in the assessment of reliability and validity of athlete training histories, there is a distinct lack of guidelines for interpreting the strength of correlation coefficients in this domain.

Similarly, as PA statistics have only been utilized in a small number of sport expertise investigations in the past, there is also a dearth of information to assist in the interpretation of these statistics to evaluate reliability and validity. Baker and colleagues (2005) reported PA values of 70 per cent as "reasonable agreement" and values above 80 per cent as "high agreement" for retrospective recall of hours involved in sport-specific training activities. Likewise, MacDonald and colleagues (2009) considered a 20 per cent difference in values reported during retrospective recall of hours involved in physical activity in a sample of master athletes acceptable, while per cent agreements of 63 per cent and 72 per cent for recall of several categorical variables relating to physical activity were deemed to be "less reliable." Even in searching the literature relating to interpretation of PA statistics in other domains, still no clear criteria for classifying the strength of agreement were evident.

Given the inherent difficulties associated with accurately recalling specific details from the past, there is a realistic possibility that athlete training history data could be unreliable and/or not valid. To ensure legitimacy of conclusions drawn from studies of sport expertise development, researchers must be certain that data are both valid and reliable; however, without a point of reference as to what are acceptable levels of reliability and validity for retrospective recall of athlete training and developmental history information, researchers must make subjective judgments on the quality of the data. To address this limitation in the current literature, Hopwood *et al.* (2013b) also developed a stringent, objective taxonomy for interpreting PA and ICC statistics, particularly in reference to the assessment of reliability and validity of retrospectively recalled athlete training and developmental history information. While the methodology and taxonomy proposed by Hopwood *et al.* (2013b) deserves scrutiny from other researchers in the field, the establishment of a clear approach to assessing and interpreting reliability and validity of athlete training and developmental history information is a significant advancement in the study of sport expertise development that addresses a range of methodological issues in this area of research.

Current understanding of reliability and validity of retrospective recall for athlete training histories

Despite the limitations of previous research discussed, it is appropriate to provide a brief summary of our current understanding of reliability and validity for various aspects of athlete training and developmental histories.

Melissa J. Hopwood

Measures typically assessed for validity and reliability include estimates of weekly practice hours (Baker *et al.*, 2003b; Helsen *et al.*, 1998; Hodges & Starkes, 1996; Moesch *et al.*, 2011; Oldenziel *et al.*, 2003; Ward *et al.*, 2007), yearly practice hours (Baker *et al.*, 2003a, 2003b; Baker *et al.*, 2005; Helsen *et al.*, 1998; Law *et al.*, 2007; Ward *et al.*, 2007), or cumulative practice hours across athletes' careers (Baker *et al.*, 2005; Memmert *et al.*, 2010; Soberlak & Côté, 2003). Occasionally, validity and reliability is assessed for age at first participation in main sport (Memmert *et al.*, 2010; Oldenziel *et al.*, 2003; Ward *et al.*, 2007) or total years of involvement in main sport (Law *et al.*, 2007; Memmert *et al.*, 2010). In studies examining participation in other organized sports and deliberate play, the number of activities reported (Baker *et al.*, 2003b; Berry *et al.*, 2008; Law *et al.*, 2007; Memmert *et al.*, 2010; Oldenziel *et al.*, 2003; Soberlak & Côté, 2003), and hours of involvement in these activities (Memmert *et al.*, 2010; Soberlak & Côté, 2003) are also assessed for validity and/or reliability.

Validity and sometimes reliability of recall for hours of involvement in practice activities is typically quite good, with Pearson correlation coefficients between the primary measure of interest and the relevant comparative measure ranging from .59–.97. Similarly, age at first participation in main sport and total years of involvement in main sport have been reported to demonstrate Pearson correlation coefficients of .79–.99, and, on occasion, even 100 per cent agreement between data sources. Measures relating to involvement in sport-specific practice activities were also generally found to have good to very good test-retest reliability, internal consistency, concurrent validity, and convergent validity with coaches, according to the statistical methodology and taxonomy proposed by Hopwood *et al.* (2013b) during the validation of a new measurement instrument known as at the Developmental History of Athletes Questionnaire (DHAQ; Hopwood, 2013). Therefore, by and large, athlete recall of sport-specific training history information is usually quite acceptable.

Agreement between primary and secondary data sources is also typically strong for number of sporting activities, with per cent agreement values reported between 88–100 per cent (Baker *et al.*, 2003b; Berry *et al.*, 2008; Memmert *et al.*, 2010); although, Oldenziel and colleagues (2003) reported a low Pearson correlation coefficient for number of sporting activities of .26. During validation of the DHAQ introduced above, Hopwood and colleagues (Hopwood, 2013; Hopwood *et al.*, 2013a) reported mixed results for reliability and validity of measures relating to involvement in sports other than athletes' main sport, with test-retest reliability, internal consistency, concurrent validity, and convergent validity with parents ranging from poor to very good for items such as number of sporting activities, hours of involvement in sporting activities other than main sport, ages of participation in these sports, and highest level of competition reached. Combined, these results suggest that further research is required to ascertain exactly which aspects of participation in sporting activities beyond their main sport athletes can recall with confidence.

Reliability and validity of retrospective recall for participation in deliberate play and informal sporting activities has only been assessed in a small number of studies; however, it appears that it may be difficult to accurately and consistently recall involvement in this type of activity, as agreement statistics and correlation coefficients for number of activities and hours of involvement in deliberate play are somewhat lower than those reported for deliberate practice activities. For example, Memmert *et al.* (2010) reported a test-retest reliability Pearson correlation coefficient of .79 for total cumulative hours of involvement in deliberate practice, but the Pearson correlation coefficient for cumulative hours of involvement in deliberate play was only .70. Similarly, Soberlak and Côté (2003) reported a 30 per cent difference between athletes and parents' accounts of time involved in deliberate play compared to just a one per cent difference for time involved in deliberate practice. Interestingly, Hopwood (2013) reported moderate or poor test-retest reliability, concurrent validity, and convergent validity with parents for almost all measures relating to participation in informal sporting play, warranting the removal of all related items from the questionnaire. The relatively poor reliability and validity of recall for details of involvement in deliberate play does not suggest that this activity is not an important contributor to the development of sport expertise, but rather reinforces the critical importance of rigorously assessing athlete recall of training history information, and indicates that further research is required to ensure more accurate collection of this information in the future.

Future directions for research involving the collection of athlete training histories

While it is positive that most studies of sport expertise involving the collection of athlete training histories have incorporated some measure of reliability and/or validity, it is clear that a number of issues in this area of research remain. In addition to limitations related to inappropriate analytical approaches and subjective interpretation of reliability and validity statistics, our understanding of the aspects of athlete training and developmental histories that can be recalled consistently and accurately is untenable.

In the majority of studies to date, establishing reliability and validity of athlete training history information has been secondary to the testing of hypotheses relating to sport expertise development. Within most investigations, reliability and validity assessments have typically only been conducted on a small number of variables, with results assumed to apply to all measures collected. Given the issues highlighted within this chapter, it is recommended that future research should focus more specifically on the assessment of reliability and validity of retrospective recall for athlete training histories. Such efforts a) would lead to a more detailed understanding of which aspects of athlete developmental histories can be unequivocally recalled, b) would inform guidelines for how to most appropriately collect athlete history information to elicit reliable, valid data, and c) could result in the creation of validated, standardized measurement tools for the collection of athlete developmental histories. In addition, it is recommended that the methodology and taxonomy proposed by Hopwood and colleagues (2013b) for assessing reliability and validity of retrospective recall for athlete developmental history information be applied, and perhaps expanded upon, in future research in this field to establish a uniform approach to the measurement and interpretation of reliability and validity analyses.

To ensure the legitimacy of debates and conclusions regarding the development of sport expertise and the factors that may influence or characterize athlete pathways, due consideration must be given to the issues highlighted concerning the collection of athlete training and developmental histories. Given the retrospective nature of research in this area, reliability and validity of recall is a key concern and deserves greater attention than it typically receives. Small improvements in the collection of athlete training histories could ultimately lead to significant advancements in the domain of sport expertise development and our understanding of what it takes to be a champion.

References

Ainsworth, B. E., Richardson, M. T., Jacobs Jr., D. R., Leon, A. S., & Sternfeld, B. (1999) 'Accuracy of recall of occupational physical activity by questionnaire', *Journal of Clinical Epidemiology*, 52: 219–27.

Atkinson, G., & Nevill, A. M. (1998) 'Statistical methods for assessing measurement error (reliability) in variables relevant to sports medicine', *Sports Medicine*, 26: 217–38.

Bahrick, H. P., Hall, L. K., & Berger, S. A. (1996) 'Accuracy and distortion in memory for high school grades', *Psychological Science*, 7: 265–71.

Baker, J., Côté, J., & Abernethy, B. (2003a) 'Learning from the experts: Practice activities of expert decision makers in sport', *Research Quarterly for Exercise and Sport*, 74: 342–7.

Baker, J., Côté, J., & Abernethy, B. (2003b) 'Sport-specific practice and the development of expert decision-making in team ball sports', *Journal of Applied Sport Psychology*, 15: 12–25.

Baker, J., Côté, J., & Deakin, J. (2005) 'Expertise in ultra-endurance triathletes early sport involvement, training structure, and the theory of deliberate practice', *Journal of Applied Sport Psychology*, 17: 64–78.

Berry, J., Abernethy, B., & Côté, J. (2008) 'The contribution of structured activity and deliberate play to the development of expert perceptual and decision-making skill', *Journal of Sport & Exercise Psychology*, 30: 685–708.

Bland, J.M., & Altman, D.G. (1986) 'Statistical methods for assessing agreement between two methods of clinical measurement', *Lancet*, 327: 307–10.

Bland, J.M., & Altman, D.G. (1999) 'Measuring agreement in method comparison studies', *Statistical Methods in Medical Research*, 8: 135–60.

Bloom, B.S. (ed) (1985) *Developing talent in young people*, New York: Ballantine Books.

Bryant, F.B. (2000) 'Assessing the validity of measurement', in L.G. Grimm & P.R. Yarnold (eds) *Reading and understanding more multivariate statistics*, Washington, DC: American Psychological Association, 99–146.

Carlson, R. (1988) 'The socialization of elite tennis players in Sweden: An analysis of the players' backgrounds and development', *Sociology of Sport Journal*, 5: 241–56.

Cohen, J. (1960) 'A coefficient of agreement for nominal scales', *Educational and Psychological Measurement*, 20: 37–46.

Costa-Santos, C., Bernardes, J., Ayres-de-Campos, D., Costa, A., & Costa, C. (2011) 'The limits of agreement and the intraclass correlation coefficient may be inconsistent in the interpretation of agreement', *Journal of Clinical Epidemiology*, 64: 264–9.

Côté, J. (1999) 'The influence of the family in the development of talent in sport', *The Sport Psychologist*, 13: 395–417.

Côté, J., Ericsson, A.K., & Law, M.P. (2005) 'Tracing the development of athletes using retrospective interview methods: A proposed interview and validation procedure for reported information', *Journal of Applied Sport Psychology*, 17: 1–19.

Durand-Bush, N., & Salmela, J.H. (2002) 'The development and maintenance of expert athletic performance: Perceptions of world and Olympic champions', *Journal of Applied Sport Psychology*, 14: 154–71.

Ford, P.R., & Williams, A.M. (2008) 'The effect of participation in Gaelic football on the development of Irish professional soccer players', *Journal of Sport & Exercise Psychology*, 30: 709–22.

Gibbons, T., Hill, R., McConnell, A., Forster, T., & Moore, J. (2002) *The path to excellence: A comprehensive view of development of U.S. Olympians who competed from 1984–1998*, Colorado Springs, CO: United States Olympic Committee.

Gould, D., Dieffenbach, K., & Moffett, A. (2002) 'Psychological characteristics and their development in Olympic champions', *Journal of Applied Sport Psychology*, 14: 172–204.

Haggard, E.A. (1958) *Intraclass correlation and the analysis of variance*, New York: The Dryden Press.

Helsen, W.F., Starkes, J.L., & Hodges, N.J. (1998) 'Team sports and the theory of deliberate practice', *Journal of Sport & Exercise Psychology*, 20: 12–34.

Hodges, N.J., Kerr, T., Starkes, J.L., Weir, P.L., & Nananidou, A. (2004) 'Predicting performance times from deliberate practice hours for triathletes and swimmers: What, when, and where is practice important?', *Journal of Experimental Psychology: Applied*, 10: 219–37.

Hodges, N.J., & Starkes, J.L. (1996) 'Wrestling with the nature of expertise: A sport specific test of Ericsson, Krampe and Tesch-Römer's (1993) theory of "deliberate practice"', *International Journal of Sport Psychology*, 27: 400–24.

Hopkins, W.G. (2000) 'Measures of reliability in sports medicine and science', *Sports Medicine*, 30: 1–15.

Hopwood, M.J. (2013) 'The developmental history of athletes questionnaire: Towards a comprehensive understanding of the development of sport expertise', doctoral dissertation, Melbourne: Victoria University. Online. Retrieved from http://vuir.vu.edu.au/id/eprint/22353 (accessed 3 June, 2014).

Hopwood, M.J., Baker, J., MacMahon, C., & Farrow, D. (2013a) 'How important is diversification for the development of sport expertise?', manuscript submitted for publication.

Hopwood, M.J., MacMahon, C., Farrow, D., & Baker, J. (2013b) 'A proposed methodology and taxonomy for assessing validity and reliability of athlete developmental history information collected via retrospective recall', manuscript submitted for publication.

Kottner, J., & Dassen, T. (2008) 'Interpreting interrater reliability coefficients of the Braden scale: A discussion paper', *International Journal of Nursing Studies*, 45: 1238–46.

Collecting athlete histories

Law, M. P., Côté, J., & Ericsson, K. A. (2007) 'Characteristics of expert development in rhythmic gymnastics: A retrospective study', *International Journal of Sport & Exercise Psychology*, 5: 82–103.

Lemmink, K.A.P.M., Elferink-Gemser, M. T., & Visscher, C. (2004) 'Evaluation of the reliability of two field hockey specific sprint and dribble tests in young field hockey players', *British Journal of Sports Medicine*, 38: 138–42.

MacDonald, D. J., Horton, S., Kraemer, K., Weir, P., Deakin, J. M., & Côté, J. (2009) 'Application and reliability of the retrospective interview procedure to trace physical activity patterns in master athletes and nonactive older adults', *Educational Gerontology*, 35: 1107–22.

Memmert, D., Baker, J., & Bertsch, C. (2010) 'Play and practice in the development of sport-specific creativity in team ball sports', *High Ability Studies*, 21: 3–18.

Moesch, K., Elbe, A. M., Hauge, M.L.T., & Wikman, J. M. (2011) 'Late specialization: The key to success in centimeters, grams, or seconds (cgs) sports', *Scandinavian Journal of Medicine & Science in Sports*, 21: e282–e290.

Müller, R., & Büttner, P. (1994) 'A critical discussion of intraclass correlation coefficients', *Statistics in Medicine*, 13: 2465–76.

Oldenziel, K., Gagné, F., & Gulbin, J. (2003) *How do elite athletes develop? A look through the 'rear-view mirror:' A preliminary report from the national athlete development survey (NADS)*, Canberra, AU: Australian Sports Commission.

Orlick, T., & Partington, J. (1988) 'Mental links to excellence', *The Sport Psychologist*, 2: 105–30.

Phillips, E., Davids, K., Renshaw, I., & Portus, M. (2010a) 'Expert performance in sport and the dynamics of talent development', *Sports Medicine*, 40: 271–83.

Phillips, E., Davids, K., Renshaw, I., & Portus, M. (2010b) 'The development of fast bowling experts in Australian cricket', *Talent Development & Excellence*, 2: 137–48.

Reis, J. P., Dubose, K. D., Ainsworth, B. E., Macera, C. A., & Yore, M. M. (2005) 'Reliability and validity of the occupational physical activity questionnaire', *Medicine and Science in Sports & Exercise*, 37: 2075–83.

Ropponen, A., Levalahti, E., Simonen, R., Videman, T., & Battie, M. C. (2001) 'Repeatability of lifetime exercise reporting', *Scandinavian Journal of Medicine and Science in Sports*, 11: 185–92.

Sloane, K. D. (1985) 'Home influences on talent development', in B. S. Bloom (ed) *Developing talent in young people*, New York: Ballantine Books, 439–76.

Soberlak, P., & Côté, J. (2003) 'The developmental activities of elite ice hockey players', *Journal of Applied Sport Psychology*, 15: 41–9.

Starkes, J.L., Deakin, J. M., Allard, F., Hodges, N. J., & Hayes, A. (1996) 'Deliberate practice in sports: What is it anyway?', in K. A. Ericsson (ed) *The road to excellence: The acquisition of expert performance in the arts and sciences, sports, and games*, Mahwah, NJ: Lawrence Erlbaum Associates, 81–106.

Strube, M. J. (2000) 'Reliability and generalizability theory', in L. G. Grimm & P. R. Yarnold (eds) *Reading and understanding more multivariate statistics*, Washington, DC: American Psychological Association, 23–66.

Ward, P., Hodges, N. J., Starkes, J. L., & Williams, A. M. (2007) 'The road to excellence: Deliberate practice and the development of expertise', *High Ability Studies*, 18: 119–53.

Weissensteiner, J., Abernethy, B., & Farrow, D. (2009) 'Towards the development of a conceptual model of expertise in cricket batting: A grounded theory approach', *Journal of Applied Sport Psychology*, 21: 276–92.

15

ISSUES IN THE MEASUREMENT OF ANTICIPATION

David L. Mann and Geert J. P. Savelsbergh

Measuring anticipation

The ability of expert athletes to better anticipate the outcomes of action sequences is well established (see Chapter 2), though there is substantial controversy about how anticipatory skill should be measured (see also Chapters 5 and 24). In particular, there is conjecture over how well performance in traditional tests of anticipation might accurately capture what skilled athletes do when acting in the natural setting.

Interest in the anticipatory ability of skilled athletes emerged largely as a result of chronometric analyses that found an incongruence between the interceptive skill observed in the natural setting and the supposed physiological limitations to reaction time (e.g., Glencross & Cibich, 1977). It was surmised on the basis of this that skilled performers in ball sports may predict event outcomes and initiate their movements prior to the availability of ball flight information. As a result, studies examining anticipatory skill based on advance information have found (and consistently confirm) that experts are better able to use the movement patterns of their opponents to predict the outcomes of those actions at an earlier point in time (Abernethy & Russell, 1987; Jones & Miles, 1978).

The majority of what is known about expert anticipation is based on studies that have employed the *temporal occlusion* technique. Using this approach, participants make a prediction of the likely outcome of a movement pattern after vision of the pattern is occluded at a critical moment in the movement sequence. For example, participants might be asked to view the movements of a soccer penalty taker (shown from the perspective of a goalkeeper) up to the point of foot-ball contact, after which vision is occluded and the participant is asked to predict the direction in which the ball would have been kicked. Occlusion is most frequently achieved using a video-based display, though more recently occlusion has also been achieved when viewing movement patterns in situ using liquid crystal occlusion goggles. A number of additional experimental paradigms have been employed – typically in combination with temporal occlusion – to further the understanding of the processes underpinning expert anticipation. We now provide a short consideration of the most popular of these experimental techniques.

Measurement of anticipation

Progressive temporal occlusion

Progressive temporal occlusion is used to establish *when* in a movement sequence skilled athletes are able to pick up useful information. Using this technique, a systematic progression of occlusion times is employed, resulting in experimental trials that temporally occlude footage at a range of time points relative to a key event (e.g., relative to foot-ball contact in the soccer penalty kick). Anticipatory skill is tested at each of these time points, with results typically demonstrating that not only are experts better able than novices to predict outcomes, but they are particularly better at doing so based on information presented earlier in the event sequence (e.g., Abernethy & Russell, 1987; Farrow & Abernethy, 2003). The ability to use information apparent at a relatively earlier point in the action sequence may provide skilled performers additional time in which to execute an appropriate response – a potentially distinct advantage in time-stressed tasks.

Spatial occlusion

Spatial occlusion relies on the systematic occlusion of particular body segments or hitting implements to make inferences about the pickup of movement behavior from each of those segments. Early studies were able to achieve spatial occlusion by masking specific features in a video display (e.g., Abernethy, 1990; Abernethy & Russell, 1987). A more recent approach has been to use video editing software to remove rather than mask this information (Müller *et al.*, 2006). These studies typically find that experts are able to make earlier decisions by picking up movements that occur earlier in the opponent's action; for example, from the playing shoulder and upper arm of a tennis server rather than the lower arm and racquet. Due to the nature of the manipulations being performed, the spatial occlusion technique is almost exclusively employed by using video-based displays rather than in situ scenarios (though for an exception see Panchuk & Vickers, 2009).

Visual search

By recording the direction of gaze when performing anticipatory judgments, the analysis of visual search behavior can be used to again make inferences about the specific locations from which information pickup takes place. Studies examining visual search patterns have generally provided support for the results of studies employing spatial occlusion, demonstrating a skilled performer's preference to attend towards bodily movements that occur earlier in the action sequence. For example, skilled tennis players spend more time directing their gaze towards the shoulder rather than the racquet of a server (Goulet *et al.*, 1989; Williams *et al.*, 2002). The registration of gaze can be performed either in lab-based or in in-situ scenarios (using mobile gaze trackers).

Despite the now almost omnipresence of gaze registration, it is important to consider two particular limitations that may restrict the usefulness of this technique. First, recordings of gaze provide an indication of the location of central vision without offering any assessment of the concurrent role of peripheral information pickup. It is entirely possible that effective pickup from other locations can also occur in the peripheral field. Second, just because central vision is directed towards a particular feature, this can in no way ensure that information has been picked up from that location. It is possible for observers to look in an appropriate location yet lack the ability to effectively pickup the meaningfulness of the movements they observe (see Chapters 3 and 16 for more discussion on gaze behavior). The use of gaze-contingent displays that are able to systematically alter the presence of central and/or peripheral vision according to the online

David L. Mann and Geert J. P. Savelsbergh

monitoring of a participant's gaze location provide a promising means of overcoming these limitations (e.g., see Ryu *et al.*, 2013).

Point-light displays

The point-light technique provides a very useful means of examining the specific role of kinematic movement patterns in the expert advantage for anticipatory skill. Point-light displays show a kinematic sequence by displaying only a series of isolated points of light at the location of important informational sources, most commonly at the location of critical joint centers. These displays necessarily remove figural and facial cues, along with contextual information including shape, contour, and color, ensuring that only the essential kinematic information remains. Studies employing point-light displays generally support the notion that expert anticipation is based largely on kinematic information; that is, the expert advantage remains even when viewing these point-light displays (Abernethy *et al.*, 2001; although see Shim *et al.*, 2005). The point-light technique provides a very simple yet advantageous means of establishing how anticipatory skill responds to systematic manipulations of movement patterns as the apparent locations of joint centers can be rather simply altered to change the appearance of the pattern.

Improving representative design when measuring anticipation

The traditional approach taken when measuring anticipatory skill has been for participants to view video-based displays of occluded movement patterns and to register their judgment by making either a verbal or pen-and-paper response. Although this approach has facilitated convenience and tight experimental control, two important and recurring concerns have been expressed that could limit the generalizability of the findings (see Abernethy *et al.*, 1993). First, the video displays used to show the movement patterns may provide a somewhat impoverished representation of the visual information available when observing a real opponent. Second, the nature of the verbal or pen-and-paper responses may fail to faithfully replicate those produced when responding in the natural setting. Collectively, these two potential limitations mean that traditional anticipatory tasks may be limited in their ability to replicate the task they are designed to represent (Brunswick, 1956; Pinder *et al.*, 2011). Abernethy *et al.* (1993) proposed that the progression towards more representative stimuli should further increase the effect size found when examining anticipation across levels of skill. More specifically, they hypothesized that improvements in representation should: (i) enhance the experiential basis of the skilled player's expertise, (ii) decrease potential floor effects in measurement, and (iii) result in responses which are more likely to be produced by the specific, dedicated processors relied on in the performer's natural setting (e.g., see Abernethy & Mann, 2008; van der Kamp *et al.*, 2008).

Display stimuli

Video-based displays provide a very convenient and reliable means of presenting actions that are repeatable and can be occluded at consistent moments in the movement pattern. This approach ensures tight experimental control and rigor, though in doing so has the potential to decrease the quality of the visual information available for the discrimination of movement patterns. For instance, movement patterns shown on video screens can be smaller, lack stereoscopic depth, have a diminished rate of sampling (frame rate), and may possess limited contrast and color. These concerns raise doubt about how well video displays represent the visual information available when observing an opponent in situ.

Measurement of anticipation

As audio-visual technologies have evolved, studies of anticipation have progressed to more closely replicate the stimuli inherent in real world scenarios. Rather than presenting stimuli on small video or computer screens, accessibility to digital video projectors has enabled testing to take place with life-sized, two-dimensional displays (e.g., Savelsbergh *et al.*, 2002). Three-dimensional video simulations allow the inclusion of stereoscopic depth information, though to date this technology has been relatively under utilised (see Ranganathan & Carlton, 2007 for a possible exception). Farrow, Rendell, and Gorman (2006) used a three-dimensional display to examine decision-making in basketball, but found only limited evidence for enhanced decision-making based on the addition of stereoscopic information.

Liquid crystal occlusion goggles offer the opportunity for observers to view the movements of real opponents in situ rather than viewing video-based displays (e.g., Abernethy *et al.*, 2001; Starkes *et al.*, 1995). By allowing observers to view actual opponents this technique offers a marked advantage in replicating the natural visual information. Whilst clearly desirable, in situ designs present significant logistical challenges, particularly in imposing heavy workloads on people recruited to act out the stimuli. Moreover, occlusion goggles can limit the experimental control in studies of anticipation by compromising both how replicable the movement pattern is between participants, and the degree of temporal precision possible for the exact moment of visual occlusion. In particular, while a video-based display will reliably occlude vision at the same moment in a movement pattern, this is not always possible when using occlusion goggles. Most studies using occlusion goggles rely on a manual trigger (by an experimenter pressing a button) to initiate occlusion, though newer methods of occlusion that are automatically triggered relative to a key moment in the movement pattern have been developed to improve the precision of occlusion in situ (e.g., Mann *et al.*, 2010c; Oudejans & Coolen, 2003).

The effect size of the expert advantage in tests of anticipation appears to increase commensurate with improvements in the fidelity of the visual information presented to participants. For instance, in a meta-analysis of perceptual-cognitive skill in sport, Mann *et al.* (2007) found a larger effect size for those studies performed in situ compared to those that used video displays. Further, Shim *et al.* (2005) examined the on-court anticipation of tennis strokes when participants observed a point-light video display, a normal video display, and an in situ opponent. Their results also demonstrated that skilled anticipation was enhanced as the display fidelity increased. Interestingly, Shim *et al.* (2005) also reported that, in contrast to the effect of display fidelity for skilled players, the performance of novice tennis players *decreased* with enhanced display fidelity. It was concluded that the increased complexity of the display may have either been distracting, or resulted in an overload of information for novice players.

Virtual reality (VR) displays provide a potentially useful compromise between experimental rigor and the quality of the visual information seen when viewing actions (see Chapter 17). VR has been successfully employed to examine expert-novice differences in movement behavior in sport (e.g., Brault *et al.*, 2012), though it is presently unclear how the effect size apparent across skill levels when using VR might compare to that observed in studies performed in situ. If proven to be effective, VR has the potential to afford specific advantages in the examination of anticipatory skill, in particular because the computer-generated movement patterns can be manipulated (much like point-light displays can be) to systematically alter selected features of the movement. These potential advantages can come at a cost though, with considerable expense and computer programming experience necessary to produce the stimuli, and the degree with which the computer-generated stimuli can accurately represent real human movement is sometimes limited.

Response characteristics

Traditional studies of anticipation have required participants to make perceptual-cognitive responses (e.g., verbal or pen-and-paper) that may fall short of accurately representing the movement responses produced in the natural setting. Decoupling action from perception facilitates experimental convenience but has been criticized as missing an important element of expert performance (Abernethy *et al.*, 1993; van der Kamp *et al.*, 2008). Gibson (1979) has highlighted the interdependency of perception and action, and claimed that any separation of the two will fail to accurately depict the true essence of expertise. This viewpoint raises serious challenges for the validity of perceptual responses being used to represent the actions produced in the natural setting.

The theoretical rationale for the inclusion of movement into testing paradigms is supported by studies of decision-making that show the incorporation of movement can enhance the suitability of action-based judgments. Oudejans *et al.* (1996a, 1996b) found that participants who were free to move were more likely to appropriately judge whether a fly ball was catchable than those participants who were stationary, and similarly that pedestrians already in a walking motion were more accurate in their road-crossing behaviors than those who were stationary. In both examples, the inclusion of action in the response enhanced decision-making accuracy, or conversely, the removal of action was detrimental to decision-making behavior.

The dual pathway theory of vision (Milner & Goodale, 1995) provides neuropsychological support for the incorporation of movement into responses made when testing anticipatory skill. In accordance with this theory it has been proposed that skilled athletes are most likely to depend on the dorsal (vision-for-action) pathway for the production of online movements, and so it is desirable to test this pathway to provide the best possible representation of skilled performance. Van der Kamp, Rivas, van Doorn, and Savelsbergh (2008) have persuasively argued though that the majority of studies examining visual anticipation in sport have tested the ventral (vision-for-perception) rather than the dorsal pathway, with the removal of movement resulting in a somewhat limited knowledge base that is biased towards conscious perceptual processing. Van der Kamp *et al.* placed a strong emphasis on the interaction between the two systems, with contributions from the ventral pathway important for both the identification of appropriate actions, and for some aspects of movement control. This in turn may aid the dorsal system for the online visual guidance of action. Within the framework presented by van der Kamp *et al.* (2008), the relative contribution of the two pathways alters across the time course of an interceptive action. Consider, for example, a tennis player receiving a serve from an opposing player. This framework proposes that the ventral system provides the predominant contribution as the service action begins; however, the ventral involvement progressively decreases while the dorsal contribution increases until the dorsal system dominates control following racquet-ball contact (see van der Kamp *et al.*, 2008, p. 109, Figure 3).

The prediction of improved expert anticipation as the response more accurately represents that produced in the real world has a sound theoretical basis, and the empirical evidence to date appears to support this. For instance, Farrow and Abernethy (2003) demonstrated that skilled tennis players were better able to anticipate the direction of serves when they moved in the anticipated direction than when they verbally predicted it. Interestingly though, this advantage when moving was found only when ball flight information was available and not when judgments were based exclusively on pre-ball flight information. More recently Mann *et al.* (2010a) demonstrated a relationship between the expert advantage for anticipation and the specificity of the action when viewing both pre- *and* post-ball flight information. Skilled and less-skilled cricket batters anticipated the movement outcomes of bowlers by using each of four response

Figure 15.1 Demonstration of a participant wearing occlusion goggles and attempting to (a) verbally predict the direction of a ball, and (b) hit a ball bowled by a cricket bowler in the study by Mann *et al.* (2010a).

types: a verbal response, a simple foot movement, a "shadowed" hitting movement (without a bat), and an interceptive movement (with a bat; see Figure 15.1). The anticipatory performance of the skilled batters improved even when performing the simple foot movement, but the largest expert advantage was seen when the interceptive movement (where participants had a chance to hit the ball) was performed (see also Dicks *et al.*, 2010a). The requirement and/or opportunity to intercept the ball may play an important role in facilitating this advantage. Conversely, Ranganathan and Carlton (2007) reported that skilled baseball batters responding to a virtual display were *disadvantaged* when responding with a movement, both when ball flight information was and was not available. They speculated that this effect could be attributable to a combination of increased task difficulty when swinging a baseball bat, and the earlier response initiation required for movement (when compared to a verbal response). It could also be that the lower fidelity of the display information and/or the lack of opportunity to intercept a target may have played a role.

Unfortunately, to date only a small number of studies of anticipatory skill have required participants to actually intercept a target (e.g., Farrow & Abernethy, 2002; Mann *et al.*, 2010b; Müller & Abernethy, 2006), primarily because of methodological and ethical concerns (e.g., for participant safety). Simulated or shadowed movements are more commonly employed to best represent natural interceptive actions (see also Chapter 24).

Future issues for consideration

Timing of the response

The ability of skilled athletes to make early anticipatory judgments in experimental tasks has often led to the assumption that experts must use this information to initiate their movements as early as possible. But the responses produced when responding to occluded actions might not necessarily reflect what an athlete does in a competitive situation when no occlusion takes place. The occlusion technique necessarily constrains participants to make responses on the basis of a limited amount of early information. It is possible that, rather than responding early, skilled athletes might wait until later visual information is available, as this information is likely to be more strongly associated with the actual movement outcome. In other words, just because athletes *can* anticipate and move earlier, it doesn't necessarily mean that they *do so* in a competitive situation.

Relatively little is known about how expert athletes use advance information to regulate their movement responses. Shim *et al.* (2005) did address this issue and found that when returning balls hit by an opponent, skilled tennis players initiated their movements earlier than they did when returning balls from a projection machine. As a result, they concluded that expert athletes use the movement patterns of their opponents to facilitate faster response times. In contrast, when asking goalkeepers to move a joystick in response to video footage of soccer penalty kicks, Savelsbergh *et al.* (2002) found that skilled goalkeepers made more accurate responses yet initiated their movements *later* and relied on less corrective movements than lesser-skilled goalkeepers. Similarly, Dicks *et al.* (2010b) found that amongst a group of skilled soccer goalkeepers attempting to save penalty kicks in situ, those who had greater action capabilities (i.e., who could move faster) waited longer before initiating their responses. These latter examples suggest that despite their ability to better anticipate action outcomes at an earlier point in time, expert athletes might actually wait longer until initiating their movements. This raises the question of if and how anticipatory information might be used to regulate actions. It seems that a key consideration must be to establish how anticipatory responses change in accordance with changes in the temporal demands of the task. More innovative measurement techniques including the use of EMG, force plates, accelerometers, and kinematic tracking may help to provide more sensitive measures of how movements change in response to manipulations in the advance information available to observers (see also Chapter 5).

Contextual information

The majority of what we know about skilled anticipation has been based on studies where anticipatory judgments are made in the absence of any information about the situational context or about the opponent performing the action. Yet, in reality, it is likely that skilled observers use contextual information (like preceding outcomes) to help them to anticipate action outcomes. For instance, Abernethy *et al.* (2001) found that skilled squash players could anticipate the likely outcome of an opponent's shot when vision was occluded *before* their opponent initiated their movement. They concluded that participants were using situational information, in that case the court position of their opponent, to help facilitate anticipatory judgments. More recently, Farrow and Reid (2012) found that skilled tennis players could use situational information (in that case serving patterns related to the game score) to facilitate the speed of their anticipatory judgments. These two examples show that contextual information can play an important role in the anticipatory judgments of skilled athletes. Surprisingly though, only a limited number of studies have so far sought to examine this effect. This gap in the research literature may have led to (i) an overestimation of the importance of kinematic information in skilled anticipation, and (ii) an overall underestimation of the nature of the expert advantage by failing to account for this seemingly important characteristic of skilled behavior.

Training anticipation

The nature of the expert advantage for anticipatory skill has led many to question whether perceptual training can be used to "speed up" the rate of anticipatory skill acquisition. As a result, a growing number of training programs have been designed to address this, and in general they find that the anticipatory skill of novice athletes can be improved as a result of perceptual training (e.g., Farrow *et al.*, 1998; Savelsbergh *et al.*, 2010; Williams *et al.*, 2002). These studies do raise, however, a number of measurement issues that are worthy of consideration if the interventions are to achieve their desired outcomes. Foremost of these concerns is whether any improvements in anticipatory skill transfer to improvements in on-field performance. Most training programs

Measurement of anticipation

show improvements in performance on video-based tests, but this does not necessarily guarantee that there will be a commensurate improvement in on-field performance. It will become increasingly important for studies evaluating perceptual training programs to demonstrate that any improvements as a result of the training lead to actual improvements in on-field movement accuracy and/or timing (e.g., Williams *et al.*, 2002). A second related consideration is whether any changes in performance as a result of training are meaningful improvements or are simply a result of a trade-off between speed and accuracy. This is an ever-present issue in tasks that concurrently prioritize the accuracy and speed of the response. Wherever possible this potential trade-off should be accounted for – for example, through the use of analysis of covariance (ANCOVA) testing to control for changes in response time (e.g., Abernethy *et al.*, 2012; Ryu *et al.*, 2012). A final consideration is that almost all studies that have evaluated the efficacy of perceptual training have done so by recruiting novice participants who possess very little or no experience in the given sporting task being trained. Although this approach provides experimental convenience in terms of access to available participants, it is problematic in that it does not evaluate whether the training will work for skilled or developmental athletes who already possess some level of proficiency in the task (and with whom these programs are most likely to be implemented). As a consequence, it is possible that the existing training studies may have overestimated the likely effect size that is possible when these interventions are implemented in practice. Further, much of what is known about the most efficacious training methods (e.g., Abernethy *et al.*, 2012) might not be accurate when the skill level of the participants is changed. These concerns highlight the need for future training studies to be implemented using participants who possess a greater level of proficiency in the chosen task (for an example, see Hopwood *et al.*, 2011).

Concluding thoughts

An important consideration in the measurement of anticipation is to choose whether to use a highly representative design that will faithfully replicate the real world skill it seeks to represent (for example, by requiring participants to make interceptive actions against real opponents), or to use a more simplified design that provides experimental convenience and control but may compromise the representativeness of the task (for example, making a verbal or pen-and-paper response to a video stimuli). A number of studies over the last 10 years have sought to address some of the key limitations of these more simplified designs. The general conclusion has been that in simplifying the task these studies may fail to fully replicate the level of performance observed in the natural setting. However, rather than providing a false representation of the findings, they may simply underestimate the true nature (and hence effect size) of the expert advantage in anticipatory skill. Future work is needed to address a number of more practical considerations in the measurement of anticipation – for example, how anticipatory skill is used and integrated with contextual information to facilitate expert performance in the natural setting.

References

Abernethy, B. (1990) 'Anticipation in squash: Differences in advance cue utilization between expert and novice players', *Journal of Sports Sciences*, 8: 17–34.

Abernethy, B., Gill, D. P., Parks, S. L., & Packer, S. T. (2001) 'Expertise and the perception of kinematic and situational probability information', *Perception*, 30: 233–52. doi:10.1068/p2872

Abernethy, B., & Mann, D. L. (2008) 'Dual pathways or dueling pathways for visual anticipation? A response to van der Kamp, Rivas, van Doorn & Savelsbergh', *International Journal of Sport Psychology*, 39(2): 136–41.

Abernethy, B., & Russell, D. G. (1987) 'Expert-novice differences in an applied selective attention task', *Journal of Sport Psychology*, 9: 326–45.

Abernethy, B., Schorer, J., Jackson, R. C., & Hagemann, N. (2012) 'Perceptual training methods compared: The relative efficacy of different approaches to enhancing sport-specific anticipation', *Journal of Experimental Psychology: Applied*, 18(2): 143–53.

Abernethy, B., Thomas, J. T., & Thomas, K. T. (1993) 'Strategies for improving understanding of motor expertise (or mistakes we have made and things we have learned)', *Advances in Psychology*, 102: 317–56.

Brault, S., Bideau, B., Kulpa, R., & Craig, C. M. (2012) 'Detecting deception in movement: The case of the side-step in rugby', *PLOS One*, 7(6): e37494.

Brunswick, E. (1956) *Perception and the representative design of psychological experiments*, 2nd ed., Berkeley: University of California Press.

Dicks, M., Button, C., & Davids, K. (2010a) 'Examination of gaze behaviors under in situ and video simulation task constraints reveals differences in information pickup for perception and action', *Attention, Perception, & Psychophysics*, 72(3): 706–20.

Dicks, M., Davids, K., & Button, C. (2010b) 'Individual differences in the visual control of intercepting a penalty kick in association football', *Human Movement Science*, 29(3): 401–11.

Farrow, D., Chivers, P., Hardingham, C., & Sachse, S. (1998) 'The effect of video-based perceptual training on the tennis return of serve', *International Journal of Sport Psychology*, 23: 231–42.

Farrow, D., & Reid, M. (2012) 'The contribution of situational probability information to anticipatory skill', *Journal of Science and Medicine in Sport*, 15(4): 368–73.

Farrow, D., Rendell, M., & Gorman, A. (2006) 'Enhancing the reality of a video simulation: Is depth information important?', *Journal of Sport & Exercise Psychology (Proceedings of NASPSPA 2006 Conference, Denver CO)*, 28(Supp): 65.

Farrow, D. T., & Abernethy, B. (2002) 'Can anticipatory skills be learned through implicit video-based perceptual training?', *Journal of Sports Sciences*, 20: 471–85.

Farrow, D. T., & Abernethy, B. (2003) 'Do expertise and the degree of perception-action coupling affect natural anticipatory performance?', *Perception*, 32: 1127–39. doi: 10.1068/p3323

Gibson, J. J. (1979) *The ecological approach to visual perception*, Boston: Houghton Mifflin.

Glencross, D. J., & Cibich, B. J. (1977) 'A decision analysis of games skills', *Australian Journal of Sports Medicine*, 9: 72–5.

Goulet, C., Bard, C., & Fleury, M. (1989) 'Expertise differences in preparing to return a tennis serve: A visual information processing approach', *Journal of Sport & Exercise Psychology*, 11: 382–98.

Hopwood, M., Mann, D. L., Farrow, D., & Nielsen, T. (2011) 'Does visual-perceptual training augment the fielding performance of skilled cricketers?', *International Journal of Sports Science and Coaching*, 6: 523–35.

Jones, C. M., & Miles, T. R. (1978) 'Use of advanced cues in predicting the flight of a lawn tennis ball', *Journal of Human Movement Studies*, 4: 231–5.

Mann, D. L., Abernethy, B., & Farrow, D. (2010a) 'Action specificity increases anticipatory performance and the expert advantage in natural interceptive tasks', *Acta Psychologica*, 135(1): 17–23.

Mann, D. L., Abernethy, B., & Farrow, D. (2010b) 'Visual information underpinning skilled anticipation: The effect of blur on a coupled and uncoupled in-situ anticipatory response', *Attention, Perception, & Psychophysics*, 72(5): 1317–26.

Mann, D. L., Abernethy, B., Farrow, D., Davis, M., & Spratford, W. (2010c) 'An event-related visual occlusion method for examining anticipatory skill in natural interceptive tasks', *Behavior Research Methods*, 42(2): 556–62. doi: 10.3758/BRM.42.2.556

Mann, D. T. Y., Williams, A. M., Ward, P., & Janelle, C. M. (2007) 'Perceptual-cognitive expertise in sport: A meta-analysis', *Journal of Sport & Exercise Psychology*, 29: 457–78.

Milner, A. D., & Goodale, M. A. (1995) *The visual brain in action*, Oxford, UK: Oxford University Press.

Müller, S., & Abernethy, B. (2006) 'Batting with occluded vision: An in situ examination of the information pick-up and interceptive skills of high- and low-skilled cricket batsmen', *Journal of Science and Medicine in Sport*, 9(6): 446–58. doi: 10.1016/j.jsams.2006.03.029

Müller, S., Abernethy, B., & Farrow, D. T. (2006) 'How do world-class cricket batsmen anticipate a bowler's intention?', *Quarterly Journal of Experimental Psychology. A Human Experimental Psychology*, 59(12): 2162–86. doi: 10.1080/02643290600576595

Oudejans, R.R.D., & Coolen, B. H. (2003) 'Human kinematics and event control: On-line movement registration as a means for experimental manipulation', *Journal of Sports Sciences*, 21: 567–76. doi: 10.1080/0264041031000101917

Oudejans, R.R.D., Michaels, C. F., Bakker, F. C., & Dolné, M. A. (1996a) 'The relevance of action in perceiving affordances: Perception of catchableness of fly balls', *Journal of Experimental Psychology: Human Perception and Performance*, 22: 879–91. doi: 10.1037/0096-1523.22.4.879

Oudejans, R.R.D., Michaels, C. F., van Dort, B., & Frissen, E. J.P. (1996b) 'To cross or not to cross: The effects of locomotion on street-crossing behavior', *Ecological Psychology*, 8: 259–67.

Panchuk, D., & Vickers, J. N. (2009) 'Using spatial occlusion to explore the control strategies used in rapid interceptive actions: Predictive or prospective control?', *Journal of Sports Sciences*, 27(12): 1249–60.

Pinder, R. A., Davids, K., Renshaw, I., & Araújo, D. (2011) 'Representative learning design and functionality of research and practice in sport', *Journal of Sport & Exercise Psychology*, 33: 146–55.

Ranganathan, R., & Carlton, L. G. (2007) 'Perception-action coupling and anticipatory performance in baseball batting', *Journal of Motor Behavior*, 39(5): 369–80. doi: 10.3200/JMBR.39.5.369-380

Ryu, D., Abernethy, B., Mann, D. L., Poolton, J. M., & Gorman, A. D. (2013) 'The role of central and peripheral vision in expert decision making', *Perception*, 42: 591–607.

Ryu, D., Kim, S., Abernethy, B., & Mann, D. L. (2012) 'Guiding attention aids the acquisition of anticipatory skill in novice soccer goalkeepers', *Research Quarterly for Exercise and Sport*, 84(2): 252–62.

Savelsbergh, G. J.P., Gastel, P. J., & Kampen, P. M. (2010) 'Anticipation of penalty kicking direction can be improved by directing attention through perceptual learning', *International Journal of Sport Psychology*, 41(1): 24–41.

Savelsbergh, G. J.P., Williams, A. M., van der Kamp, J., & Ward, P. (2002) 'Visual search, anticipation and expertise in soccer goalkeepers', *Journal of Sports Sciences*, 20: 279–87.

Shim, J., Carlton, L. G., Chow, J. W., & Chae, W. S. (2005) 'The use of anticipatory visual cues by highly skilled tennis players', *Journal of Motor Behavior*, 37(2): 164–75. doi: 10.3200/JMBR.37.2.164-175

Starkes, J. L., Edwards, P., Dissanayake, P., & Dunn, T. (1995) 'A new technology and field test of advance cue usage in volleyball', *Research Quarterly for Exercise and Sport*, 66: 162–7.

van der Kamp, J., Rivas, F., van Doorn, H., & Savelsbergh, G. J.P. (2008) 'Ventral and dorsal contributions in visual anticipation in fast ball sports', *International Journal of Sport Psychology*, 39(2): 100–30.

Williams, A. M., Ward, P., Knowles, J. M., & Smeeton, N. J. (2002) 'Anticipation skill in a real-world task: Measurement, training, and transfer in tennis', *Journal of Experimental Psychology: Applied*, 8(4): 259–70.

16

EYE TRACKING METHODS IN SPORT EXPERTISE

Derek Panchuk, Samuel Vine, and Joan N. Vickers

Introduction

Ut imago est animi voltus sic indices oculi
As the face is the image of the soul so the eyes are its revealers

(Cicero [106–43 BC], The Orator)

The idea that the eyes can reveal insight into the inner workings of the mind has been a long-standing anecdote in philosophy and has created significant scientific interest. Eminent psychologists such as James and physiologists such as Helmholtz recognized that the eyes provide insight into underlying psychological and biological processes. The development of sophisticated eye tracking technology in the 20th century has allowed scientists to begin to objectively understand the nature of eye movements and performance in a number of domains (see Wade & Tatler, 2005 for a review). In sport, the first eye tracking studies were conducted in the 1970s (Bard & Fleury, 1976), but since that time advances in technology, which have increased the freedom and flexibility of eye tracking devices, have allowed researchers to probe deeper into how gaze behavior relates to expert performance.

Of late an increasing number of psychologists and neuroscientists have identified sport as a rich domain in which to explore the attention skills important in novice to expert motor performance (Aglioti *et al.*, 2008; Yarrow *et al.*, 2009). The majority of sport is performed in a dynamic, ever-changing environment, under conditions of extreme pressure where the limits of human capability are continually challenged and extended (Ericsson, 2003). This chapter explores current trends in the area of eye tracking research within the sport domain and the attainment of expertise; we explain different types of eye movements and why eye tracking is a useful tool for studying expertise in sport. We explore various approaches to studying eye movements in sport, as well as some practical considerations and limitations.

The eye and eye movements

The eyes are the dominant sensory organs of the brain (Hubel & Weisel, 1968) and work in a complementary fashion to produce binocular vision by picking up reflections of light from objects in the visual field. Light entering the human eye is received by the retina, a light-sensitive

Eye tracking methods in sport expertise

area at the back of the eye that is lined with two types of visual receptors called rods and cones. This light is focused by the curvature of the cornea and lens, and focused upon the fovea of the retina, an area of concentrated cone cells that is responsible for the detection of color and detail. Due to the relatively small size of the fovea, the area across which we are able to see clear, detailed images is only about two to three degrees of visual angle – roughly the size of your thumb nail at arm's length (Land, 2006). This means that for humans to accurately perceive their environment they must produce purposeful movements of the eyes, head, and body to place images upon the fovea – a process known as gaze control. Gaze control constitutes a number of different eye movements that help to bring objects of interest onto the fovea (e.g., saccades) and to keep this information steady so that detail can be extracted (e.g., fixations and pursuit tracking). These eye movements are initiated by an elaborate system of muscles surrounding the eye, which are closely attuned to the head and neck through vestibular control systems. In this section we will describe the eye movements, which are commonly adopted in sport research, and also describe a specific class of fixation called the quiet eye.

Saccades

Saccades are ballistic eye movements that bring the point of maximal visual acuity onto the fovea so that an object can be seen with clarity (Thilo *et al.*, 2004). Saccades link fixations and pursuit tracking gaze together so that a cohesive view of a scene is received. In order to prevent seeing a blurry, incomprehensible world during saccades, information processing between saccades is suppressed (saccadic suppression), meaning the information between two fixated locations is not consciously perceived (Ross *et al.*, 2001), an effect that is best highlighted by the phenomena of change blindness (Grimes, 1996). Instead, visual information perceived during fixations is maintained in memory, thereby ensuring a stable, coherent scene.

Fixations

A fixation is the maintenance of steady gaze to allow processing of visual information from that location. A fixation typically ranges from one to three degrees of visual angle for 80–150 ms (see Carpenter, 1988; Vickers, 2007) and enables performers to stabilize an informative area of a scene on the fovea so that complex processing can occur. In sporting tasks, fixations allow attention to be directed to specific details from the scene, in order to guide decision-making or motor control skills.

Pursuit tracking

Pursuit tracking is the maintenance of steady gaze on a moving object or target, a skill that is particularly useful in high-speed sporting tasks (e.g., baseball or cricket). A pursuit fixation has the same temporal characteristics as a fixation, with a minimum duration of 80–150 ms of stability on the target needed to process information. Research suggests that the maximum velocity of these eye movements is around 100° per second, although dynamic acuity starts to degrade around 30° per second (Carpenter, 1988). In order to cope with this functional limitation, alternative gaze strategies are required to gather appropriate target information (e.g., predictive saccades; Land & McLeod, 2000).

Quiet eye

The quiet eye (QE) is a visuomotor variable, which has emerged from research adopting a vision-in-action approach (see below). The QE can be defined as the final fixation or tracking gaze directed to a single location or object in the visuomotor workspace within three degrees of visual angle (or less) for a minimum of 100 ms (Vickers, 1996). The onset of QE occurs before the critical movement of the motor task, and offset of the QE occurs when the final fixation deviates off the target by more than three degrees of visual angle for more than 100 ms. Research examining QE tends to involve performers of varying levels of expertise executing skills while their gaze behaviors are recorded. In order to determine the attributes of a QE fixation that correlate with sporting expertise, athletes are often asked to perform under experimental conditions in which task complexity, pressure/anxiety, and physiological arousal are manipulated. The QE is a variable that examines the complex relationship between perception and action, and has been adopted in more than 100 published studies (see Vickers, 2007; Vine *et al.*, 2014; see also Chapter 3).

Why study eye tracking?

The underlying rationale that drives the study of eye tracking in sport is the relationship between eye movements, attention, and motor performance. While attention can move independent of eye movements, or covertly (Posner, 1980), there is evidence that eye movements coincide with an obligatory shift of attention (Deubel & Schneider, 1996; Shepherd *et al.*, 1986). For example, a soccer goaltender could shift his/her attention to a player's head while fixating on the ball, but could not move his/her eyes to the hip region and attend to the head – attention would have to move with the eyes to the hips. The interdependence between eye movements and attention allows researchers to make a number of predictions about the relationship between performance and eye movements in the development of expertise.

Eye movement recordings have demonstrated how eye movements differ between experts and novices across a range of skills (see Vickers, 2007 for an overview). While the majority of these studies have used cross-sectional designs and, as such, only permit us to assume that there are differences between groups, there is evidence that eye movements change over the course of skill learning as well (Sailer *et al.*, 2005; Vine & Wilson, 2010, 2011; Vine *et al.*, 2012). Eye movement research also allows us to make predictions about the underlying structure of the task. For example, we can determine which sources of information are relevant for performance and how the sources of information that are relevant for performance change with the development of expertise (Land, 2009). Expert performers, through extended engagement within a task domain, develop the unique ability to attend to relevant information at the time when it is most necessary for task performance (Hayhoe *et al.*, 2007). Experimental studies have also demonstrated the importance that specific gaze behaviors, such as the QE, play in the performance of motor skills. Williams, Singer, and Frehlich (2002) found that when QE duration was experimentally manipulated in a billiards task to 50 per cent and 75 per cent of participants' normal QE durations, the accuracy of both experts and novices suffered, showing the superior motor system of the elite players did not insulate them from the effects of their lower than normal QE durations. Finally, insight into expert gaze behaviors can be used as a training tool to guide the behavior of novices and hasten the learning process (Harle & Vickers, 2001; Vine *et al.*, 2011).

Approaches to studying eye movements

Early research in the field of sport vision focused on questions related to visual acuity, color detection, contrast detection, depth perception, and distance judgment (Planer, 1994). However, equivocal results examining proficiency-related differences in such visual "hardware" led researchers to examine differences in "software," or how visual information is used. Knowing where and when to look is crucial for successful sport performance, yet the visual display can be large and often full of information both relevant and irrelevant to the task. Sport performers must be able to identify the most information-rich areas of the display, direct their attention appropriately, and extract meaning from these areas efficiently and effectively (Mann *et al.*, 2007; Williams *et al.*, 1999).

Visual search versus vision-in-action

The two most commonly used approaches to eye tracking in the sport domain are visual search and vision-in-action (Vickers, 2007). Visual search, which has its roots in experimental psychology, involves participants searching for targets within a visual scene that is shown using slides, videos, or virtual reality. Early experiments using the visual search approach involved participants viewing static scenes from the sport in question (Bard & Fleury, 1976). Static stimuli have since been replaced by dynamic images that present a scenario from the normal task environment and require participants to respond with either a simplified response (e.g., verbal response; Buszard *et al.*, 2012), or attempt to mimic the response typically required in the natural task (e.g., mimicking the cricket stroke; McRobert *et al.*, 2009). Studies adopting a visual search paradigm are interested in the frequency and duration of fixations, enabling the determination of a visual search strategy. Theoretically, due to the suppression of information process during saccades, a visual search strategy, which uses fewer fixations of a longer duration, is assumed to be more effective and efficient (Williams *et al.*, 1994), although this has been questioned within the literature (Moran *et al.*, 2002).

Visual search paradigms permit the researcher control over the stimuli presented to athletes and allows for visual information to be experimentally manipulated (e.g., temporal and spatial occlusion; Müller *et al.*, 2006). However, one of the criticisms of this approach is that the synthetic display used and the types of responses required by participants (e.g., manual button press or verbal response) may lead to search behaviors that are dissimilar from those displayed in real sporting environments when actual responses are required (e.g., movement; Dicks *et al.*, 2010). This limitation has been mitigated in studies that have used spatial occlusion in a more natural task environment (Panchuk & Vickers, 2009) and by using technology to combine early kinematic information to guide action and anticipation with the necessary action requirement (Panchuk *et al.*, 2013).

The vision-in-action approach (Vickers, 1992, 1996, 2007) couples athletes' movements and their gaze in one video frame, thus permitting the measurement of the gaze of individuals as they perform the different phases of a sporting task as in the real world. This approach represents an important advancement for understanding gaze behavior because the systems that support the acquisition of visual information (i.e., the eyes, head, and body) allow individuals to selectively control what information is perceived within the environment, when it is perceived, and how it is used. The advantage of using a vision-in-action approach is that it provides a relatively objective measure of the acquisition of visual information during "free viewing" that can be related temporally to the actions of the individual. Early eye movement studies were limited in the amount of movement athletes were permitted, but the advent of newer mobile eye tracking technology, such as the ASL Mobile Eye and SMI Eye Tracking Glasses, have allowed users to explore gaze behavior in tasks that would otherwise be impossible with fixed or tethered eye trackers (e.g., Vickers, 2006). When the vision-in-action approach is used, both the gaze and motor behavior vary according to a naturally occurring visual field, rather than to set stimuli that are held constant in the visual field (e.g., photos, videos, virtual reality). Because of this, both the gaze (fixations, pursuit tracking, saccades, other) and the phases of the movement are converted to a percentage of the total movement time, or relative time. Therefore, fixations and pursuit tracking gaze are generalized to the same temporal period and analyzed as a percentage (or ratio) of the total movement. In this way, fixations, pursuit tracking, saccades, and other gaze are cognitively situated relative to discrete phases of the action.

While the vision-in-action approach provides greater flexibility in terms of the range of skills that can be assessed, it does have some limitations. There is the risk of sacrificing some experimental control when measuring performance using vision-in-action; however, this can be addressed with careful planning on the part of the researcher. In more complex tasks, such as measuring decision-making in team sports (e.g., 11-on-11 in soccer), the number of participants required to create scenarios is greater and may be a limiting factor when designing tasks.

Eye tracking technology

Tracking the movements of the human eye is a relatively non-invasive technique that has been used by researchers to understand human behavior and movement for decades. Early research measuring eye movements adopted simple observation techniques (e.g., Hackman & Guilford, 1936). However, technological advancements have allowed for the development of more automated and accurate assessments of eye movements. Whereas in cognitive psychology and other psychology domains stationary, fixed eye trackers were common and indeed necessary (Richardson & Spivey, 2004), advances in eye tracking technology enabled the development of mobile eye trackers (worn by the participant). These devices (reviewed below) allow for a more representative assessment of eye movements in a range of sport environments. A major advantage of this type of system is that the location of gaze is automatically superimposed onto a video of the scene. This allows for live monitoring of the gaze data, as well as post hoc synchronization of the gaze and motor videos and the coding of exact gaze locations, rather than the analysis of x- and y-coordinates. In the section below, we review two eye trackers that have been used extensively in mobile eye tracking in sport and other motor tasks.

The Applied Sciences (ASL) Mobile Eye (ME) is a monocular system that uses lightweight glasses fitted with eye and scene cameras and a set of three light-emitting diodes (LED) that project a low-intensity, near infrared (IR) light onto the eye via a reflective "monocle" (see Figure 16.1). This light is reflected by the cornea (corneal reflection) and appears to the eye camera as a configuration of three dots at a fixed distance from each other (1b). The pupil appears black, as light does not exit the inside of the eye, enabling the system to register its position and determine its center. During saccades, the center of the pupil moves relative to the head while the corneal reflection remains in the same position. Therefore, by comparing

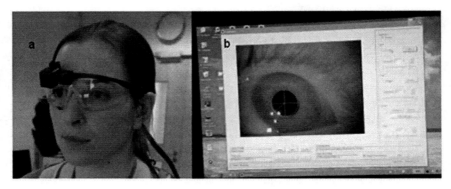

Figure 16.1 The Applied Sciences Laboratories (ASL) Mobile Eye (a) and the EyeVision software (b) user interface.

the vector (angle and distance) between the pupil and the cornea, the eye tracking system can compute the angle at which the gaze is directed on the scene video. The system also incorporates a digital recording device, which combines the two video streams from the eye and scene cameras at 30 Hz.

Calibration of the eye tracker requires that the participant hold his/her head and body still as he/she fixates specific locations within the visual field. A cursor, indicating the location of gaze in a video image of the scene (spatial accuracy ~ 0.5° visual angle; precision ~ 0.1°), is viewed in real time and can be recorded for offline analysis. The ME is lightweight, and because the optics are mounted on a pair of sport goggles, athletes find the system easy to wear and non-obtrusive. This allows them to perform sporting tasks in a normal way. The ME also functions without the need of a connecting cable, and is able to transmit the eye movement and video data wirelessly. One of the main strengths of the ASL ME is the ability to adapt the scene and eye camera and lens to accommodate different visual scenes. This is important in sport as some events have demanding visual scenes that require capturing relevant visual fields (e.g., looking down during putting or looking up to catch a ball). A drawback of the ASL ME is that it can be difficult to calibrate some subjects and requires skill to adjust the cameras and select the best lens for the task being investigated. The ASL ME therefore requires a skilled operator, and should not be given to an untrained individual.

The SensoMotoric Instruments (SMI) Eye Tracking Glasses (ETG) is a binocular system that captures the movements of both eyes, using two small cameras on the rim of the glasses, thus permitting automatic parallax compensation and accurate data acquisition over all distances with no need for manual adjustments (see Figure 16.2). The data is collected in high definition at both 30 Hz and 60 Hz, thus providing a clear image of the visual field, and features high sensitivity for low-light conditions. Live feedback of calibration on the scene video makes it easy to control the quality of recordings even with demanding subject groups. One strength of the ETG is its use of auto-calibration. Once the wearer puts the glasses on, he/she is asked to view one location in the environment for initialization. Calibration is indicated by a change in color of the gaze cursor, which occurs within a few seconds. Thus, it is easier to set up and calibrate than most eye trackers and could be managed without a high level of technical skill. A limitation of the current SMI glasses is that they cannot be adjusted to accommodate unusual task environments (e.g., the lens of the scene camera and its orientation are fixed).

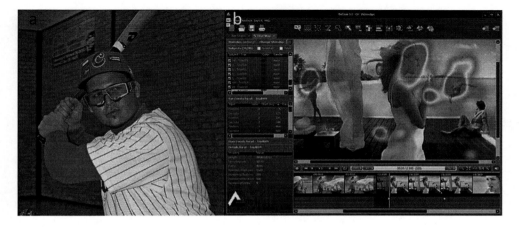

Figure 16.2 The SensoMotoric Instruments (SMI) Eye Tracking Glasses (a) and the BeGaze user interface (b).

Coding eye tracking data: defining what athletes see

The raw data captured from eye trackers must be processed in order to extract meaningful information. Two methods are currently used; one uses the digital x/y-coordinate data that all eye trackers produce and the second uses manual or semi-automatic, frame-by-frame coding of the coupled gaze and motor data.

Digital x/y coding and analysis

This approach is recommended for experiments where specific stimuli of interest are known in advance and where minimal movement is produced by the performer. Areas of interest (AOI) or regions of interest (ROI) can be defined by the experimenter, and temporal and spatial thresholds can be set for classifying each type of eye movement. The software then automatically categorizes eye movements and how often they occur in each AOI/ROI. Commercially available programs such as Gaze Tracker, ASL Results, and SMI BeGaze all have this capability. The main advantage of these programs is that results are obtained relatively easily; however, the process can also be very time consuming, as the output needs to be verified, particularly if there is any movement on the part of the participant.

Frame-by-frame coding and analysis

During vision-in-action studies, the participant moves in a natural way, and therefore critical spatial locations are not specified in advance, but instead defined by the gaze behavior of the participant. It is therefore necessary to use a frame-by-frame coding of the coupled gaze and motor data, referred to as observational coding (software with this capability include Quiet Eye Solutions and Noldus Observer). Observational coding essentially involves defining the location and type of gaze behavior for each frame of data collected. Frame numbers are used to determine the duration of the eye movement, and this is dependent upon the temporal resolution of the eye tracker. For example, the ASL Mobile Eye captures video images at 30 Hz – hence, a fixation is often calculated as three frames (99.99 ms). Locations, or areas of interest, within the scene are also determined after viewing the data of the participants, and a coding system is developed for each gaze type by location (e.g., a fixation to the head). The onset and offset of the gaze behavior can also be specified, providing the researcher with several important pieces of information: gaze type, location, onset, offset, and duration. This information can then be used for analyzing a number of important characteristics of gaze behavior during the task, including sequence, locations sampled, fixation duration, time spent fixating each location, and onset/offset of fixations relative to important events during the task. In the following section we will provide an example of how the QE is coded using the Quiet Eye Solutions software. This software is unique in that it codes the different types of gaze and the phases of the movement at the same time.

An example: calculating the QE

To calculate QE for a given task, a temporal analysis of the phases of movement is required. For the vision-in-action approach, a digital external video camera is often used to capture the actions of performers, which allows for syncing of the movement of the athlete with his/her gaze and eye videos. Figure 16.3 shows the Quiet Eye Solutions software's split-screen view of the vision-in-action video data. The software time-locks the two video files and allows for manual coding of the movement phases (position of limbs over time) from the external video, in relation to the coding of

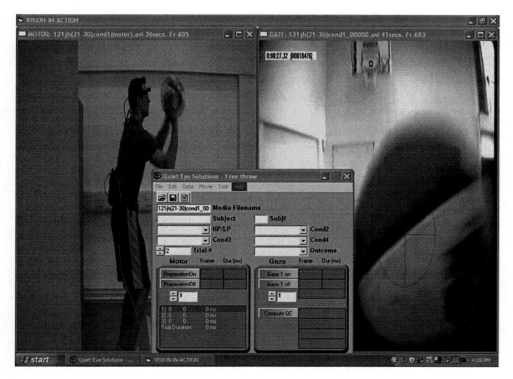

Figure 16.3 A screen grab of the Quiet Eye Solutions software analysis environment used by Vine and Wilson (2011) showing the external video of the participant (left), the view from the scene camera of the eye tracker (right), and the coding entry fields (center).

the gaze behavior (gaze location and duration) from the eye tracker. First, the temporal sequences of movements are coded by viewing the video and indicating the start and end of each phase of movement. In order to identify the phases of movement for a specific skill, researchers typically refer to biomechanic studies or the technical literature in each sport. For example, in golf putting, phases identified in QE studies are preparation, backswing, foreswing, contact, and follow through (Vickers, 1992; Vine et al., 2011). The next step is to code the eye movements of the performer, within the same time period. This is achieved by returning to the start of the video and coding the location, duration, and type (e.g., fixation, pursuit tracking, or saccade) of each gaze behavior individually by scanning backwards and forwards through the video using the previously specified "rules" (in QES this is done by clicking the onset and offset buttons, or by using the time-code information for Excel). Finally, the QES software can calculate the QE variables (including onset, offset, location, and duration) automatically using a previously determined "critical movement." In new tasks where the QE has never been determined, different critical movements can be tested and QE duration generated until QE that significantly affects skill and accuracy is determined.

Establishing the reliability

The QES software is a relatively simple piece of software to use; however, the objectivity and reliability of the coding process must be established at the outset. Code-recode reliability checks involve using a second coder to blindly code a subsection of the data for comparison with the original coder(s). Variables such as phase duration and fixation frequency and duration are then subjected to a test of interclass correlation to determine the level of agreement between the two data sets, and typically independent coding is carried out until there is 90–100 per cent agreement. This ensures that the coding methods (rules) are sound and that a high degree of objectivity is in place. Although this process can be time consuming, once the reliability of the coding system is established the coding occurs quickly. The use of observational coding methods is, in many ways, more accurate than automated coding as long as the coders are highly trained. This is because there are many complexities in the gaze of humans in sport, law enforcement, and medical tasks that cannot yet be "understood" by computers.

Limitations

The use of eye tracking technology in sport research has several limitations that researchers should be aware of before initiating a project.

Technical limitations

Despite developments in corneal reflection and dark pupil tracking, many eye trackers lack robustness in changing light conditions and often require frequent checking of the calibration. For this reason it is essential to be able to monitor the gaze of participants as the data is collected in the live experimental task. For wireless systems, such as the Mobile Eye, this is not a problem, because eye movements can be viewed online; for other systems, however, it is preferable to keep the eye tracker connected to the collection computer to ensure data integrity. When collecting in situations that do not permit constant monitoring of data researchers are encouraged to perform calibration checks frequently.

A further limitation of many mobile eye tracking systems is the capture rate. A capture rate of 30 Hz or 60 Hz allows for data to be recorded every 33.3 ms or 16.7 ms, which is significantly lower than some of its predecessors (NAC: 600 Hz; Eyelink: 500 Hz; ASL 501: 50 Hz). The benefits of capturing data whilst subjects perform in real conditions, however, potentially outweigh the sampling limitations, especially as the research questions in sport psychology tend to be related to registering fixations (>100 ms) as opposed to saccade analyses. Newer technology, such as the SMI Eye Tracking Glasses, also permit data capture at higher frequencies (60 Hz), which may be beneficial for tasks that have to contend with higher speed objects. There are studies that have questioned whether higher temporal resolutions are beneficial in terms of providing more information. For example, Helsen, Starkes, Elliott, and Ricker (1998) compared the utility of a 60 and a 120 Hz sampling frequency during a fast aiming task. No differences were found for initiation time, saccade angle, fixation duration, and overall number of saccades. They concluded that a 120 Hz sampling of the gaze and hand movements did not provide more meaningful results than a 60 Hz sampling.

Methodological limitations

The physical characteristics of an individual's eye (e.g., color of eye, position of the eye within the face, cosmetic contact lenses) can restrict the ability to calibrate the system effectively. In some cases this may lead to selective sampling of participants who have characteristics that are favorable for eye tracking studies, leading to the exclusion of other participants.

Interpretation issues

Because eye trackers are limited to measuring central foveal vision, researchers are similarly limited in the assumptions that they can make with regards to the contribution of peripheral visual information to performance and expertise. As highlighted above, attention can move independent of eye movements, so it is important when interpreting fixation data to acknowledge that the performer may be attending to other locations within the environment peripherally, or his focus of attention may be directed inwards to his own actions (e.g., he may be thinking about controlling a specific body segment). These limitations can be attenuated to some degree by carefully designed experiments. For example, the contribution of peripheral vision to performance may be explored by using novel occlusion paradigms to mask environmental locations away from the point of fixation, or verbal reporting may be used in conjunction with eye tracking to determine the athlete's intentions during the performance of the task.

When interpreting eye movement data, it is important to acknowledge the difference between looking and seeing. Simply because two athletes have similar gaze behaviors during a task does not necessarily mean that they are interpreting the information they see in the same way (Henderson, 2003). For this reason, it is important, particularly in expertise research, to identify performance and process measures that can tease apart the relationship between looking and seeing, to determine how visual information is being used by the performer.

Overall, eye tracking represents an important metric for understanding what sets experts apart and the processes that underlie the attainment of expertise. It can also provide a valuable training tool for helping novice performers develop perceptual behavior that can aide their development as they become more skilled. While there are limitations and pitfalls when collecting eye movement data, properly conducted studies with appropriate attention to detail and rigor can provide a "window" into the mind of the expert.

References

Aglioti, S. M., Cesari, P., Romani, M., & Urgesi, C. (2008) 'Action anticipation and motor resonance in elite basketball players', *Nature Neuroscience*, 11(9): 1109–16. Retrieved from www.nature.com/neuro/journal/v11/n9/suppinfo/nn.2182_S1.html

Bard, C., & Fleury, M. (1976) 'Analysis of visual search activity during sport problem situations', *Journal of Human Movement Studies*, 3(2): 14–222.

Buszard, T., Farrow, D., & Kemp, J. (2012) 'Examining the influence of acute instructional approaches on the decision-making performance of experienced team field sport players', *Journal of Sports Sciences*, 31(3): 238–47. doi: 10.1080/02640414.2012.731516

Carpenter, R.H.S. (1988) *Movements of the eyes*, London: Pion.

Deubel, H., & Schneider, W. X. (1996) 'Saccade target selection and object recognition: Evidence for a common attentional mechanism', *Vision Research*, 36(12): 1827–37. Retrieved from http://dx.doi.org/10.1016/0042–6989(95)00294–4

Dicks, M., Button, C., & Davids, K. (2010) 'Examination of gaze behaviors under in situ and video simulation task constraints reveals differences in information pickup for perception and action', *Attention, Perception, & Psychophysics*, 72(3): 706–20. doi: 10.3758/app.72.3.706

Ericsson, K. A. (2003) *Expert performance in sports: Advances in research on sport expertise*, Champaign, IL: Human Kinetics.

Grimes, J. A. (1996) 'On the failure to detect changes in scenes across saccades', in K. Akins (ed) *Perception*, Oxford: Oxford University Press, 89–110.

Hackman, B., & Guilford, J. (1936) 'A study of the "visual fixation" method of measuring attention value', *Journal of Applied Psychology*, 20(1): 44.

Harle, S. K., & Vickers, J. N. (2001) 'Training quiet eye improves accuracy in the basketball free throw', *Sport Psychologist*, 15(3): 289–305.

Hayhoe, M. M., Droll, J., & Mennie, N. (2007) 'Learning where to look', in R.P.G. van Gompel, M. H. Fischer, W. S. Murray, & R. L. Hill (eds) *Eye movements: A window on mind and brain*, Amsterdam, NL: Elsevier, 641–59.

Helsen, W., Starkes, J., Elliott, D., & Ricker, K. (1998) 'Sampling frequency and the study of eye-hand coordination in aiming', *Behavior Research Methods, Instruments, & Computers*, 30(4): 617–23. doi: 10.3758/BF03209479

Henderson, J. M. (2003) 'Human gaze control during real-world scene perception', *Trends in Cognitive Science*, 7: 498–504.

Hubel, D. H., & Wiesel, T. N. (1968) 'Receptive fields and functional architecture of monkey striate cortex', *The Journal Physiology*, 195: 215–43.

Land, M. F. (2006) 'Eye movements and the control of actions in everyday life', *Progress in Retinal and Eye Research*, 25(3): 296–324. doi: 10.1016/j.preteyeres.2006.01.002

Land, M. F. (2009) 'Vision, eye movements, and natural behavior', *Visual Neuroscience*, 26(1): 51–62. doi: 10.1017/S0952523808080899

Land, M. F., & McLeod, P. (2000) 'From eye movements to actions: How batsmen hit the ball', *Nature Neuroscience*, 3(12): 1340–5. doi: 10.1038/81887

Mann, D. T., Williams, A. M., Ward, P., & Janelle, C. M. (2007) 'Perceptual-cognitive expertise in sport: A meta-analysis', *Journal of Sport & Exercise Psychology*, 29(4): 457–78.

McRobert, A. P., Williams, A. M., Ward, P., & Eccles, D. W. (2009) 'Tracing the process of expertise in a simulated anticipation task', *Ergonomics*, 52(4): 474–83.

Moran, A., Byrne, A., & McGlade, N. (2002) 'The effects of anxiety and strategic planning on visual search behaviour', *Journal of Sports Sciences*, 20(3): 225–36.

Müller, S., Abernethy, B., & Farrow, D. (2006) 'How do world-class cricket batsmen anticipate a bowler's intention?', *The Quarterly Journal of Experimental Psychology*, 59(12): 2162–86. doi: N275211304702KUV [pii]. 1080/02643290600576595

Panchuk, D., Davids, K., Sakadjian, A., MacMahon, C., & Parrington, L. (2013) 'Did you see that? Dissociating advanced visual information and ball flight constrains perception and action processes during one-handed catching', *Acta Psychologica*, 142(3): 394–401. doi: http://dx.doi.org/10.1016/j.actpsy.2013.01.014

Panchuk, D., & Vickers, J. N. (2009) 'Using spatial occlusion to explore the control strategies used in rapid interceptive actions: predictive or prospective control?', *Journal of Sports Sciences*, 27(12): 1249–60.

Planer, P. M. (1994) *Sports vision manual*, Hamburg: International Academy of Sports Vision.

Posner, M. I. (1980) 'Orienting of attention', *The Quarterly Journal of Experimental Psychology*, 32(1): 3–25.

Richardson, D. C., & Spivey, M. J. (2004) 'Eye tracking: Characteristics and methods', *Encyclopedia of biomaterials and biomedical engineering*, 568–72.

Ross, J., Morrone, M. C., Goldberg, M. E., & Burr, D. C. (2001) 'Changes in visual perception at the time of saccades', *Trends in Neurosciences*, 24(2): 113–21. doi: http://dx.doi.org/10.1016/S0166-2236(00)01685-4

Sailer, U., Flanagan, J. R., & Johansson, R. S. (2005) 'Eye–hand coordination during learning of a novel visuomotor task', *The Journal of Neuroscience*, 25(39): 8833–42. doi: 10.1523/jneurosci.2658-05.2005

Shepherd, M., Findlay, J. M., & Hockey, R. J. (1986) 'The relationship between eye movements and spatial attention', *Quarterly Journal of Experimental Psychology. A, Human Experimental Psychology*, 38: 475–91.

Thilo, K. V., Santoro, L., Walsh, V., & Blakemore, C. (2004) 'The site of saccadic suppression', *Nature Neuroscience*, 7(1): 13–14.

Vickers, J. N. (1992) 'Gaze control in putting', *Perception*, 21(1): 117–32.

Vickers, J. N. (1996) 'Visual control when aiming at a far target', *Journal of Experimental Psychology: Human Perception and Performance*, 22(2): 342–54. doi: 10.1037/0096-1523.22.2.342

Vickers, J. N. (2006) 'Gaze of Olympic speedskaters skating at full speed on a regulation oval: Perception-action coupling in a dynamic performance environment', *Cognitive Processing*, 7(1): 102–5.

Vickers, J. N. (2007) *Perception, cognition, and decision training: The quiet eye in action*, Champaign, IL: Human Kinetics.

Vine, S. J., Moore, L., & Wilson, M. R. (2011) 'Quiet eye training facilitates competitive putting performance in elite golfers', *Frontiers in Psychology*, 2: 1–9. doi: 10.3389/fpsyg.2011.00008

Vine, S. J., Moore, L. J., & Wilson, M. R. (2012) 'The benefits of quiet eye training for the acquisition, refinement and resilient performance of targeting skills', *European Journal of Sport Science*. doi: 10.1080/17461391.2012.683815

Vine, S. J., Moore, L. J., & Wilson, M. R. (2014) 'Quiet eye training: The acquisition, refinement and resilient performance of targeting skills', *European Journal of Sport Science*, 14: S235–S242.

Vine, S. J., & Wilson, M. R. (2010) 'Quiet eye training: Effects on learning and performance under pressure', *Journal of Applied Sport Psychology*, 22(4): 361–76. doi: 10.1080/10413200.2010.495106

Eye tracking methods in sport expertise

Vine, S. J., & Wilson, M. R. (2011) 'The influence of quiet eye training and pressure on attention and visuo-motor control', *Acta Psychologica*, 136(3): 340–6. doi: 10.1016/j.actpsy.2010.12.008

Wade, N. J., & Tatler, B. W. (2005) *The moving tablet of the eye: The origins of modern eye movement research*, New York: Oxford University Press.

Williams, A. M., Davids, K., Burwitz, L., & Williams, J.G. (1994) 'Visual search strategies in experienced and inexperienced soccer players', *Research Quarterly for Exercise and Sport*, 65(2): 127–35.

Williams, A. M., Davids, K., & Williams, J.G.P. (1999) *Visual perception and action in sport*, New York: E. & F.N. Spon.

Williams, A. M., Singer, R. N., & Frehlich, S. G. (2002) 'Quiet eye duration, expertise, and task complexity in near and far aiming tasks', *Journal of Motor Behavior*, 34(2): 197–207.

Yarrow, K., Brown, P., & Krakauer, J. W. (2009) 'Inside the brain of an elite athlete: The neural processes that support high achievement in sports', *Nature Reviews Neuroscience*, 10(8): 585–96.

17

NEW METHODS FOR STUDYING PERCEPTION AND ACTION COUPLING

Cathy M. Craig and Alan Cummins

To study perception and action, Gibson advocated that "the laboratory must be like life" (Gibson, 1979, p. 3). In other words, the interactive relationship between an organism and his/her environment must be maintained so that the behavior observed in an experimental context mirrors, as closely as possible, the behavior observed in a realistic sport setting. The concept of representative design introduced by Brunswik in 1956 emphasized the need to have experimental tasks that allow the player to pick up perceptual information that specifies a property of the environment-actor system (Araújo *et al.*, 2005; see also Chapter 24). In this chapter we will provide a brief overview of the methodologies used to study perception and action in sport and present, in some detail, the opportunities new methodologies such as immersive, interactive virtual reality can offer researchers in sport expertise.

Studying perception and action

In an attempt to preserve some ecological validity, prior research looking at expertise in sport has tended to use realistic stimuli (e.g., video recordings or snapshots of a sport-related scene) to elicit sport-related behaviors, such as a response latency (Williams *et al.*, 1994) or action choice (Helsen & Pauwels, 1993). However, using stimuli that are filmed or captured from a fixed, allocentric viewpoint will not capture the dynamics of the sporting scenario from the perspective of the player (egocentric viewpoint). Petit and Ripoll (2008) showed more accurate and faster decisions when the viewpoint was presented from the player's perspective compared to that of a live broadcast (allocentric viewpoint). Furthermore, the type of display used, such as projections on small screens with no immersive capabilities to simulate motion parallax, can severely compromise the player's perception. Unlike perception in a real life environment, the optic array does not capture the environment-actor relationship, with the information presented not incorporating changes that would take place as a result of the player's own movements. Furthermore, studies have shown that where task constraints are unrepresentative of the true sporting context, the sources of information that are pertinent to performance are often absent, resulting in expert performance advantages being eroded (Abernethy *et al.*, 1993; Dicks *et al.*, 2010). In an attempt to address these issues recent studies have made considerable efforts to represent a player's viewpoint in more naturalistic settings. This has involved capturing video sequences from within the field in order to provide an "internal" viewpoint in soccer (Savelsbergh *et al.*,

New methods for studying perception

2002), tennis (Farrow & Abernethy, 2003; Williams *et al.*, 2002), rugby (Croft *et al.*, 2011), and basketball (Farrow & Fournier, 2005).

However, to properly measure perception and action we need a methodology that can adequately and accurately recreate this perception/action cycle from the player's perspective (e.g., head-mounted cameras; Croft *et al.*, 2013). In other words, we need to use technology that allows us to recreate an athlete's (egocentric) 3D perspective of an unfolding, sport-related event that can be updated in real time. At the same time, it has to also offer the possibility of precisely controlling the perceptual information presented to the observer immersed in the virtual environment, and reliably reproduce these conditions across trials (Tarr & Warren, 2002). The experience has to also be interactive, so that we can record how the observer interacts or responds to the information presented in the virtual environment (Craig & Watson, 2011; Dessing & Craig, 2010). Gibson said, "we must perceive in order to move but we must also move in order to perceive" (Gibson, 1979, p. 223). In the context of sport, players are active (rather than passive) perceivers who continuously engage in exploratory behaviors that allow them to pick up important information to guide their decisions about when and how to act. In other words, their behavior emerges from their egocentric perception of what the environment affords at a given moment in time (active perception) and what the actor is capable of doing (action capabilities) (Craig & Watson, 2011). This ability to control perceptual information in a realistic way, while precisely measuring the consequences of those changes for the subsequent regulation of action, offers an alternative way of looking at perception and action research in sport.

Immersive, interactive virtual reality

The technology that can allow us to achieve many of the aforementioned goals is immersive, interactive virtual reality (i2VR). i2VR not only offers an exciting new way of studying perception and action in sport but could also be an exciting new way of training perceptual skills in players where the perception/action loop is preserved (see Chapter 36). Virtual reality itself is an overused term that can describe many diverse and varying ways of viewing and/or interacting with a virtual environment. In fact, the definition is often determined by the technology being used to both display (perceive) and interact (move) within the virtual environment (McMenemy & Ferguson, 2007). The technology choices can be vastly different and can significantly affect the affordances available to a user within a particular application. As a result, this can act as a limiting factor when trying to use virtual reality technology for particular purposes. For example, 3D graphics generated by a computer could be displayed in many ways, such as by a 3D capable monitor, a head-mounted display, or a 3D projector where the images are projected onto a flat or curved screen. In each of these instances the scale of the images an observer perceives is very different and will influence the overarching perceptual experience. Although the quality of the display and image size are important, the most influential factor in terms of optimizing behavioral realism is the type of interaction a user can have with the virtual environment. For example, images displayed on a computer monitor are limited in terms of interactive opportunities, with no direct link available between the observer's head movements and the updating of the images displayed on the screen. Furthermore, the means of navigation through a virtual environment presented on a computer monitor often involves input devices, such as a keyboard, mouse, or joystick, that do not directly map natural movement into the virtual environment. In these cases, the applications of this technology tend to be found where the maintenance of the perception/action loop is not so important (e.g., learning a procedural task such as how to assemble a piece of furniture; Watson *et al.*, 2010).

Displaying virtual environments

The CAVE (Computer Assisted Virtual Environment) systems, or large circular displays, are often the preferred means of simulation for engineers and designers who want to visualize real life displays and virtually test drive products before production. In these cases, the large projection screens result in the observer's visual field being filled, enhancing the feeling of immersion in the virtual environment. One problem with using these systems is that the range of movement is limited to the width of the screens (Miles *et al.*, 2012; Zaal & Bootsma, 2011), which can be a major constraining factor when studying perception and action in sport. Second, the projection of the virtual images is constrained by the position of the screens, which prevents the experience from being a fully immersive one (i.e., not 360-degree immersion). Finally, to simultaneously project on multiple screens this system requires a high-performance 3D projector for each screen and a group of powerful computers to generate and update the images to be projected in real time. This technology-laden solution to generate an immersive, interactive virtual environment is often a prohibitively expensive one.

An alternative form of display that can also provide an immersive, interactive experience is a stereoscopic head-mounted display (HMD). A stereoscopic HMD is a head-worn graphic display device that has one or two small display screens placed in front of the eyes. In some HMDs the distance between the screens can be adjusted so that differences in inter-ocular distance of the user can be accommodated, improving the binocular experience. In stark contrast to the CAVE, the size of the screens is very small and the field of view is significantly reduced (about 45° diagonal in some cases). However, very recently and triggered by an increased global interest in immersive, interactive gaming, a number of low-cost HMDs have been announced. These include the Oculus Rift (www.oculusvr.com/) and the as yet unreleased Sony Morpheus project. Unlike other HMDs on the market, the Oculus Rift provides a low persistence OLED stereoscopic display with a screen resolution of 960x1080 per eye and a relatively large FoV (c.100°). It connects via an HDMI cable to one controlling PC. It is important to note that in order to have an interactive experience with the images projected in the HMD it is very important that the head movements of the user are tracked in real time and used to update the images projected within the screens of the HMD. The next section will discuss in detail different systems that facilitate head tracking and interactions in a virtual environment.

Interacting with a virtual environment

Although the quality of graphics are important, research suggests that picture realism is not a determining factor when trying to use virtual reality technology to elicit realistic sporting behaviors (Bideau *et al.*, 2003; Vignais *et al.*, 2009). Instead, research has shown that it is the extent to which the user can interact with the environment and respond as he/she would in the real world that predominates (Zahorik & Jenison, 1998). In other words, it is important that an observer's own movement (action) is incorporated into changes in the display (perception) just as it would be in real life. By preserving the perception/action loop we normally experience when we move through a real environment (Gibson, 1979), the level of behavioral realism, or functional fidelity, in a virtual environment will be significantly increased.

With this in mind, improved digital display technology must therefore be combined with appropriate interactive technology to maximize the levels of presence, or feelings of immersion, in the virtual world. For instance, by adding a tracker to an HMD, the current head position and orientation can be captured in real time and used to update, also in real time, the images rendered within the display. This means that perception in the virtual world is active, where the viewpoint is determined by the head position and orientation of the observer. In other words, the movement of the observer will bring about transformations of the available optic array to create an optic flow (Gibson, 1979). This type of immersive, interactive virtual reality experience ensures that perception enables action and action enables perception, where a strong perception/action coupling is maintained (Bideau et al., 2010). In addition to being able to actively choose where and when to sample aspects of the virtual environment, the immersive experience is complete (i.e., 360 degrees) and is not limited to the physical position of a screen. This technology not only gives the observer an egocentric perspective of an event, but also allows the experimenters to precisely control and manipulate the information presented to the participants (perception) and measure the effects on action choices. In other words, it is an ideal tool to study the perception/action cycle and how information influences decisions about when and how to act. In terms of navigating through the environment, the type of head tracker used to update the viewpoint displayed within the HMD will determine the extent of displacement in the virtual environment, which can take place using natural movement.

Tracking movement

To ensure that the perception and action loop is maintained it is important that the amplitude and speed of movement in the real world maps onto the amplitude and speed of movement perceived in the virtual world. Movement in the real, and by default the virtual, environment will be constrained by the display used (e.g., a fixed screen), the capabilities of the tracking technology (e.g., a flock of birds tracker), or a combination of both. For instance, Correia et al. (2012) created an immersive, interactive virtual environment to look at ability to perceive a gap opening in a defensive line in rugby and how the perception of a gap influenced a player's decision about his/her future choice of action. In this study, they used an HMD combined with Intersense 900 technology (ultrasonic positioning with Sonistrips) to track both head and hand position and orientation (see Figure 17.1).

Figure 17.1 Perception of an opening gap in a defensive rugby line that is used in a decision-making task.

The head tracker meant the player's viewpoint was updated in real time and corresponded to where the player wanted to look, while the hand trackers allowed for the real-time animation of virtual depictions of his/her own hands in the virtual environment. To increase the levels of realism of the task, players were asked to hold a real rugby ball. By using the real-time data from the hand trackers, the position of the virtual hands and a virtual ball directly corresponded to the real position of the player's hands and the ball they held. By having the proprioceptive information from moving and holding the ball directly correspond to the virtual, visual representation of the ball and hands in the display, a greater level of immersion was obtained through sensory coherence. Representing the action in the perceptual task space is of critical importance and increases levels of engagement and task achievement (Dessing & Craig, 2010).

In spite of perception being coupled to action, the amount of physical movement that players could perform (e.g., running) was constrained by the tracking hardware configuration (Intersense 900) and by the wired tethering of the HMD to the computer that generated the virtual environment. In an ideal scenario, the user should be immersed in an environment that allows for movement without constraint. Multidirectional moving platforms have been developed as an alternative to allow for user movement, but again the complexity of using this technology and the high costs associated with it limits their use. A potential solution at relatively low cost is the Omni treadmill by Virtuix (www.virtuix.com/), where movement is made in a fixed area. It places the user on circular, frictionless zone pads that still allow the user to walk in place. However, it is limited in terms of application to perception and action research as it yields quite an unnatural movement, despite allowing for walking and running. As HMDs are typically tethered to a control unit, which interfaces to a controlling PC to provide power, data, and display input/output, it has been suggested that tethering should be minimized to increase body engagement (Slater et al., 1995). To overcome this, researchers have previously adapted HMDs to run on adapted battery-powered supplies placed in a backpack worn by the user. Additionally, as the power of PCs increases, their size decreases, making it increasingly more feasible to place the controlling PC within the backpack. An alternative system, which is not currently in widespread use, is the implementation of wireless video and data displays. New WHDMI technology uses radio frequencies to transmit video and audio data without increasing the latency or loss of quality. For instance, Sony has introduced a wireless HMD (Sony HMZ-T3W) for consumer use only, which may provide a potential solution for untethering the user from the main PC. This would allow for an increased range of movement and further the possibility of perception and action research in sporting applications. However, care must be taken to ensure there is no loss of data through electrical interference or dropout.

Recent developments in movement-based gaming have brought image-based tracking to the fore with technologies such as the Microsoft Kinect offering low-cost full body motion tracking that can be interfaced with a virtual environment. The Kinect is a markerless camera-based system making use of a monochrome integrated complementary metal oxide semiconductor (CMOS) to obtain depth information for recognition of human full-body gestures. Although it can track a simplified skeleton with 15 joints (Microsoft Kinect 1) at 30 frames per second, the Kinect cannot be used for accurate movement data collection. First, it interprets joint segment movement patterns to estimate human gestures and second, the speed of processing is not sufficient to capture high-speed movement such as that involved in sporting applications. While researchers have attempted to use the system as a cheaper alternative to the more expensive tracking systems, the data collected only gives an estimation of movement (Fernandez-Baena et al., 2012). Despite these limitations, the introduction of a consumer-based motion tracking sensor would help to further drive down the costs of i2VR technology and provide an impetus for improving overall functionality and accuracy.

Analyzing performance in a VR context

The tracking solutions mentioned above are more concerned with rendering the virtual environments interactive. In this section we will look at techniques that can be combined with i2VR to gain more of an insight into performance. Today, motion capture techniques fall into two categories: direct methods and imaging methods. Direct methods include the use of goniometers – hinged devices that are fitted at the joints and measure the changes in angle between limb segments during movement. However, by far the most widely used methods for measuring and analyzing motor performance are imaging techniques, such as video imaging and optoelectronic imaging. Video capture, a relatively inexpensive method, combined with specialist software is widely used by sport practitioners to analyze individual and/or team performance. High-speed video capture (on average up to 1,000 frames per second) allows for a more in-depth analysis (frame by frame) of a particular technique and provides an opportunity for the player and coach to analyze performance together.

Optoelectronic methods are used widely in both research and practice due to the different levels of analysis that can be performed. This technique involves fitting markers to limbs and joints on the body. These markers are either reflective (passive) or light emitting (active). Passive marker systems, such as the popular Vicon or Qualisys, use infrared cameras and reflective markers. Full-body motion capture for one person will usually involve somewhere in the region of 40 markers and 12 cameras. Rich data relating to the change in position over time for each individual marker is fed to a computer. From there, detailed analysis of the movement can be performed and outputs produced, such as displacement plots for the elbow during throwing. For kinetic analysis of a movement, this system is often integrated with force plates that can measure the ground reaction force, the center of pressure, and the vertical moment of force generated by standing on or moving across them. The data collected from this motion capture technique can then be used to analyze the kinematics of movement performance. More importantly for i2VR applications, these systems play an important role in capturing realistic actions that can then form the basis of animated movement in perception and action studies. This was the case for the side-step in rugby where real attacker versus defender duels were captured and used in a simulation to understand what information is picked up, and used by expert players to anticipate the future running direction of an attacking rugby player (Brault et al., 2012).

Advances in development technologies

In a review, Miles et al. (2012) noted that the most important factor for using virtual reality technology in a sporting context is functional fidelity. This includes the accurate modeling of the physics of the environment (e.g., ball flight, player movement), incorporating the real-time response of the player and offering a natural means to interact with the environment. Recent game development engines such as Unity 3D, Unreal 4, and CryEngine provide access to a large range of prewritten software libraries that offer an economical way of programming and managing realistic object or person movement in a virtual environment in real time. A recently developed immersive, interactive virtual reality bowling simulator for cricket (Dhawan, in preparation) showed how an Arduino board can be used to control and synchronize other movement-based systems (Qualisys and force platforms) to get a more detailed picture of player performance (see Figure 17.2). This interface is controlled via the Uniduino library within the Unity3D game engine. Customized software combines the strengths of two separate systems to provide high-quality perception/action data for real-time and offline processing.

Figure 17.2 Avatars were created in a virtual environment based on real motion capture data of elite Australian cricketers bowling. This was used to understand how novice and elite batsmen use perceptual information to guide decisions about when and how to act. Participants wore a head-mounted display that allowed them to become immersed in the virtual environment. To increase the level of presence, the participants swung a real bat that was also tracked in real time. The position and orientation of this bat was animated in real time in the virtual environment.

Sporting expertise research

Perception and action have been studied in a variety of contexts, making use of the technologies described above. Work by Bideau *et al.* (2010) highlights not only the advantages that VR offers over video playback in decision-making research, but also the importance of this technology in terms of the emerging results. For example, in a perception-only, rugby-based task where a real defender is confronted with a virtual attacker performing a deceptive stepping movement, results showed that there was a clear expert advantage over novices, with experts (professional rugby players) being able to judge the correct final running direction much earlier than novices (see Figure 17.3).

Most interestingly, the professional players judged by the coach to play the best "heads-up" rugby were significantly better than the other professional players tested. These results suggest that certain expert players can tune into the right information that specifies the correct final running direction and not the deceptive, body-based information that is specifying the incorrect final running direction (Brault *et al.*, 2012; Brault *et al.*, 2010). Other studies have also shown how this technology can allow us to study how information picked up from a ball trajectory (e.g., a curved free kick in soccer) influences decisions about how and when to act (see Figure 17.4) (Dessing & Craig, 2010; Craig *et al.*, 2006).

Figure 17.3 Participant wearing head-mounted display and control unit, taking part in a deceptive movement task.

Figure 17.4 An expert goalkeeper immersed in a virtual interactive environment where realistic curved free kicks were presented. Decisions about when and how the goalkeeper responded were directly recorded by the tracking technology.

Again, a clear expert advantage was found where an experienced, international goalkeeper waited longer before responding, leading to less movement errors in the wrong direction (Dessing & Craig, 2010). These cases present examples where VR has been shown to be an effective means of presenting sport scenarios in a realistic yet controllable way. Furthermore, there are promising possibilities in using this technology for practitioners through the development of virtual decision-making training environments, which could be used as an off-field training tool. This may be especially beneficial for injured players in that they could still benefit from the perceptual experience without having to carry out the physical practice.

Conclusions

Immersive, interactive virtual reality is an exciting new methodology to study perception and action in sport. It offers the possibility of precisely controlling the perceptual information and directly measuring how this influences decisions about when and how to act. By using this method to further our understanding of the interplay between detecting information, decision-making, and action capabilities, we will be able to further understand performance and develop new methods of training athletes and players in sport. However, care must be taken to ensure that certain features of the perception/action cycle are preserved in the simulation to maximize functional fidelity and avoid the trap of simulating for simulation's sake. The content of the simulation and its relevance to a real sporting context is of primordial importance. Also, the mapping of movement in the real world so that it corresponds to movement in the virtual world is key. With the gaming industry developing an increased interest in movement-based games and immersive, interactive displays, the technology, in the near future, should become more accessible to everyone. Exciting new developments such as the Sony HMZ-T3W and the Oculus Rift HMDs could offer new, affordable ways of making immersive, interactive virtual reality a novel and exciting way of enhancing athlete and player performance.

References

Abernethy, B., Thomas, K. T., & Thomas, J. T. (1993) 'Strategies for improving understanding of motor expertise (or mistakes we have made and things we have learned!)', in J. L. Starkes & F. Allard (eds) *Cognitive issues in motor expertise*, Amsterdam: Elsevier Science, 317–56.

Araújo, D., Davids, K., & Serpa, S. (2005) 'An ecological approach to expertise effects in decision-making in a simulated sailing regatta', *Psychology of Sport and Exercise*, 6(6): 671–92.

Bideau, B., Kulpa, R., Menardais, S., Fradet, L., Multon, F., Delamarche, P., & Arnaldi, B. (2003) 'Real handball goalkeeper versus virtual handball thrower', *Presence: Teleoperators and Virtual Environments*, 12(4): 411–21.

Bideau, B., Kulpa, R., Vignais, N., Brault, S., Multon, F., & Craig, C. (2010) 'Using virtual reality to analyze sports performance', *IEEE Computer Graphics and Applications*, 30: 14–21.

Brault, S., Bideau, B., Craig, C., & Kulpa, R. (2010) 'Balancing deceit and disguise: How to successfully fool the defender in a 1 versus 1 situation in rugby', *Human Movement Science*, 29: 412–25.

Brault, S., Bideau, B., Kulpa, R., & Craig, C. (2012) 'Detecting deception in movement: The case of the side-step in rugby', *PLoS One*, 7(6): e37494. doi: 10.1371/journal.pone.0037494

Brunswik, E. (1956) *Perception and the representative design of psychological experiments*, 2nd ed., Berkeley: University of California Press.

Correia, V., Araújo, D., Cummins, A., & Craig, C. M. (2012) 'Perceiving and acting upon spaces in a VR rugby task: Expertise effects in affordance detection and task achievement', *Journal of Sport & Exercise Psychology*, 34: 305–21.

Craig, C., & Watson, G. (2011) 'An affordance based approach to decision making in sport: Discussing a novel methodological framework', *Revista de Psicologia Del Deporte*, 20: 689–708.

Craig, C. M., Berton, E., Rao, G., Fernandez, L., & Bootsma, R. J. (2006) 'Judging where a ball will go: The case of curved free kicks in football', *Naturwissenschaften*, 93: 97–101.

New methods for studying perception

Croft, H., Chong, A., & Wilson, B. (2011) 'Virtual reality assessment of rugby lineout throw kinematics', *Sports Technology*, 4(1–2): 2–12.

Croft, H., Kardin Suwarganda, E., & Faris Syed Omar, S. (2013) 'Development and application of a live transmitting player-mounted head camera. Development and application of a live transmitting player-mounted head camera', *Journal of Sports Technology*, 6(2): 97–110.

Dessing, J. C., & Craig, C. M. (2010) 'Bending it like Beckham: How to visually fool the goalkeeper', *PLoS ONE*, 5(10). doi: 10.1371/journal.pone.0013161

Dhawan, A. (in preparation) 'Using technology to understand performance in sport', unpublished thesis, Queen's University Belfast.

Dicks, M., Button, C., & Davids, K. (2010) 'Availability of advance visual information constrains association-football goalkeeping performance during penalty kicks', *Perception*, 39(8): 1111–24.

Farrow, D., & Abernethy, B. (2003) 'Do expertise and the degree of perception – Action coupling affect natural anticipatory performance?', *Perception*, 32(9): 1127–39.

Farrow, D., & Fournier, J. (2005) 'Training perceptual skill in basketball: Does it benefit the highly skilled?', in *Proceedings of the ISSP 11th World Congress in Sport Psychology*, Sydney: International Society of Sport Psychology.

Fernandez-Baena, A., Susin, A., & Lligadas, X. (2012) 'Biomechanical validation of upper-body and lower-body joint movements of Kinect motion capture data for rehabilitation treatments', in *Proceedings of the International Conference on Intelligent Networking and Collaborative Systems*, Bucharest: INCoS, 656–61.

Gibson, J. J. (1979) *The ecological approach to visual perception*, Boston: Houghton Mifflin.

Helsen, W. F., & Pauwels, J. M. (1993) 'The relationship between expertise and visual information processing in sport', in J. L. Starkes & F. Allard (eds) *Cognitive issues in motor expertise*, Amsterdam: Elsevier, 109–34.

McMenemy, K., & Ferguson, S. (2007) *A hitchhiker's guide to virtual reality*, Wellesley, MA: A.K. Peters Ltd.

Miles, H. C., Pop, S. R., Watt, S. J., Lawrence, G. P., & John, N. W. (2012) 'Technical section: A review of virtual environments for training in ball sports', *Journal of Computer and Graphics*, 36(6): 714–26.

Petit, J., & Ripoll, H. (2008) 'Scene perceptions and decision making in sport simulation: A masked priming investigation', *International Journal of Sport Psychology*, 39(1): 1–19.

Savelsbergh, G. J. P., Williams, M., van der Kamp, J., & Ward, P. (2002) 'Visual search, anticipation and expertise in soccer goalkeepers', *Journal of Sports Science*, 20: 279–87.

Slater, M., Usoh, M., & Steed, A. (1995) 'Taking steps: The influence of a walking technique on presence in virtual reality', *ACM Trans. Comput.-Hum. Interact.*, 2: 201–19.

Tarr, M. J., & Warren, W. H. (2002) 'Virtual reality in behavioural neuroscience and beyond', *Nature Neuroscience*, 5: 1089–92.

Vignais, N., Bideau, B., Craig, C., Brault, S., Multon, F., Delamarche, P., & Kulpa, R. (2009) 'Does the level of graphical detail of a virtual handball thrower influence a goalkeeper's motor response?', *Journal of Sports Science & Medicine*, 8(4): 501–8.

Watson, G., Butterfield, J., Curran, R., & Craig, C. (2010) 'Do dynamic work instructions provide an advantage over static instructions in a small scale assembly task?', *Learning and Instruction*, 20: 84–93.

Williams, A. M., Davids, K., Burwitz, L., & Williams, J. G. (1994) 'Visual search strategies in experienced and inexperienced soccer players', *Research Quarterly for Exercise and Sport*, 65(2): 127–35.

Williams, A. M., Ward, P., Knowles, J. M., & Smeeton, N. J. (2002) 'Perceptual skill in a real world task: Training, instruction and transfer in tennis', *Journal of Experimental Psychology Applied*, 8: 259–70.

Zaal, F. T. J. M., & Bootsma, R. J. (2011) 'Virtual reality as a tool for the study of perception action: The case of running to catch fly balls', *Presence*, 20(1): 93–103.

Zahorik, P., & Jenison, R. L. (1998) 'Presence as being-in-the-world', *Presence: Teleoperators and Virtual Environments*, 7(1): 78–89.

18

METHODS FOR MEASURING PATTERN RECALL AND RECOGNITION IN SPORT EXPERTS

Adam D. Gorman

Introduction

There are many instances in the world where objects or information are configured in such a way as to create unique, domain-specific patterns. For example, the configuration of contours on a geographical map (Gilhooly *et al.*, 1988), the arrangement of lines of program code used in computer programming (Adelson, 1981), or the structures displayed in x-ray images used for medical diagnoses (Myles-Worsley *et al.*, 1988; Sowden *et al.*, 2000) are all situations where information is arranged, either naturally or somewhat artificially, into some form of structured and ordered pattern. In each of the aforementioned examples, highly experienced individuals have been shown to be superior to their less-skilled counterparts at recalling and/or recognizing the information contained within a pattern extracted from their domain of expertise (a perceptual skill typically referred to as "pattern perception") (Adelson, 1981; Gilhooly *et al.*, 1988; Myles-Worsley *et al.*, 1988; Sowden *et al.*, 2000; see also Chapter 2).

Structured patterns have also been shown to occur in the domain of team sports (e.g., Allard *et al.*, 1980; Garland & Barry, 1991). The patterns formed by the locations of players in sports such as basketball, soccer, or handball are not only unique to the sporting domain, but in comparison to the examples outlined previously, they are also unique in that they are highly dynamic and often fast-paced (North *et al.*, 2009). These characteristics place substantial temporal demands upon team sport performers, necessitating the rapid processing of perceptual information for successful performance (North *et al.*, 2009). As in other domains, research suggests that expert sport performers are more capable than their less-skilled counterparts at accurately extracting meaningful information from the relative locations of opponents and teammates in a structured action sequence (e.g., Allard *et al.*, 1980; Gorman *et al.*, 2011; Williams & Davids, 1995). Given that such a capability may underpin other important functions such as anticipation and decision-making (Farrow *et al.*, 2010; Gorman *et al.*, 2013a; North *et al.*, 2011; Williams & Davids, 1995), the extraction of pertinent information from structured team sport patterns represents a critical component of both scientific and practical utility (see also Chapter 2).

Methods for measuring pattern recall

Researchers measuring the pattern perception capabilities of individuals recruited from a broad array of different human pursuits have commonly employed either pattern recognition or pattern recall paradigms, or a combination of both (see also Gorman, 2014). This chapter will provide an overview of the evolution of these two methodological approaches as they apply to research on expert performance – initially in chess, and later in team sports – and will outline some of the issues and considerations surrounding their use. The final section of the chapter includes suggestions for future research in pattern perception, with a distinct focus on possible methodological advancements.

The evolution of pattern recall and pattern recognition measures

Given that the initial attempts at recognition and/or recall tests were specifically targeted towards investigating expert performance in highly experienced chess players (e.g., Chase & Simon, 1973; de Groot, 1965; Goldin, 1978; see also Vicente & de Groot, 1990), a discussion of the research in the chess domain is important for understanding the evolution of these two predominant paradigms. The intention of the earlier studies, as is typically the case in more contemporary studies of pattern perception, was to determine the underlying mechanisms that subserve expert performance (Gobet, 1998; Vicente & de Groot, 1990; for early examples from other domains, see Charness, 1979; Reitman, 1976). As cited in Vicente and de Groot (1990), some of the early research in this area is attributed to a study conducted by Djakow, Petrowski, and Rudik, who examined master chess players during the Great International Chess Tournament in Moscow. One of the tests employed during the research was a recall task where master players and non-players were asked to recall the locations of chess pieces positioned on a board after having viewed the board for one minute. Despite the fact that the master players could recall, on average, the locations of three times as many pieces as the non-players, the overall average for the masters was only 66 per cent (Vicente & de Groot, 1990). However, this result may have been due to the use of artificially generated chess positions as the test stimuli (Vicente & de Groot, 1990). The unusual configuration of pieces may have attenuated the capability of the skilled players to extract realistic and meaningful information from the patterns, thereby reducing the accuracy of their recall performance (Vicente & de Groot, 1990). As will be discussed later in this chapter, the use of non-representative test stimuli in studies of pattern perception has been a major limitation in the methodological approach (Borgeaud & Abernethy, 1987; Gorman *et al.*, 2011; Williams *et al.*, 1993).

A later study conducted by de Groot (1965) also used a recall task to examine chess expertise, but improved upon the earlier design by arranging the chess pieces in the test patterns to show a typical game configuration that was likely to better reflect the processing demands experienced by players during normal competition (see also Vicente & de Groot, 1990). In addition, the presentation time permitted for viewing the locations of the chess pieces was reduced from 60 seconds to between two and 15 seconds, which, arguably, may have reduced the participants' propensity for boredom or mental fatigue during their completion of the task (see Vicente & de Groot, 1990). The results reported by de Groot (1965) were quite remarkable. The highest ranked chess player (a grandmaster) recalled an amazing 93 per cent of the chess pieces, compared to around 50 per cent for the lowest ranked player. While it is difficult to be certain, the increase in recall accuracy for the highly credentialed player may have been facilitated by the methodological improvements – namely, more representative test stimuli combined with reduced, but still manageable, presentation times (Vicente & de Groot, 1990).

The next evolutionary step in the design of the recall task is largely credited to the influential work of Chase and Simon (1973; but see Vicente & de Groot, 1990, for similar work that preceded that of Chase & Simon, 1973). The investigators followed the typical recall approach of de Groot (1965), but elected to include an additional set of test stimuli comprised of chess boards containing randomly placed chess pieces that bore only minimal resemblance to the types of configurations experienced in a typical game. The results for the representative positions once again revealed the superiority of the more advanced players at recalling structured chess positions. However, the results for the random positions were startling: the superiority of the most adept player was reduced to a level that was similar to that of a beginner. These results provided further evidence to demonstrate that the expert advantage in recall tasks is highly task specific and is therefore heavily influenced by the way in which the information in a stimulus pattern is displayed (Chase & Simon, 1973; see also Gobet, 1998; Saariluoma, 1984).

An examination of the underlying characteristics that define expert chess performance was also the focus of some of the initial studies using the pattern recognition paradigm (Goldin, 1978, 1979; Saariluoma, 1984; see also North et al., 2009; Williams et al., 2006). The general methodology, as it is now, typically involves presenting players of various skill levels with a series of chess patterns before asking those same players to identify (i.e., recognize) the presented patterns from amongst a set of previously unseen patterns (e.g., Goldin, 1978, 1979; Saariluoma, 1984). For example, Goldin (1979, experiment 2) showed high- and low-skilled players 80 diagrams of chess patterns, which comprised 40 patterns extracted from actual games and 40 random patterns showing atypical configurations that were not representative of a game. Participants were told that after viewing the full series of 80 diagrams in an initial presentation phase, they would complete a follow-up task where they would be required to differentiate those images from amongst a set of entirely new images (half of the images in the recognition test were new, and the other half were from the earlier presentation phase). Goldin (1979) found that the most experienced players were more accurate in their recognition of the patterns when compared to the less-skilled players. However, one of the interesting findings to emerge from this, and other subsequent research using the recognition paradigm (e.g., North et al., 2009; Saariluoma, 1984; Williams & Davids, 1995; Williams et al., 2006), was that the expected deterioration of the experts' recognition accuracy to that of a less-skilled player on the randomly configured patterns (as has been shown in recall tasks; e.g., Chase & Simon, 1973) was surprisingly absent. Although this result is not always evident in recognition tasks (e.g., Garland & Barry, 1991; Williams et al., 1993), the differences in the results generated by the recall and recognition paradigms for the random images may have been due to the fundamental differences between the two methodological approaches (Goldin, 1978, 1979; Saariluoma, 1984).

Given that a typical recall task requires participants to memorize and then recall the location of the entire array of elements within a stimulus pattern, whereas a recognition task can be completed by identifying only a small subsection of the pattern, it has been suggested that the two tasks may in fact measure different perceptual qualities (Allard et al., 1980; Goldin, 1978, 1979; Gorman et al., 2012; Saariluoma, 1984; Thorton & Hayes, 2004; Williams et al., 1993). Specifically, a recall task is likely to determine a performer's capability to encode the relationships that exist between each element of a given pattern within the problem space (Saariluoma, 1984). This may require a greater understanding of the underlying rules and mechanisms that constrain the overall behavior of the pattern itself (Goldin, 1979; Saariluoma, 1984). A recognition task, while still requiring some level of understanding of the typical structural behaviors of a pattern, may require only a single cue from within the overall problem space to be retrieved in order to complete the task successfully (Goldin, 1979; Saariluoma, 1984). Thus, in the case of randomly arranged patterns, the encoding processes employed during a recall task are likely to be disrupted to a far greater extent by the changes in the relationships between the elements within the pattern as compared to a recognition task (Goldin, 1979; Saariluoma, 1984). In addition, recall and recognition paradigms have different time periods between the presentation of the stimulus pattern and the subsequent initiation of the participant's response. A typical recall task requires the observed stimulus pattern to be reconstructed immediately, whereas a recognition task requires the stimulus pattern to be retained in memory over a much greater time frame (sometimes several minutes) (see Allard *et al.*, 1980; Garland & Barry, 1991; Williams *et al.*, 1993). Collectively, the aforementioned differences represent an important consideration for research designs used to examine pattern perception.

Pattern recall and pattern recognition measures in the sporting domain

Some of the early research in the sporting domain using recall and recognition tasks was conducted by Allard *et al.* (1980), who were interested in measuring the contribution of perceptual skill to expert basketball performance. The researchers applied the basic format of previous methodologies by using a series of structured and unstructured static slides ($n = 40$) extracted from an actual basketball game as their test patterns. The structured slides displayed game situations that were characteristic of normal playing patterns, whereas the random slides showed typically unstructured sequences of play such as fast breaks and turnovers. During the recall task, players and non-players were shown each slide for a period of four seconds, after which time they were required to reproduce the elements (i.e., players) within the pattern by placing magnets representing the locations of the attacking and defending players onto a scaled diagram of a basketball court. Directly after the recall task, the same participants completed a recognition task where they were presented with another set of structured and unstructured game slides (half of which had not been previously shown) and asked to identify those they had seen in the earlier recall task. The results replicated the findings reported from research into chess expertise (e.g., Chase & Simon, 1973), with the skilled players exhibiting superior recall of structured slides only. The results from the recognition test showed skilled players to be better than non-players at identifying previously seen patterns, but similar to the research in the chess domain (e.g., Goldin, 1979; Saariluoma, 1984), there were no significant skill-based effects related to the level of structure of the slides (although the authors noted a trend in the results showing superior performance by the skilled players for structured slides only).

Representative test stimuli and advanced scoring methods

Since the early work by Allard *et al.* (1980), subsequent investigations into expert pattern perception have been conducted across a diverse selection of team sports, including rugby union (Farrow *et al.*, 2010), volleyball (Borgeaud & Abernethy, 1987), and soccer (North *et al.*, 2011; Williams & Davids, 1995; see also Chapter 2). The basic method employed within the later studies has remained quite consistent with the earlier work, but, importantly, there have been a number of methodological enhancements. One of the major changes has been the introduction of video images as the test stimuli to replace the static and/or schematic images that artificially simplified and constrained the normally dynamic and environmentally rich setting that is characteristic of a team sport competition (Borgeaud & Abernethy, 1987; Gorman *et al.*, 2011; Williams *et al.*, 1993). Although static team sport images may still display many of the same performance variables as a video image (e.g., rules and court/field markings; Tenenbaum *et al.*, 1994), studies have shown that the extent of the expert advantage may increase when the image captures more of the characteristics of the natural setting (Gorman *et al.*, 2011, 2012, 2013a; Starkes *et al.*, 1994; see also Helsen & Starkes, 1999). In addition, the representation of static objects may involve different processing demands than those required during the observation of moving objects (Kourtzi & Nakayama, 2002; see also DeLucia & Maldia, 2006). Despite the fact that static images are often easier to manipulate, capture, and control for experimental purposes, and continue to be used in contemporary investigations of expert performance (e.g., Didierjean & Marmèche, 2005; Laurent *et al.*, 2006; Millslagle, 2002), the underlying nature of the expert advantage is likely to be better captured using stimuli that maintain the temporal and spatial features of the normal team sport setting (Borgeaud & Abernethy, 1987).

Another methodological advancement has occurred in the measurement techniques used to assess recall performance. Some researchers have elected to use computer-based measures (e.g., Gorman *et al.*, 2012, 2013a, 2013b; Williams *et al.*, 1993), which offer a far more objective and sensitive measure than some of the binary scoring systems (e.g., Abernethy *et al.*, 2005; Farrow, 2010) that assessed recall accuracy by manually comparing the participant's response pattern to a transparent answer template placed overhead (Gorman *et al.*, 2012). Research designs using computer-based measurements have required participants to complete recall tasks by using a computer mouse to place pattern elements onto a screen, allowing absolute error measures of recall performance to be accurately calculated for statistical analysis (e.g., Gorman *et al.*, 2012, 2013a, 2013b; Williams *et al.*, 1993).

Innovative methods for examining recall and recognition performance

Further attempts to examine the underlying features that define expert pattern perception have employed some relatively novel experimental methods. For example, Williams *et al.* (2006) used point-light displays and spatial occlusion to examine the specific sources of information used by expert soccer players when viewing video-based action sequences. For the point-light display, the players depicted in the test clips were replaced by colored dots shown on a black background. The logic behind this approach was that the superficial display features would be removed (such as the postural orientation of the players), while still maintaining the key structural information (such as the distances between players and their relative motion characteristics) (for an earlier example of the point-light display method, see Johansson, 1973). For the spatial occlusion experiment, the test images included all of the normal display features, but the two central attacking players and their immediate defenders were erased from each test clip (for an earlier example of the spatial occlusion technique in the sporting domain, see Abernethy & Russell, 1987). Results from pattern recognition tests using the point-light displays showed that skilled soccer players were able to recognize previously viewed patterns with superior speed and accuracy compared to less-skilled players. The fact that the expert advantage was maintained in the absence of superficial display information suggested that the relational information between pattern elements may be more important for facilitating expert pattern perception compared to surface features such as postural orientation (Williams *et al.*, 2006; see also North *et al.*, 2009; North *et al.*, 2011; Laurent *et al.*, 2006). The results for the spatially occluded test clips showed that the removal of key pattern features – in this instance, the central attackers and their defenders – reduced the ability of both skilled and less-skilled players to recognize soccer patterns. The decrement in performance on the spatially occluded clips was particularly pronounced for the skilled players, suggesting that certain elements within a pattern are critical for maintaining the underlying structural relationships that underpin expert perception (Williams *et al.*, 2006; see also Gorman *et al.*, 2013a, 2013b).

While novel experimental manipulations such as those just described have further advanced the understanding of pattern perception, there are some important methodological features that should be considered. In particular, when certain pattern elements are occluded, it is possible that both the overall structure of a given pattern and the nature of the interactions between

Methods for measuring pattern recall

individual pattern elements are substantially altered, even when just a single feature within the pattern is removed (see Huys *et al.*, 2009). In such instances, any decrement in recognition performance may be attributable to the changes in the relationships between the occluded element and the remaining elements, rather than being solely attributed to the single element that was removed (Huys *et al.*, 2009). For example, in the research by Williams *et al.* (2006), the removal of the centrally located players may have resulted in a decline in performance due to changes in the interactions between the occluded elements and the remaining elements (see Huys *et al.*, 2009). If this was indeed the case, it would not be possible to conclude, with absolute certainty, that the centrally located players were solely responsible for the decrement in expert recognition performance (see Huys *et al.*, 2009). In addition, Williams *et al.* (2006) instructed participants to respond both quickly *and* accurately during the completion of the recognition task. This instructional set may recreate some of the typical demands of an actual team sport competition, but it may also introduce a greater potential for a speed-accuracy trade-off (described by Abernethy *et al.*, 2005). While similar instructions have been used in other recognition studies (e.g., North *et al.*, 2009; Williams & Davids, 1995), the emphasis upon both speed and accuracy may confound the interpretation of the results if participants differ in their approach to completing the task (Abernethy *et al.*, 2005). To reduce such possibilities, participants could be instructed to simply complete the task as accurately as possible, thereby reducing the emphasis upon a rapid response (Gorman *et al.*, 2011, 2013a; see also Allard *et al.*, 1980).

Anticipatory measures of pattern recall and recognition

One of the interesting findings reported by de Groot (1965) in his investigation of chess expertise was the tendency of the master player to apply a form of anticipatory memory encoding during the completion of the recall task. De Groot (1965) reported that the chess pieces were often reproduced by placing them in a position on the board where they were likely to be moved at some point in the near future, rather than placing the pieces in the location that was displayed during the actual test (see also Goldin, 1979; Gorman *et al.*, 2012). Despite the fact that such findings suggest the presence of an anticipatory component in expert pattern perception, further investigations to explore this notion have been relatively limited in the extant literature (but see Didierjean & Marmèche, 2005; Ferrari, Didierjean, & Marmèche, 2006; Goldin, 1979; Gorman *et al.*, 2011, 2012, 2013a).

In the few studies that have investigated the anticipatory nature of expert pattern perception, the typical approach has been similar to the recognition and recall paradigms used earlier, but with some additional features embedded either within the paradigm itself, or within the scoring system used to measure performance. For example, Didierjean and Marmèche (2005) used a recognition task to examine anticipatory pattern perception in expert basketball players. The researchers created pairs of schematic basketball patterns where the second pattern in each pair showed the next likely progression of the first pattern. Using both short- and long-term recognition tasks, participants were required to either differentiate between pairs of patterns presented one after another, or identify patterns they had been asked to examine during an earlier memorization phase, respectively. During the short-term task, the two patterns in each pair were presented in three different display orders. One variation presented the two patterns in the normal chronological order of a game; the second variation presented the two patterns in reverse chronological order; the third condition simply presented two identical patterns one after the other. After viewing the first pattern in a given pair for five seconds, the second pattern was presented one second later, and participants were asked to state whether the two patterns were the same or different. The long-term task used the same set of test stimuli, but on this occasion, participants were asked to memorize a set of patterns before attempting to identify those same configurations from amongst a set of new patterns during a recognition phase. The new patterns included possible subsequent states and possible earlier states of the memorized patterns. The results from both the short- and long-term tasks showed that the experienced basketball players tended to be less accurate when attempting to differentiate between patterns that were presented in the normal progression of a game. The authors believed that the experienced players were anticipating the movements of the players depicted within the patterns and were thus encoding the first presented image as a possible subsequent state, rather than encoding the image in its original form. This, they thought, made it difficult for the experienced players to differentiate between patterns when they were presented in the usual sequence of a game (i.e., chronological order). Further advancements to this protocol by Gorman *et al.* (2011) have included more representative test stimuli involving dynamic video images showing patterns extracted from an actual game. Importantly, the results supported those of Didierjean and Marmèche (2005) by once again highlighting the anticipatory tendencies of expert basketball players when perceiving structured patterns extracted from their sport.

To further investigate the anticipatory features of pattern perception, Gorman *et al.* (2012; see also 2013a) used a typical recall paradigm to examine the extent to which expert basketball players, relative to novices, anticipated the movements of players in a structured team sport image. The methodological approach was similar to previous recall studies, where participants were asked to reproduce the locations of players shown in a structured pattern, but the technique used to measure recall accuracy provided an estimate of the magnitude of the anticipatory effect. The response patterns generated by participants were compared to the target pattern, as well as to a series of subsequent patterns that occurred immediately after the target pattern. A computer measured the distance between the participants' entered pattern elements and the actual pattern elements to produce an overall error measure of recall performance. The results showed that, on average, the response patterns entered by the experts were more closely aligned to patterns that occurred at some point in advance of the presented target patterns, with this advance being significantly further into the future than that observed for novices. The findings indicated that the experts were not only anticipating the evolution of the presented patterns, but they also suggested that, as a result of this anticipatory tendency, the recall scores reported in other studies using the recall paradigm may have been somewhat underestimated (Gorman *et al.*, 2012; see also Gorman *et al.*, 2013a).

Measurement of attentional focus in expert pattern perception

Research into pattern perception has also examined how attentional focus influences the extraction of information from a team sport action sequence. While few studies in this area currently exist, the typical approach has involved the use of carefully designed instructional sets that direct the attention of participants towards certain information within the test stimuli (e.g., Gorman *et al.*, 2013b; Weber & Brewer, 2003). For example, Weber and Brewer (2003) used patterns presented as audio recordings of field hockey playing sequences to compare the recall performance of experts and novices when attentional focus was directed to either (a) irrelevant pattern information, or (b) to information that was closely related to the underlying structure of the pattern of play. In the latter condition, participants were asked to identify the team that had the advantage or the team that was in control of the play, whereas in the former condition, participants were asked to state the names of the players described in the playing sequence. The results showed that the experts' recall accuracy declined significantly when their attention was directed towards the irrelevant pattern information, compared to when they were instructed to focus upon more game-specific information (for an example in chess, see Lane & Robertson, 1979; see also Goldin, 1978). However, given that the test stimuli were presented to participants as audio recordings, which obviously excluded all of the critical visual information, the results were somewhat limited (Gorman *et al.*, 2013b).

A different experimental design was used by Gorman *et al.* (2013b) to further examine the influence of attentional focus on pattern perception. In an attended condition, expert and novice basketball players were asked to recall the final locations of the attacking players from a series of 12 video-based basketball action sequences. Then, immediately after viewing an additional (13th) pattern in the series, participants completed an unattended condition where they were asked to recall only the locations of the defending players. The same procedure was also employed in reverse to examine the capability of participants to recall the attacking players when their attention had been focused upon the defenders. Not surprisingly, the performance of both skill groups deteriorated when they were asked to recall the unattended pattern elements. However, quite remarkably, not only were the experts able to recall more of the unattended players from the patterns than the novices, but the experts were also able to maintain their recall performance for the attacking players, even when their attentional resources were directed towards the defenders. Given the limited number of studies investigating the influence of attentional focus on expert pattern perception, this area clearly represents an intriguing avenue for further research (Gorman *et al.*, 2013b; see also Furley *et al.*, 2010; Memmert, 2009; Memmert & Furley, 2007).

Measuring transfer in recall and recognition

The recall and recognition paradigms have also been employed to examine the extent to which pattern perception skills transfer between sports. The predominant method has involved presenting expert and less-skilled team sport players with images extracted from their own sport, as well as presenting them with images extracted from one or more other team sports (e.g., Smeeton *et al.*, 2004). The underlying logic behind such approaches is quite simple. If the recall and/or recognition performance for patterns extracted from their own sport is similar to the performance exhibited for patterns from outside their preferred sport, then it is likely that some degree of transfer between the sports is evident (Abernethy *et al.*, 2005; Smeeton *et al.*, 2004). While further research in this area is required (Abernethy *et al.*, 2012), empirical evidence suggests that transfer between sports is indeed possible, provided the sports share similar structural and organizational characteristics such as rules, tactics, and playing formations (see Allard & Starkes, 1991; Gorman *et al.*, 2011; Smeeton *et al.*, 2004; see also Abernethy *et al.*, 2005). For example, pattern perception skills are more likely to transfer between soccer and hockey than between soccer and volleyball (Smeeton *et al.*, 2004; see also Gorman *et al.*, 2011).

Future directions for measuring pattern recall and pattern recognition in the sporting domain

The methodologies used to assess pattern perception in sport experts have undergone substantial changes over a period spanning several decades. However, there are a number of additional methodological changes that could continue to advance the area. Primary amongst these is the need to further enhance the representativeness of the test stimuli (Williams & Ericsson, 2005). While the use of dynamic video sequences has been a step in the right direction, two-dimensional displays, coupled with either pen-and-paper or computer-based responses, clearly fail to capture the full array of variables present in the natural setting (for a discussion of alternative methods, see Williams & Ericsson, 2005). One possible solution could be to use in situ recall and/or recognition tests where participants are required to respond to real action scenarios (Williams & Ericsson, 2005; see also Starkes & Lindley, 1994). For example, while competing in a normal basketball game, skilled players could be asked to recall the previous locations of teammates and opponents at a certain point in the game (see Starkes & Lindley, 1994; Williams & Ericsson, 2005). Similar types of in situ methods have already been employed to measure decision-making in team sports including basketball (Starkes & Lindley, 1994) and netball (Bruce *et al.*, 2012).

Another addition to the measurement of pattern perception could be the inclusion of brain imaging techniques. In particular, the advent of functional magnetic resonance imaging may allow researchers to examine the specific regions of the brain that are active during a typical recall and recognition task, and compare these to the areas that are active when subtle changes are made to the stimulus patterns. This could help to confirm whether the processing demands used by experts are indeed different when viewing random versus real patterns, or when viewing patterns that have been altered in some way through spatial occlusion or point-light displays (see Allard *et al.*, 1980; Williams *et al.*, 2006). Brain imaging may also help to identify the neural correlates relating to the underlying mechanisms that subserve the expert advantage in pattern perception (see Aglioti *et al.*, 2008; Wright *et al.*, 2010).

Finally, a potentially informative approach for exploring team sport pattern perception may be to include a combination of different, but still complementary, measures to provide a truly rich data set from which to examine the underlying attributes that contribute to skilled performance (Williams & Ericsson, 2005). Noteworthy efforts in this regard have been made by North and colleagues (North *et al.*, 2011; North *et al.*, 2009) by combining eye tracking data and verbal reports with tests of pattern recognition and anticipation. For example, eye tracking data collected from soccer players as they completed a recognition task showed that skilled players fixated upon significantly more locations in the images compared to less-skilled players, irrespective of whether the images were shown as video clips or as point-light displays (North *et al.*, 2009). This, in combination with the accuracy scores, further demonstrated that the experts were likely to be relying upon the structural information contained within the patterns in order to complete the recognition task (North *et al.*, 2009). Verbal report data collected from participants immediately after viewing each pattern during a recognition task showed that skilled participants tended to make more evaluative statements (North *et al.*, 2011). This was interpreted as evidence of the skilled players' tendency to formulate plans and strategies based upon the perceived likelihood of certain events (North *et al.*, 2011). The utility of multifactorial approaches towards the measurement of pattern perception may provide a highly fruitful methodological advancement for future investigations.

References

Abernethy, B., Baker, J., & Côté, J. (2005) 'Transfer of pattern recall skills may contribute to the development of sport expertise', *Applied Cognitive Psychology*, 19: 705–18.

Abernethy, B., Farrow, D., Gorman, A. D., & Mann, D. L. (2012) 'Anticipatory behavior and expert performance', in N. J. Hodges & A. M. Williams (eds) *Skill acquisition in sport: Research, theory and practice*, London: Routledge, 287–305.

Abernethy, B., & Russell, D. G. (1987) 'Expert-novice differences in an applied selective attention task', *Journal of Sport Psychology*, 9: 326–45.

Adelson, B. (1981) 'Problem solving and the development of abstract categories in programming languages', *Memory & Cognition*, 9: 422–33.

Aglioti, S. M., Cesari, P., Romani, M., & Urgesi, C. (2008) 'Action anticipation and motor resonance in elite basketball players', *Nature Neuroscience*, 11: 1109–16.

Allard, F., Graham, S., & Paarsalu, M. E. (1980) 'Perception in sport: Basketball', *Journal of Sport Psychology*, 2: 14–21.

Allard, F., & Starkes, J. L. (1991) 'Motor-skill experts in sports, dance, and other domains', in K. A. Ericsson & J. Smith (eds) *Toward a general theory of expertise: Prospects and limits*, Cambridge: Cambridge University Press, 126–52.

Borgeaud, P., & Abernethy, B. (1987) 'Skilled perception in volleyball defense', *Journal of Sport Psychology*, 9: 400–6.

Bruce, L., Farrow, D., Raynor, A., & Mann, D. (2012) 'But I can't pass that far! The influence of motor skill on decision making', *Psychology of Sport and Exercise*, 13: 152–61.

Charness, N. (1979) 'Components of skill in bridge', *Canadian Journal of Psychology*, 31: 1–16.

Chase, W. G., & Simon, H. A. (1973) 'Perception in chess', *Cognitive Psychology*, 4: 55–81.

de Groot, A. D. (1965) *Thought and choice in chess*, The Hague, NL: Mouton.

DeLucia, P. R., & Maldia, M. M. (2006) 'Visual memory for moving scenes', *The Quarterly Journal of Experimental Psychology*, 59: 340–60.

Didierjean, A., & Marmèche, E. (2005) 'Anticipatory representation of visual basketball scenes by novice and expert players', *Visual Cognition*, 12: 265–83.

Ericsson, K. A., & Lehmann, A. C. (1996) 'Expert and exceptional performance: Evidence of maximal adaptation to task constraints', *Annual Review of Psychology*, 47: 273–305.

Farrow, D. (2010) 'A multi-factorial examination of the development of skill expertise in high performance netball', *Talent Development & Excellence*, 2: 123–35.

Farrow, D., McCrae, J., Gross, J., & Abernethy, B. (2010) 'Revisiting the relationship between pattern recall and anticipatory skill', *International Journal of Sport Psychology*, 41: 91–106.

Ferrari, V., Didierjean, A., & Marmèche, E. (2006) 'Dynamic perception in chess', *The Quarterly Journal of Experimental Psychology*, 59: 397–410.

Furley, P., Memmert, D., & Heller, C. (2010) 'The dark side of visual awareness in sport: Inattentional blindness in a real-world basketball task', *Attention, Perception, & Psychophysics*, 72: 1327–37.

Garland, D. J., & Barry, J. R. (1991) 'Cognitive advantage in sport: The nature of perceptual structures', *American Journal of Psychology*, 104: 211–28.

Gilhooly, K. J., Wood, M., Kinnear, P. R., & Green, C. (1988) 'Skill in map reading and memory for maps', *Quarterly Journal of Experimental Psychology*, 40A: 87–107.

Gobet, F. (1998) 'Expert memory: A comparison of four theories', *Cognition*, 66: 115–52.

Goldin, S. E. (1978) 'Effects of orienting tasks on recognition of chess positions', *American Journal of Psychology*, 91: 659–71.

Goldin, S. E. (1979) 'Recognition memory for chess positions: Some preliminary research', *American Journal of Psychology*, 92: 19–31.

Gorman, A. D. (2014) 'Pattern recognition and recall', in R. C. Eklund & G. Tenenbaum (eds) *Encyclopedia of sport and exercise psychology*, vol. 2, Thousand Oaks, CA: SAGE Publications, 521–2.

Gorman, A. D., Abernethy, B., & Farrow, D. (2011) 'Investigating the anticipatory nature of pattern perception in sport', *Memory & Cognition*, 39: 894–901.

Gorman, A. D., Abernethy, B., & Farrow, D. (2012) 'Classical pattern recall tests and the prospective nature of expert performance', *The Quarterly Journal of Experimental Psychology*, 65: 1151–60.

Gorman, A. D., Abernethy, B., & Farrow, D. (2013a) 'Is the relationship between pattern recall and decision-making influenced by anticipatory recall?', *The Quarterly Journal of Experimental Psychology*, 66: 2219–36.

Gorman, A. D., Abernethy, B., & Farrow, D. (2013b) 'The expert advantage in dynamic pattern recall persists across both attended and unattended display elements', *Attention, Perception, & Psychophysics*, 75: 835–44.

Helsen, W. F., & Starkes, J. L. (1999) 'A multidimensional approach to skilled perception and performance in sport', *Applied Cognitive Psychology*, 13: 1–27.

Huys, R., Cañal-Bruland, R., Hagemann, N., Beek, P. J., Smeeton, N. J., & Williams, A. M. (2009) 'Global information pickup underpins anticipation of tennis shot direction', *Journal of Motor Behavior*, 41: 158–70.

Johansson, G. (1973) 'Visual perception of biological motion and a model for its analysis', *Perception & Psychophysics*, 14: 201–11.

Kourtzi, Z., & Nakayama, K. (2002) 'Distinct mechanisms for the representation of moving and static objects', *Visual Cognition*, 9: 248–64.

Lane, D. M., & Robertson, L. (1979) 'The generality of the levels of processing hypothesis: An application for memory to chess positions', *Memory & Cognition*, 7: 253–6.

Laurent, E., Ward, P., Williams, A. M., & Ripoll, H. (2006) 'Expertise in basketball modifies perceptual discrimination abilities, underlying cognitive processes, and visual behaviours', *Visual Cognition*, 13: 247–71.

Memmert, D. (2009) 'Pay attention! A review of visual attentional expertise in sport', *International Review of Sport and Exercise Psychology*, 2: 119–38.

Memmert, D., & Furley, P. (2007) '"I spy with my little eye!": Breadth of attention, inattentional blindness, and tactical decision making in team sports', *Journal of Sport & Exercise Psychology*, 29: 365–81.

Millslagle, D. G. (2002) 'Recognition accuracy by experienced men and women players of basketball', *Perceptual and Motor Skills*, 95: 163–72.

Myles-Worsley, M., Johnston, W. A., & Simons, M. A. (1988) 'The influence of expertise on x-ray image processing', *Journal of Experimental Psychology: Learning, Memory, and Cognition*, 14: 553–7.

North, J. S., Ward, P., Ericsson, A., & Williams, A. M. (2011) 'Mechanisms underlying skilled anticipation and recognition in a dynamic and temporally constrained domain', *Memory*, 19: 155–68.

North, J. S., Williams, A. M., Hodges, N., Ward, P., & Ericsson, K. A. (2009) 'Perceiving patterns in dynamic action sequences: Investigating the processes underpinning stimulus recognition and anticipation skill', *Applied Cognitive Psychology*, 23: 878–94.

Reitman, J. S. (1976) 'Skilled perception in go: Deducing memory structures from inter-response times', *Cognitive Psychology*, 8: 336–56.

Saariluoma, P. (1984) *Coding problem spaces in chess: A psychological study*, Helsinki: Societas Scientiarum Fennica.

Smeeton, N. J., Ward, P., & Williams, A. M. (2004) 'Do pattern recognition skills transfer across sports? A preliminary analysis', *Journal of Sports Sciences*, 22: 205–13.

Sowden, P. T., Davies, I.R.L., & Roling, P. (2000) 'Perceptual learning of the detection of features in x-ray images: A functional role for improvements in adults' visual sensitivity?', *Journal of Experimental Psychology: Human Perception and Performance*, 26: 379–90.

Starkes, J., Allard, F., Lindley, S., & O'Reilly, K. (1994) 'Abilities and skill in basketball', *International Journal of Sport Psychology*, 25: 249–65.

Starkes, J. L., & Lindley, S. (1994) 'Can we hasten expertise by video simulations?', *Quest*, 46: 211–22.

Tenenbaum, G., Levy-Kolker, N., Bar-Eli, M., & Weinberg, R. (1994) 'Information recall of younger and older skilled athletes: The role of display complexity, attentional resources and visual exposure duration', *Journal of Sports Sciences*, 12: 529–34.

Thornton, I. M., & Hayes, A. E. (2004) 'Anticipating action in complex scenes', *Visual Cognition*, 11: 341–70.

Vicente, K. J., & de Groot, A. D. (1990) 'The memory recall paradigm: Straightening out the historical record', *The American Psychologist*, 45: 285–7.

Weber, N., & Brewer, N. (2003) 'Expert memory: The interaction of stimulus structure, attention, and expertise', *Applied Cognitive Psychology*, 17: 295–308.

Williams, A. M., & Ericsson, K. A. (2005) 'Perceptual-cognitive expertise in sport: Some considerations when applying the expert performance approach', *Human Movement Science*, 24: 283–307.

Williams, A. M., Hodges, N. J., North, J. S., & Barton, G. (2006) 'Perceiving patterns of play in dynamic sport tasks: Investigating the essential information underlying skilled performance', *Perception*, 35: 317–32.

Williams, M., & Davids, K. (1995) 'Declarative knowledge in sport: A by-product of experience or a characteristic of expertise?', *Journal of Sport & Exercise Psychology*, 17: 259–75.

Williams, M., Davids, K., Burwitz, L., & Williams, J. (1993) 'Cognitive knowledge and soccer performance', *Perceptual and Motor Skills*, 76: 579–93.

Wright, M. J., Bishop, D. T., Jackson, R. C., & Abernethy, B. (2010) 'Functional MRI reveals expert-novice differences during sport-related anticipation', *NeuroReport*, 21: 94–8.

19

CAPTURING GROUP TACTICAL BEHAVIORS IN EXPERT TEAM PLAYERS

Duarte Araújo, Pedro Silva, and Keith Davids

Over the last two decades there has been increasing interest in identifying properties of sport teams that are more than the sum of the properties of their members (Eccles & Tenenbaum, 2004; Salas *et al.*, 1997). Team behaviors emerge from interactions of three or more players looking to cooperate and compete together to achieve common goals, while communicating through synergetic relations (Riley *et al.*, 2011; Silva *et al.*, 2013). Joint analysis of individual behaviors can translate to group behaviors as all players constrain and, in turn, are constrained by the dynamic, integrated system that they compose (Glazier, 2010). Expert teams are characterized by high levels of performance outcomes, achieved by the team's effective utilization of member expertise and mastery of group processes (Salas *et al.*, 2006). Research on expert, non-sport team performance (see Salas *et al.*, 2006) has revealed that: i) expert members are able to combine their individual expertise and coordinate actions to achieve a common goal, ii) the team as a whole creates a synergy, iii) expert teams solve problems quickly and accurately, iv) when faced with novel situations, members can predict events and create new procedures, and v) expert teams are adaptive.

Theories of expertise in team sports

Sport team performance has been extensively analyzed by a range of analytic performance indices (Hughes & Bartlett, 2002; James, 2006). Although some studies have investigated differences between expert and non-expert team ball players (Almeida *et al.*, 2013) or successful and unsuccessful actions (Araújo *et al.*, 2004), the vast majority of work has not examined the processes by which expert sport teams develop (e.g., the mechanisms proposed by Eccles & Tenenbaum, 2004 for sport teams were formulated on non-sport, expert team behaviors; see McGarry *et al.*, 2013 for a complete overview).

A traditional approach to understanding the mastery of group processes that culminates in team effectiveness is predicated on the notion of group cognition. This concept is based on the premise that there exist shared mental models of the performance environment, internalized among all team members (Cannon-Bowers *et al.*, 1993; Fiore & Salas, 2006; Salas *et al.*, 2008). Shared cognition is typically referred to as a state of group coordination in which each individual's specific mental expectation and representation of a performance context is similar or identical to that held by other team members (Eccles, 2010; Eccles & Tenenbaum, 2004).

Although shared cognition has tended to dominate research on coordination in groups, the mechanism to explain re-formulations of a team member's representation when changes occur in the content of another member's representation has proved difficult to verify (Mohammed *et al.*, 2000). Also, it is difficult to justify the existence of a brain that stores each player's representations (Shearer *et al.*, 2009), and it is hard to consider that representations exist beyond the boundaries of an individual organism and can be somehow shared (Riley *et al.*, 2011; Silva *et al.*, 2013).

In contrast to assumptions of putatively shared cognition, an ecological approach proposes that knowledge of the world is based upon recurrent processes of perception and action through which humans perceive *affordances* (i.e., opportunities for action; see Gibson, 1979). The concept of affordances presupposes that the environment is directly perceived in terms of what actions an organism can achieve within a performance environment (i.e., it is not dependent on a perceiver's expectations or mental representations linked to specific performance solutions) (Richardson *et al.*, 2008). As in other collective systems, performers in sport teams often have to make decisions about where to move and which actions to perform in uncertain, dynamic environmental conditions (Davids *et al.*, 2005). Affordances can be perceived by a group of individuals trained to become perceptually attuned to them (Silva *et al.*, 2013). In collective sports, both teams in opposition have the same objective (i.e., to overcome the opposition and win). Hence, the perception of collective affordances acts as a selection pressure for overcoming opponents and achieving successful performances. In this sense, collective affordances are sustained by common goals of team members who cooperate to achieve group success. From this perspective, team coordination depends on the collective attunement to shared affordances founded on a prior platform of (mainly non-verbal) communication or information exchange (Silva *et al.*, 2013). Through practice, players become perceptually attuned to affordances *of* others and affordances *for* others during competitive performance, and refine their actions (Fajen *et al.*, 2009) by adjusting behaviors to functionally adapt to those of other teammates and opponents. This process enables them to act synergistically with respect to specific team goals (Duarte *et al.*, 2012a). For example, Sampaio and Maçãs (2012), when studying the effects of a 13-week football training program on team tactical behavior, found that players showed more regular behavior with learning. This result suggests that inter-player coordination in pre-test seems to reflect individual affordances, and not shared affordances, among team players. However, post-test values showed that players became more coordinated with learning, reflecting attunement to shared affordances.

An important feature of a synergy is the ability of one of its components (e.g., a player) to lead changes in others (Riley *et al.*, 2011). Decisions and actions of players forming a synergy should not be viewed as independent, and can explain how multiple players act in accordance with dynamic performance environments in fractions of a second. Therefore, the coupling of players as independent degrees of freedom into integrated synergies is based upon a social perception-action system supported by perception of shared affordances.

This view has major implications for designing experimental research for studying team performance behaviors. For example, it implies that team tactical behaviors may not be articulated in verbal reports. There is an interdependence between perception and action, with clear differences between verbalizing and acting (Araújo *et al.*, 2010). Experimental designs need to focus on *player-player-environmental* interactions that can be elucidated in compound variables specifying functional collective behaviors of sport teams (e.g., geometrical centers), underpinned by interpersonal synergies created between players. In the next section we highlight ways of capturing group-based characteristics in team settings from existing research.

Capturing group-based characteristics in team settings

Group-based measures can be categorized by the following variables: i) team center (centroids and "weighted" centroids), ii) team dispersion (stretch index, team spread, surface area, team length per width ratio), iii) team synchrony (relative phase, cluster phase), iv) labor division (Voronoi, dominant regions, heat maps, major ranges, player-to-locus distance), and v) team communication networks (social networks).

Team center

A team's *center* (also termed centroid, center of gravity, or geometrical center) is obtained by computing the mean lateral and longitudinal positional coordinates of each performer in a team (each player contributes equally to this measure). It has been used to evaluate intra- (e.g., Gonçalves *et al.*, 2013) and inter-team coordination processes in team sports (e.g., Frencken *et al.*, 2011). Teams' centers represent the relative positioning of both teams in forward-backward and side-to-side movement displacement (see Figure 19.1 for an illustration), revealing important insights into team tactics.

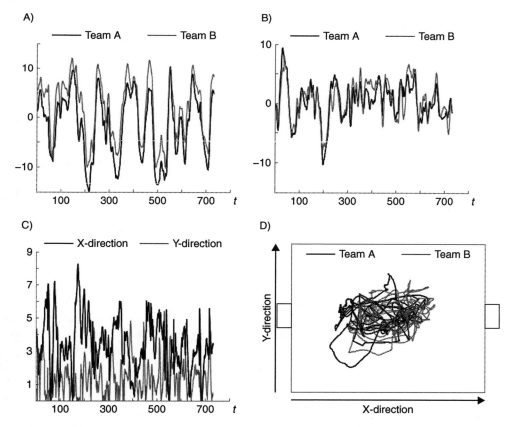

Figure 19.1 Upper panels depict the centroids' coupled oscillations of two teams during six-a-side, small-sided games in: A) X-direction, and B), Y-direction. Oscillations are more pronounced for the goal-to-goal direction. Lower panels illustrate: C) centroids' absolute distances in the X- and Y-direction and D) centroids' trajectories on the field. Distances are greater for the X-direction.

Analysis of inter-team coordination processes has considered the distance between the two teams' centroids in small-sided games as a measure of proximity between competing teams. For example, Frencken *et al.* (2011) observed that the centroid of an attacking team crossed the centroid of a defending team in several plays, ending in a goal being scored, during small-sided games. They argued that this might be a prerequisite to increase the probability of scoring. However, different results were reported by Bartlett, Button, Robbins, Dutt-Mazumder, and Kennedy (2012) in regular matches. They found no clear convergence of the teams' centroids during several plays ending with goals in 11 versus 11 football matches, likely because the positioning of players farthest from the ball compromised the influence of players nearer the ball.

Analysis of a "weighted" centroid echoes the distance of each player to the ball according to his/her influence on the play. Clemente, Couceiro, Martins, Mendes, and Figueiredo (2013b) found pronounced oscillations of both teams' weighted centroids in a lateral direction, interpreted as efforts by the team with the ball to destabilize the defensive organization of opponents by changing the flank of attack (Clemente *et al.*, 2013b). The extent to which the crossing of weighted centroids represents the creation of scoring opportunities is still to be verified.

Team dispersion

Tactics in invasion team sports are expressed by the stretching and expanding of attacking teams on the field and the contracting and reducing of distances between players of the defending team. Such collective movements are captured by specific measures of team coordination that quantify the overall spatial dispersion of players, such as the stretch index (or radius), the team spread, and the effective playing space (or surface area).

The stretch index is calculated by computing the average radial distance of all players to their team's centroid. It can also be calculated according to the axis expansion, providing distinct measures of dispersion in longitudinal and lateral directions. Using this index, Yue, Broich, Seifriz, and Mester (2008) and Bourbousson, Sève, and McGarry (2010b) highlighted the dynamics of attacking and defending, in football and basketball, by representing the intermittent expansion and contraction patterns of competing teams.

Team spread measures have been reported by Moura, Martins, Anido, Barros, and Cunha (2012), who calculated the square root of the sum of the squares of distance values between all pairs of players, except the goalkeeper. They observed a counter-phase relation between expansion in attack and contraction in defense, with greater dispersion values when teams had ball possession. However, further studies are needed to clarify how team dispersion measures are related to attacking and defending phases of play (Bartlett *et al.*, 2012).

Independently, none of the aforementioned studies have accounted for the proximity of each player to the ball, in calculations of team dispersion. In the work by Clemente, Couceiro, Martins, and Korgaokar (2012), distances of each player to the weighted centroid have been considered in calculations of the stretch index. Clemente and colleagues were able to determine a weighted stretch index that accounted for the dispersion of players in relation to the game center containing the ball. They observed a negative relationship between both teams' stretch index values and lower values of this variable without possession of the ball, compared to being in possession of the ball, in seven-a-side, under-13 (years of age) football. It seems that the expansion and contraction properties of a team are constrained by proximity of players to the ball.

The effective playing space (or surface area) is defined by the smallest polygonal area delimited by the peripheral players, containing all players in the game. It can also provide information about the surface that is being effectively covered by opposing teams, and informs how the occupation of space unfolds throughout performance and how stretched both teams are on the field. The

Capturing group tactical behaviors

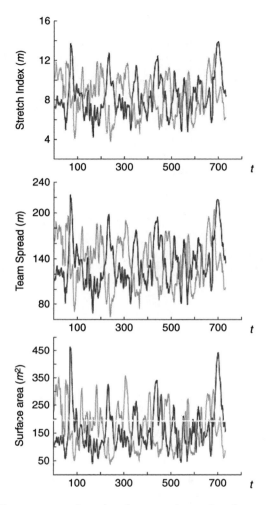

Figure 19.2 Stretch indices, team spreads, and surface areas time series of two competing teams during five-a-side games. All three quantities exhibit similar counter-phase oscillation patterns between teams.

effective playing space may also be computed as a function of attacking and defending, discriminating the surface areas of both teams in competition while representing positioning in the overall team (Frencken & Lemmink, 2008). Similar to the stretch index and team spread, the relationship between offensive and defensive surface areas can highlight the balance of the opponents' relationship during matches (Gréhaigne & Godbout, 2013). Putatively, the attacking team may occupy a larger surface area than that of the defending team, by virtue of being more stretched in the field. The suggestion is that these three variables share a similar nature (see Figure 19.2).

A different conceptualization of the effective playing area was proposed by Clemente, Couceiro, Martins, and Mendes (2013a), based on the assumption that it is important to assess the area that a team covers without intercepting the effective area of the opposing team. To this effect, Clemente and colleagues have calculated the non-overlapping triangles formed by the players of each team and the total area delimited by these triangles for the attacking and defending teams (Figure 19.3).

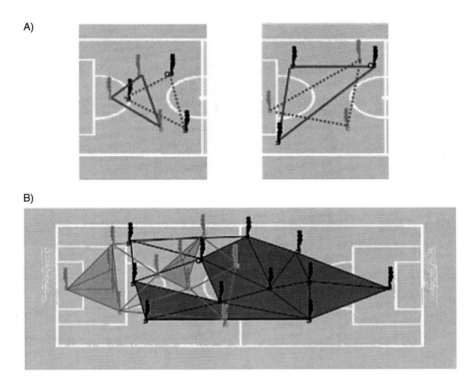

Figure 19.3 A) Examples of triangles interception. B) Effective surface area with offensive (dark grey) and defensive triangles (light grey). From Clemente, Couceiro, Martins, and Mendes (2013a), reprinted with permission of the authors.

They showed that the attacking team, in general, showed higher values of triangulations (i.e., higher number of triangles not annulled by the opponent team's triangles) and effective playing area, whereas the defending team displayed lower effective surface areas. A negative correlation between the areas of both teams was also found, indicating a counter-phase relation between both teams' effective playing areas, which did not happen in other studies that measured surface areas by the above-described means.

Team synchrony

Several tools have been used to assess coordination between two oscillatory units (e.g., the coupling of two centroids, or the phase relations of two players in a dyad). For instance, the phase synchronization of two signals has been previously studied in team sports through relative phase analysis (Bourbousson *et al.*, 2010a, 2010b) and running correlations (Duarte *et al.*, 2012b; Frencken *et al.*, 2013).

A cluster phase method has been recently proposed to analyze synchrony in systems with a small number of oscillatory units (Frank & Richardson, 2010; Richardson *et al.*, 2012). It is based on the Kuramoto order parameter conceived to examine the phase synchronization of a large set of coupled oscillators (Kuramoto, 1984), like neural synchronization in the brain. Frank and Richardson (2010) adapted this algorithm to describe the collective phase of a smaller number of oscillators into one single measure, and used it to assess group synchrony in a non-sport task. In team sports, Duarte *et al.* (2013) applied this measure to the movements of 11 football players from two teams during an English Premier League match to assess whole team and player-team synchrony. They found large synergistic relations within each team, particularly in the longitudinal direction of the field. Whole team synchrony revealed superior mean values and high levels of stability in the longitudinal direction, compared with the lateral direction of the field. Player-team synchrony revealed a tendency for a near in-phase mode of coordination. However, the cluster phase method might be useful to measure group synchrony only when it is expected that players exhibit synchrony by performing symmetric movements on the field (e.g., during a counterattack in football or a turnover in basketball). More research is needed to determine the utility of this method when players perform coordinated, but non-symmetric movement behaviors (e.g., when players switch positions).

The division of labor within teams

The behavior of each individual in a team is constrained by several factors, such as his/her position on the field (in relation to the other teammates and opponents), strategic and tactical objectives, playing phases (i.e., attacking and defending), game rules, etc. Team behavior is thus the emergent result of many individual labors in interaction (Duarte *et al.*, 2012b; Eccles, 2010).

The analysis of labor division in the field can be performed from a spatial perspective. Gréhaigne (1988) pioneered analysis of the division of individual areas, or action zones, of each player, in an attempt to assess the tactical characteristics of each player in a team. He analyzed the effective covered space of football players by registering their position on the field every 30 seconds, according to their specific location on a pitch divided into 40 equal squares. Nowadays, the reconstruction of spatial distribution maps, also known as heat maps, provides a clear picture of the distribution of each player on the field. Heat maps highlight with warmer colors the zones where each player has spent larger periods of time during performance (e.g., Lames, 2008; see also Figure 19.4).

Based on this concept, Silva *et al.* (in press) produced heat maps of youth football players of different competitive levels performing in small-sided games. They calculated entropy measures of each individual's spatial distribution, providing a value that quantified the uncertainty of locating each player in a specific location on the field. They observed that the more skillful players displayed higher spatial unpredictability on the smaller fields, compared to less-skilled players. Both groups displayed identical levels of predictability in movement trajectories on larger fields.

Another approach to assess the division of labor in team sports is by measuring the area covered by each player. Yue *et al.* (2008) proposed the calculation of a major range, defined as an

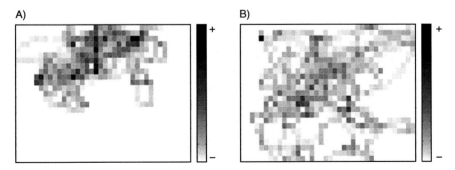

Figure 19.4 Exemplar spatial distribution maps of two players during a four-a-side game; A) regional player; B) national player. The national player presents more variability in space occupation in relation to the regional player.

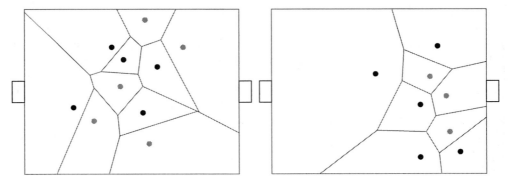

Figure 19.5 Exemplar players' Voronoi cells in two small-sided games (five versus five and five versus three) in single frames (goalkeepers excluded).

ellipse centered at each player's locus and with semi-axes being the standard deviations in the x- and y-directions, respectively. This measure identifies preferred spatial positions, major roles for each player, and playing styles.

Other spatial measures emphasizing the individual playing areas attributed to each player on a team – the Voronoi diagrams – were revised by Fonseca, Diniz, and Araújo (2014). These studies indicated that this individual spatial representation could be used to measure teamwork by assessing the dominant regions of each team. Dominant regions reflect the creation and coverage of space by teams. Given a set of n points distributed in a plane, the Voronoi diagram divides the plane into n cells (Figure 19.5), each associated with one, and only one, point. In other words, each cell corresponds to a part of the plane that is closer to one of the points. For instance, in a soccer match, the points could be the position of the players, the plane the play area, and the cells the regions associated to each player. By measuring the total area of all cells from each team, it is possible to obtain a dominant ratio of one team over the other (Kim, 2004) (see Figure 19.5).

Fonseca, Milho, Travassos, and Araújo (2012) computed the Voronoi cells of two futsal teams to understand how players of both teams coordinated their locations on the court during attack and defense. They found larger covered areas by players in attacking teams and lower regularity (measured by approximate entropy) in the areas occupied by defending teams, revealing more unpredictable interactive behaviors between defending players (see also Fonseca *et al.*, 2013 for the novel concept of superimposed Voronoi).

However, the assumption that all space inside a Voronoi cell is reachable in a shorter time by its designated player may be questioned. The position, speed, acceleration, and movement direction of the players may be determined to define which areas he/she can arrive at earlier than other players (Gréhaigne *et al.*, 1997). Taki and Hasegawa (2000) took into account these factors to calculate the dominant region of each player on a football match. They calculated deformed Voronoi cells that weighted the players' positions, movement directions, and speeds, determining with higher accuracy each player's dominant region.

Team communication networks

A team ball game can be viewed as a small-world social system in which collective behavior is sustained by interpersonal interactions among system players (Passos *et al.*, 2011). From a behavioral perspective, two players are considered to be linked when they exchange passes, or when they intentionally switch positions (Passos *et al.*, 2011). Social networks are used to analyze the

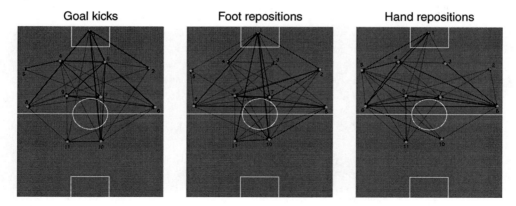

Figure 19.6 Playing patterns of one English Premier League team according to the goalkeepers' actions (courtesy of B. Travassos).

structure of such communication channels among players during subphases of play in team sports. In these networks, nodes represent players, and lines are weighted according to the number of passes or positional changes completed between players.

Using this tool, Travassos, Sá-Pinho, Marques, and Duarte (2012) analyzed the influence of different goalkeepers' actions on the attacking patterns of play of a football team. They found different patterns of play initiated by goal kicks, foot repositions, and hand repositions (Figure 19.6).

Players with major competitive roles may be easily identified through social networks, as they display a higher number and stronger connections. Additionally, different match networks can be compared to extract the general tactical and strategic features of a team (Duch et al., 2010; Passos et al., 2011).

Another approach to the analysis of networks focuses on density and centrality features, reflecting the formation of dyads between team members (Grund, 2012). Density refers to the interaction intensity of the players (e.g., passing rate), whereas centrality refers to the degree to which network positions are unequally distributed in a team. In association football it has been shown that better team performance is associated with high density and low centrality (Grund, 2012).

Conclusion

Recently, sport teams have been conceptualized as interacting social units benefiting from natural processes of self-organization among players, leading to the formation of functional group synergies, supported by perception of shared affordances. This ecological dynamics perspective has compelled sport scientists to search for measures of the behavioral expression of group processes. By means of tracked positional data, recent research has begun to reveal how players and teams continuously interact during competition (Correia et al., 2012). In this chapter we have discussed several variables that have been specifically developed to assess the tactical performance features of different teams.

From the perspective of space coverage, group variables can capture relative team positioning (team center), the degree of dispersion of players on the field (team dispersion), and the division of space into personal territories, conferring each team member specific tactical roles (division of labor). Networks expose synergies established between dyads within the team, through preferred linkages and communication channels, whereas the cluster-phase approach extended the concept of synergy to the group level.

Duarte Araújo et al.

Identification of individual key match events in time, like an assisting pass or a successful shot on target, may be crucial for understanding team behavioral changes, captured by some of the aforementioned variables, resulting in critical performance outcomes. Development of expert team analysis may benefit from approaches that contextualize and trace relevant performance processes of effective teams, as measured by time-evolving variables capturing interactions of the whole team, subgroups, individual players, or the ball and discrete events.

References

Almeida, C. H., Ferreira, A. P., & Volossovitch, A. (2013) 'Offensive sequences in youth soccer: Effects of experience and small-sided games', *Journal of Human Kinetics*, 36(1): 97–106.

Araújo, D., Davids, K., Bennett, S., Button, C., & Chapman, G. (2004) 'Emergence of sport skills under constraints', in A.M. Williams & N.J. Hodges (eds.) *Skill acquisition in sport: Research, theory and practice*, London: Routledge, Taylor & Francis, 409–33.

Araújo, D., Travassos, B., & Vilar, L. (2010) 'Tactical skills are not verbal skills: A comment on kannekens and colleagues', *Perceptual and Motor Skills*, 110(3): 1086–8.

Bartlett, R., Button, C., Robbins, M., Dutt-Mazumder, A., & Kennedy, G. (2012) 'Analysing team coordination patterns from player movement trajectories in soccer: Methodological considerations', *International Journal of Performance Analysis in Sport*, 12: 398–424.

Bourbousson, J., Sève, C., & McGarry, T. (2010a) 'Space-time coordination dynamics in basketball: Part 1. Intra- and inter-couplings among player dyads', *Journal of Sports Sciences*, 28(3): 339–47.

Bourbousson, J., Sève, C., & McGarry, T. (2010b) 'Space-time coordination dynamics in basketball: Part 2. The interaction between the two teams', *Journal of Sports Sciences*, 28(3): 349–58.

Cannon-Bowers, J. A., Salas, E., & Converse, S. (1993) 'Shared mental models in expert team decision making', in J. J. Castellan (ed) *Individual and group decision making*, Hillsdale, NJ: Erlbaum, 221–46.

Clemente, F., Couceiro, M., Martins, F., & Mendes, R. (2013a) 'An online tactical metrics applied to football game', *Research Journal of Applied Sciences, Engineering and Technology*, 5(5): 1700–19.

Clemente, F., Couceiro, M., Martins, F., Mendes, R., & Figueiredo, A. (2013b) 'Measuring collective behaviour in football teams: Inspecting the impact of each half of the match on ball possession', *International Journal of Performance Analysis in Sport*, 13: 678–89.

Clemente, F., Couceiro, M. S., Martins, F.M.L., & Korgaokar, A. (2012) 'Automatic tools of match analysis: Inspecting soccer team's dispersion', *International Journal of Applied Sports Sciences*, 24(2): 81–8.

Correia, V., Araújo, D., Vilar, L., & Davids, K. (2012) 'From recording discrete actions to studying continuous goal-directed behaviours in team sports', *Journal of Sports Sciences*, 31(5): 546–53.

Davids, K., Araújo, D., & Shuttleworth, R. (2005) 'Applications of dynamical system theory to football', in T. Reilly, J. Cabri, & D. Araújo (eds) *Science & football v*, Oxon, UK: Routledge, 556–69.

Duarte, R., Araújo, D., Correia, V., & Davids, K. (2012a) 'Sport teams as superorganisms: Implications of biological models for research and practice in team sports performance analysis', *Sports Medicine*, 42(8): 633–42.

Duarte, R., Araújo, D., Correia, V., Davids, K., Marques, P., & Richardson, M. (2013) 'Competing together: Assessing the dynamics of team-team and player-team synchrony in professional association football', *Human Movement Science*, 32: 555–66.

Duarte, R., Araújo, D., Freire, L., Folgado, H., Fernandes, O., & Davids, K. (2012b) 'Intra- and inter-group coordination patterns reveal collective behaviors of football players near the scoring zone', *Human Movement Science*, 31(6): 1639–51.

Duch, J., Waitzman, J., & Amaral, L. (2010) 'Quantifying the performance of individual players in a team activity', *PloS One*, 5(6): e10937.

Eccles, D. (2010) 'The coordination of labour in sports teams', *International Review of Sport and Exercise Psychology*, 3(2): 154–70.

Eccles, D., & Tenenbaum, G. (2004) 'Why an expert team is more than a team of experts: A social-cognitive conceptualization of team coordination and communication in sport', *Journal of Sport & Exercise Psychology*, 26: 542–60.

Fajen, B., Riley, M., & Turvey, M. (2009) 'Information, affordances, and the control of action in sport', *International Journal of Sport Psychology*, 40: 79–107.

Fiore, S., & Salas, E. (2006) 'Team cognition and expert teams: Developing insights from cross-disciplinary analysis of exceptional teams', *International Journal of Sport and Exercise Psychology*, 4(4): 369–75.

Fonseca, S., Diniz, A., & Araújo, D. (2014) 'The measurement of space and time in evolving sport phenomena', in K. Davids, R. Hristovski, D. Araújo, N. Balagué, C. Button, & P. Passos (eds) *Complex systems in sport*, London: Routledge, 125–44.

Fonseca, S., Milho, J., Travassos, B., & Araújo, D. (2012) 'Spatial dynamics of team sports exposed by Voronoi diagrams', *Human Movement Science*, 31(6): 1652–9.

Fonseca, S., Milho, J., Travassos, B., Araújo, D., & Lopes, A. (2013) 'Measuring spatial interaction behaviour in team sports using superimposed Voronoi diagrams', *International Journal of Performance Analysis in Sport*, 13: 179–89.

Frank, T. D., & Richardson, M. J. (2010) 'On a test statistic for the Kuramoto order parameter of synchronization: An illustration for group synchronization during rocking chairs', *Physica D*, 239: 2084–92.

Frencken, W., & Lemmink, K. (2008) 'Team kinematics of small-sided soccer games: A systematic approach', in T. Reilly & F. Korkusuz (eds) *Science and football vi*, Oxon, UK: Routledge, 188–93.

Frencken, W., Lemmink, K., Delleman, N., & Visscher, C. (2011) 'Oscillations of centroid position and surface area of soccer teams in small-sided games', *European Journal of Sport Science*, 11(4): 215–23.

Frencken, W., van der Plaats, J., Visscher, C., & Lemmink, K. (2013) 'Size matters: Pitch dimensions constrain interactive team behaviour in soccer', *Journal of Systems Science and Complexity*, 26(1): 85–93.

Gibson, J. (1979) *The ecological approach to visual perception*, Hillsdale, NJ: Lawrence Erlbaum Associates.

Glazier, P. S. (2010) 'Game, set and match? Substantive issues and future directions in performance analysis', *Sports Medicine*, 40(8): 625–34.

Gonçalves, B. V., Figueira, B. E., Maçãs, V., & Sampaio, J. (2013) 'Effect of player position on movement behaviour, physical and physiological performances during an 11-a-side football game', *Journal of Sports Sciences*, 32: 191–9.

Gréhaigne, J. F. (1988) 'Game systems in soccer from the point of view of coverage of space', in T. Reilly, A. Lees, K. Davids, & W. J. Murphy (eds) *Science and football*, London: E. & F.N. Spon, 316–21.

Gréhaigne, J. F., Bouthier, D., & David, B. (1997) 'Dynamic-system analysis of opponent relationships in collective actions in soccer', *Journal of Sports Sciences*, 15(2): 137–49.

Gréhaigne, J. F., & Godbout, P. (2013) 'Collective variables for analysing performance in team sports', in T. McGarry, P. O'Donoghue, & J. Sampaio (eds) *Routledge handbook of sports performance analysis*, Oxon, UK: Routledge, 101–14.

Grund, T. (2012) 'Network structure and team performance: The case of english premier league soccer teams', *Social Networks*, 34(4): 682–90.

Hughes, M., & Bartlett, R. (2002) 'The use of performance indicators in performance analysis', *Journal of Sports Sciences*, 20: 739–54.

James, N. (2006) 'Notational analysis in soccer: Past, present and future', *International Journal of Performance Analysis of Sport*, 6(2): 67–81.

Kim, S. (2004) 'Voronoi analysis of a soccer game', *Nonlinear Analysis: Modelling and Control*, 9(3): 233–40.

Kuramoto, Y. (1984) *Chemical oscillations, waves, and turbulence*, Berlin: Springer.

Lames, M. (2008) 'Coaching and computer science', in P. Dabnichki & A. Baca (eds) *Computers in sport*, Southampton, UK: WIT Press, 99–120.

McGarry, T., O'Donoghue, P., & Sampaio, J. (2013) *The Routledge handbook of sports performance analysis*, London: Routledge.

Mohammed, S., Klimoski, R., & Rentsch, J. (2000) 'The measurement of team mental models: We have no shared schema', *Organizational Research Methods*, 3(2): 123–65.

Moura, F., Martins, L., Anido, R., Barros, R., & Cunha, S. (2012) 'Quantitative analysis of brazilian football players' organisation on the pitch', *Sport Biomechanics*, 11(1): 85–96.

Passos, P., Davids, K., Araújo, D., Paz, N., Minguens, J., & Mendes, J.F.F. (2011) 'Networks as a novel tool for studying team ball sports as complex social systems', *Journal of Science and Medicine in Sport*, 14(2): 170–6.

Richardson, M., Garcia, R., Frank, T., Gergor, M., & Marsh, K. (2012) 'Measuring group synchrony: A cluster-phase method for analyzing multivariate movement time-series', *Frontiers in Psychology*, 3(Article 405): 1–10.

Richardson, M., Shockley, K., Fajen, B., Riley, M., & Turvey, M. (2008) 'Ecological psychology: Six principles for an embodied-embedded approach to behavior', in P. Calvo & A. Gomila (eds) *Handbook of cognitive science*, Amsterdam: Elsevier Inc. Academic Press, 161–87.

Riley, M., Richardson, M., Shockley, K., & Ramenzoni, V. (2011) 'Interpersonal synergies', *Frontiers in Psychology*, 2(38): 1–7.

Salas, E., Cannon-Bowers, J. A., & Johnstone, J. H. (1997) 'How can you turn a team of experts into an expert team? Emerging training strategies', in C. Zsambok & G. Klein (eds) *Naturalistic decision making: Where are we now?*, Hillsdale, NJ: Erlbaum, 359–70.

Salas, E., Cooke, N. J., & Rosen, M. A. (2008) 'On teams, teamwork, and team performance: Discoveries and developments', *Human Factors*, 50(3): 540–7.

Salas, E., Rosen, M., Burke, C. S., Goodwin, G., & Fiore, S. (2006) 'The making of a dream team: When expert teams do best', in K. A. Ericsson, N. Charness, P. Feltovich, & R. R. Hoffman (eds) *The Cambridge handbook of expertise and expert performance*, Cambridge: Cambridge University Press, 439–54.

Sampaio, J., & Maçãs, V. (2012) 'Measuring tactical behaviour in football', *International Journal of Sports Medicine*, 33(5): 395–401.

Shearer, D. A., Holmes, P., & Mellalieu, S. D. (2009) 'Collective efficacy in sport: The future from a social neuroscience perspective', *International Review of Sport and Exercise Psychology*, 2(1): 38–53.

Silva, P., Aguiar, P., Duarte, R., Davids, K., Araújo, D., & Garganta, J. (2014) 'Effects of pitch size and skill level on tactical behaviours of Association Football players during small-sided and conditioned games', *International Journal of Sports Science & Coaching*, 9(5), 993–1006.

Silva, P., Garganta, J., Araújo, D., Davids, K., & Aguiar, P. (2013) 'Shared knowledge or shared affordances? Insights from an ecological dynamics approach to team coordination in sports', *Sports Medicine*, 43: 765–72.

Taki, T., & Hasegawa, J. I. (2000) 'Visualization of dominant region in team games and its application to teamwork analysis', paper presented at the Proceedings of the International Conference on Computer Graphics in Geneva.

Travassos, B., Sá-Pinho, J., Marques, P., & Duarte, R. (2012) 'The influence of the type of goalkeeper action on the offensive patterns of play in association football', *International Journal of Performance Analysis in Sport*, 12(3): 786.

Yue, Z., Broich, H., Seifriz, F., & Mester, J. (2008) 'Mathematical analysis of a soccer game. Part i: Individual and collective behaviours', *Studies in Applied Mathematics*, 121: 223–43.

20
METHODS FOR MEASURING BREADTH AND DEPTH OF KNOWLEDGE

Doris J. F. McIlwain and John Sutton

Eccles's challenge: verbal reports of expert knowledge

In elite sport, the advantages demonstrated by expert performers over novices are sometimes due in part to their superior physical fitness or to their greater technical precision in executing specialist motor skills. However, at the very highest levels, all competitors typically share extraordinary physical capacities and have supremely well-honed techniques. Among the extra factors, which can differentiate between the best performers, psychological skills are paramount. These range from the capacities to cope under pressure and bounce back from setbacks to knowledge of themselves, opponents, and the domain, which experts access and apply in performance. In the companion chapter on breadth and depth of knowledge in expert sport (see Chapter 9), we discussed the forms or kinds of knowledge deployed by elite athletes, and described some lines of research that seek to tap and study such expert knowledge (McPherson & MacMahon, 2008; McRobert *et al.*, 2011). In this chapter we focus more directly on questions about methods for measuring or more accurately assessing expert knowledge, in particular addressing a wider range of methods to help us understand what experts know. Suggesting that sport researchers can productively adopt and adapt existing qualitative methodologies for integration with more standard quantitative methods, we introduce and survey a number of areas of qualitative research in psychology.

Since the cognitive revolution, mainstream psychologists have been increasingly cautious about the utility of verbal reports of cognitive processes. Since the bulk of processing occurs at lower levels in the cognitive system and is not consciously accessible, it is thought that we need objective observational methods to catch the system in action. But in a trenchant, recent review of work on verbal reports in sport psychology, David Eccles (2012) argues that the field has not taken this theoretical skepticism seriously enough, and is still overreliant on reports of verbal data collected in poorly controlled ways. Reviewing classical studies of people's significant inaccuracy in reporting the thoughts mediating their decisions and actions (Nisbett & Wilson 1977), Eccles argues that in general much of cognition is "inaccessible to consciousness:" he quotes Dennett's claim that "consciousness of the springs of action is the exception, not the rule" (2003, p. 246). Many apparent reports of cognitive processes are in fact confabulations, arising from implicit cultural or subculturally sanctioned theories, which involve causal claims that may be quite disconnected from the actual causal processes underlying action.

But Eccles sees this pessimism as tempered by the possibility of using clear guidelines to access what individuals can accurately report. Following Ericsson and Simon (1980; see also Fox *et al.*, 2011), Eccles suggests that the only material that can be accurately reported is that which was attended to, or heeded, in short term memory (STM) during the execution of a task. This can either be directly verbalized or recoded "into a verbal mode" (Eccles, 2012, p. 105). The best ways to elicit such legitimate verbal data are to ask practitioners to think aloud during performance ("concurrent reporting") or – as will often be required in dynamic sport tasks – collecting reports straight after task performance (immediately retrospective reporting). Experts should ideally be asked questions that are not overly directive, and do not constrain the participant to interpret his/her thoughts or to report only about some particular target interest of the researcher (like coping efforts, or self-talk strategies). Instead, undirected probes, which merely ask for the thoughts the individual remembers having, can provide information with more optimal scope and of sounder validity. Participants can be trained swiftly to report only on what they are, or have been, thinking rather than to interpret, theorize, or comment on their own cognitive processes. These methods can also aim at gathering verbal reports of specific episodes rather than general reports about how experts usually think or make decisions.

Eccles (2012) performs a critical content analysis of an array of sport research that used verbal report data in studies of psychological skill. He found that many of them did not use prompts which optimized the validity of the reports given. Most studies in his sample used interview methods, but employed directive probes, tapped only general states rather than particular episodes, and involved longer delays between the episode and the report. In summarizing the quotations provided as results in these research articles, Eccles suggests "these studies provided no evidence of a participant having recalled any actual thought from any specific episode" (2012, p. 112).

Other recent work, of course, does adhere more closely to the research guidelines Eccles outlines. In the work by McPherson and by McRobert, Roca, Ward, and colleagues, which we discussed in the chapter on breadth and depth of knowledge (Chapter 9), verbal reports are typically gathered on an immediately retrospective basis – for example, between points in tennis. In one study of anticipation and decision-making in football, for example, Roca and colleagues trained participants on how to think aloud in 30-minute sessions offering practice in "giving immediate retrospective verbal reports by solving a series of both generic and sport-specific tasks" (Roca *et al.*, 2011, p. 307). Nevertheless, Eccles's critical survey raises important questions about the degree of input a researcher should have in shaping the content of self-report, the timing of recall, and the specificity of the event under scrutiny. While we agree that sport researchers should be more aware of these think-aloud protocols, in this chapter we argue for the inclusion of a wider range of methods to tap expert knowledge by way of verbal report.

In attempting to give explanatory causal accounts of specific mechanisms underlying expertise, we may need a very specific form of verbal report. But there are many forms of knowledge relevant to expertise – knowing the background form of another player, knowing how to compensate for general personal tendencies in the face of a certain genre of challenge, recently updated knowledge of local conditions and their likely effects on particular kinds of play, and so on. Eccles's admirably narrow conception of valid self-report suggests that all one needs to discover about skill relates to a single occurrent episode, veridically described, as it unfolds in real time. If possible, this is almost self-report as a stand in for a camera. The method is explicitly set up to exclude personal meaning, context, history, experience of embodiment, or knowledge of context. Other levels of knowledge and personal insight among expert performers might, we suggest, be added to and integrated with these recommendations for optimizing valid responses. Experts are not always as ignorant of their own cognitive processes, not so constantly and consistently prone to confabulation, as is suggested by the classical literature cited by Eccles. Indeed,

Measuring breadth and depth of knowledge

they are sometimes able to open up their own knowledge base to revision, reorganization, and updating. They can access and discuss some aspects of their own cognitive processes (Chaffin *et al.*, 2002). If certain components of expert knowledge are thus more or less accessible, they are likely also to be shareable with researchers as well as with coaches and peers, provided the researcher establishes a situation of sufficient rapport, asks the right questions, and the practitioner is appropriately motivated and has no reason not to share.

Case study: Bicknell's staircase

At a 2006 Australian national cross-country mountain biking event in Thredbo, the course included a damp and muddy "staircase" section, at which riders took a range of different options. Some jumped off their bikes and ran, some pulled hard on the front brake to force the bike into a nose pivot down a wooden plank, and others slowed so much they were only just moving to steer down the edge of the stairs. Participant researcher Kath Bicknell successfully navigated this section after watching the competitors pass. She wrote later that

> if you asked me right away to describe how I had done this, I wouldn't be able to tell you exactly what I had done differently this time . . . I would probably have said what other riders had told me: "You've just gotta commit."
>
> *(Bicknell, 2010, p. 86)*

Cycling experts can often tell you what they did, even if not immediately afterwards. Bicknell (2010) notes that in cycling down such a perilous staircase, you need to "keep your body weight behind the seat of the bike [so that] the bike stays stable as it hits the flat ground at the exit – meaning the rider's body will not flip over the front wheel" (2010, pp. 87–8). This is background knowledge for most experts. In applying her knowledge to this new situation, Bicknell thinks back:

> When I had tried the stairs previously, I had slowed so much while turning that I had not believed that it was possible to complete the turn before falling off the bike, and I had put my foot out to scoot down the staircase instead. . . . By breaking the conscious direction of the movement into aiming toward the edge of the stairs, followed by looking toward the exit, I was able to successfully negotiate the turn and finish the rest of the complex manoeuvre. It is in this way that I guided my own reinvention of the correct technique. . . .
>
> *(2010, p. 88)*

So, while an expert might offer up a general maxim immediately after a ride, with patience and insightful questioning the researcher can move beyond the motto or the press release. The motto – "you've just gotta commit" – conveys the point that

> When a rider has not committed to such a move, often due to doubt, fear, or distraction, their body position will alter due to muscle tension, or looking in the wrong direction (which often affects shoulder movement, which in turn affects steering) and the movement's outcome will alter.
>
> *(Bicknell, 2010, p. 88)*

It is a "colloquial shortcut" for a complex phenomenological process of embodying a skill in which cognition is interwoven with motor skill. As Bicknell notes in reflection, her own experience "watching the men ride the staircase and then being able to do it myself has also revealed that the developmental process underpinning skilled performance does not just come from 'doing' but can be developed through cognitive experiences as well" (2010, p. 87). It is therefore something that can be captured in language and thought about, though not necessarily immediately after, the action itself.

As an expert participant observer, Bicknell has the capacity to notice and relay in language much of what a novice observer would miss. She suggests that skill embodiment

> Develops more through a process of emulation and belief rather than practice, error correction and repetition. Like jumping off a diving board for the first time, you cannot half ride a staircase, learning little components of the skill along the way. You need speed, momentum, body position and commitment to the manoeuvre at the beginning of the action, to relax during it, and to know what shape you want to feel yourself in as you finish it off.
>
> *(Bicknell, 2010, p. 87)*

When a practitioner who is also a theorist of skill gives an account of skill development, we get a window into higher levels of skill acquisition. While she is able to give a detailed description of the isolated moments of turning the bike wheel down the difficult staircase, the form of self-report offered and the levels and complexity of knowledge in play here go far beyond that alone. Here is a participant theorizing with and for you. A rare case? We suggest that the thoughtfulness of experts about their domain of expertise, or the scope of their expertise, should not be underestimated. Knowledge informs perception–action couplings through shaping what, and how much, one notices, as expert participant observation reveals.

On a wider view of skill, expert knowledge covers the core features of motor execution, perception–action coupling, and the experience of the acquisition of embodied skills. It includes response selection and strategy, which entails knowing one's own form, an opponent's form, how well one's own style has been mapped, and the current competitive context. Novices have much to learn from the moment-to-moment accounts of experience of skilled performance, including how to sustain emotional resilience in the face of stress and challenge (both long-term strain and contingent, local challenges), as well as how to handle the social consequences of fame and public scrutiny. There is on occasion more knowledge folded into a single shot or episode than could perhaps ever be conveyed in concurrent verbalization. Immediate retrospective reporting in most cases would be useful, but such access may not be possible for researchers who seek to study elite sport performance. Further, much of the knowledge may be tacit, in the sense that it is not necessarily operating explicitly at the moment of performance, but yet still informs decision and action. The expert may not be in a position to volunteer it as relevant. Because much thus relies on the insight and skill of the researcher, a wider palette of methodological tools may be useful.

Overview of qualitative methods

Qualitative research is particularly useful in breaking new ground where there is not yet an established body of knowledge or existing theoretical models of the phenomenon of interest, or where there are as yet few existing findings to generate nuanced and specific hypotheses. It can be particularly helpful when all we have to start with is a researcher with a pressing research question that may have arisen from personal experience in a field. So at that stage, to counter possible personal bias, we need to add the views of others to our own implicit theories and hunches about what might be going on. Interviews and focus groups with expert practitioners can function as a reconnaissance flight over the conceptual terrain, prior to commitment to a more detailed qualitative study, a questionnaire, or taking a relevant parameter experimentally into the lab.

Qualitative theorizing is not for everyone. The component skills are succinctly outlined by Gilgun:

> Skills required to do qualitative theory building and model testing are (a) capacities to draw detailed descriptions of phenomena of interest from respondents, from observations of settings, and from documents of various types; (b) capacities for conceptual thinking, that is, the ability to conceptualize social phenomena and identify them in data; (c) capacities for flexible thinking, where researchers are willing to challenge and undermine their own preconceptions and favorite theories, some of which may be out of their awareness; and (d) the discipline to answer questions such as, 'How do my findings add to, modify, transform, or undermine what is already known?' For many researchers, qualitative research is a way of thinking.
>
> *(2009, p. 95)*

Despite its challenges, it is worthwhile achieving expertise in this domain to supplement other methodological skills, even if one does not take the skills all the way through to theory building. For example, science requires the use of established, reliable coding schemes. However, if coding schemes are adapted from other domains or other sports, the trade-off in relevance loss may not be compensated for by the reliability sought. A researcher may need to devise a purpose-built coding scheme in ways that meet the requirements of science: the process is made public, verifiable, and replicable. So what are the relevant considerations with regards to sampling, coding, and analysis?

Moving from one research method to another requires reassessment of expectations: integrating qualitative methods into your research requires revisiting assumptions about sample size, the prior existence of precise hypotheses, at what level generalization of results is possible, and whether one can aspire to universal laws. A common error in moving from quantitative to qualitative research is to assume that sample size hinges on the number of people in a sample rather than the array of experiences sampled. Getting a large sample size is often seen as an issue, and there are often concerns about generalizability. The concern for generalizability arises because many mistakenly believe that the unit of analysis is the person, whereas the unit of analysis is in fact the element of experience. One can canvas a vast array of experiences with 15 interviews if one includes in the sample people who vary along relevant parameters.

Grounded theory (Glaser & Strauss, 1967) is one central form of qualitative method to which researchers turn as a generator of theory where existing theory is inappropriate or absent. Theory generated in this way is "derived from data, systematically gathered and analyzed through the research process" (Strauss & Corbin, 1998, p. 12). The aim "is to produce innovative theory that is 'grounded' in data collected from participants on the basis of the complexities of their lived experiences in a social context" (Fassinger, 2005, p. 157). A new field without established findings means hypotheses cannot be devised in advance. As Gilgun notes, "rather than preselecting hypotheses and the concepts on which they are based, grounded theory seeks to discover them through processes of emergence, which occur over the course of data analysis and interpretation" (1995, p. 268).

A variant methodology, which permits a researcher to enter a domain of research with formed hunches and broad hypotheses, is called modified analytic induction (MAI). According to Gilgun (1995), who champions this method, it is permissible to have hypotheses that are "rough and general approximations, prior to entry into the field or, in cases where data already are collected, prior to data analysis. These hypotheses can be based on hunches, assumptions, careful examination of research and theory, or combinations" (1995, p. 269). Hypotheses are not static, but are "revised to fit emerging interpretations of the data over the course of data collection and analysis" (1995, p. 269). An important attribute of MAI is that one searches for instances that are likely to disconfirm conclusions so far. In this way, one adds enough variability to the sample until one is sure the conclusions are robust.

If one is permitted to revise hypotheses in the light of the data, it is important that one is not just cherry-picking, modifying emphasis to find the conclusion that confirms one's prior convictions. So there are clear ways of approaching acknowledgment of the possible biases of the researcher in devising the sample and the animating question (sensitizing concepts), in interviewing the participants (writing memos about the experience of rapport or absence thereof), and in analyzing the data (via open, axial, and selective coding).

One aim of all forms of qualitative methodology is to let the data speak. Coding schemes need to arise from the data itself rather than personal hunches and pet theories. Coding has subjective elements. For example, a researcher who is also an expert in the domain under study would perhaps see more in the responses than would someone without detailed, domain-relevant, content-based expertise. The inclusion of both coders may have advantages to allow the data to disrupt and reconfigure preconceptions, which an expert may not discern as operating to shape what is seen as salient. It is optimal if, at the end of a study, conclusions do not overlap excessively with the commencing sensitizing concepts.

To address implicit theories and unconscious schemas that may bias coding, it is best to commence qualitative methodology prior to commencing the research, by writing down hunches and sources of interest in a phenomenon as well as processes thought to be operative. This is an important phase. Arcuri (2007 see also Arcuri & McIlwain, 2009) notes four advantages of doing this:

> [F]irst, to elucidate our sensitizing concepts, which would be utilized as points of departure from which to ask questions and make comparisons (but . . . not be utilized as data *per se*); second, to enable us to remain sensitive to and minimize potential areas of bias in our ways of interpreting and analyzing data (commonly referred to as bracketing; Morrow, 2005; Ponterotto, 2005); third, to begin the process of self-reflection, or *reflexivity*, which was to continue throughout the research process (Camic, Rhodes, & Yardley, 2003; Marecek, 2003); and, fourth, to contribute to the reader's ability to identify the lens through which the data were interpreted and analyzed, and thus determine the 'extent to which [he or she] is able to generalize the findings . . . to his or her own context.'
>
> *(Morrow, 2005, p. 252)*

Then one selects a sample and commences interviewing. As Eccles (2012) suggests, it is best to use non-directive probes to optimize the scope of what can be included in a response. In devising probes, the researcher decides to what degree the research focuses on the landscape of action or the landscape of meaning – whether the aim is to assemble a causal account of what happens, or to understand the person's viewpoint on the experience and why it matters to him/her to the degree it does. Sometimes, meanings have casual effects. If the experience of the yips was felt to be a devastating, career-ending moment, for example, it may well have that effect.

A researcher can then decide how much comparability across subjects is sought, and with what economy of time. Standardizing probes and prompts enhances the comparability of interviews across participants. Some interviewers see it as important to be free to go more deeply into certain issues that arise with a participant and then modify the probes for subsequent interviewees to accommodate unexpected, valuable, new material.

Measuring breadth and depth of knowledge

In addition to the advantages of non-directive probes, there is also an advantage to using a partly structured stimulus as a probe that has an open-ended element requiring the subject to respond in a way that reveals personal material (Loevinger, 1985). An example of the successful use of sentence completion stems is Rafaelli *et al.*'s (2001) exploration of the experience of "the street" by homeless, Brazilian youth. In-depth interviews might not have been possible in this research context, and shorter questions got quick replies. Examples of their sentence stems are: "In the street, I feel . . . ," "In the street, people . . . ," and "The street is not . . . ." This provides a comparability of focus across participants through the use of standard stems, while permitting individual uniqueness to be divulged in the way that stem sentences are completed by each participant. One uses both a direct and an indirect probe at the same time.

Challenges of qualitative methods

As Eccles (2012) notes, not all accounts offered in response to interview probes address the unfolding of a single event in time, even if one asks for highly specific material. Sometimes the researcher is not being told what happened, or what the player thought at the time, or even what the player thinks now. Sport experts may pass on to researchers received wisdom, or material more like "press releases" – "apparently misleading, irrelevant and stereotyped initial self-report statements [which] prevent appropriate reference to personal experience" (Wiersma, 1988, p. 205). In reporting received wisdom, an expert may avoid referring to personal experience by offering instead decontextualized maxims arising in the relevant subculture: "keep it simple," "focus on what you can control," or "move on from failure." These maxims may reflect broadly held ideals about how one should handle failure, for instance, or may be tailored to counter or optimize a particular player's existing tendencies. They do not necessarily convey how to do what the injunction conveys as ideal, such as how one moves on from failure. That aspect of experience may be lost unless there is a follow-up question. An interviewer should pursue specific, detailed content respectfully.

Yet even these "press releases" from experts may reveal much to a researcher once they are interpreted in context (Wiersma, 1988). If one has not managed to establish rapport with an interviewee, or if there is some concern about how a researcher is affiliated or where funding is from, press releases may be offered. They may be the first level of information a person offers, and patience is required to go more deeply into experience. To go more deeply, researchers need to recognize them in the moment: what is being given and (perhaps) why. Press releases may also reflect cultural taboos about acknowledging emotions, particularly negative emotions like rivalry, self-doubt, and anger; to bypass envy about being a tall poppy (Feather, 1989), luck rather than personal ability may be attributed as the cause of a player's selection.

If, as interviewer, one can establish rapport across diverse participants and a range of experience levels, interviews can open up a world of insight into skill and its context-relevant attributes. Rapport is variously defined as including a "frank and open discussion," as entailing the "acceptance of and co-operation with the research project" on the part of the interviewee, and the researcher's "capacity to engage with the language and culture of the respondent in a way that gains a level of trust" (Dundon & Ryan, 2010, p. 564). It is not just a feel-good variable; it directly affects the nature and validity of the information that the researcher is given.

Kinds of coding: integrating qualitative and quantitative methods

Once data are in hand – across grounded theory, modified analytic induction, and sentence completion stems – the next phase is coding. An appropriate starting point is often a detailed form of coding called open coding, which involves a line-by-line analysis of everything said. In open coding one identifies concepts and their properties and dimensions, before moving to axial coding, which relates concepts to each other on the basis of their properties and dimensions (Strauss & Corbin, 1998).

We can suggest how such thematic exploration might contribute to the understanding of sport expertise. Bawden and Maynard (2001) conducted a study based on semi-structured interviews of cricketers who had experienced the yips (involuntary movements occurring repeatedly in the execution of a skill). They used lead questions with standardized probes in interviews with eight bowlers to capture a broad range of experience and a wide array of parameters (level of cricket played, pace of bowling, years of experience, age). Their insightful article offers statements from each bowler that constitutes the "raw data," and then two levels of higher order themes. Above that they list the "general dimensions," which are the domains of interest and probes that they used. They do not attempt to derive a theoretical model from their data, but contribute to the literature at a descriptive level, integrating their findings with contemporary theories of the yips and of choking. Further, this research offers a vivid window into the experience of the yips with affecting specificity. There is surprise and shock at its occurrence: participants said they had no idea it was about to happen, and that helplessness was experienced, as one suggested the ball felt "stuck in his hand." In the moment, it is emotions that are highlighted, especially the emotions of trauma: pure shock, feeling destroyed, anxiety, panic, a wish to escape but an inability to "get out," "can't finish the over until you get six legal balls, and trapped until you do," negative thoughts of others' perceptions, etc. Participants found it "terrifying that they couldn't do a simple task" and reported a loss of personal agency "like I'd been taken over" and a loss of ownership, where "[your] arm feels like it isn't yours." This kind of data gives specific, experiential insight like no other.

Not every researcher wishes to devise a full theory from qualitative data. There are statistics that can take to the next level what is revealed by the frequency of codes' occurrence in light of other attributes and experiences of those in the research sample. This optimizes the generality of findings from specific interviews and codes. One can use factor analysis to look at the intercorrelation of codes to reveal strategies (Harris et al., 2011). Or, one can use cluster analysis. For this procedure one needs first to look at the relative frequency of occurrence of certain codes across the whole sample. The use of cluster analysis to do this is well represented in sport science (Ball & Best, 2007; Gaudreau & Blondin, 2004) where clusters are generated from data gathered using scales – i.e., data that are already quantitative. We could not find a mixed method approach in sports where cluster analysis was used to determine profiles based on codes derived from interview or qualitative data. Therefore, we use an example from outside the sport content domain, because Wohl, Kuiken, and Noels (2006) outline their procedure in detail and offer clear advice about selection of statistics for a cluster analysis. We briefly describe their procedure here as illustration of how clusters form and might be used. Wohl et al. analyzed narratives of forgiveness and focused on codes that were neither rare (occurring in less than 10 per cent of the narratives) nor ubiquitous (occurring in over 90 per cent of the narratives). They then carried out a cluster analysis to see how the different codes clustered. Their results gave a three-cluster solution. Each participant is accorded a cluster number as an output of this analysis. This reflects the cluster within which their narrative fits. Results show the proportion of cluster members expressing a phrase within their narratives that attracted a particular code. One can then use the cluster number as a way of forming groups that may be used in analysis of variance or t-tests to see whether there are differences between clusters on certain outcome variables like well-being, relationship satisfaction, and so on. Attributes which defined the clusters of forgiveness styles in this study illustrate how clusters differ from each other. Cluster one included those whose forgiveness began when they brought their feelings into the open with the transgressor; they

Measuring breadth and depth of knowledge

were then able to let go of their negative feelings, and to see things in light of broader well-being concerns. Those in cluster two saw forgiveness as a private moral issue, and were able to return to a normal relationship even in the absence of an apology. Cluster three included those who tried to maintain a positive relationship despite the wrong done to them, but could not forget: in contrast to the other two clusters, they did not see wider implications of forgiveness for their own well-being, and the relationship never really recovered.

Bawden and Maynard (2001) might have done a cluster analysis on their data. In addition to the qualitative codes derived from their interview data about experiences of the yips in cricket as potential clustering variables (e.g., the conditions before the yips happened, the first experience of the yips, descriptions of subsequent bowling, perceived characteristics of good bowling, and personal explanations of the yips), they might also have included, as cluster determinants, other variables they assessed like age, handedness, pace, and level of cricket. Cluster analysis would permit them to see if there were different forms of yips within their group and whether there were outcomes linked to that form of experience. By recommending integration of the use of statistics with detailed experiential studies of individuals, we hope to address two rarely integrated trends in research.

Triangulating methods: nomothetic and idiographic research

We want to understand the law-like features of performance that generalize across participants (the nomothetic approach). But we also may sometimes wish to adopt the idiographic approach: to track an individual's profile of strengths or difficulties, their ways of achieving excellence and resilience, or of experiencing performance breakdown, which may be quite unexpected and idiosyncratic. Sometimes there is a trade-off in research, but scientific understanding requires both approaches. In areas like sport where expertise often takes unique forms, involving precise, stylistic features unlikely to transfer across individuals, the mapping of the uniqueness of the individual has more to offer than in many domains. Even when abilities or difficulties are highly individual, theory may identify levels of abstraction at which seemingly unique experiences or style might generalize to other players. Really understanding the forms of expertise – what optimizes and sustains them, as well as what causes them to be momentarily lost – requires both forms of knowledge.

The triangulation of methods is a rare and joyous thing. In our chapter on breadth and depth of knowledge (Chapter 9), we discussed cases in which verbal report data are integrated with other measures such as eye movements. Sebanz and Shiffrar (2009) also found a compelling link between self-report and perception. Generalizing from literature on deceptive signals that leak out without the performer's awareness of deceptive displays that are strategies, their study used stimuli that were constructed, where the player decided in advance whether to fake or make a pass. They used as their experimental stimuli only the fakes where the defender had been completely deceived. The defender was then edited out of the videos, thus ensuring the quality of the deceptive display. Experts were better than novices when movement was present, but there were no significant differences with static posture alone. At the end of the study they distributed questionnaires, finding an overlap between self-report and observational data in terms of the emphasis on kinematics vs. postural cues in the groups. The relevance of retaining what people could actually do was still underscored: they found that only experts could detect deception from kinematics alone (point-light displays), while novices relied on chance. If Bruce, Farrow, Raynor, and Mann (2012) had only *observed* what a person had been able to do in their study that sought to determine, across three tiers of expertise, whether strategic response selection was limited by motor skill capacity, they would have missed the fact that when asked for verbal reports on the optimum strategy, even less-skilled people suggested a long pass would be optimal even where a long pass could not be reliably performed.

In an area that is already rippling with insightful research designs to capture features of a dynamically unfolding and highly contingent set of skills, it is hard to suggest that there might be supplementary methods. Yet, there are levels of skill that are beyond motor execution and perception-action coupling, but which inform them. The full picture of skill includes some dispositional forms of knowledge, which are regularly updated, about self, other, and game. Knowledge about self includes knowledge of current form, strength, speed, injury status and risk, how one handles risk and failure, and about one's capacity to come back from failure. Knowledge about one's competitors includes knowledge of their current form, stylistic strengths, and weaknesses, as well as an awareness of the degree to which they might have mapped one's own form, strengths, and weaknesses. There is also knowledge about context: the meaning of this game, what hinges on it, whether one is playing at home or away, and how much leeway there is for underperformance. Once skill is contextualized in this way, it is apparent that the motor and perceptual components of skill are an important part, embedded in a wider story. We have attempted to canvas what we can add to the methodological toolkit of research into sport expertise that addresses this wider story about forms of knowledge that feed into core skill features.

References

Arcuri, A. (2007) 'Psychotherapists' handling of sexual attraction to clients: A grounded theory', unpublished thesis, New South Wales, AU: Department of Psychology, Macquarie University.

Arcuri, A., & McIlwain, D.J.F. (2009) 'Psychotherapists' handling of sexual attraction to clients: A grounded theory', in L. Richards (ed) *Handling qualitative data*, 2nd ed., London: Sage. Retrieved from www.uk.sagepub.com/richards/homeP2.htm

Ball, K. A., & Best, R. J. (2007) 'Different centre of pressure patterns within the golf stroke I: Cluster analysis', *Journal of Sports Sciences*, 25(7): 757–70.

Bawden, M., & Maynard, I. (2001) 'Towards an understanding of the personal experience of the "yips" in cricketers', *Journal of Sport Sciences*, 19: 937–53.

Bicknell, K. (2010) 'Feeling them ride: Corporeal exchange in cross-country mountain bike racing', *About Performance*, 10: 81–91.

Bruce, L., Farrow, D., Raynor, A., & Mann, D. (2012) 'But I can't pass that far! The influence of motor skill on decision making', *Psychology of Sport and Exercise*, 13: 152–61.

Camic, P. M., Rhodes, J. E., & Yardley, L. (2003) 'Naming the stars: Integrating qualitative methods into psychological research', in P. M. Camic, J. E. Rhodes, & L. Yardley (eds) *Qualitative research in psychology: Expanding perspectives in methodology and design*, Washington, DC: American Psychological Association, 3–15.

Chaffin, R., Imreh, G., & Crawford, M. (2002) *Practicing perfection: Memory and piano performance*, New York: Lawrence Erlbaum Associates.

Dennett, D. C. (2003) *Freedom evolves*, New York: Allen Lane.

Dundon, T., & Ryan, P. (2010) 'Interviewing reluctant respondents: Strikes, henchmen, and Gaelic games', *Organizational Research Methods*, 13: 562–81.

Eccles, D. W. (2012) 'Verbal reports of cognitive processes', in G. Tenenbaum, R. Eklund, & A. Kamata (eds) *Measurement in sport and exercise psychology*, Champaign, IL: Human Kinetics, 103–17.

Ericsson, K. A., & Simon, H. A. (1980) 'Verbal reports as data', *Psychological Review*, 87: 215–51.

Fassinger, R. E. (2005) 'Paradigms, praxis, problems, and promise: Grounded theory in counseling psychology research', *Journal of Counseling Psychology*, 52: 156–66.

Feather, N. T. (1989) 'Attitudes towards the high achiever: The fall of the tall poppy', *Australian Journal of Psychology*, 41: 239–67.

Fox, M. C., Ericsson, K. A., & Best, R. (2011) 'Do procedures for verbal reporting of thinking have to be reactive? A meta-analysis and recommendations for best reporting method', *Psychological Bulletin*, 137: 316–44.

Gaudreau, P., & Blondin, J. P. (2004) 'Different athletes cope differently during a sport competition: A cluster analysis of coping', *Journal of Personality and Individual Differences*, 36: 1865–77.

Measuring breadth and depth of knowledge

Gilgun, J. (1995) 'We shared something special: The moral discourse of incest perpetrators', *Journal of Marriage and Family*, 57: 265–81.

Gilgun, J. (2009) 'Qualitative research and family psychology', in J. H. Bray & M. Stanton (eds) *The Wiley-Blackwell handbook of family psychology*, London: Wiley, 85–99.

Glaser, B. G., & Strauss, A. L. (1967) *The discovery of grounded theory: Strategies for qualitative research*, Hawthorne, NY: Aldine Publishing Company.

Harris, C. B., Keil, P. G., Sutton, J., Barnier, A. J., & McIlwain, D.J.F. (2011) '"We remember, we forget": Collaborative remembering in older couples', *Discourse Processes*, 48: 267–303.

Loevinger, J. (1985) 'Revision of the sentence completion test for ego development', *Journal of Personality and Social Psychology*, 48: 420–7.

Marecek, J. (2003) 'Dancing through minefields: Toward a qualitative stance in psychology', in P. M. Camic, J. E. Rhodes, & L. Yardley (eds) *Qualitative research in psychology: Expanding perspectives in methodology and design*, Washington, DC: American Psychological Association, 49–69.

McPherson, S. L., & MacMahon, C. (2008) 'How baseball players prepare to bat: Tactical knowledge as a mediator of expert performance in baseball', *Journal of Sport & Exercise Psychology*, 30: 755–78.

McRobert, A. P., Ward, P., Eccles, D. W., & Williams, A. M. (2011) 'The effect of manipulating context-specific information on perceptual-cognitive processes during a simulated anticipation task', *British Journal of Psychology*, 102: 519–34.

Morrow, S. L. (2005) 'Quality and trustworthiness in qualitative research in counseling psychology', *Journal of Counseling Psychology*, 52: 250–60.

Nisbett, R. E., & Wilson, T. C. (1977) 'Telling more than we can know: Verbal reports on mental processes', *Psychological Review*, 84: 231–59.

Ponterotto, J. G. (2005) 'Qualitative research in counseling psychology: A primer on research paradigms and philosophy of science', *Journal of Counseling Psychology*, 52: 126–36.

Raffaelli, M., Koller, S., Reppold, C., Kuschick, M., Krum, F., Bandeira, D., & Simões, C. (2001) 'Gender differences in Brazilian street youth's family circumstances and experiences on the street', *Child Abuse & Neglect*, 24: 1431–41.

Roca, A., Ford, P. R., McRobert, A. P., & Williams, A. M. (2011) 'Identifying the processes underlying anticipation and decision-making in a dynamic time-constrained task', *Cognitive Processing*, 12: 301–10.

Sebanz, N., & Shiffrar, M. (2009) 'Detecting deception in a bluffing body: The role of expertise', *Psychonomic Bulletin & Review*, 16: 170–5.

Strauss, A., & Corbin, J. (1998) *Basics of qualitative research: Techniques and procedures for developing grounded theory*, 2nd ed., Thousand Oaks: Sage Publications.

Wiersma, J. (1988) 'The press release: Symbolic communication in life history interviewing', *Journal of Personality*, 56: 205–38.

Wohl, M. J.A., Kuiken, D., & Noels, K. A. (2006) 'Three ways to forgive: A numerically-aided phenomenological study', *British Journal of Social Psychology*, 45: 547–61.

21

MEASURING PSYCHOLOGICAL DETERMINANTS OF EXPERTISE

Dispositional factors

Bradley Fawver, Garrett F. Beatty, and Christopher M. Janelle

Delineating the psychological factors that discriminate expertise levels is important to understanding disparate competitive outcomes. Empirically based knowledge of critical enduring psychological factors that underpin expertise will permit the advancement of evidence-based recommendations to aid in development of the psychological skills necessary to sustain consistent expert performance. Psychological factors are typically assessed using self-report interviews and questionnaires, but they can also be inferred through myriad physiological indices and overt motor behaviors. A comprehensive review of methods used to measure the psychological factors germane to sport performance could easily substantiate a separate text in and of itself (cf. Tenenbaum *et al.*, 2012). Accordingly, we have been intentionally selective to emphasize the strengths and limitations of measures of psychological factors featured in the expertise literature. We have also attempted to avoid redundancy with material featured in other sections of this book by omitting measurements pertaining to discrete attentional skills (see Chapters 6–8). General considerations for the development of sound psychometrics are overviewed, and then foundational psychological influences on sport behavior are summarized. Measures of motivational factors, dispositional characteristics, and psychological performance "profiles" are then summarized. The chapter concludes by reviewing measures of dispositional attentional characteristics.

General considerations for selecting and employing measurement tools

When researchers or practitioners select measurement tools, criteria should center on whether the selected tools: 1) are founded in sound theory, 2) accurately and consistently measure the desired psychological constructs, 3) are appropriate for the assessed population (e.g., age, gender, culture, language), and 4) are suitable for the contextual and temporal constraints of the assessment environment. Development and validation of psychological measurement tools is accomplished through statistical procedures known as exploratory factor analysis (EFA) and confirmatory factor analysis (CFA). Typically, EFA is employed when developing measurement tools and CFA when validating them. In both instances, the relationships between individual items (indicators) and psychological constructs (factors) are assessed. These tools allow researchers to test for discriminant and convergent validity. Convergent validity assesses the degree to which theoretically related measures of constructs are indeed related. Discriminant validity assesses

Measuring psychological determinants of expertise

whether measures that should not be related are truly unrelated. For a detailed review of these and other issues related to factor analysis and structural equation modeling (SEM), see Estabrook (2012) and Marsh (2007).

Construct validity is crucial to selecting appropriate measurement tools. In the simplest terms, construct validity refers to whether an instrument accurately measures the theoretical construct from which it was derived. Threats to validity come from a variety of sources. For example, the format of questions in an instrument may influence participants towards selecting extreme responses. Participants' responses may also be distorted or prone to errors when retrospectively reflecting on previous experiences (Robinson & Clore, 2002), or they may overemphasize recent experiences compared to older memories (Hedges *et al.*, 1985; Robinson & Clore, 2002; Watson & Tellegen, 2002). Also, there may be reason to believe participants unintentionally or intentionally respond in a manner that is perceived as socially desirable. While this is certainly possible, research suggests that self-ratings are no more socially desirable than the ratings of peers (Watson & Vaidya, 2003). Moreover, even when participants respond to the best of their ability, there may be reason to question the degree to which they are able to accurately self-evaluate psychological states. Woven throughout each of these are measurement issues relating to cultural differences (see Matsumoto & Yoo, 2007; Ryba *et al.*, 2012).

In addition to the validity of psychological measures, the reliability of an instrument is important to consider. Whether or not responses are steady across measurements may be related to psychometric reliability, but may also reflect the stability of the psychological factors themselves. For example, researchers in the psychological sciences are concerned with both trait (dispositional) and state (transient/contextual) characteristics. While trait factors are quite stable over time, state factors can fluctuate within a person depending on the domain (e.g., sport vs. non-sport) or activity level (e.g., arousal). Though a psychological measure may be theoretically rigorous and psychometrically sound, it may be implemented inappropriately or incorrectly. As a final, general rule of thumb, researchers should carefully select suitable measures to answer their questions, and only interpret findings within an appropriate scope of the currently accepted theoretical framework. For more information on psychometrics and measurement issues see Tenenbaum, Kamata, and Hayashi (2007) and chapters 2–8 of Tenenbaum *et al.* (2012).

Measuring motivational factors

Motivation influences sport performance in wide and varied ways (Gould *et al.*, 2002; Vallerand, 2004). Predictability of motivational impact on performance is complicated by the reality that the amount, direction, and duration of motivational influences are determined by multiple, often competing motives. At its most fundamental level, motivation serves to organize all behavior as the collective approach and avoidance tendencies that encourage attainment of pleasant or appetitive goals and avoidance of unpleasant consequences. At a more domain-specific level, motivation includes numerous intrinsic and extrinsic factors that impact sport participation. Furthermore, appropriately directed motivation is a multidimensional, idiosyncratic necessity for high-level sport achievement (Guay *et al.*, 2003; Maehr & Braskamp, 1986). Below, we review how motivational processes are measured within sport populations and, where applicable, discuss empirical findings with regard to expertise.

Motivation is a consequence of both internal and external factors that modify behavior (Vallerand, 2004). Motives are more transient than personality, more stable than discrete emotions, and directly impacted by dispositional characteristics such as trait anxiety and personality. Research generally supports the idea that task-motivated athletes perform better under stressful conditions. Younger athletes tend to believe their success is due to external factors, while older athletes have a more task-oriented focus, believing that performance is a result of motivation and effort (Duda & Nicholls, 1992; Treasure & Roberts, 1994). Therefore, as athletes mature and gain expertise, there appears to be an adaptive pattern of achievement beliefs (Roberts & Balague, 1991). Elite athletes generally view their athletic competitions as a challenge rather than a threat, a perspective that provides further motivation to succeed (Allen *et al.*, 2012). Task- or process-oriented athletes more frequently use psychological skills (e.g., imagery, goal setting, positive self-talk) to improve performance and generally perform at a superior level compared to ego-focused athletes (Harwood *et al.*, 2004). The ideal combination of ego and task orientation increases engagement in tasks that increase achievement (Hodge & Petlichkoff, 2000).

Intrinsic and extrinsic motivation

Motivation encompasses multiple intrinsic (Vallerand, 1997) and extrinsic (Deci & Ryan, 1985) factors. The hierarchical model of intrinsic and extrinsic motivation (HMIEM; Vallerand & Ratelle, 2002; Vallerand, 2007) explains motivational determinants and consequences at the global, contextual, and situational level (as well as interactions between the levels). Self-report measures have been developed to ascertain the degree to which athletes are intrinsically, extrinsically, or amotivated at each motivational level. The situational motivation scale (SIMS; Guay *et al.*, 2000) is a brief self-report instrument that measures intrinsic motivation, identified regulation, external regulation, and amotivation. At a contextual level, several measures have been developed for use in sport. The sport motivation scale (SMS; Pelletier *et al.*, 1995) and revised sport motivation scale-6 (SMS-6; Pelletier *et al.*, 2007) both measure intrinsic, extrinsic, and amotivations for participating in an activity. The scales have high levels of validity and reliability, and have been validated in multiple languages (e.g., Italian, Chinese, Japanese, Russian, Spanish). Other contextual measures include the behavioral regulation in sport questionnaire (BRSQ; Lonsdale *et al.*, 2008) and the pictorial motivation scale (PMS; Reid *et al.*, 2009). Evidence suggests that the BRSQ may have improved reliability and factorial validity compared to the SMS measures. Finally, the global motivation scale (GMS; Guay *et al.*, 2003) measures motivation towards participating in activities at the global or general level. For a more detailed review of these measures, see Vallerand, Donahue, and Lafreniere (2012).

Achievement motivation

In sport, achievement motivation represents the processes that stimulate pursuit of skill competence. Achievement motives underlie the development of superior skills that can be oriented to attainment of competitive objectives. Athletes with high task orientations tend to believe that success is dependent on interest and effort, whereas those with high ego orientations predominantly believe success depends on superior ability (for a review of achievement theory, see Elliot & Dweck, 2005; Thrash & Hurst, 2008). The hierarchical model of achievement motivation (Elliot, 1997, 1999) specifies that neurophysiological, dispositional, and contextual characteristics of the athlete (and their interactions) impact achievement goals, which manifest as achievement emotions, cognitions, and behaviors. The task and ego orientation in sport questionnaire (TEOSQ; Duda & Nicholls, 1992), based originally on the motivational orientation scales (Nicholls *et al.*, 1985; Nicholls, 1989), measures task and ego orientations in sport. The TEOSQ has shown acceptable internal consistency (Kuan & Roy, 2007) and various translated versions of the instrument are available (e.g., Barkoukis *et al.*, 2008; Wang & Liu, 2007). Although it is used frequently in sport-related fields, the TEOSQ's ability to measure dispositional traits has been questioned (Harwood & Hardy, 2001). Moreover, concerns have been raised regarding

Measuring psychological determinants of expertise

whether the task subscales encompass all task orientations (Harwood *et al.*, 2000). Notably for researchers in sport fields, task orientation may split into separate factors in non-elite populations (Duda & Whitehead, 1998), suggesting that this measure may yield confounding results when applied uniformly across levels of sport expertise.

Although not used widely to date, there are other measures that may be of value for researchers studying sport expertise. The perception of success questionnaire (POSQ; Roberts *et al.*, 1998) consists of a 12-item scale with six items based on task orientations and six items based on ego orientations. A modified version of the POSQ was created to measure the relationship between perfectionism and cognitive anxiety. Results from this version suggest that ego orientation and perfectionism made a significant contribution to the prediction of cognitive anxiety, while a task orientation significantly predicted confidence (Hall *et al.*, 1998). Other motivation and achievement measures of interest include the work and family orientation questionnaire (WOFQ; Helmreich & Spence, 1978), the sport orientation questionnaire (SOQ; Gill & Deeter, 1988), and the competitive orientation inventory (COI; Vealey, 1986). For reviews of achievement motivation processes and measures see Conroy and Hyde (2012) and Duda and Whitehead (1998).

Measuring dispositional profiles and trait factors

The role of trait psychological factors in differentiating levels of sport expertise has fascinated researchers for many years. A phenotype of personality and/or mood characteristics that distinguishes expert athletes from non-elites has yet to be discovered, but a variety of individual qualities tend to distinguish athletes of disparate expertise levels. Generally, elite athletes report increased positive personality traits (e.g., self-control, agreeableness) and mood states (e.g., vigor) compared to less successful athletes, who report increased negative personality traits (e.g., anxiety, neuroticisms) and mood states (e.g., depression, tension, fatigue). Overall, elite athletes tend to exhibit increased "hardiness" compared to non-elite competitors (Sheard & Golby, 2010), including self-belief and mental toughness (Weissensteiner *et al.*, 2012). Additionally, individual differences in domain-specific perceptual ability are important factors differentiating levels of sport expertise (Mann *et al.*, 2007). Here we review some of these and other findings, while highlighting the measurement tools used to determine stable psychological factors underpinning sport expertise.

Personality

Two commonly used psychological measures of personality are the 16 personality factor questionnaire (16PF; Cattell *et al.*, 1970) and the five factor model (FFM) of personality (McCrae & Costa, 2008; McCrae & John, 1992). Neither instrument was originally designed as a sport-specific measure, but they have been widely used in sport psychology. Research suggests that elite athletes tend to rank higher in tough-mindedness and self-control, and lower in anxiety on the 16PF questionnaire (Martin *et al.*, 2011). The most successful athletes also report lower levels of pre-game cognitive and somatic anxiety (Covassin & Pero, 2004). Work using the FFM indicates that elite athletes also tend to be higher in openness, conscientiousness, extraversion, and agreeableness, and score lower in neuroticism. The Eysenck personality inventory (EPI; Eysenck & Eysenck, 1982) can also be used to assess personality, but is limited to the dimensions of extraversion/introversion and neuroticism/stability. Higher performing athletes display higher extroversion and lower neuroticism scores when compared to athletes at lower levels.

Recently, increased attention has been directed toward understanding the role of perfectionism in the development of sport expertise. The Frost multidimensional perfectionism scale (FMPS; Frost & DiBartolo, 2002) assesses the degree to which an athlete engages in perfectionistic thinking, including subscales for concerns over mistakes, doubts about actions, parental expectations, parental criticism, and personal standards. Results suggest that scores on the FMPS are related to anxiety and obsessive thinking (Frost & DiBartolo, 2002; Hall *et al.*, 1998). A shortened version has been developed by Cox and colleagues (Cox *et al.*, 2002), with improved factorial validity. Additionally, task orientation has been shown to predict confidence, while ego orientation predicts cognitive anxiety and doubts about action (Hall *et al.*, 1998). Perfectionism scores on subscales of the shortened version of the FMPS (personal standards, organization, and concern over mistakes) may also be related to the probability of experiencing the "yips" (Roberts *et al.*, 2013). It has been suggested that domain-specific perfectionism scales may be more appropriate for use in sport (Stoeber & Stoeber, 2009). Sport-specific measures, such as the sport multidimensional perfectionism scale-2 (Sport-MPS-2; Gotwals & Dunn, 2009), are now available. Importantly, scores on the Sport-MPS-2 associate more closely with competitive trait anxiety compared to general perfectionism measures (Gotwals *et al.*, 2010).

Mood

Although the terms are sometimes used interchangeably, mood states are considered more stable than discrete emotional reactions (Davidson, 1994) and are not related to a particular acute stimulus (Frijda, 2009). In certain instances, an athlete's mood can predict performance outcomes (Beedie *et al.*, 2000). Consequently, extensive research has been conducted on mood in sport environments (LeUnes & Burger, 2000). Originally developed for psychiatric patients, the profile of mood states questionnaire (POMS; McNair *et al.*, 1971) is a classic measure of mood. In addition to stable traits, the POMS can also be used for shorter mood states lasting up to a few minutes (Payne, 2001). Six separate factors can be measured with the POMS (tension-anxiety, depression-dejection, anger-hostility, fatigue-inertia, vigor-activity, and confusion-bewilderment).

The POMS was featured in seminal investigations directed at determining stable characteristics of national and Olympic athletes (Morgan, 1978, 1980). Elite athletes tended to show the classic "iceberg profile shape," which reflects lower scores on tension, depression, anger, fatigue, and confusion, and higher scores on positive mood (i.e., vigor). Positive mood scores on the POMS are also associated with greater levels of athleticism (Terry & Lane, 2000). Contrastingly, non-elites score higher on negative moods and lower on vigor. The POMS has since been validated for work in athletic populations (Terry & Lane, 2000; Terry *et al.*, 2003). Along with the traditional iceberg profile, expertise is associated with higher levels of self-confidence and lower mood disturbances (Covassin & Pero, 2004).

It is important to note that the POMS is more successfully implemented when comparing athletes to non-athletes, and less helpful when comparing athletes at different levels (Rowley *et al.*, 1995). Moreover, meta-analytic approaches suggest that POMS is most effective when predicting performance outcomes (e.g., good or poor execution) and less accurate when predicting the level (elite vs. non-elite) of athletic achievement (Beedie *et al.*, 2000). Shorter versions of the POMS have also been developed for implementation in time-constrained environments (Biehl & Landauer, 1975; Curran *et al.*, 1995; Terry *et al.*, 1999; Terry *et al.*, 2003). Of these, the Brunel mood scale (BRUMS; Lane *et al.*, 2008) has been used in sport (Lane & Lane, 2002). Other measures of mood include the multiple affect adjective checklist (MAACL; Zuckerman & Lubin, 1965) and the four-dimension mood scale (4DMS; Gregg & Shepherd, 2009).

Dispositional anxiety

Other stable affective traits, such as dispositional anxiety, may characterize athletes of differing expertise levels, but no affective phenotype identifying elite athletes has been established. Considering the entirety of affective experience, anxiety is probably the most studied construct in the sport psychology literature. Trait anxiety represents the stable dispositional tendency to experience anxiety when encountering environmental stimuli. In general, research indicates that elite athletes often better manage anxiety levels while concurrently concentrating on the task at hand (Meyers *et al.*, 1999). Experiencing positive moods during stressful or anxiety inducing environments also contributes to experts' ability to focus. Coupled with confidence building self-talk, positive moods allow elite athletes to better cope with disappointing situations and perceive them as motivating, learning experiences (Cherry, 2005).

Several trait anxiety inventories exist for use in sporting populations. The sport competition anxiety test (SCAT; Martens, 1977) was developed as a unidimensional measure of competitive trait anxiety (cognitive and somatic factors were not distinguished), and has since produced high test-retest reliability. Another popular measure is the sport anxiety scale (SAS; Smith *et al.*, 1990), a multidimensional inventory of competitive trait anxiety. A revised version, the sport anxiety scale-2 (SAS-2; Smith *et al.*, 2006), now exists for use in all age groups. Finally, the state-trait anxiety inventory (STAI; Spielberger *et al.*, 1983), a general measure of anxiety, contains a trait scale that has frequently been used in sport (e.g., Murray & Janelle, 2003). Although not as common as anxiety measures, other affective self-report instruments can be used to measure trait dispositions in sport, such as depression (e.g., Beck's depression inventory (BDI); Beck *et al.*, 1996; the Hamilton rating scale for depression (HRSD); Hamilton, 1960), behavioral inhibition/activation (BIS/BAS scales; Carver & White, 1994), and positive/negative emotions (positive and negative affect schedule (PANAS); Watson *et al.*, 1988).

Attentional style and reinvestment

Equivocal research exists with regards to how attention differentiates athletes with varying expertise levels. Extant evidence suggests basic visual processing (e.g., innate visual acuity) does not distinguish elite athletes from non-elites (Mann *et al.*, 2010; Memmert *et al.*, 2009). Alternatively, sport-specific measures have robustly captured attentional contributors to expertise development (Laby *et al.*, 1996; Laby *et al.*, 2011). Without question, elite athletes' attentional control (Gould *et al.*, 2002; Thelwell *et al.*, 2005) and ability to focus amid distractions (Orlick, 1990; Singer *et al.*, 1991) contribute to their differentiated level of performance. In fact, differences in attentional skills among elite athletes separate the very best performers (e.g., those with multiple Olympic medals or world championships) from less accomplished elite athletes (e.g., those with only a single medal; Nideffer *et al.*, 2001). The most accomplished elite athletes score higher on measures of concentration and "focus" (Williams & Krane, 2001), and tend to direct attention to sport processes rather than outcomes (Durand-Bush & Salmela, 2001). The ability to narrowly focus on relevant cues in the visual scene while avoiding distractions is also an important component of achieving top performance (Garfield & Bennett, 1984; Gould *et al.*, 2002; Loehr, 1984; Ravizza, 1977), with more skilled players reportedly being able to narrow their focus of attention on important features better than less-skilled athletes (Kerr & Cox, 1991). Additionally, experts make better use of early cues (Abernethy & Russell, 1987) and search the visual field more effectively compared to novices. Specifically, experts make more fixations on crucial aspects of the visual scene and focus less on distracting or lower quality information. Finally, expert performers are more adept at managing limited attentional resources compared to non-experts, and they require fewer attentional resources to complete the same task (Leavitt, 1979; Beilock *et al.*, 2002). For a meta-analytic quantitative review in the area of visual search and expertise, see Mann *et al.* (2007). For more information on these and other attentional differences, including measures typically used to study attention and gaze behavior, see Chapters 6–8. Here we focus on self-report measures of attentional allocation.

The test of attentional and interpersonal style (TAIS; Nideffer, 1976), developed from Nideffer's notions of attentional style, is perhaps the most common measure of attentional selectivity used in sport research. The TAIS measures attentional focus (width: broad vs. narrow; direction: internal vs. external), concentration, selective attention, and shifting (for a review on the TAIS, see Abernethy *et al.*, 1998). Various sport-specific versions of the TAIS have been developed (Albrecht & Feltz, 1987; Bergandi *et al.*, 1990; Summers *et al.*, 1991; Van Schoyck & Grasha, 1981). Nideffer (1990, 2007) has argued that the underlying theoretical framework remains solid, and as an instrument, the TAIS holds some utility; however, researchers have called into question its discriminant (Ford & Jeffery, 1992) and construct validity (Landers, 1981).

The cognitive failures questionnaire (CFQ; Broadbent *et al.*, 1982) measures lapses in attentional control as a trait characteristic. Breaks in everyday attention are correlated with anxiety, and may be related to inhibition control (Friedman & Miyake, 2004). Although a general trait measure, the adult temperament questionnaire (ATQ; Rothbart *et al.*, 2000) has a subscale that measures attentional control. Another attentional measure, the attentional control scale (ACS; Derryberry & Reed, 2002) assesses attentional shifting, or the ability to transfer attention between tasks. Additionally, this scale assesses ability to voluntarily control attention, which has been shown to correlate with dispositional levels of anxiety. The effortful control scale (ECS; Lonigan & Phillips, 2001) measures attentional control, activational control, and inhibitory control.

Experts have the ability to adaptively exert conscious control over automatic processes (Masters & Maxwell, 2004), while novices may require increased focus on motor execution during the early stages of skill acquisition. Indeed, a hallmark of skill development is the allocation of attentional resources away from motor skills as they become increasingly automated. Still, lapses in performance among expert athletes can occur due to the reinvestment of resources into learned, controlled processes. Experts' performance suffers when controlled attentional processing is directed to automated motor skills (Beilock *et al.*, 2004; Beilock *et al.*, 2002; Rowe & McKenna, 2001), even though they may know this is a disadvantageous strategy (Baumeister & Showers, 1986). The reinvestment scale was developed by Masters and colleagues (Masters *et al.*, 1993) to measure the degree to which performers reinvest in automatic processes. The reinvestment scale contains 20 items drawn from the self-consciousness scale (Fenigstein *et al.*, 1975), the emotional control questionnaire (ECQ; Roger & Nesshoever, 1987), and the cognitive failures questionnaire (CFQ; Broadbent *et al.*, 1982). In their seminal study, Masters *et al.* (1993) found that higher scores on the scale were associated with a greater number of rules accumulated during learning. Masters and Maxwell (2004) later demonstrated that high reinvesters use more explicit knowledge than low reinvesters to control their movements during a stressed performance test. More critically, work has established a negative correlation between scores on the scale and performance under anxious conditions (Masters *et al.*, 1993; Maxwell *et al.*, 2006), revealing that high reinvesters perform poorly under pressure (Chell *et al.*, 2003). For a review of reinvestment and related notions, see Masters and Maxwell (2008).

Accumulating evidence supports the utility of reinvestment scales (Jackson *et al.*, 2006; Kinrade *et al.*, 2010), including a reinvestment scale for movement (Masters *et al.*, 2005). Further research is needed, however, to determine the mechanisms underlying the sport-specific nature of these individual differences in reinvestment (Laby *et al.*, 2011). Although no sport-specific work has been conducted concerning the susceptibility to reinvest across expertise levels, based

Measuring psychological determinants of expertise

on existing knowledge we suspect the psychological buffers (e.g., confidence) shared among most expert athletes may shield against the propensity to reinvest in controlled processes.

Summary and conclusion

Sport psychologists have developed numerous measures of psychological constructs that have been increasingly implemented to gain an understanding of the psychological factors that may be necessary for expert sport performance. We have highlighted many of the most commonly employed dispositional assessment tools within this area of research, including measures of motivation, personality, mood, and attentional style. Overall, research indicates that elite performers differ from their non-elite counterparts in the intensity and direction of motivation to participate and persist in sport, mood and personality profiles, and attentional predispositions. As empirical investigations further advance the expert sport performance knowledge base, the measures discussed here will continue to evolve and improve, revealing yet undisclosed insights into the role of psychological factors in the development of expertise in sport populations.

References

Abernethy, B., & Russell, D. G. (1987) 'The relationship between expertise and visual search strategy in a racquet sport', *Human Movement Science*, 6(4): 283–319.

Abernethy, B., Summers, J. J., & Ford, S. (1998) 'Issues in the measurement of attention', in J. L. Duda (ed) *Advances in sport and exercise psychology measurement*, Morgantown, WV: Fitness Information Technology, Inc., 173–93.

Albrecht, R. R., & Feltz, D. L. (1987) 'Generality and specificity of attention related to competitive anxiety and sport performance', *Journal of Sport Psychology*, 9(3): 231–48.

Allen, M. S., Frings, D., & Hunter, S. (2012) 'Personality, coping, and challenge and threat states in athletes', *International Journal of Sport and Exercise Psychology*, 10(4): 264–75.

Barkoukis, V., Tsorbatzoudis, H., & Grouios. G. (2008) 'Manipulation of motivational climate in physical education: Effects of a seven-month intervention', *European Physical Education Review*, 14(3): 367–87.

Baumeister, R. F., & Showers, C. J. (1986) 'A review of paradoxical performance effects: Choking under pressure in sports and mental tests', *European Journal of Social Psychology*, 16(4): 361–83.

Beck, A. T., Steer, R. A., & Brown, G. K. (1996) *Manual for the Beck depression inventory-II*, San Antonio, TX: Psychological Corporation.

Beedie, C. J., Terry, P. C., & Lane, A. M. (2000) 'The profile of mood states and athletic performance: Two meta-analyses', *Journal of Applied Sport Psychology*, 12(1): 49–68.

Beilock, S. L., Bertenthal, B. I., McCoy, A. M., & Carr, T. H. (2004) 'Haste does not always make waste: Expertise, direction of attention, and speed versus accuracy in performing sensorimotor skills', *Psychonomic Bulletin & Review*, 11(2): 373–9.

Beilock, S. L., Carr, T. H., MacMahon, C., & Starkes, J. L. (2002) 'When paying attention becomes counterproductive: Impact of divided versus skill-focused attention on novice and experienced performance of sensorimotor skills', *Journal of Experimental Psychology: Applied*, 8(1): 6–16.

Bergandi, T. A., Shryock, M. G., & Titus, T. G. (1990) 'The basketball concentration survey: Preliminary development and validation', *The Sport Psychologist*, 4(2): 119–29.

Biehl, B., & Landauer, A. (1975) *The profile of mood states (POMS)*, Mannheim, DE: Universität.

Broadbent, D. E., Cooper, P. F., FitzGerald, P., & Parkes, K. R. (1982) 'The cognitive failures questionnaire (CFQ) and its correlates', *The British Journal of Clinical Psychology*, 21(1): 1–16.

Carver, C. S., & White, T. L. (1994) 'Behavioral inhibition, behavioral activation, and affective responses to impending reward and punishment: The BIS/BAS scales', *Journal of Personality and Social Psychology*, 67(2): 319–33.

Cattell, R. B., Eber, H. W., & Tatsuoka, M. M. (1970) *Handbook for the sixteen personality factor questionnaire*, Champaign, IL: Institute for Personality and Ability Testing.

Chell, B. J., Graydon, J. K., Crowley, P. L., & Child, M. (2003) 'Manipulated stress and dispositional reinvestment in a wall-volley task: An investigation into controlled processing', *Perceptual and Motor Skills*, 97: 435–48.

Cherry, H. L. (2005) *Psychometric analysis of an inventory assessing mental toughness*, Knoxville, TN: University of Tennessee.

Conroy, D. E., & Hyde, A. L. (2012) *Achievement motivation processes*, in G. Tenenbaum, R. C. Eklund, & A. Kamata (eds) *Handbook of measurement in sport & exercise psychology*, Champaign, IL: Human Kinetics, 303–17.

Covassin, T., & Pero, S. (2004) 'The relationship between self-confidence, mood state, and anxiety among collegiate tennis players', *Journal of Sport Behavior*, 27(3): 230–42.

Cox, B. J., Enns, M. W., & Clara, I. P. (2002) 'The multidimensional structure of perfectionism in clinically distressed and college student samples', *Psychological Assessment*, 14(3): 365–73.

Curran, S. L., Andrykowski, M. A., & Studts, J. L. (1995) 'Short form of the profile of mood states (POMS-SF): Psychometric information', *Psychological Assessment*, 7(1): 80–3.

Davidson, R. J. (1994) 'On emotion, mood and related affective constructs', in P. Ekman & R. J. Davidson (eds) *The nature of emotion: Fundamental questions*, New York: Oxford University Press, 51–5.

Deci, E. L., & Ryan, R. M. (1985) *Intrinsic motivation and self-determination in human behavior*, New York: Plenum.

Derryberry, D., & Reed, M. A. (2002) 'Anxiety-related attentional biases and their regulation by attentional control', *Journal of Abnormal Psychology*, 111(2): 225–36.

Duda, J. L., & Nicholls, J. G. (1992) 'Dimensions of achievement motivation in schoolwork and sport', *Journal of Educational Psychology*, 84(3): 290–9.

Duda, J. L., & Whitehead, J. (1998) 'Measurement of goal perspectives in the physical domain', in J. L. Duda (ed) *Advances in sport and exercise psychology measurement*, Morgantown, WV: Fitness Information Technology, 21–48.

Durand-Bush, N., & Salmela, J. H. (2001) 'Becoming a world or Olympic champion: A process rather than an end result', in A. Papioannou, M. Goudas, & Y. Theodorakis (eds) *In the dawn of the new millennium: 10th World Congress of Sport Psychology*, vol. 2, Skathos, GR: Christodoul, 300–2.

Elliot, A. J. (1997) 'Integrating the "classic" and "contemporary" approaches to achievement motivation: A hierarchical model of approach and avoidance achievement motivation', in M. Maehr & P. Pintrich (eds) *Advances in motivation and achievement*, Greenwich, CT: Jai Press, 143–79.

Elliot, A. J. (1999) 'Approach and avoidance motivation and achievement goals', *Educational Psychologist*, 34(3): 169–89.

Elliot, A. J., & Dweck, C. S. (2005) *Handbook of competence and motivation*, New York: Guilford Press.

Estabrook, R. (2012) 'Measurement practice in sport and exercise psychology', in G. Tenenbaum, R. C. Eklund, & A. Kamata (eds) *Measurement in sport and exercise psychology*, Champaign, IL: Human Kinetics, 53–63.

Eysenck, H. J., & Eysenck, S.B.G. (1982) *Manual for the Eysenck personality inventory*, London: Hodder and Stoughton, 199–205.

Fenigstein, A., Scheier, M. F., & Buss, A. H. (1975) 'Public and private self-consciousness: Assessment and theory', *Journal of Consulting and Clinical Psychology*, 43(4): 522–7.

Ford, S. K., & Jeffery, J. (1992) 'The factorial validity of the TAIS attentional-style subscales', *Journal of Sport & Exercise Psychology*, 14(3): 283–98.

Friedman, N. P., & Miyake, A. (2004) 'The relations among inhibition and interference control functions: A latent-variable analysis', *Journal of Experimental Psychology: General*, 133(1): 101–35.

Frijda, N. H. (2009) 'Emotion experience and its varieties', *Emotion Review*, 1(3): 264–71.

Frost, R. O., & DiBartolo, P. M. (2002) 'Perfectionism, anxiety and obsessive-compulsive disorder', in G. L. Flett & P. L. Hewitt (eds) *Perfectionism: Theory, research and treatment*, Washington, DC: American Psychological Association, 341–71.

Garfield, C. A., & Bennett, H. Z. (1984) *Peak performance: Mental training techniques of the world's greatest athletes*, Los Angeles, CA: Tarcher.

Gill, D. L., & Deeter, T. E. (1988) 'Development of the sport orientation questionnaire', *Research Quarterly for Exercise and Sport*, 59(3): 191–202.

Gotwals, J. K., & Dunn, J.G.H. (2009) 'A multi-method multi-analytic approach to establishing internal construct validity evidence: The sport multidimensional perfectionism scale 2', *Measurement in Physical Education and Exercise Science*, 13(2): 71–92.

Gotwals, J. K., Dunn, J.G.H., Dunn, J.C., & Gamache, V. (2010) 'Establishing validity evidence for the sport multidimensional perfectionism scale-2 in intercollegiate sport', *Psychology of Sport and Exercise*, 11(6): 423–32.

Gould, D., Dieffenbach, K., & Moffett, A. (2002) 'Psychological characteristics and their development in Olympic champions', *Journal of Applied Sport Psychology*, 14(3): 172–204.

Gregg, V. H., & Shepherd, A. J. (2009) 'Factor structure of scores on the state version of the four dimension mood scale', *Educational and Psychological Measurement*, 69(1): 146–56.

Guay, F., Mageua, G., & Vallerand, R. J. (2003) 'On the hierarchical structure of self-determined motivation: A test of top-down and bottom-up, reciprocal, and horizontal effects', *Personality and Social Psychology Bulletin*, 29(8): 992–1004.

Guay, F., Vallerand, R. J., & Blanchard, C. M. (2000) 'On the assessment of situational intrinsic and extrinsic motivation: The situational motivation scale (SIMS)', *Motivation and Emotion*, 24(3): 175–213.

Hall, H. K., Alistair, W. K., & Matthews, J. (1998) 'Precompetitive anxiety in sport: The contribution of achievement goals and perfectionism', *Journal of Sport & Exercise Psychology*, 20: 194–217.

Hamilton, M. (1960) 'A rating scale for depression', *Journal of Neurology, Neurosurgery, and Psychiatry*, 23(1): 52–62.

Harwood, C., Cumming, J., & Fletcher, D. (2004) 'Motivational profiles and psychological skills use within elite youth sport', *Journal of Applied Sport Psychology*, 16(4): 318–32.

Harwood, C., & Hardy, 2001, L. (2001) 'Persistence and effort in moving achievement goal research forward: A response to Treasure and colleagues', *Journal of Sport and Exercise Psychology*, 23: 330–345.

Harwood, C., Hardy, L., & Swain, A. (2000) 'Achievement goals in sport: A critique of conceptual and measurement issues', *Journal of Sport & Exercise Psychology*, 22: 235–55.

Hedges, S. M., Jandorf, L., & Stone, A. A. (1985) 'Meaning of daily mood assessments', *Journal of Personality and Social Psychology*, 48(2): 428–34.

Helmreich, R. L., & Spence, J. T. (1978) 'The work and family orientation questionnaire: An objective instrument to assess components of achievement motivation and attitudes toward family and career [abstract]', *JSAS Catalog of Selected Documents in Psychology*, 8(2)(35): 1–27.

Hodge, K., & Petlichkoff, L. (2000) 'Goal profiles in sport motivation: a cluster analysis', *Journal of Sport & Exercise Psychology*, 22(3): 256–72.

Jackson, R. C., Ashford, K. J., & Norsworthy, G. (2006) 'Attentional focus, dispositional reinvestment, and skilled motor performance under pressure', *Journal of Sport & Exercise Psychology*, 28(1): 49–68.

Kerr, J. H., & Cox, T. (1991) 'Arousal and individual differences in sport', *Personality and Individual Differences*, 12(10): 1075–85.

Kinrade, N. P., Jackson, R. C., & Ashford, K. J. (2010) 'Dispositional reinvestment and skill failure in cognitive and motor tasks', *Psychology of Sport and Exercise*, 11(4): 312–19.

Kuan, G., & Roy, J. (2007) 'Goal profiles, mental toughness and its influences on performance outcomes among Wushu athletes', *Journal of Sports Science and Medicine*, 6(CSSI-2): 28–33.

Laby, D. M., Kirschen, D. G., & Pantall, P. (2011) 'The visual function of Olympic-level athletes – An initial report', *Eye & Contact Lens*, 37(3): 116–22.

Laby, D. M., Rosenbaum, A. L., Kirschen, D. G., Davidson, J. L., Rosenbaum, L. J., Strasser, C., & Mellman, M. F. (1996) 'The visual function of professional baseball players', *American Journal of Ophthalmology*, 122(4): 476–85.

Landers, D. M. (1981) 'Arousal attention and skilled performance: Further considerations', *Quest*, 33(2): 271–83.

Lane, A. M., & Lane, H. J. (2002) 'Predictive effectiveness of mood measures', *Perceptual and Motor Skills*, 94(3): 785–91.

Lane, A. M., Soos, I., Leibinger, E., Karsai, I., & Hamar, P. (2008) 'Validity of the Brunel mood scale for use with UK, Italian, and Hungarian athletes', in S. R. Bakere (ed) *Hot topics in sports and athletics*, New York: Science Publishers Inc., 115–27.

Leavitt, J. L. (1979) 'Cognitive demands of skating and stickhandling in ice hockey', *Canadian Journal of Applied Sport Science*, 4: 46–55.

LeUnes, A., & Burger, J. (2000) 'Profile of mood states research in sport and exercise: Past, present, and future', *Journal of Applied Sport Psychology*, 12(1): 5–15.

Loehr, J. E. (1984) 'How to overcome stress and play at your peak all the time', *Tennis*, 21: 66–76.

Lonigan, C. J., & Phillips, B. M. (2001) 'Temperamental influences on the development of anxiety disorders', in M. W. Vasey & M. R. Dadds (eds) *The developmental psychopathology of anxiety*, New York: Oxford University Press, 60–91.

Lonsdale, C., Hodge, K., & Rose, E. A. (2008) 'The behavioral regulation in sport questionnaire (BRSQ): Instrument development and initial validity evidence', *Journal of Sport & Exercise Psychology*, 30(3): 323–55.

Maehr, M. L., & Braskamp, L. A. (1986) *The motivation factor: A theory of personal investment*, Lexington, MA: Lexington Books/D.C. Heath.

Mann, D. L., Abernethy, B., & Farrow, D. (2010) 'The resilience of natural interceptive actions to refractive blur', *Human Movement Science*, 29(3): 386–400.

Mann, D.T.Y., Williams, A. M., Ward, P., & Janelle, C. M. (2007) 'Perceptual-cognitive expertise in sport: A meta-analysis', *Journal of Sport & Exercise Psychology*, 29(4): 457.

Marsh, H. W. (2007) 'Application of confirmatory factor analysis and structural equation modeling in sport and exercise psychology', in G. Tenenbaum & R.C. Eklund (eds) *Handbook of sport psychology*, 3rd ed., Hoboken, NJ: John Wiley & Sons, Inc., 774–98.

Martens, R. (1977) *Sport competition anxiety test*, Champaign, IL: Human Kinetics Publishers.

Martin, J. J., Malone, L. A., & Hilyer, J. C. (2011) 'Personality and mood in women's paralympic basketball champions', *Journal of Clinical Sport Psychology*, 5(3): 197–210.

Masters, R., & Maxwell, J. (2008) 'The theory of reinvestment', *International Review of Sport and Exercise Psychology*, 1(2): 160–83.

Masters, R.S.W., Eves, F. F., & Maxwell, J. (2005) 'Development of a movement specific reinvestment scale', in T. Morris, P. Terry, S. Gordon, S. Hanrahan, L. Levleva, G. Kolt, & P. Tremayne (eds) *Proceedings of the ISSP 11th World Congress of Sport Psychology*. Sydney, AU.

Masters, R.S.W., & Maxwell, J. P. (2004) 'Implicit motor learning, reinvestment and movement disruption: What you don't know won't hurt you?', in A. M. Williams & N. J. Hodges (eds) *Skill acquisition in sport: Research, theory and practice*, London: Routledge, 207–28.

Masters, R.S.W., Polman, R.C. J., & Hammond, N. V. (1993) '"Reinvestment": A dimension of personality implicated in skill breakdown under pressure', *Personality and Individual Differences*, 14(5): 655–66.

Matsumoto, D., & Yoo, S. H. (2007) 'Methodological considerations in the study of emotion across cultures', in J. A. Coan & J.J.B. Allen (eds) *Handbook of emotion elicitation and assessment*, Oxford, UK: Oxford University Press, 332–48.

Maxwell, J. P., Masters, R.S., & Poolton, J.M. (2006) 'Performance breakdown in sport: The roles of reinvestment and verbal knowledge', *Research Quarterly for Exercise and Sport*, 77(2): 271–6.

McCrae, R. R., & Costa, P. T. (2008) 'The five factor theory of personality', in O. P. John, R. W. Robins, & L. A. Pervin (eds) *Handbook of personality: Theory and research*, 3rd ed., New York: Guilford Press, 159–81.

McCrae, R. R., & John, O. P. (1992) 'An introduction to the five-factor model and its applications', *Journal of Personality*, 60(2): 175–215.

McNair, D. M., Lorr, M., & Droppleman, L. F. (1971) *Manual: Profile of mood states*, San Diego, CA: Educational and Industrial Testing Service.

Memmert, D., Simons, D. J., & Grimme, T. (2009) 'The relationship between visual attention and expertise in sports', *Psychology of Sport and Exercise*, 10(1): 146–51.

Meyers, M. C., Bourgeois, A. E., LeUnes, A., & Murray, N. G. (1999) 'Mood and psychological skills of elite and sub-elite equestrian athletes', *Journal of Sport Behavior*, 22(3): 399–409.

Morgan, W. P. (1978) 'Sport personality: The credulous-skeptical argument in perspective', in W. F. Straub (ed) *Sport psychology: An Analysis of athlete behavior*, Ithaca, NY: Mouvement, 218–27.

Morgan, W. P. (1980) 'The trait psychology controversy', *Research Quarterly for Exercise and Sport*, 51(1): 50–76.

Murray, N. M., & Janelle, C. M. (2003) 'Anxiety and performance: A visual search examination of the processing efficiency theory', *Journal of Sport & Exercise Psychology*, 25(2): 171–87.

Nicholls, J. G. (1989) *The competitive ethos and democratic education*, Cambridge, MA: Harvard University Press.

Nicholls, J. G., Patashnick, M., & Nolen, S. B. (1985) 'Adolescents' theories of education', *Journal of Educational Psychology*, 77(6): 683–92.

Nideffer, R. M. (1976) 'Test of attentional and interpersonal style', *Journal of Personality and Social Psychology*, 34(3): 394–404.

Nideffer, R. M. (1990) 'Use of the test of attentional and interpersonal style (TAIS) in sport', *The Sport Psychologist*, 4(3): 285–300.

Nideffer, R. M. (2007) 'Reliability and validity of the attention and interpersonal style (TAIS) inventory concentration scales', in D. Smith & M. Bar-Eli (eds) *Essential readings in sport and exercise psychology*, Champaign, IL: Human Kinetics, 265–77.

Nideffer, R. M., Sagal, M. S., Lowry, M., & Bond, J. (2001) 'Identifying and developing world class performers', in G. Tenenbaum (ed) *The practice of sport psychology*, Morgantown, WV: Fitness Information Technology, 129–44.

Orlick, T. (1990) *In pursuit of excellence*, Champaign, IL: Leisure Press.

Measuring psychological determinants of expertise

Payne, R. (2001) 'Measuring emotions at work', in R. L. Payne & C. L. Cooper (eds) *Emotions at work: Theory, research, and applications in management*, West Sussex, UK: Wiley, 107–29.

Pelletier, L. G., Fortier, M. S., Vallerand, R. J., Tuson, K. M., Briere, N. M., & Blais, M. R. (1995) 'Toward a new measure of intrinsic motivation, extrinsic motivation, and amotivation in sports: The sport motivation scale (SMS)', *Journal of Sport & Exercise Psychology*, 17: 35–53.

Pelletier, L. G., Vallerand, R. J., & Sarrazin, P. (2007) 'The revised six-factor sport motivation scale (Mallett, Kawabata, Newcombe, Otero-Forero, & Jackson, 2007): Something old, something new, and something borrowed', *Psychology of Sport and Exercise*, 8(5): 615–21.

Ravizza, K. (1977) 'Peak experiences in sport', *Journal of Humanistic Psychology*, 17: 35–40.

Reid, G., Vallerand, R. J., Poulin, C., & Crocker, P. (2009) 'The development and validation of the pictorial motivation scale in physical activity', *Motivation and Emotion*, 33(2): 161–72.

Roberts, G. C., & Balague, G. (1991) 'The development and validation of the perception of success questionnaire', *Communication to the 8th European (FEPSAC) Congress*, Cologne, DE.

Roberts, G. C., Treasure, D. C., & Balague, G. (1998) 'Achievement goals in sport: The development and validation of the perception of success questionnaire', *Journal of Sports Sciences*, 16(4): 337–47.

Roberts, R., Rotheram, M., Maynard, I., Thomas, O., & Woodman, T. (2013) 'Perfectionism and the "yips": An initial investigation', *The Sport Psychologist*, 27(1): 53–61.

Robinson, M. D., & Clore, G. L. (2002) 'Belief and feeling: Evidence for an accessibility model of emotional self-report', *Psychological Bulletin*, 128(6): 934–60.

Roger, D., & Nesshoever, W. (1987) 'The construction and preliminary validation of a scale for measuring emotional control', *Personality and Individual Differences*, 8(4): 527–34.

Rothbart, M. K., Ahadi, S. A., & Evans, D. E. (2000) 'Temperament and personality: Origins and outcomes', *Journal of Personality and Social Psychology*, 78(1): 122–35.

Rowe, R. M., & McKenna, F. P. (2001) 'Skilled anticipation in real-world tasks: Measurement of attentional demands in the domain of tennis', *Journal of Experimental Psychology: Applied*, 7(1): 60–7.

Rowley, A. J., Landers, D. M., Kyllo, L. B., & Etnier, J. L. (1995) 'Does the iceberg profile discriminate between successful and less successful athletes? A meta-analysis', *Journal of Sport & Exercise Psychology*, 16: 185–99.

Ryba, T. V., Schinke, R. J., & Stambulova, N. B. (2012) 'Cultural sport psychology: Special measurement considerations', in G. Tenenbaum, R. C. Eklund, & A. Kamata (eds) *Measurement in sport and exercise psychology*, Champaign, IL: Human Kinetics, 143–52.

Sheard, M., & Golby, J. (2010) 'Personality hardiness differentiates elite-level sport performers', *International Journal of Sport and Exercise Psychology*, 8(2): 160–9.

Singer, R. N., Cauraugh, J. H., Tennant, L. K., Murphey, M., Chen, D., & Lidor, R. (1991) 'Attention and distractors: Considerations for enhancing sport performance', *International Journal of Sport Psychology*, 22: 95–114.

Smith, R. E., Smoll, F. L., Cumming, S. P., & Grossbard, J. R. (2006) 'Measurement of multidimensional sport performance anxiety in children and adults: The sport anxiety scale-2', *Journal of Sport & Exercise Psychology*, 28(4): 479–501.

Smith, R. E., Smoll, F. L., & Schutz, R. W. (1990) 'Measurement and correlates of sport-specific cognitive and somatic trait anxiety: The sport anxiety scale', *Anxiety Research*, 2(4): 263–80.

Spielberger, C. D., Gorsuch, R. L., Lushene, P. R., Vagg, P. R., & Jacobs, G. A. (1983) *Manual for the state-trait anxiety inventory*, Palo Alto, CA: Consulting Psychologists Press.

Stoeber, J., & Stoeber, F. S. (2009) 'Domains of perfectionism: Prevalence and relationships with perfectionism, gender, age, and satisfaction with life', *Personality and Individual Differences*, 46(4): 530–5.

Summers, J. J., Miller, K., & Ford, S. K. (1991) 'Attentional style and basketball performance', *Journal of Sport & Exercise Psychology*, 13(3): 239–53.

Tenenbaum, G., Eklund, R. C., & Kamata, A. (eds) (2012) *Measurement in sport and exercise psychology*, Champaign, IL: Human Kinetics.

Tenenbaum, G., Kamata, A. and Hayashi, K. (2007) 'Measurement in Sport and Exercise Psychology: A New Outlook on Selected Issues of Reliability and Validity', in G. Tenenbaum and R. C. Eklund (Eds), *Handbook of Sport Psychology*, Third Edition John Wiley & Sons, Inc., Hoboken, NJ: USA.

Terry, P. C., Lane, A., Lane, H. J., & Keohane, L. (1999) 'Development and validation of a mood measure for adolescents: POMS-A', *Journal of Sports Sciences*, 17(11): 861–72.

Terry, P. C., & Lane, A. M. (2000) 'Normative values for the profile of mood states for use with athletic samples', *Journal of Applied Sport Psychology*, 12(1): 93–109.

Terry, P. C., Lane, A. M., & Fogarty, G. J. (2003) 'Construct validity of the profile of mood states-A for use with adults', *Psychology of Sport and Exercise*, 4(2): 125–39.

Thelwell, R., Weston, N., & Greenlees, I. (2005) 'Defining and understanding mental toughness within soccer', *Journal of Applied Sport Psychology*, 17(4): 326–32.

Bradley Fawver et al.

Thrash, T.M., & Hurst, A.L. (2008) 'Approach and avoidance motivation in the achievement domain: Integrating the achievement motivation and achievement goal traditions', in A. J. Elliot (ed) *Handbook of approach and avoidance motivation*, New York: Guilford Press, 217–33.

Treasure, D. C., & Roberts, G.C. (1994) 'Cognitive and affective concomitants of task and ego goal orientations during the middle school years', *Journal of Sport & Exercise Psychology*, 16(1): 15–28.

Vallerand, R. J. (1997) 'Toward a hierarchical model of intrinsic and extrinsic motivation', in M. P. Zanna (ed) *Advances in experimental social psychology*, vol. 29, San Diego, CA: Academic Press, 271–360.

Vallerand, R. J. (2004) 'Intrinsic and extrinsic motivation in sport', in *Encyclopedia of Applied Psychology*, Montreal, CA: Elsevier Inc., 427–35.

Vallerand, R. J. (2007) 'A hierarchical model of intrinsic and extrinsic motivation for sport and physical activity', in M.S.D. Hagger & N.L.D. Chatzisarantis (eds) *Self-determination theory in exercise and sport*, Champaign, IL: Human Kinetics, 255–79, 356–63.

Vallerand, R. J., Donahue, E.G., & Lafreniere, M.K. (2012) 'Intrinsic and extrinsic motivation in sport and exercise', in G. Tenenbaum, R.C. Eklund, & A. Kamata (eds) *Measurement in sport and exercise psychology*, Champaign, IL: Human Kinetics, 279–92.

Vallerand, R. J., & Ratelle, C. F. (2002) 'Intrinsic and extrinsic motivation: A hierarchical model', in E. L. Deci & R. M. Ryan (eds) *Handbook of self-determination research*, Rochester, NY: University of Rochester Press, 37–64.

Van Schoyck, R. S., & Grasha, A. F. (1981) 'Attentional style variations and athletic ability: The advantage of a sport-specific test', *Journal of Sport Psychology*, 3(2): 149–65.

Vealey, R.S. (1986) 'The conceptualization of sport-confidence and competitive orientation: Preliminary investigation and instrument development', *Journal of Sport Psychology*, 8(3): 221–46.

Wang, C.K.J., & Liu, W.C. (2007) 'Promoting enjoyment in girls' physical education: The impact of goals, beliefs, and self-determination', *European Physical Education Review*, 13(2): 145–64.

Watson, D., Clark, L. A., & Tellegen, A. (1988) 'Development and validation of brief measures of positive and negative affect: The PANAS scales', *Journal of Personality and Social Psychology*, 54(6): 1063–70.

Watson, D., & Tellegen, A. (2002) 'Aggregations, acquiescence, and the assessment of trait affectivity', *Journal of Research in Personality*, 36(6): 589–97.

Watson, D., & Vaidya, J. (2003) 'Mood measurement: Current status and future directions', in J.A. Schinka & W. Velicer (eds) *Comprehensive handbook of psychology: Vol. 2. Research methods*, New York: Wiley, 351–75.

Weissensteiner, J.R., Abernethy, B., Farrow, D., & Gross, J. (2012) 'Distinguishing psychological characteristics of expert cricket batsmen', *Journal of Science and Medicine in Sport*, 15(1): 74–9.

Williams, J.M., & Krane, V. (2001) 'Psychological characteristics of peak performance', in J.M. Williams (ed) *Applied sport psychology: Personal growth to peak performance*, 4th ed., Mountain View, CA: Mayfield, 137–47.

Zuckerman, M., & Lubin, B. (1965) *Manual for the multiple affect adjective check list*, San Diego, CA: Educational and Industrial Testing Service.

22

PSYCHOLOGICAL DETERMINANTS OF EXPERTISE

Emotional reactivity, psychological skills, and efficacy

Garrett F. Beatty, Bradley Fawver, and Christopher M. Janelle

Understanding coping strategies and psychological skills employed by elite athletes is paramount to the development and implementation of psychological programs that facilitate optimal performance (see Chapter 14). In Chapter 21 we provided an overview general measurement considerations in sport psychology, and summarized dispositional measures of motivation, personality, mood, anxiety, and attentional style that contribute to elite sport performance. The current chapter serves as an extension to Chapter 21 by focusing on measures of coping, emotional states, mood regulation, emotion regulation, psychological skills, and efficacy in elite sport.

Measuring how athletes cope

Athletes' ability to navigate the myriad stressors encountered throughout their career is critical in determining the capacity to achieve at the highest levels of competition. Coping skills that involve conscious cognitive and behavioral processes are used to manage external and internal demands (Aldwin, 2007; Endler & Parker, 1994; Lazarus, 2000; Lidor *et al.*, 2012; Nicholls & Polman, 2007). Coping strategies can be generally organized into categories such as problem-focused, emotion-focused, or avoidance coping functions, or they can be more specifically classified. For example, problem solving, social support, imagery, relaxation, disengagement, drug/alcohol consumption, dietary restriction, and self-blame are but a few of the many strategies employed (Lidor *et al.*, 2012).

Elite athletes have been shown to experience substantial stress in pre-competition, competition, and post-competition phases, with the majority of stress experienced in the days leading up to important competition (Kristiansen & Roberts, 2010; Pensgaard & Ursin, 1998). Additionally, elite athletes employ cognitive defense strategies (seeking social support, positive reinterpretation, acceptance, denial, religion) prior to and after competition (Kristiansen & Roberts, 2010; Pensgaard & Ursin, 1998). Elite athletes have also been shown to respond to failures with either enhanced or decreased motivation to improve (Poczwardowski & Conroy, 2002). Task-involved athletes employ more adaptive coping strategies (problem and emotion focused) compared to elite athletes who are ego oriented (Kristiansen *et al.*, 2008). Elite athletes who exhibit socially prescribed perfectionism tend to engage in avoidance coping and experience higher levels of burnout, whereas athletes who display self-oriented perfectionism engage in more problem-focused coping and experience decreased levels of burnout (Hill *et al.*, 2010). Collectively, the state of coping research highlights the complex relationship among personality factors and coping approaches in elite athletes, and identifies a need for coping measures that evaluate the external and internal demands encountered by athletes (Lidor *et al.*, 2012).

Coping measures include qualitative and quantitative assessment tools. Qualitative measures include open-ended and semi-structured interviews (e.g., Kristiansen & Roberts, 2010; Pensgaard & Roberts, 2002; Poczwardowski & Conroy, 2002) that provide rich sources of data derived from individualized accounts. Qualitative measures also provide higher levels of ecological validity than quantitative analogs, but are more time consuming to administer, may include errors of omission or commission, are inherently biased by researcher involvement, and are limited in the ability to statistically identify causal relationships.

Several standardized quantitative measures exist. Eklund, Grove, and Heard (1998) substantiated the validity of Carver, Scheier, and Weintraub's (1989) COPE inventory and Crocker and Graham's (1995) sport-specific, modified version of the COPE (MCOPE). The COPE assesses individual differences in 15 coping strategies using a 60-item inventory. In comparison, the MCOPE includes 48 items measuring the use of 12 coping strategies. The athletic coping skills inventory (ACSI-28; Smith *et al.*, 1995) includes 28 items where athletes use a four-point Likert scale to rate statements that describe their use of coping skills in athletic domains – including practice and competition. Gaudreau and Blondin (2002) developed the French language inventaire des stratégies de coping en compétition sportive (ISCCS), which has been subsequently translated and employed in English as the coping strategies in sport competition inventory (CICS; Amiot *et al.*, 2004). The CICS consists of nine four-item subscales and one three-item subscale (39 total items) that evaluate the coping strategies of mental imagery, logical analysis, relaxation, control over thoughts, effort expenditure, social support, distancing, venting of unpleasant emotions, disengagement/resignation, and mental distraction. The coping function questionnaire (CFQ; Kowalski & Crocker, 2001) consists of 18 items measuring three subscales; problem-focused, emotion-focused, and avoidance-focused coping. In addition to measuring the general coping skills of performers, work has begun to elucidate the role of specific coping skills, such as emotion regulation, in sport performance. To understand how sport performance is affected by emotion regulation coping strategies, one must first consider how emotion influences sport performance and how these effects are quantified.

Measuring discrete emotional states

Emotional states influence cognitive functioning (Eysenck *et al.*, 2007; Gray, 2004), physiological responses (Bradley & Lang, 2000), and overt motor behavior (Naugle *et al.*, 2011), which ultimately impact the efficiency and effectiveness of sport performance (Totterdell, 2000). Although emotions have been defined in many ways (Vallerand & Blanchard, 2000), we operationalize emotions as psychophysiological reactions to perceptions of discrete stimuli. The most influential emotional states tend to be personally significant, sport specific, and goal oriented (Hanin, 2004). For an athlete, emotions fluctuate across pre-performance (e.g., anxiety, fear, happiness, interest), competition (e.g., determined, excited, afraid, distressed), and post-performance (e.g., anger, satisfaction, contempt, pride) periods. Therefore, the emotional experiences of elite performers are best portrayed through assessments of multiple discrete emotions. Regardless of the discrete

Psychological determinants of expertise

emotional experience, considerable work suggests that the athlete's interpretation of symptomology and, as described later in this chapter, his/her ability to regulate emotional reactions are critical determinants of success or failure (Cheng *et al.*, 2009).

Anxiety

Experienced athletes report lower anxiety levels compared to less-experienced athletes (Avramidou *et al.*, 2007; Jones & Swain, 1995), and skilled athletes experience lower intensity of anxiety before competition (Campbell & Jones, 1997). Additionally, elite athletes interpret cognitive and somatic anxiety as more facilitative, compared to non-elites (Hanton, Thomas, & Maynard, 2004; Jones *et al.*, 1994). Cognitive anxiety (e.g., worry) may have a more detrimental impact on performance for high-skilled athletes relative to those at lower skill levels (Woodman & Hardy, 2003). Fortunately, elite athletes can control anxiety levels to recover from mistakes (Mahoney & Avener, 1977).

Many tools exist to gauge an athlete's anxiety levels, but perhaps the most widely employed in sport is the competitive state anxiety inventory-2 (CSAI-2; Martens *et al.*, 1990). This 27-item self-report instrument measures three dimensions of state anxiety: cognitive anxiety, somatic anxiety, and confidence. Cognitive anxiety consists of negative thoughts and worries related to performance (Craft *et al.*, 2003), whereas somatic anxiety refers to the perception of physiological and affective changes related to autonomic arousal (Hardy & Parfitt, 1991; Morris *et al.*, 1981). Subsequent additions to the CSAI-2 have been made to determine whether the intensity of anxiety is perceived as facilitative or debilitative (Jones & Swain, 1992). A revised version (CSAI-2R; Cox *et al.*, 2003) has since been developed amid concerns over the predictability of the subscales (Hall *et al.*, 1998) and the factor structure. Though quite popular, evidence suggests the CSAI-2R does not clearly evaluate how competition is interpreted as challenging or threatening by athletes (Cerin, 2003). Additional state anxiety measures include the three-factor anxiety inventory (TFAI; Cheng *et al.*, 2009); the anxiety rating scale (ARS; Cox *et al.*, 1996), a condensed version of the CSAI; the mental readiness form-Likert (MRF-L; Krane, 1994); the anxiety thermometer (Houtman & Bakker, 1989); and the state form of the state trait anxiety inventory (STAI; Spielberger *et al.*, 1983).

Measuring other emotional states

Researchers and practitioners in sport psychology recognize the need to account for affective states other than competitive anxiety. Both general and sport-specific measures have been used to determine how competitive environments contribute to discrete emotions. The differential emotions scale (DES-IV; Izard *et al.*, 1993) was designed to measure basic emotions (e.g., anger, contempt, disgust, fear, guilt, inner-directed hostility, interest, joy, sadness, shame, shyness, and surprise) as either state or trait characteristics. The scales are generally stable and correlate with other personality variables (Izard *et al.*, 1993), but have been applied sparingly in sport settings (Cerin, 2003). The positive and negative affect schedule (PANAS; Watson *et al.*, 1988) and subsequent expanded version of the PANAS (PANAS-X; Watson & Clark, 1994) assess the valence (pleasantness) of respondents' affective states from either a state or trait perspective. Both of these instruments show excellent test-retest reliability, validity, and internal consistency (Watson & Clark, 1997; Watson *et al.*, 1988; Watson, 2000). The profile of mood states (POMS) has also been applied over short durations to measure changes in affect due to external stimuli (Terry *et al.*, 2003). Additional measures of discrete affect include the self-assessment manikin (SAM; Bradley & Lang, 1994), the feeling scale (FS; Hardy & Rejeski, 1989), the felt arousal scale (FAS; Svebak & Murgatroyd, 1985), the affect grid (AG; Russell *et al.*, 1989), and the activation deactivation adjective checklist (AD ACL; Thayer, 1989).

Physiological and motor behavior measures

In combination with self-report measures, physiological and motoric measurement tools allow researchers to triangulate predictive indices of discrete emotional states to gain a more comprehensive understanding of affective influences on sport performance and expertise. Physiological reactions to emotionally salient stimuli can be measured through a variety of measures, including changes in the cardiovascular system (e.g., heart rate, heart rate variability, blood pressure), respiratory system (e.g., spirometry), skeletomotor system (e.g., electromyography), electrodermal system (e.g., skin conductance), brain activity (e.g., electroencephalography, positron emission tomography, functional magnetic resonance imaging), and the visual system (e.g., gaze behavior). The individual zones of optimal functioning (IZOF; Hanin, 2000) and subsequent individual affect-related performance zone models (IAPZ; Kamata *et al.*, 2002) stipulate that physiological arousal can both improve and disrupt performance. Accordingly, the ability to regulate arousal levels has been shown to improve performance when athletes are capable of placing themselves in ideal arousal states that maximize their ability to attend to performance contingent cues, and to similarly move efficiently and effectively (Janelle, 2002). Arousal regulation techniques (e.g., deep breathing, progressive muscle relaxation, positive self-talk, meditation) have been linked with modifying arousal to ideal levels for successful performance (Gould & Udry, 1994).

The effectiveness of arousal regulation has traditionally been measured by observing baseline and post-regulatory physiological values. In addition to these physiological indicators of affect, researchers also measure alterations in the motor behaviors that underlie performance outcomes. Emotional states predictably impact motor planning and motor execution, as evidenced by alterations in reaction time (e.g., Naugle *et al.*, 2011) and force error (e.g., Coombes *et al.*, 2008). By measuring behavioral outcomes, researchers can better determine how discrete emotional states potentially facilitate or debilitate performance. For a review of psychophysiological measures of emotional reactivity, see Janelle and Naugle (2012), and for further reading on measuring affective mechanisms, see Gray and Watson (2007).

Measuring regulation of affective experiences

Elite athletes are not passive recipients of emotional information. Rather, they are psychologically active when perceiving and reacting to salient stimuli within the athletic performance environment. Elite competitors spend years developing superior physical athleticism and refined motor skills. Research consistently shows that they are also more "mentally tough" than their non-elite counterparts (Cherry, 2005). When sufficient resources are available (and the athlete is motivated), coping mechanisms can help athletes overcome challenges associated with stressful training and performance environments. As such, the ability to adaptively and efficiently regulate one's affective experiences in the context of athletic competition likely differentiates expert performers (Lane *et al.*, 2012; Robazza *et al.*, 2004; Tenenbaum *et al.*, 2008).

Psychological determinants of expertise

Mood regulation

Moods are lasting affective experiences that give rise to behavioral tendencies (Gross & Thompson, 2007). Elite athletes generally score lower on negative moods (e.g., tension, anger, depression, fatigue) and higher on positive moods (e.g., vigor), but even experts experience mood fluctuations that can impede performance. Self-regulation of mood involves cognitions (e.g., thoughts) and overt behaviors aimed at altering or maintaining moods (Rusting & Nolen-Hoeksema, 1998). Most individuals employ self-regulation strategies to decrease negative mood and increase positive mood (Thayer *et al.*, 1994).

Athletes use a variety of strategies to self-regulate mood, such as listening to music, talking to others, changing environments, or physical exercise (Stevens & Lane, 2001). Mood regulation may be particularly relevant in short duration and open skill sports (Beedie *et al.*, 2000), and in team sports where one player's mood state can impact the other players (Totterdell, 2000). Increased time devoted to deliberate practice of self-regulation improves regulatory abilities (Ericsson & Charness, 1994), and the quality of self-regulation subprocesses (e.g., self-monitoring, self-reflection) has been shown to differentiate experts and non-experts in skill execution (Kitsantas & Zimmerman, 2002). Measures of mood employed in research investigating mood regulation in sport include the profile of mood states questionnaire (POMS; McNair *et al.*, 1971), the University of Wales Institute of Science and Technology mood adjective checklist (UWIST-MACL; Matthews *et al.*, 1990), and the self-regulating strategies of mood questionnaire (SRSMQ: Thayer *et al.*, 1994).

Emotion regulation

Emotions are considered dynamic psychophysiological states elicited by specific stimuli, and give rise to behavioral responses. Emotional experiences proceed through a cyclical process: perceiving an emotional situation, attending to the situation, appraising the situation, and finally, physiologically and behaviorally reacting (Gross, 2007; Selye, 1976). Behavioral responses frame subsequent situations that further inform and shape the emotional environment. Regulatory strategies can be applied throughout the full time-course of an emotional experience. For example, situational selection can be employed to avoid highly emotional, competitive environments – such as the avoidant achievement behaviors exhibited by individuals with higher fear of failure levels (Conroy & Elliot, 2004). Individuals may direct their attention towards or away from emotional stimuli during the attention phase of affective experience. Expert athletes have demonstrated an increased ability to maintain focus on performance-dependent cues, even in highly stressful environments (e.g., Causer *et al.*, 2011). Further, athletes may employ cognitive restructuring strategies, which change thoughts towards, or reinterpret, emotional situations. For example, elite athletes may perceive pre-competitive anxiety in emotionally charged performance environments as an opportunity to demonstrate expertise, as opposed to an opportunity to fail (Craft *et al.*, 2003; Hanton *et al.*, 2000). Finally, athletes may employ physiological or behavioral responses that regulate emotional experiences, such as arousal regulation techniques – including the abuse of alcohol and other drugs (Buckman *et al.*, 2011; Martens & Martin, 2010), emotional expression, or emotional suppression (Lane *et al.*, 2004).

Surprisingly little work has considered the effectiveness of regulating strategies in the context of athletic performance. Although in its infancy, existing research indicates that individual differences in the tendency to adaptively regulate emotional experiences are correlated with improved motor control (Bresin *et al.*, 2012). Additionally, meta-analytic findings suggest cognitive reappraisal, attentional deployment, and expressive suppression are effective strategies – albeit with varied attentional, cognitive, and physiological consequences (Augustine & Hemenover, 2009; Webb *et al.*, 2012). Further, within acute periods of emotional experience and performance, individuals employing expressive suppression tend to perform better at targeted ballistic motor actions, compared with attentional deployment and emotional expression strategies (Beatty *et al.*, 2014).

Although regulatory mechanisms influence attentional, cognitive, and motor processes that ultimately influence sport performance, no work to date has been conducted to delineate expertise differences in discrete emotion regulation skills and subsequent performance. A need exists, therefore, to empirically specify 1) whether and how expert and non-expert athletes differ in their emotion regulatory skills, 2) how the efficacy of specific regulatory strategies differs when employed before, during, and following competition, and 3) how emotional expertise is developed through youth sport and throughout a performer's career. The extent to which psychological expertise correlates to performance outcomes is an interesting avenue of future research. Although initial research provides promising insight into the wealth of affective and performance knowledge that can be obtained employing emotion regulation strategies, substantial empirical research – both basic and applied – is necessary to determine which emotion regulation abilities should be developed and refined. Consideration of context, including pre-season training, intensive training camps, recovery periods, pre-competition periods, active competition, and post-competition, is also critically important.

Several measurement tools demonstrating high validity and reliability have emerged in recent years to aid in assessment of emotion regulation. These tools are of particular relevance as investigators seek to fill existing gaps in the sport expertise literature and elucidate the psychological mechanisms that contribute to elite performance. The emotion regulation questionnaire (ERQ; Gross & John, 2003) is a 10-item measure that differentiates individuals' habitual use of reappraisal and suppression regulation strategies. Of particular relevance, the validity and reliability of the ERQ has been substantiated in athlete populations (Uphill *et al.*, 2012). The difficulties in emotion regulation scale (DERQ; Gratz & Roemer, 2004), also in French (Dan-Glauser & Scherer, 2013), consists of 36 items assessing difficulties in attempting to regulate emotional experiences (e.g., difficulties in adopting goal-directed behaviors, difficulties in controlling impulsive behaviors, lack of emotional awareness, limited access to emotion regulation strategies, lack of emotional identification or clarity). The cognitive emotion regulation questionnaire (CER-Q; Garnefski *et al.*, 2001) identifies the cognitive coping strategies (both adaptive and maladaptive) individuals employ during stressful life events. The questionnaire is available in a 36-item (Garnefski *et al.*, 2001) and 18-item (CERQ-short; Garnefski & Kraaij, 2006) version. In both instruments, nine scales reflect the following coping strategies: self-blame, acceptance, rumination, positive refocusing, refocus on planning, positive reappraisal, putting into perspective, catastrophizing, and other-blame. Interview style measures, such as the emotion regulation interview (ERI; Werner *et al.*, 2011) and emotion regulation profile-revised (ERP-R; Nelis *et al.*, 2011), could be modified for athletic populations to assess individuals' use of emotion regulation strategies.

Psychological skills

In addition to the coping and affective regulation skills employed by elite athletes, numerous psychological skills can be practiced, refined, and applied to improve performance (Weinberg & Forlenza, 2012). Investigations have identified that expert athletes utilize concentration, goal setting,

Psychological determinants of expertise

imagery, self-talk, and anxiety management skills (Andrew *et al.*, 2007; Durand-Bush & Salmela, 2001; Gould *et al.*, 2002) in addition to exhibiting superior decision-making, anticipation, and attentional skills (Gould *et al.*, 2002; Gould *et al.*, 1981; Williams *et al.*, 2011; see many of the Chapters in the earlier chapters of this text). Further, expert athletes with task-oriented achievement goals report using more imagery, goal setting, and positive self-talk than expert athletes with ego-oriented achievement goals (Harwood *et al.*, 2004). Compared to non-experts, experts consider the use of psychological skills as more important for success in sport (Andrew *et al.*, 2007; Macnamara *et al.*, 2010), employ more psychological skills more frequently than non-experts (Durand-Bush & Salmela, 2001; Mahoney & Avener, 1977), and engage in more deliberate, quality practice of psychological skills (Cumming & Hall, 2002; Durand-Bush & Salmela, 2001).

Measurement strategies employed to evaluate psychological skills include qualitative interviews, quantitative questionnaires, and performance profiling (Butler & Hardy, 1992). In performance profiling, athletes are asked to brainstorm the qualities/skills that are important for high-level performance. The identified qualities/skills are then organized into constructs. Athletes rate their own skills in each construct. Results are presented to athletes in a pictorial performance profile (see Butler & Hardy, 1992). Performance profiling has been successfully implemented to assess elite athletes' perceptions of psychological skills in many sports (e.g., Holland *et al.*, 2010; Jones *et al.*, 2002; Morley *et al.*, 2014; O'Brien *et al.*, 2009).

The psychological skills inventory for sports-R5 (PSIS-R5; Mahoney *et al.*, 1987) is a 45-item, five-point Likert scale questionnaire designed to distinguish the psychological skills of collegiate, pre-elite, and elite athletes. The scale is comprised of six subscales that measure anxiety control, concentration, confidence, mental preparation, motivation, and team emphasis. In spite of the theoretical premise, the PSIS-R5 has proven inconsistent in distinguishing between athletic ability levels (Murphy & Tammen, 1998; Weinberg & Forlenza, 2012). The test of performance strategies (TOPS; Thomas *et al.*, 1999) and the recently revised version (TOPS 2; Hardy *et al.*, 2010) have proven more effective in discriminating the psychological skill usage of elite athletes compared to sub-elite (Taylor *et al.*, 2008; Thomas *et al.*, 1999). TOPS 2 is a 64-item instrument designed to assess athletes' perceptions of effective implementation of psychological skills in practice and competition settings. The items are evenly dispersed between eight practice and eight competition subscales measuring self-talk, emotional control, automaticity (performance without conscious control of action), goal setting, imagery, activation (arousal/energy level), relaxation, attentional control (practice subscale only), and negative thinking (competition subscale only).

The Ottawa mental skills assessment tool-3* (OMSAT-3*) consists of 48 items that evaluate 12 subscales that discriminate between elite and sub-elite athletes (Durand-Bush *et al.*, 2001). The 12 subscales are organized into three broader components – foundation skills (goal setting, commitment, self-confidence), psychosomatic skills (stress reactions, fear control, relaxation, activation), and cognitive skills (imagery, mental practice, focusing, refocusing, competition planning). The mental toughness questionnaire (MTQ) is available in 48-item and 18-item versions that measure control, commitment, challenge, and confidence in athletes (Clough *et al.*, 2002). Initial evidence is inconclusive on the ability of the MTQ to differentiate between elite and sub-elite athletes and may suggest no real difference exists in psychological skills between competitive athletes of varying achievement levels (Nicholls *et al.*, 2009). In addition to the multidimensional measures of psychological skills, a host of measurement tools exist evaluating specific skills such as motivation (AMI; Tutko *et al.*, 1969), imagery (MIQ-R; Hall & Martin, 1997), self-talk (STUQ; Hardy *et al.*, 2005, FSTQ; Theodorakis *et al.*, 2008, and S-TQ; Zervas *et al.*, 2007), concentration (TAIS; Nideffer, 1976), and goal setting (POSQ; Roberts *et al.*, 1998). See Weinberg and Forlenza (2012) for more detail.

Garrett F. Beatty et al.

Self-confidence, self-efficacy, and collective efficacy

Self-confidence and self-efficacy in sport are often used interchangeably to describe the belief that one is capable of successfully performing necessary skills within given performance environments. In the sport psychology literature and elsewhere, self-efficacy is considered a situation- or task-specific form of self-confidence. These constructs (referred to as self-efficacy for the remainder of the chapter) are foundational to elite performance, as self-efficacy influences motivation (Hagger *et al.*, 2001), goal setting (Vancouver *et al.*, 2001), emotional states (Jones *et al.*, 2002), and ultimately performance (Beauchamp *et al.*, 2002; Moritz *et al.*, 2000; Vealey, 2001). Performance, in turn, directly influences future self-efficacy in elite athletes (Gernigon & Delloye, 2003). In comparison to self-efficacy, collective efficacy refers to the shared belief of a group in its ability to perform optimally within given performance environments. Collective efficacy is often higher in teams comprised of elite athletes compared to teams with sub-elite athletes (Shearer *et al.*, 2007). Therefore, the study of self and collective efficacy in elite sport is paramount to understanding the holistic effect of psychological constructs on performance (for reviews, see Dithurbide & Feltz, 2012; Feltz *et al.*, 2008).

The sources of sport-confidence questionnaire (SSCQ; Vealey *et al.*, 1998) contains 43 items representing nine subscales (mastery, demonstration of ability, physical/mental preparation, physical self-presentation, social support, coaches' leadership, vicarious experience, environmental comfort, and situational favorableness). Elite athletes have been shown to source efficacy from demonstration of ability, physical/mental preparation, physical self-presentation, and situational favorableness (Kingston *et al.*, 2010). Additionally, elite female athletes source efficacy from mastery, physical self-presentation, social support, environmental comfort, and coaches' leadership more than male counterparts (Kingston *et al.*, 2010). Researchers also generate custom self-efficacy measures to measure efficacy within specific performance domains (Dithurbide & Feltz, 2012). These measures can be designed as hierarchical and non-hierarchal (e.g., Hepler & Feltz, 2012) scales, with hierarchical scales asking participants to rate their belief in achieving increasingly difficult tasks (e.g., Feltz & Riessinger, 1990).

The collective efficacy questionnaire for sports (CEQS; Short *et al.*, 2005) is a 20-item measure, using a 10-point Likert scale to evaluate the five factors of ability, effort, preparation, persistence, and unity. The CEQS has proven effective in evaluating and establishing the value of promoting collective efficacy in elite team sport (Heuzé *et al.*, 2007). The collective efficacy inventory (CEI; Callow *et al.*, 2004) has also been applied with elite teams (Shearer *et al.*, 2007) and consists of 10 items. The 10 items reflect the individual athletes' beliefs in the team's ability (e.g., "I believe the team is capable of performing at a high level") and athletes' perceptions of the team's collective efficacy beliefs (e.g., "My team believes the team is capable of performing at a high level").

Summary and conclusion

Sport psychologists have developed and implemented numerous tools to measure the use of coping and psychological skills in expert sport performance. We have summarized the most commonly employed measures assessing coping, emotional states, mood regulation, emotion regulation, psychological skills, and efficacy. Extant literature indicates that elite performers employ adaptive coping strategies, adaptively experience and interpret affective experiences, effectively regulate mood, systematically and extensively employ psychological skills, and experience high levels of self and collective efficacy. Future research efforts are needed to identify how elite athletes develop and employ emotion regulation strategies in the context of training, pre-performance,

Psychological determinants of expertise

performance, and post-performance in sport, and the extent to which the development of psychological skills contributes to consistent superior performance in sport.

References

Aldwin, C. M. (2007) *Stress, coping, and development: An integrative approach*, 2nd ed., New York: Guilford Press.

Amiot, C. E., Gaudreau, P., & Blanchard, C. M. (2004) 'Self-determination, coping, and goal attainment in sport', *Journal of Sport & Exercise Psychology*, 26(3): 396–411.

Andrew, M., Grobbelaar, H. W., & Potgieter, J. C. (2007) 'Sport psychological skill levels and related psychosocial factors that distinguish between rugby union players of different participation levels', *South African Journal for Research in Sport, Physical Education & Recreation*, 29(1): 1–14.

Augustine, A. A., & Hemenover, S. H. (2009) 'On the relative effectiveness of affect regulation strategies : A meta-analysis', *Cognition and Emotion*, 23(6): 37–41.

Avramidou, E., Avramidis, S., & Pollman, R. (2007) 'Competitive anxiety in lifesavers and swimmers', *International Journal of Aquatic Research and Education*, 1(2): 108–17.

Beatty, G. F., Fawver, B., Hancock, G. M., & Janelle, C. M. (2014) 'Regulating emotions uniquely modifies reaction time, rate of force production, and accuracy of a goal-directed motor action', *Human Movement Science*, 33(1): 1–13.

Beauchamp, M. R., Bray, S. R., & Albinson, J. G. (2002) 'Pre-competition imagery, self-efficacy and performance in collegiate golfers', *Journal of Sport Sciences*, 20(9): 697–705.

Beedie, C. J., Terry, P. C., & Lane, A. M. (2000) 'The profile of mood states and athletic performance: Two meta-analyses', *Journal of Applied Sport Psychology*, 12(1): 49–68.

Bradley, M. M., & Lang, P. J. (1994) 'Measuring emotion: The self-assessment manikin and the semantic differential', *Journal of Behavior Therapy and Experimental Psychiatry*, 25(1): 49–59.

Bradley, M. M., & Lang, P. J. (2000) 'Measuring emotion: Behavior, feeling, and physiology', in R. D. Lane & L. Nadel (eds) *Cognitive neuroscience of emotion*, New York: Oxford University Press, Inc., 242–76.

Bresin, K., Fetterman, A. K., & Robinson, M. D. (2012) 'Motor control accuracy: A consequential probe of individual differences in emotion regulation', *Emotion*, 12(3): 479–86.

Buckman, J. F., Yusko, D. A., Farris, S. G., White, H. R., & Pandina, R. J. (2011) 'Risk of marijuana use in male and female college student athletes and nonathletes', *Journal of Studies on Alcohol and Drugs*, 72(4): 586–91.

Butler, R. J., & Hardy, L. (1992) 'The performance profile: Theory and application', *The Sport Psychologist*, 6(3): 253–64.

Callow, N., Hardy, L., Markland, D., & Shearer, D. A. (2004) 'The conceptualization and measurement of collective efficacy', *Journal of Sport Sciences*, 22(3): 301–2.

Campbell, E., & Jones, G. (1997) 'Pre-competition anxiety and self-confidence in elite and non-elite wheelchair sport participants', *Adapted Physical Activity Quarterly*, 14: 95–107.

Carver, C. S., Scheier, M. F., & Weintraub, J. K. (1989) 'Assessing coping strategies: A theoretically based approach', *Journal of Personality and Social Psychology*, 56(2): 267–83.

Causer, J., Holmes, P. S., Smith, N. C., & Williams, A. M. (2011) 'Anxiety, movement kinematics, and visual attention in elite-level performers', *Emotion*, 11: 595–602.

Cerin, E. (2003) 'Anxiety versus fundamental emotions as predictors of perceived functionality of precompetitive emotional states, threat, and challenge in individual sports', *Journal of Applied Sport Psychology*, 15(3): 223–38.

Cheng, W.N.K., Hardy, L., & Markland, D. (2009) 'Toward a three-dimensional conceptualization of performance anxiety: Rationale and initial measurement development', *Psychology of Sport and Exercise*, 10(2): 271–8.

Cherry, H. L. (2005) *Psychometric analysis of an inventory assessing mental toughness*, Knoxville, TN: University of Tennessee.

Clough, P., Earle, K., & Sewell, D. (2002) 'Mental toughness: The concept and its measurement', in I. Cockerill (ed) *Solutions in sport psychology*, Stamford, CT: Cengage Learning EMEA, 32–45.

Conroy, D. E., & Elliot, A. J. (2004) 'Fear of failure and achievement goals in sport: Addressing the issue of the chicken and the egg', *Anxiety, Stress, and Coping*, 17(3): 271–85.

Coombes, S. A., Gamble, K. M., Cauraugh, J. H., & Janelle, C. M. (2008) 'Emotional states alter force control during a feedback occluded motor task', *Emotion*, 8(1): 104–13.

Cox, R. H., Martens, M. P., & Russell, W. D. (2003) 'Measuring anxiety in athletics: The revised competitive state anxiety inventory-2', *Journal of Sport & Exercise Psychology*, 25(4): 519–33.

Cox, R. H., Russell, M. W.D., & Roes, M. (1996) 'Validity of the MRF and ARS competitive state anxiety rating scale for volleyball and basketball', *Research Quarterly for Exercise and Sport*, 67(1): 52–67.

Craft, L. L., Magyar, T. M., Becker, B. J., & Feltz, D. L. (2003) 'The relationship between the competitive state anxiety inventory-2 and sport performance: A meta-analysis', *Journal of Sport & Exercise Psychology*, 25(1): 44–65.

Crocker, P.R.E., & Graham, T. R. (1995) 'Coping by competitive athletes with performance stress: Gender differences and relationships with affect', *The Sport Psychologist*, 9(3): 325–38.

Cumming, J., & Hall, C. (2002) 'Deliberate imagery practice: The development of imagery skills in competitive athletes', *Journal of Sports Sciences*, 20(2): 137–45.

Dan-Glauser, E. S., & Scherer, K. R. (2013) 'The difficulties in emotion regulation scale (DERS): Factor structure and consistency of a French translation', *Swiss Journal of Psychology*, 72(1): 5–11.

Dithurbide, L., & Feltz, D. L. (2012) 'Self-efficacy and collective efficacy', in G. Tenenbaum & R. C. Eklund (eds) *Measurement in sport and exercise psychology*, Champaign, IL: Human Kinetics, 251–63.

Durand-Bush, N., & Salmela, J. H. (2001) 'Becoming a world or Olympic champion: A process rather than an end result', in A. Papioannou, M. Goudas, & Y. Theodorakis (eds) *In the dawn of the new millennium: 10th World Congress of Sport Psychology*, Skathos, GR: Christodoul, 300–2.

Durand-Bush, N., Salmela, J. H., & Green-Demers, I. (2001) 'The Ottawa mental skills assessment tool (OMSAT-3★)', *The Sport Psychologist*, 15(1): 1–19.

Eklund, R. C., Grove, R. J., & Heard, P. N. (1998) 'The measurement of slump-related coping: Factorial validity of the COPE and modified-COPE inventories', *Journal of Sport & Exercise Psychology*, 20(2): 157–75.

Endler, N. S., & Parker, J.D.A. (1994) 'Assessment of multidimensional coping: Task, emotion, and avoidance strategies', *Psychological Assessment*, 6(1): 50–60.

Ericsson, A. K., & Charness, N. (1994) 'Expert performance: Its structure and acquisition', *American Psychologist*, 49(8): 725–47.

Eysenck, M. W., Derakshan, N., Santos, R., & Calvo, M. G. (2007) 'Anxiety and cognitive performance: Attentional control theory', *Emotion*, 7(2): 336–53.

Feltz, D. L., & Riessinger, C. A. (1990) 'Effects of in vivo emotive imagery and performance feedback on self-efficacy and muscular endurance', *Journal of Sport & Exercise Psychology*, 12(2): 132–43.

Feltz, D. L., Short, S. E., & Sullivan, P. J. (2008) *Self-efficacy in sport*, Champaign, IL: Human Kinetics.

Garnefski, N., & Kraaij, V. (2006) 'Cognitive emotion regulation questionnaire – Development of a short 18-item version (CERQ-short)', *Personality and Individual Differences*, 41(6): 1045–53.

Garnefski, N., Kraaij, V., & Spinhoven, P. (2001) 'Negative life events, cognitive emotion regulation and depression', *Personality and Individual Differences*, 30(8): 1311–27.

Gaudreau, P., & Blondin, J. P. (2002) 'Development of a questionnaire for the assessment of coping strategies employed by athletes in competitive sport settings', *Psychology of Sport and Exercise*, 3(1): 1–34.

Gernigon, C., & Delloye, J. B. (2003) 'Self-efficacy, causal attribution, and track athletic performance following unexpected success or failure among elite sprinters', *The Sport Psychologist*, 17(1): 55–76.

Gould, D., Dieffenbach, K., & Moffett, A. (2002) 'Psychological characteristics and their development in Olympic champions', *Journal of Applied Sport Psychology*, 14(3): 172–204.

Gould, D., & Udry, E. (1994) 'Psychological skills for enhancing performance: Arousal regulation strategies', *Medicine and Science in Sports and Exercise*, 26(4): 478–85.

Gould, D., Weiss, M., & Weinberg, R. (1981) 'Psychological characteristics of successful and nonsuccessful big ten wrestlers', *Journal of Sport Psychology*, 3(1): 69–81.

Gratz, K. L., & Roemer, L. (2004) 'Multidimensional assessment of emotion regulation and dysregulation: Development, factor structure, and initial validation of the difficulties in emotion regulation scale', *Journal of Psychopathology and Behavioral Assessment*, 26(1): 41–54.

Gray, E. K., & Watson, D. (2007) 'Assessing positive and negative affect via self-report', in J. A. Coan & J.J.B. Allen (eds) *Handbook of emotion elicitation and assessment*, Oxford, UK: Oxford University Press, Inc., 171–83.

Gray, J.R. (2004) 'Integration of emotion and cognitive control', *Current Directions in Psychological Science*, 13(2): 46–48.

Gross, J. J. (ed) (2007) *Handbook of emotion regulation*, New York: Guilford Press.

Gross, J. J., & John, O. P. (2003) 'Individual differences in two emotion regulation processes: Implications for affect, relationships, and well-being', *Journal of Personality and Social Psychology*, 85(2): 348–62.

Gross, J. J., & Thompson, R. A. (2007) 'Emotion regulation: Conceptual foundations', in J. J. Gross (ed) *Handbook of emotion regulation*, New York: Guildford Press, 3–24.

Hagger, M. S., Chatzisarantis, N., & Biddle, S. J. (2001) 'The influence of self-efficacy and past behaviour on the physical activity intentions of young people', *Journal of Sports Sciences*, 19(9): 711–25.

Hall, C. R., & Martin, K. A. (1997) 'Measuring movement imagery abilities: A revision of the movement imagery questionnaire', *Journal of Mental Imagery*, 21(1–2): 143–54.

Hall, H. K., Alistair, W. K., & Matthews, J. (1998) 'Precompetitive anxiety in sport: The contribution of achievement goals and perfectionism', *Journal of Sport & Exercise Psychology*, 20(2): 194–217.

Hanin, Y. L. (2000) 'Individual zones of optimal functioning (IZOF) model: Emotion–performance relationships in sport', in Y. L. Hanin (ed) *Emotions in sport*, Champaign, IL: Human Kinetics, 65–89.

Hanin, Y. L. (2004) 'Emotions in sport: An individualized approach', in *Encyclopedia of applied psychology* (vol. 1), Oxford, UK: Elsevier Academic Press, 739–50.

Hanton, S., Jones, G., & Mullen, R. (2000) 'Intensity and direction of competitive state anxiety as interpreted by rugby players and rifle shooters', *Perceptual and Motor Skills*, 90(2): 513–21.

Hanton, S., Thomas, O., & Maynard, I. (2004) 'Competitive anxiety responses in the week leading up to competition: The role of intensity, direction and frequency dimensions', *Psychology of Sport and Exercise*, 5(2): 169–81.

Hardy, C. J., & Rejeski, W. J. (1989) 'Not what, but how one feels: The measurement of affect during exercise', *Journal of Sport & Exercise Psychology*, 11(3): 304–17.

Hardy, J., Hall, C. R., & Hardy, L. (2005) 'Quantifying athlete self-talk', *Journal of Sports Sciences*, 23(9): 905–17.

Hardy, L., & Parfitt, G. (1991) 'A catastrophe model of anxiety and performance', *British Journal of Psychology*, 82(2): 163–78.

Hardy, L., Roberts, R., Thomas, P. R., & Murphy, S. M. (2010) 'Test of performance strategies (TOPS): Instrument refinement using confirmatory factor analysis', *Psychology of Sport and Exercise*, 11(1): 27–35.

Harwood, C., Cumming, J., & Fletcher, D. (2004) 'Motivational profiles and psychological skills use within elite youth sport', *Journal of Applied Sport Psychology*, 16(4): 318–32.

Hepler, T. J., & Feltz, D. L. (2012) 'Path analysis examining self-efficacy and decision-making performance on a simulated baseball task', *Research Quarterly for Exercise and Sport*, 83(1): 55–64.

Heuzé, J., Bosselut, G., & Thomas, J. (2007) 'Should the coaches of elite female handball teams focus on collective efficacy or group cohesion?', *The Sport Psychologist*, 21(4): 383–99.

Hill, A. P., Hall, H. K., & Appleton, P. R. (2010) 'Perfectionism and athlete burnout in junior elite athletes: The mediating role of coping tendencies', *Anxiety, Stress, and Coping*, 23(4): 415–30.

Holland, M. J. G., Woodcock, C., Cumming, J., & Duda, J. L. (2010) 'Mental qualities and employed mental techniques of young elite team sport athletes', *Journal of Clinical Sport Psychology*, 4(1): 19–38.

Houtman, I. L., & Bakker, F. C. (1989) 'The anxiety thermometer: A validation study', *Journal of Personality Assessment*, 53(3): 575–82.

Izard, C. E., Libero, D. Z., Putnam, P., & Haynes, O. M. (1993) 'Stability of emotion expression experiences and their relations to traits of personality', *Journal of Social and Personality Psychology*, 64(5): 847–60.

Janelle, C. M. (2002) 'Anxiety, arousal and visual attention: A mechanistic account of performance variability', *Journal of Sports Sciences*, 20(3): 237–51.

Janelle, C. M., & Naugle, K. M. (2012) 'Emotional reactivity', in G. Tenenbaum, R. C. Eklund, & A. Kamata (eds) *Measurement in sport and exercise psychology*, Champaign, IL: Human Kinetics, 333–48.

Jones, G., Hanton, S., & Connaughton, D. (2002) 'What is this thing called mental toughness? An investigation of elite sport performers', *Journal of Applied Sport Psychology*, 14(3): 205–18.

Jones, G., Hanton, S., & Swain, A. B. J. (1994) 'Intensity and interpretation of anxiety symptoms in elite and non-elite sports performers', *Personal and Individual Differences*, 17(5): 657–63.

Jones, G., & Swain, A. B. J. (1992) 'Intensity and direction dimensions of competitive state anxiety and relationships with competitiveness', *Perceptual and Motor Skills*, 74(2): 467–72.

Jones, G., & Swain, A. B. J. (1995) 'Predispositions to experience debilitative and facilitative anxiety in elite and nonelite performers', *The Sport Psychologist*, 9(2): 202–12.

Jones, M. V., Bray, S. R., Mace, R. D., MacRae, A. W., & Stockbridge, C. (2002) 'The impact of motivational imagery on the emotional state and self-efficacy levels of novice climbers', *Journal of Sport Behavior*, 25(1): 57–73.

Kamata, A., Tenenbaum, G., & Hanin, Y. L. (2002) 'Individual zone of optimal functioning (IZOF): A probabilistic estimation', *Journal of Sport & Exercise Psychology*, 24(2): 189–208.

Kingston, K., Lane, A., & Thomas, O. (2010) 'A temporal examination of elite performers sources of sport-confidence', *The Sport Psychologist*, 24(3): 313–32.

Kitsantas, A., & Zimmerman, B. J. (2002) 'Comparing self-regulatory processes among novice, non-expert, and expert volleyball players: A microanalytic study', *Journal of Applied Sport Psychology*, 14(2): 91–105.

Kowalski, K. C., & Crocker, P.R.E. (2001) 'Development and validation of the coping function questionnaire for adolescents in sport', *Journal of Sport & Exercise Psychology*, 23(2): 136–55.

Krane, V. (1994) 'The mental readiness form as a measure of competitive state anxiety', *The Sport Psychologist*, 8(2): 189–202.

Kristiansen, E., & Roberts, G. C. (2010) 'Young elite athletes and social support: Coping with competitive and organizational stress in "Olympic" competition', *Scandinavian Journal of Medicine & Science in Sports*, 20(4): 686–95.

Kristiansen, E., Roberts, G. C., & Abrahamsen, F. E. (2008) 'Achievement involvement and stress coping in elite wrestling', *Scandinavian Journal of Medicine & Science in Sports*, 18(4): 526–38.

Lane, A. M., Bucknall, G., Davis, P. A., Beedie, C. J., Jones, M. V., Uphill, M., & Devonport, T. J. (2012) 'Emotions and emotion regulation among novice military parachutists', *Military Psychology*, 24(3): 331–45.

Lane, A. M., Terry, P. C., Stevens, M. J., Barney, S., & Dinsdale, S. L. (2004) 'Mood responses to athletic performance in extreme environments', *Journal of Sports Sciences*, 22(10): 886–97.

Lazarus, R. S. (2000) 'How emotions influence performance in competitive sports', *Sport Psychologist*, 14(3): 229–52.

Lidor, R., Crocker, P.R.E., & Mosewich, A. D. (2012) 'Coping in sport and exercise', in G. Tenenbaum, R. C. Eklund, & A. Kamata (eds) *Measurement in sport and exercise psychology*, Champaign, IL: Human Kinetics, 393–407.

Macnamara, Á., Button, A., & Collins, D. (2010) 'The role of psychological characteristics in facilitating the pathway to elite performance part 1 : Identifying mental skills and behaviors', *The Sport Psychologist*, 24(1): 52–73.

Mahoney, M. J., & Avener, M. (1977) 'Psychology of the elite athlete: An exploratory study', *Cognitive Therapy and Research*, 1(2): 135–41.

Mahoney, M. J., Gabriel, T. J., & Perkins, T. S. (1987) 'Psychological skills and exceptional athletic performance', *The Sport Psychologist*, 1(3): 181–99.

Martens, M. P., & Martin, J. L. (2010) 'College athletes' drinking motives and competitive seasonal status: Additional examination of the athlete drinking scale', *Addiction Research & Theory*, 18(1): 23–32.

Martens, R., Vealey, R. S., & Burton, D. (1990) *Competitive anxiety in sport*, Champaign, IL: Human Kinetics, 117–73.

Matthews, G., Jones, D. M., & Chamberlain, A. G. (1990) 'Refining the measurement of mood: The UWIST mood adjective checklist', *British Journal of Psychology*, 81(1): 17–42.

McNair, D. M., Lorr, M., & Droppleman, L. F. (1971) *Manual: Profile of mood states*, San Diego, CA: Educational and Industrial Testing Service.

Moritz, S. E., Feltz, D. L., Fahrbach, K. R., & Mack, D. E. (2000) 'The relation of self-efficacy measures to sport performance: A meta-analytic review', *Research Quarterly for Exercise and Sport*, 71(3): 280–94.

Morley, D., Morgan, G., McKenna, J., & Nicholls, A. R. (2014) 'Developmental contexts and features of elite academy football players: Coach and player perspectives', *International Journal of Sports Science and Coaching*, 9(1): 217–32.

Morris, L., Davis, D., & Hutchings, C. (1981) 'Cognitive and emotional components of anxiety: Literature review and revised worry-emotionality scale', *Journal of Educational Psychology*, 73(4): 541–55.

Murphy, S., & Tammen, V. (1998) 'In search of psychological skills', in J. L. Duda (ed) *Advances in sport and exercise psychology measurement*, Morgantown, WV: Fitness Information Technology, Inc., 195–212.

Naugle, K. M., Hass, C. J., Joyner, J., Coombes, S. A, & Janelle, C. M. (2011) 'Emotional state affects the initiation of forward gait', *Emotion*, 11(2): 267–77.

Nelis, D., Quoidbach, J., Hansenne, M., Differences, I., & Unit, I. D. (2011) 'Measuring individual differences in emotion regulation: The emotion regulation profile revised (ERP-R)', *Psychologica Belgica*, 51(1): 49–91.

Nicholls, A. R., & Polman, R. C. J. (2007) 'Coping in sport: A systematic review', *Journal of Sports Sciences*, 25(1): 11–31.

Nicholls, A. R., Polman, R. C. J., Levy, A. R., & Backhouse, S. H. (2009) 'Mental toughness in sport: Achievement level, gender, age, experience, and sport type differences', *Personality and Individual Differences*, 47(1): 73–5.

Nideffer, R. M. (1976) 'Test of attentional and interpersonal style', *Journal of Personality and Social Psychology*, 34(3): 394–404.

Psychological determinants of expertise

O'Brien, M., Mellalieu, S., & Hanton, S. (2009) 'Goal-setting effects in elite and nonelite boxers', *Journal of Applied Sport Psychology*, 21(3): 293–306.

Pensgaard, A. M., & Roberts, G. C. (2002) 'Elite athletes' experiences of the motivational climate: The coach matters', *Scandinavian Journal of Medicine & Science in Sports*, 12(1): 54–9.

Pensgaard, A. M., & Ursin, H. (1998) 'Stress, control, and coping in elite athletes', *Scandinavian Journal of Medicine & Science in Sports*, 8(3): 183–9.

Poczwardowski, A., & Conroy, D. E. (2002) 'Coping responses to failure and success among elite athletes and performing artists', *Journal of Applied Sport Psychology*, 14(4): 313–29.

Robazza, C., Pellizzari, M., & Hanin, Y. (2004) 'Emotion self-regulation and athletic performance: An application of the IZOF model', *Psychology of Sport and Exercise*, 5(4): 379–404.

Roberts, G. C., Treasure, D. C., & Balague, G. (1998) 'Achievement goals in sport: The development and validation of the perception of success questionnaire', *Journal of Sports Sciences*, 16(4): 337–47.

Russell, J. A., Weiss, A., & Mendelsohn, G. A. (1989) 'Affect grid: A single item scale of pleasure and arousal', *Journal of Personality and Social Psychology*, 57(3): 493–502.

Rusting, C. L., & Nolen-Hoeksema, S. (1998) 'Regulating responses to anger: Effects of rumination and distraction on angry mood', *Journal of Personality and Social Psychology*, 74(3): 790–803.

Selye, H. (1976) *The stress of life* (rev. ed.), New York: McGraw-Hill.

Shearer, D. A, Thomson, R., Mellalieu, S. D., & Shearer, C. R. (2007) 'The relationship between imagery type and collective efficacy in elite and non elite athletes', *Journal of Sports Science & Medicine*, 6(2): 180–7.

Short, S. E., Sullivan, P., & Feltz, D. L. (2005) 'Development and preliminary validation of the collective efficacy questionnaire for sports', *Measurement in Physical Education and Exercise Science*, 9(3): 181–202.

Smith, R. E., Schutz, R. W., Smoll, F. L., & Ptacek, J. T. (1995) 'Development and validation of a multidimensional measure of sport-specific psychological skills: The athletic coping skills inventory-28', *Journal of Sport & Exercise Psychology*, 17(4): 379–98.

Spielberger, C. D., Gorssuch, R. L., Lushene, P. R., Vagg, P. R., & Jacobs, G. A. (1983) *Manual for the state-trait anxiety inventory*, Palo Alto, CA: Consulting Psychologists Press.

Stevens, M. J., & Lane, A. M. (2001) 'Mood-regulating strategies used by athletes', *Athletic Insight*, 3(3): 1–12.

Svebak, S., & Murgatroyd, S. (1985) 'Metamotivational dominance: A multimethod validation of reversal theory constructs', *Journal of Personality and Social Psychology*, 48(1): 107–16.

Taylor, M. K., Gould, D., & Rolo, C. (2008) 'Performance strategies of US Olympians in practice and competition', *High Ability Studies*, 19(1): 19–36.

Tenenbaum, G., Edmonds, W. A., & Eccles, D. W. (2008) 'Emotions, coping strategies, and performance: A conceptual framework for defining affect-related performance zones', *Military Psychology*, 20(Suppl 1): S11–S37.

Terry, P. C., Lane, A. M., & Fogarty, G. J. (2003) 'Construct validity of the POMS-A for use with adults', *Psychology of Sport and Exercise*, 4(2): 125–39.

Thayer, R. E. (1989) *The biopsychology of mood and arousal*, New York: Oxford University Press.

Thayer, R. E., Newman, J. R., & McClain, T. M. (1994) 'Self-regulation of mood: Strategies for changing a bad mood, raising energy, and reducing tension', *Journal of Personality and Social Psychology*, 67(5): 910–25.

Theodorakis, Y., Hatzigeorgiadis, A., & Chroni, S. (2008) 'Self-talk: It works, but how? Development and preliminary validation of the functions of self-talk questionnaire', *Measurement in Physical Education and Exercise Science*, 12(1): 10–30.

Thomas, P. R., Murphy, S. M., & Hardy, L. (1999) 'Test of performance strategies: Development and preliminary validation of a comprehensive measure of athletes' psychological skills', *Journal of Sports Sciences*, 17(9): 697–711.

Totterdell, P. (2000) 'Catching moods and hitting runs: Mood linkage and subjective performance in professional sport teams', *Journal of Applied Psychology*, 85(6): 848–59.

Tutko, T., Lyon, L., & Ogilvie, B. (1969) *Athletic motivation inventory*, San Jose, CA: Institute for the Study of Athletic Motivation.

Uphill, M. A., Lane, A. M., & Jones, M. V. (2012) 'Emotion regulation questionnaire for use with athletes', *Psychology of Sport and Exercise*, 13(6): 761–70.

Vallerand, R. J., & Blanchard, C. M. (2000) 'The study of emotion in sport and exercise', in Y. L. Hanin (ed) *Emotions in sport*, Champaign, IL: Human Kinetics, 3–37.

Vancouver, J. B., Thompson, C. M., & Williams, A. A. (2001) 'The changing signs in the relationships among self-efficacy, personal goals, and performance', *Journal of Applied Psychology*, 86(4): 605–20.

Vealey, R. S. (2001) 'Understanding and enhancing self-confidence in athletes', in R. N. Singer, H. A. Hausenblas, & C. M. Janelle (eds) *Handbook of sport psychology*, 2nd ed., New York: Wiley, 550–65.

Vealey, R. S., Hayashi, S. W., Garner-Holman, M., & Giacobbi, P. (1998) 'Sources of sport-confidence: Conceptualization and instrument development', *Journal of Sport & Exercise Psychology*, 20(1): 54–80.

Watson, D. (2000) *Mood and temperament*, New York: Guilford Press.

Watson, D., & Clark, L. A. (1994) 'The PANAS-X: Manual for the positive and negative affect schedule-expanded form', unpublished manuscript, Iowa City: University of Iowa.

Watson, D., & Clark, L. A. (1997) 'Measurement and mismeasurement of mood: Recurrent and emergent issues', *Journal of Personality Assessment*, 68(2): 267–96.

Watson, D., Clarke, L. A., & Tellegen, A. (1988) 'Developmental and validation of brief measures of positive and negative affect: The PANAS scales', *Journal of Personality and Social Psychology*, 54(6): 1063–70.

Webb, T. L., Miles, E., & Sheeran, P. (2012) 'Dealing with feeling: A meta-analysis of the effectiveness of strategies derived from the process model of emotion regulation', *Psychological Bulletin*, 138(4): 775–808.

Weinberg, R., & Forlenza, S. (2012) 'Psychological skills', in G. Tenenbaum, R. C. Eklund, & A. Kamata (eds) *Measurement in sport and exercise psychology*, Champaign, IL: Human Kinetics, 381–92.

Werner, K., Goldin, P. R., Ball, T. M., Heimberg, R. G., & Gross, J. J. (2011) 'Assessing emotion regulation in social anxiety disorder: The emotion regulation interview', *Journal of Psychopathology and Behavioral Assessment*, 33(3): 346–54.

Williams, A. M., Ford, P. R., Eccles, D. W., & Ward, P. (2011) 'Perceptual-cognitive expertise in sport and its acquisition: Implications for applied cognitive psychology', *Applied Cognitive Psychology*, 25(3): 432–42.

Woodman, T., & Hardy, L. (2003) 'The relative impact of cognitive anxiety and self-confidence upon sport performance: A meta-analysis', *Journal of Sport Sciences*, 21(6): 443–57.

Zervas, Y., Stavrou, N. A., & Psychountaki, M. (2007) 'Development and validation of the self-talk questionnaire (S-TQ) for sports', *Journal of Applied Sport Psychology*, 19(2): 142–59.

23

ISSUES IN THE MEASUREMENT OF PHYSIOLOGICAL AND ANTHROPOMETRIC FACTORS

David Pyne and Naroa Etxebarria

The importance of anthropometric, physiological, and performance testing

Sport science testing is a visible element in many contemporary, high-level sporting programmes. The pace of technological advancements and innovation in sport science has greatly expanded the reach of sport science testing. Athlete testing that used to occur primarily in the laboratory can now be undertaken with a high degree of accuracy and precision in training and competition venues. With rapid advancements in digital technology, results can be obtained almost anywhere and transmitted instantaneously worldwide for processing, analysis and interpretation, and providing feedback for athletes and coaches. Sport science testing is undertaken for several purposes: to monitor short- and long-term changes in fitness and performance; to profile game and competition demands, for talent identification, selection, and development programmes; for prescription and evaluation of training drills, activities, and sessions; to assist the rehabilitation of athletes after illness, injury, or a lay-off; for observational or experimental research; to target a specific performance area needing special consideration (special projects); and occasionally for education of athletes, coaches, and support staff.

Anthropometric, physiological, and performance testing is the initial step in better understanding the characteristics, strengths, and potential weaknesses of an athlete relative to the physical and performance demands of the chosen sport. The information obtained is used to determine whether minor and/or major modifications are needed in the athlete or team's programme to meet both short- and long-term goals. Testing should always involve the athlete(s) and coach – other officials or experts can be consulted if specialist advice is required. An independent expert opinion can be useful in resolving ongoing issues, particularly plateaus or reductions in training and/or competitive performance that defy simple explanation.

Anthropometric testing can be useful throughout an athlete's career. Regular monitoring of height, mass, and body fat is informative in junior athletes who are growing and maturing quickly, occasionally reaching world-class levels in their teenage years. Frequent testing is useful in determining the effectiveness of a specific training intervention/phase, monitoring progress in fitness and performance, and/or predicting likely outcomes in competitive performance (Lamberts, 2013). Anthropometric measures in older athletes are generally monitored less frequently as changes in adults occur slowly, unless there is a specific goal of intervening and changing lean or fat body mass (Haakonsen et al., 2013). Physiological and performance profiling can be carried out in the field (training and competition venues) for greater relevance to racing or competition, and/or in the laboratory (to measure generic physiological characteristics that are difficult to control in the field), depending on the specific purpose of the testing and intended application of the results.

Specificity of physiological and performance testing is an important part of profiling athletes. The testing should be relevant and applicable to the demands of competition, the ultimate outcome of performance (Reilly et al., 2009). A high degree of specificity of testing will add meaning to the results, making them useful for the athlete and coach (see Chapter 24). The results will have more relevance if the scientist can relate them to performance, either directly or indirectly. Some studies in endurance sports such as running and cycling have correlated the results of physiological and performance testing with competitive outcomes. This is a more difficult task in team sports where a large number of factors influence the outcome of a match. To obtain sport-specific information, new approaches have emerged that customize physiological and performance testing to different sports, including endurance (Quod et al., 2010; Etxebarria et al., 2013a, 2013b) and team sports (Green et al., 2011; Mooney et al., 2011). These and other sport-specific testing and assessment approaches increase the cohesion and value of the testing programme (Pyne et al., 2013).

Testing and assessment of athletes can take different forms, depending on the level of competition and the chronological and training age of the athlete. A basic battery of tests may be appropriate for juniors and lower levels of competition. An expert athlete, especially in a senior full-time setting, often requires a more individualized testing programme, developed around special projects. Special projects may target a specific goal around a competition strategy, evaluate the effectiveness of various training and lifestyle interventions in the training domain (rather than the laboratory), address a specific environmental challenge for competition (i.e., heat, altitude), and/or develop a specific capacity/skill to gain competitive advantage over another competitor (see Figure 23.1).

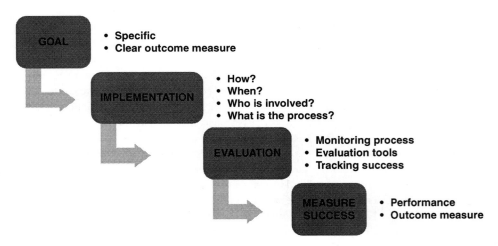

Figure 23.1 Systematic approach to the design and implementation of a special project in support of expert athletes. For example, a training load management and recovery system might be implemented for older athletes in need of more individualised recovery programmes.

Shifting from fitness testing to athlete monitoring and special projects

Fitness testing works well in talent identification programmes, junior and club-level competition, and some senior-level sports, and traditionally spans the different phases of the season, competitive calendar, or annual plan, from the pre-season through to the main competition. The rigors of pre-season testing are well known to athletes, as is the requirement to submit to testing at various stages of the early, mid-, and late season. This approach still has merit for junior and senior athletes, and individual and team sport athletes alike. Over a longer period, such as a four-year Olympic cycle, a testing programme typically involves annual testing as a team or athlete moves through a development or rebuilding phase in the initial stages (i.e., the first year of the cycle), concentrated training and competitive experience mid-cycle, during selection periods for major national and international competitions and championships, and then the final preparations for the major competition such as the world championships (or cup, depending on the sport) or the Olympic games.

However, senior athletes in both team and individual sports are often reluctant to commit to testing given the lack of time, the perception of training interruptions, or limited relevance of the results to their preparations and performance. In recent years, individualised training monitoring (Ingham *et al.*, 2012) and special projects have increased in popularity. Individualized training approaches can target young, inexperienced athletes, older athletes rehabilitating from injury back to full training, or possibly senior/veteran athletes who need reduced workloads in the latter stages of a long career. Special projects could, for example, focus on the specifics of individual competitions or tournaments to ensure that performance goals are met in challenging environments (Ross *et al.*, 2012).

Monitoring training on a regular basis has an immediate benefit for the coach and athlete. A great deal of attention has been placed on daily measures of health and well-being, including ratings of fatigue, soreness, illness, injury, training loads, and sleep quality and quantity (Montgomery & Hopkins, 2013). Physiological measures such as body mass, resting heart rate, and urine specific gravity (USG) can also be part of daily or regular monitoring. Training monitoring can be used in real time to make immediate modifications to the athlete's programme, or retrospectively to learn from both successes and/or inappropriate choices made prior to competition (Mujika, 2013). Different phases of the season or specific competition cycles also dictate the timing and frequency of fitness assessment and evaluation of the effectiveness of training interventions. Research, innovation, and experimentation with new testing or monitoring protocols are all part of the process to achieve the selected goal for each expert athlete performing at the highest level of his/her chosen sport.

Quality assurance issues in athlete preparation and standardization of protocols

Quality assurance should be a priority for all anthropometric and physiological measurements of athletes. Anecdotally, it appears that physiology laboratories in sporting institutions and universities often pay greater attention to quality assurance than do many sporting teams and individual athletes. Some countries have established quality assurance programmes for sport science testing to ensure that standardized protocols, correct procedures, and certified laboratories and staff provide consistent, accurate testing results (Tanner & Gore, 2006).

Physiological testing of athletes should take into account a range of internal and external factors. From the athlete's perspective they should present for testing in a rested state, as fatigue and/or muscle soreness might confound physiological and performance test scores. Pre-testing warm-up protocols should be established and standardized to ensure adequate preparation prior to testing to yield the best possible result and limit the risk of injury. Athletes should be given a full explanation of procedures before undertaking any testing, particularly if they have not been tested previously. Equipment and instrumentation should be calibrated and prepared as required, following standard laboratory protocols or manufacturer's recommendations. It is valuable to have any prior test results on hand so that test scores can be compared and interpreted against each athlete's historical record. Where possible, the coach should be present at testing to observe the test performance. A common discussion point is the effect of verbal encouragement by testing staff or coaches. Verbal encouragement during testing can lead to higher test scores, although conversely, athletes with a high level of conscientiousness may actually be put off with excessive encouragement and perform more poorly (Binboğa *et al.*, 2013). Junior or external staff members should be adequately briefed on protocols and procedures to ensure they are familiar with the requirements of testing.

Validity, reliability, and experimental designs

It is often said that the value or importance of a test or measurement result is highly dependent on the confidence of the coach, athlete, and staff member in the underlying accuracy and reliability. Methodological or measurement studies of testing procedures including reliability and validity are rather dry topics for most coaches and athletes. However, these are important considerations for the practitioner and researcher, and a substantial amount of work is needed behind the scenes to ensure good quality and meaningful testing results.

There are several different metrics or measures of reliability used in testing of athletes (Atkinson & Nevill, 2000; Hopkins, 2000; Hopkins *et al.*, 2009). One of the most common and familiar metrics is the simple correlation coefficient, although the typical error of measurement often works better in practical settings. For any test in which typical error has been calculated, the value should be included in reports provided to coaches or athletes. All typical error data should be reported and interpreted in absolute units (i.e., seconds, centimetres, metres, and $L.min^{-1}$). An exception to this rule is sum of skinfolds for body fat testing, given the sum of seven skinfolds could range from 30–150 mm or more, and thus per cent typical error is probably more appropriate.

Athlete test reports should also include an explanation of what typical error is and how it is interpreted. The typical error provides an indication of the typical short-term day-to-day variability of a measure. Change in a score between tests that is less than the typical error is considered to be noise (measurement error) rather than real or substantial. While a change or difference score may be real (when compared with a typical reference value), the underlying question is whether the change or difference is important (or worthwhile) in terms of a substantial improvement or decrement in performance or physiological test scores. The smallest worthwhile change is a derived reference value that permits the sport scientist to determine whether an observed change or difference score is large enough to have a substantial effect on a performance or physiological measure. The smallest worthwhile change is sport-specific, which is an attractive element for the coach, scientist, and athlete (Hopkins *et al.*, 2009). The metric is comparable to other statistical approaches in the scientific and biomedical literature, such as the meaningful clinically important difference.

In validity studies, a new test/protocol or a new instrument/device is compared with a well-established criterion or standard method. The preferred metric is the typical or standard error of the estimate. Validity can take the form of *construct validity* (to what degree

Measurement of physiological factors

does a test measure what it claims, or purports, to be measuring; for example, does a sprint test measure acceleration and maximal running velocity), *content validity* (to what extent does an anthropometric, physiological, or performance test represent all the different facets of sporting fitness and performance, giving rise to a battery of tests), and *criterion validity* (a measure of how well one variable or set of variables predicts an outcome based on information from other variables). These issues should be considered before a test is fully implemented in the field.

Approaches in analysing and interpreting testing data

Most analyses in sport science research and servicing are at a group level – either groups of research subjects or groups of individual or team sport athletes. Obviously the statistical analysis of data can become complex, but sport scientists should be familiar with basic issues such as the reliability of the testing protocols/methods, expected values, and the individual circumstances of each athlete. Deeper and more sophisticated analysis of testing data involves use of covariates in linear models to adjust for confounders, accounting for the presence, magnitude, and origins of individual differences between athletes, identifying potential mechanisms of a training effect, and identifying and dealing with outlier (unexpected) values. However, outliers in a set of testing results are often useful where they might be showcasing one or more individual athletes who can outperform almost all their peers in a particular test. Outliers are usually defined as two (top five per cent of performers) or three (top one per cent of performers) standard deviations above the mean value. The first step in dealing with an outlier is to exclude the possibility of a measurement error. However, if a test score is deemed genuine after screening, then it can be used with confidence to indicate either an expert performer and/or performance. One way to distinguish an expert performer from a performance is that the expert performer can consistently reproduce high-level performances, whereas an expert performance might just be a one-time occurrence.

Interpretation of individual athlete test scores should account for the current and recent training history, the phase of the training or competitive season, specific requirements of the sport/event, playing position (if relevant), and the presence of any underlying fatigue, soreness, illness, or medical condition. Another factor that is sometimes overlooked is the degree of familiarity that an athlete has with a particular test. This is especially important in physiological and performance tests that have a higher degree of skill or novelty. Apart from familiarization, the sport scientist should also be alert to the degree of practice, the rate of learning of new tests and skills by younger or inexperienced athletes, potentiation effects of warm-ups and/or prior exercise, and the presence of residual fatigue. Fatigue can take the form of cumulative fatigue over days, weeks, and months in the middle or latter stages of competitive season, or acute fatigue from exercise within the previous 24 hours, especially on the day of testing.

Anthropometric testing

Anthropometric measurements of height, body mass, and particularly body fat present a particular challenge to the athlete, coach, and scientist. Society places great importance on appearance, and both female and male athletes can be affected by body image concerns (Varnes *et al.*, 2013). The degree of between-subject variability in anthropometric characteristics (particularly body fat levels quantified by skinfolds testing) in a given sport is often substantially higher than variability in physiological and performance characteristics. This is not surprising given a wide range of size and shapes of athletes competing at the top level of a particular sport. In some sports such as basketball, rugby union, and rugby sevens, the effect of different playing positions means a wide range of anthropometric test scores will be obtained (Higham *et al.*, 2013). Given this degree of variability, results should be reported and interpreted on an individual level in the first instance. Body mass index often incorrectly categorizes larger size athletes as obese, and this metric should be avoided in most sports (Etchison *et al.*, 2013). Other metrics, such as the lean mass index, are useful for differentiating changes in fat mass and lean body mass in highly trained athletes (Slater *et al.*, 2006). A sport dietician is a valuable resource in addressing nutritional issues that might be impacting on dietary practices, body composition, and training/ competitive performance.

Descriptive analysis

Descriptive analysis is always informative in both individual and team sport settings. The most common metrics are obviously the mean (or average) and standard deviation (SD). Other metrics that can be informative include the minimum value, maximum value, range, and count, or the number of athletes tested. These metrics are probably more useful for the coach and sport scientist, rather than an individual athlete, in providing information about the number and distribution of test scores in the team.

Reference value

There are some sport science tests that are interpreted against a single reference value, or possibly an expert-level criterion score or value. In terms of basic anthropometric testing this might apply to height, body mass, and/or sum of skinfolds, or per cent body fat. In performance testing a football coach might set, for example, a minimum standard of 3.15 seconds for a 20 m sprint test, a multistage shuttle run score of level 12, and 100 kg for a bench press. Reference values for test scores should be sport, gender, and performance-level specific and derived from published studies, established norms in a sport, team, or programme, or pilot testing of a representative number of athletes. Expert-level reference values might, for example, distinguish national-level performance from a junior- or academy-level performance (see 40 m sprint testing data in Table 23.1).

Table 23.1 Forty metre sprint data for expert male Australian super rugby players. In this example, the Super15 players exhibit superior speed (*small difference) and momentum (**moderate to large difference) in comparison with junior and academy players. Mean ± SD

Level	40 m time(s)	Maximal velocity(m/s)	Momentum(kg·m/s)
Junior (n = 61)	5.40 ± 0.21	8.8 ± 0.3	731 ± 72
Academy (n = 48)	5.42 ± 0.25	8.9 ± 0.4	786 ± 76
Super15 (n = 18)	5.35 ± 0.19*	9.0 ± 0.4	863 ± 59**

Typical error: 10 m time = 0.04 s; 40 m time = 0.04 s; maximal velocity = 0.1 m/s, momentum = 10 kg·m/s. Reproduced with permission from Higham *et al.* (2013).

Measurement of physiological factors

Reference range or interval

An extension of the single reference value for interpreting test scores is the reference range or interval. In sports, a reference range or interval usually describes the expected range of a measurement or test score in healthy, well-trained athletes. Comparison of individual or group test scores provides the means for a sport scientist to interpret a set of results for a particular athlete or team. A key requirement in establishing a sport-specific reference range or interval is to ensure the athlete cohort used to derive the range is representative in terms of gender, age, sport, competitive level, position or event specificity, background fitness, and recent training history. For example, in high-performance swimming, a different range would need to be established for a group of senior male breaststroke swimmers preparing for the national championships compared with a second group of junior female breaststroke swimmers preparing for a local competition. The need for establishing position-specific reference values is well established in several team sports, including football (Carling & Orhant 2010), basketball (Drinkwater *et al.*, 2008), rugby union and rugby sevens (Higham *et al.*, 2014), and Australian football (Pyne *et al.*, 2006). Expert performances could be defined by level (e.g., international, national, or state) or a specified proportion of the range of test scores (e.g., the top 10 or 20 per cent of performances).

Rankings

In simple terms, ranking of test scores provides a readily accessible, ordered list of performances for the coach and player. A high ranking at a world, national, local, or even team/squad level can provide powerful feedback and motivation. Many sports have official listings of world rankings, and national sporting organizations sometimes base selection criteria of athletes for teams and competitions on a specified world ranking. For example, an athlete might need to be ranked in the top 12 in the world to be selected for a major, international championship team. In team sports, a nation might need to rank in the top 12 to make, for example, an Olympic games or world championships. While a simple ranking is intuitively appealing, the shortcomings of solely using ordinal-level data must be considered, and conveyed where appropriate to coaches and players. Simple numeric rankings of test scores may mask the actual magnitudes of differences between consecutive or specified positions in the list (see Chapter 13).

Percentile rankings

The percentile rank of a score is the percentage of scores in a frequency distribution that are the same or lower than it. For example, an athlete or player who records a test score that is greater than or equal to 90 per cent of the scores of athletes in that team or sport is said to be at the 90th percentile rank. A more accessible way of describing this result for athletes and coaches is that the athlete is ranked in the top 10 per cent. Percentile rankings are used in many team sports as a way of quickly standardising test scores across a wide range of tests. This form of ranking is more appropriate when testing large numbers of athletes rather than a smaller squad or team. For example, the draft combines of the Australian Football League (AFL), National Hockey League (NHL), and the National Football League (NFL) – where hundreds of players are tested each year – are more appropriate settings for use of percentile rankings (Tarter *et al.*, 2009).

David Pyne and Naroa Etxebarria

Supporting camps and competition

Training camps are a popular way to experience race/competition conditions and rehearse routines to be implemented before, during, and after major national and international competitions. Testing and monitoring athletes is useful during periods of high training loads to ensure athletes are fit and ready to train prior to the taper and competitive phases. Pre-season training camps in team sports often involve concentrated sport science testing to monitor adaptation and fatigue (Racinais *et al.*, 2013). Specific projects might, for example, include optimization of the warm-up, monitoring of hydration status, especially during hot and humid conditions, various post-training/competition recovery strategies including hydrotherapy (Vaile *et al.*, 2008) or monitoring of sleep quality (Hausswirth *et al.*, 2013). Recovery strategies are important in sports where athletes have to perform on multiple occasions within a short period of time (e.g., qualifiers to finals and tournament-style games). Various forms of recovery interventions can be effective (Argus *et al.*, 2013), so it is a matter of performing trials to select the most relevant, effective, or practical intervention for each particular sport or event. Tapering before a major competition, or a mini-taper rehearsal leading up to minor competition in the mid-season phase, is another area where sport science testing and monitoring can be useful (Pyne *et al.*, 2009).

Competitions are an ideal scenario for observational research and to collect information on measurable outcomes in a structured manner in the field. Sports involving competition venues with a predictable environment (i.e., swimming and track cycling) lend themselves to relatively robust race and competition race analysis. Opportunities in track cycling extend to commercially available power meters that record accurate and detailed physical/physiological information during training and competitions. In individual sports where the competition venue is less predictable (e.g., triathlon, kayaking, and sailing), case study approaches are often used to characterise race demands (Etxebarria *et al.*, 2013b). Race analysis during competition also informs the development of sport-specific assessment protocols that offer meaningful information to coaches and athletes. Furthermore, capturing expert performance in competition is important in complementing laboratory-based testing or testing conducted in routine training sessions.

Formulating feedback for coaches, athletes, and support staff

Often the challenge of effective, applied sport science and support is not the collection and interpretation of relevant information, but feedback and implementation of the outcomes. Results need to be interpreted by practitioners and researchers before the message is conveyed to coaches and athletes. This information needs to be timely, open, and representative of the results, and presented in a clear and concise manner. Reports should include details of the athlete, testing protocols, contact details of the scientist and laboratory, reference ranges or intervals, brief details of equipment and instrumentation, typical errors of measurement, and, where appropriate, environmental details (particularly for outdoors testing) (Pyne, 2013). There are three critical time points for feedback of test results: during the test if time and access permits, shortly upon completion of the testing at the training or competition venue, and same day-next day reporting if processing time is required. Delayed reporting and feedback of results should be avoided where possible so the athlete and coach can implement timely corrective actions in terms of training modification, and/or seek further specialist advice if required.

There are several different types of communication channels for giving feedback. The effectiveness of feedback for the coach, athletes, or other support staff members will depend on adequate timing, content, and form of communication. Verbal face-to-face feedback should be the first preference, but digital means such as the telephone, e-mail, SMS messaging, and social media

Measurement of physiological factors

are becoming more commonplace. The presence of coaching staff and/or support staff members can be valuable to facilitate cross-discipline discussions, although there are circumstances, particularly with anthropometric testing, where a more private and personalized approach is warranted. Written reports often follow the initial verbal interaction in order to consolidate and retain new information for future reference. Long-term analysis of trends in test results is now possible using data analytic and mining techniques.

References

Argus, C., Driller, M., Ebert, T., Martin, D., & Halson, S. (2013) 'The effects of 4 different recovery strategies on repeat sprint-cycling performance', *International Journal of Sports Physiology and Performance*, 8(5): 542–8.

Atkinson, G., & Nevill, A. (2000) 'Typical error versus limits of agreements', *Sports Medicine*, 30: 375–81.

Binboğa, E., Tok, S., Catikkas, F., Guven, S., & Dane, S. (2013) 'The effects of verbal encouragement and conscientiousness on maximal voluntary contraction of the triceps surae muscle in elite athletes', *Journal of Sports Sciences*, 31(9): 982–8.

Carling, C., & Orhant, E. (2010) 'Variation in body composition in professional soccer players: Interseasonal and intraseasonal changes and the effects of exposure time and player position', *Journal of Strength and Conditioning Research*, 24(5): 1332–9.

Drinkwater, E., Pyne, D., & McKenna, M. (2008) 'Design and interpretation of anthropometric and fitness testing of basketball players', *Sports Medicine*, 38(7): 565–78.

Etchison, W., Bloodgood, E., Minton, C., Thompson, N., Collins, M., Hunter, S., & Dai, H. (2013) 'Body mass index and percentage of body fat as indicators for obesity in an adolescent athletic population', *Sports Health*, 3(3): 249–52.

Etxebarria, N., Anson, J., Pyne, D., & Ferguson, R. (2013a) 'Cycling attributes that enhance running performance after the cycle section in triathlon', *International Journal of Sports Physiology and Performance*, 5(5): 502–9.

Etxebarria, N., D'Auria, S., Anson, J., Pyne, D., & Ferguson, R. (2013b) 'Variability in power output during cycling in international Olympic distance triathlon', *International Journal of Sports Physiology and Performance*, 9: 732–4.

Green, B., Blake, C., & Caulfield, B. (2011) 'A valid field test protocol of linear speed and agility in rugby union', *Journal of Strength and Conditioning Research*, 25(5): 1256–62.

Haakonsen, E., Martin, D., Burke, L., & Jenkins, D. (2013) 'Increased lean mass with reduced fat mass in an elite female cyclist returning to competition: Case study', *International Journal of Sports Physiology and Performance*, 8(6): 699–701.

Hausswirth, C., Louis, J., Aubry, A., Bonnet, G., Duffield, R., & Le Meur, Y. (2013) 'Evidence of disturbed sleep and increased illness in overreached endurance athletes', *Medicine and Science in Sports and Exercise*, 46: 1036–45.

Higham, D., Pyne, D., Anson, J., Dziedzic, C., & Slater, G. (2014) 'Distribution of fat, non-osseous lean and bone mineral mass in international rugby union and rugby sevens players', *International Journal of Sports Medicine*, 35: 575–82.

Higham, D., Pyne, D., Anson, J., & Eddy, A. (2013) 'Physiological, anthropometric, and performance characteristics of rugby sevens players', *International Journal of Sports Physiology and Performance*, 8(1): 19–27.

Hopkins, W. (2000) 'Measures of reliability in sports medicine and science', *Sports Medicine*, 30: 1–15.

Hopkins, W., Marshall, S., Batterham, A., & Hanin, J. (2009) 'Progressive statistics for studies in sports medicine and exercise science', *Medicine and Science in Sports and Exercise*, 41(1): 3–13.

Ingham, S., Fudge, B., & Pringle, J. (2012) 'Training distribution, physiological profile and performance for a male international 1500-m runner', *International Journal of Sports Physiology and Performance*, 7(2): 193–5.

Lamberts, R. (2013) 'Predicting cycling performance in trained to elite male and female cyclists', *International Journal of Sports Physiology and Performance*, 9: 610–14.

Montgomery, P., & Hopkins, W. (2013) 'The effects of game and training loads on perceptual responses of muscle soreness in Australian football', *International Journal of Sports Physiology and Performance*, 8: 312–8.

Mooney, M., O'Brien, B., Cormack, S., Coutts, A., Berry, J., & Young, W. (2011) 'The relationship between physical capacity and match performance in elite Australian football: A mediation approach', *Journal of Science and Medicine in Sport*, 14(5): 447–52.

Mujika, I. (2013) 'Olympic preparation of a world-class female triathlete', *International Journal of Sports Physiology and Performance*, 9: 727–31.

Pyne, D. (2013) 'Data collection and analysis', in R. Tanner & C. Gore (eds) *Physiological tests for elite athletes*, 2nd ed., Champaign, IL: Human Kinetics, 35–42.

Pyne, D., Gardner, A., Sheehan, K., & Hopkins, W. (2006) 'Positional differences in fitness and anthropometric characteristics in Australian football', *Journal of Science and Medicine in Sport*, 9(1–2): 143–50.

Pyne, D., Mujika, I., & Reilly, T. (2009) 'Peaking for optimal performance: Research limitations and future directions', *Journal of Sports Sciences*, 27(3): 195–202.

Pyne, D., Spencer, M., & Mujika, I. (2013) 'Improving the value of fitness testing for football', *International Journal of Sports Physiology and Performance*, 9: 511–14.

Quod, M., Martin, D., Martin, J., & Laursen, P. (2010) 'The power profile predicts road cycling MMP', *International Journal of Sports Medicine*, 6: 397–401.

Racinais, S., Buchheit, M., Bilsborough, J., Bourdon, P., Cordy, J., & Coutts, A. (2014) 'Physiological and performance responses to a training-camp in the heat in professional Australian football players', *International Journal of Sports Physiology and Performance*, 9(4): 598–603.

Reilly, T., Morris, T., & Whyte, G. (2009) 'The specificity of training prescription and physiological assessment: A review', *Journal of Sports Sciences*, 27(6): 575–89.

Ross, M., Jeacocke, N., Laursen, P., Martin, D., Abbiss, C., & Burke, L. (2012) 'Effects of lowering body temperature via hyperhydration, with and without glycerol ingestion and practical precooling on cycling time trial performance in hot and humid conditions', *Journal of the International Society of Sports Nutrition*, 9(1): 55.

Slater, G., Duthie, G., Pyne, D., & Hopkins, W. (2006) 'Validation of a skinfold based index for tracking proportional changes in lean mass', *British Journal of Sports Medicine*, 40(3): 208–13.

Tanner, R., & Gore, C. (2006) 'Quality assurance in Australian exercise physiology laboratories in quest of excellence', *International Journal of Sports Physiology and Performance*, 1(1): 58–60.

Tarter, B., Kirisci, L., Tarter, R., Weatherbee, S., Jamnik, V., McGuire, E., & Gledhill, N. (2009) 'Use of aggregate fitness indicators to predict transition into the National Hockey League', *Journal of Strength and Conditioning Research*, 23(6): 1828–32.

Vaile, J., Halson, S., Gill, N., & Dawson, B. (2008) 'Effect of hydrotherapy on recovery from fatigue', *International Journal of Sports Medicine*, 29(7): 539–44.

Varnes, J., Stellefson, M., Janelle, C., Dorman, S., Dodd, V., & Miller, M. (2013) 'A systematic review of studies comparing body image concerns among female college athletes and non-athletes, 1997–2012', *Body Image*, 10(4): 431–2.

24

ISSUES AND CHALLENGES IN DEVELOPING REPRESENTATIVE TASKS IN SPORT

Ross A. Pinder, Jonathon Headrick, and Raôul R. D. Oudejans

Introduction

Our understanding and development of expertise in sport relies on the capture and assessment of performers in various performance environments, and the design of appropriate practice conditions. To truly understand sport expertise we must ensure that we accurately describe and measure performance under specific task constraints that effectively capture the functional responses of performers in representative situations (e.g., competition), before attempting to develop knowledge and expertise within this context (Araújo & Davids, 2009). The aims of this chapter are to discuss a range of issues and considerations in developing representative tasks in sport research and practice, and provide tangible examples, applied insights, and advice for researchers and practitioners.

The big issue

Expert performances in sport are characterized by attributes such as better anticipation (see Chapter 2), more efficient decision-making (see Chapter 6), and superior physiological performance (see Chapter 11). Recently, however, it has been highlighted that much of our current understanding may be based on research data gained from situations that do not fully capture performers demonstrating sport-specific movement, knowledge, and expertise (Dicks *et al.*, 2010; Pinder *et al.*, 2011b; van der Kamp *et al.*, 2008). Furthermore, traditional methods of learning motor skills in sport have focused on breaking down skills and developing "drills" away from the performance environment (see Magill, 2007). Such instances have typically been characterized by the decomposition of perceptual and action processes, impoverished information sources, use of restrictive training methods (such as treadmills or ball projection machines), or isolated tasks. Indeed, two-thirds of all published sport science research completed in Australia between 1983 and 2003 is reported to have been completed in laboratory settings (Williams & Kendall, 2007). Studying expertise in sport provides unique and fascinating insights into the limits of human performance; however, with this comes a range of issues and challenges for practitioners to consider.

Two settings commonly referred to in expertise research are (i) laboratory (generally allowing high degrees of experimental control) and (ii) field (often referred to as in situ, where experimental control is more difficult, but can allow for a better replication of performance conditions). The choice of setting is not always straightforward, and changes in data collection and analysis methods have led and will continue to lead to changes in research designs (e.g., the development of portable GPS units has revolutionized the role of player workload tracking in team sports; see Chapter 11). In situations where such methods are not available or appropriate, the manipulation of task constraints in laboratory studies may allow for performances to emerge that reflect expertise advantages in competition. In contrast, the completion of research within a field setting does not necessarily guarantee representative performance will be captured. A growing number of studies, however, are providing influential evidence demonstrating significant and meaningful differences in movement and visual behavior between traditional methods of capturing expertise in laboratory settings and contexts that are more representative of the participants' performance environment. For example, the use of decomposed tasks (including different degrees of coupling of perception to action; see Farrow & Abernethy, 2003) for assessing perceptual expertise in soccer goalkeeping led to significant changes in visual search behavior compared to an in situ task where goalkeepers physically moved and attempted to intercept the ball as they would in a game (Dicks *et al.*, 2010). Such findings reinforce previous warnings that small changes in task constraints in the design of an experiment can lead to substantial changes in aspects of visual and movement behavior, as well as physiological performance, and may in fact be limiting our progress in understanding expertise in sport-specific contexts – a consideration researchers and practitioners should keep in mind throughout the rest of this chapter and when designing representative tasks in the future.

Representative learning design: a framework for practitioners

The concerns raised above have been highlighted numerous times within the literature while slowly gaining traction and evidence over the past 10 years, primarily in perceptual-motor research in sport (Dhami *et al.*, 2004; Dicks *et al.*, 2008; Fajen *et al.*, 2009) and more recently in general sport science (Robertson *et al.*, 2013) and across other domains of expert human performance (Colin *et al.*, 2014). Recent expertise studies (particularly those comparing perceptual-motor attributes of skilled and novice performers) have demonstrated that an expert's advantage is maximized under conditions that more closely replicate the competitive context (e.g., Mann *et al.*, 2010; Müller *et al.*, 2009). Whereas this premise allows researchers to allude to the ideas of representative design, a framework has been specifically developed to guide researchers and practitioners in designing various research and practice tasks (Pinder *et al.*, 2011b).

Concerns of non-representative experimental design have been considered akin to the design of learning environments in practice. Here, and previously, we have used the case study of ball projection machines in sport to demonstrate the commonalities between designing research tasks and practice tasks that attempt to simulate aspects of competition for athletes to develop sport-specific expertise (see *Applied insight – A*). Developed using concepts emanating from an ecological dynamics approach to understanding expertise in human behavior (see Chapter 12), the assessment of representative learning design has been proposed to help guide sport scientists, coaches, and students in recognizing benefits and limitations of specific tasks in an attempt to optimize the balance between experimental control, representativeness, generalizability, transfer of performance, and practical (applied) considerations (for comprehensive discussions of these concepts, see Araújo *et al.*, 2007; Dicks *et al.*, 2008; Pinder *et al.*, 2011b; Pinder *et al.*, 2014).

Applied insight – A: considering the impact beyond experimental design

Experimental work has begun to critically evaluate the role of ball projection machines, which had previously been used to assess aspects of interceptive expertise, including visual (Croft *et al.*, 2010; Land & McLeod, 2000) and kinematic measures in cricket batting (Weissensteiner *et al.*, 2009). It was hypothesized that comparing cricket batting performance against a ball projection machine with a more representative task of a bowler (similar to pitcher in baseball) would clearly exemplify limitations of current experimental designs, and the need for tasks to faithfully simulate the task constraints of the performance environment of interest. Results showed that each distinct task led to variations in emergent patterns of movement control, with removal of advanced information when using a ball projection machine resulting in significant reductions in performance and delays in movement timing (Pinder *et al.*, 2011a; Renshaw *et al.*, 2007) and significant changes in visual search patterns (Pinder, 2012) – findings replicated in tennis (Shim *et al.*, 2005). With the prominence of ball projection machines in practice, these findings demonstrate commensurate concerns for the design of learning programs, which overemphasize the use of non-representative tasks. Just as experimental tasks need to attempt to "simulate" all key aspects of performance to allow for generalizability of research findings (see below), practice tasks designed to develop expertise should be considered simulations that maximize transfer between practice and competition. Practitioners and coaches should carefully consider the advantages and disadvantages of particular practice tasks; for example, the use of ball projection machines can alleviate bowling workloads, but may lead to significant changes in performance and movement coordination.

In the design of research and practice tasks researchers and practitioners should consider the action fidelity and functionality provided in specific experimental and practice tasks (Pinder *et al.*, 2011b). In practice, coaches may have to rely on face validity to question if the practice task adequately replicates competition (due to time constraints; also see below); the more a task looks and feels like competitive performance, the higher likelihood we will see functional performances (i.e., allowing similar levels of performance based on the same information sources) transfer beyond the current task. Researchers and practitioners should initially consider questions such as: (i) what are the key features of the competition environment that need to be simulated? (ii) what are the critical perception and action processes within the task? (iii) does the task allow the performer to achieve a similar level of performance to that measured under competitive conditions? or (iv) what factors could affect performance or behavior?

The strength of these theoretical advances are evident in the adaptability of the concepts for a variety of distinct areas of sport expertise (for a case study in sailing, see Pluijms *et al.*, 2013), and application within a range of sports (e.g., cricket, sailing, soccer, diving), in addition to a global framework to guide practitioners. Furthermore, such a theoretical and methodological advance holds implications for a range of subdisciplines of sport expertise, such as talent identification and development (Davids *et al.*, 2013; Pinder *et al.*, 2012), coaching science (Greenwood *et al.*, 2012), and sports technology (cf. Portus & Farrow, 2011; Stone *et al.*, 2013). Next we expand upon some of the key issues and challenges for developing expertise in sport, providing examples, considerations, and suggestions for future experimentation and practice design.

Ross A. Pinder et al.

Issues and challenges in designing representative tasks

Experimental control, representative conditions, and learning design

It is widely accepted that laboratory settings allow for a greater degree of experimental control compared with in situ designs, exemplified by a large proportion of sport science and motor learning research adopting these contexts (Dhami *et al.*, 2004; Williams & Kendall, 2007). By testing performers under strictly controlled laboratory conditions, researchers can be more confident that any findings are a result of the manipulation of a singular and specific variable (e.g., the effect of pre-cooling on performance in distance running, or the amount of visual information required for successful shot prediction in tennis or cricket); essentially, these studies provide insight into critical aspects of expertise isolated by the manipulation of experimental variables.

For example, a common method of assessing anticipatory expertise has been through the use of video-based occlusion techniques, in which participants of differing skill levels attempt to predict the outcome of an opponent's action based on manipulated amounts of visual information before a key event is occluded (e.g., racquet-ball contact during a serve in tennis), typically using verbal, written, or simplified movement responses. This controlled format ensures that only the influence of the manipulated variable (information provided) is examined (Lucas, 2003), and ensures stimulus consistency across tests and participants – an important and valid consideration of researchers (Pluijms *et al.*, 2013), particularly given the stringent process of peer review and publishing of experimental research (see below). The major benefit of control, however, has been proposed as a false dilemma, where experimentation restricts performers' responses and requires behavior that is not representative of their competitive performance. Studies using approaches such as video-based temporal occlusion have consistently concluded that expertise in interceptive sport is characterized by the ability to process earlier visual information, anticipate more effectively, and pick up useful information from kinematics of an opponent's movement (for a review, see Farrow *et al.*, 2005). However, in a recent example, prediction accuracies of cricket batters only exceeded chance levels under no occlusion conditions, with hours of cricket-specific practice explaining only a modest percentage (13.3 and 14.4 per cent for ball type and length, respectively) of the total variance in anticipatory skill (Weissensteiner *et al.*, 2008). Van der Kamp *et al.* (2008) proposed that, whereas previous experimental designs may have provided some limited insights into expertise, behavioral tasks which lack representative design (originally confused with ecological validity, see Pinder *et al.*, 2011b) may not have allowed perception and action to function as evolved (and as learned in context; for an early example, see Oudejans *et al.*, 1996) – in such instances our understanding of the true mechanisms of expertise may be limited, biased, or misleading (Savelsbergh & van der Kamp, 2009; van der Kamp *et al.*, 2008). Importantly, the reactions produced by participants bear no relation to the complex, coupled responses coordinated in dynamic sport environments. Despite these increasing concerns and discussed evidence, these methods remain prominent in research in perceptual-motor expertise, often with little acknowledgment of limitations or potential generalizability of research findings (e.g., Loffing & Hagemann, 2014; also see below). Research has shown that small (and seemingly insignificant) changes in task constraints can lead to substantial changes in performance outcomes and movement responses (Hristovski *et al.*, 2006), including changes in practice environment (Barris *et al.*, 2013), changes to practice tasks (Pinder *et al.*, 2011a), the location of experimental tasks in situ (Headrick *et al.*, 2012), and the presence of significant others (e.g., defenders/team members) in practice (Orth *et al.*, 2014). Advances in technology are providing researchers practical options for assessing expertise (for examples, see Mann *et al.*, 2010; Panchuk & Vickers, 2006). However,

Developing representative tasks

the issue of experimental control remains a "thorny issue" (Pluijms *et al.*, 2013). One clear and necessary advancement is the increased possibility to measure aspects such as gaze behavior on the (training) field, rather than in the laboratory (e.g., in basketball jump shooting, soccer goal-keeping, or other areas of perceptual-motor expertise).

As outlined above, the isolation of specific components in reductionist experimental designs can result in behavior that is not representative of competitive performance, limiting our understanding of expertise. Decomposing tasks in this way is also a major concern for practice. As highlighted in *Applied insight – B*, the traditional method of developing skills in sport has been to break them down into component parts, before reintegrating these components into a whole skill or competition – a method still common in high-performance sport. This insight demonstrates how the concerns of training design are synonymous with those of experimentation. For example, in springboard diving athletes spend a large proportion of time practicing their approach and hurdle steps into foam pits rather than a pool environment (Barris *et al.*, 2013), which has been shown to alter the kinematics of the approach phase. Similar to the use of ball projection machines, the role of "dry land" environments in sport may be to establish basic coordination before applying these skills in representative conditions, and potentially reducing their use later in learning.

In general, practitioners should strive for a balance between quantity and quality of training (see *Applied insight – B*). Some researchers have argued that individuals need many hours of deliberate practice (e.g., Ericsson, 1996) and hundreds of thousands of repetitions to become an expert. In this regard, traditional approaches have looked to progress from basic coordination training with an emphasis on volume and many repetitions (i.e., to develop skill automatization) to game-specific training. For example, in developing the basketball shot, first the technique is learned in a stable environment, before learning to execute this shot consistently under different circumstances (e.g., after a dribble, after a pass, with and without defenders, under high time pressure). While these methods have provided a level of success (and hence coaches are reluctant to move away from them), they have recently been questioned from a theoretical viewpoint, as well as through experiential and empirical work. Preliminary evidence is demonstrating the potential consequences of changing the physical, environmental, and contextual constraints and employing practice designs that are not representative of the performance context (e.g., Dicks *et al.*, 2010). Research is also suggesting that greater gains in learning may be achieved through variable practice earlier in learning during coordination and control phases (Ranganathan & Newell, 2013), and through the use of task simplification over task decomposition; however, more research is desperately needed in this area.

Applied insight – B: designing training activities

The challenges involved in creating representative training activities are numerous. For example, one of the traditional approaches to teach a motor skill is to break the skill down into smaller parts or to reduce or remove defensive pressure to make the different phases of the skill easier to manage (Ford *et al.*, 2010; Renshaw *et al.*, 2009). While this approach is often employed, it is possible that the resultant degradation in features such as perception-action coupling may in fact be detrimental to learning (Renshaw *et al.*, 2009). Similarly, creating representative tasks can sometimes make it more difficult to monitor and control the number of repetitions and the amount of physical loading in a training session (Farrow *et al.*, 2008). It may also require a much higher level of coaching/teaching expertise to be able to balance physiological needs with skill needs in order to implement a truly representative task that satisfies all of the objectives of the training session (Farrow *et al.*, 2008). Irrespective of the approach, one of the most important factors is for the practitioner and/or scientist to be aware of the potential consequences of any changes that are made to a given training task, and perhaps use that as the basis for determining the extent to which a more representative task could, or should, be employed.

(Adam Gorman – lecturer and skill acquisition specialist, University of the Sunshine Coast)

Researchers and practitioners should look to identify as many influential and environmental factors as possible, provide situations in which performances are less restricted, and categorize experimental trials by environmental conditions after collection (Pluijms *et al.*, 2013). With this goal comes a range of new issues, which include the development of complex tasks or competition simulation, increased coaching experience/knowledge requirements, collection of large and complex data sets that increase analysis and feedback time, and management of injury and workload. For example, traditional training methods such as using drills or isolated conditioning work allow for the assessment of tangible changes in performance (albeit if just under conditions of the drill), and for the detailed tracking of workloads. Again, the issues highlighted with training design are synonymous with those of experimental designs; there is a need to consider the degree of action fidelity (i.e., the degree to which actions in practice replicate those in competition) for typical practice tasks. While the benefits of providing practice tasks that are representative of competition are intuitive, applied case studies are required to demonstrate the benefits to learning in representative situations over traditional approaches, providing specific guidelines for the management of workloads and assessing progression. It is important that researchers, sport scientists, and coaches work closely together to maximize theoretical and practical outputs and to cumulatively "pool" their expertise (Greenwood *et al.*, 2012; Phillips *et al.*, 2010; Pluijms *et al.*, 2013). *Applied insight – C* provides a personal account of a coach's approach to these challenges.

Applied insight – C: science and practice working together in designing representative training methods

Developing training materials on the basis of scientifically supported and substantiated ideas has had an enormous influence within the last five years on the CTO women's basketball program, myself, and the performance of the players during competition. The questions that remain are whether the investment in time leads to sufficient results for research and training, and whether it actually successfully replaces more traditional forms of training. In my own experience I do not have many restrictions regarding the use of all kinds of training material. For example, I often use a big mat as a screen or a rack of balls as a defender over which the players should shoot. It takes time and experience to teach yourself to think outside the box and use all kinds of constraints during practice to achieve specific goals. In collaboration with a good scientist you will come to conclusions and training methods that go beyond your own blind spot(s). Coaches have the tendency to stick to those safe strategies that have yielded good results in the past. Nowadays you have to keep moving forward in order to get and stay in touch with international competition, and to be able to structurally perform at that level.

From personal experience I dare to say that the investment in time is certainly worth it, and that mutual trust and understanding between coach and scientist leads to more space to tackle certain

> other issues yourself while science takes care of tests during training. In the end it is the quality of
> the coach that determines the degree to which scientific ideas transfer to specific sport practice and
> the output this generates. If you take the time for these processes they will certainly pay off in time.
>
> *(Remy de Wit – head coach CTO Amsterdam, women's basketball)*

Generalizability and transfer beyond experimental and practice tasks

Another crucial and related consideration in designing representative tasks is the extent to which research findings can be generalized beyond the experimental conditions. External validity came to reference the amount to which research findings from a specific study could be generalized, both beyond the specific constraints of the experimental situation or task (Bryman, 1988; Lucas, 2003) and to a wider population (Bracht & Glass, 1968). Some researchers have argued that the simplification of experimental designs allows for the required control, simplification of competitive situations, and increases in generalization of results (Lucas, 2003). However, as we have highlighted previously, in many instances it is a combination of decomposition and simplification, which reduces the potential transfer for experimental results into meaningful applications. For example, in occlusion studies highlighted above, it is typical for participants of multiple skill levels to view clips of one skilled participant performing a series of actions and then perform a simple response; this control may actually bias the results, as well as severely limit the ability to generalize beyond the experimental conditions, or performers sampled.

The peer-reviewed process itself creates a number of challenges for researchers, where the currently accepted scientific paradigm emphasizes statistical power and large numbers of participants, statistically rather than practically meaningful results, and generalizable data to a wide range of domains (i.e., value to the journal and chance of future citations). Consequently, researchers in sport have often been concerned with ensuring that representative populations are sampled (often based on available participants), rather than ensuring that representative conditions are provided. For example, as discussed, much of the early literature on anticipation compared novices with experts, as such a comparison fits well with scientific standards. Novices are typically participants who have no experience with the task in question, whereas experts are those who were available for scientific testing, and as a result of which they are often intermediate to skilled, at best. Expert participants tend to be hard to get for research, with group numbers that are by their definition small, possibly too small for sound experimental testing. For example, to attain acceptable participant numbers researchers in wheelchair sports have often used able-bodied participants and one-off snapshot performances, such as when assessing the effect of glove type on skill and performance in wheelchair rugby (Lutgendorf *et al.*, 2009). Given the distinct and individual changes in function of elite athletes with disabilities such as quadriplegia, such results cannot even be generalized to a specific class of athlete eligible to compete in the sport.

The key problem with smaller subsets of skilled performers is that differences will be smaller and therefore harder to detect in experimental settings. Existing research has provided valuable insights into characteristics of experienced participants. Currently, however, it is important to emphasize that expert-novice differences are no longer that interesting, as the differences have been shown very often. Assessment of finer skill development levels (e.g., development, skilled, true experts) may provide more and valuable insights into the development of expertise, with the learning process characterized by non-linear exploration and transitions (Davids, 2012). However, this is easier said than done, especially in the light of the common requirements for scientific research (including the use of control groups). In the end, it may be more beneficial for the development of expertise in specific domains to capture small groups of skilled participants (including truly expert participants) in a series of representative performances (cf. Pluijms *et al.*, 2013). This asks for more creativity and flexibility in research designs, by using and accepting, for example, case studies and single-participant designs in which each participant also functions as its own control or baseline reference during interventions and longitudinal investigations.

The reductionist nature of experimental tasks may therefore be a key barrier in translating research findings into applied outputs and meaningful recommendations for practitioners and coaches. Often, findings will not result in applied outcomes focused on further shaping expertise, or indeed will already be behind current coaching knowledge. In elite sport settings, practitioners very rarely have time to wait for empirical evidence, and rely on developing their own evidence in practice. A change to the use of more representative experimental situations may invite more coaches to open their programs for research purposes, where the application of research findings may be more obvious. Related to this, there is an additional consideration of the language used in scientific publications, especially with an increase in the use of complexity sciences to explain complex and dynamic interactions in sport, an issue akin to the reporting of complex data analysis methods (see above). Practitioners working to develop sport expertise are interested in maximizing performance, while researchers may be more interested in addressing related theoretical and applied questions and developing cumulative knowledge (Williams & Kendall, 2007); it should be acknowledged that research funding also requires projects to be largely theory driven, limiting applied possibilities and reductions in experimental control. Researchers should continue to consider the best outputs for research findings and the use of alternative mediums for quick and concise feedback for practitioners, coaches, and athletes.

Context and emotion in capturing and developing expert performances

The pathway to developing expertise in sport requires athletes to frequently deal with intermittent periods of success, uncertainty, and failure across various timescales (Collins & MacNamara, 2012; Davids, 2012; Seifert *et al.*, 2013). Through these periods the methods for planning, implementing, observing, and evaluating representative tasks have tended to focus on the physical performance outcomes and movement responses of athletes in isolation (Barris *et al.*, 2013; Hristovski *et al.*, 2006; Pinder *et al.*, 2011a). While these approaches do provide vital information concerning the manipulation of constraints in learning and performance tasks, a somewhat neglected aspect to consider when developing a representative task is the influence of psychological factors, in combination with physical performance outcomes. More specifically, this refers to the importance of considering context, situational constraints, and engaging individuals emotionally in representative tasks to enhance the overall development of expertise.

A major challenge for the design and implementation of representative tasks in sport is ensuring that the acquisition and evaluation of skills takes place under constraints that appropriately simulate a specific performance task. As discussed in previous sections, laboratory-based and decomposed tasks will rarely capture the physical and visual constraints of the actual performance environments that they intend to simulate (Dhami *et al.*, 2004; Pinder *et al.*, 2011b). Similarly, these isolated settings provide little sport-specific, contextual information that is essential to inform decision-making and performance outcomes. For example, in Australian football practice sessions, open drills (increased specificity) were found to correspond with higher physical and cognitive loads when compared with closed drills (Farrow *et al.*, 2008). This finding implies that open skill drills provide key contextual information that more closely resembles the demands of a game or competition. Further game subphase work investigated player interactions in team

Developing representative tasks

sports when contextual information was manipulated, thus influencing the intentions of players in relation to match scenarios. In football, differing field positions representing attacking, midfield, and defending contexts were found to influence the intentions of direct (attacker-defender) opponents and their interaction with the ball (Headrick *et al.*, 2012). Also in football, the presence and distance of a chasing defender to a wing player influenced the performance characteristics of a cross into the penalty area (Orth *et al.*, 2014). In both these examples the context created by the inclusion of game-specific information (field position, presence of a defender) constrained performance without a reliance on prescribed verbal instruction from a coach. By providing contextual information, athletes are free to interact with the informational constraints of a performance environment, rather than conforming to potentially "artificial" instructions from a coach, which would not be available in a match (Ford *et al.*, 2010).

Representative sport tasks that include contextual information have the associated benefit of creating the potential for athletes to be engaged in a task emotionally (Pinder *et al.*, 2014). Emotion-laden tasks are considered to facilitate a "deeper" engagement, which is integral for effective learning and performance (Jones, 2003; Solomon, 2008). The role of emotion during the development of expertise in sport has often been neglected because emotional responses are considered irrational, instinctive, and difficult to control (Hutto, 2012). Therefore, emotion (and performance) has been considered, mistakenly, as unwanted "noise" that researchers, practitioners, and coaches attempt to remove or limit (Davids *et al.*, 2003; Seifert & Davids, 2012). Suppressing emotions suggests a focus on manufacturing predictable performance outcomes rather than allowing individual athletes to be exposed to both positive and negative experiences that may be paralleled in competition. Emotions should also be considered as part of a holistic, representative approach to developing expertise on account of the relationship between emotion, behavior, and cognition (feeling, acting, and knowing, respectively) (Breckler, 1984; Hilgard, 1980). The intertwined relationship between cognitions, emotions, and actions can provide a more comprehensive understanding of an athlete's perceptions, intentions, and action tendencies corresponding to situational constraints (Davids *et al.*, 2001; Lewis, 2004). For example, gymnasts attempting balance beam routines on beams of increasing height were found to display performance decrements, elevated heart rate, and increased prevalence of perceived dysfunctional emotions, particularly on the first attempt at a new height (Cottyn *et al.*, 2012). Furthermore, climbing traverses that were identical in design but differing in height from the ground were found to influence anxiety, heart rate, climbing completion times, and the number of exploratory movements in participants (Pijpers *et al.*, 2005). Similar studies have investigated the benefits of training with induced anxiety for dart-throwing and basketball shooting tasks (Oudejans & Pijpers, 2009, 2010). Performance in these sport-specific tasks was found to be enhanced following training in induced anxiety conditions, even though participants were observed to have elevated heart rates, perceived exertion ratings, and anxiety scores. Similar findings have been obtained in experiments with police officers who trained and performed handgun shooting under pressure (Nieuwenhuys & Oudejans, 2011; Oudejans, 2008), and sport practitioners should continue to look to other domains for advances in experimental and learning design for the development of expertise. Such findings exhibit how changes in performance outcomes and movement responses are accompanied by emotional and cognitive tendencies that become recognized as characteristic responses for specific situations. Therefore, truly representative tasks in sport should aim to include contextual and situational information that engages athletes emotionally.

Applying the above ideas and conceptualizations provides many challenges for coaches and practitioners, given the individualized characteristics and responses of each athlete and sport (see *Applied insight – D*). One approach is developing practice "vignettes" that simulate sport-specific scenarios, game contexts, or challenges. For example, in basketball subphases, vignettes specifying game score and time scenarios (e.g., one point behind with 10 seconds to play) were implemented to observe how attacking and defending players acted under these situational constraints (Cordovil *et al.*, 2009). Furthermore, of particular importance in team games is the relationship between the number of players and the available playing area. By manipulating these factors a coach can create representative game types that simulate the intensity (space-time characteristics) of match, or approaching match conditions (game intensity index, see Chow *et al.*, 2013). Similar techniques are alluded to in *Applied insight − D* in the form of implementing time restrictions, creating uncertainty, and simulating unpredictable competition situations in practice sessions for elite athletes with physical disabilities. The benefit of incorporating such approaches centers on creating intentionality and emotional engagement in tasks, as opposed to decomposed, generic tasks where athletes merely "go through the motions."

Applied insight − D: preparation for competition in Paralympic sport

The majority of boccia athletes have the physical disability of cerebral palsy, ranging in levels from moderate to severe. Typically, this affects the athlete's muscle function in either a commonly described "flight or fight" affect. Consequently, his/her physical reactions to external stimuli can be extreme and unpredictable. For example, the sound of applause from one competition court can cause a physical reaction in athletes performing on another court, as if a loud, low-flying plane was going past. Athletes with cerebral palsy have to perform accurate and precise tasks within an environment which their senses, and hence muscles, interpret as being one that is highly unstable and unpredictable. The key task for the coach is to recreate this in training to prepare them for performance. This can be achieved in a number of ways by creating challenging modified games and introducing unpredictable variables. Some obvious examples to achieve this include setting multiple targets, complicating the victory conditions, creating pressure of time restrictions, or just manipulating any dimension of the formal game that creates uncertainty. The options for introducing unpredictable variables is only limited to your imagination − for example, equipment being changed without notice, a fire alarm going off, a simulated opponent doing something unusual. While it is important to not let any "flight or fight" variable lessen focus, or unproductively corrupt the essential game skills, it can successfully enable an athlete to be prepared for any eventuality, or situation of high stress, that would normally derail his/her performance.

(Peter King − boccia head coach, Australian Paralympic Committee)

Summary

Here, we have provided a brief overview of some of the key issues and challenges in the development of representative tasks in sport. Researchers and practitioners should look to advance understanding of areas identified through:

1 the use of principled approaches and assessment of action fidelity and functionality of a range of existing experimental and practice tasks;
2 embracing technology for the assessment of performance in representative and competitive contexts;
3 assessment of expertise throughout developmental pathways, using a series of case studies or small-group designs; and
4 increased use of contextual information, scenarios, and emotion in the design of tasks.

References

Araújo, D., & Davids, K. (2009) 'Ecological approaches to cognition and action in sport and exercise: Ask not only what you do, but where you do it', *International Journal of Sport Psychology*, 40(1): 5–37.

Araújo, D., Davids, K., & Passos, P. (2007) 'Ecological validity, representative design, and correspondence between experimental task constraints and behavioral setting: Comment on Rogers, Kadar, and Costall (2005)', *Ecological Psychology*, 19(1): 69–78.

Barris, S., Davids, K., & Farrow, D. (2013) 'Representative learning design in springboard diving: Is dry-land training representative of a pool dive?', *European Journal of Sport Science*. doi: 10.1080/17461391.2013.770923

Bracht, G. H., & Glass, G. V. (1968) 'The external validity of experiments', *American Educational Research Journal*, 5(4): 437–74.

Breckler, S. J. (1984) 'Empirical validation of affect, behaviour, and cognition as distinct components of attitude', *Journal of Personality and Social Psychology*, 47(6): 1191–1205. doi: 10.1037/0022–3514.47.6.1191

Bryman, A. (1988) *Quantity and quality in social research*, London: Unwin Hyman.

Chow, J. Y., Davids, K., Renshaw, I., & Button, C. (2013) 'The acquisition of movement skill in children through nonlinear pedagogy', in J. Côté & R. Lidor (eds) *Conditions of children's talent development in sport*, Morgantown, WV: FIT, 41–59.

Colin, L., Nieuwenhuys, A., Visser, A., & Oudejans, R.R.D. (2014) 'Positive effects of imagery on police officers' shooting performance under threat', *Applied Cognitive Psychology*, 28: 115–21.

Collins, D., & MacNamara, A. (2012) 'The rocky road to the top: Why talent needs trauma', *Sports Medicine*, 42(11): 907–14. doi: 10.2165/11635140-000000000-00000

Cordovil, R., Araújo, D., Davids, K., Gouveia, L., Barreiros, J., Fernandes, O., & Serpa, S. (2009) 'The influence of instructions and body-scaling as constraints on decision-making processes in team sports', *European Journal of Sport Science*, 9(3): 169–79.

Cottyn, J., De Clercq, D., Crombez, G., & Lenoir, M. (2012) 'The interaction of functional and dysfunctional emotions during balance beam performance', *Research Quarterly for Exercise and Sport*, 83(2): 300–7.

Croft, J. L., Button, C., & Dicks, M. (2010) 'Visual strategies of sub-elite cricket batsmen in response to different ball velocities', *Human Movement Science*, 29: 751–63.

Davids, K. (2012) 'Learning design for nonlinear dynamical movement systems', *The Open Sports Sciences Journal*, 5(Suppl 1): 9–16. doi: 10.2174/1875399X01205010009

Davids, K., Araújo, D., Vilar, L., Renshaw, I., & Pinder, R. A. (2013) 'An ecological dynamics approach to skill acquisition: Implications for development of talent in sport', *Talent Development & Excellence*, 5(1): 21–34.

Davids, K., Glazier, P., Araújo, D., & Bartlett, R. (2003) 'Movement systems as dynamical systems: The functional role of variability and it's implications for sports medicine', *Sports Medicine*, 33(4): 245–60.

Davids, K., Williams, A. M., Button, C., & Court, M. (2001) 'An integrative modelling approach to the study of intentional movement behavior', in R. N. Singer, H. A. Hausenblas, & C. M. Janelle (eds) *Handbook of sport psychology*, 2nd ed., New York: John Wiley & Sons, 144–73.

Dhami, M. K., Hertwig, R., & Hoffrage, U. (2004) 'The role of representative design in an ecological approach to cognition', *Psychological Bulletin*, 130(6): 959–88.

Dicks, M., Button, C., & Davids, K. (2010) 'Examination of gaze behaviors under in situ and video simulation task constraints reveals differences in information pickup for perception and action', *Attention, Perception & Psychophysics*, 72(3): 706–20.

Dicks, M., Davids, K., & Araújo, D. (2008) 'Ecological psychology and task representativeness: Implications for the design of perceptual-motor training programmes in sport', in Y. Hong & R. Bartlett (eds) *The Routledge handbook of biomechanics and human movement science*, London: Routledge, 129–39.

Ericsson, K. A. (1996) 'The acquisition of expert performance: An introduction to some of the issues', in K. A. Ericsson (ed) *The road to excellence: The acquisition of expert performance in arts and sciences, sports, and games*, Mahwah, NJ: Lawrence Erlbaum Associates, Inc., 1–50.

Fajen, B. R., Riley, M. A., & Turvey, M. T. (2009) 'Information, affordances and the control of action in sport', *International Journal of Sport Psychology*, 40: 79–107.

Farrow, D., & Abernethy, B. (2003) 'Do expertise and the degree of perception-action coupling affect natural anticipatory performance?', *Perception*, 32(9): 1127–39.

Farrow, D., Abernethy, B., & Jackson, R. C. (2005) 'Probing expert anticipation with the temporal occlusion paradigm: experimental investigations of some methodological issues', *Motor Control*, 9(3): 332–51.

Farrow, D., Pyne, D. B., & Gabbett, T. (2008) 'Skill and physiological demands of open and closed training drills in Australian football', *International Journal of Sports Science & Coaching*, 3(4): 485–95. doi: 10.1260/174795408787186512

Ford, P. R., Yates, I., & Williams, A. M. (2010) 'An analysis of practice activities and instructional behaviours used by youth soccer coaches during practice', *Journal of Sports Sciences*, 28(5): 483–95. doi: 10.1080/02640410903582750

Greenwood, D., Davids, K., & Renshaw, I. (2012) 'How elite coaches' experiential knowledge might enhance empirical research on sport performance', *International Journal of Sports Science and Coaching*, 7(2): 411–22.

Headrick, J., Davids, K., Renshaw, I., Araújo, D., Passos, P., & Fernandes, O. (2012) 'Proximity-to-goal as a constraint on patterns of behaviour in attacker-defender dyads in team games', *Journal of Sports Sciences*, 30(3): 247–53. doi: 10.1080/02640414.2011.640706

Hilgard, E. R. (1980) 'The trilogy of the mind: Cognition, affection, and conation', *Journal of the History of the Behavioral Sciences*, 16: 107–17.

Hristovski, R., Davids, K., Araújo, D., & Button, C. (2006) 'How boxers decide to punch a target: Emergent behaviour in nonlinear dynamical movement systems', *Journal of Sports Science & Medicine*, CSSI: 60–73.

Hutto, D. D. (2012) 'Truly enactive emotion', *Emotion Review*, 4(2): 176–81. doi: 10.1177/1754073911430134

Jones, M. V. (2003) 'Controlling emotions in sport', *The Sport Psychologist*, 17: 471–86.

Land, M. F., & McLeod, P. (2000) 'From eye movements to actions: How batsmen hit the ball', *Nature Neuroscience*, 3(12): 1340–45.

Lewis, M. D. (2004) 'The emergence of mind in the emotional brain', in A. Demetriou & A. Raftopoulos (eds) *Cognitive developmental change*, New York: Cambridge University Press, 217–40.

Loffing, F., & Hagemann, N. (2014) 'Skill differences in visual anticipation of type of throw in team-handball penalties', *Psychology of Sport and Exercise*, 15(3): 260–7.

Lucas, J. W. (2003) 'Theory-testing, generalization, and the problem of external validity', *Sociological Theory*, 21(3): 236–53.

Lutgendorf, M., Mason, B. R., van der Woude, L., & Goosey-Tolfrey, V. L. (2009) 'Effect of glove type on wheelchair rugby sports performance', *Sports Technology*, 2: 121–8.

Magill, R. A. (2007) *Motor learning and control: Concepts and applications*, 8th ed., Boston: McGraw-Hill.

Mann, D., Abernethy, B., Farrow, D., Davis, M., & Spratford, W. (2010) 'An event-related visual occlusion method for examining anticipatory skill in natural interceptive tasks', *Behavior Research Methods*, 42(2): 556–62. doi: 10.3758/brm.42.2.556

Müller, S., Abernethy, B., Reece, J., Rose, M., Eid, M., McBean, R., . . . Abreu, C. (2009) 'An in-situ examination of the timing of information pick-up for interception by cricket batsmen of different skill levels', *Psychology of Sport and Exercise*, 10(6): 644–52.

Nieuwenhuys, A., & Oudejans, R. R. (2011) 'Training with anxiety: Short-and long-term effects on police officers' shooting behavior under pressure', *Cognitive processing*, 12(3): 277–88.

Orth, D., Davids, K., Araújo, D., Renshaw, I., & Passos, P. (2014) 'Effects of a defender on run-up velocity and ball speed when crossing a football', *European Journal of Sport Science*, 14(sup1): S316–S323. doi: 10.1080/17461391.2012.696712

Oudejans, R. (2008) 'Reality-based practice under pressure improves handgun shooting performance of police officers', *Ergonomics*, 51(3): 261–73.

Oudejans, R.R.D., Michaels, C. F., Bakker, F. C., & Dolné, M. A. (1996) 'The relevance of action in perceiving affordances: Perception of catchableness of fly balls', *Journal of Experimental Psychology: Human Perception and Performance*, 22(4): 879–91.

Oudejans, R.R.D., & Pijpers, J. R. (2009) 'Training with anxiety has a positive effect on expert perceptual-motor performance under pressure', *The Quarterly Journal of Experimental Psychology*, 62(8): 1631–47. doi: 10.1080/17470210802557702

Oudejans, R.R.D. & Pijpers, J. R. (2010) 'Training with mild anxiety may prevent choking under higher levels of anxiety', *Psychology of Sport and Exercise*, 11: 44–50. doi: 10.1016/j.psychsport.2009.05.002

Panchuk, D., & Vickers, J. N. (2006) 'Gaze behaviors of goaltenders under spatial-temporal constraints', *Human Movement Science*, 25: 733–52.

Phillips, E., Davids, K., Renshaw, I., & Portus, M. R. (2010) 'Expert performance in sport and the dynamics of talent develoment', *Sports Medicine*, 40(4): 271–83.

Pijpers, J. R., Oudejans, R.R.D., & Bakker, F. C. (2005) 'Anxiety-induced changes in movement behaviour during the execution of a complex whole-body task', *The Quarterly Journal of Experimental Psychology*, 58A(3): 421–45. doi: 10.1080/02724980343000945

Pinder, R. A. (2012) 'Representative learning design in dynamic interceptive actions', unpublished thesis, Queensland University of Technology.

Pinder, R. A., Davids, K., Renshaw, I., & Araújo, D. (2011a) 'Manipulating informational constraints shapes movement reorganization in interceptive actions', *Attention, Perception & Psychophysics*, 73(4): 1242–54.

Pinder, R. A., Davids, K., Renshaw, I., & Araújo, D. (2011b) 'Representative learning design and functionality of research and practice in sport', *Journal of Sport & Exercise Psychology*, 33: 146–55.

Pinder, R. A., Renshaw, I., & Davids, K. (2012) 'The role of representative test design in talent development: A comment on "talent identification and promotion programmes of Olympic athletes"', *Journal of Sports Sciences*, 31(8): 803–806.

Pinder, R. A., Renshaw, I., Headrick, J., & Davids, K. (2014) 'Skill acquisition and representative task design', in K. Davids, R. Hristovski, D. Araújo, N. Balagué, C. Button, & P. Passos (eds) *Complex systems in sport*, London: Routledge, 319–33.

Pluijms, J. P., Canal-Bruland, R., Kats, S., & Savelsbergh, G. J. P. (2013) 'Translating key methodological advancements when running in-situ experiments in sports: An example from sailing', *International Journal of Sport Science & Coaching*, 8(1): 89–103.

Portus, M. R., & Farrow, D. (2011) 'Enhancing cricket batting skill: Implications for biomechanics and skill acquisition research and practice', *Sports Biomechanics*, 10: 294–305.

Ranganathan, R., & Newell, K. M. (2013) 'Changing up the routine: Intervention-induced variability in motor learning', *Exercise and sport sciences reviews*, 41(1): 64–70.

Renshaw, I., Davids, K., Shuttleworth, R., & Chow, J. Y. (2009) 'Insights from ecological psychology and dynamical systems theory can underpin a philosophy of coaching', *International Journal of Sport Psychology*, 40(4): 580–602.

Renshaw, I., Oldham, A.R.H., Davids, K., & Golds, T. (2007) 'Changing ecological constraints of practice alters coordination of dynamic interceptive actions', *European Journal of Sport Science*, 7(3): 157–67.

Robertson, S. J., Burnett, A. F., & Cochrane, J. (2013) 'Tests examining skill outcomes in sport: A systematic review of measurement properties and feasibility', *Sports Medicine*, 44: 501–518.

Savelsbergh, G. J. P., & van der Kamp, J. (2009) 'Catching two visual systems at once', in D. Araújo, H. Ripoll, & M. Raab (eds) *Perspectives on cognition and action in sport*, New York: Nova Science Publishers, Inc., 15–26.

Seifert, L., Button, C., & Davids, K. (2013) 'Key properties of expert movement systems in sport: An ecological dynamics perspective', *Sports Medicine*, 43(3): 167–78. doi: 10.1007/s40279-012-0011-z

Seifert, L., & Davids, K. (2012) 'Intentions, perceptions and actions constrain functional intra – and inter – individual variability in the acquisition of expertise in individual sports', *The Open Sports Sciences Journal*, 5(Suppl 1): 68–75. doi: 10.2174/1875399X01205010068

Shim, J., Carlton, L. G., Chow, J. W., & Chae, W. K. (2005) 'The use of anticipatory visual cues by highly skilled tennis players', *Journal of Motor Behavior*, 37(2): 164–75.

Solomon, R. C. (2008) 'The philosophy of emotions', in M. Lewis, J. M. Haviland-Jones, & L. Feldman Barrett (eds) *Handbook of emotions*, 3rd ed., New York: The Guilford Press, 3–16.

Stone, J. A., Panchuck, D., Davids, K., North, J. S., Fairweather, I., & Maynard, I. W. (2013) 'An integrated ball projection technology for the study of dynamic interceptive actions', *Behavior Research Methods*, 46: 948–91.

van der Kamp, J., Rivas, F., van Doorn, H., & Savelsbergh, G. (2008) 'Ventral and dorsal contributions in visual anticipation in fast ball sports', *International Journal of Sport Psychology*, 39(2): 100–30.

Weissensteiner, J., Abernethy, B., & Farrow, D. (2009) 'Examining the development of technical skill in cricket batting', paper presented at the 7th Australasian Biomechanics Conference, Gold Coast, AU-QLD.

Weissensteiner, J., Abernethy, B., Farrow, D., & Müller, S. (2008) 'The development of anticipation: A cross-sectional examination of the practice experiences contributing to skill in cricket batting', *Journal of Sport & Exercise Psychology*, 30(6): 663–84.

Williams, S. J., & Kendall, L. R. (2007) 'A profile of sport science research (1983–2003)', *Journal of Science and Medicine in Sport*, 10: 193–200.

25

CHALLENGES TO CAPTURING EXPERTISE IN FIELD SETTINGS

Ian Renshaw and Adam D. Gorman

Capturing expertise is a challenging task, particularly given the inherently complex environment of the typical performance setting. Current research findings continue to highlight the importance of creating representative research methodologies, designed to assess the continuous and unobtrusive interactions that occur between the expert performer and the vast array of sensory information that surrounds him/her (Pluijms *et al.*, 2013; see also Pinder *et al.*, 2011). The need to ensure the presence of all key information sources that guide a performer's actions in tests of expertise (Pinder *et al.*, 2011) demands the adoption of integrative, interdisciplinary approaches (e.g., see Millar *et al.*, 2013). Fortunately, advances in technology where data are able to be collected in situ are providing unprecedented opportunities for sport scientists to achieve these goals. However, the vast amounts of information that can be collected often present some additional problems, given the wide range of variables from which to choose. One of the possible approaches for selecting and delimiting the list of experimental variables, in a principled way, is for skill acquisition scientists, coaches, and performers to work collaboratively to design tests that accommodate the needs of all of the key stakeholders. As such, this chapter will propose that capturing expertise in field settings requires sport scientists to base experimental designs on an interdisciplinary theoretical foundation that utilizes the expertise of practitioners (e.g., coaches and athletes) to identify the key variables upon which to focus (e.g., Millar *et al.*, 2013). We propose that an ecological dynamics framework based around Newell's (1986) notion of constraints, where the critical interactions between task, environmental, and organismic constraints are maintained in their natural state, may allow motor learning and performance to be examined in a more representative manner (Zelaznik, 2014). Given that other chapters in this book focus more specifically on the ecological dynamics theory and the application of representative research designs (see Chapters 5, 12, and 24), we will only offer a perfunctory discussion of the key principles of these concepts to ensure that we focus on the challenges of measuring expertise in field settings. We initially contextualize this discussion by considering the problem from the point of view of a "new" skill acquisition scientist charged with measuring the performance of an elite cohort of athletes. We will include a brief overview of previous approaches to capturing expertise, as well as some of the problems associated with these approaches, before providing some suggestions and theoretical principles that can guide sport scientists' practice going forward.

Capturing expertise in the field

The new girl: working at the coalface

Consider for a moment the following scenario. You are a young graduate sport scientist emerging from the "ivory towers" of academia into the real world of high-performance sport. In this cutthroat world, everyone is trying to find an edge and identify the "one per centers" that will hopefully result in a gold medal-winning performance. Full of knowledge and enthusiasm, the new graduate is looking forward to making a real difference; she expects her contribution may even result in a few medals at the upcoming championships. Her first assignment seems relatively straightforward; she is asked to devise a test that is able to (i) differentiate between the levels of expertise of athletes in an elite developmental squad and (ii) identify possible future champions. The young graduate decides that her first task should be to determine the "characteristics, skills, and knowledge distinguishing experts from novices" in the chosen sport (Ericsson, 2006, p. 3). She soon finds, however, that although this proposal appears to be quite simple, and there has been a plethora of research across different sports to offer some insights, the problem has not proven to be an easy one for scientists to solve. In fact, sport science has often struggled to provide appropriate methods to measure the performance of experts, leading many practitioners to dismiss the usefulness of sport science support staff, including those who specialize in the area of skill acquisition (see Steel *et al.*, 2013 for a more in-depth discussion). To further compound the issue, much of the early research in skill acquisition employed non-representative, laboratory-based tasks, making it difficult for practitioners to apply the research generated by sport scientists (Williams & Ford, 2009).

The problem with non-representative testing

An early example of the use of non-representative tests was recently described by former Olympic table tennis player Matthew Syed. Syed (2011) cites the example of his initial exposure to sport science testing at Brighton University, shortly after he joined the national team. Given that a key requirement of table tennis players is the need for fast reactions, the sport scientists, quite logically, elected to implement a test of the players' reaction times. It was anticipated that the player who showed the fastest reactions in gameplay and who was the best player in the squad, Desmond Douglas, would achieve the best score in the test. However, despite the logic of their predictions, the results revealed that Douglas achieved the lowest test scores. As a consequence, the players lost faith in the scientists, believing that the test was either measuring the wrong variable or the machine itself was faulty; subsequently, the sport science staff were informed that their services were no longer required (see also Chapter 2).

Other examples of non-representative tests of expert performance are those that are used in talent identification of future experts. For example, in a study designed to examine the utility of general mental ability tests, Lyons, Hoffman, and Michel (2009) reported that, as part of the drafting process for the National Football League (NFL) in North America, draftees have been routinely administered with generalized mental tests to assess their capability to perform the necessary mental functions required for successful performance in the NFL. Lyons *et al.* (2009) hypothesized that such tests may provide a useful predictor of performance, particularly given that the game requires players to learn and understand a large volume of playing strategies that need to be constantly adapted to suit the specific tendencies of different opponents and situations. Moreover, given the decision-making demands of a typical NFL game, Lyons *et al.* (2009) predicted that the players likely to require the most mental intelligence – and therefore, the players who were most likely to achieve the best scores on the test – would be the quarterbacks.

However, the results from a series of analyses showed that test scores and NFL performance were not significantly correlated for *any* of the playing positions (Lyons *et al.*, 2009). In fact, as highlighted by Ankersen (2012), two of the best quarterbacks in history, Terry Bradshaw and Dan Marino, are actually among the seven worst performers on the test (throughout its history). Thus, as evidenced by other research, the types of performance attributes measured by generalized and non-representative tests tend to provide information that is not directly related to the attributes required during actual performance (Helsen & Starkes, 1999; Starkes, 1987). It is therefore not surprising that Ankersen has argued that "every year NFL coaches and scouts manage to get selection absolutely wrong, with only half of the 40 top-rated performers over the past four years still in the league" (2012, p. 56). Academics who are interested in expertise and, in particular, identifying future experts have also recently lamented the wastage of talent through the use of inappropriate testing methods (MacNamara & Collins, 2011; Pinder *et al.*, 2013).

It is therefore not surprising that many practitioners see little value in employing sport science specialists in motor learning to support their work (see Ericsson & Williams, 2007; Steel *et al.*, 2013; Williams & Ford, 2009). While the extant research clearly highlights the fallacy of using such generic performance tests to examine the highly specific skills required of expert performers (e.g., Helsen & Starkes, 1999), many current testing methods may still be failing to capture the true characteristics of expertise (Williams & Ericsson, 2005).

Traditional approaches to measuring expertise

As one would expect, most studies on expertise through the 1980s and 90s adopted the predominant theory of the time – namely, the cognitive information-processing theory (see Summers, 2004; Zelaznik, 2014). Whereas much of this research added to the understanding of expertise, it also tended to be criticized, particularly in terms of the lack of consideration of actions when assessing anticipation (see van der Kamp *et al.*, 2008; see also Chapters 2 and 15). Given that one of the basic premises of information-processing theories was that perception and action could be examined separately, much of the research took place in laboratory settings using tasks that often shared limited resemblance to real world tasks (see Summers, 2004). However, there were also examples of more applied studies that examined actual sport movements, in an attempt to shed more light on the underlying processes associated with expert performance. These studies could involve biomechanical analyses of movement patterns to compare novices and experts in closed skill environments (e.g., Anderson & Sidaway's (1994) seminal paper on kicking a football), but they still sometimes neglected to include all of the key information sources on which performers would be typically attuned (see Williams & Ericsson, 2005). While this might seem reasonable (especially when viewing skills from a motor programming perspective), recent evidence is showing that the interaction of individual, environmental, and task constraints results in a change in the actions of experts (see Renshaw *et al.*, 2009). Essentially, ecological constraints determine the couplings between perception and action (see Davids *et al.*, 2001; Williams & Ericsson, 2005). A good example of the importance of examining expertise in a representative performance environment can be seen in the recent examination of the drives of nine elite field hockey players (three defenders, three midfielders, three attackers) (Brétigny *et al.*, 2011). Coordination profiles for five drives from each player were undertaken, with players being asked to hit the ball as hard as possible at a target. Upon first inspection this task would appear to be a somewhat poor representation of the natural setting. However, the important inclusion was the consideration of the players' extensive experience in interacting with their environment. That is, if the expert players adapted their techniques to suit the demands of their normal playing position (defender, midfielder, or attacker), it would be expected that the constraints of playing in a specific position would act to shape the coordination patterns displayed by the players. The results supported this assumption by showing individual differences that were likely to have been influenced by the nature of the players' normal playing roles. For example, midfield and attacking players exhibited less preparation time when hitting the ball (possibly due to the greater risk of the ball being stolen) and had shorter backswings to allow a faster stroke, albeit with reduced power of the hit. In contrast, defenders tended to execute longer and wider swings, presumably because they were accustomed to executing their hits with more time and could therefore hit the ball with increased power. In effect, the task constraints encountered during matches, such as different time-space pressures in different areas of the field, led to the emergence of different coordination profiles from the respective roles that each participant typically filled in matches. Players had essentially learned to calibrate their movements to fit their performance environments (Bretigny *et al.*, 2011).

Another fruitful area for those interested in studying the processes underlying expertise has been sporting run-ups; first in athletics, and later in gymnastic vaulting and cricket bowling (e.g., Berg *et al.*, 1994; Lee *et al.*, 1982; Montagne *et al.*, 2000b; Renshaw & Davids, 2004; Scott *et al.*, 1997). The seminal study that shaped the direction of many subsequent run-up studies was undertaken by Lee *et al.* (1982), who examined the run-ups of three experienced female long jumpers. The results showed that the locomotor control strategy of all three jumpers could be broken down into two distinct phases. The first phase comprised an initial "accelerative phase," involving a relatively consistent and stereotyped stride pattern, which was followed by the second phase – a "zeroing-in phase" where the athletes switched to a pattern that involved regulating their strides via their visually perceived relationship to the board (Lee *et al.*, 1982). Subsequent work (Hay, 1988; Scott *et al.*, 1997) corroborated the results of Lee *et al.* (1982) and led to the acceptance of a "two phase" run-up control strategy. Consequently, the understanding of run-ups became bi-theoretical, with the first phase seen as preprogrammed (i.e., planned and executed with minimal change) and the second phase viewed as prospectively controlled (i.e., continuously regulated) (see Beek *et al.*, 2003; Lee *et al.*, 1982). The result of this interpretation was that subsequent studies focused almost exclusively (but for a notable exception, see Glize & Laurent, 1997) on the final phase of the run-up, because it was largely concluded that there was little need for scientists to conduct further research on the first phase. In the zeroing-in phase, the belief was that the athletes made the adjustments to stride length by using time-to-contact information from the takeoff board to manipulate the vertical impulse of running strides near the board (Lee *et al.*, 1982). However, no studies were able to demonstrate that steps were in fact regulated using time-to-contact information (Montagne *et al.*, 2000a), a problem Montagne suggested might be due to the choice of inferential statistical analysis used in the original study that emphasized pooled data over participants and trials. Montagne *et al.* (2000b) addressed this issue by adopting a trial-by-trial analysis, reporting the existence of a prospective control strategy in the run-ups of long jumpers. In line with the thoughts of Lee *et al.* (1982) – who had suggested that the greater the error built up in the first phase of the run-up, the sooner this error would become detectable (by the athlete) and the sooner the commencement of the zeroing-in phase – the step number at which regulation occurred was found not to be constant, but a function of the amount of adjustment required to successfully contact the board. As predicted, the prospective control of gait led to earlier adjustments in the run-up sequence being made when a greater amount of adjustment was required within any one run-up trial. However, it is important to mention that Montagne *et al.* (2000b) still chose to focus on the last six strides of the run-up, a methodological decision consistent with previous findings that visual regulation only occurs in the last few strides in long jumping.

The findings outlined by Lee *et al.* (1982) and Montagne *et al.* (2000b) have provided crucial information to help guide theoretical frameworks regarding the visual regulation of human locomotion. Despite these advancements, an important question for sport scientists is the extent to which these ideas are important for examining locomotor control strategies in the natural setting. Recent evidence suggests that gait patterns differ as a function of the environmental and task constraints nested onto the end of the run-up (Renshaw & Davids, 2004; Greenwood, 2014). That is, the nature of the task at the end of the run-up significantly constrains the specific implementation of the visual regulation strategy employed by the athlete throughout the full phase of the run-up. However, due to the research emphasis placed upon the final phase of the run-up, the finding that continuous perception-action coupling occurs throughout the whole of the run-up was only found as late as 2004 (see Renshaw & Davids, 2004). Since then, further work on whole run-ups has begun to reveal the significant impact of changes to practice environments that remove specifying information (e.g., Greenwood, 2014). For example, when specifying information is present in performance environments in the immediate vicinity of the nested task (i.e., the bowler's delivery or the takeoff for the long jumper) adjustments are (i) spread more evenly across the run-up, causing less disruption to nested actions and (ii) the run-up speed is greater (Greenwood, 2014; see also Chapter 5).

Collectively, the empirical evidence suggests that research into expert performance should carefully consider the influence of the constraints that guide performance, including, but not necessarily limited to, (i) the task constraints, (ii) the physical, cultural, or environmental constraints, and (iii) the action capabilities that impact upon perception (Dicks *et al.*, 2010; see also Newell, 1986). In fact, failing to test perception *in* action may represent a critical limitation of laboratory-based studies, because the mechanisms relied upon by participants in a laboratory setting may not replicate the mechanisms that are relied upon by sport performers in a more realistic performance environment (Oudejans & Coolen, 2003; Montagne *et al.*, 2008). For example, Oudejans, Michaels, Bakker, and Dolné (1996) found that perceptual judgments of whether a fly ball is catchable or not were better when participants were allowed to move compared to when they were required to make judgments from a stationary position. In situ experimental studies in team sports also highlight the importance of ensuring the presence of key information sources available in performance environments. The presence of opponents (Orth *et al.*, 2014), pitch markings (Headrick *et al.*, 2012), and contextual information such as the state of the game (Cordovil *et al.*, 2009) all have an impact upon the actions executed by participants as they attempt to coadapt to the interacting constraints to meet performance goals.

Thus, the overreliance on studies that fail to fully capture the richness of the typical performance environment may not only limit the conclusions derived from their results, but they may also limit the capability of practitioners to apply those findings to real world situations (Ericsson & Williams, 2007; Williams & Ford, 2009). Moreover, the focus on generalized mechanisms, rather than applied research, has not permitted substantial contributions to our understanding of how complex skills and expertise are acquired (Williams & Hodges, 2005), and highlights the need to provide guidelines to help skill acquisition scientists design more effective tests of expertise in the real world of high-performance sport (see also Pinder *et al.*, 2011; Renshaw *et al.*, 2009).

The predominance of research findings generated by laboratory-based studies represents an obvious challenge for sport scientists working in applied settings (see Williams & Ericsson, 2005). In fact, it is not uncommon for coaches or athletes to ask real world questions for which there is little real world empirical evidence that can be used to provide a definitive answer (see Button & Farrow, 2012). For instance, many of the questions generated by coaches working with elite athletes are often directed towards factors such as the optimal number of practice trials to enhance performance, the ideal amount of variable practice compared to constant practice, and the optimal duration of training sessions. While such questions have tended to be addressed in laboratory-based studies (for examples, see Magill & Anderson, 2014), there is comparatively little research evidence generated from highly applied research conducted in representative experimental settings (Button & Farrow, 2012; Williams & Ericsson, 2005). Similarly, the continued use of generalized tests in applied settings (such as that described by Lyons *et al.*, 2009) may have influenced the expectations of sporting practitioners, encouraging them to persist with such tests in the belief that other, more real world tests are either not available or are somewhat unconventional. As we describe later, a possible solution to this challenge is to involve practitioners in the design stages of skill-based tests so that the tests themselves are likely to contain a higher degree of real world utility, and the practitioners may also be more inclined to implement the tests as a regular part of their schedule. In the next section of this chapter, we will outline a theoretical model of performance that could potentially lead to the design of more effective tests that satisfy the needs of scientists, practitioners, and performers alike (but see also Pinder *et al.*, 2011).

An ecological dynamics approach to expertise

In order to consider the methods that can be adopted to measure expertise in the field, Seifert, Button, and Davids' (2013) definition of expertise provides a useful starting point. These authors described expertise within an ecological dynamics framework that sees the performer-environment relationship as the appropriate basis for understanding expert performance. As such, they argue that expertise is predicated on continuous, functional coadaptation of behaviors to dynamic, interacting constraints to achieve specific, intended performance goals. This definition emphasizes that the level of expertise demonstrated by performers is reflective of their improved fit as they interact with their (performance) environments (Araújo *et al.*, 2009), resulting in the emergence of adaptive perception-action couplings as individuals attempt to meet specific task goals (Warren, 2006). Expert performance is therefore the optimal satisfaction of unique, interacting constraints on each individual in specific performance domains (Phillips *et al.*, 2014). Essentially, the development of expert performance requires initially establishing a reciprocal, functional link between information and movement, before refining or calibrating these links in the longer term (Araújo *et al.*, 2007). Key to establishing this link is the process of education of attention (Gibson & Pick, 2000) as experts attune to key affordances specifying information sources within performance environments (Fajen *et al.*, 2008). Affordances are opportunities for action where appropriately attuned individuals are able to directly perceive the world in relation to their own action capabilities (Gibson, 1986). The mutuality of the individual and the environment in this definition highlights that changes in intrinsic dynamics, such as attunement to specifying information sources or increased speed or strength, means that the same performance situation has a different meaning for different individuals at any one time, but can also mean different things for the same individual over short and long time scales (Araújo & Davids, 2011; see also Chapters 12 and 19).

The dynamic nature of the calibration of the perceptual-motor system to information has some important implications for capturing expertise. Adopting this theoretical approach means that identifying and then tracking unchanging performance variables over each phase of an athlete's development, from their initial introduction into the domain through to attainment of expert levels, is difficult to achieve (Williams & Ericsson, 2008), because expertise is an adaptive, emergent process where changes in action capabilities lead to changes in the environmental properties, leading to further changes in actions (Araújo & Davids, 2011; Warren, 2006). In the following section, we propose that using Gibson's (1986) concept of "events," in conjunction with principles of ecological dynamics, would allow skill acquisition scientists to capture individual experts' superior knowledge *of* the environment – i.e., the ability to know what needs to be done based on direct perception through "sensitivity to the events that convey information for his/her aims in any instance of the game" (Araújo & Davids, 2011, p. 120). Knowledge *of* the environment captures the capability of performers to perceive the properties of the environment in the scale of body and action capabilities (Araújo *et al.*, 2009). Therefore, the expert performer becomes more attuned to the environment through direct learning via task-specific experiences where the variables picked up become more subtle, elaborate, and precise (Araújo & Davids, 2011; Araújo *et al.*, 2009). Knowledge *of* the environment is therefore different to knowledge *about* the environment, where the latter refers to indirect perception mediated by language, pictures, or other media (Gibson, 1986). In order to truly test expertise, it is therefore essential to capture the individual acting in his/her performance habitat (i.e., the performance environment) as he/she participates in events (see also Pinder *et al.*, 2011). A good example of a study that was able to fully capture expertise as an event was undertaken by Triolet, Benguigui, Runigo, and Williams, (2013), who analyzed 3,000 incidents of tennis players in International Tennis Federation matches. Interestingly, and against conventional wisdom that expert tennis performance would require high levels of anticipatory skill, they found that only six to 13 per cent of shots relied on anticipation. In all other shots, the receiver waited for his opponent to hit the ball before making his response. These results further highlight the capability of representative test designs to reveal critical sources of information used by expert performers that may otherwise have gone unnoticed in more tightly controlled laboratory settings (see also Williams & Ericsson, 2005).

Designing field tests to capture expertise: some pointers

Capturing expertise: why it should be an event

Given the complexity of performance environments, a useful approach to capturing expertise could be to consider the whole event and incorporate the concept of nested tasks advocated by ecological psychologists (Gibson, 1986), rather than focus on an isolated component of performance such as anticipation. Gibson argues that "the flow of ecological events consists of natural units that are nested within one another – episodes within episodes, subordinate ones and superordinate ones" (1986, p. 101). Adopting this viewpoint means that each rally in a tennis match, each pitch in a game of baseball, and each one-on-one situation in soccer does not take place in isolation, but instead, perception and action can naturally emerge as the environment demands. In effect, an episode such as a rally or an attacking phase in an invasion game is nested in the whole event, which may be a game, a set, a match, or even a series of matches in a tournament. When assessing a performer's expertise, the sport scientist ideally needs to track behavior across the whole event and avoid making judgments on isolated snapshots. For example, when analyzing a cricket batter's dismissal in a match, it is necessary to consider factors such as the previous balls faced, the state of the game, and the environmental conditions. As former cricketing great and expert coach Greg Chappell elaborates,

> The video replays [of the dismissal] only tell you part of the story. They tell you it's a snapshot of that instant . . . the wicket may have come from something that happened two balls, three balls, six balls, eighteen balls before.
>
> *(Renshaw & Chappell, 2010, p. 161)*

By assessing performance across the whole event, the skill acquisition scientist can evaluate the emergent behaviors of the performer, assessing how he/she has adapted to the interacting constraints during the whole event. Assessing expertise throughout an event also allows practitioners to evaluate a performer's capability to utilize his/her knowledge *of* the environment (Araújo &

Davids, 2011; Araújo *et al.*, 2007; Gibson, 1986). Adopting an ecological dynamics approach to understanding expertise suggests that the most appropriate way to assess performance is by observation and analysis of the events that take place in the normal habitat of the performer. However, this can often be problematic, and so skill acquisition scientists need to design suitable experimental tasks that capture the key components of performance and allow repeatability, but do so in an unobtrusive manner and without compromising the need for experimental control (Pinder *et al.*, 2011; Williams & Ericsson, 2005). To that end, we now discuss how skill acquisition scientists can design performance vignettes, primarily using a collaborative approach, to capture representative events commensurate with the performance environment (see also Chapters 19 and 24).

Integrating sport scientist, coach, and performer knowledge of and about expertise to design effective tests and training tasks

Whereas improvements in technology and equipment have their advantages for sport scientists attempting to capture expertise, they have also created the problem of producing a large number of primary and derived variables from which to choose. The selection of which variables to consider was Kelso's "inspired guess" or choosing problem (Kelso, 1995). Adopting a positivistic, reductionist approach would see multiple relationships examined in an eliminative fashion, with the risk of certain patterns emerging due to chance. How then do we choose? One strategy that has recently been adopted in empirical research programs is the accessing of experiential knowledge of experts to initially identify key variables that can then be tested in representative performance tasks. The rich data, provided via qualitative interviews by expert coaches and performers in the studies of Greenwood, Davids, and Renshaw (2013) and Millar *et al.* (2013), demonstrate the value of accessing the experience of expert practitioners. The ideas and views of expert coaching practitioners have been tested over time and suggest that a mimetic approach to knowledge generation via the symbiotic relationship of practitioners and coaches might enrich understanding of sport performance. Millar *et al.* (2013) asked rowing coaches specific questions about the nature of expert performance in their sport (e.g., "what makes a boat go fast?"), which allowed a principled approach, ensuring that only those variables that the experts identified as key information sources were considered in the emergent research program. The use of this qualitative data led to the generation of new knowledge with respect to expertise in the movement tasks. For example, the results from Millar *et al.* (2013) led to a new understanding of timing in pairs rowing and revealed that high-performance rowers exploit visual regulation in a novel way to achieve interpersonal coordination by *extra-personal coordination* (a process where rowers timed their movements with the water and the boat). Expert rowers and coaches stated that while interpersonal coordination between rowers is crucial for performance, it is not achieved by direct coupling to each other's actions as was generally thought, but instead, it was achieved indirectly through individual rowers who were timing their movements with invariant information provided by the boat and water. The connection with the boat and water was termed by experts as "rowing with the boat." Hence, if both rowers can row in time with the boat, they will be in time with each other, even though they do not actively seek to row in time with each other. These findings formed the basis of a series of studies that allowed the researchers to use a combination of biomechanics and motor learning to test these ideas in representative vignettes of rowing performance to empirically verify the experts' assumptions (see Chapter 8).

Earlier in the chapter we highlighted the need for an interdisciplinary approach to studies of expertise and highlighted how the advances in technology have made in situ data collection much easier to achieve. However, there are few published studies that have meshed theory and a combination of technologies to examine expertise in action. An exception is the study of sailing expertise by Pluijms *et al.* (2013) that can act as an exemplar of what is possible and provide some guidance moving forward. Based on pilot work, key events in a sailing regatta were identified; namely, rounding a "mark." Technology included an online video camera to capture sailor movement behaviors, a portable eye tracker to capture visual search behaviors, a wind monitor to record the environmental conditions, and importantly, a global positioning system to record the performance of the boat itself. This setup allowed the researchers to capture sailing performance under interacting individual, environmental, and task constraints that facilitated and enhanced understanding of sailing expertise. Pluijms and colleagues' (2013) study shows that when methodological design is based on a theory, as well as on the collaboration of coaches, scientists, and performers, the understanding of expertise in complex sports can be advanced in ways that offer real world benefits.

Other examples of applied research that employed a collaborative approach involving the expertise of coaches and sport scientists included two projects implemented in a high-performance sport setting. The first example is based upon a project conducted by Gorman and Maloney (in preparation) to measure the shooting performance of basketball players. Discussions with coaches and sport scientists revealed that the main challenges surrounding the design of an appropriate shooting test were to ensure that the test required minimal amounts of time and resources, and that the test was able to provide representative scenarios from which coaches could gain a better understanding of players' shooting skill. Given that many existing tests tended to involve non-representative situations where shooting performance was examined in the absence of a defender, the new test was designed to include both defended and undefended scenarios so that the contrasting conditions could be used to provide important information regarding the extent to which players' shooting techniques changed in response to defensive pressure. To further approximate the demands of a game, shots were performed from a range of different court locations where no two shots were performed consecutively from the same location. The total duration of the test was approximately 20 minutes for each condition (i.e., defended and undefended conditions; although subsequent tests for ongoing monitoring of players could possibly be performed using only the defended condition), with digital cameras used to record each test trial. These latter features were important because they allowed the test to be implemented on a regular basis without requiring excessive amounts of time, and without the need for specialized or cumbersome equipment. The data are still in preparation; however, the preliminary results have already provided valuable feedback. In particular, the comparison between defended and undefended conditions highlighted specific technical issues in players' shooting technique that may have otherwise gone unnoticed in a less representative test. This information has since been used to guide the design of shooting training sessions.

The second example of a collaborative approach towards the design of appropriate testing and training protocols is based upon an applied project with three elite swimmers, outlined by Gorman (2012; see also Farrow, 2012). The main intention of the project was simple: design and implement short-duration, pool-based training sessions to enhance starting technique and starting speed off the blocks. Throughout the project, regular discussions between coaches and sport scientists helped to provide direction on the specific nature of the technical changes required for each athlete, as well as ideas regarding possible strategies that could be used to promote those changes. The regularity of the discussions helped to ensure that the objectives of the coaches and sport scientists were in close agreement, and also provided the opportunity to continually refine the structure of the training sessions. In a similar vein to the basketball shooting example outlined earlier, the main challenges of the project were to design training sessions that were time efficient, but to also include representative tasks that were based upon sound skill acquisition principles. To manage the time constraint, the skill-based sessions for each athlete (approximately one session of 20 minutes per athlete, twice per week) were interspersed within normal squad training at appropriate times, so that the disruption to the main training set was minimal and so that the athletes were not required to attend additional sessions outside of normal training times. To maintain representative training tasks, technical issues were addressed by employing a constraints-led approach (see Davids *et al.*, 2008; Newell, 1986). For example, to encourage a deeper knee bend (and hence, a more forceful start) when pushing off the blocks, flexible foam strips were strapped to the posterior lower leg of the swimmer at a point where the foam would touch the athlete's upper leg when sufficient knee bend had been achieved. This essentially provided the athlete with a reference point, allowing him/her to sense the point at which the desired knee angle had been achieved. By preserving the task in its natural form, the constraints-led approach retained the important couplings between perception and action, thereby helping to provide a representative training activity (see Renshaw *et al.*, 2009). To help determine the efficacy of the training sessions, the data collected from starts performed on an instrumented starting block were examined. The results (although not statistically significant) gathered from the instrumented block revealed improvements in entry angle and entry distance for all three athletes, and enhanced starting speed for two out of the three athletes.

Conclusion

Ecological dynamics, with its emphasis on the interdependence of performer and environment, and the mutuality of perception and action, intuitively appears to be a more relevant and appropriate approach to understanding sport expertise. Unfortunately, there has been limited application of the key ideas of this approach within applied sport science and coaching. Skill acquisition requires a radical paradigm shift where research is driven by the same types of questions as those posed by practitioners working in the field (Williams & Ericsson, 2008). Undertaking testing that measures key performance variables under real world constraints can help shed more light on the key characteristics and common features that contribute to expert performance in the natural setting. For example, how does pressure affect decision-making for the key playmaker in a soccer world cup final? How do rowers adapt their technique to different wind and water conditions? How do opponents influence intentions and actions? This can help to identify the most functional action solutions for a given environment. However, based upon the theoretical perspective we have adopted, it is also necessary to make an important point concerning the generalizability of research findings when testing experts. Adopting an ecological dynamics perspective means that the focus is on the individual, and so this requires a nomothetic approach to analysis, meaning that scientists and coaches must show extreme caution in presuming that all experts will have the same expertise (Williams & Ericsson, 2005). By default, experts will solve problems in ways that are unique to their individual, intrinsic dynamics as they interact with task and environmental constraints. Ideally, this requires a historical knowledge of the previous experiences of the performer that have led to his/her coordination tendencies, as they may act to explain individual approaches to solving performance problems. For example, a squash player who has previously played badminton is more likely to have developed cooperative movement patterns, whereas previously playing tennis is more likely to lead to competitive movement patterns (Magill & Anderson, 2014). Despite this, studies may also reveal laws of control and common features of experts in specific situations that can, and perhaps should, be used to guide skill acquisition principles.

References

Anderson, D. I., & Sidaway, B. (1994) 'Coordination changes associated with practice of a soccer kick', *Research Quarterly for Exercise and Sport*, 65: 93–9.

Ankersen, R. (2012) *The gold mine effect: Crack the secrets of high performance*, London: Icon Publishing.

Araújo, D., & Davids, K. (2011) 'What exactly is acquired during skill acquisition?', *Journal of Consciousness Studies*, 18: 7–23.

Araújo, D., Davids, K., Cordovil, R., Ribeiro, J., & Fernandes, O. (2009) 'How does knowledge constrain sport performance? An ecological perspective', in D. Araújo, H. Ripoll, & M. Raab (eds) *Perspectives on cognition and action in sport*, New York: Nova Science Publishers Inc., 157–69.

Araújo, D., Davids, K., & Passos, P. (2007) 'Ecological validity, representative design, and correspondence between experimental task constraints and behavioral setting: Comment on Rogers, Kadar, and Costall (2005)', *Ecological Psychology*, 19: 69–78.

Beek, P. J., Dessing, J. C., Peper, C. E., & Bullock, D. (2003) 'Modelling the control of interceptive actions', *Philosophical Transactions of the Royal Society of London. Series B, Biological Sciences*, 358: 1511–23.

Berg, W. P., Wade, M. G., & Greer, N. L. (1994) ,Visual regulation of gait in bipedal locomotion: Revisiting Lee, Lishman, and Thomson (1982)', *Journal of Experimental Psychology: Human Perception and Performance*, 20: 854–63.

Brétigny, P., Leroy, D., Button, C., Chollet, D., & Seifert, L. (2011) 'Coordination profiles of the expert field hockey drive according to field roles', *Sports Biomechanics*, 10: 339–50.

Button, C., & Farrow, D. (2012) 'Working in the field (southern hemisphere)', in N. J. Hodges & A. M. Williams (eds) *Skill acquisition in sport: Research, theory and practice*, London: Routledge, 367–80.

Cordovil, R., Araújo, D., Davids, K., Gouveia, L., Barreiros, J., Fernandes, O., & Serpa, S. (2009) 'The influence of instructions and body-scaling as constraints on decision-making processes in team sports', *European Journal of Sport Science*, 9: 169–79.

Davids, K., Button, C., & Bennett, S. (2008) *Dynamics of skill acquisition: A constraints-led approach*, Champaign, IL: Human Kinetics.

Davids, K., Kingsbury, D., Bennett, S., & Handford, C. (2001) 'Information-movement coupling: Implications of the organization of research and practice during acquisition of self-paced extrinsic timing skills', *Journal of Sports Sciences*, 19: 117–27.

Dicks, M., Davids, K., & Button, C. (2010) 'Individual differences in the visual control of intercepting a penalty kick in association football', *Human Movement Science*, 29: 401–11.

Ericsson, K. A. (2006) 'An introduction to Cambridge handbook of expertise and expert performance: Its development, organization, and content', in K. A. Ericsson, N. Charness, P. J. Feltovich, & R. R. Hoffman (eds) *The Cambridge handbook of expertise and expert performance*, Cambridge: Cambridge University Press, 3–19.

Ericsson, K. A., & Williams, A. M. (2007) 'Capturing naturally occurring superior performance in the laboratory: Translational research on expert performance', *Journal of Experimental Psychology: Applied*, 13: 115–23.

Fajen, B. R., Riley, M. A., & Turvey, M. T. (2008) 'Information, affordances, and the control of action in sport', *International Journal of Sport Psychology*, 40: 79–107.

Farrow, D. (2012) 'Applied skill acquisition: Working with elite athletes – Introduction', *Journal of Sport & Exercise Psychology*, 34 (Suppl.): S28.

Gibson, E. J., & Pick, A, D. (2000) *An ecological approach to perceptual learning and development*, Oxford: Oxford University Press.

Gibson, J. J. (1986) *The ecological approach to visual perception*, London: LEA Publishers.

Glize, D., & Laurent, M. (1997) 'Controlling locomotion during the acceleration phase in sprinting and long jumping', *Journal of Sports Sciences*, 15: 181–9.

Gorman, A. D. (2012) 'The application of augmented feedback and a constraints-led approach in an elite sports setting', *Journal of Sport & Exercise Psychology*, 34 (Suppl.): S29.

Gorman, A. D., & Maloney, M. A. (in preparation) *Representative design: Does the addition of a defender change the execution of a basketball shot?*, manuscript in preparation.

Greenwood, D. (2014) 'Informational constraints on performance of dynamic interceptive actions', unpublished thesis, Brisbane: Queensland University of Technology.

Greenwood, D., Davids, K., & Renshaw, I. (2013) 'Experiential knowledge of expert coaches can help identify informational constraints on performance of dynamic interceptive actions', *Journal of Sports Sciences*, 32: 328–35.

Hay, J. G. (1988) 'Approach strategies in the long jump', *International Journal of Sport Biomechanics*, 4: 114–29.

Headrick, J. J., Davids, K., Renshaw, I., Araújo, D., Passos, P., & Fernandes, O. (2012) 'Proximity-to-goal as a constraint on patterns of behaviour in attacker-defender dyads in team games', *Journal of Sports Sciences*, 30: 247–53.

Helsen, W. F., & Starkes, J. L. (1999) 'A multidimensional approach to skilled perception and performance in sport', *Applied Cognitive Psychology*, 13: 1–27.

Kelso, J.A.S. (1995) *Dynamic patterns: The self-organization of brain and behavior*, Cambridge: MIT press.

Lee, D. N., Lishman, J. R., & Thomson, J. A. (1982) 'Regulation of gait in long jumping', *Journal of Experimental Psychology: Human Perception and Performance*, 8: 448–59.

Lyons, B. D., Hoffman, B. J., & Michel, J. W. (2009) 'Not much more than g? An examination of the impact of intelligence on NFL performance', *Human Performance*, 22(3): 225–45.

MacNamara, A., & Collins, D. (2011) 'Comment on "Talent identification and promotion programmes of Olympic athletes"', *Journal of Sports Sciences*, 29: 1353–6.

Magill, R. A., & Anderson, D. I. (2014) *Motor learning and control: Concepts and applications*, 10th ed., New York: McGraw-Hill.

Millar, S. K., Oldham, A. R., & Renshaw, I. (2013) 'Interpersonal, intrapersonal, extrapersonal? Qualitatively investigating coordinative couplings between rowers in Olympic sculling', *Nonlinear Dynamics, Psychology, and Life Sciences*, 17: 425–43.

Montagne, G., Bastin, J., & Jacobs, D. M. (2008) 'What is visual anticipation and how much does it rely on the dorsal stream?', *International Journal of Sport Psychology*, 39: 149–56.

Montagne, G., Cornus, S., Glize, D., Quaine, F., & Laurent, M. (2000b) 'A perception-action coupling type of control in long jumping', *Journal of Motor Behavior*, 32: 37–43.

Montagne, G., Fraisse, F., Ripoll, H., & Laurent, M. (2000a) 'Perception–action coupling in an interceptive task: First-order time-to-contact as an input variable', *Human Movement Science*, 19: 59–72.

Newell, K. M. (1986) 'Constraints on the development of coordination', in M. Wade & H.T.A Whiting (eds) *Motor development in children: Aspects of coordination and control*, Dordrecht: Martinus Nijhoff, 341–60.

Orth, D., Davids, K., Araújo, D., Renshaw, I., & Passos, P. (2014) 'Effects of a defender on run-up velocity and ball speed when crossing a football', *European Journal of Sports Sciences*, 14: S316-S323.

Oudejans, R.R.D., & Coolen, B. H. (2003) 'Human kinematics and event control: On-line movement registration as a means for experimental manipulation', *Journal of Sports Sciences*, 21: 567–76.

Oudejans, R.R.D., Michaels, C. F., Bakker, F.C., & Dolné, M. A. (1996) 'The relevance of action in perceiving affordances: perception of catchableness of fly balls', *Journal of Experimental Psychology: Human Perception and performance*, 22: 879–91.

Phillips, E., Davids, K. W., Araújo, D., & Renshaw, I. (2014) 'Talent development and expertise in sport', in K. Davids, R. Hristovski, D. Araújo, N. Balagué Serre, C. Button, & P. Passos (eds) *Complex systems in sport*, London: Routledge, 241–60.

Pinder, R. A., Davids, K., Renshaw, I., & Araújo, D. (2011) 'Representative learning design and functionality of research and practice in sport', *Journal of Sport & Exercise Psychology*, 33: 146–55.

Pinder, R. A., Renshaw, I., & Davids, K. (2013) 'The role of representative design in talent development: A comment on "Talent identification and promotion programmes of Olympic athletes"', *Journal of Sports Sciences*, 31(8): 803–6.

Pluijms, J. P., Cañal-Bruland, R., Kats, S., & Savelsbergh, G.J.P. (2013) 'Translating key methodological issues into technological advancements when running in-situ experiments in sports: An example from sailing', *International Journal of Sports Science & Coaching*, 8: 89–103.

Renshaw, I., & Chappell, G.S. (2010) 'A constraints-led approach to talent development in cricket', in L. Kidman & B. Lombardo (eds) *Athlete-centred coaching*, 2nd ed., Christchurch: Innovative Publishing, 161.

Renshaw, I., & Davids, K. (2004) 'Nested task constraints shape continuous perception-action coupling control during human locomotor pointing', *Neuroscience Letters*, 369: 93–8.

Renshaw, I., Davids, K., Shuttleworth, R., & Chow, J. Y. (2009) 'Insights from ecological psychology and dynamic systems. Theory can underpin a philosophy of coaching', *International Journal of Sport Psychology*, 40: 580–602.

Scott, M. A., Li, F. X., & Davids, K. (1997) 'Expertise and the regulation of gait in the approach phase of the long jump', *Journal of Sports Sciences*, 15: 597–605.

Seifert, L., Button, C., & Davids, K. (2013) 'Key properties of expert movement systems in sport: An ecological dynamics perspective', *Sports Medicine*, 43: 167–78.

Starkes, J. L. (1987) 'Skill in field hockey: The nature of the cognitive advantage', *Journal of Sport Psychology*, 9: 146–60.

Steel, K. A., Harris, B., Baxter, D., & King, M. (2013) 'Skill acquisition specialists, coaches and athletes: The current state of play?', *Journal of Sport Behavior*, 36: 291–305.

Summers, J. J. (2004) 'A historical perspective on skill acquisition', in A. M. Williams & N. J. Hodges (eds) *Skill acquisition in sport: Research, theory and practice*, London: Routledge, 1–26.

Syed, M. (2011) *Bounce: The myth of talent and the power of practice*, New York: Harper Collins Publishers.

Triolet, C., Benguigui, N., Le Runigo, C., & Williams, A. M. (2013) 'Quantifying the nature of anticipation in professional tennis', *Journal of Sports Sciences*, 31: 820–30.

van der Kamp, J., Rivas, F., van Doorn, H., Savelsbergh, G. (2008) 'Ventral and dorsal system contributions to visual anticipation in fast ball sports', *International Journal of Sport Psychology*, 39: 100–30.

Warren, W. H. (2006) 'The dynamics of perception and action', *Psychological Review*, 113: 358–89.

Williams, A. M., & Ericsson, K. A. (2005) 'Perceptual-cognitive expertise in sport: Some considerations when applying the expert performance approach', *Human Movement Science*, 24: 283–307.

Williams, A. M., & Ericsson, K. A. (2008) 'From the guest editors: How do experts learn?', *Journal of Sport & Exercise Psychology*, 30: 653–62.

Williams, A. M., & Ford, P. R. (2009) 'Promoting a skills-based agenda in Olympic sports: The role of skill-acquisition specialists', *Journal of Sports Scientists*, 27: 1381–92.

Williams, A. M., & Hodges, N. J. (2005) 'Practice, instruction and skill acquisition in soccer: Challenging tradition', *Journal of Sports Sciences*, 23: 637–50.

Zelaznik, H. N. (2014) 'The past and future of motor learning and control: What is the proper level of description and analysis?', *Kinesiology Review*, 3: 38–43.

26

GENOMICS OF ELITE SPORTING PERFORMANCE

Yannis P. Pitsiladis and Guan Wang

Sporting performance is a complex phenotype, and it is acknowledged that to become an elite athlete, a synergy of physiological, behavioral, and other environmental factors is required. It is nevertheless widely accepted that there will be many genes involved in sporting performance. To date, over 200 single nucleotide polymorphisms (SNPs; i.e., variation in a genetic sequence of a single nucleotide, which can be found in at least one per cent of the population) and quantitative trait loci associated with some performance- and fitness-related traits have been reported in the literature and were summarized on a yearly basis until 2009 in "The Human Gene Map for Performance and Health-Related Fitness Phenotypes" (Bray *et al.*, 2009). The large increase in genetic studies and limited resources from the few dedicated teams able to manage these continuously expanded data entries have resulted in the publication of only the most important findings each year since 2010 in "Advances in Exercise, Fitness, and Performance Genomics" (Pérusse *et al.*, 2013). In a review of 133 studies involving athletic cohorts published during the period 1997–2012, 59 genetic markers were reported to be associated with endurance performance, 20 with power/strength-related performance, whereas 25 per cent of these markers were positively associated with performance in at least two studies (Ahmetov & Fedotovskaya, 2012).

The data reviewed have been generated using classical genetic methods such as candidate gene analysis and primarily applied to cohorts with small sample sizes (usually n < 300) and therefore especially prone to type one error. Apart from the alpha-actinin-3 (ACTN3) R577X (Alfred *et al.*, 2011) and possibly angiotensin-converting enzyme (ACE) insertion/deletion (I/D) (Puthucheary *et al.*, 2011), the vast majority of the candidate genes for sporting performance discovered to date are not the resulting variants responsible for the phenotypes of interest. It is widely acknowledged that there will be many genes involved in performance phenotypes and hence it is timely that genetic research has moved to the genomics era; for example, doing genetic studies at a genome-wide level by simultaneously testing a large number of genetic variants across the entire human genome without specific prior hypotheses. Priority should therefore be given to applying whole genome technology to sufficiently large study cohorts of world-class athletes with adequately measured phenotypes where it is possible to increase statistical power. Some of the elite athlete cohorts summarized in Table 26.1 (and described in Pitsiladis *et al.*, 2013) might suffice, and collectively, these cohorts could be used for replication purposes. Genome-wide association studies (GWASs) are ongoing in some of these cohorts (i.e., genathlete, Russian, Spanish, Japanese, US, and Jamaican cohorts). Preliminary and unpublished findings include the

Table 26.1 Major study cohorts in genetics of elite performance.

Study	Design	Subjects
GENATHLETE	Candidate gene case-control multicenter study	~ 300 endurance athletes with high $\dot{V}O_2$max ~ 300 untrained controls with low to average $\dot{V}O_2$max
Russian cohort	Candidate gene case-control study involving 24 different athletic disciplines	1,423 Russian endurance athletes of regional or national competitive standard 1,242 Russian controls
East African cohort	Candidate gene case-control study	291 Kenyan endurance athletes of national/international competitive standard 85 Kenyan controls 76 Ethiopian endurance athletes from the junior/senior national athletic teams 315 Ethiopian controls
Jamaican and USA cohort	Candidate gene case-control study and GWAS	116 Jamaican sprint athletes of national/international competitive standard 311 Jamaican controls 114 African American sprint athletes of national/international competitive standard 191 African American controls
Australian cohort	Candidate gene case-control study involving 14 different sports	429 elite white athletes 436 white controls
Japanese cohort	Candidate gene case-control study and GWAS	717 Japanese athletes of national/international competitive standard (including 381 track and field athletes, 166 swimmers, and 170 Olympians from various sports) 814 Japanese controls
European and Asian swimming cohort	Candidate gene case-control study	200 Caucasian swimmers of world-class status 158 Japanese of national/international competitive standard 649 Japanese controls 168 Taiwanese swimmers of national/international competitive standard 603 Taiwanese controls
Spanish cohort	Candidate gene case-control study	100 Spanish male endurance athletes of world-class status 54 Spanish male rowers of world-class status 108 all-time best Spanish judo male athletes 88 swimmers of national level 53 power athletes of national/international competitive standard 343 Spanish controls
Israeli cohort	Candidate gene case-control study	74 Israeli endurance athletes of national/international competitive standard 81 power athletes of national/international competitive standard 240 Israeli controls
Chinese cohort	Candidate gene case-control study	241 Chinese (Han) endurance athletes 504 Chinese (Han) controls
Polish cohort	Candidate gene case-control study involving 20 different athletic disciplines	660 Polish athletes of national or international competitive standard 684 Polish controls

Genomics of elite sporting performance

identification of one SNP (among more than a million SNPs analyzed) that associates with sprint performance in Japanese, US (i.e., African American), and Jamaican cohorts with a combined effect size of approximately 2.6 ($P = 4.66$ x 10^{-7}) and good concordance with endurance performance between select cohorts. Further validation of these signals in independent cohorts will be required, including any replicated SNPs taken forward for fine mapping/targeted resequencing and other sets of functional studies to uncover the underlying biological mechanisms.

Despite the emergence of some potentially interesting, yet unreplicated, associations from ongoing GWASs, none of the associations are of sufficient magnitude to warrant further investigation after applying the mostly recognized and conventional criterion of $P = 5x10^{-8}$, which is calculated by dividing the value of alpha 0.05 by one million SNPs that are thought to be effectively independent across the genome based on linkage disequilibrium patterns of non-Africans (Pe'er *et al.*, 2008; Stranger *et al.*, 2011). Irrespective of where one sets the significance threshold (i.e., $P = 5x10^{-8}$, etc.), the implications of these first GWASs are that elite/world-class sporting performance is not significantly linked to a few common genetic variance with strong effect. It is unsurprising therefore that no genes/SNPS have been discovered with any worthwhile predictive capacity, despite numerous publications in sport genetics (Pitsiladis *et al.*, 2013). The focus of this chapter is on current knowledge in sport genetics and necessary advances.

The occurrence of rare variants that are not captured by GWASs may help explain the limited success in determining the genetic associations with a complex trait such as sporting performance. In the field of genetic epidemiology of common and complex traits, identification of underlying genetic structure by GWAS initially relied on the common disease-common variant hypothesis (known as the CDCV hypothesis), which assumed that the risk of common and complex traits are largely explained by a moderate number of common variants (Botstein & Risch, 2003; Lander, 1996; Pritchard & Cox, 2002; Reich & Lander, 2001). However, the small fraction of genetic variation revealed in the ongoing GWAS raises the issue of missing heritability (Maher, 2008; Manolio *et al.*, 2009). For example, human height is a highly heritable, quantitative trait (up to 90 per cent of variation is most likely explained by genetic factors) (Macgregor *et al.*, 2006; Perola *et al.*, 2007; Preece, 1996; Silventoinen *et al.*, 2000), as well as stable and easy to measure. One of the largest studies (n = 183,727) to date identified at least 180 loci associated with adult height (explaining only 10 per cent of the phenotypic variation in height) (Lango Allen *et al.*, 2010). There have been suggestions that common variants do explain up to 45 per cent of the variance in height (Yang *et al.*, 2010), but the small effect size of these variants may render them undetectable by common study designs (Manolio *et al.*, 2009). Furthermore, the identified common variants associated with the most complex diseases do not show predictive utility (Talmud *et al.*, 2010). Thus, much of the heritability of complex traits remains hidden or missing (Gibson, 2010; Manolio *et al.*, 2009) and several models have been proposed to account for this missing heritability (Gibson, 2012). These include: 1) the infinitesimal model, in which genetic variance is attributable to numerous common variants with small effects (Visscher *et al.*, 2008); 2) the rare allele model, in which genetic variance is attributable to many rare variants (allele frequency is typically less than one per cent) with large effects (Cirulli & Goldstein, 2010); and 3) the broad sense heritability model (relative to the narrow sense heritability that refers to the additive portion of the genetic variance), in which genetic variance is attributable to the non-additive components – the gene-gene interactions (i.e., epistasis), gene-environment interactions, and epigenetics (e.g., the effect of DNA methylation, histone modification, and microRNA expression on a genotype without change of the DNA sequence) (Eichler *et al.*, 2010; Feldman & Lewontin, 1975; Gibson, 2012). An intuitive illustration of the above three models as well as the CDCV hypothesis model is displayed in Figure 26.1 (Gibson, 2012). It remains unclear which elements contribute to an inferred genetic variance and in what proportion, but a useful way

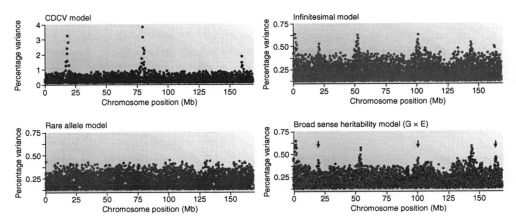

Figure 26.1 Genome-wide association signals for elucidation of four models related to common and complex traits (Gibson, 2012). Each plot represents an expected distribution of SNP effects for a study of 2,000 cases and controls. The y-axis shows the percentage of genetic variance explained by each SNP for a trait in a population, and the x-axis refers to the chromosomal location for each SNP. In the plot of the CDCV model, a small number of SNPs show strong effects on the trait being studied (i.e., the expended scale of the percentage of variance on the y-axis compared to other plots). In the plot of the infinitesimal model, the strongly associated signals are explained by a large number of SNPs with small effects. In the plot of the rare allele model, rare causal variants (shown in yellow) may have a large effect in a few individuals, although they are not common in a population to explain a reasonable amount of variance and to result in genome-wide significance. In the plot of the broad sense heritability model, for associations that are only present under certain conditions (e.g., influenced by environmental factors, shown as green and orange signals), the overall effect will be reduced in a mixed population at such loci (see arrows, bottom right), and this would lead to few associations being detected, hence less variance observed (Gibson, 2012).

forward is to consider how these proposed hypotheses interact and build the genetic foundation of a complex trait (Schork *et al.*, 2009).

In addition to the previous explanations, structural variations (e.g., copy number variants, inversions, and translocations) may also explain some of the missing heritability (Manolio *et al.*, 2009). Although common variants of small to modest effect size are likely to be revealed by GWAS, there are no published GWASs of elite human performance to date, and therefore the true genetic architecture underlying elite athlete status remains unclear. Despite a study of 4,488 adult British female twins showing athlete status is highly heritable (h^2 = 66 per cent) (De Moor *et al.*, 2007), the proportion of phenotypic variation that can be explained by GWAS markers is currently unclear. For example, the heritability of elite sprint athlete status that can be explained by the handful of unconfirmed SNPs being identified in the ongoing GWAS may be extremely limited, given the polygenic nature of elite performance. Except that common variants of small to modest effect and rare variants of large effect may contribute to genetic variance in elite human performance, common variants of large effect as well as rare variants of small effect may also exist (see Figure 26.2; Manolio *et al.*, 2009).

Unlike most other common and complex traits, large genetic studies involving DNA samples collected from tens of thousands of athletes are practically impossible to achieve due to limited resources. An alternative strategy would be to conduct GWASs involving as many of the world's greatest athletes (i.e., the "special" ones) as possible in order to reduce the required sample size. A cohort of world-class athletes – involving Olympians, world champions, holders of world records, and the like – is thought to increase the efficiency of identifying genetic

Genomics of elite sporting performance

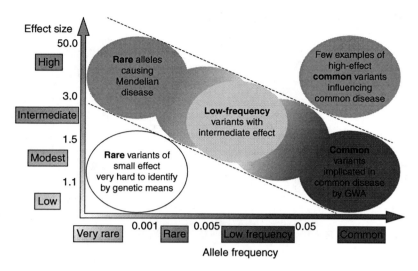

Figure 26.2 Feasibility of identifying genetic variants by risk allele frequency and strength of genetic effect (Manolio et al., 2009).

variants associated with elite athlete status by comparing allele frequencies in the elite athletes who are at one extreme of the phenotype distribution to their geographically matched controls. The allele frequency may be enriched in one or both phenotype extremes, and this may circumvent the need for very large samples (Lanktree et al., 2010; Pitsiladis & Wang, 2011). In a similar way, the first GWAS in age-related macular degeneration (AMD) revealed an intronic and common variant (with an effect size of 7.4) significantly related to AMD by comparing 96 cases to 50 controls, and subsequently a functional polymorphism (in linkage disequilibrium with the risk allele of this common variant) in the complement factor H (CFH) gene was identified by resequencing (Klein et al., 2005), suggesting that it is not unreasonable to expect that variants with large effects may be detected in small but unique cohorts. Statistical power is a function of sample size, effect size, correlation between the marker and the causal variant, as well as allele frequencies. When effect size of a variant is large and the variant is frequent enough to be detected in a population, the power for detecting a novel variant is also increased. Statistical power for GWAS has been estimated by simulation using 100 cases and 100 controls (in line with current ongoing GWASs of elite sprint performance), with marker minor allele frequency (MAF) varying from 0.05 to 0.5 and assuming low prevalence of the trait at 0.1 (see Figure 26.3). Under these conditions, to achieve 80 per cent power, minimum effect sizes range from 3.02 to 6.07 under the four different genetic models (i.e., the multiplicative, additive, dominant, and recessive models). Whereas power calculations such as these can improve gene discovery prospects in association studies, data cleaning at the discovery phase and appropriate meta-analysis for combining several discovery studies (to increase the sample size, where applicable) are also very important and would help improve power. The estimated effect sizes from the ongoing discovery GWASs are likely to be somewhat inflated due to inadequate power (Ioannidis, 2008; Xiao & Boehnke, 2009; Yu et al., 2007; Zhong & Prentice, 2008). The application of meta-analysis across several independent GWASs is ongoing and an essential strategy to greatly increase sample size and statistical power.

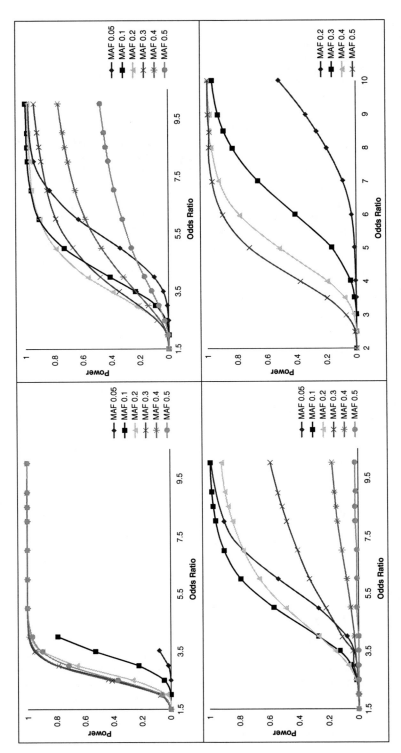

Figure 26.3 Power vs. effect size for 100 cases and 100 controls under the multiplicative (top left), additive (top right), dominant (bottom left), and recessive (bottom right) models, assuming a low prevalence of the trait at 0.1 for MAF varied from 0.05 to 0.5.

Conclusions

GWAS has been able to detect many loci that implicate biologically related genes and pathways. At present, GWAS remains the most effective way to discover genetic variants associated with complex and multifactorial traits such as sporting performance. The association signals to be identified from GWAS may also highlight the genomic regions harboring other forms of variation, such as rare and structural variants. Following GWAS, additional approaches, such as fine mapping and sequencing, may be used to find other common variants with larger effect sizes than GWAS, tag SNPs, and identify rare variants across GWAS loci. Considerable efforts such as these will be required in order to decipher the missing heritability for sporting performance and elite athlete status. The first positive findings from ongoing GWASs involving world-class athletes will provide the first tangible evidence of genetic predisposition to elite human performance. GWAS of elite athletes, as well as the application of meta-analysis across the several initial GWASs, will be required to help circumvent the need for very large cohorts of elite athletes and increase statistical power. While significant progress can be expected from current GWASs, major progress will require new, large, well-funded, international collaborations using larger cohorts of elite/world-class athletes in order to explore further the genetic architecture underlying elite human performance. Such initiatives will allow gene-gene and gene-environment interactions to be explored, as well as the predictive utility of sport genomics research.

Practical implications

The general consensus amongst researchers in sport and exercise genetics is that direct-to-consumer (DTC) genetic tests based on current knowledge have little or no role to play in talent identification or the individualized prescription of training to maximize performance (Pitsiladis *et al.*, 2013). Despite this, genetic tests related to sport and exercise are widely available on a commercial basis (e.g., Figure 26.4); there are at least 22 companies providing DTC genetic

Figure 26.4 DNA test (sport gene) being offered at Tallinn Airport, Estonia *(continued).*

Figure 26.4 (Continued)

Genomics of elite sporting performance

tests marketed in relation to human sport or exercise performance or injury. Taking a charitable view, the information provided by the tests currently available might be of personal interest to some people, and might help individuals (e.g., sports coaches) attempt to "better understand" observed physical limitations to performance or training adaptations – even though the data provide no answer at present as to how to overcome those limitations. There is little doubt that the future of sport and exercise science will become increasingly focused on "omics" (i.e., genomics, transcriptomics, metabolomics, proteomics, and the like) as these technologies become faster, cheaper, and more widely available and as the data these technologies produce are translated into practical tools for sport and exercise scientists. Two promising, recent examples with diagnostic potential include the 21 SNPs that appear to capture the heritable component (approximately 50 per cent of total inter-individual variability) of the responsiveness to endurance training (Bouchard et al., 2011) and the use of molecular signatures to detect recombinant human erythropoietin doping (Durussel et al., 2013). Consequently, scientists and medical practitioners involved in sport need to ensure they are sufficiently familiar with "omics" technologies to capitalize on such findings in an ethically acceptable manner. Scientists associated with companies offering DTC genetic tests related to sport and exercise should also ensure that they are responsible in their activities.

References

Ahmetov, I. I., & Fedotovskaya, O. N. (2012) 'Sports genomics: Current state of knowledge and future directions', *Cellular and Molecular Exercise Physiology*, 1(1): e1.

Alfred, T., Ben-Shlomo, Y., Cooper, R., Hardy, R., Cooper, C., Deary, I. J., . . . HALCyon study team (2011) 'ACTN3 genotype, athletic status, and life course physical capability: Meta-analysis of the published literature and findings from nine studies', *Human Mutation*, 32(9): 1008–18.

Botstein, D., & Risch, N. (2003) 'Discovering genotypes underlying human phenotypes: Past successes for mendelian disease, future approaches for complex disease', *Nature Genetics*, 33 (Suppl): 228–37.

Bouchard, C., Sarzynski, M. A., Rice, T. K., Kraus, W. E., Church, T. S., Sung, Y. J., . . . Rankinen, T. (2011) 'Genomic predictors of the maximal O_2 uptake response to standardized exercise training programs', *Journal of Applied Physiology*, 110(5): 1160–70.

Bray, M. S., Hagberg, J. M., Pérusse, L., Rankinen, T., Roth, S. M., Wolfarth, B., & Bouchard, C. (2009) 'The human gene map for performance and health-related fitness phenotypes: The 2006–2007 update', *Medicine and Science in Sports and Exercise*, 41(1): 35–73.

Cirulli, E. T., & Goldstein, D. B. (2010) 'Uncovering the roles of rare variants in common disease through whole-genome sequencing', *Nature Reviews Genetics*, 11(6): 415–25.

De Moor, M. H., Spector, T. D., Cherkas, L. F., Falchi, M., Hottenga, J. J., Boomsma, D. I., & De Geus, E. J. (2007) 'Genome-wide linkage scan for athlete status in 700 British female DZ twin pairs', *Twin Research and Human Genetics*, 10(6): 812–20.

Durussel, J., McClure, J. D., McBride, M. W., Wondimu, D. H., Crawford, W., Daskalaki, E., & Chatterji, T. (2013) 'Blood gene expression profiles of Kenyan and Caucasian endurance trained males after rHuEpo administration', paper presented at the American College of Sports Medicine Annual Meeting, Indianapolis.

Eichler, E. E., Flint, J., Gibson, G., Kong, A., Leal, S. M., Moore, J. H., & Nadeau, J. H. (2010) 'Missing heritability and strategies for finding the underlying causes of complex disease', *Nature Reviews Genetics*, 11(6): 446–50.

Feldman, M. W., & Lewontin, R. C. (1975) 'The heritability hang-up', *Science*, 190(4220): 1163–68.

Gibson, G. (2010) 'Hints of hidden heritablity in GWAS', *Nature Genetics*, 42(7): 558–60.

Gibson, G. (2012) 'Rare and common variants: Twenty arguments', *Nature Reviews Genetics*, 13(2): 135–45.

Ioannidis, J. P. (2008) 'Why most discovered true associations are inflated', *Epidemiology*, 19(5): 640–8.

Klein, R. J., Zeiss, C., Chew, E. Y., Tsai, J. Y., Sackler, R. S., Haynes, C., . . . Hoh, J. (2005) 'Complement factor H polymorphism in age-related macular degeneration', *Science*, 308(5720): 385–9.

Lander, E. S. (1996) 'The new genomics: Global views of biology', *Science*, 274(5287): 536–9.

Lango Allen, H., Estrada, K., Lettre, G., Berndt, S. I., Weedon, M. N., Rivadeneira, F., . . . Hirschhorn, J. N. (2010) 'Hundreds of variants clustered in genomic loci and biological pathways affect human height', *Nature*, 467: 832–8.

Lanktree, M. B., Hegele, R. A., Schork, N. J., & Spence, J. D. (2010) 'Extremes of unexplained variation as a phenotype: An efficient approach for genome-wide association studies of cardiovascular disease', *Circulation: Cardiovascular Genetics*, 3(2): 215–21.

Macgregor, S., Cornes, B. K., Martin, N. G., & Visscher, P. M. (2006) 'Bias, precision and heritability of self-reported and clinically measured height in Australian twins', *Human Genetics*, 120(4): 571–80.

Maher, B. (2008) 'Personal genomes: The case of the missing heritability', *Nature*, 456(7218): 18–21.

Manolio, T. A., Collins, F. S., Cox, N. J., Goldstein, D. B., Hindorff, L. A., Hunter, D. J., & McCarthy, M. I. (2009) 'Finding the missing heritability of complex diseases', *Nature*, 461(7265): 747–53.

Pe'er, I., Yelensky, R., Altshuler, D., & Daly, M. J. (2008) 'Estimation of the multiple testing burden for genomewide association studies of nearly all common variants', *Genetic Epidemiology*, 32(4): 381–5.

Perola, M., Sammalisto, S., Hiekkalinna, T., Martin, N. G., Visscher, P. M., Montgomery, G. W., & Benyamin, B. (2007) 'Combined genome scans for body stature in 6,602 European twins: Evidence for common Caucasian loci', *PLoS Genetics*, 3(6): e97.

Pérusse, L., Rankinen, T., Hagberg, J. M., Loos, R. J., Roth, S. M., Sarzynski, M. A., . . . Bouchard, C. (2013) 'Advances in exercise, fitness, and performance genomics in 2012', *Medicine and Science in Sports and Exercise*, 45(5): 824–31.

Pitsiladis, Y., & Wang, G. (2011) 'Necessary advances in exercise genomics and likely pitfalls', *Journal of Applied Physiology*, 110(5): 1150–1.

Pitsiladis, Y., Wang, G., Wolfarth, B., Scott, R., Fuku, N., Mikami, E., . . . Lucia, A. (2013) 'Genomics of elite sporting performance: What little we know and necessary advances', *British Journal of Sports Medicine*, 47(9): 550–5.

Preece, M. A. (1996) 'The genetic contribution to stature', *Hormone Research*, 45(Suppl 2): 56–8.

Pritchard, J. K., & Cox, N. J. (2002) 'The allelic architecture of human disease genes: Common disease-common variant . . . or not?', *Human Molecular Genetics*, 11(20): 2417–23.

Puthucheary, Z., Skipworth, J. R., Rawal, J., Loosemore, M., Van Someren, K., & Montgomery, H. E. (2011) 'The ACE gene and human performance: 12 years on', *Sports Medicine*, 41(6): 433–48.

Reich, D. E., & Lander, E. S. (2001) 'On the allelic spectrum of human disease', *Trends in Genetics*, 17(9): 502–10.

Schork, N. J., Murray, S. S., Frazer, K. A., & Topol, E. J. (2009) 'Common vs. rare allele hypotheses for complex diseases', *Current Opinion in Genetics & Development*, 19(3): 212–9.

Silventoinen, K., Kaprio, J., Lahelma, E., & Koskenvuo, M. (2000) 'Relative effect of genetic and environmental factors on body height: Differences across birth cohorts among Finnish men and women', *American Journal of Public Health*, 90(4): 627–30.

Stranger, B. E., Stahl, E. A., & Raj, T. (2011) 'Progress and promise of genome-wide association studies for human complex trait genetics', *Genetics*, 187(2): 367–83.

Talmud, P. J., Hingorani, A. D., Cooper, J. A., Marmot, M. G., Brunner, E. J., Kumari, M., . . . Humphries, S. E. (2010) 'Utility of genetic and non-genetic risk factors in prediction of type 2 diabetes: Whitehall II prospective cohort study', *British Medical Journal*, 340: b4838.

Visscher, P. M., Hill, W. G., & Wray, N. R. (2008) 'Heritability in the genomics era – Concepts and misconceptions', *Nature Reviews Genetics*, 9(4): 255–66.

Xiao, R., & Boehnke, M. (2009) 'Quantifying and correcting for the winner's curse in genetic association studies', *Genetic Epidemiology*, 33(5): 453–62.

Yang, J., Benyamin, B., McEvoy, B. P., Gordon, S., Henders, A. K., Nyholt, D. R., & Madden, P. A. (2010) 'Common SNPs explain a large proportion of the heritability for human height', *Nature Genetics*, 42(7): 565–9.

Yu, K., Chatterjee, N., Wheeler, W., Li, Q., Wang, S., Rothman, N., & Wacholder, S. (2007) 'Flexible design for following up positive findings', *American Journal of Human Genetics*, 81(3): 540–51.

Zhong, H., & Prentice, R. L. (2008) 'Bias-reduced estimators and confidence intervals for odds ratios in genome-wide association studies', *Biostatistics*, 9(4): 621–34.

27

DIVERSIFICATION AND DELIBERATE PLAY DURING THE SAMPLING YEARS

Jean Côté and Karl Erickson

Specialization in one sport and intense investment in sport-specific practice is, without any doubt, a prerequisite for the attainment of expertise. The timing of specialization and the consequences of early specialization on athlete development are, however, questions that have created debates in the last several years (Baker *et al.*, 2009; Malina, 2010; Wiersma, 2000). Governing bodies around the world face the challenge of structuring a youth sport system that regularly develops elite athletes at the professional and international levels. To reach this goal, governing bodies are adapting models of development that focus on long-term athlete development, institutionalization, elitism, early selection, and early specialization, instead of focusing on the inherent enjoyment of participating in various forms of sport and the natural challenges and skill development opportunities that result from playing sports during childhood (Côté *et al.*, 2011).

The restricted number of available spots on professional and national teams limits the odds of competing at an elite level of performance in sport, even for young athletes who are investing in sport at an early age. As an example, we will use statistics from the United States to depict the low odds of a pathway from youth and college sport to a professional career in sport. According to recent numbers published by ESPN, there are approximately 30 million youths between the ages of six and 17 who play organized sport each year in the United States (Kelley & Carchia, 2013). At the other end of the spectrum, the number of professional athletes in the United States is estimated to be around 18,000 (Wiki Answers, 2013). Based on average career lengths (4.8 years) in the major professional sports (RAM Financial Group, 2013), we can make an educated guess that approximately 3,600 professional athletic positions are available every year in the United States. If we consider the number of youths involved in sport (i.e., 30 million), the conversion rate from youth sport participation to professional sport is therefore slightly over 0.01 per cent. These low odds are also very conservative considering that youths from all over the world, and not only the United States, will compete for spots on professional teams in leagues like the NHL, NBA, and MLB. Whichever way we look at the numbers, the pathway from youth sport participation to elite performance is a rare occurrence and very unpredictable.

We recognize that not all 30 million youth sport participants in the United States dream of a professional sport career; however, when examining the odds of becoming a professional athlete from programs that are specifically designed for elite performance in specific sports (e.g., high school sport programs in the United States) the numbers do not get much better, with percentages that vary between 0.02 per cent in women's basketball to 0.46 per cent in the MLB (Malina,

305

2010). The odds of achieving a professional status in elite sport in the United States illustrates a situation that is similar for ice hockey players in Canada (Parcells, 2002) and would likely be paralleled in other countries around the world. Therefore, the conversion rate, even from specialized elite sport programs for youths of older ages (13 and up), to professional sport remains very low.

These statistics provide uncomfortable facts about the structure of youth sport systems that are based on early specialization, intensity of practice, and sole focus on the development of sport skills during childhood. Implicit with an approach that focuses on elite performance in youth sport is the assumption that earlier and increased training during childhood will provide a performance advantage to children by allowing them to be chosen for "select" teams and will eventually increase their chance to climb to the top in adult sports. This approach to youth sport organization is based on an adult competitive sport model that is characterized by a limited number of available spots in the highest level of competition, whether it be professional leagues or Olympic teams. It is important to consider the consequences of such an approach on more than 99 per cent of youths who participate in these programs. Youth sport programs should not be built solely around the variables that affect skill development and performance (e.g., amount of practice), but need to be considered from a psychosocial perspective (e.g., enjoyment, personal development) as well, especially considering the impact of youth sport programs on the quality of the experience and retention of all the young people involved. The psychosocial environment of youth sport affects the experience of young athletes and, of particular relevance to the consistent development of sport expertise, eventually the talent pool of committed athletes that are willing to invest in elite performance.

There are a number of problems with youth programs that focus solely on skill acquisition at a young age and on the performance of a few athletes who reach the pinnacle of elite sport 15 to 20 years after their first involvement in sport. Several review articles (Baker, 2003; Côté et al., 2009a, 2009b; Hill & Hansen, 1988; Malina, 2010; Martindale et al., 2005) have been published in the last several years that highlight the negative effects of early specialization and the positive impact of sampling (including diversity of sport and deliberate play) during childhood. These reviews reinforce the idea that youth sport programs that focus solely on skill development in one sport during childhood limit their impact on expertise development by negatively affecting the overall number of children who participate in sport and reducing the pool of talented teenagers.

The developmental model of sport participation (DMSP; Côté, 1999; Côté & Abernethy, 2012) provides a flexible developmental framework that focuses on the transitions from play to practice and from diversity to intensity throughout development. The DMSP consists of three stages of development towards sport expertise, including the 1) sampling years (ages six through 12), 2) specializing years (ages 13–15), and 3) investment years (ages 16+). The original conceptualization of the DMSP resulted from interviews with parents, coaches, and athletes (Côté, 1999). This model was in line with results from other qualitative studies of athletes' development (e.g., Bloom, 1985; Carlson, 1988) and provided explicit and original propositions that could be quantified and tested empirically. Two new concepts regarding sport involvement throughout the life span emerged from this first step: diversity and deliberate play. The concept of diversity described a level of involvement in different types of sport experiences during childhood, before specialization and intense training in one sport. Indeed, biographical studies of elite athletes in different sports and from different backgrounds support the idea that being involved in different sports during childhood is linked to long-term participation and elite performance in sport (Bloom, 1985). The concept of deliberate play was described by elite athletes (Côté, 1999) as sport activities they engaged in during childhood that were inherently enjoyable and differed from organized sport and adult-led practices. Deliberate play activities were a distinctive form

Diversification and deliberate play

of sport activities that added to the breadth of contexts and experiences of the youth sport environment. The concepts of diversity and deliberate play were the main elements of the proposed DMSP and together form the backbone of the sampling years. Several studies of elite athletes have supported the concept of diversity and deliberate play as important elements of youth sport that lay the foundation to the achievement of elite performance (e.g., Baker *et al.*, 2003a; Baker *et al.*, 2005; Berry *et al.*, 2008; Bridge & Toms, 2013; Gulbin *et al.*, 2010; Leite & Sampaio, 2012; Lidor & Lavyan, 2002; Soberlak & Côté, 2003).

The most important aspect of diversity and deliberate play during the sampling years is that these components of sport programs reduce the intensity of involvement in one sport and the need to have selective teams that favor only a chosen number of athletes during childhood. Furthermore, youth sport programs built around the concepts of diversity and play have a protective effect against burnout, dropout, and injuries (Fraser-Thomas *et al.*, 2008a, 2008b; Law *et al.*, 2007; Wall & Côté, 2007). The diversity and play elements of the sampling years remind adults to focus on the needs of all children involved in sport, instead of a "selected" number of children that have been unreliably chosen.

Early specialization has often been described as a preferable pathway to elite performance, since this approach explicitly focuses on the activities that lead to skill development in one sport (Ford *et al.*, 2009). More specifically, early specialization is consistent with Ericsson, Krampe, and Tesch-Römer's (1993) view of deliberate practice suggesting that higher level of performance is achieved when involvement in sport-specific practice starts early and is continued at high-intensity levels. This approach to youth sport involvement focuses on intense and explicit training with the goal of achieving success and long-term elite performance. However, sampling is a more comprehensive concept that implies early involvement in sporting activities that focus on diversity and play and the immediate rewards associated with sport participation. The concepts of diversity and deliberate play as fundamental components of sampling will be described in the following sections.

Diversity

The DMSP suggests a progression in sport for both expert and recreational athletes that is based on a diversity of sport experiences during childhood. The main tenet of the DMSP is that diversity should precede specialization in sport (Côté *et al.*, 2009a, 2009b). The diversity of experiences in the sampling years has not been suggested as a variable that distinguishes between expert and non-expert athletes, but rather as the foundation to future participation in sport at a recreational or elite level (Côté & Abernethy, 2012; Côté *et al.*, 2009a, 2009b). Diversity during childhood sport allows young athletes to experience a range of opportunities and then select (or be selected to) a specific path during adolescence, entering either the recreational years or the specializing years. The advantage of a diversified foundation in sport during the sampling years provides young athletes with a breadth of experience first, without an intense focus on skill acquisition and performance in one sport. Empirical evidence (Busseri *et al.*, 2006; Fredricks & Eccles, 2006; Rose-Krasnor *et al.*, 2006) shows that a breadth of experiences in early development is an indicator of continued involvement in more intense activities later in life and of successful development. Although most sport expertise studies have focused on the absolute amount of time spent in an activity, researchers have acknowledged the importance of understanding better the motivational factors and developmental variables related to why and how a person does certain things (Bloom, 1985; Côté & Abernethy, 2012; Starkes, 2000) – the line of research that focuses on breadth and intensity of youth activites sheds light on this issue.

Reconceptualizing diversity

This interpretation of diversity as opposed to intensity of training in one sport during the sampling years broadens the scope of indicators of early specialization from simply counting the number of sports participated in to including variables related to intensity and precocity of performance. Bohnert, Fredricks, and Randall (2010) suggested in a recent review article that using the total number of activities as the sole indicator of breadth or diversity is problematic because it does not account for the different contexts and different types of experiences within a larger category of activities. For example, children can play soccer on the beach with friends, in a park, or in an organized game with teammates and a coach; although these three activities could be counted as "playing soccer," they take place in three different settings and provide children with different experiences and outcomes. Therefore, indicators of diversity should include variation in settings within the same sport to account for differences in activities, such as level of competition, opportunities for skill building, and social interaction with peers and adults. All in all, the variations in the nature of participation in a specific sport activity should be the marker of early diversity, instead of the crude number of sporting activities one is involved in. Accordingly, a diversity of choice involves participation in multiple sports or different versions of the same sports on a yearly basis, delaying the intensity of one type of training in one sport.

Diversity before specialization

When diversity precedes specialization in sport, it creates conditions that impact the commitment of the young athlete to later invest in sport. In an article that reviews the impact of breadth and intensity in extracurricular activities for the development of youth, Busseri and Rose-Krasner (2009) suggested that diversity before intensity (or specialization) promoted the development of a healthy identity, provided participants the opportunity to self-regulate their involvement, and promoted a wide range of interpersonal skills through exposure to various social settings. Their theoretical suggestions will be adapted below to the context of the DMSP and the achievement of elite performance in sport.

First, being involved in a diversity of sports during childhood can be related to the development of an "achieved identity" (Busseri & Rose-Krasner, 2009; Marcia, 1993). According to Marcia (1993), an "achieved identity" results from the dual processes of exploration first and commitment second, and is linked positively to intra and interpersonal competences. Accordingly, a diversity of sport contexts and experiences during the sampling years provides children with opportunities to experiment with different situations, such as different sports and various positions within a sport, to learn about different sporting demands and abilities, and to find out more about one's own personal abilities and preferences. These diverse experiences help children to transition from exploring different alternatives to making an informed commitment to a specific sport and intense training during adolescence. This "achieved identity," resulting from an initial period of exploration of different activities, provides the strongest foundation for intrapersonal (e.g., confidence, motivation) and interpersonal (e.g., communication, social relationships) competences (Marcia, 1993), both of which are crucial characteristics of expert performers in sport.

Second, diversity of experiences during development is linked to improved self-regulation (Baltes, 1997; Lerner et al., 2001). Consequently, a diversity of sporting experiences during the sampling years will allow children to explore different sports, positions, peer groups, and so on, to eventually select (or be selected in) a specific pathway towards elite performance (specialization years) or recreational participation (recreational years). The exploration of various sport activities during the sampling years helps children to build a flexible repertoire of sport skills, human resources, and personal capabilities that will strengthen their self-regulation and commitment to a specific pathway of sport participation (e.g., elite performance or recreational participation). Research on the development of expertise in music and sport supports the role of self-regulatory and self-initiated motivational processes as critical personal skills of elite performers (Zimmerman, 2006).

Third, a diversity of sport activities is associated with a wider range of exposure to various social settings, ultimately supporting the development of social assets and interpersonal skills (Mahoney *et al.*, 2005). Experiencing sporting activities in different contexts allows children to experiment with a broad range of social contexts, coaches, and peers and to collect valuable information about what these different contexts have to offer in terms of elite performance in sport. The social assets (e.g., connection with others) that are associated with the experimentation of a diversity of experiences in sport during childhood may have multiplicative and compensatory effects that contribute to future elite performance in sport. In fact, being immersed in different social settings during childhood has been acknowledged in the DMSP and different models of expertise (e.g., Bloom, 1985) as a way of focusing and sparking the interests of youth in a specific activity.

Although studies have shown that both early diversity and early specialization pathways can lead to talent development under optimal conditions (e.g. Bridge & Toms, 2013; Ford *et al.*, 2009; Ford & Williams, 2012; Leite & Sampaio, 2012; Lidor & Lavyan, 2002; Moesch *et al.*, 2011; Surya *et al.*, 2012), the review by Busseri and Rose-Krasner (2009) supports the idea that diversity should precede specialization to positively impact personal development and thus affect the long-term retention of young athletes in sport. At a population level, youth sport programs that focus on diversity before specialization may maximize the potential impact that youth sport activities can have on youth development and adult performance in sport. As suggested by the different pathways of the DMSP, the diversity of sport activities during the sampling years should not be seen as a discriminating factor that predicts sport expertise but rather as a foundation to optimal development in an elite performance or recreational pathway. The nurturing of talent through the diversification of sports without an intense focus on performance in one sport during childhood can have more positive outcomes and less negative consequences for all children involved in sport, while still facilitating development toward expertise.

Implications of diversity for successful youth sport programs

Despite the benefits of early diversity and the risks associated with early specialization (Côté *et al.*, 2009a, 2009b; Malina, 2010), the success of sport programs for the development of elite performers continues to be measured, in many countries, by the performance of young athletes who reach elite performance in adulthood – with little attention being provided to more than 99 per cent of young athletes who participate in these sport programs without going on to elite performance. Ford and colleagues (2009; 2012) proposed an early engagement pathway to sport expertise that included "minimal diversity in other sports and high levels of play and practice in the primary domain" (2009, p. 73). This early engagement pathway suggests that young athletes who achieve an elite status in sport early have more chance to achieve elite performance in adulthood.

Several lines of research would not be supportive of the "early engagement" hypothesis by showing that early intensity of training and peak performance is linked to more dropout (Fraser-Thomas *et al.*, 2008a; Wall & Côté, 2007) and early peak performance that does not translate into adult expertise (Barreiros *et al.*, 2012, 2013; Moesh *et al.*, 2011). Because the early engagement hypothesis focuses only on variables related to skill acquisition and performance, it fails to consider variables that affect "disengagement" in sport. The early engagement hypothesis may be supported in sports with a large base of participants, such as soccer in England, where dropout rates and disengagement are seen as natural consequences or "collateral damage" that result from an effective system of talent development (Brown & Potrac, 2009). However, the selection of certain athletes at a young age for more intense training regimes excludes a large number of children from opportunities for developing into elite athletes and reduces the pool of potential elite athletes from an early age (Côté et al., 2011). Considering that performance in a given sport during childhood is a poor predictor of later adult performance (Vaeyens et al., 2009), it is more important that sport programs in childhood focus on *retaining* athletes than on achieving a high level of current performance.

Just as diversity is to be considered in light of the different contexts in which sport participation takes places, so too must the nature and characteristics of the activities constituting participation in a given sport context be considered. Whereas deliberate practice has received considerable attention in the study of sport expertise, the remainder of this chapter is devoted to discussion of a sport activity of particular relevance to the sampling years and sport expertise development – i.e., deliberate play.

Deliberate play

Several authors have analyzed and discussed the type of activities that have the most significant impact on talent development in sport. Côté, Erickson, and Abernethy (2013) recently reviewed this literature and suggested a taxonomy of activities that could be generally categorized as either practice or play. The fundamental difference between practice and play resides in the goal that the activity aims to achieve in a specific sporting situation. The goal of practice activities is to improve performance, whereas the goal of play activities is to have fun. The various practice and play activities that constitute sport fulfill different needs in youth and ultimately affect their current and future sport involvement. The intrinsically motivating and self-directed nature of primarily play-oriented activities contrasts with the outcome-oriented and often adult-driven nature of mainly practice-oriented activities.

Côté and colleagues (2013) suggested that the developmental activities of youth in sport can be categorized along two axes; first, the social structure of the activity and second, the personal value the activity provides to the participants. The first axis shows the amount of instruction and input that is vested by supervising adult(s) (i.e., the coach) vs. the participating youth. At one end of this axis there are sport activities where adults have minimal roles in providing instructions, as in play activities. At the other end of the axis there are sport activities in which adults set the direction and provide instruction in a structured environment, such as the structured practices of organized sport. A second axis relates to the personal values associated with an activity, varying from extrinsic to intrinsic values. Extrinsic values describe activities that are performed with the goal of improving skills or performance (e.g., practice), whereas intrinsic values symbolize activities that are done for inherent enjoyment (e.g., play). When combined, these two axes form a matrix in which the prototype activities of youth sport can be located, and a distinct learning context emerges. Accordingly, the prototype activities of deliberate practice (Ericsson et al., 1993), play practice (Griffin & Butler, 2005; Launder, 2001), spontaneous practice (Livingstone, 2002), and deliberate play (Côté, 1999; Côté et al., 2007) result from the intersection of these two axes. While much has been written about the effect of practice on skill development and performance, we will focus here on the role of intrinsically valued, youth-led activity (e.g., play) on the development of talent in sport.

Contribution of deliberate play to expertise development

Support for the positive role of youth-led activities such as deliberate play in the development of sport expertise is found within several bodies of literature. First, researchers have examined the occurrence of these activities during the development of current sport experts. A number of studies employing retrospective designs to examine the developmental histories of elite and expert athletes have reported high levels of participation in deliberate play activities during childhood (e.g., Baker *et al.*, 2003a, 2003b; Berry *et al.*, 2008; Soberlak & Côté, 2003). For example, in their retrospective study of the developmental activities of expert vs. less-skilled tactical decision makers in professional Australian football, Berry and colleagues (2008) found that athletes in both groups had accumulated well over 1,000 hours of deliberate play on average before the initiation of their professional careers. Additionally, expert decision makers accumulated significantly more hours of deliberate play in invasion-type games during their development than did the less-skilled decision makers. Taken together, these retrospective data from multiple studies suggest that participation in high amounts of deliberate play and relatively low amounts of deliberate practice during childhood can contribute to, or at least does not impede, the eventual acquisition of sport expertise (Côté *et al.*, 2009b).

While studies tracing the developmental pathways of sport experts suggest a role for deliberate play activities during the early stages of talent development, the nature of this role – that is, how participation in play contributes to sport expertise development – is also of interest. One aspect of this contribution may include setting a motivational, psychological, and social foundation for continued sport participation and future engagement in necessary deliberate practice activities. Motivationally, it has been suggested that individuals' motivational orientation is largely set by age 12 (Fry, 2001). Given the strong motivational requirements of expertise development (Abbott & Collins, 2004; Baker & Horton, 2004) and the well-established influence of contextual factors on children's motivation (Weiss & Amorose, 2008), the activities of childhood and the social environments in which these activities take place may thus have a substantial, lasting impact on athletes' long-term willingness and desire to pursue an expertise development pathway. In particular, Côté, Lidor, and Hackfort (2009b) postulated that participation in high amounts of deliberate play – autonomously regulated and targeted purely at in-the-moment enjoyment – during childhood provides a solid base of intrinsic motivation on which to ground self-regulated participation in future sport activities that may not be as inherently enjoyable.

Psychologically, the study of children's play has highlighted the potential for participation in play contexts to foster what might be termed "metaskills" (Lester & Russell, 2008; Pellegrini *et al.*, 2007; Smith, 2010). Rather than specific, structured response patterns, these metaskills include the capacity to adapt and adjust to new circumstances, to productively seek solutions in unpredictable circumstances, and to self-regulate engagement with other people and the environment. In essence, play helps children learn how to learn. This then sets the stage for functional adaptation to future learning demands, as sport performance becomes increasingly complex and challenging on the path toward expertise (Abbott & Collins, 2004; Jonker *et al.*, 2012). Studies of the psychological characteristics of expert athletes often describe this ability to deal with challenging circumstances (e.g., resilience, mental toughness, etc.) as a key feature of expert performance (e.g., Durand-Bush & Salmela, 2002; Gould *et al.*, 2002).

Socially, the child-led nature of deliberate play is a key component of its unique contribution to development. Without a coach to organize, structure, and regulate both the task and social environment, children in play are exposed to more uncontrolled and diverse social situations unmediated by adult intervention (for good or bad) (Lester & Russell, 2008; Smith, 2010). Inherent in this experience then is the autonomy to negotiate social interactions for both social and functional (i.e., keep the game running, work with teammates, etc.) aims (Jarvis, 2007). Children themselves are thus afforded the opportunity to develop and practice taking responsibility for the nature of their own social participation. Based on an extensive review of peer and group research in youth sport, Bruner, Eys, and Turnnidge (2013) suggested that these early social experiences with peers in sport are particularly influential for both continued sport participation and the development of interpersonal skills. Later in development these interpersonal skills become critical to expert performance (Gould *et al.*, 2002), with respect to both intra-team processes in team sports and the ability to work with and establish productive relationships with significant others in the performance domain (i.e., coaches). Thus, rather than competing with deliberate practice as contributors to expertise development, participation in high amounts of sport play during childhood (i.e., sampling years) may actually facilitate participation in, and benefit, deliberate practice at later stages of development. Such a view may explain the transition from high play and low practice to low play and high practice seen in the developmental histories of a number of expert athletes (e.g., Berry *et al.*, 2008; Soberlak & Côté, 2003).

In addition to the role child-led activities may play in setting an early foundation for future sport participation and practice activities, deliberate play may in and of itself represent a developmentally functional skill acquisition process or mechanism. The particular characteristics of child-led play activities create a unique context for technical and tactical learning, particularly suited to the developmental level of children. For example, by nature, play contexts expose children to unpredictable situations, and their intrinsically motivated objectives provide the freedom from actual or perceived performance pressure constraints to explore, experiment, and occasionally fail within this unpredictability. Non-sport studies of children's play (see Lester & Russell, 2008; Pellegrini *et al.*, 2007; Smith, 2010) have highlighted flexibility and adaptability in problem solving, and increased understanding of the possibility of multiple solutions for any given situation, as a critical outcome of extended participation in these contexts.

Similar associations between time spent in unstructured play activities and increased creativity in sport were noted by Memmert, Baker, and Bertsch (2010), whereas Chow and colleagues (2013) argued from a nonlinear pedagogy perspective that unstructured sport play during childhood provides optimal conditions for the encouragement of variability, flexibility, and adaptability in motor skill performance that is key to successful athletic performance. Further, studies of motor learning and skill acquisition in sport (Masters & Maxwell, 2004) have revealed performance advantages, particularly in conditions of stress or pressure, for motor skills learned implicitly. Implicit (as opposed to explicit) motor learning refers to performance improvements through practice or repetition but without conscious processing or effort to that end. Thus it is possible, and can be beneficial, to acquire new skills or improve execution of current skills without consciously setting or adhering to performance enhancement objectives. This would seem a consistent fit with the intrinsic, enjoyment-based values driving children's participation in sport play, where children experience high exposure to skill practice opportunities but without the performance improvement objectives typical of coach-led deliberate practice activities (Côté *et al.*, 2013). In this vein, Masters, van der Kamp, and Capio (2013) argue that implicit approaches to motor skill acquisition may be particularly suited to children's levels of cognitive maturity. These authors highlight the significant load placed on executive cognitive functions by explicit (i.e., rule-based) approaches to learning, and suggest that "given the limitations associated with verbal development and rule use by children, skill acquisition approaches that avoid loading working memory are likely to have greater efficacy for motor performance" (Masters *et al.*, 2013, p. 27).

In sum, deliberate play can offer a unique contribution to sport expertise development during the sampling years, as evidenced by high participation in these activities during the development of many sport experts. While further empirical evidence is still needed, the contribution of deliberate play during early stages of expertise development appears to be functional with respect to: 1) providing a motivational, psychological, and social foundation for later stages of expertise development and 2) facilitating developmentally appropriate skill acquisition contexts.

Conclusion

In this chapter, we have attempted to present a developmental account of sport expertise, with particular focus on the early stages of athlete development during childhood. We summarized evidence relating to two aspects of sport participation during childhood: diversity and deliberate play. Both aspects have important long-term implications for sport participation and can make significant contributions to the development of sport expertise.

Just as children are different from adults, any sport expertise development system must also be differentiated to account for these changes through time and the unique maturational demands of child athletes. The model presented in this chapter, highlighting the changing developmental environment of athletes who achieved a high level of performance in sport, has many implications for the design of sport programs. The choice of learning objectives, curriculum sequencing, and teaching methods will need to vary greatly for athletes of different ages. Early sport diversification, high amounts of deliberate play, child-centered coaches and parents, and being around peers that are involved in sport appear to be essential characteristics of environments for young children that encourage their later investment in deliberate practice activities. Accordingly, we suggest that an optimal, developmental progression for producing elite athletes should include diversity and exploration before specialization and intense training in one sport. Within the diversity of early sport experiences, this optimal, developmental progression should also incorporate high levels of participation in deliberate play activities prior to transitioning to an emphasis on deliberate practice activities with specialization. While expert performance can be reached without early diversification and deliberate play, we argue that the incorporation of these two critical elements into the early stages of sport development pathways effectively facilitates expert performance development at a much lower social cost.

Author notes

The writing of this chapter was supported by a standard research grant from the Social Sciences and Humanities Research Council of Canada (SSHRC Grant # 410-2014-0038). This chapter was written while Jean Côté was a visiting professor in Florianopolis, Brazil, at Universidade Federal de Santa Catarina, Centro De Desporto.

References

Abbott, A., & Collins, D. (2004) 'Eliminating the dichotomy between theory and practice in talent identification and development: Considering the role of psychology', *Journal of Sports Sciences*, 22: 395–408.
Baker, J. (2003) 'Early specialization in youth sport: A requirement for adult expertise?', *High Ability Studies*, 14: 85–94.
Baker, J., Cobley, S., & Fraser-Thomas, J. (2009) 'What do we know about early sport specialisation? Not much!', *High Ability Studies*, 20: 77–90.
Baker, J., Côté, J., & Abernethy, B. (2003a) 'Learning from the experts: Practice activities of expert decision makers in sport', *Research Quarterly for Exercise and Sport*, 74: 342–7.
Baker, J., Côté, J., & Abernethy, B. (2003b) 'Sport-specific practice and the development of expert decision-making in team ball sports', *Journal of Applied Sport Psychology*, 15: 12–25.
Baker, J., Côté, J., & Deakin, J. (2005) 'Expertise in ultraendurance triathletes early sport involvement, training structure, and the theory of deliberate practice', *Journal of Applied Sport Psychology*, 17: 64–78.

Baker, J., & Horton, S. (2004) 'A review of primary and secondary influences on sport expertise', *High Ability Studies*, 15: 211–28.

Baltes, P. B. (1997) 'On the incomplete architecture of human ontogeny', *American Psychologist*, 32: 366–80.

Barreiros, A., Côté, J., & Fonseca, A. M. (2012) 'Early to adult sport success: Analyzing athletes' progression in national squads', *European Journal of Sport Science,* (ahead of print): 1–5.

Barreiros, A., Côté, J., & Fonseca, A. M. (2013) 'Training and psychosocial patterns during the early development of Portuguese national team athletes', *High Ability Studies*, 24(1): 49–61.

Berry, J., Abernethy, B., & Côté, J. (2008) 'The contribution of structured activity and deliberate play to the development of expert perceptual and decision-making skill', *Journal of Sport & Exercise Psychology*, 30: 685–708.

Bloom, B. S. (1985) *Developing talent in young people*, New York: Ballantine.

Bohnert, A., Fredricks, J., & Randall, E. (2010) 'Theoretical and methodological considerations capturing unique dimensions of youth organized activity involvement', *Review of Educational Research*, 80: 576–610.

Bridge, M. W., & Toms, M. R. (2013) 'The specialising or sampling debate: A retrospective analysis of adolescent sports participation in the UK', *Journal of Sports Sciences*, 31: 87–96.

Brown, G., & Potrac, P. (2009) '"You've not made the grade, son": De-selection and identity disruption in elite level youth football', *Soccer & Society*, 10: 143–59.

Bruner, M. W., Eys, M. A., & Turnnidge, J. (2013) 'Peer and group influences in youth sport', in J. Côté & R. Lidor (eds) *Conditions of children's talent development in sport*, Morgantown, WV: Fitness Information Technology, 157–78.

Busseri, M. A., & Rose-Krasnor, L. (2009) 'Breadth and intensity: Salient, separable, and developmentally significant dimensions of structured youth activity involvement', *British Journal of Developmental Psychology*, 27: 907–33.

Busseri, M. A, Rose-Krasnor, L., Willoughby, T., & Chalmers, H. (2006) 'A longitudinal examination of breadth and intensity of youth activity involvement and successful development', *Developmental Psychology*, 42: 1313–26.

Carlson, R. C. (1988) 'The socialization of elite tennis players in Sweden: An analysis of players' backgrounds and development', *Sociology of Sport Journal*, 5: 241–56.

Chow, J. Y., Davids, K., Renshaw, I., & Button, C. (2013) 'The acquisition of movement skill in children through nonlinear pedagogy', in J. Côté & R. Lidor (eds) *Conditions of children's talent development in sport*, Morgantown, WV: Fitness Information Technology, 41–60.

Côté, J. (1999) 'The influence of the family in the development of talent in sport', *The Sport Psychologist*, 13: 395–417.

Côté, J., & Abernethy, B. (2012) 'A developmental approach to sport expertise', in S. Murphy (ed) *The Oxford handbook of sport and performance psychology*, New York: Oxford University Press, 435–47.

Côté, J., Baker, J., & Abernethy, B. (2007) 'Practice and play in the development of sport expertise', in R. Eklund & G. Tenenbaum (eds) *Handbook of sport psychology*, 3rd ed., Hoboken, NJ: Wiley, 184–202.

Côté, J., Coakley, C., & Bruner, M. W. (2011) 'Children's talent development in sport: Effectiveness or efficiency?', in S. Dagkas & K. Armour (eds) *Inclusion and exclusion through youth sport*, London, UK: Routledge, 172–85.

Côté, J., Erickson, K., & Abernethy, B. (2013) 'Practice and play in sport development', in J. Côté & R. Lidor (eds) *Condition of children's talent development in sport*, Morgantown, WV: Fitness Information Technology, 9–20.

Côté, J., Horton, S., MacDonald, D., & Wilkes, S. (2009a) 'The benefits of sampling sports during childhood', *Physical and Health Education Journal*, 74: 6–11.

Côté, J., Lidor, R., & Hackfort, D. (2009b) 'ISSP position stand: To sample or to specialize? Seven postulates about youth sport activities that lead to continued participation and elite performance', *International Journal of Sport and Exercise Psychology*, 9: 7–17.

Durand-Bush, N., & Salmela, J. H. (2002) 'The development and maintenance of expert athletic performance: Perceptions of world and Olympic champions', *Journal of Applied Sport Psychology*, 14: 154–71.

Ericsson, K. A., Krampe, R. T., & Tesch-Römer, C. (1993) 'The role of deliberate practice in the acquisition of expert performance', *Psychological Review*, 100(3): 363.

Ford, P. R., Ward, P, Hodges, N. J., & Williams, A. M. (2009) 'The role of deliberate practice and play in career progression in sport: The early engagement hypothesis', *High Ability Studies*, 20: 67–75.

Diversification and deliberate play

Ford, P. R., & Williams, A. M. (2012) 'The developmental activities engaged in by elite youth soccer players who progressed to professional status compared to those who did not', *Psychology of Sport and Exercise*, 13: 349–52.

Fraser-Thomas, J., Côté, J., & Deakin, J. (2008a) 'Understanding dropout and prolonged engagement in adolescent competitive sport', *Psychology of Sport and Exercise*, 9: 645–62.

Fraser-Thomas, J., Côté, J., & Deakin, J. (2008b) 'Examining adolescent sport dropout and prolonged engagement from a developmental perspective', *Journal of Applied Sport Psychology*, 20: 318–33.

Fredricks, J. A., & Eccles, J. S. (2006) 'Extracurricular involvement and adolescent adjustment: Impact of duration, number of activities, and breadth of participation', *Applied Developmental Science*, 10: 132–46.

Fry, M. D. (2001) 'The development of motivation in children', in G. C. Roberts (ed) *Advances in motivation in sport and exercise*, Champaign, IL: Human Kinetics, 51–78.

Gould , D., Dieffenbach, K., & Moffett, A. (2002) 'Psychological characteristics and their development in Olympic champions', *Journal of Applied Sport Psychology*, 14: 172–204.

Griffin, L. L., & Butler, J. I. (eds) (2005) *Teaching games for understanding: Theory, research, and practice*, Champaign, IL: Human Kinetics.

Gulbin, J. P., Oldenziel, K. E., Weissensteiner, J. R., & Gagné, F. (2010) 'A look through the rear view mirror: Developmental experiences and insights of high performance athletes', *Talent Development & Excellence*, 2: 149–64.

Hill, G. M., & Hansen, G. F. (1988) 'Specialization in high school sports – The pros and cons', *Journal of Physical Education, Recreation, & Dance*, 59: 76–9.

'How many professional athletes are there in the US?', *Wiki Answers*. Online. Retrieved from http://wiki. answers.com/Q/How_many_professional_athletes_are_there_in_the_US#slide2 (accessed 16 November, 2013).

Jarvis, P. (2007) 'Dangerous activities within an invisible playground: A study of emergent male football play and teachers' perspectives of outdoor free play in the early years of primary school', *International Journal of Early Years Education*, 15: 245–59.

Jonker, L., Elferink-Gemser, M. T., de Roos, I. M., & Visscher, C. (2012) 'The role of reflection in sport expertise', *The Sport Psychologist*, 26: 224–42.

Kelley, B., & Carchia, C. (2013) '"Hey, data data – Swing!" The hidden demographics of youth sports', *ESPN*. Online. Retrieved from http://espn.go.com/espn/story/_/id/ 9469252/hidden-demographics-youth-sports-espn-magazine (accessed 10 October, 2013).

Launder, A. G. (2001) *Play practice: The games approach to teaching and coaching sports*, Champaign, IL: Human Kinetics.

Law, M. P., Côté, J., & Ericsson, K. A. (2007) 'Characteristics of expert development in rhythmic gymnastics: A retrospective study', *International Journal of Sport and Exercise Psychology*, 5: 82–103.

Leite, N., & Sampaio, J. (2012) 'Long-term athletic development across different age groups and gender from Portuguese basketball players', *International Journal of Sports Science and Coaching*, 7: 285–300.

Lerner, R. M., Freund, A. M., De Stefanis, I., & Habermas, T. H. (2001) 'Understanding developmental regulation in adolescence: The use of the selection, optimization, and compensation model', *Human Development*, 44: 29–50.

Lester, S., & Russell, W. (2008) 'Play for a change: Play, policy and practice: A review of contemporary perspectives – Summary report', *Play England*. Online. Retrieved from www.playengland.org.uk/resources/play-for-a-change-symmary.pdf (accessed 15 November, 2013).

Lidor, R., & Lavyan, N. Z. (2002) 'A retrospective picture of early sport experiences among elite and near-elite Israeli athletes: Developmental and psychological perspectives', *International Journal of Sport Psychology*, 33: 269–89.

Livingstone, D. W. (2002) 'Mapping the iceberg'. Online. Retrieved from www.nall.ca/res/54David Livingstone.pdf (accessed 15 November, 2013).

Mahoney, J. L., Larson, R. W., Eccles, J. S., & Lord, H. (2005) 'Organized activities as developmental contexts for children and adolescents', in J. L. Mahoney, R. W. Larson, & J. S. Eccles (eds) *Organized activities as contexts for development: Extracurricular activities, after-school and community programs*, Mahwah, NJ: Erlbaum, 3–22.

Malina, R. M. (2010) 'Early sport specialization: Roots, effectiveness, risks', *Current Sports Medicine Reports*, 9: 364–71.

Marcia, J. E. (1993) 'The ego identity status approach to ego identity', in J. E. Marcia, A. S. Waterman, D. R. Matteson, S. L. Archer, & J. L. Orlofsky (eds) *Ego identity: A handbook of psychosocial research*, New York: Springer-Verlag, 3–41.

Martindale, R. J., Collins, D., & Daubney, J. (2005) 'Talent development: A guide for practice and research within sport', *Quest*, 57(4): 353–75.

Masters, R., van der Kamp, J., & Capio, C. (2013) 'Implicit motor learning by children', in J. Côté & R. Lidor (eds) *Conditions of children's talent development in sport*, Morgantown, WV: Fitness Information Technology, 21–40.

Masters, R.S.W., & Maxwell, J.P. (2004) 'Implicit motor learning, reinvestment and movement disruption: What you don't know won't hurt you?', in A. M. Williams & N. J. Hodges (eds) *Skill acquisition in sport: Research, theory and practice*, London: Routledge, 207–28.

Memmert, D., Baker, J., & Bertsch, C. (2010) 'Play and practice in the development of sport-specific creativity in team ball sports', *High Ability Studies*, 21: 3–18.

Moesch, K., Elbe, A. M., Hauge, M.L.T., & Wikman, J. M. (2011) 'Late specialization: The key to success in centimeters, grams, or seconds (cgs) sports', *Scandinavian Journal of Medicine and Science in Sports*, 21: 282–90.

Parcells, J. (2002) 'Chances of making it in pro hockey', *Ontario Minor Hockey Association*. Online. Retrieved from www.nepeanhockey.on.ca/Docs/General/MakingIt.pdf (accessed 7 January, 2013).

Pellegrini, A. D., Dupuis, D., & Smith, P. K. (2007) 'Play in evolution and development', *Developmental Review*, 27: 261–76.

RAM Financial Group. 'Athlete services', Retrieved from www.ramfg.com/RAM-Financial-Group-Solutions-Professional-Athletes-Athletes-Services (accessed 16 November, 2013).

Rose-Krasnor, L., Busseri, M.A., Willoughby, T., Chalmers, H. (2006) 'Breadth and intensity of youth activity involvement as contexts for positive development', *Journal of Youth and Adolescence*, 35: 385–499.

Smith, P. K. (2010) *Children and play*, Chichester, UK: Wiley-Blackwell.

Soberlak, P., & Côté, J. (2003) 'The developmental activities of elite ice hockey players', *Journal of Applied Sport Psychology*, 15: 41–9.

Starkes, J. L. (2000) 'The road the expertise: Is practice the only determinant?', *International Journal of Sport Psychology*, 31: 431–51.

Surya, M., Bruner, M. W., MacDonald, D., & Côté, J. (2012) 'A comparison of developmental activities of elite athletes born in large and small cities', *Physical & Health Education Academic Journal*, 4: 1–8.

Vaeyens, R., Gullich, A., Warr, C.R., & Philippaerts, R. (2009) 'Talent identification and promotion programmes of Olympic athletes', *Journal of Sports Sciences*, 27: 1367–80.

Wall, M., & Côté, J. (2007) 'Developmental activities that lead to drop out and investment in sport', *Physical Education and Sport Pedagogy*, 12: 77–87.

Weiss, M. R., & Amorose, A. J. (2008) 'Motivational orientations and sport behavior', in T. S. Horn (ed) *Advances in sport psychology*, 3rd ed., Champaign, IL: Human Kinetics, 115–55.

Wiersma, L.D. (2000) 'Risks and benefits of youth sport specialization: Perspectives and recommendations', *Pediatric Exercise Science*, 12: 13–22.

Wiki Answers (2013). How many professional atheletes are there in the US?, Retrieved from http://wiki. answers.com/Q/How_many_professional_athletes_are_there_in_the_US#slide2 (accessed 16 November, 2013).

Zimmerman, B. J. (2006) 'Development and adaptation of expertise: The role of self-regulatory processes and beliefs', in K. A. Ericsson, N. Charness, P. J. Feltovich, R. R. Hoffman (eds) *The Cambridge handbook of expertise and expert performance*, New York: Cambridge, 705–22.

28

PSYCHOLOGICAL CHARACTERISTICS AND THE DEVELOPING ATHLETE

The importance of self-regulation

Laura Jonker, Marije T. Elferink-Gemser, E. J. Yvonne Tromp, Joseph Baker, and Chris Visscher

The myth of sport expertise

Sport participation and sport expertise are highly valued in many societies. Given the considerable funds countries and sports devote to athlete development, improving our accuracy in identifying those athletes who have a greater potential to reach the highest levels of expertise has become increasingly important. There are several critical questions to consider. How do elite athletes learn to perform at this exceptional level? How can coaches and trainers facilitate athletes' way to the top? Can our knowledge of the development of exceptional performers benefit less-gifted athletes?

The process of developing talent

In order to reach high levels of expertise, athletes not only have to outperform their peers during training and games in youth competition, but also have to fulfill their full potential towards senior competitive levels (Elferink-Gemser & Visscher, 2011). In a relatively long but nevertheless restricted time period (approximately 10 years of training; Ericsson, 1996; Ericsson *et al.*, 1993), youth athletes need to improve sport-specific characteristics enough to be able to not only compete at a high standard as juniors but also actively increase their likelihood of reaching senior elite levels in their sport.

A model of the development of a talented athlete's sport performance over time is shown in Figure 28.1. Modified after Newell (1986), this model shows the hypothetical contribution of person-related, task-related, and environmental characteristics to sport performance in talented athletes. This model is based on the assumption that an athlete needs a specific combination of person-related and environmental characteristics to successfully perform a given sport-specific task. Multidimensional performance characteristics such as anthropometric, physiological, technical, tactical, and psychological factors are considered person-related characteristics (Elferink-Gemser & Visscher, 2011).

Environmental characteristics apply across several levels; for instance, the macrolevel includes variables such as the sport federation or the sport's competition structure, while meso-level and

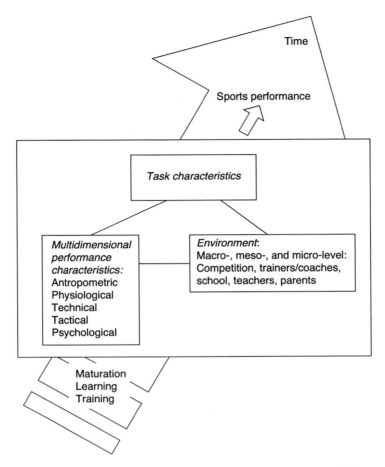

Figure 28.1 Talent development model, including personal, task-related, general characteristics and environment-related characteristics.

microlevel variables include variables such as training facilities and parents or coaches, respectively. As the road to the top is long, to be successful in sports a talented athlete has to continuously improve his or her sport performance over time. The interrelationships between the demands of the task, personal characteristics, and the environment, along with a component of chance define an athlete's development. Along the road to the top, maturation, learning, and training are important components influencing the above mentioned interrelationships. While performance change over time is clearly influenced by maturation (Malina *et al.*, 2005), one of the most powerful determinants of performance improvement is the athlete's exposure to opportunities for learning and training.

The importance of psychological characteristics

Models of skill acquisition and expertise (Baker & Horton, 2004; Ericsson *et al.*, 1993) have emphasized the need for athletes to possess specific psychological characteristics. Baker and Horton (2004) note that differing psychological characteristics are necessary for the acquisition of skill/expertise (e.g., long-term motivation) and the demonstration of this expertise (e.g., the

Importance of self-regulation

ability to regulate emotion and stress). In this chapter we focus on psychological characteristics that appear to facilitate the acquisition of skill over an extended period of time.

Given the extended period of time required to attain expertise (see Ericsson & Towne, 2010), a beneficial motivational profile is clearly necessary. While contemporary motivation researchers have considered this issue from the lens of attribution theory (e.g., Allen, 2012), achievement goal theory (e.g., Harwood *et al.*, 2008), self-efficacy theory (e.g., Feltz *et al.*, 2008), and self-determination theory (e.g., Standage, 2012), among others, what seems clear across these accounts is that a focus on long-term outcomes (e.g., mastery) is superior to a focus on short-term results (Weiss & Chaumeton, 1992). Moreover, studies from personality researchers have suggested differences in the personality traits of expert athletes compared to athletes at lower levels of skill (see Allen *et al.*, 2013 for a review). Regardless of the theoretical perspective taken, without the proper psychological characteristics (e.g., motivation, personality, etc.) an athlete is unlikely to stay involved long enough to acquire the skills necessary for expertise (Ericsson *et al.*, 1993).

However, simple involvement does not seem to be enough to guarantee maximal skill development (Ericsson, 2003; Jonker *et al.*, 2012). In sports with a broad population base of athletes, developing experts must use training and learning opportunities in the most efficient way possible. Over the last decade, an emerging evidence base suggests that a measure of efficient learning is related to an athlete's ability to regulate his or her own learning – in other words, to the athlete's self-regulatory skills. Our studies show that talented athletes who set clear goals and take responsibility for their own learning process in reaching those goals are more successful in fulfilling their potential than athletes who fail to do so (Jonker, 2011).

Self-regulatory skills and talent development

Self-regulation in the context of learning and development reflects an individual's capacity to control his or her learning behavior. Zimmerman defined self-regulation as "the degree to which learners are metacognitively, motivationally and behaviorally proactive participants in their own learning process" (1986, p. 308; 1989, p. 329). In this definition, the metacognitive component relates to awareness of, and knowledge about, one's personal thoughts and feelings (Zimmerman, 1990). Skills such as reflection (i.e., ability to appraise what has been learned and to adapt past knowledge and experiences to improve), planning (i.e., awareness of task demands prior to its execution), self-monitoring (i.e., awareness of actions during task execution), and evaluation (i.e., ability to assess both the processes employed and the finished product after task completion) are frequently mentioned metacognitive skills (Ertmer & Newby, 1996; Hong & O'Neil, 2001; Peltier *et al.*, 2006; Zimmerman, 1990, see Figure 28.2).

The motivational component refers to the degree to which learners are self-efficaciously, autonomously, and intrinsically motivated to attain a specific goal (Zimmerman, 1990), with effort (i.e., willingness to apply oneself to attain the set goal) and self-efficacy (i.e., judgment of capabilities to organize and execute the required actions successfully) as the critical elements (Hong & O'Neil, 2001; Zimmerman, 1990). Through the frequent use of self-regulatory skills, one can optimize the time spent on learning due to an improved ability to prioritize what has to be learned and how it must be learned (Toering *et al.*, 2009). In other words, self-regulatory skills help athletes to learn more efficiently.

The use of self-regulatory skills is associated with success in a range of domains, including sports (Anshel & Porter, 1996; Jonker *et al.*, 2011; Kitsantas & Zimmerman, 2002) and academics (Nota *et al.*, 2004). For example, 12–16-year-old elite athletes use self-regulatory skills more frequently than their peers competing at lower competitive levels (Anshel & Porter, 1996; Jonker

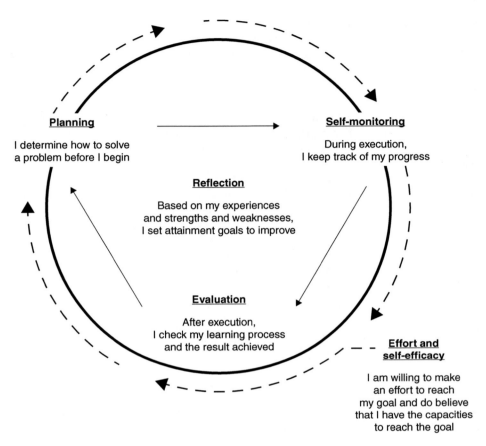

Figure 28.2 The self-regulatory process in phases.

et al., 2011), and more successful students (i.e., higher academic level) outscore their less successful counterparts on self-regulatory skills (Nota et al., 2004). Furthermore, research has shown that most elite athletes are also high academic achievers, and it has been proposed that their increased use of self-regulatory skills may be an underlying mechanism for both their sport and academic achievements (Jonker et al., 2009). Recently, the use of self-regulatory skills has also been related to success in the attainment of senior elite status in sport (Jonker et al., 2012).

The development of self-regulatory skills

Previous studies suggest that metacognitive skills arise as early as four to six years of age and grow in the years thereafter (McCabe et al., 2004; Veenman & Spaans, 2005). From the age of 11 to 12 years, the metacognitive skills of children further develop and transform from a set of domain-specific skills to a more general repertoire that can be used across performance domains (Van der Stel & Veenman, 2008; Veenman & Spaans, 2005). With respect to the motivational component, the age of 12 seems critical for the use of motivational skills, as children after 12 years of age are better able to balance their efforts to succeed and to interpret their capabilities (Boekaerts, 1997; Nicholls, 1978).

Importance of self-regulation

Even though it has been assumed that self-regulatory skills start to develop at a very young age and increase thereafter (McCabe *et al.*, 2004), evidence suggests they do not occur naturally (Boekaerts, 1997). Children are best able to develop self-regulatory skills in a powerful, inspiring, and goal-oriented environment (Boekaerts, 1997), with youth sport proposed to be an optimal setting. Prior work of Perry (1998) subdivides four contextual aspects fostering the development of self-regulation. A context has to 1) have complex tasks, 2) allow students to have a choice in task and level of challenge, 3) provide opportunities for evaluation, and 4) offer opportunities for collaboration. Given its inherent complexity, sport fulfills all or most of these contextual requirements. Regarding the first aspect, a soccer player, for example, has to be familiar with the rules of the game, apply those rules during the game, and meanwhile has to handle the ball and make the right decision at the right moment while facing an opponent who differs from game to game. The second aspect is fulfilled by the fact that athletes can choose the sport in which they want to participate and, to a certain extent, the level of competition (Hidi & Harackiewicz, 2000; Vallerand & Rousseau, 2001). With regard to the third aspect, during their training sessions athletes can be flexible in the extent to which they monitor their performances and their levels of effort related to their goals. Goal setting and appropriate feedback, in particular, are suggested to help athletes develop self-regulatory skills that assist them in positively modifying their learning (Boekaerts & Corno, 2005; Pintrich & Zusho, 2002). In sports, athletes learn from an early age to set short- and long-term attainment goals or to strive to reach for the goals set by the coach. In addition, they receive constant feedback about their performance, not just from the end result of their skill execution (i.e., success vs. failure) but also from the process via feedback from trainers, parents, peers, and other participants. With respect to the fourth aspect, the interplay between trainers, parents, peers, other participants, and the athlete during training sessions requires collaboration. Common behavior among athletes is to coach each other and to collaborate with the coach (Orlick & Partington, 1988; Toering *et al.*, 2011). Furthermore, academic studies investigating the development of self-regulatory skills have shown that environments where students have high levels of control over their learning process are best for developing self-regulatory skills (Eshel & Kohavi, 2003), which is also the case in sports.

Collectively, these studies emphasize the importance of self-regulatory skills for youth in sports. Nevertheless, many athletes and students between 12 and 16 years of age fail to self-regulate effectively (Boekaerts, 1997). Although the existing evidence is relatively robust in emphasizing the importance of self-regulation in distinguishing between elites and non-elites, research examining how these skills develop is surprisingly limited. From 2007 to 2010, our research team tracked over 600 12–17 year-old student-athletes in the 11 most popular sports in The Netherlands (i.e., soccer, field-hockey, volleyball, handball, basketball, baseball, tennis, judo, gymnastics, swimming, speed-skating) to assess their use of self-regulatory skills in general learning contexts (Jonker, 2011). Multilevel modeling (Rasbash *et al.*, 1999) was used to examine the longitudinal development of the use of self-regulatory skills in sport (competitive sport level, number of training hours per week) and academic (academic level) domains (Table 28.1).

The development of reflection and sport expertise

Our data showed that elite athletes (i.e., those who outscore their peers during training and games) outscored their regional peers on reflection and effort at all ages. Studies of talent development in sport have noted the importance of reflection with internationally competing athletes discriminating themselves from their peers competing nationally (Jonker *et al.*, 2010) suggesting that reflection may be a key characteristic for learning among elite athletes, enabling them to comprehend knowledge and skills they have learned and to turn this knowledge and

Laura Jonker et al.

Table 28.1 Means and standard deviations for number of training hours per week, reflection and effort, n and % for academic level and repeating class for the number of measurements per age group subdivided by competitive level.

	n	Sport training▪ (hours/week)		Academic level				Repeating class				Reflection~		Effort~	
				Pre-university		Pre-vocational		Never		Once					
		M	SD	n	%	n	%	n	%	n	%	M	SD	M	SD
Elite athletes[x]															
12-13 years	224	8.1	4.5	176	78.6	48	21.4	207	92.4	17	7.6	4.01	.05	2.98	.04
14 years	279	8.8	4.6	225	80.6	54	19.4	257	92.1	22	7.9	4.04	.05	2.96	.05
15 years	260	9.0	4.7	200	76.9	60	23.1	224	86.2	36	13.8	4.06	.06	2.94	.06
16 years	153	8.9	4.3	123	80.4	30	19.6	128	83.7	25	16.3	4.07	.06	2.91	.06
17 years	69	9.2	4.5	66	95.7	3	4.3	55	79.7	14	20.3	4.09	.06	2.89	.07
Regional athletes[x]															
12-13 years	38	3.2	2.1	26	68.4	12	31.6	36	94.7	2	5.3	3.85	.04	2.84	.04
14 years	79	3.0	2.0	55	69.6	24	30.4	69	87.3	10	12.7	3.85	.04	2.79	.05
15 years	97	3.1	1.8	69	71.1	28	28.9	83	85.6	14	14.4	3.85	.04	2.75	.05
16 years	82	3.5	2.8	54	65.9	28	34.1	62	75.6	20	24.4	3.86	.05	2.71	.05
17 years	38	2.4	1.2	27	71.1	11	28.9	20	52.6	18	47.4	3.84	.03	2.64	.04
Non-athletes[x]															
12-13 years	13	0.0	0.0	8	61.5	5	38.5	12	92.3	1	7.7	3.74	.00	2.72	.03
14 years	27	0.0	0.0	15	55.6	12	44.4	19	70.4	8	29.6	3.73	.00	2.66	.05
15 years	34	0.0	0.0	20	58.8	14	41.2	27	79.4	7	20.6	3.72	.00	2.62	.04
16 years	32	0.0	0.0	18	56.3	14	43.8	21	65.6	11	34.4	3.72	.00	2.57	.05
17 years	20	0.0	0.0	15	75.0	5	25.0	12	60.0	8	40.0	3.71	.00	2.52	.05

Notes: ^ 1 missing value. # 2 missing values. [x] The database of the Netherlands Olympic Committee * Netherlands Sports Federation (NOC*NSF) was used to deter mine the competitive level of the athletes. ▪ Sport training was subdivided into four training categories (i.e., category 0: ≤ 3 hours per week, category 1: > 3 hours per week, category 2: > 6 hours per week, category 4: > 9 hours per week). 68.8% of the elite youth athletes spent more than 6 hours per week on training (i.e., upper 2 training categories), 73.3% of the non-elite athletes spent less than 3 hours per week on training (i.e., lowest training category). [+] The schools' databases were used to recruit whether athletes were involved in the pre-university or pre-vocational system and the respondents answered questions on whether they had ever had to repeat class. Repeating class means that they have had to repeat a full year of study because of insufficient grades on two or more classes. ~ Mean scores of reflection and effort are based on multilevel model parameters (i.e., age x competitive level x training category for reflection and age x competitive level x training category x repeating class for effort).

experience into action to improve future performances (Ertmer & Newby, 1996; Jonker *et al.*, 2010; Peltier *et al.*, 2006; Toering *et al.*, 2009). Through the use of reflection, athletes can optimize time spent on learning, which may be necessary for realizing one's potential, particularly in high-performance athletes (Ericsson, 2003).

Extending this work, our longitudinal data showed that elite athletes increase their scores on reflection between 12 and 17 years – the reflection scores of regional athletes and non-athletes were more stable over this time period in interaction with the number of hours athletes spend on training per week. Relative to skill development in sports and the attainment of expertise, this is an interesting finding, as prior research suggested that reflection at junior ages (12–18 years of age for most sports) predicts those who go on to attain senior international status. In a study examining how reflection scores among athletes at a junior competitive level (i.e., 2.5 years before the transition to senior level) affected the likelihood of attaining expertise at senior ages, Jonker and colleagues (2010) proposed that those who become senior (i.e., elite adult) athletes used greater reflection as junior athletes to make use of prior experiences, set goals of improvement accordingly, and reach these goals in an innovative manner to outdo their competitors. Another interesting result was related to training hours and the development of reflection – athletes who spent more hours per week on training showed an increased use of reflection.

The development of effort and sport expertise

A similar result was observed for effort. Although the use of effort declined for all athletes between 12 and 17 years of age, athletes who spent more time on training per week and were performing at a higher competitive level (elite athletes) showed a less steep decline in the development of effort. Although this may seem counterintuitive, the general decline in effort between 12 and 17 years of age may be related to the fact that, from the age of 12, people in general are better able to balance their efforts to succeed and to interpret their capabilities related to the task (Bandura, 1997; Boekaerts, 1997; Multon et al., 1991; Nicholls, 1978). In relation to the development of effort, reflection, competitive level, and training hours, it may well be the case that elite athletes are very conscious about how much effort they have to put forth within their available time frame to reach their goals. More specifically, elite athletes do not put forth effort mindlessly, but seem to use reflective thinking to be able to do more within a similar number of training hours, or have similar results in fewer hours by putting forth effort consciously related to their goals.

The importance of effort in elite sports has been highlighted in prior research; Anshel and Porter (1996) reported that elite athletes were more willing to practice regularly and with optimal effort and concentration than regional athletes. Toering and colleagues (2009) showed that 12–16-year-old elite youth soccer players were more willing to put forth effort than their regional peers. Ericsson and colleagues' deliberate practice framework (1993) emphasizes the need for developing experts to maintain optimal effort through their commitment to deliberate practice. These findings were extended by Ford and colleagues (Ford et al., 2009), who reinforced the relationship between accumulated training hours during the talent years (15 years of age) and performance level reached by the adult (i.e., senior) athlete. In our research, elite athletes outperformed their less-gifted peers on effort at all ages.

Practical implications

In the introduction of this chapter we asked a few questions. How do elite athletes learn to perform at exceptional level? How can coaches facilitate talented athletes on their way to the top? And how can knowledge from exceptional performers benefit less-gifted athletes? Based on research examining the use of self-regulatory skills, we can make well-educated guesses about the answers to these questions.

How do elite athletes learn to perform at exceptional levels?

This chapter suggests the possibility of measuring the learning potential of 12–17-year-old elite athletes. Through continuous research in the field of talent development, we seem better and better able to distinguish between more and less talented athletes, but still struggle to determine which athletes have the most potential to become future internationals. Ensuring talented athletes fulfill their potential is related to multiple tasks and personal and environment-related characteristics (Huijgen *et al.*, 2009; Kannekens *et al.*, 2011; Roescher *et al.*, 2010). From a self-regulation perspective, learning more efficiently by means of reflection and putting forth effort into aspects most closely related to performance goals have obvious benefits. Scoring high on reflection is beneficial in knowing which task characteristics are required to perform well and setting clear goals. It also helps in directing focus to improve those personal performance characteristics that are required for top performance and figuring out how to convince environmental agents (e.g., parents, trainers, coaches) to provide the help needed.

Scoring high on effort is obviously needed to sustain the multiple hours of training required for adult expertise. Data from our research program underscore this proposition with talented athletes striving to attain senior elite status, outscoring their regional and non-athletic peers on reflection and effort. In their teenage years, their scores on these psychological characteristics increased with age. Moreover, the potential for athletes to learn and improve by using reflection seems to be an important characteristic of athletes who are more likely to make it to senior international level (Jonker *et al.*, 2012).

How can coaches and trainers assist talented athletes on their way to the top?

Trainers and coaches play an important role in stimulating athletes to set improvement goals and providing them with the high-quality feedback necessary to improve their sport performance. This way of coaching may also help in the development of effort and reflection (Jonker *et al.*, 2012).

Autonomy-supportive coaching practices that involve athletes in the processes of goal setting and feedback, and that take athletes' developmental phases into account, seem advantageous (Van Ark *et al.*, 2010). We recommend that coaches involve their athletes in the process of goal setting and feedback from a young age, instead of trying to impose their performance standards on the athletes. One way to do so is by asking open questions before, during, and after training about sport-specific aspects and how to improve them. This autonomy-supportive way of coaching is assumed to stimulate young athletes to develop reflection skills, keeping them motivated and willing to put forth effort from which they benefit during their talent years. In this perspective, the value of taking an individual approach in the field of talent development must be emphasized. Not only do athletes differ in their use of reflective thinking, as athletes with lower levels of reflection and effort should be stimulated to be reflective and effortful, the very best athletes seem not to be satisfied with just meeting the demands of the commonly established standards in their sport and make use of reflective thinking even more, as they continuously look for new ways to reinvent themselves.

Coaches must be sensitive enough to recognize those athletes, value their learning process objectively, and provide them with space to follow their own developmental path. In addition, the value of taking an individual perspective is not only related to the athletes' levels of reflection and effort; athletes all have personal characteristics and operate in individual environments that interact as a dynamical system (Newell, 1986). More specifically, based on athletes' prior experiences and personal strengths and weaknesses, the achievement goals set in order to progress differ between athletes. Every individual has his or her own personal characteristics, and is considered to be part of a personal environment (e.g., coach, peers, parents, school). Based on the tenets of dynamical systems theory (Newell, 1986; see also Chapter 3), sport performance is ultimately composed of several interacting factors, such as the task, multidimensional performance characteristics, and the environment (Elferink-Gemser *et al.*, 2004). This individual approach during training challenges coaches to design individual training schemes for athletes to further personal development.

Furthermore, athletes should be stimulated to use their reflective thinking skills outside the sport environment, as this fosters their performances in other domains (e.g., academics).

Nowadays, another way to provide athletes with direct high quality feedback may be by the use of video feedback or other digital tools. For example in Dutch youth national soccer teams, feedback after training and games is provided by showing athletes clips related to the individual and team goals set in advance.

Can knowledge from exceptional performers benefit less-gifted athletes?

This last question relates to how mainstream youth can benefit from the way elite athletes approach learning and performance. It is important to emphasize that developing athletes not only operate in sporting domains, but also in education and other social domains that are elements of normal development. The sport context is considered an optimal environment for youth to develop self-regulatory skills and benefit from goal setting and feedback. In sports, athletes learn from an early age to set short- and long-term goals, or to reach the goals set by the coach. These skills may have relevance for other domains of life, as supported by studies showing that talented athletes not only perform well in sports but also at school (Jonker *et al.*, 2009).

In academia, however, an above average number of mainstream students have difficulty using self-regulatory skills (Veenman *et al.*, 2005) and most mainstream students have trouble deciding what the most important material to learn is. In addition, the feedback provided by the teacher is more often absent or delayed and based on the performance outcome (e.g., as expressed in final grades). By using self-regulatory skills, students may be better able to recognize the most important parts of the study material, and to match these demands to their own strengths and weaknesses, instead of learning everything mindlessly (Martín *et al.*, 2008). Our studies show that regardless of the level at which sport is played, 12–17-year-old athletes who spent close to three to six hours a week on training showed an increased use of self-regulatory skills (Jonker *et al.*, 2011). Training at a young age can be considered a learning process in which the main focus is on the development of new skills (Côté, 1999), which includes self-regulation.

Future directions for research on the role of psychological factors in developing expertise

Despite the overwhelming acceptance that psychological characteristics are critically important for the development of expertise, there is surprisingly little research exploring these factors. In this final section we highlight several limitations to current understanding and note areas for future research.

The need for more and better study designs

Much of the research exploring the role of psychological characteristics in elite and high-performance sport has been cross-sectional, exploring athlete characteristics at a single point in time. Designs of this nature are highly valuable; however, their potential to increase our understanding of cause and effect is limited. Research by our group (e.g., Jonker, 2011; Jonker *et al.*, 2011; Jonker *et al.*, 2012) has begun to examine these research questions longitudinally, but more work is needed. The present chapter sheds light on whether elite athletes are able to compete at a high competitive level because of an innate ability to self-regulate, or whether they have developed their self-regulatory skills as a consequence of being active in elite sports. Developmental trends in the relationship between competitive level and sport participation, measured by number of training hours per week, and development of reflection and effort have been observed. However, high-quality intervention studies are necessary to conclusively determine the size and direction of these relationships over developmental time.

Furthermore, future studies should examine whether developing athletes with higher levels of reflection and effort are more likely to make it to elite status as an adult. This is interesting, as prior research shows that talented athletes often struggle with the transition to senior levels of competition. This is a harsh phase in their careers as, for example, they have to perform while "the world is watching" and are no longer protected by two-year age categories. It is also a phase in which athletes are faced with important transitions psychologically and academically (Wylleman et al., 2004). Athletes should therefore be prepared for the transition to senior levels, and reflection may assist them in making this transition (MacNamara & Collins, 2010). From this perspective, investigating the development of reflection and effort as they relate to making a successful transition to senior competitive levels may also be of interest.

In addition, much of the work on psychological factors and sport expertise has considered the relevant research questions from a single theoretical perspective. However, this may not capture the dynamic processes occurring at any point in an athlete's development. For example, understanding how self-regulatory skills change over time is important, but a more comprehensive approach considers how this change over time relates to athletes' personality or motivation and/ or to behavioral changes in training microstructure. In the absence of a global framework that captures the myriad psychological factors at play across expertise development, there is a great need for research that combines several theoretical approaches.

References

Allen, M. S. (2012) 'A systematic review of content themes in sport attribution research: 1954–2011', *International Review of Sport and Exercise Psychology*, 5: 1–8.

Allen, M. S., Greenlees, I., & Jones, M. (2013) 'Personality in sport: A comprehensive review', *International Review of Sport and Exercise Psychology*, 6: 184–208.

Anshel, M. H., & Porter, A. (1996) 'Efficacy of a model for examining self-regulation with elite and non-elite male and female competitive swimmers', *International Journal of Psychology*, 27: 321–36.

Baker, J., & Horton, S. (2004) 'A review of primary and secondary influences on sport expertise', *High Ability Studies*, 15: 211–28.

Bandura, A. (1997) *Self-efficacy: The exercise of control*, New York: Freeman.

Boekaerts, M. (1997) 'Self-regulated learning: A new concept embraced by researchers, policy makers, educators, teachers, and students', *Learning and Instruction*, 7: 161–86.

Boekaerts, M., & Corno, L. (2005) 'Self-regulation in the classroom: A perspective on assessment and intervention', *Applied Psychology: An International Review*, 54: 199–231.

Côté, J. (1999) 'The influence of the family in the development of talent in sport', *The Sports Psychologist*, 13: 395–417.

Elferink-Gemser, M. T., & Visscher. C. (2011) 'Who are the superstars of tomorrow?', in J. Baker, S. Cobley, & J. Schorer (eds) *Talent identification and development in sport, international perspectives*, New York: Routledge, 95–105.

Elferink-Gemser, M. T., Visscher, C., Lemmink, K.A.P.M., & Mulder, T. W. (2004) 'Relation between multidimensional performance characteristics and level of performance in talented youth field hockey players', *Journal of Sports Sciences*, 22: 1053–63.

Ericsson, K. A. (1996) 'The acquisition of expert performance: An introduction to some of the issues', in. K. A. Ericsson (ed) *The road to excellence. The acquisition of expert performance in the arts and sciences, sports and games*, Mahwah, NJ: Lawrence Erlbaum Associates, 1–50.

Ericsson, K. A. (2003) 'Development of elite performance and deliberate practice. An update from the perspective of the expert performance approach', in J. L. Starkes & K. A. Ericsson (eds) *Expert performance in sports. Advances in research expertise*, Champaign, IL: Human Kinetics, 49–87.

Importance of self-regulation

Ericsson, K. A., Krampe, R. T., & Tesch-Römer, C. (1993) 'The role of deliberate practice in the acquisition of expert performance', *Psychological Review*, 100: 363–406.

Ericsson, K. A., & Towne, T. J. (2010) 'Expertise', *Wiley Interdisciplinary Reviews: Cognitive Science*, 1: 404–16.

Ertmer, P. A., & Newby, T. J. (1996) 'The expert learner: Strategic, self-regulated, and reflective', *Instructional Science*, 24: 1–24.

Eshel, Y., & Kohavi, R. (2003) 'Perceived classroom control, self-regulated learning strategies, and academic achievement', *Educational Psychology*, 23: 249–60.

Feltz, D., Short, S., & Sullivan, P. (2008) 'Self-efficacy in sport: Research and strategies for working with athletes, teams and coaches', *International Journal of Sport Science and Coaching*, 3: 293–5.

Ford, P. R., Ward, P., Hodges, N. J., & Williams, A. M. (2009) 'The role of deliberate practice and play in career progression in sport: The early engagement hypothesis', *High Ability Studies*, 20: 65–75.

Harwood, C, Spray, C. M., & Keegan, R. (2008) 'Achievement goal theories in sport', in T. S. Horn (ed) *Advances in sport psychology*, 3rd ed., Champaign, IL: Human Kinetics, 157–85.

Hidi, S., & Harackiewicz, J. M. (2000) 'Motivating the academically unmotivated: A critical issue for the 21st century', *Review of Educational Research*, 70: 151–79.

Hong, E., & O'Neil, H. F., Jr. (2001) 'Construct validation of a trait self-regulation model', *International Journal of Psychology*, 36: 186–94.

Huijgen, B.C.H., Elferink-Gemser, M. T., Post, W. J., & Visscher, C. (2009) 'Soccer skill development in professionals', *International Journal of Sports Medicine*, 30: 585–91.

Jonker, L. (2011) *Self-regulation in sport and education. Important for sport expertise and academic achievement for elite youth athletes*, Groningen, NL: Ipskampr Drukkers B.V.

Jonker, L., Elferink-Gemser, M. T., de Roos, I. M., & Visscher, C. (2012) 'The role of reflection in sport expertise', *The Sports Psychologist*, 26: 224–42.

Jonker, L., Elferink-Gemser, M. T., & Visscher, C. (2009) 'Talented athletes and academic achievements: A comparison over 14 years', *High Ability Studies*, 22: 55–64.

Jonker, L., Elferink-Gemser, M. T., & Visscher, C. (2010) 'Differences in self-regulatory skills among talented athletes: The significance of competitive level and type of sport', *Journal of Sports Sciences*, 28: 901–8.

Jonker, L., Elferink-Gemser, M. T., & Visscher, C. (2011) 'The development of reflection and attainment of senior international status', abstract presented at the 16th Annual Congress of the European Congress for Sports Sciences (ECSS), Liverpool.

Kannekens, R., Elferink-Gemser, M. T., & Visscher, C. (2011) 'Positioning and deciding: Key factors for talent development in soccer', *Scandinavian Journal of Medicine & Science in Sports*, 21(6): 846–52.

Kitsantas, A., & Zimmerman, B. J. (2002) 'Comparing self-regulatory processes among novice, non-expert, and expert volleyball players: A microanalytic study', *Journal of Applied Sport Psychology*, 14: 91–105.

MacNamara, A., & Collins, D. (2010) 'The role of psychological characteristics in managing the transition to university', *Psychology of Sport and Exercise*, 11: 353–62.

Malina, R. M., Cumming, S. P., Kontos, A. P., Eisenmannd, J. C., Ribeiro, B. & Aroso, J. (2005) 'Maturity-associated variation in sport-specific skills of youth soccer players aged 13–15 years', *Journal of Sports Sciences*, 23: 515–22.

Martín, E., Martínez-Arias, R., Marchesi, A., & Pérez, E. M. (2008) 'Variables that predict academic achievement in the Spanish compulsory secondary education system: A longitudinal multi-level analysis', *The Spanish Journal of Psychology*, 11: 400–13.

McCabe, L. A., Cunnington, M., & Brooks-Gunn, J. (2004) 'The development of self-regulation in young children: Individual characteristics and environmental contexts', in R. F. Baumeister & K. Vohs (eds) *Handbook of self-regulation: Research, theory and applications*, New York: Guilford Press, 340–56.

Multon, K. D., Brown, S. D., & Lent, R. W. (1991) 'Relation of self-efficacy beliefs to academic outcomes: A meta-analytic investigation', *Journal of Counseling Psychology*, 38: 30–8.

Newell, K. M. (1986) 'Constraints on the development of coordination', in M. G. Wade & H.T.A. Whiting (eds) *Motor skill acquisition in children: Aspects of coordination and control*, Amsterdam: Martinus Nijhoff, 341–60.

Nicholls, J. G. (1978) 'The development of the concepts of effort and ability, perceptions of academic attainment, and the understanding that difficult tasks require more ability', *Child Development*, 49: 800–14.

Nota, L., Soresi, S., & Zimmerman, B. J. (2004) 'Self-regulation and academic achievement and resilience: A longitudinal study', *International Journal of Educational Research*, 41: 198–215.

Orlick, T., & Partington, J. (1988) 'Mental links to excellence', *The Sport Psychologist*, 2: 105–30.

Peltier, J. W., Hay, A., & Drago, W. (2006) 'Reflecting on reflection: Scale extension and a comparison of undergraduate business students in the United States and the United Kingdom', *Journal of Marketing Education*, 28: 5–16. doi: 10.1177/0273475305279658

Perry, N. (1998) 'Young children's self-regulated learning and contexts that support it', *Journal of Educational Psychology*, 90: 715–29.

Pintrich, P. R., & Zusho, A. (2002) 'The development of academic self-regulation. The role of cognitive and motivational factors', in A. Wigfield & J. S. Eccles (eds) *Development of achievement motivation*, San Diego, CA: Academic Press, 249–84.

Rasbash, J., Browne, W., Goldstein, H., Yang, M., Plewis, I., & Draper, D., . . . Woodhouse, G. (1999) *A user's guide to MlwiN*, London: Institute of Education.

Roescher, C. R., Elferink-Gemser, M. T., Huijgen, B.C.H., & Visscher, C. (2010) 'Soccer endurance development in professionals', *International Journal of Sports Medicine*, 31: 174–9.

Standage, M. (2012) 'Motivation: Self-determination theory and performance in sport', in S. Murphy (ed) *The Oxford handbook of sport and performance psychology*, Oxford: Oxford University Press, 233–49.

Toering, T., Elferink-Gemser, M., Jordet, G., Jorna, C., Pepping, G. J., & Visscher, C. (2011) 'Self-regulation of practice behavior among elite youth soccer players: An exploratory observation study', *Journal of Applied Sport Psychology*, 23: 11–128.

Toering, T. T., Elferink-Gemser, M. T., Jordet, G., & Visscher, C. (2009) 'Self-regulation and performance level of elite and expert youth soccer players', *Journal of Sports Sciences*, 27: 1509–17.

Vallerand, R. J., & Rousseau, F. L. (2001) 'Intrinsic and extrinsic motivation in sport and exercise: A review using the hierarchical model of intrinsic and extrinsic motivation', in R. N. Singer, H. A. Hausenblas, & M. C. Janelle (eds) *Handbook of sport psychology*, 2nd ed., New York: John Wiley & Sons, 389–416.

Van Ark, M., Elferink-Gemser, M. T., Roskam, A., & Visscher, C. (2010) 'Important features of talent coaches for talent development in sports', in. M. J. Coelho e Silva, A. J. Figueiredo, M. T. Elferink-Gemser, & R. M. Malina (eds) *Youth sports. Growth, maturation and talent*, Coimbra, PT: Coimbra University Press, 179–206.

Van der Stel, M., & Veenman, M. V. J. (2008) 'Relation between intellectual ability and metacognitive skillfulness as predictors of learning performance of young students performing tasks in different domains', *Learning and Individual Differences*, 18: 128–34.

Veenman, M. V. J., Kok, R., & Blöte, A. W. (2005) 'The relation between intellectual and metacognitive skills in early adolescence', *Instructional Science*, 33: 193–211.

Veenman, M. V. J., & Spaans, M. A. (2005) 'Relation between intellectual and metacognitive skills: Age and task differences', *Learning and Individual Differences*, 15: 159–76.

Weiss, M. R., & Chaumeton, N. (1992) 'Motivational orientations in sport', in T. Horn (ed) *Advances in sport psychology*, Champaign, IL: Human Kinetics, 61–100.

Wylleman, P., Alfermann, D., & Lavallee, D. (2004) 'Career transitions in sport: European perspective', *Psychology of Sport and Exercise*, 5: 7–20.

Zimmerman, B. J. (1986) 'Becoming a self-regulated learner: Which are the key subprocesses?', *Contemporary Educational Psychology*, 11: 307–13.

Zimmerman, B. J. (1989) 'A social cognitive view of self-regulated academic learning', *Journal of educational Psychology*, 81: 329–39.

Zimmerman, B. J. (1990) 'Self-regulated learning and academic achievement: An overview', *Educational Psychologist*, 25: 3–17.

29

FAMILY AND PEER INFLUENCES IN THE DEVELOPMENT OF SPORT EXPERTISE

Jessica Fraser-Thomas and Theresa Beesley

At the 2014 Olympics in Sochi, Russia, three women represented Canada in the freestyle skiing moguls event, earning two podium finishes (gold and silver) and a 12th place finish. Most remarkable, these three women were sisters: Justine, Chloé, and Maxime Dufour-Lapointe. One cannot help but be curious about the upbringing and home environment that would lead all three siblings to be the most successful in their discipline in the world. When and how were they introduced to sport? How did they influence each other growing up? What was the nature of dinner hour conversations? International media outlets eagerly embraced their story, uncovering details of a family built on genuine support and care for each other, calling them "Canada's first family of emotion . . . Platinum winners in family bonding" (MacGregor, 2014). Balanced within this tightly connected family were strong values of work ethic, discipline, and fearless competition. When their father, Yves Lapointe, was asked about "sacrifices," he corrected the interviewer, suggesting his family had made "choices" – which included mother Johanne Dufour putting her master's education on hold, and the family spending every weekend on ski hills, even before youngest sister Justine (Olympic gold medalist) was competing in the sport (MacGregor, 2014). When asked about competing against each other, the eldest, Maxime (non-medalist), explained, "we don't have rivalry. We push and support each other to be the best that we can be" (Canadian Broadcasting Corporation, 2014a).

The case of the Dufour-Lapointe sisters presents an excellent backdrop to introduce our discussion on family and peer influences in the development of expertise. Among elite athletes, family members, particularly parents, are often the first to be thanked for their support through the years, yet social networks, and specifically the influences of siblings and peers, have received much less attention in the literature than other more salient "nature" and "nurture" elements of expert athlete development such as genetic makeup, physiological characteristics, sport training patterns, coaching influences, and psychological characteristics (e.g., Côté *et al.*, 2007; Davis & Meyer, 2008). As such, in this chapter we focus on the roles that family members (i.e., parents and siblings) and peers (i.e., teammates, competitors, non-sport peers) play throughout development in optimizing athletes' opportunities to reach the highest levels in their sport. We focus on both family and peers, given past literature highlighting their unique but complimentary roles in providing social support and calls for further examination of how these relationships may coexist (Fredricks & Eccles, 2004; Hassell *et al.*, 2010; Ullrich-French & Smith, 2006, 2009), while using a developmental lens, given calls for investigation of athletes' changing experiences over time (Fraser-Thomas *et al.*, 2013; Lauer *et al.*, 2010).

We begin with an overview of the developmental model of sport participation (DMSP; Côté, 1999; Côté et al., 2007; Côté & Fraser-Thomas, 2011; Côté & Hay, 2002; Durand-Bush & Salmela, 2002), which we use as a framework to guide our discussion. We then present literature that speaks to the roles of parents, siblings, and peers throughout each stage of the DMSP – the sampling, specializing, investment, and maintenance phases of expert athlete development. Throughout our review, we draw upon common social support typologies (Hardy & Crace, 1993; Holt & Hoar, 2006) to explain families and peers' influential roles, including the provision of emotional support (e.g., listening and comforting), information support (e.g., sport-specific feedback), tangible support (e.g., financial and practical resources), esteem support (e.g., encouragement and praise), and network support (e.g., integrated support of a group). Finally, we conclude with a discussion of future research directions and potential implications related to parents, siblings, and peers' influence in expert athlete development.

The developmental model of sport participation

The developmental model of sport participation (DMSP) was first proposed by Côté (1999), following a study involving four elite Canadian junior athletes (i.e., rowers and tennis players) and their families. Findings yielded the establishment of three phases of sport participation: the sampling (age six to 13), specializing (age 13–15), and investment years (age 15 and over). During the sampling years parents focused on providing their children with opportunities to experience fun and excitement through their engagement in sport and physical activity. During the specializing years, child athletes were involved in fewer extracurricular activities, while sport-specific skill development became of increasing importance over fun and excitement. During this phase, parents often increased financial and time commitments while developing a growing interest in their child's sport, but also continued emphasizing school achievement alongside sport accomplishments; older siblings often acted as role models of work ethic. Finally, within the investment years, adolescent athletes committed to developing an elite level of performance in one sport, with increased focus on strategy, commitment, competition, and skills. During this phase parents often treated the talented athlete differently than other children in the family and often helped the athlete work through sport-related challenges and obstacles, while siblings sometimes showed bitterness and jealousy toward their athlete siblings. Côté's (1999) findings aligned closely with previous work done by Bloom (1985), which examined the processes that enabled talented children in the arts, sciences, and athletics to reach their full capabilities, but offered an important advancement by examining children's key psychosocial influences anchored within sport-specific theoretical concepts.

Extensive research with athletes involved in diverse sports and levels (e.g., Baker et al., 2003a; Fraser-Thomas et al., 2008a) has resulted in several modifications and advancements to Côté's (1999) original DMSP. Côté and Fraser-Thomas (2011) identify two trajectories towards elite sport performance – one through sampling, specializing, and investment, and the second through early specialization, whereby the athlete bypasses the sampling stage, and moves directly into specializing and/or investment stages. Further, Durand-Bush and Salmela's (2002) study examining the developmental paths of world and Olympic champions found the existence of a fourth stage following the investment years, beginning as the athlete reaches the pinnacle in his/her sport in early adulthood; the maintenance stage was associated with perfection and maintenance of optimal performance, and while family members did not play an extremely active role, their support was nonetheless considered critical. Throughout the chapter we interpret the chronological age associated with the four phases of sampling, specializing, investment, and maintenance years, to align approximately with childhood, early adolescence, later adolescence, and early adulthood.

Family and peer influences

We make this loose interpretation given past research showing considerable range in starting age of each stage, and transitions between stages sometimes occurring over extended periods of time (e.g., Lauer *et al.*, 2010), in addition to suggestions of fluidity between trajectories (e.g., an athlete initially involved at a recreational level may begin investing in elite sport during adolescence) (Côté & Fraser-Thomas, 2011).

The sampling years

Research on the earliest phases of expert athletes' development is often the most challenging to conduct, given that childhood sport experiences typically occur years prior to athletes' attainment of expert status. For this reason, in this section, we draw upon research conducted among expert athletes, most often involving data collected retrospectively, but we also draw upon more generic literature related to children's healthy socialization and development in sport.

Introduction to sport

Expert athletes, like all young sport participants, need first be introduced to their sport. Past research suggests this often occurs through "sponsored recruitment" (Stevenson, 1990), whereby parents enroll and support their young children in sport programs (Côté, 1999; Morgan & Giacobbi, 2006; Stevenson, 1990). According to Eccles's expectancy-value model, parents can play important roles in initiating, as well as supporting and encouraging, young athletes' sport involvement (Eccles & Harold, 1991; Fredricks & Eccles, 2004). More specifically, when parents demonstrate an interest in a sport, children may internalize their parents' values and beliefs, leading to their own choice behaviors and expression of interest in a particular activity. The DMSP was built upon these principles, as parents of talented junior athletes in Côté's (1999) seminal study believed sport was an important factor in their children's overall development, and thus provided opportunities for their children to develop an interest in sport. While little research has focused on mother-father differences, there is some evidence to suggest fathers may play a greater role in the introduction of sport to expert athletes (e.g., Blazo *et al.*, 2014).

Siblings have also been found to act as sport "recruitment sponsors" (Stevenson, 1990) through role modeling and companionship (Côté, 1999; Gould *et al.*, 2002; Hopwood *et al.*, in press; Morgan & Giacobbi, 2006; Stevenson, 1990; Whiteman *et al.*, 2007). Hopwood and colleagues' (in press) recent investigation of more than 600 Canadian and Australian athletes and their siblings found an over-representation of elite athletes among later-born children, with their older siblings more likely to have participated in sport activities than older siblings of non-elite athletes. Authors suggested younger siblings likely spent a large amount of time in their older sibling's sport environment, leading to increased interest or opportunity to pursue sport. Interestingly, these propositions are exemplified by the Dufour-Lapointe sisters, who described how Justine, the youngest sister, was often treated to hot chocolate as a child, so that she would agree to stay at the ski hill a few hours longer while her older sisters continued training (MacGregor, 2014).

Peers have consistently been identified as key sources of children's sport motivation (Duncan, 1993; Smith, 2003; Ullrich-French & Smith, 2006, 2009; Weiss *et al.*, 1996). In exploring the early careers of international athletes in Canada and the United Kingdom, Stevenson (1990) found that while cross-gender sponsoring existed among siblings (i.e., siblings influenced the involvement of both their same and opposite gender siblings), this was not the case among peers, where only same-gender sponsoring existed (i.e., boys influenced boys' involvement, and girls influenced girls' involvement). While additional research focusing on the processes by which peers may influence children's initial participation is necessary, the DMSP suggests the sampling years involve modified and child-directed sport play (Côté & Fraser-Thomas, 2011), whereby engagement by and interactions with peers are essential to the sport participation experience (MacPhail *et al.*, 2003).

Continued motivation

Once enrolled in sport, parents can be critical in facilitating future expert athletes' continued motivation. Research consistently highlights the importance of parents who demonstrate supportive behaviors and avoid pressuring behaviors to assure children's enjoyment and continued motivation in sport (Keegan *et al.*, 2009; Wuerth *et al.*, 2004); however, the question of what these constructs "look like" during childhood remains an issue of much discussion and debate, as well-intentioned behaviors from parents can often be perceived as controlling or pressuring by child athletes (Wolfenden & Holt, 2005). Several models of motivation highlight parents' roles influencing their children's competence beliefs (Eccles & Harold, 1991; Fredricks & Eccles, 2004; Harter, 1978) and subsequent sport enjoyment and commitment (Scanlan *et al.*, 1993; Weiss *et al.*, 2001). However, as Horn and Harris (2002) point out, significant others' feedback must be adjusted according to developmental stage, and in childhood, parents' frequent, positive, performance-contingent feedback is associated with higher competence beliefs, enjoyment, and intrinsic motivation (Babkes & Weiss, 1999; Power & Woolger, 1994). Consistent with this contention, Gould and colleagues' (2002) study of Olympic champions found parents often showed an unfaltering belief in their children's abilities to succeed.

While parents often have the greatest influence on young children's competence beliefs, these beliefs shift during early to later childhood and begin to focus to a greater extent on accomplishment and effort through peer comparison and judgment (Horn & Harris, 2002; Horn & Hasbrook, 1986; Horn & Weiss, 1991). Ongoing participation in sport is often motivated by children's desire to be accepted by and affiliated with a larger peer group, while satisfying their need to belong (Allen, 2003; Weiss & Ferrer-Caja, 2002). Past work highlights that peer acceptance (i.e., social standing and worthiness within a peer group; Weiss *et al.*, 1996) can provide children with information to facilitate social comparison, feedback, and judgment about their abilities within a larger peer group (Horn & Hasbrook, 1986; Horn & Weiss, 1991), in turn influencing children's competence beliefs and subsequent motivation (Brustad *et al.*, 2001; Scanlan *et al.*, 1989; Ullrich-French & Smith, 2006; Weiss *et al.*, 1996). Interestingly, studies describe children's negative peer interactions in their sport contexts, ranging from teammates failing to support them in times of stress or anxiety, to peers emphasizing their poor performances or putting them down with insulting comments (McCarthy & Jones, 2007); however, it is unclear how these experiences may influence children's sport motivation and persistence.

Friendships (i.e., dyadic relationships involving interactions between two individuals) are also of significant interest to understanding children's motivation in sport (Weiss *et al.*, 1996). Friendships can offer influences on sport motivation unique and independent of peer acceptance, as children may be engaged in a friendship while simultaneously being rejected by their peer group, or vice versa (Ladd *et al.*, 1997). It has been suggested that sport friendships can function to stimulate skill acquisition and learning and improve young athletes' self-perceptions and positive experiences (Bukowski, 2001). Specifically, similar to peer groups, individual friends' companionship plays an important role in children's beliefs about their physical competence and success, positive global affect, enjoyment, and desire to participate and continue in sports (Duncan, 1993; MacPhail *et al.*, 2003; Ullrich-French & Smith, 2006, 2009); however, gender differences have been highlighted, showing girls are less likely to participate in sport without an accompanying friend, while boys are less inclined to require the involvement of a friend to participate (Coakley & White, 1992).

Family environment

Recent work has also begun to recognize the importance of a positive family environment in children's early sport development. In particular, Trussell's (2012) study of Canadian, sport-involved sibling dyads and triads aged nine through 17 uncovered the notion of "team family," whereby sport served as a backdrop for the development of healthy sibling relationships and rapport, as a result of enhanced opportunities to spend time together (e.g., practicing skills), communicate with each other (e.g., formal and informal mentoring), and establish a connection (e.g., shared identity). In line with Trussell's findings, studies of expert athletes show that during childhood, parents often spend extensive quality time playing with or coaching their child in their chosen sport, leading to close parent-child relationships, and continued commitment for sport (Bloom, 1985; Côté, 1999, Lauer *et al.*, 2010; Stevenson, 1990). In the same vein, studies also show that siblings often engage in sport together, modeling and teaching skills, and instilling positive and healthy values and attitudes surrounding sport (Blazo *et al.*, 2014; Gould *et al.*, 2002; Trussell, 2012).

While past work has also highlighted conflict and tensions within expert athletes' family dynamics, these do not appear to be concerning issues during the sampling phase (Bloom, 1985; Côté, 1999; Trussell, 2012). This may be in part due to parents' aim to support all their children's participation in various extracurricular activities, and distribute resources similarly across the family (Côté, 1999). Trussell (2012) found children were acutely aware of this challenge, assessing "fairness" and "equality" according to how many teams each sibling participated in, or the number of evenings that they were involved. Hopwood and colleagues (in press) also found that younger sibling expert athletes often participated in a different sport than their older siblings, possibly allowing them to minimize competition for parental resources and seek a unique niche in the family environment (see Sulloway, 1996). Also noteworthy is that some of the parents in Côté's (1999) study recognized during the sampling years that their child athlete had a "gift," but did not immediately act on this acknowledgment by increasing investment in the child.

Specializing years

Transition from the sampling to the specializing phase is perhaps the most challenging to navigate for young athletes and their key social influences, likely due in part to the significant social, cognitive, and emotional developmental changes occurring during this time (Kohlberg, 1969; Piaget, 1971). In this section, we discuss the complexity of parents, siblings, and peers' behaviors and relationships with athletes during this phase.

Transitioning and committing

The decision to commit to, or specialize in a sport, has consistently been found to be a child-directed decision among expert athletes; however, this decision is often indirectly influenced by significant others such as teammates, friends, siblings, and parents (Côté, 1999; Gould *et al.*, 2002; Holt & Dunn, 2004; Morgan & Giacobbi, 2006; Stevenson, 1990). For example, Stevenson's (1990) study of international athletes found that youths' affinity to the people in the sport, or aversion to people in another sport, were often factors in athletes' decisions to commit to a particular sport. Similarly, studies among talented and high-investment adolescent athletes have shown that unfulfilling peer relationships or a lack of a "best friend" within sport are associated with withdrawal, particularly among females (Fraser-Thomas *et al.*, 2008a; Patrick *et al.*, 1999). These findings are in line with additional work showing that friendship, affiliation, group identity, and perceived belonging have the potential to endorse or discourage motivation, commitment, and perseverance in sport (Keegan *et al.*, 2010; Vazou *et al.*, 2005; Weiss *et al.*, 1996). Parents may also indirectly influence adolescents' sport investments, as athletes may feel a sense of obligation to commit, given their parents' enthusiasm and emotional support (Fraser-Thomas *et al.*, 2008b). Ullrich-French and Smith's (2009) work highlights the collective influences of parents and peers during late childhood and early adolescence, finding the combination of mother relationship quality, peer acceptance, and friendship quality predicted athletes' continued sport participation one year later.

A grey area begins to emerge with regard to parents' optimal behaviors when athletes may be lacking motivation in the specializing phase. MacPhail and Kirk's (2006) ethnographic study in an English athletic (i.e., track and field) club found some parents pushed or pressured their children to continue by taking away other opportunities, or going to great lengths to assure they attended training sessions. However, in other cases, parents seemed to achieve the same outcome through a more gentle "nudging" approach, whereby parents prompted, encouraged, and helped motivate their children to attend training sessions (Gould *et al.*, 2002; Lauer *et al.*, 2010; MacPhail & Kirk, 2006). Parent-child communication and interactions related to participation and commitment in this phase of sport development appear to have substantive implications; past findings among high-investment adolescent competitive swimmers found dropout athletes felt pressure by parents to continue swimming when considering dropping out, while engaged athletes reflected on how their parents encouraged them to continue, but provided options for how that continuation could optimally unfold (Fraser-Thomas *et al.*, 2008b).

Families' tangible support

Perhaps the most significant marker of young athletes' transition from sampling to specializing phase is the increased tangible support required from parents. In the introduction, we highlighted that Yves Lapointe spoke of the family's "choices" rather than "sacrifices" following his daughters' outstanding Olympic performances. In line with these comments, research suggests parents of expert athletes have few regrets regarding their investment in their high-performing athletes' sport, with increased time spent together being associated with special, meaningful, and particularly close relationships (Fraser-Thomas & Côté, 2009; Keegan *et al.*, 2010). However, there is little doubt that considerable adaptations to what is considered "normal" family life are made by families in the name of children's high-performance sport, with potential emotional, social, and financial repercussions. Adaptations may include the family routine being determined by children's training schedule (e.g., disappearance of family meals), holidays being rearranged or cancelled, decreased shared family leisure time, parents' work schedules adapted or changing/quitting their jobs to accommodate training schedules, and the selling or remortgaging of homes to finance or relocate for sport (Kay, 2000; Kirk *et al.*, 1997b; Morgan & Giacobbi, 2006; Wolfenden & Holt, 2005). In their study of NCAA division I collegiate athletes, coaches, and parents, Morgan and Giacobbi found families experience tremendous financial strain and practical challenges as a result of their child's involvement, with one parent suggesting "it was a giant effort by both of us . . . a very expensive affair" (2006, p. 303). Financial costs are associated primarily with coaching, competition, equipment, and travel (Côté, 1999; Hassell *et al.*, 2010; Kay, 2000; Kirk *et al.*, 1997a). One participant in Kay's (2000) study of talent-developing families in England directly addressed the critical importance of tangible resources, saying, "I believe there must be a lot of talented swimmers who do not get the chance to compete seriously because their parents do not support them, whether because of financial reasons or time constraints" (2000, p. 161).

Family and peer influences

While expert athletes consistently recognize and appreciate parents' commitments and investments, suggesting they make them feel loved and valued, these feelings are sometimes accompanied by a sense of guilt and pressure to continue and/or excel in the sport (Fraser-Thomas *et al.*, 2008b; Hassell *et al.*, 2010; Lauer *et al.*, 2010), potentially leading to a sense of entrapment, lack of control, decreased enjoyment, and burnout (Coakley, 1992; Raedeke, 1997). Clearly, parents' decisions are made to optimize their child athletes' sport development, but sometime these decisions (e.g., moving the child and/or family to a central training location) may not always be in the best interest of the family or the psychosocial health of the athlete (Lauer *et al.*, 2010). Parents in Kay's (2000) study spoke of investment increasing incrementally and progressively, yet expressed concern about their ability to continue maintaining such a sport-centered family lifestyle, whereas Wolfenden and Holt (2005) highlighted that mothers typically played a greater role in daily transportation and logistics, in turn making more sacrifices to their own personal well-being. Parents' unequal distribution of resources across children is also increasingly evident at this stage, leading to potential jealousy, rivalry, decreased competence, identity loss, and sport dropout among less-accomplished siblings (Blazo *et al.*, 2014; Côté, 1999; Davis & Meyer, 2008; Fraser-Thomas *et al.*, 2008b; Kay, 2000; Trussell, 2012; Wolfenden & Holt, 2005). Trussell (2012) found these concerns to be particularly problematic when star athletes were same-sex younger siblings, and/or on the same team as their siblings. However, younger siblings in Blazo and colleagues' (2014) study believed they experienced personal benefits as a result of their older sibling's sport involvement (e.g., traveling, meeting new people, college recruitment). Collectively, these findings illustrate the challenges and complexities of parents' providing appropriate tangible support, particularly during the specializing stage of expert athletes' development.

Parents' informational support

Parents' provision of informational support is also an intricate process during the specializing years. While during childhood, parents' feedback is critical to building athletes' sense of competence and motivation; research among high-performance adolescent athletes indicates parents demonstrate diverse behaviors. As such, recent research has focused on parent-child interactions in training, competition, and other contexts, as well as the conditions surrounding these interactions. For example, adolescent athletes have typically shown an aversion to parents' provision of sport-specific advice (e.g., parents playing a coaching role, correcting errors, offering technical feedback), as they do not believe their parents are credible sources of information; as such, these behaviors are perceived to be frustrating, confusing, ineffective, and have even been linked to dropout (Fraser-Thomas *et al.*, 2008b; Hassell *et al.*, 2010; Keegan *et al.*, 2010; Knight *et al.*, 2010; Knight *et al.*, 2011; Lauer *et al.*, 2010; Wolfenden & Holt, 2005). There is, however, some evidence to suggest quite the opposite – that adolescents appreciate receiving sport-related advice and guidance from parents – but this is most often the case when parents have extensive sport-specific knowledge and expertise (Gould *et al.*, 2002; Holt & Dunn, 2004; Knight *et al.*, 2010).

Additional considerations are noteworthy when considering the above findings. First, regardless of their sport background, parents often believe they possess expertise, allowing them to make very specific, coaching-like comments to their children (Holt *et al.*, 2008). Second, athletes whose parents have an extensive sport background (i.e., played in their youth) have been found to experience greater pressure and demands from their parents, attain lower levels of success, and be more prone to dropout (Carlson, 1988; Fraser-Thomas *et al.*, 2008a). In sum, parents who believe they have sport expertise may interact with their child athletes in a unique manner, but athletes may respond differently to their parents' feedback, depending on their own perception of their parents' expertise. Further, few studies have focused on differences in mother-father and daughter-son interactions, yet past work suggests that fathers are often primary providers of instructional feed-back (e.g., Hassell *et al.*, 2010; Holt & Dunn, 2004; Knight *et al.*, 2011), highlighting the need for further research exploring parents' behaviors through the lens of gender.

Although there is not one simple group of behaviors that will successfully guide all parents (Knight *et al.*, 2010; Wolfenden & Holt, 2005), a growing body of research highlights some con-sistencies. In particular, adolescents appear to appreciate parents' offering feedback about effort and attitude and providing guidance and assistance on practical preparation for performance (e.g., resting, nutrition, hydration, staying warm), in addition to attending or spectating at competitions, providing verbal feedback that is genuine and honest (i.e., matches their body language), and offering feedback at the appropriate time and place (e.g., constructive criticism removed from teammates and coaches) (Keegan *et al.*, 2010; Knight *et al.*, 2010; Knight *et al.*, 2011; Woodcock *et al.*, 2011).

Emotional climate created by parents

During the specializing phase, expert athletes often begin to experience greater sport and life stresses, with research showing that parents play an important role in demonstrating uncon-ditional care, concern, love, comfort, empathy, understanding, optimism, and sense of security during what can be turbulent times – whether in the form of a listening ear, a hug, or a perspec-tive-giving conversation (Côté, 1999; Fraser-Thomas & Côté, 2009; Gould *et al*, 2002; Holt & Dunn, 2004; Keegan *et al.*, 2010). Lauer and colleagues' (2010) study among professional tennis players found the nature of parents' "intelligent conversations" changed gradually from the sam-pling to specializing years, as parents responded to children's maturation, emotional highs and lows, and repercussions of their victories and loses, learning to manipulate conversation quantity and quality. Family members appear to be in an optimal position to offer emotional support, as they are willing to address complex personal issues for which coaches may have less tolerance, and are skilled in "reading" their child, given their intimate awareness of the child's personality, behaviors, and emotional states (Hassell *et al.*, 2010; Knight *et al.*, 2011; Wolfenden & Holt, 2005).

Much literature also highlights that some high-performing athletes experience a less support-ive emotional climate throughout the specializing phase, with parents demonstrating "negative" behaviors such as yelling, being critical, pushing or pressuring their child athlete to win, and punishing their child athlete for losing (Fraser-Thomas & Côté, 2009; Gould *et al.*, 2008; Has-sell *et al.*, 2010). An obvious question, which remains very difficult to address, is whether these behaviors hinder athletes' sport and personal development by undermining athletes' motivation and fostering frustration, or alternatively, contribute to their motivation through an "I'll show you" attitude (Fraser-Thomas *et al.*, 2013; Keegan *et al.*, 2010; Lauer *et al.*, 2010). Csikszentmi-halyi, Rathunde, and Whalen's (1993) seminal study of talented American teenagers found that complex family environments – ones that were stable, supportive, and consistent, while also promoting the taking on of new challenges – were associated with the most positive outcomes (e.g., teenagers were excited about their activities and had a sense of fulfillment and accomplish-ment). While one must assume that all parents are acting in a manner that they believe to be in the best interest of their child, Gould and colleagues (2008) found junior tennis coaches per-ceived that 36 per cent of parents negatively influenced their child's development. One possible explanation is that parents simply do not understand how their behaviors influence their child, particularly from an emotional perspective, as they are often ill equipped to handle their sudden thrust into high-performance sport (Fraser-Thomas & Côté, 2009; Lauer *et al.*, 2010). As such, parents may benefit from engaging their child athletes in discussions to better understand how to optimize their development (Knight *et al.*, 2010), while the provision of resources for parents of high-performance athletes could help them better navigate their roles (Kay & Bass, 2011).

Family and peer influences

Complex dynamics of peer relationships

Given extensive training and performance demands, it follows that adolescents spend large amounts of time with teammates and sport-related peers during the specializing years; however, the dynamics of these relationships are diverse. Athletes generally appreciate their networks of support among teammates, built upon a sense of acceptance, shared experiences, similar work ethic, parallel struggles, and contagious enthusiasm (Fraser-Thomas & Côté, 2009; Fraser-Thomas *et al.*, 2008b; Patrick *et al.*, 1999). For example, MacPhail and Kirk (2006) found adolescent track and field teammates offered each other esteem support by sharing leadership roles, acknowledging each others' abilities, and pushing each other in training, and offered emotional support by being able to read and understand each other and knowing how to best navigate difficult sport experiences (e.g., distraction strategies such as humor, or non-verbal communication such as a smile).

However, peers also continue to serve as key sources of feedback by which to judge competence, and while this information often includes praise and encouragement, it can also include criticism and negative feedback, making positive peer relationships in sport sometimes dependent on athletes' levels of competence (Keegan *et al.*, 2010; Vazou *et al.*, 2005). A participant in Patrick *et al.*'s study described the awkwardness of competing with friends, as she reported her best friend saying, "Geez, you're good! I'm so scared that you're going to take my place" (1999, p. 755). Issues such as boasting, pressuring, rivalry, jealousy, conflict, showing off, and poor role modeling often arise among peer competitors (Fraser-Thomas *et al.*, 2008b; Keegan *et al.*, 2010; Vazou *et al.*, 2005); however, they are often short lived, as sport requires rapid resolutions, serving as inflated grounds for common adolescent peer conflicts (Fraser-Thomas & Côté, 2009; Weiss *et al.*, 1996).

Training and performance demands also lead high-performing adolescents to spend less time with non-sport peers (Csikszentmihalyi *et al.*, 1993; Hassell *et al.*, 2010; Holt & Dunn, 2004; Patrick *et al.*, 1999). Research has highlighted challenges of maintaining peer relationships outside sport, as school friends sometimes show ambivalence towards athletes' sport involvement, isolating them in their school contexts (Fraser-Thomas *et al.*, 2008b; MacPhail & Kirk, 2006). Despite this, adolescent athletes may have a positive sense of identity associated with being the high-performing athlete within their school, and feel their peers recognize their accomplishments and respect their commitments (Fraser-Thomas *et al.*, 2008b; Holt & Dunn, 2004; MacPhail & Kirk, 2006; Stevenson, 1990). Further, research by Patrick and colleagues (1999) found non-sport peers contributed to athletes' sport commitment through increased relationship satisfaction, when athletes were effective in balancing social opportunities outside of sport with their training.

Personal and social development

Family members and peers also play important roles in expert athletes' personal and social development throughout the specializing years, espousing values related to achievement, respect, altruism, hard work, success, and persistence (Bloom, 1985; Csikszentmihalyi *et al.*, 1993; Gould *et al.*, 2002; Stevenson, 1990; Trussell, 2012). The high-performance context appears to provide a backdrop for the modeling and learning of key skills and attributes, such as effective communication, time management, independence, emotional control (e.g., learning appropriate reactions following mistakes), self-awareness (e.g., learning constructive reflection following performances), and resilience (Fraser-Thomas & Côté, 2009; Keegan *et al.*, 2010; Lauer *et al.*, 2010; Woodcock *et al.*, 2011).

Parents also play key roles in assuring adolescents' healthy psychological development by offering esteem support – showing pride in accomplishments, confirming and reinforcing their child athlete's identity, and contributing to their overall self-worth (Harter, 1978; Hassell *et al.*, 2010; Scanlan *et al.*, 1989; Stevenson, 1990); however, these roles must be balanced with helping athletes keep perspective in relation to their sport, assuring privileges are not afforded to their child athlete, and emphasizing academic success and engagement in other activities (Côté, 1999; Lauer *et al.*, 2010; Woodcock *et al.*, 2011). As an example, in Lauer and colleagues' (2010) study of professional tennis players, one participant explained that she'd just returned from Wimbledon, but was nonetheless expected to do the dishes. Parents may sometimes work collaboratively to achieve this balance, whereby one parent has the dominant role in their child athlete's sport development, and the other focuses to a greater extent on non-sport elements in the child's life (Fraser-Thomas *et al.*, 2008b; Gould *et al.*, 2002; Lauer *et al.*, 2010).

Positive facilitation of personal and social development is again not unanimous, as some parents have been found to be poor models of responsibility and weak communicators (e.g., failing to demonstrate emotional regulation), while maintaining excessive control of their child's development (e.g., restricting social life) and breeding a sense of unhealthy dependence (e.g., packing his/her training bag) (Gould *et al.*, 2002; Lauer *et al.*, 2010). It remains unclear how such behaviors influence expertise development, as athletes reflecting retrospectively in these studies suggested parents' behaviors may have contributed to their achievements. As Coakley (2006) suggests, it is likely that many well-intentioned parents lose perspective of how to best foster their child athlete's development, particularly during the specializing phase, as they get caught up in their child's success, their tangible investments in their child, and judgments of their self-worth as a parent.

Investment and maintenance years

Parents and peers continue to have changing roles in expert athletes' development during the transition from the specializing to investment and maintenance years. While parents provide ongoing tangible and emotional support, their involvement is less direct, with athletes often living away from home in a central training location, and siblings, peers, and teammates' roles also evolving (Côté, 1999; Durand-Bush & Salmela, 2002).

Parents and athletes' adversity

One parental role of continued importance during the investment and maintenance years is that of supporting athletes through setbacks, which has been associated with athletes' increased acceptance of adversity and use of positive coping strategies (Lafferty & Dorrell, 2006). Experiences of adversity may include training difficulties (e.g., fatigue, decreased motivation), coaching conflicts (e.g., favoritism), transition adjustments (e.g., freshman year), injury (e.g., decisions regarding surgery), or burnout (Côté, 1999; Durand-Bush & Salmela, 2002; Gould *et al.*, 2002; Morgan & Giacobbi, 2006). Past research with Olympians suggests family members could be unequivocally trusted with sensitive issues (e.g., injury, coach pressure) in the sometimes hyperpolitical climate of elite sport, and were helpful in providing optimism balanced with constructive feedback, given their understanding of the "whole person" (Durand-Bush & Salmela, 2002; Gould *et al.*, 2002).

Tamminen and Holt (2012) highlight parents' key roles in helping adolescent athletes cope, outlining how parents can offer a supportive context for learning by establishing a psychologically safe environment for discussion, monitoring athletes' reactions throughout discussions, questioning and reminding athletes of past successful coping strategies, sharing their own experiences, and encouraging independence (i.e., not running to fix problems every time they arise); however, not all parents in their study played facilitative roles, as some athletes were uncomfortable approaching their parents to discuss stress and coping, while other parents limited athletes'

Family and peer influences

exposure to stressors, in turn inhibiting their ability to learn to cope. Similarly, a study of injured inter-university swimmers found that many athletes felt removed from their home environment, and failed to draw upon parents' support (Abgarov *et al.*, 2012), highlighting the need for further examination of situational and personal factors that might influence parents' facilitation of athletes' coping experiences.

Unique role of siblings

The case of the Dufour-LaPointe sisters presented in the introduction reinforces Côté and Hay's (2002) argument that siblings' mutual socialization must be a consideration in talent development. Whereas peers typically become increasingly important socializing agents during later adolescence and young adulthood (Horn & Harris, 2002; Horn & Weiss, 1991), recent studies suggest that families of high-performing athletes may be more cohesive given tremendous time spent together, and that siblings may play unique roles in fostering expertise, beyond those of peers and teammates (Blazo *et al.*, 2014; Davis & Meyer, 2008). Specifically, Davis and Meyer's (2008) study of same-sex, same-sport sibling competitors found positive relationship functions including emotional support (i.e., cheering, displaying pride, encouraging) and informational support (i.e., providing technical/mental advice), with siblings' motivation to beat each other at the forefront of relationships. Older siblings were driven by a need to maintain their superior athletic status, while younger siblings aspired to move out of the shadow of their older siblings and establish their own sport identity. While rivalries involved warmth and closeness (i.e., concern for siblings' feelings and well-being), they also led siblings to experience negative emotions such as anxiety, anger, annoyance, and frustration. Collectively, these findings speak to the paradoxical nature of siblings' relationships (Furman & Buhrmester, 1985), and the need for continued investigation and understanding.

Relationships with teammates and peers

Teammates and competitors in this stage are often critical in optimizing talented athletes' performance, whether directly through modeling, or indirectly through the provision of an optimal training and competitive environment (Durand-Bush & Salmela, 2002; Gould *et al.*, 2002; Morgan & Giacobbi, 2006). Olympic champions highlighted teammates' roles in facilitating athletes' learning by fostering, nurturing, and instilling key psychological skills, and helping athletes gain perspective within the climate of high-performance sport (Gould *et al.*, 2002). Teammates are also important in challenging and inspiring athletes to work harder, as well as encouraging and supporting them emotionally during stressful situations, with older/veteran team members often serving like older siblings (Bruner *et al.*, 2008; Gould *et al.* 2002; Morgan & Giacobbi, 2006). However, the dynamics of peer relationships remain complex at this stage, with some athletes highlighting the drawbacks and challenges of interacting with competitors, as ordinary conversations (e.g., discussing training, competition schedules, injury status, etc.) could potentially be used against them (Durand-Bush & Salmela, 2002). Athletes have also struggled to maintain genuine relationships with teammates when they experience injury, feeling a lesser part of the team and judged for "bringing [their] negative energy to practice" (Abgarov *et al.*, 2012, p. 218).

While little work has focused on expert athletes' peer relationships outside high-level sport, such relationships appear to be generally healthy contributors to athletes' development. Gould and colleagues' (Gould *et al.*, 1999) work with Olympians found that having non-sport peers who were aware and accepting of the demands of high-performance sport facilitated more successful performances, given their roles as supporters and confidence builders. Further, while some Olympians experienced teasing from friends, this often served as a positive influence in keeping life normality and fostering determination. These athletes also spoke of the value of seeing their non-sport peers achieve success in other domains, as this fostered their own belief in their ability to be successful.

Future research directions and potential implications

This chapter's aim was to advance understanding of parents, siblings, and peers' roles throughout development in optimizing young athletes' opportunities to reach the highest levels in their sport, using the DMSP (Côté, 1999; Côté & Fraser-Thomas, 2011; Durand-Bush & Salmela, 2002) as a framework to guide our discussion. Broadly speaking, our review yielded many commonalities across expert athletes' career paths with regard to parents, siblings, and peers as networks of support, but also uncovered a range of athletes' experiences that did not always appear supportive of athletes' talent development, despite leading to expertise. We reiterate Stevenson's early conclusion following his investigation of international athletes – that there is enormous diversity in career paths of each individual, and "success in sport, is not entirely the product of a rational system" (1990, p. 250). Starkes, Helsen, and Jack (2001) suggested the goal of talent development research was to advance understanding of talent development, to in turn shorten athletes' journeys to expertise, and elongate the duration of time that they perform at their peak; it appears that much research is still necessary, regarding the roles of family and peers, in reaching this goal. Throughout our review, we made suggestions regarding specific areas in need of further research. In this section, we highlight five broader issues that we feel warrant particular attention moving forward, to in turn lead to more robust practical implications in expertise development.

Methodological: longitudinal, prospective, and innovative research

Given the very nature of expertise development (i.e., attainment of high levels of achievement over time), the outcome of expertise remains unknown for much of the time that is of ultimate interest for study, creating extensive methodological challenges (see Chapter 14). Many of the studies reviewed in this chapter relied on retrospective methodologies, whereby athletes who had attained expertise in adulthood reflected on their childhood and adolescent experiences, which were susceptible to memory bias (Gabbe *et al.*, 2003). While logistically challenging and time intensive, it is essential that future researchers use prospective and longitudinal methodologies to better understand social influences at each stage of development, rather than only after expertise attainment (Kremer-Sadlik & Kim, 2007). A related issue is the need to study highly invested athletes who are less successful in their attainment of expertise, to better understand potential nuances in social support between those who reach the highest levels and those who do not (Lauer *et al.*, 2010). While there is benefit in using phenomenological research designs such as ethnography (Fraser-Thomas & Côté, 2009), the potentially evasive nature of studying athletes' intimate relationships throughout development requires future researchers to draw upon innovative methodologies such as diaries, logs, social networking sites, and photo journaling to capture the essence of regular dynamic interactions.

Whole family dynamics – including siblings

The study of the dynamics of entire families in fostering sport expertise is also important, as there is a need to consider reciprocal effects parents, children, and brothers and sisters may have on one another (Blazo *et al.*, 2014; Côté, 1999; Kremer-Sadlik & Kim, 2007; Trussell, 2012). Siblings are grossly overlooked in the study of expertise development, given their role as a major family

Family and peer influences

subsystem affecting the entire family climate (Côté & Hay, 2002). In particular, enhanced understanding of the processes underlying siblings' positive and negative interactions is necessary, and whether these interactions ultimately facilitate or hinder elite athletes' development (e.g., Blazo *et al.*, 2014; Davis & Meyer, 2008). In addition, research focused on studying diverse factors that may moderate sibling experiences, including birth order, proximity of birth, gender, sport trajectories, and parent behaviors within the family context, is warranted. Further investigation of situations where siblings are also teammates, competitors, peers, and/or friends would also be beneficial, given the potential complexities of athletes' engaging in these multiple diverse roles (Trussell, 2012).

The study of entire families may begin to tease out issues of diverse perspectives encountered when examining only athletes or parents' experiences (Keegan *et al.*, 2009; Knight *et al.*, 2011; Lauer *et al.*, 2010; Wuerth *et al.*, 2004), while also facilitating better understanding of bi-directional relationships that may exist between families' sport involvement, families' healthy development, and elite athletes' development. Given past research suggesting family relationships are both stronger and more strained as a result of children's sport investment (e.g., Blazo *et al.*, 2014; Kay, 2000; Kirk *et al.*, 1997b; Morgan & Giacobbi, 2006; Trussel, 2012), further investigation is necessary to examine underlying elements of sport that may optimize family health and athlete expertise. In essence, how does a family such as the Dufour-Lapointes become "platinum winners in family bonding" (MacGregor, 2014), while others seem the picture of dysfunction?

Athletes' healthy psychosocial development

Greater focus is also necessary to examine family and peer influences in expert athletes' development through the lens of healthy psychosocial development. A comment by a participant in Holt and Dunn's study of international adolescent soccer players speaks to this issue: ". . . I don't know if I sacrificed growing up, my childhood. I definitely had fun, but I don't really feel I had a childhood" (2004, p. 208). As children are being encouraged to become involved in sport at increasingly early ages (e.g., as advocated by models such as Canadian Sport for Life), and potentially staying involved in high-performance sport further into adulthood (Wylleman & Lavallee, 2004), additional consideration should be given to the healthy socialization of these individuals throughout and following their careers (Lauer *et al.*, 2010). At the youth level, for example, only a handful of studies have focused on parents as coaches of their child athletes, despite youth programs' extensive reliance on volunteer parent coaches, and many expert athletes' recalling this experience (e.g., Bloom, 1985; Stevenson, 1990). Parent coach-child athlete studies highlight complexities around parental pressure, challenging communication, inflated emotions, and conflicting demands (Jowett *et al.*, 2007; Weiss & Fretwell, 2005), indicating a need for greater understanding of the dynamics, interactions, challenges, and benefits of these relationships within the context of healthy psychosocial development. In later stages, additional understanding of peer groups and friendships among high-performance athletes is necessary, given preliminary evidence of overlapping roles as teammates and competitors, leading to layered and sometimes dysfunctional relationships (Durand-Bush & Salmela, 2002). Also of critical value would be research examining optimal roles of family and peers as high-performance athletes transition out of sport, at a time of numerous life changes when athletes' psychological and social health may be particularly vulnerable (Wylleman & Lavallee, 2004).

Changing social landscape

Families' influences in expert athletes' development must also be contextualized within the changing social landscape. Given extensive reliance on retrospective methodologies, much of our knowledge is built upon sport experiences that occurred in past decades. Kay (2000) highlights numerous factors that suggest families' roles in talent development may differ from those in past decades, including changing family structures (i.e., increases in lone parenting, reconstituted households, smaller families), changing parent demographics (i.e., older parents, both parents working, same-sex parents, decline of middle class), and changing parenting expectations (i.e., "intensive" parenting, roles and contributions of male and females). As such, past research conducted among intact middle class families (e.g., Côté, 1999; Fraser-Thomas *et al.*, 2008a, 2008b) may not be representative of current expert athletes' experiences, and future researchers should be particularly cognizant of these changing social factors. For instance, current families of high socioeconomic status may have the financial resources to support their child athletes, but they may struggle more than in the past to provide other forms of tangible support (e.g., time, transportation) if both parents are working. Further, given changing expectations in parenting roles, and increased occurrence of reconstituted families and same-sex parents, past calls for examination of differences in mother and father interactions with their high-performing child athletes (e.g., Hassell *et al.*, 2010; Knight *et al.*, 2011) are of increased importance. In addition, given past findings' suggesting large families, divorce, and lone-parent families may contribute to expert athletes' development of key life skills and psychological characteristics (e.g., teamwork, resilience, work ethic) (Gould *et al.*, 2002), examination of the role of changing family structures in relation to expert athletes' development would also be of interest.

Assuring tangible support

We began the chapter by discussing the incredible performances of the Dufour-Lapointe sisters who gained international attention following their gold, silver, and 12th place finishes in freestyle moguls in the Olympics in Sochi, Russia. When asked about "sacrifices," the girls' father corrected his interviewer, outlining that the family had made "choices about what [we] want to do" (MacGregor, 2014). Yet some may disagree with this comment, arguing that the pursuit of high-performance sport is not a choice for many families. As the mother of a gymnast in Kay and colleagues' study outlined, "it didn't matter how talented you were, you needed to be rich" (2006, p. 9, as cited in Kay, 2000). Evidence suggests that parents' provision of tangible support may be a prerequisite for children's sport involvement, rather than a factor distinguishing experts (Fraser-Thomas *et al.*, 2013; Kirk *et al.*, 1997a; Lauer *et al.*, 2010; Wolfenden & Holt, 2005), as children of lower income and lone-parent families are less likely to be involved in high-performance sports, due to barriers such as cost, transportation, and proximity to facilities (e.g., Kirk *et al.*, 1997a, 1997b; Rowley, 1992; Yang *et al.*, 1996).

Kay (2000) asks whether this should be a policy issue. On the one hand, family matters tend to be a private sphere; on the other, athletes' performances in major games have become of increasing interest in public spheres, with nations having a strong sense of ownership in their high-performing athletes. Green's (2005) suggestion – increasing broad-based participation would increase the pool of competitive sport athletes from which the higher performers could develop – reiterates the fundamental principles of the sport participation pyramid. While some policy initiatives have taken steps towards assuring all children have equal opportunity for sport involvement by increasing families' access to tangible support, research assessing the effectiveness of these initiatives shows they are used primarily by more affluent families, essentially negating their intended purpose (Collins & Buller, 2003; Spence *et al.*, 2010). Baker and colleagues (Baker *et al.*, 2003b) suggest the road to expertise development is likely qualitatively different for those for whom emotional and financial resources are not accessible; however, evidence suggests the road to expertise is taken by very few who have limited resources.

Family and peer influences

Clearly, while extensive research has contributed to substantial growth in knowledge over the past few decades regarding family and peer influences in the development of expert athletes, one of the greatest limitations to optimizing talent remains at the most grassroots level – parents being able to offer their children initial sport opportunities and subsequent tangible support. As such, further advancement of expertise research at an applied level will be dependent on researchers' focusing to a greater extent on evidence-based initiatives and intervention studies to determine how to assure supportive contexts for talent development from family to policy levels, so that all families are able to support their children in aspiring to become expert athletes.

References

Abgarov, A., Fraser-Thomas, J., Baker, J., & Jeffery-Tosoni, S. (2012) 'Understanding social support throughout the injury process among interuniversity swimmers', *Journal of Intercollegiate Sport*, 5(2): 213–39.

Allen, J. B. (2003) 'Social motivation in youth sport', *Journal of Sport & Exercise Psychology*, 25: 551–67.

Babkes, M. K., & Weiss, M. R. (1999) 'Parental influence on cognitive and affective responses in children's competitive soccer participation', *Pediatric Exercise Science,* 11: 44–62

Baker, J., Côté, J., & Abernethy, B. (2003a) 'Learning from the experts: Practice activities of expert decision makers in sport', *Research Quarterly for Exercise and Sport*, 74: 342–7.

Baker, J., Horton, S., Robertson-Wilson, J., & Wall, M. (2003b) 'Nurturing sport expertise: Factors influencing the development of elite athletes', *Journal of Sport Science and Medicine*, 1: 1–9.

Blazo, J. A., Carson, S., Czech, D. R., & Dees, W. (2014) 'A qualitative investigation of the sibling sport achievement', *The Sport Psychologist*, 28: 36–47.

Bloom, B. S. (1985) *Developing talent in young people*, New York: Ballantine Books.

Bruner, M. W., Munroe-Chandler, K. J., & Spink, K. S. (2008) 'Entry into elite sport: A preliminary investigation into the transition experiences of rookie athletes', *Journal of Applied Sport Psychology*, 20: 236–52.

Brustad, R. J., Babkes, M. L. & Smith, A. L. (2001) 'Youth in sport: Psychological considerations', in R. N. Singer, H. A. Hausenblas, & C. M. Janelle (eds) *Handbook of sport psychology*, New York: John Wiley, 604–35.

Bukowski, W. M. (2001) 'Friendship and the worlds of childhood', in D. W. Nangle & C. A. Erdley (eds) *The role of friendship is psychological adjustment: Vol. 91. New direction for child and adolescent development*, San Francisco: Jossey-Bass, 93–106.

Canadian Broadcasting Corporation (2014a). 'Dufour-Lapointe family speaks to Ron MacLean', Retrieved from http://olympics.cbc.ca/videos/video/seoname=the-dufour-lapointe-family interview-olympic-primetime.html (accessed 9 February, 2014).

Carlson, R. (1988) 'The socialization of elite tennis players in Sweden: An analysis of the players' backgrounds and development', *Sociology of Sport Journal*, 5: 241–56.

Coakley, J. (1992) 'Burnout among adolescent athletes: A personal failure or social problem', *Sociology of Sport Journal*, 9: 271–85.

Coakley, J. (2006) 'The good father: Parental expectations and youth sports', *Leisure Studies*, 25: 153–63.

Coakley, J., & White, A. (1992) 'Making decisions: Gender and sport participation among British adolescents', *Sociology of Sport Journal*, 9: 20–35.

Collins, M. F., & Buller, J. R. (2003) 'Social exclusion from high-performance sport. Are all talented young sports people being given and equal opportunity of reaching the Olympic podium?', *Journal of Sport & Social Issues*, 27: 420–42.

Côté, J. (1999) 'The influence of family in the development of talent in sport', *The Sport Psychologist*, 13: 395–417.

Côté, J., Baker, J., & Abernethy, B. (2007) 'Practice and play in the development of sport expertise', in R. Eklund & G. Tenebaum (eds) *Handbook of sport psychology*, 3rd ed., Hoboken, NJ: Wiley, 184–202.

Côté, J., & Fraser-Thomas, J. (2011) 'Youth involvement and positive development in sport', in P.R.E. Crocker (ed) *Sport psychology: A Canadian perspective*, 2nd ed., Toronto: Pearson Prentice Hall, 226–55.

Côté, J., & Hay, J. (2002) 'Children's involvement in sport: A developmental perspective', in J.M. Silva & D. E. Stevens (eds) *Psychological foundations of sport*, Boston: Allyn & Bacon, 484–502.

Csikszentmihalyi, M., Rathunde, K., & Whalen, S. (1993) *Talented teenagers: The roots of success and failure*, Cambridge: Cambridge University Press.

Davis, N. W., & Meyer, B. B. (2008) 'When sibling becomes competitor: A qualitative investigation of same-sex sibling competitive in elite sport', *Journal of Applied Sport Psychology*, 20(2): 220–35.

Duncan, S. C. (1993) 'The role of cognitive appraisal and friendship provisions in adolescents' affect and motivation towards activity in physical education', *Research Quarterly for Exercise and Sport*, 64: 314–23.

Durand-Bush, N., & Salmela, J. H. (2002) 'The development and maintenance of expert athletic performance: Perceptions of world and Olympic champions', *Journal of Applied Sport Psychology*, 14: 154–71.

Eccles, J. S., & Harold, R. D. (1991) 'Gender differences in sport involvement: Applying the Eccles' expectancy-value model', *Journal of Applied Sport Psychology*, 3: 7–35.

Fraser-Thomas, J. L., & Côté, J. (2009) 'Understanding adolescents' positive and negative developmental experiences in sport', *The Sport Psychologist*, 23: 3–23.

Fraser-Thomas, J., Côté, J., & Deakin, J. (2008a) 'Examining adolescent sport dropout and prolonged engagement from a developmental perspective', *Journal of Applied Sport Psychology*, 20: 318–33.

Fraser-Thomas, J., Côté, J., & Deakin, J. (2008b) 'Understanding dropout and prolonged engagement in adolescent competitive sport', *Psychology of Sport and Exercise*, 9: 645–62.

Fraser-Thomas, J., Strachan, L., & Jeffery-Tosoni, S. (2013) 'Family influence on children's involvement in sport', in J. Côté & R. Lidor (eds) *Conditions of children's talent development in sport*, Morgantown, WV: Fitness Information Technology, 179–96.

Fredricks, J. A., & Eccles, J. S. (2004) 'Parental influences on youth involvement in sports', in M. R. Weiss (ed) *Developmental sport and exercise psychology: A lifespan perspective*, Morgantown, WV: Fitness Information Technology, 145–64.

Furman, W., & Buhrmester, D. (1985) 'Children's perceptions of the qualities of sibling relationships', *Child Development*, 56: 448–61.

Gabbe, B. J., Finch, C. F., Bennell, K. L., & Wajswelner, H. (2003) 'How valid is a self reported 12 month sports injury history?', *British Journal of Sports Medicine*, 37: 545–7.

Gould, D., Dieffenbach, K., & Moffatt, A. (2002) 'Psychological characteristics and their development in Olympic champions', *Journal of Applied Sport Psychology*, 14: 172–204.

Gould, D., Guinan, D., Greenleaf, C., Medbery, R., & Peterson, K. (1999) 'Factors affecting Olympic performance: Perceptions of athletes and coaches from more less successful teams', *The Sport Psychologist*, 13: 371–94.

Gould, D., Lauer, L., Rolo, C., Jannes, C., & Pennisi, N. (2008) 'The role of parents in tennis success: Focus group interviews with junior coaches', *The Sport Psychologist*, 22: 18–37.

Green, C. B. (2005) 'Building sport programs to optimize athlete recruitment, retention and transition: Toward a normative theory of sport development', *Journal of Sport Management*, 19: 233–53.

Hardy, C. J., & Crace, R. K. (1993) 'The dimensions of social support when dealing with sport injuries', in D. Paragman (ed) *Psychological bases of sport injury*, Morgantown, WV: Fitness Information Technology, 121–44.

Harter, S. (1978) 'Effectance motivation reconsidered. Toward a developmental model', *Human Development*, 21: 34–64.

Hassell, K., Sabiston, C. M., & Bloom, G. A. (2010) 'Exploring the multiple dimensions of social support among elite female adolescent swimmers', *International Journal of Sport Psychology*, 41: 340–59.

Holt, N. L., & Dunn, J.G.H. (2004) 'Toward a grounded theory of the psychosocial competencies and environmental conditions associated with soccer success', *Journal of Applied Sport Psychology*, 16: 199–219.

Holt, N. L., & Hoar, S. (2006) 'The multidimensional construct of social support', in S. Hanton & S. Mellalieu (eds) *Literature reviews in sport psychology*, Hauppauge, NY: Nova Science, 199–225.

Holt, N. L., Tamminen, K. A., Black, D. E., Sehn, Z. L., & Wall, M. P. (2008) 'Parental involvement in competitive youth sport settings', *Psychology of Sport and Exercise*, 9: 663–85.

Hopwood, M. J., Farrow, D., MacMahon, C., & Baker, J. (in press) *Sibling dynamics and sport expertise*, manuscript under review.

Horn, T. S., & Harris, A. (2002) 'Perceived competence in young athletes: Research findings and recommendations for coaches and parents', in F. L. Smoll & R. E. Smith (eds) *Children and youth in sport: A biopsychosocial perspective*, 2nd ed., Dubuque, IA: Kendall-Hunt, 435–64.

Horn, T. S., & Hasbrook, C. A. (1986) 'Informational components influencing children's perceptions of their physical competence', in M. R. Weiss & D. Gould (eds) *Sport for children and youths*, Champaign, IL: Human Kinetics, 81–8.

Horn, T. S., & Weiss, M. R. (1991) 'A developmental analysis of children's self-ability judgments in the physical domain', *Pediatric Exercise Science*, 3: 310–26.

Jowett, S., Timson-Katchis, M., & Adams, R. (2007) 'Too close for comfort? Dependence in the dual role of parent/coach-child/athlete relationship', *International Journal of Coaching Science*, 1: 59–78.

Kay, T. (2000) 'Sporting excellence: A family affair?', *European Physical Education Review*, 6: 151–69.

Family and peer influences

Kay, T., & Bass, D. (2011) 'The family factor in coaching', in I. Stafford (ed) *Coaching children in sport*, New York: Routledge, 169–80.

Keegan, R., Harwood, C., Spray, C., & Lavallee, D. (2009) 'A qualitative investigation exploring the motivational climate in early career sports participants: Coach, parent and peer influences on sport motivation', *Psychology of Sport and Exercise*, 10: 361–72.

Keegan, R., Spray, C., Harwood, C., & Lavallee, D. (2010) 'The motivational atmosphere in youth sport: Coach, parent and peer influences on motivation in specializing sport participants', *Journal of Applied Sport Psychology*, 22: 87–105.

Kirk, D., Carlson, T., O'Connor, A., Burke, P., Davis, K., & Glover, S. (1997a) 'The economic impact on families of children's participation in junior sport', *Australian Journal of Science and Medicine in Sport*, 29: 27–33.

Kirk, D., O'Connor, A., Carlson, T., Burke, P., Davis, K., & Glover, S. (1997b) 'Time commitments in junior sport: Social consequences for participants and their families', *European Journal of Physical Education*, 2: 51–73.

Knight, C. J., Boden, C. M., & Holt, N. L. (2010) 'Junior tennis players' preferences for parental behaviours', *Journal of Applied Sport Psychology*, 22: 377–91.

Knight, C. J., Neely, K. C., & Holt, N. L. (2011) 'Parental behaviours in team sports: How do female athletes want parents to behave?', *Journal of Applied Sport Psychology*, 23: 76–92.

Kohlberg, L. (1969) 'Stage and sequence: The cognitive developmental approach to socialization', in D. A. Goslin (ed) *Handbook of socialization theory and research*, Chicago, IL: Rand McNally, 347–80.

Kremer-Sadlik, T., & Kim, J. L. (2007) 'Lessons from sports: Children's socialization to values through family interaction during sports activities', *Discourse and Society*, 18: 35–52.

Ladd, G. W., Kochenderfer, B. J., & Coleman, C. (1997) 'Classroom peer acceptance, friendship and victimization: Distinct relational systems that contribute uniquely to children's school adjustment?', *Child Development*, 68: 1181–97.

Lafferty, M. E., & Dorrell, K. (2006) 'Coping strategies and the influence of perceived parental support in junior national age swimmers', *Journal of Sport Sciences*, 24: 253–9.

Lauer, L., Gould, D., Roman, N., & Pierce, M. (2010) 'Parental behaviors that affect junior tennis player development', *Psychology of Sport and Exercise*, 11: 487–96.

MacGregor, R. (2014, February 9) 'Dufour-Lapointe family bonds over medal wins', *The Globe and Mail*. Online. Retrieved from www.theglobeandmail.com/sports/olympics/dufour-lapointe-family-bonds-over-medal-wins/article16772511/#dashboard/follows/ (accessed 31 July, 2014).

MacPhail, A., Gorely, T., & Kirk, D. (2003) 'Young people's socialization into sport: A case study of an athletics club', *Sport, Education and Society*, 8: 251–76.

MacPhail, A., & Kirk, D. (2006) 'Young people's socialization into sport: Experiencing the specializing phase', *Leisure Studies*, 25: 57–74.

McCarthy, P. J., & Jones, M. V. (2007) 'A qualitative study of sport enjoyment in the sampling years', *The Sport Psychologist*, 21: 400–16.

Morgan, T. K. & Giacobbi, P.R., Jr. (2006) 'Toward two grounded theories of the talent development and social support process of highly successful collegiate athletes', *The Sport Psychologist*, 20: 295–313.

Patrick, H., Ryan, A. M., Alfeld-Liro, C., Fredricks, J. A., Hruda, L. Z. & Eccles, J. S. (1999) 'Adolescents' commitment to developing talent: The role of peers in continuing motivation for sports and the arts', *Journal of Youth and Adolescence*, 28: 741–63.

Piaget J. (1971) 'The theory of stages in cognitive development', in D. R. Green, M. P. Ford, & G. B. Flamer (eds) *Measurement and Piaget*, New York: MacGraw-Hill, 1–11.

Power, T.G., & Woolger, C. (1994) 'Parenting practices and age-group swimming. A correlational study', *Research Quarterly for Exercise and Sport*, 65: 59–66.

Raedeke, T. D. (1997) 'Is athlete burnout more than just stress? A sport commitment perspective', *Journal of Sport & Exercise Psychology*, 19: 396–417.

Rowley, S. (1992) *TOYA (Training of young athletes study): Identification of talent*. London: The Sports Council.

Scanlan, T. K., Carpenter, P. J., Schmidt, G. W., Simons, J., & Keeler, B. (1993) 'An introduction to the sport commitment model', *Journal of Sport & Exercise Psychology*, 15: 1–15.

Scanlan, T. K., Stein, G. L., & Ravizza, K. (1989) 'An in-depth study of former elite figure skaters II: Sources of enjoyment', *Journal of Sport & Exercise Psychology*, 11: 65–83.

Smith, A. L. (2003) 'Peer relationships in physical activity contexts: A road less traveled in youth sport and exercise psychology research', *Psychology of Sport and Exercise*, 4: 25–39.

Spence, J. C., Holt, N. L., Dutove, J. K., & Carson, V. (2010) 'Uptake and effectiveness of the children's fitness tax credit in Canada: The rich get richer', *BMC Public Health*, 10: 356–61.

Starkes, J., Helsen, W., & Jack, R. (2001) 'Expert performance in sport and dance', in R. N. Singer, H. A. Hausenblas, & C. M. Janelle (eds) *Handbook of sport psychology*, New York: Wiley, 174–201.

Stevenson, C. L. (1990) 'The early careers of international athletes', *Sociology of Sport Journal*, 7: 238–53.

Sulloway, F. J. (1996) *Born to rebel: Birth order, family dynamics, and creative lives*, New York: Pantheon.

Tamminen, K. A., & Holt, N. L. (2012) 'Adolescent athletes' learning about coping and the roles of parents and coaches', *Psychology of Sport and Exercise*, 13: 69–79.

Trussell, D. E. (2012) 'Contradictory aspects of organized youth sport: Challenging and fostering sibling relationships and participation experiences', *Youth and Society*. doi: 10.1177/0044118X12453058.

Ullrich-French, S., & Smith, A. L. (2006) 'Perceptions of relationships with parents and peers in youth sport: Independent and combined predictions of motivational outcomes', *Psychology of Sport and Exercise*, 7: 193–214.

Ullrich-French, S., & Smith, A. L. (2009) 'Social and motivational predictors of continued youth sport participation', *Psychology of Sport and Exercise*, 10: 87–95.

Vazou, S., Ntoumanis, N., & Duda, J. L. (2005) 'Peer motivational climate in youth sport: A qualitative inquiry', *Psychology of Sport and Exercise*, 6: 497–516.

Weiss, M. R., & Ferrer-Caja, E. (2002) 'Motivational orientations in sport', in T. Horn (ed) *Advances in sport and exercise psychology*, Champaign, IL: Human Kinetics, 347–79.

Weiss, M. R., & Fretwell, S. D. (2005) 'The parent-coach/child-athlete relationship in youth sport. Cordial, contentious, or conundrum?', *Research Quarterly for Exercise and Sport*, 76: 286–305.

Weiss, M. R., Kimmel, L. A., & Smith, A. L. (2001) 'Determinants of sport commitment among junior tennis players: Enjoyment as a mediating variable', *Pediatric Exercise Science*, 13: 131–44.

Weiss, M. R., Smith, A. L., & Theeboom, M. (1996) '"That's what friends are for": Children's and teenagers' perceptions of peer relationships in the sport domain', *Journal of Sport & Exercise Psychology*, 18: 347–79.

Whiteman, S. D., Mchale, S. M., & Crouter, A. C. (2007) 'Explaining sibling similarities: Perceptions of sibling influences', *Journal of Youth and Adolescence*, 36: 963–72.

Wolfenden, L. E., & Holt, N. L. (2005) 'Talent development in elite junior tennis: Perceptions of players, parents, and coaches', *Journal of Applied Sport Psychology*, 17: 108–26.

Woodcock, C., Holland, M. J.G., Duda, J. L., & Cumming, J. (2011) 'Psychological qualities of elite adolescent rugby players: Parents, coaches, and sport administration staff perceptions and supporting roles', *The Sport Psychologist*, 25: 411–43.

Wuerth, S., Lee, M. J., & Alfermann, D. (2004) 'Parental involvement and athletes' career in youth sport', *Psychology of Sport and Exercise*, 5: 21–33.

Wylleman, P., & Lavallee, D. (2004) 'Career transitions in sport: European perspectives', *Psychology of Sport and Exercise*, 5: 7–20.

Yang, X., Telama, R., & Laakso, L. (1996) 'Parents physical activity, socioeconomic status and education as predictors of physical activity and sport among children and youths: A 12-year follow-up study', *International Review for Sociology of Sport*, 31: 272–89.

30

DELIBERATE PRACTICE IN SPORT

Paul R. Ford, Edward K. Coughlan, Nicola J. Hodges, and A. Mark Williams

Many observers wonder how expert athletes are able to achieve, maintain, and improve upon their outstanding performances. The majority of people agree that engagement in practice is an important part of this process. In this chapter, we review a particular type of practice activity known as *deliberate practice*. Deliberate practice is both an activity in sport and a scientific theory. We begin the chapter with an outline of the theory and a review of the original research study that introduced it (Ericsson, Krampe, and Tesch-Römer, 1993). In the second section, we briefly define deliberate practice as an activity in sport and review the research on it with athletes. In recent times, deliberate practice has become a somewhat maligned activity and theory (e.g., Hambrick *et al.*, 2013; Tucker & Collins, 2012). We believe the scientific interrogation of theories and concepts is an important part of their development, and should be encouraged. Therefore, in the third section of the chapter, we review the concepts associated with deliberate practice that have been subject to criticism. We address some misinterpretations of the research findings from studies that have examined deliberate practice. In the final section, we detail the concepts of deliberate practice that we consider essential parts of the acquisition and improvement of expert performance in sport.

Deliberate practice theory and supporting data

The theory of deliberate practice is a framework that details how practice can lead to improvements in performance and the attainment of expertise. The theory has been detailed in several articles and book chapters elsewhere by Ericsson (1996, 2003, 2006, 2007; Ericsson *et al.*, 1993; Ericsson & Towne, 2010). The seminal paper published by Ericsson *et al.* in 1993 introduced and provided tests of deliberate practice theory. They examined the activities that violinists and pianists who were enrolled at a music academy in Berlin had engaged in since starting in the domain. In a first study, two of the groups were students studying the violin in the West Berlin Music Academy. These students were divided into "best" and "good" violinists based on assessments of current performance by the professors, with the "best" group expected to make a professional career as members of the top orchestras in the world. They were compared to the lowest skill group who were studying to be music teachers in the education department. A fourth group took part, comprised of middle-aged professional violinists playing in world-class orchestras in order to provide data on a current expert group. In a second study, two groups of pianists were studied, who were either young adult experts from the music academy or age-matched amateurs.

The data from these studies was intended to inform about two key aspects of deliberate practice theory: first, the *monotonic benefits assumption*, or how practice increases over time and its relation to performance and attainment and second, the *ratings of deliberate practice*, or how this activity is defined.

Monotonic benefits assumption

A key part of deliberate practice theory is the monotonic benefits assumption, which holds "... that the amount of time an individual engages in deliberate practice activities is monotonically related to that individual's acquired performance level" (Ericsson *et al.*, 1993, p. 368). Monotonic means that two or more variables increase or decrease together, so that in this case when deliberate practice amounts increase, so will performance (Everitt & Skrondal, 2012). Experience alone is not thought to be sufficient for improvements in performance to occur, and typically the attainment of expertise in a domain requires engagement in deliberate practice across 10 years or more. Based on this assumption the central claim of their framework is that "... the level of performance an individual attains is directly related to the amount of deliberate practice accumulated" (Ericsson et al., 1993, p. 370). In the two studies of musicians, participants retrospectively recalled in interviews and diaries the amount of hours spent in music activities between starting in the domain and the current time. The amount of hours accumulated in solitary music practice by 18 years of age was compared between groups. The focus on solitary deliberate practice activities was due to it being rated by the violinists as the most relevant to improving their performance. There were other activities that were rated by the violinists as being highly relevant to improving performance, including group practice, taking lessons, and music theory, but these were not included in the accumulated hours analyzed in these studies.

The mean start age of participants in violin practice was 7.9 years of age (5.8 years of age for experts pianists), providing some support for the idea that the attainment of expertise requires engagement across 10 years or more. Figure 30.1 shows that by 18 years of age the best violinists in the academy and the middle-aged professional violinists had accumulated 7,410 and 7,336 hours in solitary deliberate practice activities, respectively. In comparison, by the same age, the

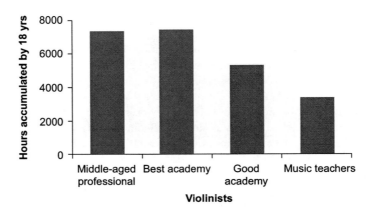

Figure 30.1 Hours accumulated in solitary deliberate practice by 18 years of age for violinists who are middle-aged professionals, best in academy, good in academy, and music teachers (adapted from Ericsson *et al.*, 1993).

Deliberate practice in sport

good violinists had accumulated 5,301 hours, whereas the music teachers had accumulated only 3,420 hours. The accumulated, solitary deliberate practice for each violinist group was positively related to their current level of attainment, supporting the central prediction that performance level is directly related to the amount of deliberate practice accumulated. For all four groups, the reported amount of practice increased monotonically with age. In their second study, expert pianists had accumulated 7,606 hours of solitary deliberate practice by 18 years of age, which was significantly more than the amateur pianists, who had accumulated only 1,606 hours. Moreover, accumulated solitary practice hours by 18 years of age were highly related to current performance by the pianists on music tasks (e.g., tapping and movement coordination measures), independent of skill group.

In summary, these data reported in Ericsson *et al.* (1993) provided support for the positive relationship between accumulated deliberate practice and performance or attainment level. Moreover, both weekly and accumulated practice amounts increased in a monotonic fashion with age. However, there was no data collected to show that practice amounts increased in a monotonic relationship with performance, in accord with the monotonic benefits assumption. The measures of performance and attainment were only determined at one time point (i.e., current skill level), not across development. The researchers state that sports, such as individual track and field events, may provide an opportunity to repeatedly measure the performance of individuals as they develop; however, researchers are yet to do this and relate it to practice amounts.

Ratings of deliberate practice

Deliberate practice was predicted to differ from other activities by being more relevant to improving key aspects of current performance, more effortful, yet relatively low in inherent enjoyment (Ericsson *et al.*, 1993). To test these predictions, the musicians were asked to rate various activities that were either music related (e.g., solo performance, group performance, solitary practice, practice with others) or everyday activities believed to be common to everyone (e.g., household chores, shopping, leisure, sleep). These activities were presented to all violinists who were required to estimate how much time they had spent on each activity for "the most recent typical week" (Ericsson *et al.*, 1993, p. 373). Participants were required to rate on a scale of one to 10 how relevant each activity was to improving their musical performance, how much effort was required to do the activity, and their level of enjoyment experienced when engaging in the activity (without allowing the outcome of the activity to influence their rating). There were no between-group differences in the activity ratings for relevance, effort, and enjoyment. Rating scores for each activity were collapsed across groups and compared against the grand mean for all activities to determine whether they were significantly higher or lower.

For the musical activities, solitary practice had the highest rating for relevance to improving performance. In comparison, solitary playing for fun was given one of the lowest ratings for relevance. The other musical activities that were rated higher for relevance than the grand mean rating of all activities were practice with others, taking lessons, solo and group performance, music theory, and listening to music. All of the musical activities that were rated higher than the grand mean for relevance to improving performance were rated higher than the grand mean for effort, except for listening to music. These same music activities were not rated differently for enjoyment compared to the grand mean for all activities, except for group performance and listening to music, which were rated higher. Sleep was the only everyday activity that scored higher for relevance than the grand mean. These ratings formed the criteria for defining the characteristics of deliberate practice.

The ratings are linked to three potential constraints inherent in long-term engagement in deliberate practice (Ericsson *et al.*, 1993). The motivational constraint is based on the premise that performers are motivated to engage in deliberate practice because of its value to improving their performance and that engaging in that activity is not inherently enjoyable. Therefore, beginning engagement in deliberate practice requires that performers are already participating in the domain and are motivated to improve performance. The effort constraint holds that engaging in deliberate practice requires the full attention of the performer to be maintained across the entire period of the activity. Therefore, antinomy exists between the requirement to maximize the amount of deliberate practice engaged and the somewhat limited duration that full attention and high effort can be maintained during bouts of this activity. The need to be able to quickly recover from bouts of deliberate practice so that more of this activity can be engaged in was made particularly salient by Ericsson *et al.* (1993). They showed that the best violinist groups tended to sleep more than the music teachers, particularly taking short naps in the afternoon. The associated prediction was that being unable to recover would lead to exhaustion in the form of mental and physical fatigue, as well as injury. Finally, the resource constraint is related to support from the family and significant others, such as coaches and teachers suitable for the stage of development of the performer. Other resources in terms of facilities, time, and equipment are required in order to engage in deliberate practice activities.

In recent versions of the theory, the notion of "arrested development" has been included to describe the plateau in performance that occurs for many performers (Ericsson, 2003, 2007). Some performers become competent at a task or domain and are satisfied to remain at that current level of performance. In contrast, current and future expert performers are not satisfied with being merely competent and, as a consequence, they plan and engage in deliberate practice activities that are highly relevant to improving their current performances and their weaknesses. Moreover, only some individuals have the motivation to consistently engage in deliberate practice to improve their performance (Ericsson, 2013a). It is their engagement in this activity (and motivation to do so) that continues to improve their performance beyond its current level or plateau. These differences in the quality and quantity of deliberate practice between expert performers and other performers illustrate how experts continue to improve performance across time. They are hypothesized to maintain cognitive control over their performance so that they can consistently improve it, with only some parts of performance being automated (Ericsson, 2013a).

Deliberate practice studies with athletes

Deliberate practice in sport is an activity engaged in by some athletes with the intention of improving specific aspects of competition performance. It is usually sport-specific activity (e.g., tennis activity for tennis players), but this depends on the aspect of performance being improved. It can include more generic activities, such as strength, fitness, or mental skill training. It requires a prior analysis of competition performance so that key aspects that are limiting performance and require improvement are identified and improved (e.g., Jones, 2012). These aspects include any of the physical, psychological, tactical, or skill aspects of the sport and athlete, as well as the equipment used by the athlete in the sport.

The first test of deliberate practice theory using athletes was a comparison of adult male Canadian international and club-level Olympic-style wrestlers (Hodges & Starkes, 1996). Wrestlers started the sport at 13 years of age on average, later than Ericsson *et al.*'s (1993) musicians who had started around seven or eight years of age. 10 years later, the international wrestlers had accumulated 5,882 hours of practice compared to 3,571 hours for the club wrestlers, demonstrating the same positive relationship between practice and attainment shown by Ericsson *et al.* (1993). When practice data were examined as a function of years wrestling, hours per week increased in a monotonic fashion with age and differentiated across the skill groups after about six years in the sport. It was practice time with others that differentiated the groups, however, rather than solitary practice as reported for the musicians. Moreover, two of the four practice activities that were rated highest for their relevance to improving performance by the wrestlers were also rated as highly enjoyable (i.e., mat work and working alone with the coach). These data served to question the hypothesis that deliberate practice comprises activities that are not high in inherent enjoyment. Fitness activities (weights, running) were, however, rated high for relevance and low for enjoyment. These findings were subsequently replicated in a study of Belgian international, national, and provincial soccer and hockey players (Helsen *et al.*, 1998). Across the two sports, nine of the 14 sport-specific practice activities (e.g., technical skills, tactical skills, games, practice alone with a coach) were rated significantly higher than the overall mean for their relevance to improving performance and for inherent enjoyment. Again, fitness activities rated high for relevance were rated as less enjoyable (e.g., running).

The deliberate practice studies conducted with athletes since 2000 have generally used the same methods as Ericsson *et al.* (1993). The data has generally supported the idea that practice and skill level are positively related, and that practice amounts increase in a monotonic fashion with age, supporting deliberate practice theory. In general, more skilled athlete groups have accumulated more hours in practice in their sport compared to less-skilled athlete groups (for recent reviews, see Baker & Young, 2014; Ward *et al.*, 2004). Moreover, fitness activities (e.g., weights, flexibility) have again been rated high as for relevance, but low for enjoyment, whereas sport-specific practices rated high for relevance are also rated high for enjoyment (e.g., Law *et al.*, 2007; Young & Salmela, 2002). Other researchers have examined the practice activities of elite youth or adolescent athletes (e.g., Ford *et al.*, 2009; Ford *et al.*, 2012; Hendry *et al.*, 2014; Ward *et al.*, 2007; Weissensteiner *et al.*, 2008). Despite the contribution of this research to models of skill development, it is somewhat limited by the possibility that many of the athletes studied will not become adult elites (yet see Ford *et al.*, 2009 for a longitudinal follow-up).

Criticisms of deliberate practice research

In this section, we review some concepts that have been associated with deliberate practice and that have been subject to criticism. These include the "10,000-hour rule," the idea that all practice and training is deliberate, the enjoyment tenet of the theory, and the belief that children should engage in deliberate practice.

The 10,000-hour rule

In 2008, a popular science book entitled *Outliers* (Gladwell, 2008) was published. In that book, the author reviewed Ericsson *et al.*'s (1993) study in a chapter entitled the "The 10,000-Hour Rule." In that chapter, Gladwell stated that "researchers have settled on what they believe is the magic number for true expertise: ten thousand hours" (Gladwell, 2008, p. 40). The book was hugely successful and the idea that it takes 10,000 hours of practice to become an expert performer became popular. That is, if someone does 10,000 hours of practice they will become an expert, whereas if one does not, then they will not. The "10,000-hour rule" text appears to have emanated erroneously from two parts of the Ericsson *et al.* (1993) paper. First, the average amount of hours of solitary deliberate practice that the best and professional violinists had reached by the age of 20 years was approximately 10,000 hours (Ericsson *et al.*, 1993). Second, based on previous research in other domains, most notably Simon and Chase's study of chess (1973), it was predicted that "expert performance is not reached with less than 10 years of deliberate practice" (Ericsson *et al.*, 1993, p. 372), also known as the "10-year rule" (Simon & Chase, 1973). In 2013, Ericsson (2013b) responded that the "10,000-hour rule" should not be attributed to him, and that he does not use the term in his papers.

The main method used by researchers to study accumulated practice is to have current expert athletes retrospectively recall the number of hours they have spent in practice since they began in their sport. Generally, researchers have shown that the number of hours accumulated by expert athletes in deliberate practice and other activities in their sport by the time they reach expert levels is significantly greater than that accumulated by less-skilled athletes, but is less than 10,000 hours. For example, international Belgium professional soccer players had accumulated around 7,000 hours in practice activities by 20 years of age (Helsen *et al.*, 1998), whereas Australian national team sport players had accumulated on average 3,939 hours by 19 years of age (Baker *et al.*, 2003a). There have been a few exceptions where "10,000 hours" have been exceeded. For example, Olympic gymnasts in Canada had accumulated 18,835 hours in practice activities by the age of 16 years (Law *et al.*, 2007). The "10,000-hour rule" as the "magic" amount of time required to become an expert athlete does not appear to be supported by research evidence from sport, although between sports there is considerable variability in accumulated hours.

Researchers have shown that the number of hours accumulated in practice in a sport before becoming an expert not only varies between sports, but also varies within the same sample of athletes in the same sport. For example, in the study cited above with Australian national team sport players (Baker *et al.*, 2003a), the standard deviation was 1,770 hours (almost half the size of the mean), ranging from 600 to 6,026 hours of practice by the age of 19 years. The variation of accumulated hours between expert athletes in the same sample suggests problems exists in the method of counting practice hours, or that other factors contribute to the development of expert performance. Tucker and Collins (2012) have calculated that hours accumulated in deliberate practice explained only 28 per cent of the variance in dart performance at 15 years into the career of the professional and regional dart players examined by Duffy *et al.* (2004). Several factors have been forwarded to explain the remaining variance, including genetic differences between individuals (e.g., Tucker & Collins, 2012). In the original Duffy *et al.* (2004) study, however, the sample size was relatively small ($n = 36$), so the 95 per cent confidence intervals for the correlation of 0.53 were 0.24 and 0.73. Moreover, the number of hours accumulated by the dart players showed large between-subject variation, with the professional male players accumulating 12,839 hours at 15 years into their career with a standard deviation of 7,780 hours. In a study of Canadian recreational, near elite, and elite swimmers, practice hours again accounted for only 31 per cent and 29 per cent of the variance in the 100 m and 200 m sprint events, respectively (Hodges *et al.*, 2004). However, this increased to 63 per cent of the variance as the distance of the event increased (i.e., 400 m). In the same paper, practice hours for triathletes who swam 1.5 km as part of an Olympic triathlon event accounted for 53 per cent of the variance in times in the swim event, albeit this decreased to 38 per cent for the overall triathlon event. The amount of explained variance increased as the emphasis on speed and power decreased, supporting the suggestion that certain sports or events might be more or less amenable to change with practice.

A potential limitation of previous research on deliberate practice is that very few, if any, researchers have addressed differences in the quality or efficiency of the deliberate practice engaged in, which might be expected to explain a substantial proportion of variance in eventual attainment. Researchers have not taken into account what is being practiced, including the aspect of performance being focused upon, how practice is structured, the coaching delivered, or the athlete's current status. Variance in these factors occurring across many practice sessions is likely to magnify differences in the number of hours required to reach expert levels of performance. Because the monotonic benefits assumption is not falsifiable when the quality of practice is used to excuse cases that do not support the premise (Tucker & Collins, 2012), it has been argued that researchers must incorporate more fine-grained measures of the quality of practice into future assessments of practice.

Several other limitations exist in the research conducted on accumulated hours in deliberate practice in sport. First, variation exists across studies for the age at which the number of hours accumulated in practice is totaled. Many researchers have totaled the hours across career to date, which is from start age in the sport to current age. For example, the mean start age for Belgian elite soccer players was five years and their practice hours were totaled to their current mean age of 25 years (Helsen et al., 1998). In comparison, Canadian international and club wrestlers had a mean start age of 13 years and a mean current age of 23 years (Hodges & Starkes, 1996). A 20-year career span (Helsen et al., 1998) compared to a 10-year career span (Hodges & Starkes, 1996) is likely to lead to significant disparities in accumulated practice amounts. Therefore, we recommend that researchers sum accumulated practice hours to the first meaningful milestone achievement of expertise (e.g., first professional contract in sport) or later milestones (e.g., winning world championships) (for an example, see Baker et al., 2003b). Second, and related to this point, the definition of expertise varies considerably between studies, with some participants being only semi-professional or national competitors rather than of international caliber, or junior/youth level rather than adult elite. Both of these limitations could lead to unnecessary variation in the reported number of hours accumulated in practice by athletes in these studies. Third, participants in these studies are required to recall hours engaged in practice that occurred many years ago, which may lead to memory errors and bias that will impact variance in the total number of hours accumulated. Fourth, the sports themselves contain a range of characteristics that may affect the number of practice hours needed to be an elite performer. These characteristics include the nature and popularity of the sport, the attributes required to be an expert performer in the sport, the age when peak performance is typically reached, and the extent to which other performers accumulate practice in the domain.

Not all practice is deliberate

In Table 30.1 we have differentiated four types of practice activities that are engaged in by athletes during training. Researchers have shown that a lot of athlete training is not deliberate practice. Based on estimates from weekly activity diaries, Hodges and Starkes (1996) reported that wrestlers invested significantly less practice time in sparring activities, which they rated as their most relevant activity for performance improvement, when compared to other activities that were deemed less relevant, such as warm-up. During training, many athletes engage in *maintenance practice activities*. These activities are designed to maintain their current level of performance, rather than improve it through deliberate practice (Krampe & Ericsson, 1996). During training, athletes also engage in *play activities* with the intention of fun and enjoyment or *competition activities*, in which the intention is to win. Researchers have generally tallied the amount of time athletes have spent in all forms of training, as opposed to just deliberate practice activities. Given that training can consist of maintenance, play, competition, and deliberate practice, it is likely that the amount of actual deliberate practice engaged in by athletes has been overestimated.

Competition activities are where the athlete must demonstrate their current performance, such as during match play in basketball. Ericsson et al. (1993) categorised competition as work activity and differentiated it from deliberate practice because it is time-constrained, motivated by external rewards,

Table 30.1 Four different types of practice activities that potentially comprise sport training but that differ with respect to the intention of the activity.

Activity	Main intention	Other main characteristics
Deliberate practice	To improve aspects of current performance	Relevant to improving performance, effortful, not necessarily enjoyable
Maintenance practice	To maintain current performance level	Unknown
Play practice	To experience fun, enjoyment, and improvement	Enjoyable
Competition	To win	Effortful, enjoyable

lacks repeated experiences or experimentation, and may lead to less performance improvement. However, a few researchers (e.g., Abernethy, Farrow, & Berry, 2003; Singer & Janelle, 1999) have stated that engagement in competition activity might contribute to the development and improvement of expert performance in sport. Many characteristics of competition activity in sport are difficult to recreate in practice. These include opponent characteristics, the size and structure of the activity, the influence of travel, venue and the crowd, or the frequent bouts of competition activity that occur over a relatively short period of time, such as in tennis. Indeed, team sport athletes rate competition activity as highly relevant to improving their decision making and physical fitness (Baker et al., 2003), which may be consequences of its unique characteristics. Moreover, athletes who maintain cognitive control over their performance (Ericsson, 2013a) may improve more so from competition compared to those who do not, but research is required on this activity to test these hypotheses.

Deliberate practice in sport and the enjoyment tenet

In a number of studies, researchers have shown that athletes rate some types of practice as high for both their relevance to improving performance and for enjoyment (e.g., Helsen *et al.*, 1998; Hodge & Deakin, 1998; Hodges & Starkes, 1996; Starkes *et al.*, 1996). These data do not fit with the original definition of deliberate practice as being an activity that is highly relevant to improving performance and not inherently enjoyable when compared to other activities. In these early studies, athletes rated sport-specific games and practice as enjoyable, as well as working with a coach. In contrast, it was only general fitness activities (e.g., strength or flexibility training) that fitted the original definition of deliberate practice as being high in relevance and low in inherent enjoyment. A number of reasons have been forwarded to explain why athletes retrospectively rate sport-specific practice activities as enjoyable. First and as above, training can consist of maintenance, play, competition, and deliberate practice activities, so that many activities do not meet the definition of deliberate practice, but are included in these ratings. Second, Ericsson (1996) stated that sport is an inherently social activity, and athletes might be rating this social interaction during the activity as enjoyable. Counter to this argument, however, sport-specific practice in individual sports, such as figure skating, has also been rated as highly enjoyable. Third, it is possible that athletes might be rating the consequences of the activity as enjoyable, such as improved performance, rather than their in-the-moment enjoyment during the activity (Ericsson, 1996). When these two variables have been differentiated, ratings of enjoyment are generally lower (Hodges *et al.*, 2004; Ward *et al.*, 2007). Fourth, it is possible that the method of retrospectively rating activities that have been engaged in some time ago into a single aggregate score might lead to misperceptions (Coughlan *et al.*, 2014).

In the study of elite triathletes and swimmers detailed earlier, a diary study of all physical activities engaged in during a typical training week revealed enjoyment to be only weakly or not at all correlated to relevance and effort ($rs < 0.1$; Hodges *et al.*, 2004). For example, a run on one day was perceived as high in effort and relevant to improving performance, but not enjoyable, whereas a similar run the following day received similar ratings for relevance and effort, yet this time was perceived as enjoyable. These ratings were collected soon after the event was completed, were verified with questionnaire data, and the inherent enjoyment of the activity was separated from general feelings of satisfaction with its outcome. Based on these data there is reason to recommend that enjoyment should not be seen as a defining criteria for whether practice is "deliberate" or not. Certain deliberate practice activities, such as those designed to improve weaknesses (e.g., Coughlan *et al.*, 2014) or physical attributes (e.g., weight training; Hodges & Starkes, 1996), are generally not perceived as inherently enjoyable, whereas others are generally rated as more enjoyable, such as sport-specific tactical practice (e.g., Helsen *et al.*, 1998).

Children and deliberate practice

The monotonic benefits assumption has led to the popular belief that the start of engagement in deliberate practice in a sport should occur very early in childhood. However, in the theory, Ericsson *et al.* (1993) explicitly outline a pre-deliberate practice phase of participation. The first phase of participation in a domain was argued to ". . . begin with an individual's introduction to activities in the domain and end with the start of instruction and deliberate practice" (Ericsson *et al.*, 1993, p. 369). It was proposed that ". . . interested individuals need to be engaging in the domain and motivated to improve performance before they begin deliberate practice" (p. 371). The inclusion of this early, pre-deliberate practice stage was mainly based on a collection of interviews edited by Bloom (1985) about the personal skill development of young adult expert performers across a range of domains in North America. The interviewees included professional tennis players (Monsaas, 1985) and Olympic swimmers (Kalinowski, 1985). Across domains, playful, exploratory, and fun activities defined the early or childhood stage of participation, with more serious training starting later in childhood or in early adolescence.

A number of researchers have recommended that youth athletes delay the start of engagement in deliberate practice in a single sport until early adolescence (for reviews, see Côté *et al.*, 2003, 2007; Côté *et al.*, 2012). Childhood engagement in intense deliberate practice and competition in a single sport (known as the "early specialization" pathway) has been hypothesized to lead to negative motivational consequences, including reduced enjoyment, overtraining, dropout, burnout, and overuse injuries (Baker, 2003; Baker *et al.*, 2009; DiFiori *et al.*, 2014; Wiersma, 2000). Some researchers have investigated the consequences for athletes who engaged in an "early specialization" pathway. For example, Olympic gymnasts in Canada who engaged in this pathway reported health and injury problems (Law *et al.*, 2007), whereas elite adolescent tennis players cited high training loads, spending too much time in the sport, and a sole focus as some of the multiple reasons for their burnout and dropout (Gould *et al.*, 1996; see also Kenttä *et al.*, 2001; Strachan *et al.*, 2009).

In contrast to early engagement in deliberate practice in a single sport, a recommendation has been to keep childhood engagement in playful activity until early adolescence (for reviews, see Côté *et al.*, 2003, 2007; Côté *et al.*, 2012). Playful activity in sport is fun and enjoyable, intrinsically motivating, led by the child, and often involves modified versions of the competition format of the sport to meet their needs (also termed deliberate play; Côté, 1999; Côté & Hay, 2002). It includes activities such as street soccer, backyard basketball, or mini versions of golf and tennis. Initial and childhood engagement in sport-specific playful activity is hypothesized to benefit skill acquisition, attainment, and the intrinsic motivation of participants (e.g., Côté *et al.*, 2012). In soccer, there has been some evidence in support of the relationship between early engagement in soccer-specific play and later attainment of skill. The amount of soccer-specific play in childhood was greater for adult players with superior decision-making skills compared to those with inferior skills (Roca *et al.*, 2012), and those that signed professional contracts in late adolescence compared to those who did not (Ford *et al.*, 2009). Moreover, both Australian-rules football players (Berry *et al.*, 2008) and Australian Olympic team sport players (Baker *et al.*, 2003a) who had superior decision-making skills engaged in more playful activities across a number of similar sports during childhood when compared to those with inferior skills. However, Ward *et al.* (2007) failed to show a relationship between amount of time in play and skill level among elite and recreational youth players. It has been argued that modified versions of the competition format of the sport (e.g., small-sided games) that occur during playful activity contain conditions that promote acquisition of the skills required during later competition performance. Moreover, the "power law of practice" describes the repeated finding that in the early stages of engagement in a domain there is a relatively rapid improvement in performance, whereas later performance improvement begins to plateau (Newell & Rosenbloom, 1981). It may be that in sport, childhood engagement in playful activity leads to a relatively rapid improvement in performance and motivation. When performance begins to plateau sometime later, future expert performers start to plan and engage in deliberate practice to continue improving their performance.

Childhood sport engagement in playful activity has been hypothesized to lead to positive motivational consequences, including enhanced enjoyment, intrinsic motivation, commitment, and perseverance. Few researchers have examined the motivational consequences of childhood engagement in playful activity, particularly for expert adult athletes. An exception to this was a study of elite adolescent soccer players in the United Kingdom (Hendry *et al.*, 2014). Based on estimates of practice and play across three different age groups (up until age 17), no relationship was shown between measures of intrinsic motivation and the amount of childhood engagement in soccer-specific play or practice. There was evidence that among the oldest age group only (i.e., aged 17 years), the years in the elite system were negatively related to current measures of intrinsic motivation, although this might simply be related to the development system, rather than a lack of time in play, or too much practice. Further research is needed to study the link between early childhood engagement in playful activity and motivational outcomes. Longitudinal studies would be the best method to chart the relationship between activity amounts and their impact on both later success and motivation.

Another proposal has been that childhood engagement should entail the sampling of a number of different sports ("early diversification;" Côté *et al.*, 2003, 2007; Côté *et al.*, 2012; see also Jayanthi *et al.*, 2012; Mostafavifar *et al.*, 2013; Wojtys, 2013). The childhood activities of some expert athletes have been characterized by engagement in a number of sports, including the primary sport in which they became an expert (Baker *et al.*, 2003b; Berry *et al.*, 2008; Côté, 1999; Monsaas, 1985; Soberlak & Côté, 2003). In some sports, such as the winter sport of skeleton (Bullock *et al.*, 2009), a late start age in adolescence is relatively common, being preceded by earlier activity in other sports that presumably develops attributes later required in the primary sport (e.g., sprinting transferring to skeleton). Diversity in activities during childhood is predicted to foster motivation by protecting participants against burnout, dropout, and overuse injuries, whilst benefitting skill acquisition through the transfer of attributes between sports. Some transfer of attributes has been shown to occur between sports with similar elements, but less so between those with different elements (e.g., Causer & Ford, 2014). The link between engagement in a number of sports in childhood and motivation is yet to receive systematic attention.

Deliberate practice in sport in the 21st century

In this final section, we detail the parts of deliberate practice that we consider to be the essential components of the acquisition and improvement of expert performance in sport.

Deliberate practice is necessary to improve performance beyond plateaus

For expert adult and elite adolescent athletes, systematic and consistent engagement in effortful deliberate practice activity is the optimal way to improve upon performance and achievements. It is well established that practice and performance show a strong positive relationship, and it is one of the most robust findings in behavioral science (Davids & Baker, 2007). There is a need for researchers to show how deliberate practice causes improvements in performance and its underlying attributes that are beyond those found from engagement in other types of practice activities. For example, performance improvements were examined in expert and intermediate Gaelic football players' practicing two different types of kick across pre-, post-, and retention tests surrounding four practice sessions (Coughlan et al., 2014). During the practice sessions, the expert Gaelic football players self-selected to practice the kick they were weaker at. In the delayed retention test that occurred six weeks after practice finished, they had significantly improved their weaker kick score by 17 per cent when compared to their pre-test score. In contrast, the intermediate group self-selected to practice their stronger kick and did not improve between the pre- and retention test (see Figure 30.2). Moreover, the expert players rated their practice as more

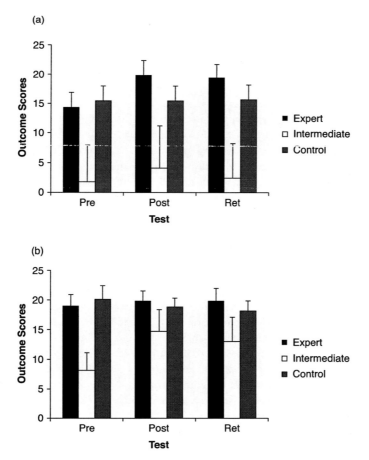

Figure 30.2 Mean (SD) outcome scores (out of 30 points) for the (a) weaker and (b) stronger kicks of the expert, intermediate, and expert control groups for the pre-test, post-test, and retention test (Coughlan et al., 2014).

Paul R. Ford et al.

effortful and less enjoyable compared to the intermediate group, supporting those predictions in deliberate practice theory. Measuring deliberate practice activity whilst athletes engage in it and recording the associated adaptations, perhaps in a longitudinal manner, are arguably preferable methods to measuring it retrospectively.

Deliberate practice has to be of sufficient quality

The quality of practice will have a major effect on the amount of performance improvement achieved. Factors influencing the quality of the activity include the relevance to improving current performance of the aspect being practiced. It includes the effort invested in the activity and the associated recovery. Moreover, the quality of the activity is influenced by the structure of the practice and the augmented information provided during practice, as well as the athlete's current state in terms of skill level, age, fitness, etc. Expert adult and elite adolescent athletes should be engaging in high amounts of quality deliberate practice during training each day, week, month, and year. Measuring the quality of practice and providing clear hypotheses about how it differentiates those who become expert performers from those who do not should be a key focus for future research.

Expert athletes engage in a deliberate environment, not just in practice

Researchers have generally taken the view that deliberate practice in sport only occurs during training sessions. However, other activities can be made to and do contain the characteristics of deliberate practice, particularly the intention to improve performance. These include team meetings and reflective team debriefs (Richards *et al.*, 2012), athletes observing their sport live or on television, physical fitness training (e.g., Baker *et al.*, 2003b; Helsen *et al.*, 1998), competition (e.g., Singer & Janelle, 1999), reflection (e.g., Coughlan *et al.*, in preparation), recovery practices (e.g., Gill *et al.*, 2006; Versey *et al.*, 2013), diet and nutrition (e.g., Taylor *et al.*, 2013), and performance analysis sessions (Baker *et al.*, 2003b; Helsen *et al.*, 1998; Richards *et al.*, 2012). When the intention of these activities is the improvement of specific and key aspects of current performance and the engagement is effortful, then these activities contain the characteristics of deliberate practice. Expert adult and late adolescent elite athletes are hypothesized to engage in all of these activities with the intention of performance improvement. Many of these activities occur during an athlete's time at their sport's organization, whereas some of these activities occur during the athlete's personal life, such as diet and nutrition, recovery, and sleep. These activities in combination have been termed the *deliberate environment* (Ford *et al.*, 2013). In a deliberate environment, the majority of decisions and behaviors made by and for athletes across their sporting and personal life are goal directed and optimized towards improving their competition performance. There has been anecdotal evidence that expert athletes engage in such a deliberate environment during their careers (e.g., Farah, 2013; White, 2013). Professional sport organizations play a key role in designing, creating, supporting, managing, and improving this deliberate environment (e.g., *deliberate programming*; Bullock *et al.*, 2009). In a deliberate environment, the hours spent in all of these activities, including recovery from them, are predicted to be relatively high, increasing from lower amounts in adolescence to higher amounts in adulthood. The "litmus test" of each activity is the amount of improvement in competition performance and the underlying attributes that it causes.

Summary

Deliberate practice is both a scientific theory and an activity engaged in by some athletes. As a scientific theory, it has led to a large body of research and has entered popular culture. The main focus of the research and its translation to popular culture has been on the number of hours that expert performers engage in practice across their development. The theory and this research have done much to advance understanding of how expert performance in a domain is acquired and improved upon. Generally, expert performers in sport have accumulated more hours in practice and other developmental activities by the time they achieve that milestone when compared to less-skilled performers. The focus on counting the number of hours has led to criticisms of the theory and research, as well as misunderstandings of it in popular culture (i.e., the "10,000-hour rule").

Another focus of the research has been on the characteristics of deliberate practice when compared to other activities. It was originally rated as being more relevant to improving key aspects of current performance, more effortful, yet relatively low in inherent enjoyment (Ericsson *et al.*, 1993). Researchers have shown that athletes rate fitness activities as highly relevant to improving performance and as less enjoyable than other activities, in line with original conceptions of enjoyment in deliberate practice theory. However, most researchers have shown that expert athletes rate sport-specific practice as relevant to improving future performance, but as highly enjoyable. Moreover, expert athletes often have a period of engagement in enjoyable, playful activity in their sport or across sports during childhood and prior to the start of meaningful engagement in deliberate practice in their primary sport.

In the near future, researchers will continue to debate the merits and weaknesses of deliberate practice theory. It is likely that there will be new research designs that allow better insight into the types of practice and activities that best predict performance over short and long timescales, as well as continuation in sport (e.g., motivation). Researchers should seek to measure deliberate practice and its effects as athletes engage in it, preferably across long timescales. Another area for further research is to determine the optimal developmental time points to specialize and engage in deliberate practice activities, as well as the continued investigation of the consequences of childhood engagement in a variety of sports or activities that vary in their formal structure and goals, such as play or competition.

References

Abernethy, B., Farrow, D., & Berry, J. (2003). Constraints and issues in the development of a general theory of expert perceptual-motor performance: A critique of the deliberate practice framework. In J. L. Starkes & K. A. Ericsson (Eds.), Expert performance in sports: Advances in research on sport expertise (pp. 349–369). Champaign, IL: Human Kinetics.

Baker, J. (2003) 'Early specialization in youth sport: A requirement for adult expertise?', *High Ability Studies*, 14: 85–94.

Baker, J., Cobley, S., & Fraser-Thomas, J. (2009) 'What do we know about early sport specialization? Not much!', *High Ability Studies*, 20: 77–89.

Baker, J., Côté, J., & Abernethy, B. (2003a) 'Sport specific practice and the development of expert decision-making in team ball sports', *Journal of Applied Sport Psychology*, 15: 12–25.

Baker, J., Côté., J., & Abernethy, B. (2003b) 'Learning from the experts: Practice activities of expert decision makers in sport', *Research Quarterly for Exercise and Sport*, 74: 342–7.

Baker, J., & Young, B. (2014) '20 years later: Deliberate practice and the development of expertise in sport', *International Review of Sport and Exercise Psychology*, 7: 135–57.

Berry, J., Abernethy, B., & Côté., J. (2008) 'The contribution of structured activity and deliberate play to the development of expert perceptual and decision-making skill', *Journal of Sport & Exercise Psychology*, 30: 685–708.

Bloom, B. S. (1985) *Developing talent in young people*, New York: Ballantine.

Bullock, N., Gulbin, J. P., Martin, D. T., Ross, A., Holland, T., & Marino, F. (2009) 'Talent identification and deliberate programming in skeleton: Ice novice to winter Olympian in 14 months', *Journal of Sports Sciences*, 27: 397–404.

Causer, J., & Ford, P. R. (2014) '"Decisions, decisions, decisions": Transfer and specificity of decision making skill between sports', *Cognitive Processing*. doi: 10.1007/s10339–014–0598–0

Côté, J. (1999) 'The influence of the family in the development of talent in sport', *The Sport Psychologist*, 13: 395–417.

Côté, J., Baker, J., & Abernethy, B. (2003) 'From play to practice: A developmental framework for the acquisition of expertise in team sports', in J. Starkes & K. A. Ericsson (eds) *Expert performance in sports: Advances in research on sport expertise*, Champaign, IL: Human Kinetics, 89–110.

Côté, J., Baker, J., & Abernethy, B. (2007) 'Play and practice in the development of sport expertise', in G. Tenenbaum & R. C. Eklund (eds) *Handbook of sport psychology*, 3rd ed., New York: Wiley, 184–202.

Côté, J., & Hay, J. (2002) 'Children's involvement in sport: A developmental perspective', in J. M. Silva & D. Stevens (eds) *Psychological foundations of sport*, Boston: Allyn and Bacon, 484–502.

Côté, J., Murphy-Mills, J., & Abernethy, B. (2012) 'The development of skill in sport', in A. M. Williams & N. J. Hodges (eds) *Skill acquisition in sport: Research, theory and practice*, 2nd ed., London: Routledge, 269–86.

Coughlan, E. K., Williams, A. M., & Ford, P. R. (in preparation) 'Deliberate practice and reflective practice during skill acquisition by expert and intermediate performers', manuscript in preparation.

Coughlan, E. K., Williams, A. M., McRobert, A. P., & Ford, P. R. (2014) 'How experts practice: A novel test of deliberate practice theory', *Journal of Experimental Psychology: Learning, Memory, and Cognition*, 40: 449–58.

Davids, K., & Baker, J. (2007) 'Genes, environment and sport performance: Why the nature-nurture dualism is no longer relevant', *Sports Medicine*, 37: 961–80.

DiFiori, J. P., Benjamin, H. J., Brenner, J. S., Gregory, A, Jayanthi, N, Landry, G. L., Luke, A. (2014) 'Overuse injuries and burnout in youth sports: A position statement from the American Medical Society for Sports Medicine', *British Journal of Sports Medicine*, 48: 287–8.

Duffy, L. J., Baluch, B., & Ericsson, K. A. (2004) 'Dart performance as a function of facets of practice amongst professional and amateur men and women players', *International Journal of Sport Psychology*, 35: 232–45.

Ericsson, K. A. (ed) (1996) *The road to excellence: The acquisition of expert performance in the arts and sciences, sports and games*, Hillsdale, NJ: Lawrence Erlbaum.

Ericsson, K. A. (2003) 'The development of elite performance and deliberate practice: An update from the perspective of the expert-performance approach', in J. Starkes & K. A. Ericsson (eds) *Expert performance in sport: Recent advances in research on sport expertise*, Champaign, IL: Human Kinetics, 49–81.

Ericsson, K. A. (2006) 'The influence of experience and deliberate practice on the development of superior expert performance', in K. A. Ericsson, N. Charness, P. Feltovich, & R. R. Hoffman (eds) *Cambridge handbook of expertise and expert performance*, Cambridge, UK: Cambridge University Press, 685–706.

Ericsson, K. A. (2007) 'Deliberate practice and the modifiability of body and mind: Toward a science of the structure and acquisition of expert and elite performance', *International Journal of Sport Psychology*, 38: 4–34.

Ericsson, K. A. (2013a) 'Why expert performance is special and cannot be extrapolated from studies of performance in the general population: A response to criticisms', *Intelligence*. doi: http://dx.doi.org/10.1016/j.intell.2013.12.001

Ericsson, K. A. (2013b) 'Training history, deliberate practice and elite sports performance: An analysis in response to Tucker and Collins review – What makes champions?', *British Journal of Sports Medicine*, 47: 533–5.

Ericsson, K. A., Krampe, R. T., & Tesch-Römer, C. (1993) 'The role of deliberate practice in the acquisition of expert performance', *Psychological Review*, 100: 363–406.

Ericsson, K. A., & Towne, T. J. (2010) 'Expertise', *WIREs Cognitive Science*, 1: 404–16.

Everitt, B. S., & Skrondal, A. (2012) *The Cambridge dictionary of statistics*, Cambridge, UK: Cambridge University Press.

Farah, M. (2013, 7 October) 'Mo Farah: Moving into a house full of Kenyan runners changed my whole attitude to training and racing', *The Telegraph*. Online. Retrieved from www.telegraph.co.uk/sport/othersports/athletics/10361777/Mo-Farah-moving-into-a-house-full-of-Kenyan-runners-changed-my-whole-attitude-to-training-and-racing.html (accessed 14 July, 2014).

Deliberate practice in sport

Ford, P. R., Carling, C., Garces, M., Marques, M., Miguel, C., Farrant, A., . . . Williams, M. (2012) 'The developmental activities of elite soccer players aged under-16 years from Brazil, England, France, Ghana, Mexico, Portugal and Sweden', *Journal of Sports Sciences*, 30: 1653–63.

Ford, P. R., Hodges, N. J., & Williams, A. M. (2013) 'Creating champions: The development of expertise in sports', in S. B. Kaufman (ed) *Beyond talent: The complexity of greatness*, Oxford: Oxford University Press, 391–414.

Ford, P. R., Ward, P., Hodges, N. J., & Williams, A. M. (2009) 'The role of deliberate practice and play in career progression in sport: The early engagement hypothesis', *High Ability Studies*, 20: 65–75.

Gill, N. D., Beaven, C. M., & Cook, C. (2006) 'Effectiveness of post-match recovery strategies in rugby players', *British Journal of Sports Medicine*, 40: 260–3.

Gladwell, M. (2008) *Outliers: The story of success*, Boston: Little, Brown and Company.

Gould, D., Tuffey, S., Udry, S., & Loehr, J. (1996) 'Burnout in competitive junior tennis players: A quantitative psychological assessment', *The Sport Psychologist*, 10: 322–40.

Hambrick, D. Z., Oswald, F. L., Altmann, E. M., Meinz, E. J., Gobet, F., & Campitelli, G. (2013) 'Deliberate practice: Is that all it takes to become an expert?', *Intelligence*. doi: http://dx.doi.org/10.1016/j.intell.2013.04.001

Helsen, W. F., Starkes, J. L., & Hodges, N. J. (1998) 'Team sports and the theory of deliberate practice', *Journal of Sport & Exercise Psychology*, 20: 12–34.

Hendry, D. T., Crocker, P. R. E., & Hodges, N. J. (2014) 'Practice and play as determinants of self-determined motivation in youth soccer players', *Journal of Sports Sciences*. doi: 10.1080/02640414.2014.880792

Hodge, T., & Deakin, J. (1998) 'Deliberate practice and expertise in the martial arts: The role of context in motor recall', *Journal of Sport & Exercise Psychology*, 20: 260–79.

Hodges, N. J., Kerr, T., Starkes, J. L., Weir, P. L., & Nananidou, A. (2004) 'Predicting performance times from deliberate practice hours for triathletes and swimmers: What, when, and where is practice important?', *Journal of Experimental Psychology: Applied*, 10: 219–37.

Hodges, N. J., & Starkes, J. L. (1996) 'Wrestling with the nature of expertise: A sport-specific test of Ericsson, Krampe and Tesch-Römer's (1993) theory of "deliberate practice"', *International Journal of Sport Psychology*, 27: 400–24.

Jayanthi, N., Pinkham, C., Dugas, L., Patrick, B., & LaBella, C. (2012) 'Sports specialization in young athletes: Evidence-based recommendations', *Sports Health*, 5: 251–7.

Jones, C. (2012, July 4) 'How Andy Murray turned a second serve into his lethal weapon', *The London Evening Standard*. Online. Retrieved from www.standard.co.uk/sport/wimbledon/how-andy-murray-turned-a-second-serve-into-his-lethal-weapon-7908115.html (accessed 14 July, 2014).

Kalinowski, A. G. (1985) 'The development of Olympic swimmers', in B. S. Bloom (ed) *Developing talent in young people*, New York: Ballantine, 139–92.

Kenttä, G., Hassmén, P., & Raglin, J. S. (2001) 'Training practices and over-training syndrome in Swedish age-group athletes', *International Journal of Sports Medicine*, 22: 460–5.

Krampe, R. T., & Ericsson, K. A. (1996) 'Maintaining excellence: Deliberate practice and elite performance in young and older pianists', *Journal of Experimental Psychology: General*, 125: 331–59.

Law, M., Côté, J., & Ericsson, K. A. (2007) 'Characteristics of expert development in rhythmic gymnastics: A retrospective study', *International Journal of Sport and Exercise Psychology*, 5: 82–103.

Monsaas, J. A. (1985) 'Learning to be a world-class tennis player', in B. S. Bloom (ed) *Developing talent in young people*, New York: Ballantine, 211–69.

Mostafavifar, A. M., Best, T. M., & Myer, G. D. (2013) 'Early sport specialisation, does it lead to long-term problems?', *British Journal of Sports Medicine*, 47: 1060–1.

Newell, A., & Rosenbloom, P. S. (1981) 'Mechanisms of skill acquisition and the law of practice', in J. R. Anderson (ed) *Cognitive skills and their acquisition*, Hillsdale, NJ: Erlbaum, 1–55.

Richards, P., Collins, D., & Mascarenhas, D. R. D. (2012) 'Developing rapid high-pressure team decision-making skills. The integration of slow deliberate reflective learning within the competitive performance environment: A case study of elite netball', *Reflective Practice*, 13: 407–24.

Roca, A., Williams, A. M., & Ford, P. R. (2012) 'Developmental activities and the acquisition of superior anticipation and decision making in soccer players', *Journal of Sports Sciences*, 30: 1643–52.

Simon, H. A., & Chase, W. G. (1973) 'Skill in chess', *American Scientist*, 61: 394–403.

Singer, R. M., & Janelle, C. M. (1999) 'Determining sport expertise: From genes to supremes', *International Journal of Sport Psychology*, 30: 117–50.

Soberlak, P., & Côté, J. (2003) 'The developmental activities of professional ice hockey players', *Journal of Applied Sport Psychology*, 15: 41–9.

Starkes, J. L., Deakin, J., Allard, F., Hodges, N. J., & Hayes, A. (1996) 'Deliberate practice in sports: What is it anyway?', in K. A. Ericsson (ed) *The road to excellence: The acquisition of expert performance in the arts and sciences, sports, and games*, Mahwah, NJ: Earlbaum, 181–206.

Strachan, L., Côté, J., & Deakin, J. (2009) '"Specializers" versus "samplers" in youth sport: Comparing experiences and outcomes', *The Sport Psychologist*, 23: 77–92.

Taylor, C., Bartlett, J. D., Soler van de Graaf, C., Louhelainen, J., Coyne, V., Iqbal, Z., . . . Morton, J. P. (2013) 'Protein ingestion does not impair exercise-induced AMPK signalling when in a glycogen-depleted state: Implications for train-low compete-high', *European Journal of Applied Physiology*, 113: 1457–68.

Tucker, R., & Collins, M. (2012) 'What makes champions? A review of the relative contribution of genes and training to sporting success', *British Journal of Sports Medicine*, 46: 555–61.

Versey, N. G., Halson, S. L., & Dawson, B. T. (2013) 'Water immersion recovery for athletes: Effect on exercise performance and practical recommendations', *Sports Medicine*, 43: 1101–30.

Ward, P., Hodges, N. J., Starkes, J. L., & Williams, A. M. (2007) 'The road to excellence: Deliberate practice and the development of expertise', *High Ability Studies*, 18: 119–53.

Ward, P., Hodges, N. J., Williams, A. M., & Starkes, J. L. (2004) 'Deliberate practice and expert performance: Defining the path to excellence', in A. M. Williams & N. J. Hodges (eds) *Skill acquisition in Sport: Research, theory and practice*, London: Routledge, 231–58.

Weissensteiner, J., Abernethy, B., Farrow, D., & Muller, S. (2008) 'The development of anticipation: A cross-sectional examination of the practice experiences contributing to skill in cricket batting', *Journal of Sport & Exercise Psychology*, 30: 663–84.

White, J. (2013, 4 July) 'Andy Murray's appliance of science', *The Telegraph*. Online. Retrieved from www.telegraph.co.uk/sport/tennis/andymurray/10159973/Andy-Murrays-appliance-of-science.html (accessed 14 July, 2014).

Wiersma, L. D. (2000) 'Risks and benefits of youth sport specialization: Perspectives and recommendations', *Pediatric Exercise Science*, 12: 13–22.

Wojtys, E. M. (2013) 'Sports specialization vs. diversification', *Sports Health*, 5: 212–3.

Young B. W., & Salmela, J. H. (2002) 'Perceptions of training and deliberate practice of middle distance runners', *International Journal of Sport Psychology*, 33: 167–81.

31
DEVELOPMENT OF TACTICAL CREATIVITY IN SPORTS

Daniel Memmert

Tactically optimal and creative solutions are of outstanding relevance to success in high-performance sport (Memmert, 2015) and a component of talent development and selection systems (Williams, 2013). In soccer, for example, the midfield players have the responsibility of controlling the buildup play with smart, tactical choices. Similarly, playmakers in handball and basketball are able to initialize the closing option of their teammates with creative solutions.

In this chapter a discussion focused on tactical creativity and its quality is developed. I start by contextualizing the value of tactical creativity, using current statements from world soccer coupled with empirical data. Subsequent to this, the term "tactical creativity" is operationally defined and theoretically considered as it relates to current process models of cognition. After a short description of the assessment of creativity in team and racket sports, the development of tactical creativity is centrally discussed, and a detailed description of various methods used in current creativity research is provided. In the concluding section, future fields of research in the field of creativity are addressed.

Relevance of tactical creativity in team and racket sports

To highlight the value of tactical creativity in high-performance sport, I provide examples from international soccer. Statements from German national coach Jogi Löw substantiate the special meaning of creativity in this sport: "creativity should be the new German virtue." Matthias Sammer, the chairman of the Champions League winner in 2013, Bayern Munich, emphasizes the meaning of creativity in sports:

> the first impulse to increase the flexibility in your own team always originates from the coach. . . . We just had the feeling that our game had to become more flexible . . . then our way of playing was unpredictable and modern – extremely creative.

Internationally, it appears that highly creative soccer players make a difference. For example, Lionel Messi, who is described as highly creative, was appointed the world soccer player of the year for the third time in 2012. Similarly, Frank Ribéry was appointed the soccer player of the year in Europe in 2013, and his Bayern Munich teammate Arjen Robben scored the winning goal in the Champions League final in 2013. Louis Van Gaal has said about Arjen Robben: "next

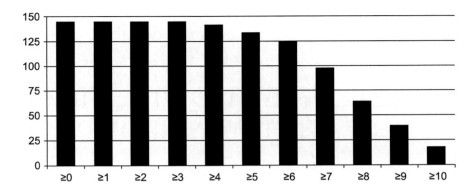

Figure 31.1 The evaluation of the individual eight actions in front of the goal concerning their tactical creativity (from 0 to 10, 0 = not creative, 10 = highly creative). Each bar represents the percentage of all 145 analyzed goals (see the text for more information). For example, 12% of one of all last eight actions before a goal was scored were highly creative (=10).

to Ribéry we have one more that brings creativity in a tight space into the game. We want to improve. This only works with extraordinary players." Franz Beckenbauer has said about Arjen Robben: "he makes the difference, he brings the unpredictable into the game and carries the team with him."

Empirical evidence for the value of creativity in soccer can be drawn from Memmert, Vogelbein, Nopp, and Knievel (2013). They qualitatively examined all goals in the soccer World Cup 2010 in South Africa. In these games, 159 goals were scored overall with 11 goals resulting from penalty shootouts. Three experts evaluated the last eight actions before each goal, using a creativity scale ranging from zero to 10 (zero = not creative, 10 = highly creative). The results showed that the closer the actions were to the goal (i.e., temporally from one to eight actions from the goal), the more creative they were evaluated as. Eighty-six per cent of all goals included at least one of the eight actions in the high creative area (cf. Figure 31.1). Forty-four per cent of all goals included at least one of the eight actions in the highest creative area. Further, teams that moved into more advanced rounds of the tournament demonstrated more creativity in the seventh action (second last pass) than teams that failed to advance past the preliminary round. To sum up, tactical creativity seems to be a more and more important factor in both team and racket sports, especially at the highest levels of performance.

Definition and theoretical background of tactical creativity

Tactical creativity and tactical intelligence are concepts based on the theoretical distinction between divergent and convergent thinking by Guilford (1967; for a recent overview, see Runco, 2007). Tactical creativity in team and racket sports can be defined as the generation of several solutions of problems in specific individual groups or in team tactical game situations, which can be denoted as surprising, rare, and/or original (Memmert, 2015). It differs from tactical intelligence, game sense, or game ability where the main task is to find the ideal solution to a given problem (Memmert & Roth, 2007).

The special meaning of tactical creativity is clarified when you consider divergent thinking ability in the whole process of human decision-making processes (also see Sternberg & Lubart, 1999). First of all, a situation is anticipated and perceived based on past experiences (memory), then attention is paid to specific targets of the situation, and finally a range of ideas is collected

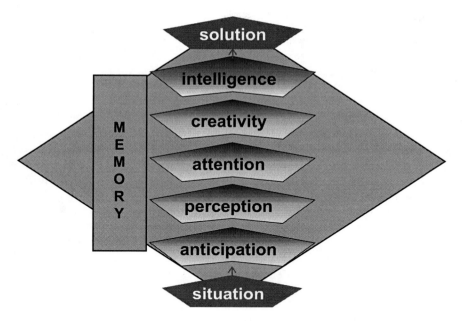

Figure 31.2 Overview of the central cognitive performance factors that underlie all actions in team and racket sports.

(creativity) and one of them is chosen (intelligence) to be a solution for the situation. The presentation of the individual psychological processes generally follows a temporal course, although all perceptive-cognitive phases may not be run through (cf. Figure 31.2). While doing so it becomes obvious that the cognitive process of solving problems runs similarly in all sport games, and a key role belongs to the tactical creativity.

Human beings – and therefore sportsmen – often find themselves in situations where they have to search for the most appropriate decision from a range of possible options. More specifically, since human beings have been using their experience (memory) to make anticipatory decisions in different situations, individual environmental factors are perceived consciously or unconsciously, and attention is paid to them. Therefore, it is not surprising that several studies emphasize the strong influence of attention on decision-making, especially divergent thinking (Kasof, 1997; Memmert, 2010a). After the intellectual generation of a certain number of solution options (divergent thinking) from long-term or working memory, a solution is finally chosen. The proportion of variability accounted for general creativity and general intelligence lies between 20 and 30 per cent (cf. Runco & Albert, 1986). Empirical data from a longitudinal study in team and racket sports (for an overview, see Memmert, 2015) show that higher tactical intelligence is associated with higher tactical creativity.

Testing tactical creativity

Operationalization of tactical creativity is often based on the characteristics of originality, flexibility, and fluency identified by Guilford (1967) using factor analysis.

- Originality: the unusualness of tactical elements of decision-making can be rated by experts.

- Flexibility: the variety of tactical elements of decision-making is determined by action and response diversity of the players.
- Fluency: the number of tactical elements of decision-making that the players generate for certain situational constellations.

The most common approaches to rating tactical creativity in team and racket sports by means of these three factors are performed via video tests or game test situations (Memmert, 2013). Video test scenarios are relatively highly standardized (Williams, Davids, & Williams, 1999; Memmert, 2010a) and require subjects to watch sport-specific videos that end with a frozen image. They then have to imagine themselves as the acting player and report all possibilities that might lead to a goal. The answers are evaluated according to the criteria of originality, flexibility, and fluency. In contrast, game test situations may have a higher degree of authenticity with regards to complex game situations, which may not be the case for standardized video tests due to the "artificialness" of the lab environment. Game test situations contain contextual, real world representations that provoke creative, tactical actions. In comparable tactical situations, this ecologically valid setting evokes reliable and repeated creative behavior in specific match situations (Memmert, 2007, 2010b). During game test situations, the general game purpose, number of players, rules, skill execution (hand, foot, or hockey stick), and environmental conditions are given. In order to analyze creative solutions, a video of the recorded tactical behavior is rated with regard to specific concepts by several independent evaluators (Memmert & Roth, 2007). The specific advantages and disadvantages of both approaches (i.e., standardized video test and game test situations) are discussed in more detail by Memmert (2011).

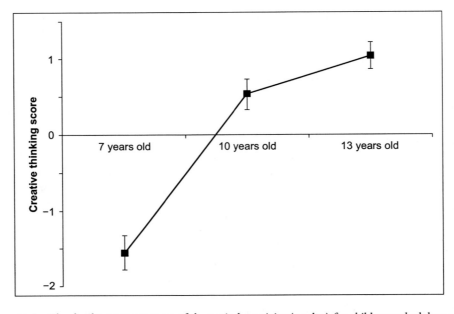

Figure 31.3 The development processes of the tactical creativity (z-value) for children and adolescents at the age of seven, 10, and 13 years.

Development of tactical creativity

Research in psychology indicates that divergent thinking has to be learned and developed early in life (Milgram, 1990). A few empirical studies have pursued the development of tactical creativity in sport. In a cross-sectional study (peer group: seven, 10, and 13 years) Memmert (2010a) suggested that children and adolescents do not develop linearly (cf. Figure 31.3). While meaningful increases of tactical creativity were found between the ages of seven to 10, such creativity seemed to develop much slower at older ages. Findings from neuroscience support these results, suggesting that the absolute number of synapses and synaptic density reach their maximum in this age range (Huttenlocher, 1990). Moreover, the number and density of synapses in the human primary visual cortex are associated with creativity (Ashby *et al.*, 2002).

To examine this phenomenon, Memmert (2010b) used a longitudinal design to analyze intra-individual improvements of German Soccer Foundation (DFB) talents according to soccer-specific tactical creativity. Talents aged 12 and 13 years were actively controlled by an additional "Monday training day" of the DFB talent promotion program, as well as the usual soccer club training during the week. The results across all four DFB bases indicated that, on average, no deterioration or improvement in tactical creativity (as evaluated by game test situations) was evident after a six-month observation period. However, there was a slight tendency for younger athletes to become more creative. A more specific inspection of the data, however, showed that although the study period only comprised six months, more than half of the DFB talents improved with respect to their tactical creativity. Twelve subjects improved by more than five per cent and 20 by more than 10 per cent, with regard to divergent thinking. Three players who were born in 1992 and two players born in 1991 even improved their creative performance by more than 20 per cent. However, the development of nine players decreased by more than 20 per cent, creating the overall impression that the development of tactical creativity stagnates above the age of 13. This suggests a large potential for intra-individual improvements with regard to tactical, divergent thinking. The results of Memmert (2010b) revealed that very different processes of change were observed within the DFB players. On the one hand, some adolescents reacted very positively during the training units at the club and at the bases. On the other hand, other adolescents reacted negatively, or in a neutral way, to these training units.

To sum up, teachers and coaches should integrate tasks that concentrate on the development of divergent, tactical thinking abilities in their training units as early as possible. After childhood, the effect of training activities for tactical creativity may decrease, but improvements are still possible.

Factors affecting the process of tactical creativity development

In this section, varying factors affecting the process of tactical creativity development are discussed, ranging across training-related variables such as quantity of deliberate practice and play, diversification, and the quality of coaching and motivational instructions throughout talent development. According to the tactical creativity approach (TCA) by Memmert (2015), different factors affect the development of tactical creativity (cf. Figure 31.4) during training in team and racket sports.

The theoretical framework of the TCA is based on the "investment approach to creativity: buy low, sell high" integration model by Sternberg and Lubart (1995). Sport psychological studies show that unspecific divergent thinking is not the only relevant factor – cognition (attention), expertise, and environmental influences also have a decisive effect on the process of developing tactical creativity in sports (for detailed description, see Memmert, 2015). The order – starting on the top with deliberate play – of the six training principles shown in Figure 31.4 indicates a

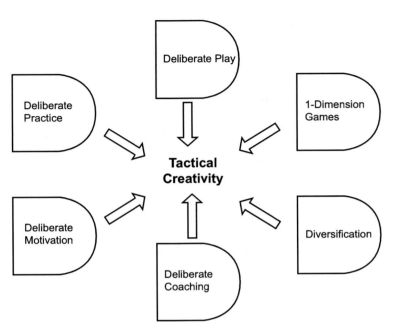

Figure 31.4 The six Ds fostering tactical creativity in team and racket sports (see tactical creativity approach by Memmert, 2014).

chronological system from child and youth training to adolescent and adult training. While the first four principles are more suited for younger age groups, all principles are useful for older age groups.

Deliberate play

Uninstructed games and unstructured activities during childhood have been categorized as "deliberate play" (Baker, 2003; Côté et al., 2003, 2007; also see Chapter 27). Sport biographical studies indicate that "deliberate play" during youth influences the development of creativity in national team and national league players (Memmert et al., 2010). Uninstructed operating can lead to trying out different response variations; Greco, Memmert, and Morales (2010) had youth basketball players complete two different kinds of basketball training, one according to the deliberate play approach, and the other according to a traditional basketball approach with structured game forms and specific routines. The authors demonstrated that a deliberate play training program leads to greater improvements of tactical creativity than the traditional training group.

One-dimension games

While small-sided games have become more and more popular for the improvement of technical skills and aerobic fitness components of performance (see Hill-Haas et al., 2011; Clemente et al., 2012), one-dimension games can develop general and sport-specific tactical skills (for a review, see Memmert, 2015). Recent research has demonstrated that one-dimension games foster the development of tactical components (Memmert & König, 2007), train players in creating creative solutions (Memmert, 2007; Memmert & Roth, 2007), and have a structure that is easily applied to team and racket sports that have a non-specific format (Memmert & Harvey, 2010).

The main aim of one-dimension games is to have players learn divergent, tactical thinking in complex and dynamic situations, which means that they train single basic tactical components through a great amount of continuously repeating comparable tactical constellations (cf. "representative learning design" in Pinder *et al.*, 2011; see also Chapter 4). However, one-dimension games have clearly defined game ideas, a stable number of players, as well as defined rules and environmental conditions. Non-specific one-dimension games were developed and validated in the context of team and racket sports (cf. Griffin *et al.*, 1997; Memmert & Harvey, 2010). They can be used to train elementary basic tactics, which are of importance in many different team and racket sports. In addition, specific one-dimension games exist in youth soccer, especially for group tactical abilities (Memmert *et al.*, 2011).

Diversification

Participation in many different sport/game situations seems to have a positive influence on the transferability of cognitive skills like pattern recognition (Abernethy *et al.*, 2005), as well as on the development of tactical creativity (Memmert & Roth, 2007). Studies of highly creative athletes (Memmert *et al.*, 2010) emphasize that creative players were given the possibility to try different sports and develop a breadth of movement experience, in contrast to less creative athletes.

Therefore, for the generation of original ideas to sport problems, it is important that children and adolescents get into contact with different balls in their "ball game life" as early as possible, learn to adequately operate with hand, foot, and tennis/hockey racket, and think of situations in a different or new manner again. Thus, clubs and associations should encourage their coaches at an early stage, especially during the training of beginners and talent promotion, to train tactical creativity by using wide-ranging sport games that overlap regular training, thereby letting the children learn to solve tasks with a variety of solutions.

Deliberate coaching

A wide focus of attention (Memmert & Furley, 2007) is necessary to perceive unexpected objects like unguarded teammates, which could be the starting point of original solution operations. Reduced instruction on the side of the coach leads to children and adolescents' – due to a wider focus of attention – more frequently being able to generate original solution possibilities with many variations than children and adolescents who were frequently confronted with attention-leading hints during practice (Memmert, 2007). This suggests that the coach who continuously stops the training game and constantly gives tactical instructions to his youth players may not be designing their training for optimal creativity development (Furley *et al.*, 2010).

Psychological experiments also demonstrate that a wider focus of attention facilitates the production of creative performance, because different, spatially further away, and secondarily relevant stimuli can be included in the task solution (Kasof, 1997). A narrow focus of attention results in less original methods of solution, since not all of the relevant information is noted.

Generally, coaches have two possibilities to influence their players' scope of attention: a) directly through instructions, or b) indirectly by inventing forms of games or exercises that provoke a wider focus of attention for the players. Through certain instruction possibilities and providing external (implicit) stimuli, attention focusing can be controlled (Memmert & Furley, 2007). Another training goal should be that the coach or teacher provides the children with the possibility to perceive and search for unexpected and (potentially) better solution variations through reduced instruction parallel to his own solution demands.

Deliberate motivation

Current models and empirical results from social psychology highlight that creative accomplishments can be directly influenced by the simplest instructions, which, for example, manipulate the emotional conditions of the participants (Friedman & Förster, 2000, 2001; Hirt *et al.*, 1997; Isen, 2000; Isen *et al.*, 1987). A promotion focus, which regulates pleasure as the achievement of positive results of action and suffering as an absence of those positive results (cf. Higgins, 1997), facilitates the generation of creative solutions more than a prevention focus, which expresses the successful avoidance of unpleasant, negative results and their arrival as suffering.

Memmert, Hüttermann, and Orliczek (2013) were able to show that divergent decision-making in sports also benefits from a promotion focus. In this study, soccer players had to name as many decision options as possible per video clip with a standardized video soccer test. Analogous to the work of Friedman and Förster (2001), the players were shown identical labyrinths with different framing in the run-up: half of the players had to find the way for a mouse to reach the cheese ("promotion" focus), whereas the other participants had to solve the labyrinth with the goal that the mouse would not be caught by the owl ("prevention" focus). In the "promotion" condition, soccer players generated more original and flexible solutions than in the "prevention" manipulation. On the whole, all results emphasize that coaches and teachers should try to optimize the divergent thinking of the athletes with suitable promotion focus instructions ("my wish is that every third ball is kicked through gaps," *not* "I expect you to kick every third ball through gaps").

Deliberate practice

Working with instructions in exercise-centered and more structured situations with the goal to effectively improve specific individual performance criteria is referred to as "deliberate practice" (Côté *et al.*, 2003, 2007; also see Chapter 28). Expertise research has demonstrated that experts spend more than 10 years of extensive effort in the acquisition of decision-making and skill execution in their sports (see Chapter 30). According to the theory of deliberate practice (see Ericsson *et al.*, 1993), expertise in a given sport like soccer and basketball is the final result of extended engagement in high-quality training. Memmert and colleagues (2010) showed that creative athletes practiced much longer in their main sport in a goal-oriented way than less creative players. The quantity of hours of deliberate practice makes the difference between more and less creative team sport players, especially for top team players in the national teams. National league athletes began their specific sport later than players in the next highest level of competition. Therefore, deliberate practice seems to be an important characteristic for the support of tactical creativity, especially in later childhood and the beginning of adolescence.

Future directions of the development of tactical creativity

Earvin "Magic" Johnson and Wayne Gretzky have delighted us with their skill and imaginativeness. Kobe Bryant, Ricky Rubio, Rajon Rondo, Chris Paul, Sidney Crosby, and Lionel Messi currently enchant us again and again by providing us new solutions that are surprising for their opponents, fans, audience, television commentators, and sometimes even their teammates. Given the data-rich environment of current professional and elite sport, match preparation involves more and more information about an opposing team and its players. As a result, future success

Development of tactical creativity

will likely depend on players' capability to find creative solutions in the match that are hard for the opponent players to anticipate.

Research on tactical creativity is certainly at an early stage. Further activity is necessary to refine the theoretical framework, to develop and validate new, sport-specific creativity tasks, as well as to experimentally examine additional methodological guidelines for fostering tactical creativity in team and racket sports. The cognitive skills of attention and motivation certainly present the biggest potential due to their influence on tactical creativity. Furthermore, working memory has to be considered in future studies of divergent tactical thinking. Recent empirical evidence based on the dual pathway to creativity model indicate that general working-memory capacity benefits general creativity because it allows people to maintain attention on the task itself and avoids unwanted mind processing (De Dreu *et al.*, 2012). Finally, including the sporting organizations for team and racket sports is necessary, since talent selection tests in many invasion games are still primarily focused on technical and physical attributes. Here, a process of rethinking has to take place, so that tactical creativity is respected and considered as a talent indicator at an early stage. This is certainly not as easy as measuring variables such as sprint performances, but it is possible and surely desirable.

References

Abernethy, B., Baker, J., & Côté, J. (2005) 'Transfer of pattern recall skills may contribute to the development of sport expertise', *Applied Cognitive Psychology*, 19: 705–18.

Ashby, F. G., Valentin, V. V., & Turken, A. U. (2002) 'The effects of positive affect and arousal on working memory and executive attention: Neurobiology and computational models', in S. Moore & M. Oaksford (eds) *Emotional cognition: From brain to behaviour*, Amsterdam: John Benjamins, 245–87.

Baker, J. (2003) 'Early specialization in youth sport: A requirement for adult expertise?', *High Ability Studies*, 14: 85–94.

Clemente, F., Couceiro, M., Martins, F.M.L., & Mendes, R. (2012) 'The usefulness of small-sided games on soccer training', *Journal of Physical Education and Sport*, 12: 93–102.

Côté, J., Baker, J., & Abernethy, B. (2003) 'From play to practice: A developmental framework for the acquisition of expertise in team sports', in K. A. Ericsson & J. L. Starkes (eds) *Expert performance in sports: Advances in research on sport expertise*, Champaign, IL: Human Kinetics, 184–202.

Côté, J., Baker, J., & Abernethy, B. (2007) 'Practice and play in the development of sport expertise', *Handbook of sport psychology*, 3: 184–202.

De Dreu, C. K., Nijstad, B. A., Baas, M., Wolsink, I., & Roskes, M. (2012) 'Working memory benefits creative insight, musical improvisation, and original ideation through maintained task-focused attention', *Personality and Social Psychology Bulletin*, 38: 656–69.

Ericsson, K. A., Krampe, R. T., & Tesch-Römer, C. (1993) 'The role of deliberate practice in the acquisition of expert performance', *Psychological Review*, 100: 363–406.

Friedman, R. S., & Förster, J. (2000) 'The effects of approach and avoidance motor actions on the elements of creative insight', *Journal of Personality and Social Psychology*, 79: 477–92.

Friedman, R. S., & Förster, J. (2001) 'The effects of promotion and prevention cues on creativity', *Journal of Personality and Social Psychology*, 81: 1001–13.

Furley, P., Memmert, D., & Heller, C. (2010) 'The dark side of visual awareness in sport – inattentional blindness in a real-world basketball task', *Attention, Perception, & Psychophysics*, 72: 1327–37.

Goal.com (2009). 'Bayern-Pressekonferenz – Louis van Gaal spricht über Robben und Ribery [Bayern Munich news conference – Louis van Gaal talks about Robben and Ribery]. Retrieved from www. goal.com/de/news/827/bundesliga/2009/08/28/1466292/bayern-pressekonferenz-louis-van-gaal-spricht-%C3%BCber-robben (accessed January 22, 2015).

Greco, P., Memmert, D., & Morales, J.C.P. (2010) 'The effect of deliberate play on tactical performance in basketball', *Perceptual & Motor Skills*, 110: 849–56.

Griffin, L. A., Mitchell, S. A., & Oslin, J. L. (1997) *Teaching sport concepts and skills: A tactical games approach*, Champaign, IL: Human Kinetics.

Guilford, J. P. (1967) *The nature of human intelligence*, New York: McGraw-Hill.

Higgins, E. T. (1997) 'Beyond pleasure and pain', *American Psychologist*, 52: 1280–300.

Hill-Haas, S. V., Dawson, B., Impellizzeri, F. M., & Coutts, A. J. (2011) 'Physiology of small-sided games training in football. A systematic review', *Sports Medicine*, 41: 199–220.

Hirt, E. R., Levine, G. M., McDonald, H. E., Melton, R. J., & Martin, L. L. (1997) 'The role of mood in quantitative and qualitative aspects of performance: Single or multiple mechanisms?', *Journal of Experimental Social Psychology*, 33: 602–29.

Huttenlocher, P. R. (1990) 'Morphometric study of human cerebral cortex development', *Neuropsychologia*, 28: 517–27.

Isen, A. M. (2000) 'Positive affect and decision making', in M. Lewis & J. Haviland-Jones (eds) *Handbook of emotions*, 2nd ed., New York: Guilford, 417–35.

Isen, A. M., Daubman, K. A., & Nowicki, G. P. (1987) 'Positive affect facilitates creative problem solving', *Journal of Personality and Social Psychology*, 52: 1122–31.

Kasof, J. (1997) 'Creativity and breadth of attention', *Creativity Research Journal*, 10: 303–15.

KICKER, 22.01.2013.

Memmert, D. (2007) 'Can creativity be improved by an attention-broadening training program? An exploratory study focusing on team sports', *Creativity Research Journal*, 19: 1–12.

Memmert, D. (2010a) 'Creativity, expertise, and attention: Exploring their development and their relationships', *Journal of Sports Sciences*, 29: 93–104.

Memmert, D. (2010b) 'Testing of tactical performance in youth elite soccer', *Journal of Sports Science and Medicine*, 9: 199–205.

Memmert, D. (2011) 'Sports and creativity', in M. A. Runco & S. R. Pritzker (eds) *Encyclopedia of creativity*, 2nd ed., vol. 2, San Diego: Academic Press, 373–8.

Memmert, D. (2013) 'Tactical creativity', in T. McGarry, P. O'Donoghue, & J. Sampaio (eds) *Routledge handbook of sports performance analysis*, Abingdon, UK: Routledge, 297–308.

Memmert, D. (2015) *Teaching tactical creativity in team and racket sports: Research and practice*, Abingdon, UK: Routledge.

Memmert, D., Baker, J., & Bertsch, C. (2010) 'Play and practice in the development of sport-specific creativity in team ball sports', *High Ability Studies*, 21: 3–18.

Memmert, D., Bischof, J., Endler, S., Grunz, A., Schmid, M., Schmidt, A., & Perl, J., (2011) 'World-level analysis in top level football. Analysis and simulation of football specific group tactics by means of adaptive neural networks', in C.L.P. Hui (ed) *Artificial neural networks – Application*, 3–12. doi: 10.5772/14919

Memmert, D., & Furley, P. (2007) '"I spy with my little eye!": Breadth of attention, inattentional blindness, and tactical decision making in team sports', *Journal of Sport & Exercise Psychology*, 29: 365–81.

Memmert, D., & Harvey, S. (2010) 'Identification of non-specific tactical problems in invasion games', *Physical Education and Sport Pedagogy*, 15: 287–305.

Memmert, D., Hüttermann, S., & Orliczek, J. (2013) 'Decide like Lionel Messi! The impact of regulatory focus on divergent thinking in sports', *Journal of Applied Social Psychology*, 43: 2163–7.

Memmert, D., & König, S. (2007) 'Teaching games at elementary schools', *International Journal of Physical Education*, 44: 54–67.

Memmert, D., & Roth, K. (2007) 'The effects of non-specific and specific concepts on tactical creativity in team ball sports', *Journal of Sports Sciences*, 25: 1423–32.

Memmert, D., Vogelbein, M., Nopp, S., & Knievel, G. (2013, in preparation) 'Good, better, creative! The relevance of tactical creativity in world class soccer'.

Milgram, R. M. (1990) 'Creativity: An idea whose time has come and gone', in M. A. Runco & R. S. Albert (eds) *Theory of creativity*, Newbury Park, CA: Sage, 215–33.

Hamburger Morgenpost (2009). Van Gaal will «frische Köpfe» [Van Gaal would like to have «fresh heads»]. Retrieved from www.mopo.de/news/fussball-van-gaal-will—frische-koepfe-,5066732,5330016.html (accessed January 22, 2015).

Pinder, R. A., Davids, K. W., Renshaw, I., & Araújo, D. (2011) 'Representative learning design and functionality of research and practice in sport', *Journal of Sport & Exercise Psychology*, 33: 146–55.

Runco, M. A. (2007) *Creativity. Theories and themes: Research, development, and practice*, San Diego, CA: Academic Press.

Runco, M. A., & Albert, R. S. (1986) 'The threshold theory regarding creativity and intelligence: An empirical test with gifted and nongifted children', *Creative Child & Adult Quarterly*, 11: 212–8.

Sternberg, R. J., & Lubart, T. I. (1995) *Defying the crowd: Cultivating creativity in a culture of conformity*, New York: Free Press.

Sternberg, R. J., & Lubart, T. I. (1999) 'The concept of creativity: Prospects and paradigms', in R. J. Sternberg (ed) *Handbook of creativity*, Cambridge: Cambridge University Press, 3–15.

Williams, A. M., Davids, K., & Williams, J. G. (1999). *Visual perception and action in sport*. London: E & F. N Spon.

Williams, M. (2013) *Science and soccer: Developing elite performance*, Abingdon, UK: Routledge.

32

BIRTHDATE AND BIRTHPLACE EFFECTS ON EXPERTISE ATTAINMENT

Nick Wattie, Dany J. MacDonald, and Stephen Cobley

While factors such as genetics and practice are primary influences in producing sport expertise, resources and environmental characteristics have been identified as important secondary factors that can constrain the influence of primary factors (see Baker & Horton, 2004). Failure to address secondary factors, which are pertinent to the *actual* lives of expert performers, may decrease the ecological validity of sport expertise models (e.g., Bronfenbrenner, 2005). In this chapter we review two such secondary factors, namely relative age and birthplace. Research on both these topics highlights how they can constrain the process of expertise development, and both phenomena demonstrate that sport expertise, like other developmental outcomes, is the result of interactions between individuals and their developmental environments (e.g., Lerner, 2006).

Relative age

Relative age describes a potential difference in age of nearly 12 months between youth eligible for the same level of sport participation (Wattie *et al.*, 2008).[1] An individual's relative age depends on his/her birthdate relative to the selection date (cutoff date) policy used by his/her specific sport. A selection date of December 31, stipulating that an athlete must be a specific age (e.g., six years old) by December 31 of the current playing season, ensures that those born just prior to the cutoff date in December will be younger (relatively younger) than those born in January of the same calendar year. Although selection dates can and do vary, those born in the months immediately proceeding a selection date will be "relatively older" than those born later in the selection date (i.e., the "relatively younger"). Relative age effects (RAEs) refer to the participation, selection, and attainment discrepancies that have been observed in various contexts of youth and adult sport, which then affect the process of expertise development.

RAEs and youth sport

The first studies of relative age in the context of competitive youth sport were in Canadian ice hockey (Barnsley & Thompson, 1988; Grondin *et al.*, 1984). In these studies, researchers observed repeated over-representations of youth ice hockey players born in the first three months after the selection date (referred to as quartile 1: Q1) compared to the last three months before the selection date (i.e., quartile 4: Q4) in age categories from eight to 15 years of age. Results highlighted that Q1 players could be two to four times over-represented compared to Q4 players, with the largest discrepancies associated with higher tiers of competitive play (Barnsley & Thompson, 1988; Grondin et al., 1984).

Since these initial studies, RAEs have been identified across numerous male competitive team and individual youth sport contexts. These include soccer (Helsen et al., 2005; Simmons & Paull, 2001), basketball (e.g., Delorme & Raspaud, 2009), handball (Schorer et al., 2009), both codes of rugby (e.g., Till et al., 2010b; Wilson, 1999), Australian-rules football (van den Honert, 2012), tennis (Edgar & O'Donoghue, 2005), swimming (Costa et al., 2013), and a variety of strength, endurance, and technique-based sports at the youth Olympic games (Raschner et al., 2012). Across these studies, Q1:Q4 ratios have ranged from 1.5:1 to as high as 8.5:1.

In female youth sport contexts, fewer studies have been conducted and the prevalence of RAEs has been inconsistent, with either no or lower discrepancies between Q1 and Q4. Relatively older girls were more likely to be participants on provincial youth volleyball teams (i.e., ages 14–15; Q1:Q4 = 2.25:1); however, samples at lower skill and other age groups (e.g., 12–19 years old) did not show significant discrepancies (Grondin et al., 1984). In German handball, relatively older females were over-represented (i.e., Q1 vs. Q4) on regional and national youth teams (ages 13–20; Schorer et al., 2009), and other studies have reported RAEs for particular age groups in swimming (Costa et al., 2013) and soccer (Romann & Fuchslocher, 2011). Overall, RAEs appear prevalent in youth sport contexts, although sex appears to moderate the likelihood and size of the effect (see Cobley et al., 2009).

RAEs and elite sport

What is particularly salient from a sport expertise perspective is that RAEs at youth levels of participation can have long-term effects; RAEs are still observed at elite international and professional levels of sport (Musch & Grondin, 2001), although the effect sizes tend to be smaller compared to youth levels (see Cobley et al., 2009). RAEs have been most notably observed at elite levels of men's ice hockey (Barnsley et al., 1985; Grondin et al., 1984; Wattie et al., 2007) and soccer (see Helsen et al., 2012), although effects have also been observed in sports such as basketball (Esteva & Drobnic, 2006; Hoare, 2000) and tennis (Loffing et al., 2010).

RAE mechanisms

There are likely several interacting processes that might explain the occurrence of RAEs. One of the principal mechanisms reflects advantages associated with physical size during selection processes. For example, one study of nine- and 10-year-old competitive ice hockey players found that selected players were at the 75th percentile (or higher) for weight and stature, *and* that a significant RAE existed among those youths (Baker et al., 2010). However, no differences in anthropometric measures were observed between relatively older and younger players. Similar results have been observed in older samples of youth ice hockey (Sherar et al., 2007), soccer (Baxter-Jones, 1995; Hirose, 2009), and rugby league players (Till et al., 2010a). As such, there is convincing evidence that a driving mechanism of RAEs may be the advantages associated with greater physical size and/or maturity. Relatively older youths are more likely to have greater weight and stature than relatively younger peers, because physical growth and maturation correlate with chronological age (Malina et al., 2004). In addition, Votteler and Höner (2014) have suggested that relatively older youths may have greater explosive power, independent of height and weight differences. It has been hypothesized that the above advantages, which result in a greater likelihood of selection to competitive sport, subsequently lead to further advantages as a result of exposure to better coaching, increased practice, and competition (Musch & Grondin, 2001).

While physical maturation may be the main mechanism responsible for the creation of RAEs (see Helsen *et al.*, 2000), research also highlights that sport-specific constraints may influence RAEs (see Wattie *et al.*, 2015). For example, in some sports being left-handed can be an advantage (see Hagemann, 2009); because so few people are left-handed (10–13 per cent), it can be more difficult for right-handed athletes to perceive and interpret the movements of left-handed athletes. As such, being left-handed can provide a tactical advantage that outweighs the potential advantage typically associated with relative age. The result is that RAEs remain prevalent among right handed-players but *not* among left-handed players, in sports such as tennis and handball (Loffing *et al.*, 2010; Schorer *et al.*, 2009). Sport-specific conditions may also differently constrain RAEs for males and females. While women's ice hockey emphasizes a benefit from greater physical size, the opposite is true in women's gymnastics where delayed maturation and more diminutive physical size are beneficial to performance. As such, contrary to women's ice hockey (see Weir *et al.*, 2010), women's gymnastics favor relatively *younger* athletes, resulting in inverse RAEs (see Hancock *et al.*, in press; Wattie *et al.*, 2012).

Further complicating our understanding of RAEs is evidence that relative age may influence the predisposition for initial participation in certain sports. Delorme and Raspaud (2009), as well as Hancock, Ste-Marie, and Young (2013), have observed RAEs at the introductory level of basketball and ice hockey, respectively. Both studies stress that the introductory stage does not contain any formal selection; participation is open to all youths interested and able to play. The reasons for these trends are not clear, but may include informal selection processes. Parents may withhold their relatively younger, and perhaps physically smaller, children from sports where size is important. Alternatively, these trends may reflect relatively younger children's prior negative experiences in sport or physical education, and the motivation to avoid further negative experiences. Indeed, evidence suggests that athletes of different relative age have different experiences in sport. Research suggests that relatively younger boys are more likely to drop out of sport (regarding soccer, see Helsen *et al.*, 1998; regarding ice hockey, see Lemez *et al.*, 2013). While these findings are likely not sufficient to explain the prevalence and magnitude of RAEs in adolescent and adult levels of high-performance sport, they may contribute to the influence of the longitudinal process of relative age on athlete development.

Other outcomes also cloud our understanding of the influence of relative age on the process of expertise development. In particular, between the emergence of RAEs at youth levels and the end of elite athletes' careers, paradoxical trends emerge wherein relatively *younger* athletes appear to develop into more talented and valued athletes. Relatively younger athletes have been found to receive higher monetary value contracts in professional German soccer (Ashworth & Heyndels, 2007), and have longer careers in German handball (Schorer *et al.*, 2009). In the case of North American professional ice hockey, relatively younger players are selected earlier in entry drafts (Baker & Logan, 2007) and may be more productive during their careers (Deaner *et al.*, 2013). Collectively, these findings suggest that relative age is actively involved in the long-term process of athlete development past the initial emergence of RAEs within a sport system. At the moment, it is unclear what types of constraints (i.e., individual, environmental, and/or sport-specific characteristics) are responsible for these paradoxical trends. However, identifying the mechanisms of these trends will be important to understanding how RAEs influence the entire process of athlete development.

Nick Wattie et al.

Birthplace

This section describes how the characteristics of different developmental environments can also act as important secondary influences on the process of attaining sport expertise. While the previous section of this chapter reviewed microlevel phenomena (i.e., relative age), this section shifts focus towards a more macrolevel influence on sport expertise: geographic environment. Specifically, a growing body of research has investigated how a person's birthplace can act as a secondary influence on expertise development. Generally speaking, the birthplace effect stipulates that the size of the city in which an individual is born, or first introduced to sport, is related to future attainment of expertise.

Although the majority of the research investigating the birthplace effect has occurred within the last decade, early conceptualization of the topic can be traced back to the work of Rooney (1969), Curtis and Birch (1987), and Carlson (1988). Without providing strong statistical evidence that a birthplace effect was present, these researchers investigated the environment of athletes to further understand how it relates to expert development. Rooney (1969) studied American football players and identified talent hotbeds that produced disproportionate amounts of professional players. Although the work by Rooney (1969) did not investigate city size per se, it provided preliminary evidence suggesting that certain geographic areas were more conducive to developing elite athletes than others. In an attempt to expand this work, Curtis and Birch (1987) compared proportions of professional and Olympic ice hockey players in Canada and the United States across different city sizes to the number of residents within these cities. They concluded that there were disproportionate amounts of players from certain city sizes. More specifically, very large and very small cities produced fewer professional athletes than expected, whereas medium-sized cities produced higher than expected rates of professional athletes. Further support for these findings was provided by Carlson (1988). His qualitative study of elite tennis players concluded that athletes from small- to medium-sized cities benefitted from their environment by having easy and constant access to the facilities needed to train.

More recently, research has attempted to understand the birthplace effect across different sports and countries. In a review of the literature, MacDonald and Baker (2013) outlined how birthplace effects have been investigated across different sports and countries. Table 32.1 summarizes the results of these studies and identifies the city sizes that have been shown to produce significantly more and less elite athletes than expected. The information presented in Table 32.1 outlines some consistent findings across countries with respect to city size and attainment of elite levels. When we consider the findings across North American countries, results indicate that city sizes between 5,000 and 500,000 produce higher than expected rates of professional athletes, whereas cities of less than 5,000 and more than five million produce less than expected rates. Mixed findings are reported for cities between 500,000 and one million. When we look at European countries, results suggest that cities between 50,000 and 200,000, along with cities of 2.5 to five million, produce more professional athletes than expected, whereas cities of less than 50,000 seem less favorable to athlete development. For example, although approximately 1.1 per cent of the US population live in towns with 50,000–99,999 residents, 10–17 per cent of professional hockey, basketball, baseball, and football athletes are from such towns (Côté *et al.*, 2006; MacDonald *et al.*, 2009a, 2009b). Similarly, although 13 per cent of the Canadian population resides in cities with populations from 100,000–499,999, 33 per cent of NHL players emerge from such cities (Côté *et al.*, 2006).

Although the evidence indicates that birthplace effects are an important factor in the attainment of expertise, less is known about the mechanisms that produce the effects. MacDonald and Baker (2013) stipulated that the birthplace effect may be related to the big-fish-little-pond effect

Birthdate and birthplace effects

Table 32.1 Summary of city sizes that are over- and under-represented across the studies that investigated the birthplace effect.

Sport	Country	Over-representation	Under-representation
American football[1]	United States	< 500K	> 500K
Baseball[2]	United States	< 500K	> 500K
Basketball[2–4]	Israel	–	2K – 50K
	United States	< 500K	> 500K
Golf (male)[2]	United States	< 500K	> 500K
Golf (female)[1]	United States	< 250K	> 250K
Handball[3,5]	Germany	30K – 1M;2.5M – 5M	< 30K
	Israel	50K – 200K	< 2K – 50K
Handball (female)[4]	Israel	50K – 200K	< 2K – 50K
Ice hockey (professional)[2,6]	Canada	100K – 250K;500K – 1M	< 10K
	United States	< 500K;30K – 2.5M	> 500K; < 2.5K
Ice hockey (junior elite)[7]	Canada	<100K;100K – 500K	> 100K
	Finland	10K – 30K	–
	United States	30K – 500K	–
	Sweden	< 10K	> 10K
Olympians[8]	Canada	100K – 250K;> 500K	< 5K
	United Stated	30K – 2.5M	< 2.5K; > 5M
	United Kingdom	10K – 30K	500K – 1M
	Germany	30K – 250K;2.5M – 5M	<10K
Rugby[9]	Australia	<20K;100K – 400K	> 1M
Soccer (female)[1,4]	United States	< 1M	> 5M
	Israel	50K – 200K	< 50K
Soccer (male)[3]	Israel	50K – 200K	< 50K
Volleyball (male)[3]	Israel	< 2K	2K – 50K
Volleyball (female)[4]	Israel	< 2K	2K – 50K

M = million; K = thousand; [1]MacDonald *et al.*, 2009b; [2]Côté *et al.*, 2006; [3]Lidor *et al.*, 2010; [4]Lidor *et al.*, 2014; [5]Schorer *et al.*, 2010; [6]Baker & Logan, 2007; [7]Bruner *et al.*, 2011; [8]Baker *et al.*, 2009; [9]Cobley *et al.*, 2014.

(BFLPE; Marsh *et al.*, 2008) in that athletes from small- to medium-sized centers have the right amounts of competition to develop their skills. Conversely, athletes in very small centers may not have adequate competition against which to play, whereas athletes in large urban centers may be overlooked due to the volume of individuals competing for limited spots on a team. In addition, Bale (2003) suggests that the cultural identity of those in smaller cities is much more explicitly connected to local sport than those in larger cities. As such, cities of particular sizes may be more likely to socialize athletes and parents towards particular sports, and may have unique resources (e.g., sport facilities) that facilitate expertise development.

Although these explanations are reasonable, the different findings across North American and European countries also suggest that city size alone is not a sufficient factor in explaining geographic trends of elite athletes. Within European countries, cities of less than 50,000 are under-represented in athlete production, whereas larger cities seem favorable to athlete development. This contrasts with North American countries where the largest (more than five million) and smallest (less than 10,000) cities seem to inhibit expertise development. Therefore, it appears that different mechanisms are operating, and it would be of interest to investigate other theoretical propositions for explaining the effect. For example, population density, which differs considerably between North American and European cities (see Baker *et al.*, 2009), could constrain the influence of birthplace effects in different regions. In addition, distances between cities are much larger in North America compared to Europe, which may uniquely influence access to important resources. Overall, these findings suggest that we must consider constraints specific to broader geographic location as well. However, further research is needed in this area to understand contextual differences related to birthplace.

One attempt to contextualize and explain different international spatial patterns has been to isolate what is of greater influence, birthplace *or* junior location where skill development takes place. For example, Schorer *et al.* (2010) investigated location of first club in elite handball players from Germany. Their results were mostly consistent with previous findings related to birthplace with respect to over- and under-representation of athletes. Although the results do not indicate differences between birthplace and location of first club, findings may relate to geographical proximity to urban centers in Europe. In another recent investigation of location of first club in Australian rugby players, Cobley *et al.* (2014) also found results consistent with previous birthplace findings. Combined, these results indicate that both first club location and actual birthplace produce similar influences on attainment of expertise. While it is unclear how location of first club and birthplace correlate, further studies are warranted to investigate additional mechanisms offered by first club location. In particular, it would be of interest to investigate the location of first club in North American countries to determine if similar findings arise given the differences in geographic makeup between the countries.

In another attempt to understand how spatial patterns influence talent development, Woolcock and Burke (2013) recently utilized a unique approach in a study of professional Australian Football League (AFL) players. Rather than comparing the proportion of professional players that emerged from a specific region to general population estimates for that region, they used geographic information systems (GIS) to compare the proportion of players that emerged from a region to the *actual* number of registered athletes participating in AFL in that region. This allowed the authors to calculate national averages of *talent yield* (professional athletes produced per 1,000 youth participants) and region-specific estimates of talent yield. Interestingly, not only do Woolcock and Burke's (2013) results support geographic differences in talent yield between regions of Australia and between cities, they also identify spatial differences in talent yields *within* cities. Going forward, methods such as these may make it possible to isolate specific regional constraints that influence birthplace effects, such as socio-demographic trends, physical resources, and participation rate thresholds for BFLPE.

Overall, results from the studies conducted on birthplace demonstrate that the location of birth and the location of the first club affect the development of expertise across different countries and sports. Although it has been consistently demonstrated that certain city sizes are more favorable than others, little information is currently known about the processes by which birthplace effects operate. If location of first club can be considered a proxy to birthplace, it may explain part of the process related to the development of expertise; however, further information is needed to further conceptualize the mechanisms involved. In addition, testing the BFLPE more directly, along with other possible mechanisms (e.g., talent yield), would help explain how and why birthplace effects occur. In an attempt to explore a possible mechanism of birthplace effects, researchers have considered whether an interaction exists between relative age and population size (Bruner *et al.*, 2011; Côté *et al.*, 2006). Although no significant inter-action has been found between relative age and birthplace, studies that acknowledge birthplace alongside other constraints have the potential to provide insights into birthplace effects. Overall, the field needs to move beyond identifying sports and countries where the effect is present by investigating mechanistic properties of the effect.

Conclusion

The research outlined herein demonstrates that relative age and birthplace are widespread factors that influence the process of expertise development in sport. While relative age and birthplace are distinct secondary influences on expertise attainment, both factors ultimately influence who has a better chance to enter high-performance sport and who is exposed to resources that facilitate expertise development. However, the reality is that RAEs are nei-ther homogenous in the nature of their outcomes *nor* in terms of the etiological processes which ultimately influence respective outcomes. Similarly, while birthplace effects exist in different sports and countries, unique processes may be responsible for spatial patterns in expertise development in different regions.

Overall, a substantial amount of relative age research, and the majority of birthplace research, have been largely descriptive. While this is typical of research still in its early stages (Bickhard, 2008), the next step, providing a detailed, mechanistic account of how both phenomena influence the process of expertise development, is essential. As relative age and birthplace effects are inher-ently complicated, understanding both secondary influences on athlete development will neces-sitate that researchers and practitioners consider individual, environmental, and sport-specific constraints. Ultimately, a better understanding of the processes inherent to RAEs and birthplace effects could be used to better inform high-performance selection and participation structures, and the distribution of resources important for athlete development.

Note

1 Relative age also exists in education (see Wattie & Baker, 2013), and a form also emerges at Masters (i.e., older adult) levels of sport participation (see Medic *et al.*, 2007). Schorer, Wattie & Baker (2013) also describe how a variety of different manifestations of relative age can exist in sport.

References

Ashworth, J., & Heyndels, B. (2007) 'Selection bias and peer effects in team sports: The effect of age group-ing on earnings of German soccer players', *Journal of Sports Economics*, 8: 355–77.

Baker, J., Cobley, S., Montelpare, W. J., Wattie, N., Faught, B., & The Ontario Hockey Research Group (2010) 'Exploring proposed mechanisms of the relative age effect in Canadian minor hockey', *International Journal of Sport Psychology*, 41: 148–59.

Baker, J., & Horton, S. (2004) 'A review of primary and secondary influences on sport expertise', *High Ability Studies*, 15: 211–28.

Baker, J., & Logan, A. J. (2007) 'Developmental contexts and sporting success: Birthdate and birthplace effects in NHL draftees 2000–2005', *British Journal of Sports Medicine*, 41: 515–17.

Baker, J., Schorer, J., Cobley, S., Schimmer, G., & Wattie, N. (2009) 'Circumstantial development and athletic excellence: The role of date of birth and birthplace', *European Journal of Sport Sciences*, 9: 329–39.

Bale, J. (2003) *Sports geography*, Oxford, UK: Routledge.

Barnsley, R. H., & Thompson, A. H. (1988) 'Birthdate and success in minor hockey: The key to the NHL', *Canadian Journal of Behavioural Science*, 20: 167–76.

Barnsley, R. H., Thompson, A. H., & Barnsley, P. E. (1985) 'Hockey success and birthdate: The RAE', *Canadian Assocation of Health, Physical Education and Recreation Journal*, 51: 23–8.

Baxter-Jones, A. (1995) 'Growth and development of young athletes: Should competition levels be age related?', *Sports Medicine*, 20: 59–64.

Bickhard, M. H. (2008) 'Issues in process metaphysics', *Ecological Psychology*, 20: 252–6.

Bronfenbrenner, U. (2005) *Making human beings human: Bioecological perspectives on human development*, London: Sage.

Bruner, M. W., MacDonald, D. J., Pickett, W., & Côté, J. (2011) 'Examination of birthplace and birthdate in world junior ice hockey players', *Journal of Sports Sciences*, 29: 1337–44.

Carlson, R. C. (1988) 'The socialization of elite tennis players in Sweden: An analysis of player's backgrounds and development', *Sociology of Sport Journal*, 5: 241–56.

Cobley, S., Baker, J., Wattie, N., & McKenna, J. (2009) 'Annual age-grouping and athlete development: A meta-analytical review of relative age effects in sport', *Sports Medicine*, 39: 235–56.

Cobley, S., Hanratty, M., O'Connor, D., & Cotton, W. (2014) 'First club location and relative age as influences on being a professional Australian rugby league player', *International Journal of Sport Science and Coaching*, 9: 335–346.

Costa, A. M., Marques, M. C., Louro, H., Ferreira, S. S., & Marinho, D. A. (2013) 'The relative age effect among elite youth competitive swimmers', *European Journal of Sport Science*, 13: 437–44.

Côté, J., MacDonald, D. J., Baker, J., & Abernethy, B. (2006) 'When size matters: Birthplace effects on the development of expertise', *Journal of Sport Science*, 24: 1065–73.

Curtis, J. E., & Birch, J. S. (1987) 'Size of community of origin and recruitment to professional and Olympic hockey in North America', *Sociology of Sport Journal*, 4: 229–44.

Deaner, R. O., Lowen, A., & Cobley, S. (2013) 'Born at the wrong time: Selection bias in the NHL draft', *PLoS ONE*, 8. doi: 10.1371/journal.pone.0057753

Delorme, N., & Raspaud, M. (2009) 'The relative age effect in young French basketball players: A study on the whole population', *Scandinavian Journal of Medicine and Science in Sport*, 19: 235–42.

Edgar, S., & O'Donoghue, P. (2005) 'Season of birth distribution of elite tennis players', *Journal of Sports Sciences*, 23: 1013–20.

Esteva, S., & Drobnic, F. (2006) 'Birthdate and basketball success', *FIBA Assist Magazine*, 18: 64–6.

Grondin, S., Deschaies, P., & Nault, L. P. (1984) 'Trimester of birth and school output [in French]', *Apprentissage Social*, 16: 169–74.

Hagemann, N. (2009) 'The advantage of being left-handed in interactive sports', *Attention, Perception, & Psychophysics*, 71: 1641–8.

Hancock, D. J., Starkes, J. L., & Ste-Marie, D. M. (in press) 'The relative age effect in female gymnastics: A flip-flop phenomenon', *International Journal of Sport Psychology*.

Hancock, D. J., Ste-Marie, D. M., & Young, B. W. (2013) 'Coach selections and the relative age effect in male youth ice hockey', *Research Quarterly for Exercise and Sport*, 84: 126–30.

Helsen, W. F., Baker, J., Michiels, S., Schorer, J., van Winckel, J., & Williams, A. M. (2012) 'The relative age effect in European professional soccer: Did ten years of research make any difference?', *Journal of Sports Sciences*, 30: 1665–71.

Helsen, W. F., Hodges, N. J., van Winckel, J., & Starkes, J. L. (2000) 'The roles of talent, physical precocity and practice in the development of soccer expertise', *Journal of Sports Sciences*, 18: 727–36.

Helsen, W. F., Starkes, J. L., & Van Winckel, J. (1998) 'The influence of relative age on success and dropout in male soccer players', *American Journal of Human Biolology*, 10: 791–8.

Helsen, W. F., Van Winckel, J., & Williams, M. A. (2005) 'The relative age effect in youth soccer across Europe', *Journal of Sports Sciences*, 23: 629–36.

Hirose, N. (2009) 'Relationships among birth-month distribution, skeletal age and athropometric characteristics in adolescent elite soccer players', *Journal Sports Sciences*, 27: 1159–66.

Hoare, D. (2000) 'Birthdate and basketball success: Is there a relative age effect?', in *Proceedings of the Pre-Olympic Congress: Sports Medicine and Physical Education International Congress on Sports Science*, Brisbane, AU-QLD.

Lemez, S., Baker, J., Horton, S., Wattie, N., & Weir, P. (2013) 'Examining the relationship between relative age, competition level, and dropout rates in male youth ice-hockey players', *Scandinavian Journal of Medicine and Science in Sport*. doi: 10.1111/sms.12127

Lerner, R. M. (2006) 'Developmental science, developmental systems, and contemporary theories of human developmental', in W. Damon & R. M. Lerner (eds) *Handbook of child psychology, volume 1: Theoretical models of human development*, 6th ed., Hoboken, NJ: John Wiley & Sons, 1–17.

Lidor, R., Arnon, M., Maayab, Z., Gershon, T., & Côté, J. (2014) 'Relative age effect and birthplace effect in division 1 female ballgame players – The relevance of sport-specific factors', *International Journal of Sport and Exercise Psychology*, 12: 19–33.

Lidor, R., Côté, J., Arnon, M., Zeev, A., & Cohen-Maoz, S. (2010) 'Relative age and birthplace effects in division 1 players: Do they exist in a small country?', *Talent Development and Excellence*, 2: 181–92.

Loffing, F., Schorer, J., & Cobley, S. P. (2010) 'Relative age effects are a developmental problem in tennis: But not necessarily when you're left-handed!', *High Ability Studies*, 21: 19–25.

MacDonald, D. J., & Baker, J. (2013) 'Circumstantial development: Birthdate and birthplace effects on athlete development', in J. Côté & R. Lidor (eds) *Conditions of children's talent development in sport*, Morgantown, WV: Fitness Information Technology, 197–208.

MacDonald, D. J., Cheung, M., Côté, J., & Abernethy, B. (2009a) 'Place but not date of birth influences the development and emergence of athletic talent in American football', *Journal of Applied Sport Psychology*, 21: 80–90.

MacDonald, D. J., King, J., Côté, J., & Abernethy, B. (2009b) 'Birthplace effects on the development of female athletic talent', *Journal of Science and Medicine in Sport*, 12: 234–7.

Malina, R. M., Bouchard, C., & Bar-Or, O. (2004) *Growth, maturation, and physical activity*, 2nd ed., Champaign, IL: Human Kinetics.

Marsh, H. W., Seaton, M., Trautwein, U., Lüdtke, O., Hau, K. T., O'Mara, A. J., & Craven, R. G. (2008) 'The big-fish-little-pond-effect stands up to the critical scrutiny: Implications for theory, methodology, and future research', *Educational Psychology Review*, 20: 319–50.

Medic, N., Starkes, J. L., & Young, B. W. (2007) 'Examining relative age effects on performance achievement and participation rates in masters athletes', *Journal of Sports Sciences*, 25: 1377–84.

Musch, J., & Grondin, S. (2001) 'Unequal competition as an impediment to personal development: A review of the relative age effect in sport', *Developmental Review*, 21: 147–67.

Raschner, C., Müller, L., & Hildebrandt, C. (2012) 'The role of relative age effects in the first winter youth Olympic games in 2012', *British Journal of Sports Medicine*, 46: 1038–43.

Romann, M., & Fuchslocher, J. (2011) 'Influence of the selection level, age and playing position on relative age effects in Swiss women's soccer', *Talent Development & Excellence*, 3: 239–47.

Rooney, J. F., Jr. (1969) 'Up from the mines and out from the prairies: Some geographical implications of football', *Geographical Review*, 59: 471–92.

Schorer, J., Baker, J., Lotz, S., & Büsch, D. (2010) 'Influence of early environmental constraints on achievement motivation in talented young handball players', *International Journal of Sport Psychology*, 41: 42–57.

Schorer, J., Cobley, S., Büsch, D., Bräutigam, H., & Baker, J. (2009) 'Influences of competition level, gender, player nationality, career stage and playing position on relative age effects', *Scandinavian Journal of Medicine and Science in Sport*, 19: 720–30.

Schorer, J., Wattie, N., & Baker, J. R. (2013) 'A new dimension to relative age effects: Constant year effects in German youth handball', *PLoS ONE*, 8(4): e60336. doi: 10.1371/journal.pone.0060336

Sherar, L. B., Baxter-Jones, A.D.G., Faulkner, R. A., & Russell, K. W. (2007) 'Does physical maturity and birth date predict talent in male youth ice hockey players?', *Journal of Sports Science*, 25: 879–86.

Simmons, C., & Paull, G. C. (2001) 'Season-of-birth bias in assocation football', *Journal of Sports Sciences*, 19: 677–86.

Till, K., Cobley, S., O'Hara, J., Chapman, C., & Cooke, C. (2010a) 'Anthropometric, physiological and selection characteristics in high performance UK junior rugby league players', *Talent Development & Excellence*, 2: 193–207.

Till, K., Cobley, S., Wattie, N., O'Hara, J., Cooke, C., & Chapman, C. (2010b) 'The prevalence, influential factors and mechanisms of relative age effects in UK rugby league', *Scandinavian Journal of Medicine & Science in Sports*, 20: 320–9.

van de Honert, R. (2012) 'Evidence of the relative age effect in football in Australia', *Journal of Sports Sciences*, 30: 1365–74.

Votteler, A., & Höner, O. (2014) 'The relative age effect in the German football TID programme: Biases in motor performance diagnostics and effects on single motor abilities and skills in groups of selected players', *European Journal of Sport Science*, 14: 433–442.

Wattie, N., & Baker, J. (2013) 'Happy birthday? Relative age and its influence on human development', *The Psychologist*, 26: 110–13.

Wattie, N., Baker, J., Cobley, S., & Montelpare, W. J. (2007) 'A historical examination of relative age effects in Canadian hockey players', *International Journal of Sport Psychology*, 38: 178–86.

Wattie, N., Cobley, S., & Baker, J. (2008) 'Toward a unified understanding of relative age effects', *Journal of Sports Sciences*, 26: 1403–9.

Wattie, N., Schorer, J., & Baker, J. (2015) 'The relative age effect in sport: A developmental systems model', *Sports Medicine*, 45: 83–94.

Wattie, N., Tietjens, M., Schorer, J., Cobley, S., Baker, J., & Kurz, D. (2012) 'Relative age-related participation and dropout trends in German youth sports clubs', *European Journal of Sport Science.* doi: 10.1080/17461391.2012.681806

Weir, P. L., Smith, K. L., Paterson, C., & Horton, S. (2010) 'Canadian women's ice hockey – Evidence of a relative age effect', *Talent Development & Excellence*, 2: 209–17.

Wilson, G. (1999) 'The birthdate effect in school sports teams', *Physical Education & Sport Pedagogy*, 4: 139–45.

Woolcock, G., & Burke, M. (2013) 'Measuring spatial variations in sports talent development: The approach, methods and measures of "talent tracker"', *Australian Geographer*, 44: 23–9.

33

CAREER LENGTH, AGING, AND EXPERTISE

Sean Horton, Joseph Baker, and Patricia Weir

Introduction

One of the most remarkable near misses in the world of sports occurred in 2009, when golfer Tom Watson, at age 59, had an eight-foot putt on the 72nd hole to win the British Open. Watson missed the putt, and then subsequently lost the three-hole playoff. Watson's remarkable performance was one for the ages, and the aged, for he was at the time more than a decade older than Tom Morris – who is the oldest winner of what is arguably the world's most prestigious golf tournament (R&A championships limited). "Old" Tom Morris won the 1867 British Open at age 46, at a time when the level of competition was far inferior to what it is today.

In the 2008 Beijing Olympics, Dara Torres won three silver medals at the age of 41. In the 50 m sprint, Torres finished 1/100th of a second behind the gold medalist, and set a personal best in that event. Beijing was Torres's 5th Olympic games. Previous to Torres, the oldest medal winner in swimming was 38-year-old William Robinson, whose win occurred in the 1908 Olympic games in London, England (Clarey, 2008).

In the strike-shortened National Hockey League (NHL) season of 2013, Martin St. Louis won the scoring title, which is awarded to the player with the highest point total (goals and assists combined). At age 38, he is the oldest player in history to win this award (Duhatschek, 2013). St. Louis has been battling the odds his whole life; he was initially ignored by all NHL teams, going undrafted as a junior player, and at 5'8" was always considered to be too small to play in the NHL. Yet St. Louis has now won the scoring title twice, won a Stanley Cup, an Olympic Gold medal, and continues to excel at an age at which most players have retired from the game.

Steve Redgrave is England's most decorated rower. Redgrave won gold medals at five successive Olympic games, the last at age 38. He is just the fourth person to win gold at five straight Olympics. In addition, Redgrave was victorious in nine world rowing championships over an 18-year time span (Benedict, 2014). These four individuals exemplify extraordinary accomplishment at an age normally considered to be beyond peak performance. We are, however, living longer lives, so perhaps it is inevitable that superior performance, and potentially career length, would drift upwards as well. Oeppen and Vaupel (2002) have depicted the remarkable linear trend of increasing human lifespan. Since 1840, human longevity has increased by three months each year on average, to the point that children born today in advanced, industrialized countries can expect to live upwards of 80 years. This is having wide-sweeping societal effects, both positive

383

and negative. For instance, many countries are reducing retirement benefits as people live longer, and the corresponding declining birthrates mean fewer workers to support retirees (Pension crisis a global problem, 2013). Unless drastic adjustments are made to social programs and policy, a rapidly aging population has the potential to wreak havoc with government finances.

The sporting world has experienced substantial increases in participation by older athletes; participation rates in events like the World Masters games have grown considerably since their inauguration in 1985 (Weir *et al.*, 2010). Physiological evidence suggests that adults in their 70s, provided they maintain high-quality training, will have body composition and muscle fiber measures comparable to athletes in their 40s (Wroblewski *et al.*, 2011). Septuagenarians now achieve running times that would have garnered Olympic medals in the early part of the 20th century. Distance runner Ed Whitlock has run multiple sub-three-hour marathons after the age of 70. Those times would have contended for an Olympic gold medal in 1908 (Official Olympic games results). Similarly, men over the age of 50 achieve comparable 100 m times to those winning medals in this event in the early 20th century (World Masters Athletics).

It remains an open question, however, as to whether improved performance at later ages necessarily translates into longer careers, or that this performance is considered "expert" (see also Chapter 13). As fields advance, training techniques improve, and athletes become more specialized, performance standards continue to evolve. While this will vary by domain, experts of yesteryear are perhaps no more than very good by modern standards. This raises important questions about career length and maintaining expert performance. To this end, this chapter will examine two separate yet related questions concerning aging, career length, and expertise. The first examines career length as it relates to maintaining performance at the expert or professional level. The second investigates the extent to which high performance can be maintained in later life. Research on Masters athletes is particularly relevant with respect to the degree individuals can limit age-related decline. For each of these questions, however, the available quantitative data do not tell the whole story. Social factors invariably influence opportunities for participation, thus affecting performance data for athletes both at the peak of their careers, and as they age.

How long can someone stay expert?

Despite the obvious importance of understanding the length of time athletes are able to spend at the highest levels of performance, very little research has been done in this area. Several models of athlete development have been proposed (Côté *et al.*, 2007; Starkes *et al.*, 2004; see Chapter 27 for more on early stages of development), with most focusing on early periods of skill development and very little attention given to factors influencing the duration and/or quality of the expert stage of development. Unfortunately, this has left researchers, coaches, and athletes with a limited understanding of the average length of time an athlete can spend at his/her "peak" or what supports can be put in place to maximize the amount of time an athlete can spend at this level. One of the reasons these issues have been rarely examined relates to the difficulty obtaining samples of athletes at this exceptional level of achievement. Studies that have been conducted have typically focused on medical treatments that might prolong playing careers (e.g., Brophy *et al.*, 2010) or social concerns, such as racial inequality in length of careers in football (Best, 1987) and basketball (Hoang & Rascher, 1999). Few have examined length of professional/elite career as it relates to models of skill acquisition and maintenance over the lifespan.

In a recent study, Baker and colleagues examined career length (defined as the duration of time spent as a professional athlete) among athletes who had careers in the four major North American professional sport leagues (NBA, NHL, NFL, and MLB; Baker *et al.*, 2013). NBA players had the longest professional careers (mean = 8.2 years) and NFL players had the shortest (mean = 5.5 years), although there was considerable variability across all of the sports. There were also differences in professional career length across the various positions in baseball and football that suggested those with greater risk of injury (e.g., defensive lineman in football) had shorter careers than those not at elevated risk. Interestingly there were no positional differences in basketball and ice hockey. Finally, and as would be expected, superior performance was related to longer professional careers. While research in this area is in its early stages, it emphasizes the importance of understanding the highest levels of performance in order to inform more sophisticated lifespan models of skill development that adequately bridge the gap between skill acquisition and age-related decline. In-depth interviews with athletes approaching the end of their careers that explore the various factors that influence retirement decisions and the ultimate exit from their sport would prove to be valuable.

Career length and expert performance in a social context

One of the most fascinating aspects of human development and our collective accomplishments is that notions of biological and physiological constraints are consistently surpassed. While there are undoubtedly constraints to what humans can achieve, history suggests that we are likely to underestimate those boundaries. Breaking the four-minute mile barrier is perhaps the most notable example of surpassing perceived biological thresholds. For a number of years, runners had come tantalizingly close to eclipsing the four-minute mark (Klawans, 1998). At the time, however, many believed it was a physical impossibility, and that attempts to break the barrier would result in serious physiological consequences (Epstein, 2013). Roger Bannister's historic run in 1954 shattered that notion permanently. Amazingly, Bannister was a 25-year-old medical student and essentially a part-time runner, although his scientific approach to the event was notable (Klawans, 1998). After Bannister broke the barrier, several other runners did so shortly thereafter, and today the record is almost 17 seconds under four minutes (The world record).

Such examples raise questions as to what extent factors are at work other than biological constraints that affect achievement and career length. The increasing popularity of professional sports over the past 100 years, and the corresponding rise in both the number of teams (i.e., league expansion) and salaries has created opportunities for participation in these particular endeavors, potentially extending career length (Whitnauer et al., 2007). Other factors such as racism, ageism, homophobia, and sexism play out in the athletic arena, and likely distort the analysis related to the achievement and maintenance of expert performance. Athletes barred from participating, or athletes themselves withdrawing from an inhospitable environment in the face of discrimination, has been commonplace. For example, Fusco (1998) investigated the discrimination that lesbian athletes experience from fellow athletes, coaches, or teammates that can lead to feelings of isolation, maladaptive behaviors such as alcohol abuse, and ultimately dropping out of a sport.

While Witnauer and colleagues (Witnauer et al., 2007) examined the career length of Major League Baseball (MLB) players over the 20th century, it is not inconsequential to their analysis that black players were excluded from participation in the league until 1947, when the color barrier was first breached by Jackie Robinson. The Professional Golfers' Association had a caucasians-only rule until 1960, and it was not until 1975 that a black golfer played in the Master's golf tournament (Schupak, 2010). Tiger Woods, born in 1976, and victorious in the Master's on four occasions, might have never played the event had he been born 40 years earlier.

Indeed, evidence from a number of sports indicates that racism has an influence on career length. Goodard and Wilson's (2009) study of English football from 1986–2001 intimated the possibility of hiring discrimination affecting opportunities for black players to play professionally. Gandelman (2009) found evidence of discrimination against non-white players in the Uruguayan

Soccer League. Hoang and Rascher (1999) found that white players could expect NBA (National Basketball Association) careers two seasons longer than similarly skilled black players. Similarly, Khan and Shaw (2005) reported discrimination in the NBA against marginal, non-white players. Indigenous Australian footballers appear to be under-represented in the Australian Football League draft (Mitchell *et al.*, 2011). Jiobu (1988) found evidence of discrimination against black athletes in MLB, but not Hispanic athletes, in examining player retention by teams between 1971 and 1985. Of interest is the fact that a subsequent study by Groothuis and Hill (2008) found no discrimination against black baseball players in the major leagues between the years of 1990 and 2004. The authors speculated that market competition might have overcome this discrimination.

This may as yet be a premature conclusion to draw. Discrimination continues to exist at a more subtle level, as "stacking" has distorted the career opportunities for minority players. Stacking systematically excludes certain groups from specific positions due to perceived intellectual shortcomings. This practice has been seen in baseball (Jiobu, 1988; Sack *et al.*, 2005), but perhaps most notably in American football, where black players were systematically excluded from certain positions thought to be more cognitively challenging (Berri & Simmons, 2009). Black players tended to be stacked in the position of wide receiver or running back, based on notions that these are highly athletic positions. At the same time, they were excluded from the quarterback position, due to perceptions of the cognitive challenge associated with this task. This perpetuated and reinforced stereotypes of superior black athleticism, but inferior cognitive skills and decision-making abilities compared to white athletes.

While black quarterbacks are still under-represented in the National Football League and college ranks (Bopp & Sagas, 2014), stacking is less pronounced than it once was, potentially replaced by an even more subtle form of discrimination – namely "racial tasking," which suggests that blacks and whites play the quarterback position differently (Berri & Simmons, 2009). Bopp and Sagas (2014) found the black quarterbacks ran the ball more and passed less frequently than their white counterparts. Team offences appear to be structured differently depending on the race of the quarterback. Running is considered to require more natural athleticism, akin to the position of running back, whereas throwing is more cognitively complex, due to the fact that it involves keeping track of multiple receivers and defenders. Throwing is also riskier, due to the chance of an interception (McGarrity & Linnen, 2010).

Bopp and Sagas (2014) argue that such practices have consequences, both for skill acquisition and for the ability of black athletes to obtain jobs as coaches after their playing careers. The practice of stacking, or more recently, tasking, may perpetuate the stereotype that black athletes do not have the requisite knowledge to take on the demanding cognitive challenge that is coaching. Bopp and Sagas assert that those who play the most cognitively challenging positions tend to be the most likely to move into coaching, and that systematic exclusion from those positions, or even playing those positions differently, can affect the development of pattern recognition and cognitive skills essential to being a successful coach.

While individual sports have their own extensive history of racism, sexism, and homophobia, they may provide an easier environment to navigate than team sports, particularly if the sport has very objective measures of performance. If Tom Watson shoots a score low enough, he wins golf tournaments. Similarly, if Dara Torres swims fast enough, she wins medals. While there are undoubtedly barriers that athletes face in individual sports, which historically have included even the most basic forms of access, individual sport athletes may not face the same type of coach/management irrationality that they would in team environments (Lewis, 2004; Mitchell *et al.*, 2011).

Of interest, however, is how irrationality on the part of some organizations allows others to exploit the inefficiencies that are created. Lewis (2004) detailed the scientific approach that

Oakland A's manager Billy Beane utilized to identify baseball players that were overlooked by other organizations. Despite working with one of the smallest budgets in major league baseball, Beane has led Oakland to considerable success over a number of years. Beane's scientific approach to the game, and to talent identification in particular, has led to other teams' employing saberme-tricians in an attempt to replicate Beane's success. A byproduct of this scientific approach may be a lessening of inefficient and often discriminatory practices. Part of the reason that Branch Rickey signed Jackie Robinson was to help the Brooklyn Dodgers win baseball games. While data on career length and expertise have historically been distorted by a number of social factors, the evidence suggests that this may be decreasing, particularly as the cost of such irrationality is revealed by systematic analysis.

Beyond peak performance – managing the decline

As with peak performance, notions of age, biological limits, and how they relate to performance have evolved over time. Data presented by Oeppen and Vaupel (2002) exemplify this phenome-non. The consistent, linear increase in life span over the past 170 years has been punctuated with perceived limits postulated by researchers who thought that the human life span had reached its biological ceiling. These perceived boundaries were each proven wrong as, generally within a very short time after the prediction, life span extended well past that postulated ceiling (Oeppen & Vaupel, 2002). That peak performance will decline is inevitable, although the rate of decline and the extent to which highly learned skills can be maintained is debatable. Bortz and Bortz (1996) proposed that 0.5 per cent per year after peak performance represented a general bio-marker of the aging process. This value was based on their summary of age-related decline in out-comes ranging from rate of DNA repair and fingernail growth to various physiological systems and sporting events. However, there has been considerable debate regarding whether this value represents the hard limits to the maintenance of skill in humans, since the aging process is also typically reflective of changes in behavior patterns (e.g., sport involvement declines with age in both sexes; Statistics Canada, 2013), which may confound any analysis of functioning/perfor-mance over time. Specific to sport, recent Canadian data indicate that participation rates are high-est in young Canadians, with 54 per cent between the ages of 15 and 19 taking part in sporting activity. This declines precipitously with age, and by age 55 only 17 per cent of individuals are engaging in sport (Statistics Canada, 2013).

One population that maintains high levels of training and competitive involvement is com-prised of Masters athletes. Masters sport is a rapidly growing domain, providing opportunities for competition at advanced ages. The accuracy and availability of results from Masters competitions provide a rich data source for examining changes in performance with age. Moreover, due to their commitment to ongoing training, these performance changes have been suggested to reflect important indicators of physiological aging (Anton *et al.*, 2004).

Tracking changes over time: endurance and power events

Modeling performance changes in older adults has coincided with the initiation and growth of Masters events, which have exploded in popularity in the last 30 years (Weir *et al.*, 2010). Stones and Kozma (1981, 1984) were the early leaders in this regard, modeling performance changes in cross-sectional, semi-longitudinal, and longitudinal samples. This early research suggested that cross-sectional samples showed steeper rates of performance decline than longitudinal samples, generally beginning at approximately 60 years of age. Given the heterogeneity of cross-sectional samples this might not be surprising; participation in athletic events at late ages was uncommon

30 years ago, thus performance decline in cross-sectional analysis was likely due to the small number of participants as much as to the physical and physiological variables involved. More recent research has found less of a distinction between longitudinal and cross-sectional results. Moreover, the recent, stable patterns of performance seen in longitudinal within-subject analyses speak to the ongoing nature and quality of training in which elite Masters athletes are participating (Young & Starkes, 2005; Young *et al.*, 2008b).

Tanaka and Seals (1997) examined the top 10 times for both men and women from 1991–1995 United States Masters swimming championships (USMS), using cross-sectional data. Over a 50-year age span up to age 70, the authors reported performance declines of 38 per cent in women and 31 per cent in men. Fairbrother (2007) extended these findings and determined that performance deteriorated across both genders by approximately one per cent per year up to age 70, whereas from ages 70–83 this decline accelerated to approximately two per cent per year. Importantly, Fairbrother (2007) clarified that the presence of more swimmers in younger age groups, and thus more swimming times contributing to the prediction equations, had no impact on the declines in swimming performance up to age 83. Beyond 83 years of age the number of participants competing drops substantially and becomes a limiting factor in analyzing age-related performance declines. Moving from cross-sectional to longitudinal samples, Donato *et al.* (2003) examined swimming performance across a group of top-10 1,500 m swimmers who had competed in the USMS over a 12-year period. Akin to previous findings, this longitudinal analysis showed that performance times declined in a comparable fashion and at similar rates – linearly to age 70, after which this deterioration accelerated.

Anton *et al.* (2004) examined weightlifting and powerlifting for both men and women and found that performance declines with increasing age were more pronounced for weightlifting. Weightlifting events such as the clean and jerk, which requires the combination of two different muscular efforts (the weight is raised to shoulder height, held momentarily, and then quickly thrust overhead usually with a lunge or a spring from the legs), are thought to involve more complex movements and to be more sensitive to physiological changes with age than powerlifting moves, which tend to be planar in nature (e.g., bench press). Across sexes, women experienced a greater decline in weightlifting performance than men. While both men and women declined in a linear fashion in powerlifting, for women in weightlifting events this decline accelerated at age 50. Of interest is the fact that there were no significant differences in age-related decreases in upper- and lower-body strength; the decline appears to be a systemic effect on the entire body.

Baker and Tang (2010) investigated changes in weightlifting performances across age and, similar to Anton *et al.* (2004), found that women deteriorated at a more rapid rate. Weightlifting performance decreased by 75 per cent between age 30 and age 67 for women, with further exponential declines into the early 70s as performance drops off markedly. In contrast, in the men's data there is a performance decline of 75 per cent from age 30 to 82, with similar exponential deterioration thereafter into the late 80s. Baker and Tang (2010) also reported a more rapid decline in weightlifting compared to all other sports (with the exception of women's sprint cycling). In men's and women's rowing, a 75 per cent decline in performance is generally not seen until past age 100. The authors note that this is in spite of the fact that rowing is considered to be perhaps the most physiologically strenuous of sports. While rowing and weightlifting test different components of an aging body, it is likely that social, economic, and lifestyle factors play a role in these drastic differences between sports. Baker and Tang note that participation rates will invariably influence the analysis of performance decline and likely account for some of the gender differences witnessed in weightlifting. Considering the recent growth of Masters events, Baker and Tang's compilation of data may underestimate performance, given the smaller number of participants in the oldest age groups of their analyses.

Skill-based sports

A different profile of maintenance emerges with skill-based sports (i.e., sports where performance reflects relatively complex acquired skills rather than more biologically determined qualities like speed, power, or endurance). Although there is still some decrease in elements of performance with age, the rate of decline is relatively small and in some cases can be counterbalanced with improvements in other areas. Baker and colleagues' (Baker *et al.*, 2005; Baker *et al.*, 2007) examination of professional golfers highlights the stability of skilled performance over time (Figure 33.1). In a sample of 17 elite professional golfers whose performance spanned the Professional Golfers' Association (PGA; open to all ages) and Champions' Tour (open to players 50 years old and older) performance was relatively stable, declining at a rate of just 0.07 per cent per year on the PGA Tour and accelerating moderately to 0.25 per cent on the Champions' Tour (Baker *et al.*, 2005). A more comprehensive analysis (Baker *et al.*, 2007) found that some components of golf performance (e.g., putting, driving accuracy) were remarkably stable with age, while other elements (e.g., driving distance, greens in regulation) declined at a faster rate. However, none of the markers of golf skill declined at the 0.5 per cent rate proposed by Bortz and Bortz (1996).

Preliminary data from Schorer and Baker's (2009) study of perceptual performance in handball goalkeepers also found stability over time. Interestingly, when retired handball goalkeepers'

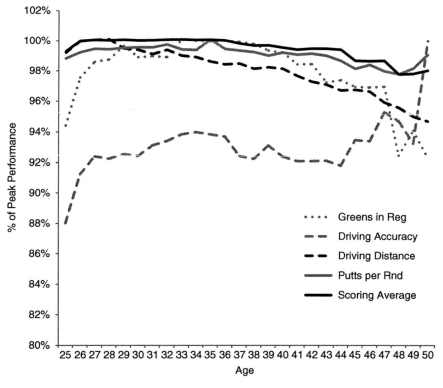

Figure 33.1 Performance of elite PGA golfers from 25 to 50 years of age relative to peak performance (100%). These data show the dynamics of performance over time. While scoring average remained relatively stable, the components of performance varied. Putting remained relatively stable while driving distance and greens in regulation declined and driving accuracy showed modest improvement. Changes in equipment technology were controlled for by accounting for improvements in the PGA tour as a whole. Adapted from Baker *et al.*, (2007).

perceptual skills were examined, performance was maintained despite the fact that the older players' involvement in the game was limited to the role of coach or team manager (i.e., no physical practice). These results suggest that skills such as identifying critical sources of perceptual information from an opponent (i.e., the type used for skilled anticipation) may be maintained with advancing age even without continued practice in the domain.

Studies from other domains of cognitive/motor expertise have shown similar trends. For instance, Salthouse (1984) found that performance of skilled typists was virtually unchanged with advanced age, similar to results from Charness (1981) in elite chess players. In an extensive investigation of age and musical skill, Krampe and Ericsson (1996) measured young and old expert pianists along with young and old amateurs on a range of specific (i.e., to piano) and general parameters. While the results were similar to those found in chess and typing – in the sense that measures of piano playing skill were maintained for the experts – there was a significant age effect for the general measures of processing speed (e.g., choice RT and digit symbol substitution); older performers showed normal rates of decline, regardless of skill level. Krampe and Ericsson hypothesized that through selective maintenance – that is, continued engagement in high-quality practice – musical experts were able to maintain piano-specific skills. In the section below, we consider this and other explanations for the maintenance of experts' skill with age.

Theoretical explanations for stability of performance with advancing age

Francis Galton is generally considered to have initiated some of the earliest and most influential work into the study of high achievement. Galton (1881) outlined innate capacity, zeal, and the ability to work hard as the primary determinants of excellence. Initial forays into explaining high achievement focused on the first of the three determinants: innate capacity. The *preserved differentiation* (or general factor) account is a genetic explanation of superior performance, and suggests that experts have this innate capacity that facilitates performance across all stages of the life span. These inherent advantages existed prior to the development of high performance and help to sustain that performance across the age spectrum.

In contrast, the theory of *selective maintenance* suggests that the retention of skill with age is the result of concentrated training on the most relevant components of the task (Krampe & Ericsson, 1996). Ericsson (1990) showed that for elite athletes many physiological changes (e.g., cardiovascular adaptations) were likely acquired over long periods of practice and not inherited. Although contemporary models of skilled performance have challenged the simple dichotomy of nature vs. nurture, the expertise approach and its associated research developed over the last 40 years has provided important evidence that performance in a wide variety of domains is robustly predicted by time spent in high-quality practice (Bloom, 1985; Chase & Simon, 1973; Ericsson *et al.*, 1993).

In a longitudinal analysis of long distance runners, Young and colleagues demonstrated that ongoing weekly training explained substantially more variance in running performance ($R^2 = 0.28$) than age alone ($R^2 = 0.15$); similarly, training over the last five years ($R^2 = 0.32$) explained more unique variance (Young *et al.*, 2008a). While the evidence suggests that the training patterns of Masters athletes are different than that of younger athletes (i.e., older athletes train fewer hours per week and primarily for endurance), the level of training is substantial enough to maintain superior performances (Starkes *et al.*, 1999; Weir *et al.*, 2002).

Despite the fact that older athletes train for fewer hours per week, they may train "smarter," in that they focus on the most important aspects of training. This is consistent with Baltes and Baltes's (1990) suggestion that when resources are limited the individual copes by using a combination of *selection* (i.e., a conscious choice of where to invest resources), *optimization* (i.e.,

Career length, aging, and expertise

making choices that optimize performance), and *compensation* (i.e., adapting to accommodate for restrictions). Compensation represents a third major theory of performance preservation, and is a method of dealing with age-related declines in cognitive or physiological resources. One of the most noteworthy studies in this area was Salthouse's (1984) work with expert typists. Salthouse found that typing performance of older experts (i.e., domain-specific functioning) was equivalent to the young experts in spite of the fact that choice reaction time, finger tapping speed, and performance on the digit symbol substitution test (i.e., related general measures of functioning) all declined. The larger eye-hand span displayed by the older typists led Salthouse to postulate that older experts compensated for these declines by scanning further ahead in the text. Similarly, athletes involved in sports such as basketball that involve explosive movements may develop other components of their game (i.e., refining their jump shot) to make up for an age-related loss in jumping ability. As noted earlier, aging golfers seem to compensate for a decline in power associated with driving distance by maintaining, or improving, their short game (Baker *et al.*, 2007).

Masters sport represents an important model for studying the influence of advancing age on skill maintenance, and the available research provides intriguing data on the extent to which performance can be maintained at late ages. There are, however, important social factors at work in addition to the biological and physiological constraints on the aging body. What are perceived to be biological limits in an athletic activity may reflect low participation numbers at very advanced ages. If Masters sport continues to grow in popularity it may have a profound effect on theories of performance and its associated decline. Moreover, Masters games tend to be dominated by those who have the time and money to train for and travel to these events (Dionigi *et al.*, 2013). Additional expenses include the equipment and coaching associated with the sport itself. This will vary by sport, but it necessarily influences participation rates and reinforces notions that class is an important variable in this research.

A myriad of social factors interact with biological limits to influence performance measures across the age spectrum, from our youngest citizens to our very oldest. Understanding career length and performance maintenance requires an appreciation for the complexity of the interactions amongst a number of variables, which includes global social influences like race and class, to individual factors such as training volumes and how they might be influenced by biological or genetic constraints.

References

Anton, M. M., Spirduso, W. W., & Tanaka, H. (2004) 'Age-related declines in anaerobic muscular performance: Weightlifting and powerlifting', *Medicine and Science in Sports and Exercise*, 36(1): 143–7.

Baker, A. B., & Tang, Y. Q. (2010) 'Aging performance for masters records in athletics, swimming, rowing, cycling, triathlon, and weightlifting', *Experimental Aging Research*, 36(4): 453–77.

Baker, J., Deakin, J., Horton, S., & Pearce, G. W. (2007) 'Maintenance of skilled performance with age: A descriptive examination of professional golfers', *Journal of Aging and Physical Activity*, 15: 299–316.

Baker, J., Horton, S., Pearce, W., & Deakin, J. (2005) 'A longitudinal examination of performance in champion golfers', *High Ability Studies*, 16: 179–85.

Baker, J., Koz, D., Kungl, A. M., Fraser-Thomas, J., & Schorer, J. (2013) 'Staying at the top: Playing position and performance affect career length in professional sport', *High Ability Studies*, 24: 63–76.

Baltes, P. B., & Baltes, M. M. (1990) 'Psychological perspectives on successful aging: The model of selective optimization with compensation', in P. B. Baltes & M. Baltes (eds) *Successful aging: Perspectives from the behavioral sciences*, Cambridge: Cambridge University Press, 1–34.

Benedict, L. (2014, February 5) 'Hall of fame . . . Sir Steve Redgrave: The British bulldog who refused to lose and who set the gold standard for our Olympians', *The Daily Mail*. Online. Retrieved from www.dailymail.co.uk/sport/othersports/article-2552244/Hall-Fame-Sir-Steve-Redgrave-The-British-Bulldog-refused-lose-set-gold-standard-Olympians.html (accessed 31 July, 2014).

Berri, D. J., & Simmons, R. (2009) 'Race and the evaluation of signal callers in the National Football League', *Journal of Sport Economics*, 10: 23–43.

Best, C. (1987) 'Experience and career length in professional football: The effect of positional segregation', *Sociology of Sport Journal*, 4: 410–20.

Bloom, B. S. (1985) *Developing talent in young people*, New York: Ballantine.

Bopp, T., & Sagas, M. (2014) 'Racial tasking and the college quarterback: Redefining the stacking phenomenon', *Journal of Sport Management*, 28: 136–42.

Bortz, W. M., & Bortz, W. M. (1996) 'How fast do we age? Exercise performance over time as a biomarker', *Journal of Gerontology: Medical Sciences*, 51: 223–5.

Brophy, R. H., Gill, C. S., Lyman, S., Barnes, R. P., Rodeo, S. A., & Warren, R. F. (2010) 'Effect of shoulder stabilization on career length in National Football League athletes', *American Journal of Sports Medicine*, 39: 704–9.

Charness, N. (1981) 'Search in chess: Age and skill differences', *Journal of Experimental Psychology: Human Perception and Performance*, 7: 467–76.

Chase, W. G., & Simon, H. A. (1973) 'Perception in chess', *Cognitive Psychology*, 4(1): 55–81.

Clarey, C. (2008, August 10) 'With silver, Torres sets age record for medalist', *The New York Times*. Online. Retrieved from www.nytimes.com/2008/08/10/sports/olympics/10finals.html?_r=1& (accessed 31 July, 2014).

Côté, J., Baker, J., & Abernethy, B. (2007) 'Play and practice in the development of sport expertise', in G. Tenenbaum & R. C. Eklund (eds) *Handbook of sport psychology*, Hoboken, NJ: John Wiley & Sons, 184–202.

Dionigi, R. A., Horton, S., & Baker, J. (2013) 'How do older masters athletes account for their performance preservation? A qualitative analysis', *Ageing and Society*, 33: 297–319.

Donato, A. J., Tench, K., Glueck, D. H., Seals, D. R., Eskurza, I., & Tanaka, H. (2003) 'Declines in physiological functional capacity with age: A longitudinal study in peak swimming performance', *Journal of Applied Physiology*, 94: 764–9.

Duhatschek, E. (2013, August 27) 'St. Louis proves he was never too small and now not too old', *The Globe and Mail*. Online. Retrieved from www.theglobeandmail.com/sports/hockey/duhatschek-st-louis-proves-he-was-never-too-small-and-now-not-too-old/article13961558/ (accessed 31 July, 2014).

Epstein, D. (2013) *The sports gene*, New York: Penguin.

Ericsson, K. A. (1990) 'Peak performance and age: An examination of peak performance in sports', in P. B. Baltes & M. Baltes (eds) *Successful aging: Perspectives from the behavioral sciences*, Cambridge: Cambridge University Press, 164–95.

Ericsson, K. A., Krampe, R. T., & Tesch-Römer, C. (1993) 'The role of deliberate practice in the acquisition of expert performance', *Psychological Review*, 100(3): 363–406.

Fairbrother, J. T. (2007) 'Prediction of 1500-m freestyle swimming times for older masters all-American swimmers', *Experimental Aging Research*, 33(4): 461–71.

Fusco, C. (1998) 'Lesbians and locker rooms: The subjective experiences of lesbians in sport', in G. Rail (ed) *Sport and modern times*, New York: State University of New York Press, 87–116.

Galton, F. (1881) *Hereditary genius: An inquiry into its laws and consequences*, New York: D. Appleton and Company.

Gandelman, N. (2009) 'Selection biases in sports markets', *Hospitality, Sport, Leisure & Tourism*, 10: 502–21.

Goodard, J., & Wilson, J. (2009) 'Racial discrimination in English professional football: Evidence from an empirical analysis of players' career progression', *Cambridge Journal of Economics*, 33: 295–316.

Groothuis, P. A., & Hill, J. R. (2008) 'Exit discrimination in major league baseball: 1990–2004', *Southern Economic Journal*, 75: 574–90.

Hoang, H., & Rascher, D. (1999) 'The NBA, exit discrimination and career earnings', *Industrial Relations*, 38: 69–91.

Jiobu, R. M. (1988) 'Racial inequality in a public arena: The case of professional baseball', *Social Forces*, 67: 524–34.

Khan, L. M., & Shaw, M. (2005) 'Race, compensation and contract length in the NBA: 2001–2002', *Industrial Relations: A Journal of Economy and Society*, 44: 444–62.

Klawans, H. (1998) *Why Michael couldn't hit*, New York: W. H. Freeman and Company.

Krampe, R. T., & Ericsson, K. A. (1996) 'Maintaining excellence: Deliberate practice and elite performance in young and older pianists', *Journal of Experimental Psychology: General*, 125: 331–59.

Lewis, M. (2004) *Moneyball: The art of winning an unfair game*, New York: W. W. Norton & Company Inc.

Career length, aging, and expertise

McGarrity, J. P., & Linnen, B. (2010) 'Pass or run: An empirical test of the matching pennies game using data from the National Football League', *Southern Economic Journal*, 76: 791–810.

Mitchell, H., Stavros, C., & Stewart, M. F. (2011) 'Does the Australian football league draft undervalue indigenous Australian footballers?', *Journal of Sport Economics*, 12: 36–54.

Oeppen, J., & Vaupel, J. W. (2002) 'Broken limits to life expectancy', *Science*, 296: 1029–31.

'Official Olympic games results'. Online. Retrieved from www.olympic.org/olympic-results (accessed 31 July, 2014).

'Pension crisis a global problem' (2013, December 31) *CBC*. Online. Retrieved from www.cbc.ca/news/business/pension-crisis-a-global-problem-1.2478858 (accessed 31 July, 2014).

'R&A championships limited', *The Open Championship*. Online. Retrieved from www.theopen.com/en/History/Do-You-Know.aspx (accessed 5 February, 2014).

Sack, A. L., Singh, P., & Thiel, R. (2005) 'Occupational segregation on the playing field: The case of Major League Baseball', *Journal of Sport Management*, 19: 300–18.

Salthouse, T. A. (1984) 'Effects of age and skill in typing', *Journal of Experimental Psychology: General*, 113: 345–71.

Schorer, J., & Baker, J. (2009) 'Aging and perceptual–motor expertise in handball goalkeepers', *Experimental Aging Research*, 35: 1–19.

Schupak, A. (2010, April 4) 'Recalling Lee Elder's trip down magnolia lane', *Golfweek*. Online. Retrieved from http://golfweek.com/news/2010/apr/04/lee-elder-his-trip-down-magnolia/ (accessed 31 July, 2014).

Starkes, J. L., Cullen, J. D., & MacMahon, C. (2004) 'A lifespan model of skill acquisition and retention of expert perceptual–motor performance', in A. M. Williams & N. J. Hodges (eds) *Skill acquisition in sport: Research, theory and practice*, London: Routledge, 259–81.

Starkes, J. L., Weir, P. L., Singh, P., Hodges, N. J., & Kerr, T. (1999) 'Aging and the retention of sport expertise', *International Journal of Sport Psychology*, 30(2): 283–301.

Statistics Canada (2013) 'Sport participation 2010', Canadian Heritage, Sports Canada. http://publications.gc.ca/collections/collection_2013/pc-ch/CH24-1-2012-eng.pdf (accessed January 15, 2015).

Stones, M. J., & Kozma, A. (1981) 'Adult age trends in athletic performances', *Experimental Aging Research*, 7(3): 269–80.

Stones, M. J., & Kozma, A. (1984) 'Longitudinal trends in track and field performances', *Experimental aging research*, 10(2): 107–10.

Tanaka, H., & Seals, D. R. (1997) 'Age and gender interactions in physiological functional capacity. Insight from swimming performance', *Journal of Applied Physiology*, 82(3): 846–51.

'The world record for the mile run', *Mathematical Association of America*. Online. Retrieved from www.maa.org/sites/default/files/images/upload_library/3/osslets/100multiParameterAnimation/mile_record_scatter.html (accessed 5 February, 2014).

Weir, P., Baker, J., & Horton, S. (2010) 'The emergence of masters sport: Participatory trends and historical developments', in J. Baker, S. Horton, & P. Weir (eds) *The masters athlete: Understanding the role of exercise in optimizing aging*, London UK: Routledge, 7–14.

Weir, P. L., Kerr, T., Hodges, N. J., McKay, S. M., & Starkes, J. L. (2002) 'Master swimmers: How are they different from younger elite swimmers? An examination of practice and performance patterns', *Journal of Aging & Physical Activity*, 10(1): 41–63.

Whitnauer, W. D., Rogers, R. G., & Saint Onge, J. M. (2007) 'Major league baseball career length in the 20th century', *Population Research Policy Review*, 26: 371–86.

'World Masters Athletics', *World Association of Masters Athletes*. Online. Retrieved from www.world-masters-athletics.org/records/outdoor-men (accessed 5 February, 2014).

Wroblewski, A. P., Amati, F., Smiley, M. A., Goodpaster, P., & Wright, V. (2011) 'Chronic exercise preserves lean muscles mass in masters athletes', *The Physician and Sportsmedicine*, 39(3): 172–8.

Young, B. W., Medic, N., Weir, P. L., & Starkes, J. L. (2008a) 'Explaining performance in elite middle-aged runners: Contributions from age and from ongoing and past training factors', *Journal of Sport & Exercise Psychology*, 30(6): 737–54.

Young, B. W., & Starkes, J. L. (2005) 'Career-span analyses of track performance: Longitudinal data present a more optimistic view of age-related performance decline', *Experimental Aging Research*, 31(1): 69–90.

Young, B. W., Weir, P. L., Starkes, J. L., & Medic, N. (2008b) 'Does lifelong training temper age-related decline in sport performance? Interpreting differences between cross-sectional and longitudinal data', *Experimental Aging Research*, 34(1): 27–48.

34

CHANGING ROLE OF COACHES ACROSS DEVELOPMENT

Clifford J. Mallett and Steven Rynne

Coaches are considered the key actors in the delivery of instruction to participants in a range of sporting contexts. In synthesizing the literature, the International Council for Coaching Excellence (ICCE) purports that the motives, aspirations, and needs of all sport participants change throughout the life span and therefore, coaches' ideologies, knowledge, and competence should reflect these varying needs (ICCE, 2013). Indeed, all forms of coaching should be valued for the potential contribution to the learning and development of sport participants throughout their life span (Mallett, 2013). The ongoing learning of coaches in all contexts is essential so that they might become more expert practitioners and better placed to deliver the potential benefits of sport engagement.

There are several classifications of sport involvement in the literature. For the purposes of this chapter we have focused on four contexts in which sport coaching work is undertaken: coaches of (a) young children, (b) emerging athletes, (c) performance athletes, and (d) high-performance athletes. On the basis of these different contexts in which coaches operate, we consider the needs of sport participants in each context to guide the discussion about the specific nature of coaching and how they learn their craft. Although we acknowledge the various roles of coaches in sport (e.g., sport teacher/instructor, assistant coaches, senior coach, master coach) for the purposes of this chapter, the coach-in-charge and the development of his/her expertise is the focus of attention in each sporting context.

It is worthwhile noting that we have also made the decision that coaches working with "diverse," "marginalized," and "special" groups may be appropriately viewed as forms of participation coaches, development coaches, performance coaches, or high-performance coaches. This is not to suggest that there are not complexities and subtleties associated with coaching disabled athletes for instance, but we also feel that it is doing those coaches and athletes somewhat of a disservice to position them as being separate from other coaches in a chapter that broadly considers the changing role of coaches across development. Of course, there are many more subtleties and complexities that exist in sport coaching than can be addressed here (e.g., the notion of early and late maturation sports). It is for this reason that such issues as the lack of female coaches at all levels of coaching and the dominant culture of autocratic styles in most sports are unable to attract more than a minor reference in this chapter. Despite these limitations, the aim in this chapter is to provide some account of the role of coaches of children, emerging athletes, performance athletes, and high-performance athletes through a consideration of what the context involves, the nature of the coach-athlete relationship, and how coaches develop their craft.

Coaching children

In thinking about young children in sport we focus our attention towards what is termed a participation sport setting. Young children are introduced into organized sporting activities from about four to eight years of age, although some may commence at an earlier age. Exceptions to this notion of a participation setting for young children are those who are engaged in early specialization sports such as gymnastics and who likely engage in more deliberate practice preschool. Many parents likely value the potential contribution of sport to the healthy and holistic development of their children, including physical, psychological, social, and emotional aspects (Trost, 2005). Highly competent coaches, who deliver these biophysical and psychosocial outcomes, are considered necessary to retain young participants in the sport pathways (Côté et al., 2013).

Several developmental and pathway models chart this initial foray into sport, including Côté and colleagues' developmental model of sport participation (DMSP; Côté, 1999; Côté & Hay, 2002) and Gulbin, Croser, Morley, and Weissensteiner's (2013) foundations, talent, elite, and mastery model (FTEM). This initiation into sport is aligned with the notion of "sampling" sports and may also include some modified sports such as "Auskick" (short duration introductory program for Australian football). It is also aligned with the development of fundamental movement skills (Booth et al., 1999) and Gulbin et al.'s (2013) F1 and F2 stages. This first stage (F1) in the FTEM model is associated with many movement experiences, which might be broadly classified as (a) locomotor and (b) manipulating objects such as bats (Gulbin et al., 2013). In transitioning to the second stage (F2), young children are further engaged in fundamental motor and manipulative skills through formal and informal play activities (e.g., modified games), which is also consistent with Côté et al.'s sampling phase in their DMSP model. In this transition from F1 to F2 it is likely that young children access more qualified instruction either through school or community sporting clubs (Gulbin et al., 2013). Access to guided development (e.g., teacher) complements young children's free play activities (Côté, 1999; DMSP) and fosters the acquisition of fundamental motor skills (Davids et al., 2008).

The Development Coach and Child Relationship

The International Council for Coaching Excellence (ICCE) has underscored the importance of having expert coaches work with children due to the inherent complexity associated with development (e.g., age-related assumptions; see Burrows, 2009) and context (ICCE, 2013). For this reason it is crucial that the child's introduction to sport is associated with the scaffolded development of fundamental motor and manipulative skills within a supportive learning environment (ICCE, 2013).

Coaches are the architects of the learning environment and therefore should take responsibility for creating an environment that fosters healthy and holistic development (Mallett, 2005, 2013). Central to the design of a supportive learning environment is the manner in which coaches interact with young children and how they explicitly attempt to deliver on the agreed learning outcomes (e.g., the four Cs of positive youth development) (Vierimaa et al., 2012). Coaches are implicit role models for young children, and they can either foster healthy development or contribute to attrition from sport at an early age (Côté & Gilbert, 2009). Coaches should deliver activities that are enjoyable, challenging, and promote perceptions of competence and belonging (Mageau & Vallerand, 2003; Wall & Côté, 2007). These outcomes can be achieved through an emphasis on (a) deliberate play activities (Côté & Fraser-Thomas, 2007) that are fun and enjoyable (Wall & Côté, 2007) to promote player engagement (frequent time on task) and subsequently develop fundamental motor and manipulative skills, and (b) coach feedback focused on self-referencing rather than normative comparisons (Fraser-Thomas & Côté, 2006) to promote internal motivation (Mageau & Vallerand, 2003). In particular, the lack of fun has been reported as a frequently cited reason for attrition from sport (Gould *et al.*, 1982; Butcher *et al.*, 2002).

Parents are also key actors in this initiation phase in sport. How they interact with coaches and children influences the quality of their athletes' sporting experience (Mallett & Rynne, 2012). To date, we do not have a clear understanding of the complex relations between all adult actors in the sporting context (Mallett & Rynne, 2012). For instance, it is considered necessary for parents to be involved in young children's sport participation; however, the nature of that involvement needs to be balanced to minimize the risk of either under- or over-involvement that might have the potential to contribute to negative sporting experiences and potential attrition (Côté, 1999).

How coaches of young children develop their competence

There is a paucity of research examining the learning and development of coaches of young children. Often these coaches are included in larger data sets with coaches of emerging athletes (discussed in the next section). What we do know about coaches of young children is that they are (a) often untrained, with only approximately 50 per cent reporting some formal introductory coach education (Trudel & Gilbert, 2006), and (b) itinerant, usually volunteering parents, who are likely time poor, and have limited access to learning opportunities to develop their coaching skills (Trudel & Gilbert, 2006). Coaches of young children develop their craft mostly through informal learning situations to complement their own sporting experiences in how they deliver coaching (Mallett *et al.*, 2009; Trudel & Gilbert, 2006). Those coaches who have been trained through formal coach education programs have been found to be more supportive of young children in sport compared with untrained coaches (see Smoll & Smith, 2002 for a review of coach effectiveness training studies). Nevertheless, formal coach education programs differentially contribute to the development of coaches of young children (Lemyre *et al.*, 2007). Most coaches of young children probably rely upon their own sporting experiences to inform their practice (Trudel & Gilbert, 2006). It is suggested that coaches of young children are in need of mediated or guided training even though they are not career coaches, because of their role in fostering continued sport involvement or dropout for children. A corollary of dropout is a potential decrease in the talent pool along the pathway to high performance and likely an overall reduction in the quality of those that remain because of a lack of "late maturing" athletes (i.e., not remaining in the sport long enough to demonstrate their potential). This is a key concern in a number of developed nations where involvement in organized sport is at somewhat of a crisis point; for example, only one in three young children participate in sport in the Australian context, and participation peaks between nine and 11 years of age (Trost, 2013). A key challenge for the training of time-poor coaches of young children is the need to minimize the administrative load (e.g., marketing, health and safety, medical forms, contact details) that volunteering (and mostly parental) coaches undertake (Cronin & Armour, 2013) to comply with various regulatory bodies.

Coaching emerging athletes

In this section, and those that follow, we start to move the discussion away from participation sport settings towards a consideration of coaches and athletes involved in performance sport settings. To begin with, we discuss "emerging athletes" and "development coaches." Emerging athletes are typically receiving specialized, sport-specific training in ways that resemble the "specialization stage" of athlete development in Côté and colleagues' (Côté, 1999; Côté & Hay, 2002)

DMSP and the transition from "foundation 2" to "foundation 3" in Gulbin *et al.*'s (2013) FTEM model. This is a time where a child generally starts to spend greater time in one or two sporting activities, often at the expense of other sporting pursuits or non-sporting interests (Strachan *et al.*, 2009; Trudel & Gilbert, 2006).

Despite the increased attention given to formal practices and competitions, there is still a strong emphasis on participation and fun, suggesting a balance between the various forms of play and practice (Côté *et al.*, 2013). In sum, the activities undertaken by emerging athletes are sometimes referred to as a combination of deliberate play and deliberate practice (Côté *et al.*, 2003; Ericsson *et al.*, 1993). As part of their involvement in sports at this stage, emerging athletes are generally identified as being on some kind of performance "pathway," whereby they may be selected to representative (junior/regional/academy) squads in their sport. Importantly, this progress is often overseen by one or more designated coaches.

The development coach and emerging athlete relationship

Previous research has shown the importance of appropriately structured programs for emerging athletes, as their experiences at this stage have a large bearing on their continued engagement in sport (Fraser-Thomas *et al.*, 2008; Smoll & Smith, 2002). Indeed, development coaches have a large bearing on factors leading to drop out, such as pressure to move up skill levels too quickly, too much emphasis on winning, lack of playing time, and showing favoritism (Fraser-Thomas *et al.*, 2008). Conversely, development coaches have been shown to be important to the sustained engagement of emerging athletes through offering care and support, demonstrating excellent people skills, and possessing sound technical expertise. The research on coaches and athletes at this stage shows that it is important for development coaches to both challenge (technical and skill-oriented sessions) and support their athletes (personable, mastery approaches), as this facilitates adaptive forms of motivation and can enhance perseverance (Fraser-Thomas *et al.*, 2008; North, 2008).

Clearly, the role of the development coach requires far more than just the development of physical skills in emerging athletes. Unfortunately, many practices that are ingrained in sports seem counterproductive for long-term athlete engagement and well-being. This context is one in which arguably the greatest amount of harm can be done to athletes (physically and psychologically) by inappropriately adopting high–performance coaching and athletic models (Mallett & Rynne, 2012). Development coaches may experience internal role conflict between athlete personal development and the desire to produce winning athletes (Gilbert & Trudel, 2004); this is a delicate balancing act. Compounding these potentially competing goals is the fact that there is often little guidance regarding how best to coach at a developmental level. As such, development coaches are generally left to come to their own conclusions about how much emphasis they will place on winning and technical development compared to how much they will emphasize fun and the development of psychosocial skills (Gilbert & Trudel, 2004).

How development coaches develop competence

The educational background of development coaches tends to vary considerably. Trudel and Gilbert (2006) noted that development coaches may have some form of tertiary education (college/university). There are many development coaches, however, who have no tertiary education to underpin their practice. Despite this, the majority of development coaches have engaged in some kind of coaching clinic or program of coach education. Most sports have a system of coach education (primarily under the banner of accreditation/certification), and learning in these contexts has been referred to as formal (because it is a program of study) and mediated (because the national body determines what is in the curriculum) (Wright *et al.*, 2007). However, coaches have raised concerns about the value and impact of such offerings (Stephenson & Jowett, 2009).

As a result, many development coaches are left to draw on their experiences as athletes (in the sport they now coach, as well as others that they played) and develop their coaching practice through learning by experience. Learning in this way has been described as informal (because it is primarily incidental, unregulated, and sometimes unintended) and unmediated (because the coach is wholly responsible for the direction and intensity of the development) (Gilbert *et al.*, 2009; Mallett *et al.*, 2009; Trudel & Gilbert, 2006; Wright *et al.*, 2007).

Performance athletes

Building upon the conceptualization of emerging athletes and development coaches in the previous section, we now move to a discussion of "performance athletes" and "performance coaches." Like emerging athletes, performance athletes typically receive specialized, sport-specific training. However, the nature of their sport engagement is more prolonged and intense such that it resembles the movement from Côté and colleagues' (Côté, 1999; Côté & Hay, 2002) "specializing stage" of sport participation to the "investment stage." Emerging athletes can also be thought of as being across the "talent" section of Gulbin *et al.*'s (2013) FTEM model (especially T2-T3). Performance athletes are generally only participating in one sport and are committed to higher levels of sport-specific training (deliberate practice, including ancillary activities like specialized gym programs), with less emphasis on deliberate play (Côté *et al.*, 2003; Ericsson *et al.*, 1993; Gulbin *et al.*, 2013).

Those often charged with the responsibility of accelerating the development of performance athletes are coaches – sometimes referred to as "performance coaches." Performance coaches and athletes generally have a very stable relationship (Lyle, 2002; Trudel & Gilbert, 2006) and in certain sports (typically individual ones) the coach that an athlete has at this stage may be his/her coach for the rest of his/her athletic career. Representative sport settings are the obvious exception where the coaches and athletes may only be together for a relatively short period, such as for a state or national championship (Lyle, 2002). The most common role for performance coaches, however, is in traditional club sport settings as the coaches in charge of the top teams (variously known as A teams or first teams, etc.).

The performance coach and performance athlete relationship

For performance athletes, the emphasis is very much on performance outcomes through systematic training and competition scheduling. As such, performance coaches assume a central role in the development of these athletes. Also, perceptions of coaching quality are closely tied to athletic outcomes for coaches at this level. Regardless of the form (individual, team, representative), the coach-athlete relationship tends to be quite intensive, with both parties being committed to their sporting endeavors. The nature of leadership and motivational style varies somewhat for performance coaches, but as with most forms of coaching, autocratic styles are often favored (with varying results) (Trudel & Gilbert, 2006).

Given the increased importance placed on "talent development" and "talent acceleration" with respect to performance athletes and performance coaches, one factor that has been shown to be important to this group is the issue of expectancy. Athletes who are expected to perform at a high level tend to perceive their coaches to be more positive, and through a variety of mechanisms tend to perform better than their low-expectancy peers (Trudel & Gilbert, 2006). Like their other coaching colleagues, performance coaches typically mention maintaining a connection with the sport they once played as the primary reason that they choose to coach. Other reasons that are often cited include working with future elite athletes and sporting staff and serving as a role model in their sport (Trudel & Gilbert, 2006).

How performance coaches develop competence

Performance coaches often have some form of tertiary education (college/university). Some performance coaches have attained graduate and doctoral degrees (Trudel & Gilbert, 2006). Virtually all performance coaches engage in formal coach education programs and clinics during their careers (formal and mediated). In part, this is a reflection of the expectations that national sporting bodies have of their performance coaches, but the reality is also that performance coaches tend to view their coaching as more than just a hobby, and they are prepared to spend time, money, and energy in developing their craft (Rynne, 2012). Many hope to extend their work to a full-time basis in the future and view professional development as a necessary part of improving their practice and employability.

Performance coaches also report a variety of informal learning situations that they access (Mallett *et al.*, 2009; Rynne *et al.*, 2010), and these likely change and increase over the course of their careers (Mallett *et al.*, in press). Indeed, performance coaches are often afforded greater opportunities for development than their development coaching counterparts. Because of their role as "feeder coaches," pushing athletes along the pathway to high-performance sport, performance coaches are also regularly granted access to high-performance contexts to observe or be actively "mentored" by established high-performance coaches (generally informal learning). These experiences are highly valued by performance coaches, as they are viewed as being authentic and relevant to their current coaching practices. So just like the development coaches, performance coaches are able to draw on their time as an athlete in the sport they coach and their practical experiences. The difference for the performance coaches is that they are also able to take advantage of a broader range of observational experiences and their direct interactions with a greater variety of coaching mentors (Wright *et al.*, 2007).

High-performance athletes

High-performance athletes are highly committed to a long-term and intensive program of preparation. This group of athletes can be considered to be firmly in the "investment stage" of Côté and colleagues' (Côté, 1999; Côté & Hay, 2002) model of sport participation. In keeping with this position, high-performance athletes span the "talent," "elite," and "mastery" sections of Gulbin *et al.*'s (2013) FTEM model (notably T4–M). As opposed to their performance athlete peers who may be able to balance full-time work and study with their sporting commitments, the increased training, recovery, and travel requirements of high-performance athletes means that they are generally only able to sustain casual work or part-time study and sometimes neither.

Several personnel support high-performance athletes and the coach to improve athlete performances. In short, these athletes are generally afforded significant support in pursuing their athletic ambitions. Those responsible for guiding the continued development of high-performance athletes and coordinating the team of support personnel are high-performance coaches. High-performance coaches are almost always employed on a full-time basis and include those coaching in national and international (Olympics, Paralympics, world championships) contexts, as well as in professional sport leagues (Trudel & Gilbert, 2006). High-performance coaches employ a series of clear performance benchmarks supported by highly sophisticated planning structures (Gulbin *et al.*, 2013; Lyle, 2002; Mallett, 2010). As with performance coaching, representative coaching positions also exist within the high-performance coaching context. It should be noted that for high-performance coaches, their prospects for continued employment (reappointment) and the performance of their athletes and teams are virtually inseparable.

The high-performance coach and high-performance athlete relationship

As alluded to above, the high-performance coach and high-performance athlete relationship is extremely intense. It is typically a long-term commitment between a stable group of actors with a high frequency and duration of engagement (the exception being concentrated, representative sport engagements, such as when athletes from professional teams join national squads for world championships or the Olympics). Given the typically full-time nature of the high-performance athletes and high-performance coaches, during the peak of their performance period they may spend more time together than with any other person (including partners, children, and friends). As such, the ideal relationship is almost always founded on trust and mutual respect.

The athlete relies upon the coach to support and guide his/her development while navigating the many tensions and challenges that exist in high-performance sport. Similarly, the coach relies upon the athlete(s) to engage with training, provide feedback, and ultimately perform to their potential. Mallett (2013) noted that because of the importance of athletic performance to future sport funding and coach employment, high-performance coaches face dilemmas that challenge their values and beliefs. This serves to direct their behavior, with some high-performance coaches moved to behave in unacceptable and inappropriate ways (examples include playing concussed athletes, engaging in emotional abuse, physically striking athletes). For this group of coaches (potentially more than any other described in this chapter) there are far more ethical and moral dimensions to their work because the stakes are so high (Rynne & Mallett, 2014).

How high-performance coaches develop competence

High-performance coaches have been shown to have a strong desire for continual learning (Trudel & Gilbert, 2006). They tend to have some form of tertiary education (college/ university) (Trudel & Gilbert, 2006). A study by Rynne, Mallett, and Tinning (2010) found that those who completed tertiary qualifications in a coaching-specific field highly valued their experiences in formal study. In particular, they valued the higher order thinking skills promoted in tertiary study and the exposure to concepts and terminology that allow them to interact more professionally with support staff in their programs (e.g., sport scientists; Mallett *et al.*, 2014). Other formal and mediated educational experiences reported by high-performance coaches include formal coach education (accreditation and certification). Unfortunately, high-performance coaches tend to be less enthusiastic about these offerings, generally reporting that they have somewhat limited impact on their high-performance coaching work.

Like the development and performance coaches, high-performance coaches also find value in a variety of informal learning situations that increase over their careers (Mallett *et al.*, 2014). Common learning sources reported include time spent as an athlete, previous coaching experience, and discussions with other coaches (Rynne *et al.*, 2010). The potential value of these sources may be enhanced in the high-performance coaching group because of the access that these coaches have to virtually all levels of the coaching pathway. There is also increasing acceptance that high-performance athletes serve as both a stimulus and source for high-performance coaches' learning. However, this aspect tends to be marginalized in empirical and anecdotal accounts of coach learning and development.

Role of coaches across development

Individual and team sport variations

While we have tried to provide some general commentary regarding different categories of athletes and coaches, of course there is much variation in terms of real life practice. A key variation is with respect to the type of sport in which athletes and coaches are involved. There is a range of ways this can be conceptualized, but at the most basic of levels, there are fundamental differences between team and individual sports. For example, training dynamics and athletic performance benchmarks are conceptualized in very different ways between team and individual sports (Lyle, 2002). Similarly, assessments of coaching practice vary between team and individual sports; individual sports permit a higher degree of assessment regarding the value-added contributions of the coach, whereas this is often lost in the group processes found in team sports. Even the specific planning and training processes tend to be different, with individualization being foundational to individual sports but somewhat problematic in team sports.

Future research

There has been a dearth of studies that examine the changing role of coaches across development; however, there seems to be increased interest in coaching research, especially in young children, emerging youth, and high-performance athletes. This area of inquiry is considered important because of the central role of coaches to the quality of the athletes' sporting experience and their subsequent continued engagement in the sporting pathways.

Given the emphasis on athlete-centered work in previous research, an obvious direction for future work would be to examine: (a) the coach as performer in the coach-athlete performance relationship; (b) coaching behaviors across different contexts (i.e., further differentiation between coaching roles); (c) the relative value of interventions that focus on quality coaching; (d) how high-performance coaches learn and develop (including greater consideration of those with elite playing backgrounds); (e) the contribution of coaches to athletic development; and (f) the dynamics of the coach-athlete performance relationship (rather than examining coaches or athletes in isolation).

Summary

In this chapter we focused on four athletic coaching contexts: (a) young children, (b) emerging athletes, (c) performance athletes, and (d) high-performance athletes. In each of the above contexts, coaches should be mindful of the needs, motives, and challenges of sport participants to guide their practice, learning, and development.

Coaches are considered central to the quality of sport participants' engagement. We reiterate the importance of valuing all forms of coaching and the differential contribution of blended formal, non-formal, and informal learning experiences to developing the craft of coaching in all contexts. We are also mindful of the inherent complexity associated with human development and its interdependence with the sporting and familial contexts that make the work of coaches challenging and problematic in delivering quality coaching.

The professionalization of the vocation of sport coaching (including the significant volunteer cohort) necessitates the ongoing learning of coaches through guidance from knowledgeable others and self-reflection to contribute to their becoming an expert. To contribute to this professionalization of sport coaching there is significant need for high-quality research to inform the development of coach expertise. The provision of mediated learning opportunities is central to the development of coach expertise. However, it is the responsibility of coaches to exert their agency in seeking and maximizing varied learning opportunities to develop their craft and pursue the notion of becoming an expert.

References

Booth, M. L., Okely, T., McLellan, L., Phongsavan, P., Macaskill, P., Patterson, J., Holland, B. (1999) 'Mastery of fundamental motor skills among New South Wales schools students: Prevalence and sociodemographic distribution', *Journal of Science and Medicine in Sport*, 2: 93–105.

Burrows, L. (2009) 'Developing' athletes', in, T. Cassidy, R. L. Jones, & P. Potrac (eds) *Understanding sports coaching: The social, cultural, and pedagogical foundations of coaching practice*, 2nd ed., London: Routledge, 85–92.

Butcher, J., Lindner, K. J., & Johns, D. P. (2002) 'Withdrawal from competitive youth sport: A retrospective ten-year study', *Journal of Sport Behaviour*, 25(2): 145–63.

Côté, J. (1999) 'The influence of the family in the development of talent in sport', *The Sport Psychologist*, 13: 395–417.

Côté, J., Baker, J., & Abernethy, B. (2003) 'From play to practice: A developmental framework for the acquisition of expertise in team sports', in J. L. Starkes & K. A. Ericsson (eds) *Expert performance in sports: Advances in research on sport expertise*, South Australia: Human Kinetics, 89–114.

Côté, J., Erickson, K., & Abernethy, B. (2013) 'Play and practice during childhood', in J. Côté & R. Lidor (eds) *Conditions of children's talent development*, Morgantown, WV: Fitness Information Technology, 9–20.

Côté, J., & Fraser-Thomas, J. (2007) 'Youth involvement in sport', in P.R.E. Crocker (ed) *Introduction to sport psychology: A Canadian perspective*, Toronto: Pearson Prentice Hall, 266–94.

Côté, J., & Gilbert, W. (2009) 'An integrative definition of coaching effectiveness and expertise', *International Journal of Sports Science & Coaching*, 4: 307–23.

Côté, J., & Hay, J. (2002) 'Children's involvement in sport: A developmental perspective', in J. M. Silva & D. E. Stevens (eds) *Psychological foundations of sport*, Sydney: Allyn and Bacon, 484–502.

Cronin, C., & Armour, K. M. (2013) 'Lived experience and community sport coaching: A phenomenological investigation', *Sport, Education and Society*. doi: 10.1080/13573322.2013.858625

Davids, K. W., Button, C., & Bennett, S. J. (2008) *Dynamics of skill acquisition: A constraints-led approach*, Champaign, IL: Human Kinetics.

Ericsson, K. A., Krampe, R. T., & Tesch-Römer, C. (1993) 'The role of deliberate practice in the acquisition of expert performance', *Psychological Review*, 100(3): 363–406.

Fraser-Thomas, J., & Côté, J. (2006, September) 'Youth sports: Implementing findings and moving forward with research', *Athletic Insight*, 8, Article 2. Online. Retrieved from www.athleticinsight.com/Vol8Iss3/YouthSports.htm (accessed 1 February, 2014).

Fraser-Thomas, J., Côté, J., & Deakin, J. (2008) 'Understanding dropout and prolonged engagement in adolescent competitive sport', *Psychology of Sport and Exercise*, 9: 645–62.

Gilbert, W., Lichtenwaldt, L., Gilbert, J., Zelenzny, L., & Côté, J. (2009) 'Developmental profiles of successful high school coaches', *International Journal of Sports Science and Coaching*, 4(3): 415–31.

Gilbert, W., & Trudel, P. (2004) 'Role of the coach: How model youth team sport coaches frame their roles', *The Sport Psychologist*, 18: 21–43.

Gould, D., Feltz, D., Horn, T., & Weiss, M. (1982) 'Reasons for attrition in competitive youth swimming', *Journal of Sport Behaviour*, 5: 155–65.

Gulbin, J. P., Croser, M. J., Morley, E. J., & Weissensteiner, J. R. (2013) 'An integrated framework for the optimisation of sport and athlete development: A practitioner approach', *Journal of Sport Sciences*, 31(12): 1319–31. doi: 10.1080/02640414.2013.781661

International Council for Coaching Excellence (ICCE), Association of Summer Olympic International Federations (ASOIF), & Leeds Metropolitan University (LMU) (2013) *International sport coaching framework version 1.2*, Champaign, IL: Human Kinetics.

Lemyre, F., Trudel, P., & Durand-Bush, N. (2007) 'How youth-sport coaches learn to coach', *The Sport Psychologist*, 21: 191–209.

Lyle, J. (2002) *Sports coaching concepts: A framework for coaches' behaviour*, London: Routledge.

Mageau, G. A., & Vallerand, R. J. (2003) 'The coach-athlete relationship: A motivational model', *Journal of Sport Sciences*, 21: 883–904.

Mallett, C. J. (2005) 'Self-determination theory: A case study of evidence-based coaching', *The Sport Psychologist*, 19: 417–29.

Mallett, C. J. (2010) 'High performance coaches' careers and communities', in J. Lyle & C. Cushion (eds) *Sports coaching: Professionalism and practice*, London: Elsevier, 119–33.

Mallett, C. J. (2013) 'Roles and responsibilities of the coach', in F. Pyke (ed) *Coaching excellence*, Champaign, IL: Human Kinetics.

Mallett, C. J., & Rynne, S. B. (2012) *Junior sports framework review – Briefing paper topic: Role of adults in junior sport*, prepared for the Australian Sports Commission, St Lucia, AU: UniQuest Pty Ltd.

Mallett, C. J., Rynne, S. B., & Billett, S. (2014) 'Valued learning experiences of early career and experienced high performance coaches', *Physical Education and Sport Pedagogy*. DOI: 10.1080/17408989.2014.892062

Mallett, C. J., Trudel, P., Lyle, J., & Rynne, S. B. (2009) 'Formal vs. informal coach education', *International Journal of Sports Science and Coaching*, 4(3): 325–34.

North, J. (2008) 'Increasing participation in sport: The role of the coach', Leeds, UK: Sports Coach UK.

Rynne, S. B. (2012) '"Fast track" and "traditional path" coaches: Affordances, agency and social capital', *Sport, Education and Society*, 19: 1–15. doi: 10.1080/13573322.2012.670113

Rynne, S. B., & Mallett, C. J. (2014) 'Coaches' learning and sustainability in high performance sport', *Reflective Practice*, 15: 1–15. doi: 10.1080/14623943.2013.868798

Rynne, S. B., Mallett, C. J., & Tinning, R. (2010) 'Workplace learning of high performance sports coaches', *Sport, Education and Society*, 15(3): 315–30.

Smoll, F. L., & Smith, R. E. (2002) 'Coaching behavior research and intervention in youth sports', in F. L. Smoll & R. E. Smith (eds) *Children and youth in sport: A biopsycho-social perspective*, 2nd ed., Dubuque, IA: Kendall/Hunt, 211–33.

Stephenson, B., & Jowett, S. (2009) 'Factors that influence the development of English youth soccer coaches', *International Journal of Coaching Science*, 3(1): 3–16.

Strachan, L., Côté, J., & Deakin, J. (2009) '"Specializers" versus "samplers" in youth sport: Comparing experiences and outcomes', *The Sport Psychologist*, 23: 77–92.

Trost, S. G. (2005) 'Discussion paper for the development of recommendations for children's and youth's participation in health promoting physical activity', a report prepared for the Commonwealth Department of Health and Ageing, Canberra: Australian Government.

Trost, S. G. (2013) 'Junior sports framework review – Briefing paper topic: Trends in sport and physical activity participation in Australian children and youth', prepared for the Australian Sports Commission, St Lucia, AU: UniQuest Pty Ltd.

Trudel, P., & Gilbert, W. (2006) 'Coaching and coach education', in D. Kirk, D. Macdonald, & M. O'Sullivan (eds) *The handbook of physical education*, London: Sage, 516–39.

Vierimaa, M., Erickson, K., Côté, J., & Gilbert, W. (2012) 'Positive youth development: A measurement framework for sport', *International Journal of Sports Science and Coaching*, 7(3): 601–14. doi: 10.1260/1747–9541.7.3.601

Wall, M., & Côté, J. (2007) 'Developmental activities that lead to dropout and investment in sport', *Physical Education and Sport Pedagogy*, 12(1): 77–87.

Wright, T., Trudel, P., & Culver, D. M. (2007) 'Learning how to coach: The different learning situations reported by youth ice hockey coaches', *Physical Education and Sport Pedagogy*, 12(2): 127–44.

35

THE USE OF OBSERVATION AS A METHOD TO DEVELOP EXPERTISE IN COACHING AND OFFICIATING

Diane M. Ste-Marie and David J. Hancock

The journey toward expert performance in sport is long and complicated, with many variables impacting the final outcomes. Baker and Horton (2004) categorized these variables as primary and secondary factors. Primary factors are those that have a direct impact on one's ability to attain expert status. Included among these are genetics (e.g., height), training (e.g., amount of deliberate practice), and psychological factors (e.g., intrinsic motivation). Secondary factors moderate or mediate primary factors, thus the impact on one's expert development is indirect. The most discussed secondary factors in research are sociocultural (e.g., the value a society places on a sport) and contextual influences (e.g., one's birthdate/birthplace). While most researchers are primarily concerned with understanding the primary and secondary factors that impact athletes' expertise, a smaller group of researchers dedicate their attention to coaches and officials, which will be the populations of focus in this chapter. Specifically, we are interested in the secondary factor of the use of observation by coaches and officials for their personal development along the pathways to expertise.

Defining coaches and officials

Before continuing, it is important to delineate the particular population of coaches and officials of interest in this chapter. Beginning with coaches, there are multiple types of coaches identified in the literature. Côté and Gilbert (2009) narrowed this scope to (1) participation coaches for children, (2) participation coaches for adolescents/adults, (3) performance coaches for young adolescents, and (4) performance coaches for older adolescents/adults. Each type of coach has different requisite duties; for instance, participation coaches should focus on fun and prolonged engagement, whereas performance coaches for older adolescents, not surprisingly, should focus on performance accomplishments. For the purposes of this chapter, we focus on performance coaches for adolescents or adults.

Regarding officials, there are three types identified in the research: (1) interactors are those who navigate many perceptual cues and have a high level of interaction with the athletes, such as basketball and soccer referees, (2) monitors attend to many perceptual cues, but have few interactions with the athletes, such as gymnastic and figure skating judges, and (3) reactors have comparatively fewer perceptual cues to which they attend and less interactions with athletes,

The use of observation

such as tennis and volleyball line judges (MacMahon & Plessner, 2008). As with coaches, officials also perform at recreational and competitive levels, which makes for a broad category of officials. Given the limited research on officials' use of observation, however, we have included all three types in this chapter.

Observation and expert development

The career pathway to becoming an expert coach or official has been shown to include a variety of sources of knowledge (Erickson *et al.*, 2008; Lemyre *et al.*, 2007; MacMahon & Ste-Marie, 2002; Mascarenhas *et al.*, 2005a; Wright *et al.*, 2007). These sources of knowledge accrue through formal mechanisms, like that of coaching/officiating clinics and education programs, as well as informal mechanisms (Catteeuw *et al.*, 2009; Cushion *et al.*, 2003; Gould *et al.*, 1990; MacMahon *et al.*, 2007; Werthner & Trudel, 2006). These informal learning experiences can take many forms, such as the use of communities of practice, Internet sources, and interactions with peers in the same role (Culver & Trudel, 2008; Erickson *et al.*, 2007; Gilbert *et al.*, 2006; Hancock *et al.*, 2011). Of specific interest in this chapter is the use of observational learning by coaches/officials as a significant source of knowledge within these more informal learning contexts. Indeed, in the literature on coaching expertise, observation of other coaches has often emerged as one of the primary elements in their professional development (e.g., Gould *et al.*, 1990; Jones *et al.*, 2003); thus, a better understanding of these observational experiences in coaches and officials is important.

To better understand observation for coaches and officials, we have chosen to work within a framework that was used by Ste-Marie and colleagues (2012) in their development of an applied model for the use of observation. Although that applied model does not map exactly onto the context presented here, there is usefulness in adopting their basic approach of considering the five Ws (when, who, why, what, where) and one H (how) in regard to the use of observation. Hence, the next sections of this chapter examine the research within this framework.

When

Considering the applied model developed by Ste-Marie and colleagues (2012), the *when* component referred to the specific time during which an athlete might use observation. For instance, an athlete could use video observation before, during, or after physical practice of a given motor skill. The literature on observation for coaches and officials does not align exactly with this reference point. Thus, in contrast to the model, we use *when* to denote the varied points in time during which elite coaches and officials could use observation along their career pathways.

Coaches

Beginning with the coaching literature, a number of researchers have interviewed experienced coaches to learn of their developmental experiences as they advanced to expert levels. Salmela and colleagues' research (e.g., Salmela, 1994, 1995; Schinke *et al.*, 1995) in the mid-1990s was some of the first research that involved interviewing expert coaches in varied team sports to better understand their developmental pathways. Since then, other researchers have also used this qualitative methodology to interview successful coaches about their previous experiences (e.g., Erickson *et al.*, 2007; Gilbert *et al.*, 2006; Lynch & Mallett, 2006). Varied developmental pathways were presented by these different researchers. For example, Schinke and colleagues (1995) identified seven steps that began with initial sport involvement and led to elite national and then international coaching. Erickson and colleagues (2007), in comparison, described five levels; the first two levels involved early sport experience and the last two involved moves from being a part-time coach to a full-time head coach in high-performance sport.

Despite the variations in the developmental pathways, common themes emerged from the research. First, all highlight that coaches initially started as athletes, typically in a variety of sports before narrowing down to the sport in which they were now coaching. A second commonality was the transition from being an athlete to the involvement in coaching at a lower level, often as an assistant coach or in a developmental coaching setting, before moving forward as a head coach in a performance-based setting. Relevant to this chapter, a third consistency is that across each of these developmental steps it was acknowledged that learning experiences were gained from observing coaches. For example, Gilbert and colleagues (2006) argued that pre-coaching experience as an athlete likely provided an "apprenticeship of observation," which enabled a coach to gain tacit knowledge about the sport in general and coaching roles in particular. Similarly, the role of assistant coach would certainly provide numerous observational learning opportunities of one's head coach. Finally, head coaches often spoke of observing other coaches, as well as highlighting the importance of mentors in their development.

Although not the purpose of this chapter, it is important to mention that mentoring was often cited as one of the most significant factors in a coach's development (Bloom *et al.*, 1998; Erickson *et al.*, 2008). The manner in which mentors facilitate this development, however, is difficult to disentangle from observation. Indeed, many of the authors include the importance of "observing" the mentor in action (e.g., Bloom *et al.*, 1998; Irwin *et al.*, 2004) when speaking about the role that mentors played. This can also been seen from the perspective of the coach in the following quote extracted from Irwin and colleagues' work: "You learn all your basic coaching strategies or whatever, philosophies from mentor coaches ... you look at how they are doing it, what they are saying and tend to mirror it, you may not understand why" (2004, p. 430).

Thus, a clear separation of observing and mentoring is hard to accomplish, and future research that seeks to better understand the relative contributions of what a mentor provides, such as observation opportunities, sage advice, and/or transmission of coaching philosophies, for example, would be useful. The main point of this section, however, was to denote that the time frame in which expert coaches have been observing other coaches extends from when they were athletes into their early years of coaching and right through until they become experts.

Officials

As with coaches, research indicates that the majority of elite officials were athletes prior to becoming officials (Fratzke, 1975; Furst, 1989, 1991). Unlike coaches, however, there is no current evidence to suggest that officials begin observing other officials during their athletic careers. Possibly, athletes who later become officials are motivated to do so during the later stages of their athletic careers; so it would not be surprising to discover that observation begins as an athlete. However, there is no empirical support for this statement. Once beginning as officials, observation begins to be incorporated. In the literature, officials have been shown to use observation early in their careers (e.g., Hancock *et al.*, 2011), as well as later in their careers when they begin to incorporate more deliberate practice hours and commit to the profession, particularly through self-observation using video analysis (e.g., Catteeuw *et al.*, 2010; Catteeuw *et al.*, 2009; MacMahon *et al.*, 2007; Ollis *et al.*, 2006). It would be important for researchers to identify when officials begin using observational learning, and also to delineate when they begin self-observation on video compared to observing others either live or on video.

The use of observation

Who

In their model, Ste-Marie and colleagues (2012) described *who* in terms of various characteristics of the individual being observed. To start, individuals can observe themselves using video, or they can observe others either live or on video. When observing others, one can watch a coping model (model begins low in confidence, but this builds over time) or a mastery model (model begins with, and maintains, high confidence). Furthermore, models can be skilled (perfect execution), unskilled (some performance errors), or learning (progresses from unskilled to skilled) (see McCullagh *et al.*, 2013 for further elaboration on model types). Herein, we mainly describe the characteristics of who is observed, but also provide some details on the types of models observed.

Coaches

Knowing that coach development occurs during an extended time frame, one can question who it is coaches are observing and how this can impact their development. As noted in the previous section, coaches' observations begin from their time as athletes. Given that these coaches are described as having engaged in sport for a fair number of years and having competed at elite levels (e.g., Erickson *et al.*, 2007; Gilbert *et al.*, 2006; Schinke *et al.*, 1995), they would have had opportunities to observe a wide variety of coaching approaches and expertise. Interestingly, observation of coaches was said to have shaped their own coaching practices not only in the identification of behaviors and attitudes they would want to have as a coach themselves, but also in those they would want to avoid (Schinke *et al.*, 1995). During this early developmental phase, little choice is available in terms of who is observed; however, this likely changes as they move into the early and middle years of coaching experience.

Wright and colleagues (2007) examined different learning situations of ice hockey coaches and noted that four coaching groups were identified in terms of whom those coaches could learn from through observation: coaches on the same team, coaches from the same association, and those outside the association, as well as coaches at a more elite level. In these four groups, we see varied levels of expertise, from coaches who are at the same level (e.g., peers from within and outside the association), to those that are at a higher level (e.g., those on the same team, with the assumption that the observation is of the head coach, and elite coaches). Similar testimony was identified in other research (Mesquita *et al.*, 2010). In drawing a parallel to the observational learning literature, one could argue that peer coaches provide a "learning" model, whereas the more advanced coaches serve as a "mastery" model. Of note is that both these types of models have been shown to provide informative motor learning experiences (see review by McCullagh *et al.*, 2012), and thus there is likely great value in not only observing elite coaches, but also observing ones' peers. Future research should examine the specific benefits that are gained by "peer" observation vs. "mastery" observation. In terms of determining which of these groups of coaches would be considered the most important there is evidence to suggest that observing expert coaches is deemed as most constructive to a coach's own expertise development (Gould *et al.*, 1990; Mesquita *et al.*, 2010; Salmela, 1994).

As we move into the observational experiences of expert coaches, there is less literature concerning who expert coaches observe to continue their development. Schempp, Webster, McCullik, Busch, and Mason (2007) examined top golf coaches to identify how they maintained their self-reported strengths and addressed their weaknesses. It was noted that to maintain their strengths, these high-level coaches looked to the expertise of other coaches by, among other things, watching them coach. These coaches also spoke of watching themselves on videotape to gain insight for improving their own coaching. This self-as-model procedure is similar to self-observation techniques used in motor skill learning (see Franks & Miller, 1991) and is an interesting avenue for further research as the self-as-model has been shown to be effective in many learning situations (Ste-Marie, 2013). Finally, Irwin and colleagues' (2004) study with elite artistic gymnastic coaches in Britain revealed that observing foreign coaches was valued, as foreign coaches were seen to have greater knowledge and more practical experience than coaches in the same country.

Overall, coaches observe varied coaching groups to develop their expertise. Little research is available to discern the benefits obtained from these varied sources of observation, and it is likely that each coaching group may serve different purposes that aid expertise development. This idea that the observational experience may afford different sources of information speaks to the varied functions that observation can serve, which are elaborated upon in the section on *why* coaches and officials observe others.

Officials

For officials, the research on who is observed is quite scarce. While many studies test whether referee performance can be improved through video training (e.g., Catteeuw *et al.*, 2010; Mascarenhas *et al.*, 2005b; Schweizer *et al.*, 2011), typically these studies use videos where the referee is absent or occluded; thus, no observational learning occurs. This is not to say observation never happens. In fact, in two studies where participants completed activity questionnaires, officials indicated that video training was part of their off-field activities (Catteeuw *et al.*, 2009; MacMahon *et al.*, 2007). This was further supported in an ethnographic study of officials (Ollis *et al.*, 2006). However, the nature of these studies did not allow for an explanation of the type of video analysis being used by participants (e.g., who was observed on video), as the studies were primarily concerned with creating an account of all activities that contributed to deliberate practice for officials, rather than understanding the characteristics of each activity. Likely, officials observe themselves and others; but making any specific conclusions about the percentage of time dedicated to viewing the self vs. others, or the type of model being observed (e.g., mastery vs. coping models) is too speculative. Clearly *who* is observed requires more dedicated attention from researchers to understand how observational learning can shape officials' development.

Why

Most of the observational learning research in the context of motor learning was focused on the outcome of improved skill technique for athletes as a result of observing others or the self. Cumming, Clark, Ste-Marie, McCullagh, and Hall (2005) were the first to suggest that there may be more to observation than just benefits to technical skill learning. In that paper, Cumming and colleagues presented a series of studies that examined the development and psychometrics of the functions of observational learning questionnaire (FOLQ). While it was determined that athletes did use observation mostly for skill learning (skill function), athletes also reported using it to learn strategies (strategic function), and, to a lesser extent, they used it to control arousal and psychological states for performance (performance function). As we only have knowledge of one paper examining the functions of observation for coaches and officials (Hancock *et al.*, 2011), we examine coaches and officials together below.

Coaches and officials

Hancock and colleagues (2011) had athletes, coaches, and officials involved in team interactive sports complete the FOLQ. Similar to the data of Cumming and colleagues (2005), athletes showed greater use of the skill function, followed by the strategy function, and then that of performance; coaches and officials also showed the same pattern of results for the three functions.

The use of observation

These findings were significant, as they intimated that coaches and officials were using observation for varied reasons. While this descending pattern was similar across the three sport groups, differences still emerged within each of the functions. Coaches, for example, scored significantly higher on both the skill and strategy functions than athletes and officials; meanwhile, officials scored significantly higher than coaches on the performance function.

The higher strategy function was anticipated by the authors, as coaches of team interactive sports are in charge of creating, implementing, and adjusting game strategies, and this increased responsibility may well heighten their desire to observe the strategies other coaches utilize, compared to athletes and officials. The finding of a higher skill function for the coaches, however, was more of a surprise, and the authors argued that the unexpected finding may be due to the more elaborate skill set needed of an effective coach. That is, coaches do not only need to know the technical skills of the sport, they must also understand how to organize practice, how to prepare athletes for competition, and how to implement effective training (Côté *et al.*, 1995). These additional requirements may result in their seeking out observational experiences of other coaches more so than athletes or officials, though this explanation has yet to be examined.

For officials, the main finding was that the performance function was rated significantly higher compared to coaches. This result was explained by the authors as a function of the pressure and scrutiny of the position. Referees, particularly at elite levels, are under tremendous scrutiny, and any incorrect decision is deconstructed and criticized (often times even the correct decisions are criticized). Fans do not have to think long to recall an egregious mistake by an official that impacted the outcome of a game. This pressure is an inherent and unique component of officiating, and being able to stay calm and focused during these stressful situations is paramount to success. As such, it is not surprising to find that officials have a greater propensity than coaches to observe other officials in order to learn effective coping skills for performance. Understanding why coaches and officials observe others now leads us to the particulars of what is observed and where it is observed.

What and where

Within Ste-Marie and colleagues' (2012) applied model of the use of observation, the *what* component considered two main factors. The first centered on what information was being observed by skill learners to learn and optimize the observed movement pattern, with the main finding pointing to the importance of relative motion information. Second, additional instructional features with observation were considered, such as verbal cueing or rehearsal strategies. Neither relative motion information nor instructional features combined with observation, however, are likely relevant in the coaching and officiating context. Consequently, our focus will be on what information coaches and officials are seeking to learn when observing other coaches/officials. Combined with this, we consider what is specifically observed in the various contexts that would constitute the *where* component, which we propose to include their own training sessions (i.e., coach training), as well as when they are involved in practice and competition settings with their athletes. While these three contexts are relevant for coaches, they are not all applicable to officials. In particular, officials do not engage in traditional practice sessions, so we direct our attention to observations in the competitive environment or other training settings (e.g., officials' meetings).

Coaches

Little variation was noted in what was observed by coaches during practice/training compared to competition; consequently, we speak to both of these settings, for the most part, at the same time. Moreover, to follow in line with the *why* section, we frame what is being observed by coaches in the context of the skill, strategy, and performance functions. Also of note is that none of the reviewed literature had the specific research question of *what* was being observed; rather, it was mainly through reading the quotes of the expert coaches that we identified what they said they observed, and often there was insufficient information to clearly discern the particular function of observation. For example, in a study by Wilson, Bloom, and Harvey (2010), a coach drew attention to the fact that when he was at games he watched the coach rather than the game because he was more interested in seeing what the coach was trying to accomplish. Thus, there is clearly a decision by the coach to observe another coach in the game context; yet the specific features being observed are unknown. As such, further investigation into what aspects are being directly observed would be warranted.

Beginning with the skill function, team coaches reported watching drills and exercises that were executed during practices, warm-ups, and/or competitions (Jones *et al.*, 2003; Sage, 1989; Wilson *et al.*, 2010; Wright *et al.*, 2007). Gymnastic coaches reported observing other coaches to gain information about the particular technique they were teaching for given movement skills (Irwin *et al.*, 2004). The strategy function was also shown to be used by both individual coaches, such as gymnastic coaches seeking information on determining the age to best introduce particular motor skills (Irwin *et al.*, 2004), as well as team coaches in their observations of tactical plays being practiced and used in game play (Jones *et al.*, 2003; Wright *et al.*, 2007). The performance function relates to controlling arousal and other psychological factors necessary for optimal performance. As it is difficult to observe another person and know their emotions and coping mechanisms, it is challenging to tease out the use of observation for the performance function. It may be that the observation of communication skills ties in with the performance function as interactions with athletes often involve getting them in the right frame of mind for optimal training and competition. In fact, coaches stated that they observed communication skills used by others in terms of how they interacted with players during practice (Jones *et al.*, 2003; Sage, 1989), as well as before and during games (Jones *et al.*, 2003).

Coaches also reported that they learned about coaching philosophies, beliefs, and values through observation (Irwin *et al.*, 2004; Jones *et al.*, 2003), as well as the culture of coaching (Jones *et al.*, 2003). These latter examples are difficult to place in any of the functions identified by Cumming and colleagues (2005), which coincides with a criticism made by McCullagh and colleagues (2012) in terms of the FOLQ possibly not capturing all the potential functions of observation. Hence, continued investigation is needed into what is captured by coaches through observation, and for what purpose.

Officials

Once again, the amount of literature addressing what and where officials observe is scant. Many officials attend regular monthly or yearly meetings (Catteeuw *et al.*, 2009; MacMahon *et al.*, 2007), and this appears to be one context in which observation occurs (Ollis *et al.*, 2006). Ollis and colleagues' (2006) ethnographic account of rugby referees indeed demonstrated that referees would watch video of other referees during monthly meetings to discuss referee decisions; however, the details of this observational method have yet to be well explained. The other setting that might be ripe for observation is during competitions. The second author can anecdotally speak to the fact that, during live competitive performance as an ice hockey referee, he observed other officials and was observed by officials. Observations included skill (e.g., conducting face-offs), strategy (e.g., proper positioning), and performance (e.g., maintaining composure) functions. To the authors' knowledge, however, there is no published empirical evidence that describes this type of observation for officials. The only support the authors could find for observation was a quote

The use of observation

from the second author's unpublished[1] doctoral dissertation (Hancock, 2011). In the dissertation, Hancock interviewed ice hockey referees, one of whom spoke of observing other referees: "It's really neat to learn from guys that have more experience than I do and guys that have [refereed] higher hockey than I do. So they've been in the position where I've been before." This quote indicates that observation in competitive environments is present; but again, more research is required to grasp a full understanding of the process.

How

The *how* component refers to such factors as the frequency of observation, the viewing angle one assumes, and the viewing speed one implements when watching a model on video. Understanding and incorporating these elements is important to improving the effectiveness of observation. In Ste-Marie and colleagues' (2012) review of literature, it is interesting to note that approximately eight per cent of the research had investigated questions related to *how* to make the observation experience effective. We consider this a very low percentage, given the importance of understanding the efficacy of a method; but the case is even worse within the research on coaching and officials, as we were unable to find any literature specifically addressing this component. Certainly, this is quite surprising given the strong support for observation as a meaningful source for acquiring knowledge and expertise in coaching and officiating. Obviously, investigation into *how* coaches and officials can optimize their observation experiences is merited.

Discussion of observation for coaches and officials

By integrating Ste-Marie and colleagues' (2012) applied model for observational learning, we have presented evidence for observation by coaches and officials with regard to the five Ws and one H. It seems evident from the literature that coaches and officials implement observation to help them improve their effectiveness. Collating this literature has helped us to understand that coaches: (1) use observation during their athletic and coaching careers, (2) observe coaches from within and outside of their associations, (3) use observation for skill, strategy, and performance improvements, and (4) observe other practices and games. For officials, the research is limited; but we were still able to glean some results, including officials' use of observation during monthly meetings and at competitions to improve skill, strategy, and especially performance. It is less clear when observation begins, as well as who is observed. For both coaches and officials, there is a paucity of information on the *how* of observation.

A point not yet made about learning via observation is that, at least for coaches, not all want to be observed and enable other coaches to learn from them. Certainly, when one is trying to get athletes to win, sharing knowledge on the process being undertaken could jeopardize chances of future success. This idea was highlighted by a quote presented in Lemyre and colleagues' research, in which a soccer coach indicated that he would spy on other coaches at soccer tournaments and said that "coaching is being able to steal from other coaches. You take what you like and what you find relevant for your team" (2007, p. 201). This is an important consideration, as one of the applications of this research concerns how information about observational learning can improve the expert development of coaches and officials; thus, open sharing of knowledge may be a prerequisite.

Conclusions

Having presented a five Ws and one H approach to coaches' and officials' observations, it is evident that much more research is required to fully understand how observation improves performance. Likely, there is more to coaching and officiating than meets the eye. That is to say, observation of other coaches and officials, or of the self, could be critical to performance improvements; but that observation should not stand alone – it needs to be supplemented by direct interactions with observed coaches and officials. Moreover, not everything can be learned through observation. For instance, it is probably quite difficult to observe the organizational methods that coaches implement, which Côté and colleagues (1995) suggest are critical to coaching expertise. Therefore, practical experiences and formal education complement the observational learning process. Identifying the scope and magnitude of observational experiences for coaches and officials along the pathway to excellence would be a fruitful future endeavor.

Note

1 Parts of the dissertation were published (Hancock & Ste-Marie, in press), though the particular quote to which we refer is not found in the publication.

References

Baker J., & Horton, S. (2004) 'A review of primary and secondary influences on sport expertise', *High Ability Studies*, 15: 211–28.

Bloom, G. A., Durand-Bush, N., Schinke, R. J., & Salmela, J. (1998) 'The importance of mentoring in the development of coaches and athletes', *International Journal of Sport Psychology*, 29: 267–81.

Catteeuw, P., Gilis, B., Jaspers, A., Wagemans, J., & Helsen, W. (2010) 'Training of perceptual-cognitive skills in offside decision making', *Journal of Sport & Exercise Psychology*, 32: 845–61.

Catteeuw, P., Helsen, W., Gilis, B., & Wagemans, J. (2009) 'Decision-making skills, role specificity, and deliberate practice in association football refereeing', *Journal of Sports Sciences*, 27: 1125–36.

Côté, J., & Gilbert, W. (2009) 'An integrative definition of coaching effectiveness and expertise', *International Journal of Sports Science and Coaching*, 4: 307–23.

Côté, J., Salmela, J., Trudel, P., Baria, A., & Russell, S. (1995) 'The coaching model: A grounded assessment of expert gymnastic coaches' knowledge', *Journal of Sport & Exercise Psychology*, 17: 1–17.

Culver, D., & Trudel, P. (2008) 'Clarifying the concept of communities of practice in sport', *International Journal of Sports Science and Coaching*, 3: 1–10.

Cumming, J., Clark, S. E., Ste-Marie, D. M., McCullagh, P., & Hall, C. (2005) 'The functions of observational learning questionnaire (FOLQ)', *Psychology of Sport and Exercise*, 6: 517–37.

Cushion, C. J., Armour, K. M., & Jones, R. L. (2003) 'Professional development: Experience and learning to coach', *Quest*, 55: 215–30.

Erickson, K., Bruner, M. W., MacDonald, D., & Côté, J. (2008) 'Gaining insight into actual and preferred sources of coaching knowledge', *International Journal of Sports Science & Coaching*, 3: 527–38.

Erickson, K., Côté, J., & Fraser-Thomas, J. (2007) 'Sport experiences, milestones, and educational activities associated with high-performance coaches' development', *The Sport Psychologist*, 21: 302–16.

Franks, I., & Miller, G. (1991) 'Training coaches to observe and remember', *Journal of Sports Sciences*, 9: 285–97.

Fratzke, M. R. (1975) 'Personality and biographical traits of superior and average college basketball officials', *The Research Quarterly*, 46: 484–8.

Furst, D. M. (1989) 'Sport role socialization: Initial entry into the subculture of officiating', *Journal of Sport Behavior*, 12: 41–52.

Furst, D. M. (1991) 'Career contingencies: Patterns of initial entry and continuity in collegiate sports officiating', *Journal of Sport Behavior*, 14: 93–102.

Gilbert, W., Côté, J., & Mallet, C. (2006) 'Developmental paths and activities of successful sport coaches', *International Journal of Sports Science and Coaching*, 1: 69–76.

Gould, D., Gianani, J., Krane, V., & Hodge, K. (1990) 'Educational needs of elite U.S. national team, pan American, and Olympic coaches', *Journal of Teaching in Physical Education*, 9: 332–4.

Hancock, D. J. (2011) 'Examining perceptual differences amongst elite, intermediate, and novice ice hockey referees: Visual attention and eye movement recordings', unpublished thesis, University of Ottawa. Online. Retrieved from www.ruor.uottawa.ca/en/bitstream/handle/10393/20260/Hancock_David_2011_Thesis.pdf?sequence=1 (accessed 2 December 2013).

Hancock, D. J., Rymal, A. M., & Ste-Marie, D. M. (2011) 'A triadic comparison of the use of observational learning amongst team sport athletes, coaches, and officials', *Psychology of Sport and Exercise*, 12: 236–41.

The use of observation

Hancock, D. J., & Ste-Marie, D. M. (2014). Describing strategies used by elite, intermediate, and novice ice hockey referees. *Research Quarterly for Exercise and Sport, 85*, 351–364.

Irwin, G., Hanton, S., & Kerwin, D. (2004) 'Reflective practice and the origins of elite coaching knowledge', *Reflective Practice*, 5: 425–42.

Jones, R. L., Armour, K. M., & Potrac, P. (2003) 'Constructing expert knowledge: A case study of a top-level professional soccer coach', *Sport, Education, and Society*, 8: 213–29.

Lemyre, F., Trudel, P., & Durand-Bush, N. (2007) 'How youth sport coaches learn to coach', *The Sport Psychologist*, 21: 191–209.

Lynch, M., & Mallett, C. (2006) 'Becoming a successful high performance track and field coach', *Modern Athlete and Coach*, 44: 15–20.

MacMahon, C., Helsen, W. F., Starkes, J. L., & Weston, M. (2007) 'Decision-making skills and deliberate practice in elite association football referees', *Journal of Sports Sciences*, 25: 65–78.

MacMahon, C., & Plessner, H. (2008) 'The sport official in research and practice', in D. Farrow, J. Baker, & C. MacMahon (eds) *Developing sport expertise: Lessons from theory and practice*, New York: Routledge, 172–90.

MacMahon, C., & Ste-Marie, D. M. (2002) 'Decision-making by experienced rugby referees: Use of perceptual information and episodic memory', *Perceptual and Motor Skills*, 95: 570–2.

Mascarenhas, D.R.D., Collins, D., & Mortimer, P. (2005a) 'Elite refereeing performance: Developing a model for sport science support', *The Sport Psychologist*, 19: 364–79.

Mascarenhas, D.R.D., Collins, D., Mortimer, P., & Morris, B. (2005b) 'Training accurate and coherent decision making in rugby union referees', *The Sport Psychologist*, 19: 131–47.

McCullagh, P., Law, B., & Ste-Marie, D. M. (2012) 'Modeling and performance', in S. Murphy (ed) *The Oxford handbook of sport and performance psychology*, New York: Oxford University Press, 250–72.

McCullagh, P., Ste-Marie, D. M., & Law, B. (2013) 'Modeling: Is what you see what you get?', in J. L. Van Raalte & B. W. Brewer (eds) *Exploring sport and exercise psychology*, 3rd ed., Washington, DC: American Psychological Association, 139–62.

Mesquita, I., Isidro, S., & Rosado, A. (2010) 'Portuguese coaches' perceptions of and preferences for knowledge sources related to their professional background', *Journal of Sports Science and Medicine*, 9: 480–9.

Ollis, S., MacPherson, A., & Collins, D. (2006) 'Expertise and talent development in rugby refereeing: An ethnographic enquiry', *Journal of Sports Sciences*, 24: 309–22.

Sage, G. H. (1989) 'Becoming a high school coach: From playing sports to coaching', *Research Quarterly for Exercise and Sport*, 60: 81–92.

Salmela, J. (1994) 'Learning from the development of expert coaches', *Journal of Coaching and Sport Science*, 1: 1–11.

Salmela, J. (1995) 'Learning from the development of expert coaches', *Coaching and Sport Science Journal*, 2: 3–13.

Schempp, P. G., Webster, C., McCullik, B. A., Busch, C., & Mason, I. S. (2007) 'How the best get better: An analysis of the self-monitoring strategies used by expert golf instructors', *Sport, Education, and Society*, 12: 175–92.

Schinke, R. J., Bloom, G. A., & Salmela, J. (1995) 'The career stages of elite Canadian basketball coaches', *Avante*, 1: 48–62.

Schweizer, G., Plessner, H., Kahlert, D., & Brand, R. (2011) 'A video-based training method for improving soccer referees' intuitive decision-making skills', *Journal of Applied Sport Psychology*, 23: 429–42.

Ste-Marie, D. M. (2013) 'Self-as-a-model interventions situated within an applied model for the use of observation', *Movement & Sport Sciences-Sciences & Motricité*, 79: 33–41.

Ste-Marie, D. M., Law, B., Rymal, A. M., O, J., Hall, C., & McCullagh, P. (2012) 'Observation interventions for motor skill learning and performance: An applied model for the use of observation', *International Review of Sport and Exercise Psychology*, 5: 145–76.

Werthner, P., & Trudel, P. (2006) 'A new theoretical perspective for understanding how coaches learn to coach', *The Sport Psychologist*, 20: 198–212.

Wilson, L. M., Bloom, G. A., & Harvey, W. J. (2010) 'Sources of knowledge acquisition: Perceptions of high school teacher/coach', *Physical Education and Sport Pedagogy*, 15: 383–99.

Wright, T., Trudel, P., & Culver, D. (2007) 'Learning how to coach: The different learning situations reported by youth ice hockey coaches', *Physical Education and Sport Pedagogy*, 12: 127–44.

36

FIVE EVIDENCE-BASED PRINCIPLES OF EFFECTIVE PRACTICE AND INSTRUCTION

David T. Hendry, Paul R. Ford, A. Mark Williams, and Nicola J. Hodges

Introduction

Around the world thousands of coaches lead practice or training sessions for youth athletes every week. One of the major goals of coaching is to encourage the acquisition of skills. Over the last few decades, the scientific study of practice and instruction has enhanced our understanding of how skill and expert performance is acquired. A considerable body of research now exists, showing the importance of investing vast amounts of time in practice in order to attain skill and expertise in sports (for reviews, see Ericsson, 2003, 2007; Ford *et al.*, 2013; Hodges & Baker, 2011; Ward *et al.*, 2004). Popular science books such as *The Talent Code* (Coyle, 2009) and *Outliers* (Gladwell, 2008) have provided information relating to the quantity of practice required to attain a high level of skill in sport and have reached practitioners in the field. However, much less scientific information has reached practitioners with respect to the type or quality of practice. For example, recent analysis of activities during coaching sessions in youth sports indicates that there is a significant gap between scientific research evidence and the methods employed by coaches in the field (Farrow *et al.*, 2008; Ford *et al.*, 2010; Low *et al.*, 2013; Williams & Hodges, 2005).

The aim of this chapter is to provide five evidence-based principles of effective practice and instruction to help guide practitioners who work with athletes to create efficient, challenging, and engaging practice sessions. Expert performance in most sports requires a high level of perceptual, cognitive, and motor skill, including visual search, decision-making, and motor skill execution (for a review, see Williams *et al.*, 2011). In this chapter, we address how practice and instruction can be used to help athletes acquire the perceptual, cognitive, and motor skills required for expert performance in sport. We first present principles related to practice organization and its optimization, followed by principles on instructional strategies. We conclude with a final section on motivation and its impact on engagement in practice and motor learning.

Practice activity

In the following sections, we briefly detail two evidence-based principles related to how practice should be organized to best aid skill acquisition. We have titled the first principle: "Use the game as the learning tool." This principle is about ensuring that athletes are active decision makers during practice in the same or similar manner as they would be during competition. The second principle is about ensuring that the difficulty of practice is set at an appropriate level of challenge for the skill and age of the learners in order to best optimize learning and engagement. We have titled this section: "Setting the bar." In these sections, we refer to ideas from the *constraints-led approach* to skill acquisition (Davids et al., 2008; Newell, 1986) and draw on more traditional motor learning research and theories related to contextual interference, variability of practice, and the challenge-point hypothesis.

"Use the game as the learning tool"

Ensure that athletes are active decision makers as per the competition format of the sport

The main goal of practice is for participants to acquire skill that transfers to improved performance in the competition format of the sport. The type of practice that athletes engage in can have a profound effect on that skill acquisition. Researchers have shown that coaches have their youth athletes spend more time engaging in drill-type activities during practice compared to games-based activities. For example, in England, youth soccer players (Ford et al., 2010) and youth cricket players (Low et al., 2013) were shown to spend two-thirds of practice time in drill-type activity (see Figure 36.1 for an illustration). Traditional, drill-type activities are usually characterized by repetitions of a single skill (e.g., practice turning or practice hitting the same types of shots). They are often conducted alone or in small groups with limited, if any, pressure from opponents (also referred to as "training form" activities; Ford et al., 2010). While these practices are used with best intentions to reduce the difficulty of the sport for athletes by breaking the skill down into its constituent parts, they are often devoid of key features from the competition format of the sport, such as opposition pressure and unpredictability. Therefore, drill-type activities are unlikely to promote positive transfer of the skills from practice to competition (Farrow et al., 2008; Low

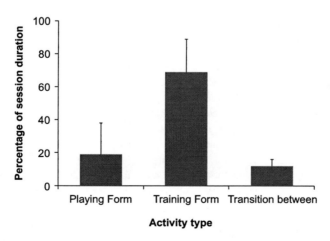

Figure 36.1 Percentage of time in a practice session spent in playing form (i.e., play- or game-type activities), training form (i.e., drill-type activities), and transitions between these across 36 coaching sessions in English youth cricket (adapted from Low et al., 2013).

et al., 2013). For numerous reasons, it has been recommended that drill-type practices should be kept to a minimum, and instead, coaches should look to use the game as the learning tool. This aim is achieved through the use of modified games, matches, or the competition format of the sport (referred to as "playing form" activities, Ford *et al.*, 2010). When athletes practice in games, the situations have similar underlying structures to those encountered in competition, so the transfer of skill to competition is likely to be high. One reason for this positive transfer is that it should help athletes acquire the necessary perceptual and cognitive skills, which give rise to the appropriate selection and execution of motor skills in competition (for a review, see Williams *et al.*, 2011).

Game activities place participants into more random and variable practice conditions. During these games, athletes must switch between different skills, such as passing, dribbling, and shooting in soccer, which is referred to as a more "random ordered" type of practice. They must use variations of the same skill, such as making a shot or a pass from different distances or to different targets, which is referred to as a more "variable" type of practice. Organizing practice in this manner is supported by one of the most robust findings in the motor learning literature; i.e., the contextual interference (CI) effect (for a review, see Lee, 2012). The CI effect is a learning phenomenon associated with how a person practices multiple skills. Skills that are practiced in a mixed or random order (or high CI practice) slow the rate of acquisition, but lead to better retention of the skills. In contrast, blocked practice order (or low CI practice), in which the same skill is practiced multiple times in succession, such as in drill-type practices, leads to better performance during acquisition, but results in poorer learning/retention when assessed at a later date. One mechanistic explanation for the CI effect is that it is beneficial to "forget" and "recall" skills across practice attempts, so that retrieval processes are strengthened. During blocked practice conditions, there is not the same cognitive effort required to retrieve and remember what to do as there is for random practice (Lee & Magill, 1985). Although the CI effect is a relatively robust phenomenon, in the early stages of learning or for particularly difficult skills or tasks, there are not the same advantages associated with random practice. A less random order of skill executions in practice (at least initially) appears to help individuals stabilize a motor skill (Porter & Magill, 2010; Shea *et al.*, 1990); however, practice should still involve active, game-like decision-making (Low *et al.*, 2013).

Games-based activities contain what is known as variable practice conditions, in which each attempt at a skill is slightly different in some manner to the other attempts. The opposite of variable practice is constant practice, in which a singular skill is performed with no variations in conditions. There is empirical support for the learning advantages associated with variable rather than constant practice conditions, particularly for transfer of skills within the range of variations practiced (e.g., Lee *et al.*, 1985). For example, shooting towards the basket or net from various distances, towards different targets, or with different ball types helps to facilitate skill acquisition within the practiced parameters (Salmoni *et al.*, 1984). The adjustments that learners need to make in variable practice results in more adaptable movement patterns and skills that should aid transfer to dynamic conditions of competition.

The constraints-led approach to skill teaching (e.g., Davids *et al.*, 2008) holds that coaches can harness the inherent variability in their sport and use it to bring about robust skill acquisition in learners. According to this approach, what is important in practice is the interactive relationship between the performer and the environment. Changes to the context or environment where an individual performs or trains, such as playing surface, weather, or the audience, can affect the performance of the athlete in desirable and non-desirable ways. More specific task modifications to the rules of a game, the size of the playing area, ball, or bat, or the opposition characteristics also impact on the performer and the types of skills displayed. Skill acquisition is considered as a continual and varied adaptation to these changing task and environmental constraints that are fluctuating factors inherent in the sport (Davids *et al.*, 2012; Seifert *et al.*, 2013). Coaches can

Principles of effective practice

systematically vary all of the many factors inherent in the sport to have their athletes experience and learn how to perform successfully under each of these conditions.

In summary, game activities promote variability in how skills are practiced and appear to provide a number of benefits for athletes in terms of long-term retention and effective transfer to competitive environments where variability is to be expected. Structuring practice to bring in conditions that would typify competition, such as pressure, opponents, and uncertainty, is likely to benefit transfer of skills to game situations.

"Setting the bar"

Provide the learner with the optimal challenge for their skill and age

Setting an appropriate level of challenge during practice is arguably one of the most critical aspects of coaching. The reason that coaches use drill-type activities is to reduce the challenge of the sport for learners. In contrast, games-based activities might be considered by coaches as too challenging for learners. However, the key for coaches is to ensure that athletes are making active decisions during practice in the same manner as the competition format of the sport, with games-based activities being the simplest way for coaches to achieve this aim (Low *et al.*, 2013). The challenge-point hypothesis (Guadagnoli & Lee, 2004) provides a framework for conceptualizing how to reduce the difficulty of games-based and other practice activities to the appropriate level for the learner. Accordingly, practitioners should consider both the constant amount of task difficulty, irrespective of the athlete or condition (termed *nominal* task difficulty), and the degree of task difficulty in relation to a performer's skill level (termed *functional* task difficulty). Guadagnoli and Lee (2004) suggest that there exists a theoretical "optimal challenge point," in which the nominal and functional task difficulties interact to produce the greatest learning and performance benefits. For example, a certain pitch in baseball (either type of pitch or speed of pitch) will be relatively more or less challenging, depending on the age, size, and experience of the batter.

Although there has not been direct research conducted on the challenge-point principle during practice, the systematic manipulation of it appears to be a key part of skill acquisition. Performers who are allowed to self-select practice conditions tend to adopt practice conditions that are adaptively suited to their skills and needs, such as switching practice to new skills once errors on another skill start to decrease (referred to as performance-contingent switching; Keetch & Lee, 2007). However, learners who are in control of their practice tend towards lower challenging environments, thinking erroneously that they learn more from blocked- rather than random-type practices, and spend time on already mastered skills, potentially reinforcing their beliefs in their existing ability, rather than looking to improve on harder skills (Huang *et al.*, 2008). For these reasons, the coach needs to be aware of the principles of challenge-point and active decision-making as per the competition format of the sport, so that they can ensure practice remains optimal.

In games-based activities, the challenge point can be modified through the manipulation of task constraints to decrease (e.g., reduce number of opposition, increase size of area, reduce opponent pressure) or increase difficulty (e.g., reduce playing area, increase opponent pressure) (Davids *et al.*, 2008). For beginners, the challenge point of games-based activities can be reduced to an appropriate level at which the game or practice facilitates success, whilst it is ensured that athletes remain active decision makers as per the competition format of the sport. For example, in mini-tennis, the court is smaller, the net is lower, the racket is scaled to the participant, and the ball is bigger and much slower, all of which counteract some of the difficulties encountered in normal tennis, such as a fast ball and a high net (Buszard *et al.*, 2014). Activities that serve to reduce the amount of errors in practice for beginners also have the potential advantage of aiding the robustness of these skills in the face of later pressures (Masters & Poolton, 2012). These "errorless learning" conditions (where errors are low, not absent) are based on the principle of limiting the accumulation of explicit rules via the hypothesis testing that occurs when errors are made. The accumulation of explicit rules early in practice is problematic when performers are later placed under stressful conditions, such as in competition. Under these stressful conditions, they tend to "reinvest" attention towards previously learned explicit rules, disrupting automatic processes and causing a decrement in performance (e.g. Baumeister, 1984; Deschamp *et al.*, 2004; Fuchs, 1962.

Games with a lowered challenge point, such as mini-tennis, are ideal ways for learners to acquire sports skills, but may be too difficult for completely novice players or too easy for more skilled players. For novice players who find games with the lowest challenge point too difficult, coaches would normally regress to drill-based activity (Ford *et al.*, 2010). However, coaches should ensure that when doing so, learners remain active decision makers as per the competition format of the sport (Low *et al.*, 2013). By being active decision makers, learners are likely to acquire all the necessary components of a skill (i.e., perceptual, cognitive, and motor) that are required for competition performance in most sports (for a review, see Williams *et al.*, 2011). For example, in tennis, the main goal is to hit the ball into space away from the opponent – so all practice should contain this aim and a moving "opponent." An example drill in tennis is for the complete novice to serve the larger ball from closer to the lowered net, attempting to hit the ball into the larger opposite court away from the moving "opponent." For more skilled players, the challenge point can be raised to an appropriate level by systematically manipulating key task and environmental constraints to increase the difficulty; for example, in tennis, using a higher net or a normal tennis ball, or opposition with the specific characteristics and tactics of upcoming competition opponents.

The key goal for practitioners is to carefully balance constraints to provide game-like conditions while considering the learner's phase of skill development. For advanced learners, constraints should be manipulated to maximize the information available (promoting variability and resultant options), whereas for novices fewer options should be presented (or more constraints) to allow learners to develop and stabilize skills (e.g., Davids *et al.*, 2012; Guadagnoli & Lee, 2004).

Instructional strategies

In this section, we briefly detail two evidence-based principles related to instructional strategies. The first principle is about ensuring variation in the use of demonstrations, whereas with the second principle we advocate that in the early stages of learning, a "hands-off" approach to instruction and feedback should be adopted (Williams & Hodges, 2005).

"Mixing it up"

Mixing up demonstrations with physical practice leads to learning benefits

Watching others, or even oneself, is considered a key component of skill learning. Demonstrations can help convey strategies simply and hence reduce the cognitive effort that might be associated with processing verbal instruction. This type of observational practice provides learners with a visual template or reference for learning, such that they are alerted to movement features and strategies that potentially promote goal attainment (such as shooting a ball through a net or correctly landing a jump on the ice; see Hodges & Franks, 2002).

Demonstrations can be given before, during, or after a period of physical practice. Recently, researchers have shown that adopting a mixed schedule of observation and physical practice can

Principles of effective practice

lead to learning benefits equal to those derived from physical practice alone (Ong *et al.*, 2011; Shea *et al.*, 2000; Vinter & Chartrel, 2010; for a review see Ong & Hodges, 2012). Interspersing demonstrations with physical practice allows the learner to integrate strategies derived from observational practice into physical practice, promoting enhanced movement execution (e.g., Deakin & Proteau, 2000). For novices, "mixing it up" allows the learner to devote greater attentional resources to strategic components of the skill that may not have been possible during physical practice (Wulf & Shea, 2002). Findings suggest that observational practice can, to an extent, compensate for the absence of physical practice (Shea *et al.*, 2000), which is beneficial in sports that are highly demanding physically and mentally or incur high financial costs. With respect to how demonstrations should be interspersed effectively during practice, there is evidence that during practice of novel skills they should be provided early in learning and then gradually faded out as practice progresses (e.g., Badets & Blandin, 2004; Badets *et al.*, 2006; Weeks & Anderson, 2000).

Traditionally, demonstrations are performed by a skilled performer (e.g., the coach/instructor) to convey movement goals before physical practice. Mixing up when observational practice is provided, so that demonstrations occur *after* a practice attempt (retroactive) rather than *before* an attempt (proactive), can facilitate learning by encouraging the athletes to think and engage more in the learning process. In this case, "retroactive" demonstrations function more like feedback and are assumed to aid retention through enhanced cognitive effort and what is termed "retrieval practice" (Richardson & Lee, 1999; Patterson & Lee, 2008). Similarly, viewing a combination of correct and incorrect learning models, such as watching a peer and the coach, has been shown to aid learning (e.g., Shebilske *et al.*, 1992; Shea *et al.*, 1999). In this case, mixing up the type of model viewed allows the goals of the action to be accurately conveyed (through a correct model) whilst enhancing the observer's problem-solving capabilities (though a model with error). In this latter instance, the observer is engaged in figuring out what to do through observation of errors and corrections of these errors (e.g., Andrieux & Proteau, 2013; McCullagh & Caird, 1990; Rohbanfard & Proteau, 2011). Variability in demonstration type can also alert the learner to a number of potential movement solutions, promoting individualized solutions based on the athlete's current capabilities, body constraints, or learning goals. In directing attention towards a particular model or one "correct" technique the individual has less chance to vary his/her practice or may be inhibited creatively (Davids *et al.*, 2008).

"Use a 'hands-off' approach to instruction and feedback"

Minimizing the amount and frequency of instruction and feedback reduces "overthinking" of movements

INSTRUCTION

Providing relevant and accurate instructions is often the de facto starting point for teaching sport skills. Of course, there will be significant variability in what technical information is delivered in this process. In this section, we aim to point out that more information is not always better and that subtleties in how technical information is delivered can have significant implications for skill learning and performance.

In order to understand the mechanisms behind effective instruction, we must first consider that humans can only process or remember a limited amount of information. Early research shows that people have difficulty processing more than five to nine verbal items at a time (Miller, 1956). Since the general purpose of instructions is to provide a framework to support movement execution, providing verbal instructions that contain more information than the upper limits of an individual's processing capacity can complicate and potentially impede learning. Magill and Anderson (2012) have recently suggested that an instructor should consider using the minimum amount of information that a performer needs to achieve a desired movement or movement outcome. This habit of providing the minimum amount of instruction to learners of motor skills, admittedly not necessarily an easy task and one that is likely to require adaptation across skill levels and ages, should help prevent any tendency to over-solve or over-talk through the skill. As further encouragement for this method, there is evidence that more discovery-based approaches to learning motor skills, which encourage the learner to problem solve and arrive at their own motor solutions, are more effective than being told what to do, with games-based activities being a good method to achieve this aim. Reducing the amount of prescriptive guidance is thought to encourage learners to engage more in the learning process, as well as to encourage greater flexibility and variability in movements, promoting adaptation across varying conditions (Davids *et al.*, 2008; Hodges & Franks, 2004; Seifert *et al.*, 2013). Even delaying when to give instructions (i.e., later in practice rather than right at the start) has been shown to benefit learning (Ong *et al.*, 2011; Poolton *et al.*, 2005) and supports the idea that instruction should be minimized, particularly early in skill learning.

Sport is frequently performed under conditions of high psychological stress. Consequently, learners must acquire skills that are resistant to such pressures. A body of research exists showing how instructional techniques that are more "explicit" (e.g. conscious, rule-based, verbalizable) rather than "implicit" (i.e. no or low conscious awareness, non-verbalizable) can affect performance negatively under pressure (for a recent review, see Masters & Poolton, 2012). When placed under stressful conditions, performers tend to "reinvest" attention towards previously learned explicit, technical aspects of an action, disrupting automatic processes and causing a regression in performance back to an earlier level (e.g., Baumeister, 1984; Deschamp *et al.*, 2004; Fuchs, 1962). The greater the number of explicit rules acquired during practice, the greater is this inclination to reinvest, resulting in performance decrements during pressure situations (Liao & Masters, 2002; Masters & Maxwell, 2004; Maxwell *et al.*, 2006). Conversely, learning implicitly can be less resistant to distraction, psychological pressure, and physiological fatigue (Masters & Poolton, 2012). Therefore, keeping the amount of instruction to a minimum helps to limit the amount of explicit knowledge acquired by the performer.

A number of instructional methods have been proposed to reduce explicit learning and encourage the acquisition of more implicit knowledge. These techniques generally involve practice that prevents or reduces the chance to generate or remember rules (e.g., performing a math task during practice; see Masters & Poolton, 2012). However, this type of practice can slow the rate of acquisition and may not be very practical in a sport setting, despite its potential resistance to psychological pressure. Analogy learning (e.g., "shoot as if you are trying to put cookies into a jar on the top shelf;" Liao & Masters, 2001) is one relatively simple instructional technique that serves the purpose of reducing the amount of explicit knowledge conveyed to an athlete, resulting in learning that is more resistant to psychological stress (Liao & Masters, 2001; Lam *et al.*, 2009).

Closely tied to the amount of information that is provided during instruction is the manner in which instructions are presented. Relatively minor differences in the wording of instructions have repeatedly been shown to impact performance and learning. Specifically, subtle changes in the focus of instructions from the body (internal) onto the effects of the action (external) can change how a skill is acquired and, importantly, retained (Lohse *et al.*, 2012; Wulf, 2007; Wulf & Lewthwaite, 2009; see also Chapter 4). In throwing tasks, such as the forehand Frisbee disc throw, internally focused instructions might be: "accelerate first your elbow and then your wrist." The same instructions could be conveyed without this internal

Principles of effective practice

focus, instead directing attention externally to the object, such as: "release the disc as though you are snapping a wet towel" (Ong *et al.*, 2010). Generally, an external focus of attention has been shown to benefit (relative to no instructions and internal focus instructions) both skilled and novice athletes. Instructions that direct attention onto the movement (e.g., the foot in soccer dribbling) are harmful for skilled performers, relative to control conditions (Beilock *et al.*, 2002a; Ford *et al.*, 2005; Gray, 2004), but familiarity with a particular attentional focus condition (i.e., tendency to focus internally or externally) can moderate these effects (Maurer & Munzert, 2013). The constrained action hypothesis is the most common explanation for advantages associated with focusing externally during motor skill execution and learning (McNevin *et al.*, 2003; Wulf, 2007). According to this hypothesis, an external focus of attention encourages the operation of automatic-type processes during the movement that are assumed to be more efficient and effective than processes encouraged when attention is directed internally. An internal focus of attention disrupts this low level of control, instead promoting more conscious movement control (see also the "deautomization of skills" hypothesis; Beilock *et al.*, 2002b; Ford *et al.*, 2005).

The automization of movements and actions appears to be the goal for athletes, so that during performance effective and efficient movement execution occurs without conscious thought or attention-demanding control. This is not to say that athletes do not acquire explicit, domain-specific knowledge as they develop, such as tactical and strategic knowledge, but that knowledge relating to movement execution and the "how to" of the action is relatively less available during action and/or less specific (Beilock *et al.*, 2002a). In a recent study, elite netball players showed positive transfer of tactical decision-making knowledge that was acquired through off-court, explicit, instructional strategies to practice and later to competition (Richards *et al.*, 2012). Therefore, it is possible that only certain types of knowledge are subject to performance breakdowns, although further research is required to better understand optimal instructional strategies for the acquisition of different types of knowledge (e.g., tactical) and how these strategies might interact with skill and age.

In summary, we recommend that coaches be thrifty with their words and that they pay attention to how their instructions affect an athlete's focus of attention. Keeping it simple, either not providing instruction or providing only the minimum needed to encourage change in a relatively efficient manner, should serve as a good practice principle. Simple cues or analogies that direct attention to the intended effects can be used to help shape how skills are acquired or improved, as well as to help stave off the potential harmful effects of psychological pressure.

FEEDBACK

Intrinsic feedback is a naturally available consequence of performing a skill. Information from the sensory systems of vision, muscle proprioceptors, joint angles, and the vestibular system is relayed automatically to the performer. Coaches often add to the sensory feedback by providing augmented, extrinsic feedback, which can be verbal, visual, or tactile information about how a skill was performed and its overall effectiveness. This additional feedback is becoming ever more popular as personal computers or devices allow for relatively economical and easy to use, real time feedback, such as video analysis software.

Similar to instruction and observational practice, the content and presentation of feedback can significantly impact learning (for recent reviews, see Magill & Anderson, 2012; Phillips *et al.*, 2013; Williams & Hodges, 2005; Wulf & Shea, 2004). The most critical finding to underline with respect to augmented feedback provision is the need for it to be provided sparingly, particularly for skills that are low in sources of intrinsic feedback or that do not allow the augmented feedback to be provided during competition. For example, in archery, biofeedback pertaining to breath or heart rate is a common technique in practice, but this type of feedback is not allowed during competition.

Providing augmented feedback after every trial can accelerate performance during practice, yet this methodology can result in an overreliance on feedback, such that when it is no longer available decrements in performance occur. The guidance effect holds that sustained and substantial provision of augmented feedback reduces learners' ability to attend to and use intrinsic feedback, negatively impacting the capacity to engage in the learning process (e.g., Salmoni *et al.*, 1984). With respect to feedback frequency, coaches must consider both the complexity of the skill to be practiced and the skill of the learner before deciding on the correct amount and schedule of feedback. Although feedback may be required more frequently early in learning (Wulf *et al.*, 1998), feedback should be "faded out" over time, so that learners become self-equipped to detect and correct errors. To reduce the amount of feedback provision, practitioners would be best advised to delay the provision of feedback over trials (Anderson *et al.*, 1994), provide it in summary form (Lavery, 1962), as an average (Young & Schmidt, 1992), after the learner has personally estimated the success or accuracy of their performance, or offer additional performance feedback only when performance deviates significantly from "acceptable" parameters (Sherwood, 1988). Providing incrementally less feedback as learners progress will help them to acquire the fundamental elements of the skill, reduce the likelihood of an overreliance on feedback, and maintain motivation for continued practice through competency attainment (i.e., acknowledgment of correct performance; see Deci & Ryan, 2008).

Giving learners the opportunity to self-select when they receive augmented feedback has been shown to facilitate motor learning (for a review, see Sanli *et al.*, 2013). One key finding from this research is that when novice learners have control over feedback, they tend to ask for feedback after perceived "good" trials (Chiviacowsky & Wulf, 2002; Patterson & Carter, 2010). These findings run contrary to traditional notions of feedback, whereby augmented feedback is generally provided after errors (i.e., Adams, 1971). However, this trend does not continue with more skilled performers, who tend to ask for augmented feedback after unsuccessful attempts (Hodges *et al.*, 2011). It may be that feedback plays more of a motivational role (through positive reinforcement) during the early stages of learning, but more of an informational role later in practice, although further research is required to better understand the relationship between feedback provision and performance.

Learning can also be affected by the nature and precision of feedback. Providing individuals with prescriptive feedback about what to do next, in order to compensate for errors in performance or technique, reduces the problem-solving activities of players to a greater extent than descriptive feedback that refers only to what went wrong with the skill (Wulf & Shea, 2004). During the early stages of learning, or with more complex tasks, participants may require more prescriptive feedback to improve performance and maintain motivation, whereas later in learning the feedback should be more descriptive (Wulf *et al.*, 1998). With more advanced tasks, or as performance improves, the precision of feedback should become more precise in order to match the goals of performance (Magill & Wood, 1986).

Overall, augmented feedback is a potent learning tool if used sparingly and in a way that promotes cognitive engagement of the learner. In general, feedback provision should become less frequent, more descriptive, and increase in precision as skill develops, albeit much less is known about feedback for development and refinement of skills in highly skilled performers. The methods outlined above can facilitate learners' ability to detect and correct errors, allowing athletes to take ownership over their learning.

Principles of effective practice

Motivational strategies

"Give the learner the reins and enable success"

Ensure that athletes' basic psychological needs of competency, autonomy, and relatedness are met during practice

Until recently it has been assumed that motivation has a rather temporary and indirect influence on learning (Schmidt & Lee, 2011, p. 425). Yet researchers have started to show that motivational factors have an enduring, positive impact on motor learning (for a review, see Lewthwaite & Wulf, 2012). Self-determination theory (Deci & Ryan, 2000, 2008) has the satisfaction of basic needs as a key subcomponent, and underpins much of the emergent research in this area. Three basic psychological needs of competency, autonomy, and social relatedness are thought to be main drivers of continued behavior (e.g., Deci & Ryan, 2000, 2008). Experiencing and exhibiting competence, having control over one's behavior, and feeling connected to others encapsulates these three needs.

Learning environments that promote feelings of competency (even falsely) can enhance learning. For example, providing participants with positive feedback that indicates they are doing better than average leads to better retention than situations where this type of feedback was not provided, or feedback indicating below average performance was given (Avila *et al.*, 2012; Lewthwaite & Wulf, 2010; Wulf *et al.*, 2010). Because learners have shown a preference to receive feedback after perceived successful (or low error) trials (Chiviacowsky & Wulf, 2002, 2005), this has been seen as evidence that during practice, reinforcement of competency is valued. What is important here is that it is not actual competency that matters, but perceptions of success, underscoring the key role for the instructor as a competency-enhancing coach in learning environments that are potentially moderate to high in challenge (with the caveat that these competency-enhancing instructions or feedback need to be believable/realistic and not undermine effort in practice).

There is a significant body of research that shows how performers benefit from practice schedules that give them control over how much feedback or instruction is received during practice, how the practice should be scheduled, and even how much practice is needed (for a review, see Sanli *et al.*, 2013). Although the mechanisms underpinning these potential benefits are somewhat debated, one hypothesis is that giving the performer choice over how he/she learns might satisfy the need for autonomy and hence benefit motivation. In these studies, self-selected (autonomous) conditions are compared against matched conditions that mimic the practice schedule adopted by the autonomous learner. Overall, motor learning is improved when the learner has perceived control over a variety of different practice parameters, including: augmented feedback (Janelle *et al.*, 1997; Janelle *et al.*, 1995), use of physical assistance devices (Hartman, 2007; Wulf *et al.*, 2001; Wulf & Toole, 1999), the number of demonstrations (Wrisberg & Pein, 2002), and practice scheduling (Hodges *et al.*, 2011; Keetch & Lee, 2007). However, these findings do not mean that coaches have become redundant. When learners are given full control over practice, they prefer to select relatively easier tasks than those practiced in formal, deliberate practice conditions (e.g., Pachman *et al.*, 2013). That is, they do not participate in practice activities that adequately stretch their limits and improve existing performance (Ericsson, 1996).

Practicing with a partner is commonplace within many sports, and there is some evidence to support its effectiveness relative to practicing alone (e.g., Shea *et al.*, 1999). In addition to picking up informational cues relevant to improving performance and co-representing actions of a partner (for a review, see Eskenazi *et al.*, 2012), learning in pairs may help to satisfy the need for social relatedness and enhance motivation (Lewthwaite & Wulf, 2012). Working with a partner

David T. Hendry et al.

can serve to motivate learners through social comparison and support, and may even facilitate learning through enhanced team cohesion. To date, most of the research on joint action has focused on immediate performance rather than learning (cf. Karlinsky & Hodges, in press).

In addition to the studies presented, there are a myriad of other motivational factors (e.g., motivational climate, practice microstructure, coach behaviors) that are likely to influence need satisfaction and skill acquisition (see also Chapters 22 and 29). For example, some researchers have hypothesized that intrinsic motivation is enhanced through childhood engagement in sport activity that is fun and enjoyable, with engagement in deliberate practice activities explicitly focused on improving performance being delayed until early adolescence (for a review, see Côté *et al.*, 2007; although, see also Hendry *et al.*, 2014). Overall, there is growing evidence that techniques that impact autonomy (i.e., choice about how and what to practice), feelings of competency (such as reward/feedback), and, to a lesser degree, relatedness directly affect both performance and learning. We still know very little about these various motivational techniques on practice behaviors of skilled performers, yet there is reason to hypothesize that these methods will have a similar impact among more seasoned learners.

Conclusions

In this chapter, we have synthesized the motor learning and skill acquisition literature to provide five evidence-based principles of effective practice. Our aim in presenting these principles was to help provide an evidence-based guide for coaches, athletes, and other practitioners in sports. In the earlier stages of learning, the goal of practice and instruction should be to create a performer who executes motor and technical skills relatively automatically with little conscious thought or explicit rules about how to do so. The goal should be to develop a performer who selects and makes correct decisions in the competition format of the sport. Performers should be able to use vision appropriately to extract and recognize situations in the performance environment in order to make good decisions. Much of the motor learning research focuses on the earlier stages of learning, when novice or relatively inexperienced performers are practicing novel skills. Far less research has been conducted on the optimal practice and instructional strategies for skilled athletes. This is particularly notable when considering acquisition of perceptual-cognitive skills and the type of practice structure that might best aid acquisition of these skills. The research that does exist on more elite performers shows that skilled athletes should be engaging in effortful practice that is designed to improve specific aspects of performance (i.e., deliberate practice; Ericsson *et al.*, 1993). However, there are reasons to suspect that the principles detailed in this chapter will apply across the skill spectrum, given their broad and mechanistic nature and because even highly skilled athletes will still encounter situations that require (re)learning of components of skill and new techniques.

In Figure 36.2 we have provided a schematic summary of the main principles outlined in this chapter. Games-based and modified versions of the competition format of the sport ("Use the game as the learning tool") that contain a lowered challenge point through the systematic manipulation of task constraints encapsulate activities which best achieve the goals of learning for beginners. For more skilled athletes, obviously, the degree of challenge will be higher in order to attain improvements in skills, and hence the game-based training format should more closely approximate actual competition, with time pressures, opponents, and potentially consequences associated with errors. Minimizing the amount of instruction and feedback ("Use a 'hands-off' approach to instruction and feedback"), varying the timing of instruction or demonstrations

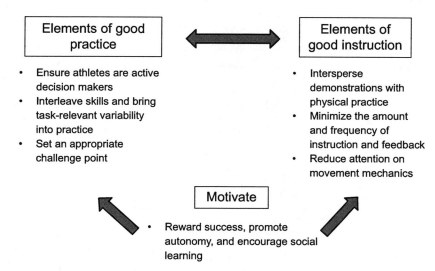

Figure 36.2 Summary schematic highlighting the key principles of effective practice organization and instruction and how these are moderated by motivational influences.

as well as the content of demonstrations ("Mixing it up") are also principles and methods for effective learning across the spectrum of skill. Within practice, consideration of motivation and factors that impact motivation, such as feelings of competency and autonomy, will impact what is retained and facilitate long-term engagement in practice ("Give the learner the reins and reward success"), which is certainly one of the most critical factors in attainment and maintenance of high levels of skill in sport.

References

Adams, J. A. (1971) 'A closed-loop theory of motor learning', *Journal of Motor Behavior*, 3: 111–50.
Anderson, D. I., Magill, R. A., & Sekiya, H. (1994) 'A reconsideration of the trials-delay of knowledge of results paradigm in motor skill learning', *Research Quarterly for Exercise and Sport*, 65: 286–90.
Andrieux, M., & Proteau, L. (2013) 'Observation learning of a motor task: Who and when?', *Experimental Brain Research*, 229: 125–37.
Ávila, L.T.G., Chiviacowsky, S., Wulf, G., & Lewthwaite, R. (2012) 'Positive social-comparative feedback enhances motor learning in children', *Psychology of Sport and Exercise*, 13: 849–53.
Badets, A., & Blandin, Y. (2004) 'The role of knowledge of results frequency in learning through observation', *Journal of Motor Behavior*, 36: 62–70.
Badets, A., Blandin, Y., Wright, D. L., & Shea, C. H. (2006) 'Error detection processes through observational learning', *Research Quarterly for Exercise and Sport*, 77: 177–84.
Baumeister, R. F. (1984) 'Choking under pressure: Self-consciousness and paradoxical effects of incentives on skillful performance', *Journal of Personality and Social Psychology*, 46: 610–20.
Beilock, S. L., Carr, T. H., MacMahon, C., & Starkes, J. L. (2002b) 'When paying attention becomes counterproductive: Impact of divided versus skill-focused attention on novice and experienced performance of sensorimotor skills', *Journal of Experimental Psychology Applied*, 8: 6–16.
Beilock, S. L., Wierenga, S. A., & Carr, T. H. (2002a) 'Expertise, attention, and memory in sensorimotor skill execution: Impact of novel task constraints on dual-task performance and episodic memory', *The Quarterly Journal of Experimental Psychology (A)*, 55: 1211–40.

Buszard, T., Farrow, D., Reid, M., & Masters, R.S.W. (2014) 'Modifying equipment early in skill development: A tennis perspective', *Research Quarterly for Exercise and Sport*, 85: 218–25.

Chiviacowsky, S., & Wulf, G. (2002) 'Self-controlled feedback: Does it enhance learning because performers get feedback when they need it?', *Research Quarterly for Exercise & Sport*, 73: 408–15.

Chiviacowsky, S., & Wulf, G. (2005) 'Self-controlled feedback is effective if it is based on the learner's performance', *Research Quarterly for Exercise & Sport*, 76: 42–8.

Coyle, D. (2009) *The talent code: Greatness isn't born, it's grown. Here's how*, New York: Bantam Dell, Random House Books.

Côté, J., Baker, J., & Abernethy, B. (2007) 'Play and practice in the development of sport expertise', in G. Tenenbaum & R. C. Eklund (eds) *Handbook of sport psychology*, 3rd ed., New York: Wiley, 184–202.

Davids, K., Araújo, D., Hristovski, R., Passos, P., & Chow, J. Y. (2012) 'Ecological dynamics and motor learning design sport', in A. M. Williams & N. J. Hodges (eds) *Skill acquisition in sport: Research, theory and practice*, 2nd ed., London: Routledge, 112–30.

Davids, K., Davids, K., Button, C., & Bennett, S. (2008) *Dynamics of skill acquisition: A constraints-led approach*, Champaign, IL: Human Kinetics.

Deakin, J. M., & Proteau, L. (2000) 'The role of scheduling in learning through observation', *Journal of Motor Behaviour*, 32: 268–76.

Deci, E. L., & Ryan, R. M. (2000) 'The "what" and "why" of goal pursuits: Human needs and the self-determination of behavior', *Psychological Inquiry*, 11: 227–68.

Deci, E. L., & Ryan, R. M. (2008) 'Self-determination theory: A macrotheory of human motivation, development, and health', *Canadian Psychology*, 49: 182–5.

Deschamps, T., Nourrit, D., Caillou, N., & Delignières, D. (2004) 'Influence of a stressing constraint on stiffness and damping functions of ski simulator's platform motion', *Journal of Sport Sciences*, 2: 867–74.

Ericsson, K. A. (1996) 'The acquisition of expert performance: An introduction to some of the issues', in K. A. Ericsson (ed) *The road to excellence: The acquisition of expert performance in the arts and sciences, sports and games*, Mahwah, NJ: Erlbaum, 1–50.

Ericsson, K. A. (2003) 'Development of elite performance and deliberate practice: An update from the perspective of the expert performance approach', in J. L. Starkes & K. A. Ericsson (eds) *Expert performance in sports: Advances in research on sport expertise*, Champaign: IL, Human Kinetics, 49–84.

Ericsson, K. A. (2007) 'Deliberate practice and the modifiability of body and mind: Toward a science of the structure and acquisition of expert and elite performance', *International Journal of Sport Psychology*, 38: 4–34.

Ericsson, K. A., Krampe, R. Th., & Tesch-Roemer, C. (1993). 'The role of deliberate practice in the acquisition of expert performance', *Psychological Review*, 100: 363–406.

Eskenazi, T., van der Wel, R., & Sebanz, N. (2012) 'Mechanisms of skilled joint action performance', in A. M. Williams & N. J. Hodges (eds) *Skill acquisition in sport: Research, theory and practice*, 2nd ed., New York: Routledge, 229–46.

Farrow, D., Baker, J., & McMahon, C. (eds) (2008) *Developing sports expertise: Researchers and coaches put theory into practice*, London: Routledge.

Ford, P. R., Hodges, N. J., & Williams, A. M. (2005) 'Online attentional-focus manipulations in a soccer-dribbling task: Implications for the proceduralization of motor skills', *Journal of Motor Behaviour*, 37: 386–94.

Ford, P. R., Hodges, N. J., & Williams, A. M. (2013) 'Creating champions: The development of expertise in sports', in S. B. Kaufman (ed) *The complexity of greatness: Beyond talent or practice*, New York: Oxford University Press, 391–413.

Ford, P. R., Yates, I., & Williams, A. M. (2010) 'An analysis of practice activities and instructional behaviours used by youth soccer coaches during practice: Exploring the link between science and application', *Journal of Sports Sciences*, 28: 483–95.

Fuchs, A. H. (1962) 'The progression-regression hypotheses in perceptual-motor skill learning', *Journal of Experimental Psychology*, 63: 177–82.

Gladwell, M. (2008) *Outliers: The story of success*, New York: Little & Brown.

Gray, R. (2004) 'Attending to the execution of a complex sensorimotor skill: expertise differences, choking, and slumps', *Journal of Experimental Psychology Applied*, 10: 42–54.

Guadagnoli, M. A., & Lee, T. D. (2004) 'Challenge point: A framework for conceptualizing the effects of various practice methods in motor learning', *Journal of Motor Behavior*, 36: 212–24.

Principles of effective practice

Hartman, J. M. (2007) 'Self-controlled use of a perceived physical assistance device during a balancing task', *Perceptual and Motor Skills*, 104: 1005–16.

Hendry, D. T., Crocker, P.R.E., & Hodges, N. J. (2014) 'Practice and play as determinants of self-determined motivation in youth soccer players', *Journal of Sports Sciences*, 32(11): 1091–9.

Hodges, N. J., & Baker, J. (2011) 'Expertise: The goal of performance development', in D. Collins, A. Button, H. Richards (eds) *Performance psychology: A practitioner's guide*, Oxford: Elsevier Publishers, 31–46.

Hodges, N. J., Edwards, C., Luttin, S., & Bowcock (2011) 'Learning from the experts: Gaining insights into best practice during the acquisition of three novel motor skills', *Research Quarterly for Exercise & Sport*, 82: 178–87.

Hodges, N. J., & Franks, I. M. (2002) 'Modelling coaching practice: The role of instruction and demonstration', *Journal of Sport Sciences*, 20: 793–811.

Hodges, N. J., & Franks, I. M. (2004) 'Instructions, demonstrations and the learning process: Creating and constraining movement options', in N. J. Hodges & A. M. Williams (eds) *Skill acquisition in sport: Research, theory and practice*, Oxford: Routledge, 145–74.

Huang, V. S., Shadmehr, R., & Diedrichsen, J. (2008) 'Active learning: Learning a motor skill without a coach', *Journal of Neurophysiology*, 100: 879–87.

Janelle, C. M., Barba, D. A., Frehlich, S. G., Tennant, L. K., & Cauraugh, J. H. (1997) 'Maximizing performance effectiveness through videotape replay and a self-controlled learning environment', *Research Quarterly for Exercise & Sport*, 68: 269–79.

Janelle, C. M., Kim, J. G., & Singer, R. N. (1995) 'Subject-controlled performance feedback and learning of a closed motor skill', *Perceptual and Motor Skills*, 81: 627–34.

Karlinsky, A., & Hodges, N. J. (in press) '"Self" or "other" directed learning in pairs: Isolating autonomy in practice', *Journal of Motor Learning and Development*.

Keetch, K., & Lee, T. D. (2007) 'The effect of self-regulated and experimenter-imposed practice schedules on motor learning for tasks of varying difficulty', *Research Quarterly for Exercise & Sport*, 78: 476–86.

Lam W. K., Maxwell, J. P., & Masters, R.S.W. (2009) 'Analogy versus explicit learning of a modified basketball shooting task: Performance and kinematic outcomes', *Journal of Sports Sciences*, 27: 179–91.

Lavery, J. J. (1962) 'Retention of simple motor skills as a function of type of knowledge of results', *Canadian Journal of Psychology*, 16: 300–11.

Lee, T. D. (2012) 'Scheduling practice', in A. M. Williams & N. J. Hodges (eds) *Skill acquisition in sport: Research, theory and practice*, 2nd ed., London: Routledge, 79–93.

Lee, T. D., & Magill, R. A. (1985) 'Can forgetting facilitate skill acquisition?', in D. Goodman, R. B. Wilberg, & I. M. Franks (eds) *Differing perspectives in motor learning, memory and control*, Amsterdam: North-Holland, 3–22.

Lee, T. D., Magill, R. A., & Weeks, D. J. (1985) 'Influence of practice schedule on testing schema theory predictions in adults', *Journal of Motor Behavior*, 17: 283–99.

Lewthwaite, R., & Wulf, G. (2010) 'Social-comparative feedback affects motor skill learning', *Quarterly Journal of Experimental Psychology*, 63: 738–49.

Lewthwaite, R., & Wulf, G. (2012) 'Motivation and skill learning', in A. M. Williams & N. J. Hodges (eds) *Skill acquisition in sport: Research, theory and practice*, 2nd ed., London: Routledge, 173–91.

Liao, C. M., & Masters, R.S.W. (2001) 'Analogy learning: A means to implicit motor learning', *Journal of Sports Sciences*, 19: 307–19.

Liao, C. M., & Masters, R.S.W. (2002) 'Self-focused attention and performance failure under psychological stress', *Journal of Sport & Exercise Psychology*, 24: 289–305.

Lohse, K. R., Wulf, G., & Lewthwaite, R. (2012) 'Attentional focus affects movement efficiency', in A. M. Williams & N. J. Hodges (eds) *Skill acquisition in sport: Research, theory and practice*, 2nd ed., London: Routledge, 40–58.

Low, J., Williams, A. M., McRobert, A. P., & Ford, P. R. (2013) 'The microstructure of practice activities engaged in by elite and recreational youth cricket players', *Journal of Sport Sciences*, 31: 1242–50.

Magill, R. A., & Anderson, D. I. (2012) 'The roles and uses of augmented feedback in motor skill acquisition', in A. M. Williams & N. J. Hodges (eds) *Skill acquisition in sport: Research, theory and practice*, 2nd ed., London: Routledge, 3–21.

Magill, R. A., & Wood, C. A. (1986) 'Knowledge of results precision as a learning variable in motor skill acquisition', *Research Quarterly for Exercise and Sport*, 57: 170–3.

Masters, R.S.W., & Maxwell, J. P. (2004) 'Implicit motor learning, reinvestment and movement disruption: What you don't know won't hurt you?', in A. M. Williams & N. J. Hodges (eds) *Skill acquisition in sport: Research, theory and practice*, London: Routledge, 207–28.

Masters, R.S.W., & Poolton, J. M. (2012) 'Implicit motor learning', in A. M. Williams & N. J. Hodges (eds) *Skill acquisition in sport: Research, theory and practice*, 2nd ed., London: Routledge, 59–75.

Maxwell, J. P., Masters, R.S.W., & Poolton, J. M. (2006) 'Performance breakdown in sport: The roles of reinvestment and verbal knowledge', *Research Quarterly for Sport and Exercise*, 77: 271–6.

Maurer, H., & Munzert, J. (2013) 'Influence of attentional focus on motor skill performance: Performance decrements under unfamiliar conditions', *Human Movement Science*, 32: 730–40.

McCullagh, P., & Caird, J. K. (1990) 'Correct learning models and use of knowledge of results in the acquisition and retention of a motor skill', *Journal of Human Movement Studies*, 18: 107–16.

McNevin, N. H., Shea, C. H., & Wulf, G. (2003) 'Increasing the distance of an external focus of attention enhances learning', *Psychological Research*, 67: 22–9.

Miller, G. A. (1956) 'The magical number seven plus or minus two: Some limits on our capacity for processing information', *Psychological Review*, 62: 81–97.

Newell, K. M. (1986) 'Constraints on the development of coordination', in M. G. Wade & H.T.A. Whiting (eds) *Motor development in children. Aspects of coordination and control*, Dordrecht, NL: Martinus Nijhoff, 341–60.

Ong, N. T., Bowcock, A., & Hodges, N. J. (2010) 'Manipulations to the timing and type of instructions to examine motor skill performance under pressure', *Frontiers in Psychology*, 1: 1–13.

Ong, N. T., & Hodges, N. J. (2012) 'Mixing it up a little: How to schedule observational practice', in A. M. Williams & N. J. Hodges (eds) *Skill acquisition in sport: Research, theory and practice*, 2nd ed., London: Routledge, 22–39.

Ong, N. T., Larsson, B., & Hodges, N. J. (2011) 'In the absence of physical practice, observation and imagery do not result in the updating of internal models for aiming', *Experimental Brain Research*, 291: 9–19.

Pachman, M., Sweller, J., & Kalyuga, S. (2013) 'Levels of knowledge and deliberate practice', *Journal of Experimental Psychology: Applied*, 19: 108–19.

Patterson, J. T., & Carter, M. (2010) 'Learner regulated knowledge of results during the acquisition of multiple timing goals', *Human Movement Science*, 29: 214–27.

Patterson, J. T., & Lee, T. D. (2008) 'Organizing practice: The interaction of repetition and cognitive effort for skilled performance', in D. Farrow, J. Baker, & C. McMahon (eds) *Developing sports expertise: Researchers and coaches put theory into practice*, London: Routledge, 119–34.

Phillips, E., Farrow, D., Ball, K., & Helmer, R. (2013) 'Harnessing and understanding feedback technology in applied settings', *Sports Medicine*, 43: 919–25.

Poolton, J. M., Masters, R.S.W., & Maxwell, J. P. (2005) 'The relationship between initial errorless learning conditions and subsequent performance', *Human Movement Science*, 24: 362–78.

Porter, J. M., & Magill, R. A. (2010) 'Systematically increasing contextual interference is beneficial for learning sport skills', *Journal of Sports Sciences*, 28: 1277–85.

Richards P., Collins, D., & Mascarenhas, D.R.D. (2012) 'Developing rapid high-pressure team decision-making skills. The integration of slow deliberate reflective learning within the competitive performance environment: A case study of elite netball', *Reflective Practice: International and Multidisciplinary Perspectives*, 13: 407–24.

Richardson, J.R., & Lee, T.D. (1999) 'The effects of proactive and retroactive demonstrations on learning signed letters', *Acta Psychologica*, 101: 79–90.

Rohbanfard, H., & Proteau, L. (2011) 'Learning through observation: A combination of expert and novice models favors learning', *Experimental Brain Research*, 215: 183–97.

Salmoni, A. W., Schmidt, R. A., & Walter, C. B. (1984) 'Knowledge of results and motor learning: A review and critical reappraisal', *Psychological Bulletin*, 95: 355–86.

Sanli, E. A., Patterson, J. T., Bray, S. R., & Lee, T. D. (2013) 'Understanding self-controlled motor learning protocols through the self-determination theory', *Frontiers in Psychology*, 3: 1–17.

Schmidt, R. A., & Lee, T. D. (2011) *Motor learning and control*, 5th ed., Champaign, IL: Human Kinetics Publishers.

Seifert, L., Button, C., & Davids, K. (2013) 'Key properties of expert movement systems in sport: An ecological dynamics perspective', *Sports Medicine*, 43: 167–78.

Shea, C.H., Kohl, R., & Indermill, C. (1990) 'Contextual interference: Contributions of practice', *Acta Psychologica*, 73: 145–57.

Shea, C. H., Wright, D. L., Wulf, G., & Whitacre, C. (2000) 'Physical and observational practice afford unique learning opportunities', *Journal of Motor Behavior*, 32: 119–25.

Shea, C. H., Wulf, G., & Whitacre, C. (1999) 'Enhancing training efficiency and effectiveness through the use of dyad training', *Journal of Motor Behavior*, 31: 119–25.

Principles of effective practice

Shebilske, W. L., Regian, J. W., Arthur, W., & Jordan, J. A. (1992) 'A dyadic protocol for training complex skills', *Human Factors*, 34: 369–74.

Sherwood, D. E. (1988) 'Effect of bandwidth knowledge of results on movement consistency', *Perceptual & Motor Skills*, 66: 535–42.

Vinter, A., & Chartrel, E. (2010) 'Effects of different types of learning on handwriting movements in young children', *Learning and Instruction*, 20: 476–86.

Ward, P., Hodges, N. J., Williams, A. M., & Starkes, J. L. (2004) 'Deliberate practice and expert performance: Defining the path to excellence', in A. M. Williams & N. J. Hodges (eds) *Skill acquisition in sport: Research theory and practice*, New York: Routledge, 231–58.

Weeks, D. L., & Anderson, L. P. (2000) 'The interaction of observational learning with overt practice: Effects on motor skill learning', *Acta Psychologica*, 104: 259–71.

Williams, A. M., Ford, P. R., Eccles, D. W., & Ward, P. (2011) 'Perceptual-cognitive expertise in sport and its acquisition: Implications for applied cognitive psychology', *Applied Cognitive Psychology*, 25: 432–42.

Williams, A. M., & Hodges, N. J. (2005) 'Practice, instruction and skill acquisition in soccer: Challenging tradition', *Journal of Sports Sciences*, 23: 637–50.

Wrisberg, C. A., & Pein, R. L. (2002) 'Note on learners' control of the frequency of model presentation during skill acquisition', *Perceptual & Motor Skills*, 94: 792–4.

Wulf, G. (2007) *Attention and motor skill learning*, Champaign, IL: Human Kinetics.

Wulf, G., Chiviacowsky, S., & Lewthwaite, R. (2010) 'Normative feedback effects on learning a timing task', *Research Quarterly for Exercise and Sport*, 81: 425–31.

Wulf, G., Clauss, A., Shea, C. H., & Whitacre, C. (2001) 'Benefits of self-control in dyad practice', *Research Quarterly for Exercise and Sport*, 72: 299–303.

Wulf, G., & Lewthwaite, R. (2009) 'Conceptions of ability affect motor learning', *Journal of Motor Behavior*, 41: 461–7.

Wulf, G., & Shea, C. H. (2002) 'Principles derived from the study of simple skills do not generalize to complex skill learning', *Psychonomic Bulletin & Review*, 9: 185–211.

Wulf, G., & Shea, C. H. (2004) 'Understanding the role of augmented feedback: The good, the bad, and the ugly', in A. M. Williams & N. J. Hodges (eds) *Skill acquisition in sport: Research, theory and practice*, London: Routledge, 121–44.

Wulf, G., Shea, C. H., & Matschiner, S. (1998) 'Frequent feedback enhances complex motor skill learning', *Journal of Motor Behavior*, 30: 180–92.

Wulf, G., & Toole, T. (1999) 'Physical assistance devices in complex motor skill learning: Benefits of a self-controlled practice schedule', *Research Quarterly for Exercise and Sport*, 70: 265–72.

Young, D. E., & Schmidt, R. A. (1992) 'Augmented feedback for enhanced skill acquisition', in G. E. Stelmach & J. Requin (eds) *Tutorials in motor behavior II*, Amsterdam: Elsevier, 677–93.

37

EFFICACY OF TRAINING INTERVENTIONS FOR ACQUIRING PERCEPTUAL-COGNITIVE SKILL

Jörg Schorer, Florian Loffing, Rebecca Rienhoff,
and Norbert Hagemann

Numerous expert-nvice studies have confirmed that expert athletes possess special perceptual-cognitive skills (Mann *et al.*, 2007; Williams *et al.*, 1999). These skills are particularly necessary in racket and ball sports where performance is decisively codetermined by cognitive factors. Perceptual-cognitive skills can be defined as involving a selective intake of information from the surroundings and the use of elaborate memory structures to produce a situationally adequate outcome of play (Mann *et al.*, 2007). The differences in perceptual-cognitive skills between experts and novices have led to the development of specific training interventions designed to improve these skills. Over the past decade, a central focus has been to determine the best way to organize the training of perceptual-cognitive skills and to ascertain how best to transfer the results of laboratory studies on such skills to the field. Training interventions have frequently been carried out in the laboratory where (video) simulations were presented on a PC or a large screen. Athletes view sequences of situations in the field that have typically been recorded from the same perspective as they would take (i.e., a first-person perspective). Typically, these videos stop at a certain stage (temporal occlusion; Abernethy & Russell, 1987), and the athletes have to use the available information (before being supplied with adequate feedback) to either predict the direction of the opponent's move or indicate what they would do in this situation. The features of the field situation are selected to train special components of perceptual-cognitive skills such as anticipation and decision-making, "quiet eye" behavior, or pattern perception.

Because of the enormous significance of perceptual and decision-making processes for top-ranking athletic performance, there have also been attempts to improve basic visual abilities such as depth perception, visual acuity, and peripheral vision (Williams & Grant, 1999). However, when it comes to improving task-specific performance (e.g., correctly interpreting the sequence of movement to predict the direction of a tennis serve), the utility of such programs is doubtful and has not been confirmed empirically (Abernethy & Wood, 2001). Although some studies have indicated that experts score better than novices on certain basic cognitive components (Overney *et al.*, 2008; Voss *et al.*, 2010), previous work in this field suggests that there generally tend to be no experience-dependent differences (Helsen & Starkes, 1999; Ward *et al.*, 2000; Yarrow *et al.*, 2009). For example, in an expert-novice study of youth soccer players, Ward *et al.* (2000) were unable

Efficacy of training interventions

to confirm any relation between general visual perception performance and sport performance (however, see Laby *et al.*, 1996, regarding baseball).

This chapter provides an overview of training interventions that apply task-specific interventions to improve perceptual-cognitive skills. In addition, it focuses on athletes and does not consider training programs to improve perceptual-cognitive skills in other groups (e.g., referees; Put *et al.*, 2013; Schweizer *et al.*, 2011). For reasons of space, we do not present an in-depth discussion of the suspected influence of motor competence on the processes involved in perceiving and reaching decisions on human movements (Aglioti *et al.*, 2008; Bruce *et al.*, 2012; Casile & Giese, 2006) or report on approaches for comparing laboratory-based visual perception interventions with field-based procedures (Hagemann & Memmert, 2006).

Training anticipation and decision-making

Unlike general training programs, the training of perceptual-cognitive skills through task-specific simulations can draw on a large body of empirical research (for reviews, see Abernethy *et al.*, 1998; Ward *et al.*, 2008; Ward *et al.*, 2006; Williams *et al.*, 2011; Williams & Grant, 1999; Williams & Ward, 2003). These interventions generally follow the expert performance approach by using testing and training conditions designed to deliver the closest possible simulation of the real perceptual and cognitive demands facing the athlete (Williams & Ericsson, 2005). Programs focus on training anticipatory and decision-making skills, which are an essential element of sport performance in racket and ball games and where robust differences have been found in expert-novice studies (Mann *et al.*, 2007). In comparison, the majority of training programs have tried to improve anticipatory skills, possibly because it is relatively easy to record simulation videos from an athlete's perspective to obtain a high-fidelity measure that closely matches simulations with real field situations (Hays & Singer, 1989). For decision-making skills, often relevant field situations are recorded from an unnatural overview perspective (e.g., from behind or above), and study participants are asked to place themselves in the position of one particular person in the video (e.g., Lorains *et al.*, 2013; Raab, 2003; Starkes & Lindley, 1994). Such procedures somewhat impair fidelity, because the perspective does not match that of the athlete during execution of the task.

Particularly in racket sports, experts stand out because they are better at anticipating the actions or reactions of their opponent (Williams *et al.*, 1999). Therefore, task-specific training studies try to train the perception of typical movement patterns (e.g., the serve in tennis). The goal is to recognize differences in the way the opponent executes early phases of a movement, to link these differences to different action outcomes (e.g., direction of serve) and use this information to optimize one's own subsequent action. Drawing on earlier research on anticipation, potential anticipation-relevant sources of information for predicting the direction of the ball flight in tennis serves have been identified (Cauraugh & Janelle, 2002). Anticipation training can also be used to familiarize athletes with less common movement patterns (e.g., left-handed 7 m throws in handball; Schorer *et al.*, 2012) in order to counteract potential performance disadvantages (Hagemann, 2009; Loffing *et al.*, 2012).

Looking at training studies to improve anticipatory and decision-making skills, it is worth noticing that they frequently recruit novices or less-skilled players as participants. Of course, it is easier to achieve performance gains at a lower skill level, and some studies note the difficulty in improving anticipatory and decision-making skills in experts (Gorman & Farrow, 2009; Hagemann *et al.*, 2006). For example, Hagemann *et al.* (2006) reported that a 45-minute perception intervention that was successful with novices and local league players failed to produce any improvements in anticipatory performance in badminton players from the first and second national leagues. However, other evidence indicates that even high-performance athletes such as

431

international cricket players may benefit from perceptual training; see, for example, a cricket-specific field test after a six-week, video-based training program (Hopwood *et al.*, 2011).

How should athletes be instructed in these training programs?

Numerous studies have examined the effects of different instructions on the efficacy of perceptual training (e.g., Abernethy *et al.*, 2012; Farrow & Abernethy, 2002; Poulter *et al.*, 2005; Smeeton *et al.*, 2005; Williams *et al.*, 2002a). The question is whether one can identify a single superior instruction method that will get athletes in a specific sport to pay attention to the most relevant movement characteristics (see Memmert *et al.*, 2009; on the influence of feedback: Schorer *et al.*, 2010). Basically, instruction methods in visual perception interventions vary according to how explicitly they inform participants about the relevant movement characteristics in a specific type of sport (Jackson & Farrow, 2005).

This relates more generally to the discussion on implicit vs. explicit learning methods in motor learning (Masters, 2000). For example, Farrow and Abernethy (2002) studied the influence of explicit and implicit instructions on prediction of tennis serves. An explicit learning group completed 12 training sessions with 50 video clips that emphasized the relations between certain movement characteristics (e.g., ball toss, service grip, and shoulder rotation) and the direction of the serve. The implicit learning group viewed the same video clips and had to estimate the speed of the serve. Compared to the explicit group and the control and placebo groups (no video training or viewing excerpts from professional tennis matches), the implicit learning group was able to improve prediction performance significantly in a post-test. However, this increase could not be replicated in a retention test 32 days later.

Williams *et al.* (2002b) studied the efficacy of two different instruction methods by assessing performance in predicting groundstrokes in tennis. An explicitly instructed group received information on the most important movement characteristics and how they related to the direction of the shot. Members of another group (guided discovery) had the movement characteristics pointed out to them, but had to find out the relation between body posture and the direction of the shot by themselves. Results showed no differences in efficacy between the two groups. However, both groups were able to reduce their reaction times compared to a placebo group and a control group, in both a laboratory test and an anticipation test in the field.

Hagemann *et al.* (2006) studied the effects of an attention cue in video clips on novices' performance in predicting overhead strokes in badminton, using a pre-post-retention test design. The attention cue was a transparent red patch that highlighted the critical regions (torso, racket, and arm). Compared to controls, the video-based (without attention cues) and the attention-cueing training group markedly improved their prediction performance over the three measurement times. However, a difference between the two training groups became apparent in the retention test. Participants who trained with the attention-cueing video clips showed a further marked improvement in performance compared to the post-test. Novices receiving attention cues pointing to the relevant body areas were able to recognize the differences in the movement patterns associated with different stroke directions more quickly than novices not receiving such cues (see Ryu *et al.*, 2013, and Savelsbergh *et al.*, 2010, for similiar positive effects of visual guidance).

Abernethy *et al.* (2012), in contrast, found no advantage to this kind of instruction compared to controls in a video-based, anticipatory intervention of 7 m throws in handball. They found that initially (from pre- to post-test), explicit and verbal cueing (as a kind of guided discovery) learning groups showed the largest increase in learning, and that the implicit learning group had an advantage under stress conditions (see also Smeeton *et al.*, 2005), as well as in a retention test five months later.

Efficacy of training interventions

The results of studies on training are encouraging. They confirm that task-specific perceptual processes can be improved through focused training interventions. However, it is still necessary to clarify how far the effects on performance achieved in the laboratory can be transferred to performance in the field.

Can effects of training be confirmed in the field?

Williams, Ward, and Chapman (2003) studied the effect of a video-based intervention on novice female field hockey goalkeepers' anticipation of penalty flicks, with the aim of finding a potential transfer to real field conditions. The group completing the video-based training program sped up its reaction times by about 100 milliseconds while not making more mistakes than in the pre-test. Such positive effect was confirmed in the field test where this group reached its decisions, on average, 50 milliseconds earlier (a significant difference) and made fewer mistakes (a non-significant trend). In the placebo and control group, no changes were found in both laboratory and field testing.

Farrow and Abernethy (2002) reported similar findings when examining the effect of implicit, video-based training of return of tennis serves on reaction behavior on the tennis court. Even though video-based training programs did not link the perceptual component directly to the sporting action, they still influenced the sporting reaction under real conditions (Farrow & Abernethy, 2002).

The results underline the effect of video-based training on perceptual or anticipatory performance in sport and confirm some transfer of the performance gains acquired and measured in the laboratory to real field conditions (see also Gabbett *et al.*, 2007; Hopwood *et al.*, 2011; Williams *et al.*, 2002b). Nonetheless, it has to be acknowledged that some of the field tests represent a restriction of real playing conditions and that the task structure frequently overlaps with that in the laboratory test. Therefore, improved transfer tests are required to evaluate future training studies (see Williams & Grant, 1999).

Looking to stabilize – training of quiet eye

The "quiet eye," as a characteristic of perceptual expertise and its methodological issues, has been described in more detail in earlier chapters (cf. Chapters 7 and 19). As a reminder, the quiet eye is defined as the final fixation or tracking gaze on a specific location or object in the visuomotor workspace within three degrees of visual angle for a minimum of 100 milliseconds. Furthermore, onset of the quiet eye period occurs prior to the initiation of the final movement in the task, and offset occurs when the gaze deviates off the location by more than three degrees of visual angle for a minimum of 100 milliseconds (Vickers, 2007). In studies focusing on *inter*-individual differences, skill was associated with longer quiet eye durations and an earlier onset of the final fixation prior to conducting the task (e.g., Causer *et al.*, 2010; Vickers, 1996; Vickers & Williams, 2007; Williams *et al.*, 2002a). In addition, studies on *intra*-individual differences (e.g., comparison of made and missed shots in basketball) demonstrated longer and specifically timed quiet eye durations associated with better performance (Harle & Vickers, 2001; Janelle *et al.*, 2000; Vickers, 1996; Vickers & Adolphe, 1997). These findings suggest that quiet eye training should aim to either prolong the quiet eye duration or to adjust the timing of the quiet eye duration.

In quiet eye training, two main lines of research have been conducted. The first investigates whether findings from the motor learning literature can be transferred to the training of quiet eye, the focus being on instructions, schedule of practice, or feedback (cf. Adolphe *et al.*, 1997; Causer *et al.*, 2011; Harle & Vickers, 2001). The second line of research focuses on whether quiet eye training can reduce the perception of anxiety and pressure or even prevent phenomena like choking under pressure (cf. Moore *et al.*, 2012a, 2012b; Vine *et al.*, 2011; Vine & Wilson, 2010, 2011; Wood & Wilson, 2011, 2012). The two lines of research will be elaborated on in the following subsections.

Instructions, practice schedules, and feedback in quiet eye training

Causer, Holmes, and Williams (2011) investigated the role of instructions in improving efficiency of gaze behavior through perceptual training. Two groups of elite shotgun shooters were compared. One group trained under specific quiet eye protocols and another without explicit instruction on gaze behavior. After an eight-week training intervention, the quiet eye training group demonstrated superior performance in shooting accuracy, quiet eye duration, and quiet eye onset. The authors suggested that improvements resulted from an extended period for motor programming and optimal arousal control.

In comparison, Horn and colleagues (2012) studied the role of schedule of practice, demonstrating that dart novices were responsive to variability of practice and changes in target axis. More specifically, longer quite eye durations were elicited by both random practice conditions and changes of targets along the horizontal axis (as compared to target changes along the vertical axis). Surprisingly, neither of those factors affected the novices' throwing performance, which might be explained by the overall high variability of novices' throwing performance.

With regard to the impact of feedback on the efficacy on quiet eye training, Adolphe *et al.* (1997) conducted a six-week intervention with elite volleyball players, noting that provision of video feedback on the players' gaze behavior resulted in an earlier tracking onset and an improved tracking duration from pre- to post-test. In another study, Harle and Vickers (2001) conducted a two-season training intervention on basketball free throws with near-experts. Participants received feedback on their own gaze behavior in comparison to an elite model. The training program led to an improvement (> 20 per cent) in throwing performance and to longer, more stable quiet eye durations.

Pressure situations and quiet eye training

The second line of research on quiet eye training under specific conditions was conducted by Mark Wilson and his research group (Moore *et al.*, 2012b; Vine *et al.*, 2011; Vine & Wilson, 2010, 2011; Wood & Wilson, 2011, 2012). In a series of studies, they investigated whether quiet eye training expedites the learning of motor skills in novices and if the acquired skills are more robust in pressure situations (Moore *et al.*, 2012b; Vine & Wilson, 2010, 2011). For basketball free throws, for example, Vine and Wilson (2011) demonstrated that a quiet eye training group performed significantly better than a control group (technical instructions only) in both a retention and a pressure test. In a golf putting study, Moore and colleagues (2012b) replicated these findings and extended our understanding of quiet eye training effects through considering kinematic and physiological parameters. Kinematic analyses of club head acceleration revealed a mediation of between-group differences, indicating that a seven-day quiet eye training intervention resulted in a more accurate putter-ball interaction. Additionally, heart rate and muscle activity were reduced in the quiet eye training group as opposed to the technical training group in both retention and pressure tests.

Many of the above findings with novices have also been replicated with advanced athletes (Vine *et al.*, 2011; Wood & Wilson, 2011, 2012). Vine and colleagues (2011) conducted a quiet eye intervention with elite golfers and tested their performance in comparison to a control

Efficacy of training interventions

group under pressure in the lab, as well as in real competition. In line with earlier findings on novices, the training group showed longer quiet eye durations under pressure. Additionally, they demonstrated better performance in lab and in field situations. Similarly, in a study by Wood and Wilson (2011), a seven-week intervention on soccer penalty shooting led to more effective visual-attentional control in a quiet eye training group compared to a placebo group. Additionally, the quiet eye training group had more accurate shots and 50 per cent fewer shots saved by the goalkeeper. Differences in quiet eye were maintained under pressure situations; however, shooting performance deteriorated in both training groups. Moreover, Wood and Wilson (2012) examined the impact of quiet eye training on experienced soccer players' perceived (psychological) control beliefs in soccer penalty shooting. Compared to a practice group (i.e., practice without instruction), a quiet eye training group demonstrated better performance and longer quiet eye durations, which came with a reduction in perceived contingency (outcome uncertainty) and an increase in perceived competence (shooting stability) and control (ability to cope under pressure). Furthermore, players with high control beliefs aimed more optimally and further away from the goalkeeper.

Training of pattern recall and recognition

The role of pattern recall and recognition for sporting expertise has been documented (cf. Chapter 18). However, as noted by Williams and Ward (2003), research on its trainability is scarce, and, somewhat surprisingly, little effort has been made to advance our understanding. To our knowledge, there is only one training study that has investigated the effects of pattern recall or recognition training. Schorer and colleagues (under review) recently tested the efficacy of a combined field and lab training program for improving tactical skills. Two groups of skilled youth football players received normal field training on tactical positioning in specific game situations twice per week for four weeks. A third group (placebo group) also received normal field training that was not related to the specific game situations. In addition, one of the two groups that received tactical training in specific game situations underwent a 30-minute, lab-based intervention in addition to the normal field training session. In each lab-based training session, videos of game situations similar to those experienced during the field training were presented. These videos stopped at unpredictable time points, and participants were then asked to recall playing positions. Compared to the other two groups, the additional lab training group demonstrated the largest improvements in recall performance from pre- to post-test and was superior at retaining its pattern recall knowledge after four weeks of unfilled retention.

Conclusion

Recent perceptual-cognitive training programs try to create a situation that is as close as possible to the real world environment where the task-specific (re)actions are required (Williams *et al.*, 2004). Technological progress is likely to increase the use of virtual realities in future training programs in order to improve their fidelity (Miles *et al.*, 2012). Moreover, these programs may be used to selectively train individual aspects of a perceptual-cognitive skill or to draw athletes' attention to unfamiliar movement patterns (Schorer *et al.*, 2012). Implicit forms of training (e.g., self-discovery learning of the relations between the characteristics and the outcome of movements during anticipation training) appear to be as effective as explicit instructions in the form of, for example, if-then rules, and even beneficial in terms of performance stability under stress conditions (Jackson & Farrow, 2005). Collectively, task-specific training interventions may assist athletes in acquiring or improving perceptual-cognitive skill. However, the extent to which these

Jörg Schorer et al.

positive effects are a) sustainable, b) transferable to the field, and c) able to facilitate high achievement in sports remains insufficiently addressed in current research.

References

Abernethy, B., & Russell, D.G. (1987) 'Expert-novice differences in an applied selective attention task', *Journal of Sport Psychology*, 9: 326–45.

Abernethy, B., Schorer, J., Jackson, R.C., & Hagemann, N. (2012) 'Perceptual training methods compared: The relative efficacy of different approaches to enhancing sport-specific anticipation', *Journal of Experimental Psychology: Applied*, 18: 143–53.

Abernethy, B., Wann, J.P., & Parks, S.L. (1998) 'Training perceptual-motor skills for sport', in B. Elliott (ed) *Training in sport: Applying sport science*, Chichester, UK: Wiley, 1–68.

Abernethy, B., & Wood, J.M. (2001) 'Do generalized visual training programmes for sport really work? An experimental investigation', *Journal of Sports Sciences*, 19: 203–22.

Adolphe, R.M., Vickers, J.N., & La Plante, G. (1997) 'The effects of training visual attention on gaze behaviour and accuracy: A pilot study', *International Journal of Sports Vision*, 4: 28–33.

Aglioti, S.M., Cesari, P., Romani, M., & Urgesi, C. (2008) 'Action anticipation and motor resonance in elite basketball players', *Nature Neuroscience*, 11: 1109–16.

Bruce, L., Farrow, D., Raynor, A., & Mann, D. (2012) 'But I can't pass that far! The influence of motor skill on decision making', *Psychology of Sport and Exercise*, 13: 152–61.

Casile, A., & Giese, M.A. (2006) 'Nonvisual motor training influences biological motion perception', *Current Biology*, 16: 69–74.

Cauraugh, J.H., & Janelle, C.M. (2002) 'Visual search and cue utilisation in racket sports', in K. Davids, G.J.P. Savelsbergh, S.J. Bennett, & J. van der Kamp (eds) *Interceptive actions in sport*, London: Routledge, 64–89.

Causer, J., Bennett, S.J., Holmes, P.S., Janelle, C.M., & Williams, A.M. (2010) 'Quiet eye duration and gun motion in elite shotgun shooting', *Medicine and Science in Sports and Exercise*, 42: 1599–1608.

Causer, J., Holmes, P.S., & Williams, A.M. (2011) 'Quiet eye training in a visuomotor control task', *Medicine and Science in Sports and Exercise*, 43: 1042–9.

Farrow, D., & Abernethy, B. (2002) 'Can anticipatory skills be learned through implicit video-based perceptual training?', *Journal of Sports Sciences*, 20: 471–85.

Gabbett, T., Rubinoff, M., Thorburn, L., & Farrow, D. (2007) 'Testing and training anticipation skills in softball fielders', *International Journal of Sports Science and Coaching*, 2: 15–25.

Gorman, A., & Farrow, D. (2009) 'Perceptual training using explicit and implicit instructional techniques: Does it benefit skilled performers?', *International Journal of Sports Science & Coaching*, 4: 193–208.

Hagemann, N. (2009) 'The advantage of being left-handed in interactive sports', *Attention, Perception, & Psychophysics*, 71: 1641–8.

Hagemann, N., & Memmert, D. (2006) 'Coaching anticipatory skill in badminton: Laboratory versus field-based perceptual training', *Journal of Human Movement Studies*, 50: 381–98.

Hagemann, N., Strauss, B., & Cañal-Bruland, R. (2006) 'Training perceptual skill by orienting visual attention', *Journal of Sport & Exercise Psychology*, 28: 143–58.

Harle, S.K., & Vickers, J.N. (2001) 'Training quiet eye improves accuracy in the basketball free throw', *Sport Psychologist*, 15: 289–305.

Hays, R.T., & Singer, M.J. (1989) *Simulation fidelity in training system design. Bridging the gap between reality and training*, New York: Springer.

Helsen, W.F., & Starkes, J.L. (1999) 'A multidimensional approach to skilled perception and performance in sport', *Applied Cognitive Psychology*, 13: 1–27.

Hopwood, M., Mann, D., Farrow, D., & Nielsen, T. (2011) 'Does visual-perceptual training augment the fielding performance of skilled cricketers?', *International Journal of Sports Science and Coaching*, 6: 523–35.

Horn, R.R., Okumura, M.S., Alexander, M.G.F., Gardin, F.A., & Sylvester, C.T. (2012) 'Quiet eye duration is responsive to variability of practice and to the axis of target changes', *Research Quarterly for Exercise and Sport*, 83: 204–11.

Jackson, R.C., & Farrow, D. (2005) 'Implicit perceptual training: How, when, and why?', *Human Movement Science*, 24: 308–25.

Janelle, C.M., Hillman, C.H., Apparies, R.J., Murray, N.P., Meili, L., Fallon, E.A., & Hatfield, B.D. (2000) 'Expertise differences in cortical activation and gaze behavior during rifle shooting', *Journal of Sport & Exercise Psychology*, 22: 167–82.

Efficacy of training interventions

Laby, D. M., Rosenbaum, A. L., Kirschen, D. G., Davidson, J. L., Rosenbaum, L. J., Strasser, C., & Mellman, M. F. (1996) 'The visual function of professional baseball players', *American Journal of Ophthamology*, 122: 476–85.

Loffing, F., Schorer, J., Hagemann, N., & Baker, J. (2012) 'On the advantage of being left-handed in volleyball: Further evidence of the specificity of skilled visual perception', *Attention, Perception, & Psychophysics*, 74: 446–53.

Lorains, M., Ball, K., & MacMahon, C. (2013) 'An above real time training intervention for sport decision making', *Psychology of Sport and Exercise*, 14: 670–974.

Mann, D. Y., Williams, A. M., Ward, P., & Janelle, C. M. (2007) 'Perceptual-cognitive expertise in sport: A meta-analysis', *Journal of Sport & Exercise Psychology*, 29: 457–78.

Masters, R.S.W. (2000) 'Theoretical aspects of implicit learning in sport', *International Journal of Sport Psychology*, 31: 530–41.

Memmert, D., Hagemann, N., Althoetmar, R., Geppert, S., & Seiler, D. (2009) 'Conditions of practice in perceptual skill learning', *Research Quarterly for Exercise and Sport*, 80: 32–43.

Miles, H. C., Pop, S. R., Watt, S. J., Lawrence, G. P., & John, N. W. (2012) 'A review of virtual environments for training in ball sports', *Computers and Graphics (Pergamon)*, 36: 714–26.

Moore, L. J., Vine, S. J., Cooke, A., Ring, C., & Wilson, M. R. (2012b) 'Quiet eye training expedites motor learning and aids performance under heightened anxiety: The roles of response programming and external attention', *Psychophysiology*, 49: 1005–15.

Moore, L. J., Vine, S. J., Wilson, M. R., & Freeman, P. (2012a) 'The effect of challenge and threat states on performance: An examination of potential mechanisms', *Psychophysiology*, 49: 1417–25.

Overney, L. S., Blanke, O., & Herzog, M. H. (2008) 'Enhanced temporal but not attentional processing in expert tennis players', *PLoS ONE*, 3: e2380.

Poulter, D. R., Jackson, R. C., Wann, J. P., & Berry, D. C. (2005) 'The effect of learning condition on perceptual anticipation, awareness, and visual search', *Human Movement Science*, 24: 345–61.

Put, K., Wagemans, J., Jaspers, A., & Helsen, W. F. (2013) 'Web-based training improves on-field offside decision-making performance', *Psychology of Sport and Exercise*, 14: 577–85.

Raab, M. (2003) 'Implicit and explicit learning of decision making in sports is affected by complexity of situation', *International Journal of Sport Psychology*, 34: 273–88.

Ryu, D., Kim, S., Abernethy, B., & Mann, D. L. (2013) 'Guiding attention aids the acquisition of anticipatory skill in novice soccer goalkeepers', *Research Quarterly for Exercise and Sport*, 84: 252–62.

Savelsbergh, G. J.P., van Gastel, P. J., & van Kampen, P. M. (2010) 'Anticipation of penalty kicking direction can be improved by directing attention through perceptual learning', *International Journal of Sport Psychology*, 41: 24–41.

Schorer, J., Cañal-Bruland, R., & Cobley, S. (2010) 'Frequency of knowledge of results does not influence perceptual learning and retention in novices', *International Journal of Sport Psychology*, 41: 107–17.

Schorer, J., Habben, J., Fischer, L., & Baker, J. (under review) 'Augmented pattern recall training supports learning and retention of tactical skills', manuscript under review.

Schorer, J., Loffing, F., Hagemann, N., & Baker, J. (2012) 'Human handedness in interactive situations: Negative perceptual frequency effects can be reversed!', *Journal of Sports Sciences*, 30: 507–13.

Schweizer, G., Plessner, H., Kahlert, D., & Brand, R. (2011) 'A video-based training method for improving soccer referees' intuitive decision-making skills', *Journal of Applied Sport Psychology*, 23: 429–42.

Smeeton, N. J., Williams, A. M., Hodges, N. J., & Ward, P. (2005) 'The relative effectiveness of various instructional approaches in developing anticipation skill', *Journal of Experimental Psychology: Applied*, 11: 98–110.

Starkes, J. L., & Lindley, S. (1994) 'Can we hasten expertise by video simulation?', *Quest*, 46: 211–22.

Vickers, J. N. (1996) 'Control of visual attention during the basketball free throw', *American Journal of Sports Medicine*, 24: S93-S97.

Vickers, J. N. (2007) *Perception, cognition and decision training: The quiet eye in action*, Champaign, IL: Human Kinetics.

Vickers, J. N., & Adolphe, R. (1997) 'Gaze behaviour while tracking an object and aiming at a far target', *International Journal of Sports Vision*, 4: 18–27.

Vickers, J. N., & Williams, A. M. (2007) 'Performing under pressure: The effects of physiological arousal, cognitive anxiety, and gaze control in biathlon', *Journal of Motor Behavior*, 39: 381–94.

Vine, S. J., Moore, L., & Wilson, M. R. (2011) 'Quiet eye training facilitates competitive putting performance in elite golfers', *Frontiers in Psychology*, 2: 1–9.

Vine, S. J., & Wilson, M. R. (2010) 'Quiet eye training: Effects on learning and performance under pressure', *Journal of Applied Sport Psychology*, 22: 361–76.

Vine, S. J., & Wilson, M. R. (2011) 'The influence of quiet eye training and pressure on attention and visuo-motor control', *Acta Psychologica*, 136: 340–6.

Voss, M. W., Kramer, A. F., Basak, C., Prakash, R. S., & Roberts, B. (2010) 'Are expert athletes "expert" in the cognitive laboratory? A meta-analytic review of cognition and sport expertise', *Applied Cognitive Psychology*, 24: 812–26.

Ward, P., Farrow, D., Harris, K. R., Williams, A. M., Eccles, D. W., & Ericsson, K. A. (2008) 'Training perceptual-cognitive skills: Can sport psychology research inform military decision training?', *Military Psychology*, 20: S71–S102.

Ward, P., Williams, A. M., & Hancock, P. A. (2006) 'Simulation for performance and training', in K. A. Ericsson, N. Charness, P. J. Feltovich, & R. R. Hoffman (eds) *The Cambridge handbook of expertise and expert performance*, New York: Cambridge University Press, 243–62.

Ward, P., Williams, A. M., & Loran, D.F.C. (2000) 'The development of visual function in elite and sub-elite soccer players', *International Journal of Sports Vision*, 6: 1–11.

Williams, A. M., Davids, K., & Williams, J. G. (1999) *Visual perception and action in sport*, London: Routledge.

Williams, A. M., & Ericsson, K. A. (2005) 'Perceptual-cognitive expertise in sport: Some considerations when applying the expert performance approach', *Human Movement Science*, 24: 287–307.

Williams, A. M., Ford, P. R., Eccles, D. W., & Ward, P. (2011) 'Perceptual-cognitive expertise in sport and its acquisition: Implications for applied cognitive psychology', *Applied Cognitive Psychology*, 25: 432–42.

Williams, A. M., & Grant, A. (1999) 'Training perceptual skill in sport', *International Journal of Sport Psychology*, 30: 194–220.

Williams, A. M., Singer, R. N., & Frehlich, S. G. (2002a) 'Quiet eye duration, expertise, and task complexity in near and far aiming tasks', *Journal of Motor Behavior*, 34: 197–207.

Williams, A. M., & Ward, P. (2003) 'Perceptual expertise: Development in sport', in J. L. Starkes & K. A. Ericsson (eds) *Expert performance in sports*, Champaign, IL: Human Kinetics, 219–49.

Williams, A. M., Ward, P., & Chapman, C. (2003) 'Training perceptual skill in field hockey: Is there transfer from the laboratory to the field', *Research Quarterly for Exercise and Sport*, 74: 98–103.

Williams, A. M., Ward, P., Knowles, J. M., & Smeeton, N. J. (2002b) 'Anticipation skill in a real-world task: Measurement, training, and transfer in tennis', *Journal of Experimental Psychology: Applied*, 8: 259–70.

Williams, A. M., Ward, P., Smeeton, N. J., & Allen, D. (2004) 'Developing anticipation skills in tennis using on-court instruction: Perception versus perception and action', *Journal of Applied Sport Psychology*, 16: 350–60.

Wood, G., & Wilson, M. R. (2011) 'Quiet-eye training for soccer penalty kicks', *Cognitive Processing*, 12: 257–66.

Wood, G., & Wilson, M. R. (2012) 'Quiet-eye training, perceived control and performing under pressure', *Psychology of Sport and Exercise*, 13: 721–8.

Yarrow, K., Brown, P., & Krakauer, J. W. (2009) 'Inside the brain of an elite athlete: The neural processes that support high achievement in sports', *Nature Reviews Neuroscience*, 10: 585–96.

38

THE FUTURE OF SPORT EXPERTISE RESEARCH

Barriers and facilitators in theory and practice

Damian Farrow and Joseph Baker

Depending on your reading habits you have arrived at this chapter in one of a few ways. You have either systematically digested the vast array of information presented (in chapter order) that details the characteristics of sport expertise, the process it takes to develop expertise, and the associated methodological issues in gathering such information. Or you may have "cherry-picked" particular chapters before opening up here for the conclusions and recommendations. Whatever method you have used to get here, this chapter is devoted toward discussing the key factors we believe will facilitate or hinder the further evolution of sport expertise research. We draw on key issues identified in many of the preceding chapters to illustrate our point and encourage you to refer to the associated chapters (if you haven't already). The underpinning theme that will be considered in all of the issues discussed is the importance of not only designing research that drives the development of better theory, but the need for translational work that will lead to genuine changes in practice. Perhaps unlike some other fields of research, we argue that the imperative to connect with the population we are studying and the associated stakeholders we seek to influence (i.e., coaches, sports administrators, other sport scientists and parents) is particularly critical.

Better theory and superior designs

As demonstrated throughout this text, the field of sport expertise has evolved from a number of underpinning scientific disciplines. The field's early adoption of a cognitive psychology framework has meant the vast majority of work has tended to evolve from cognitive psychology's underpinning theoretical assumptions and methodological approaches (e.g., Abernethy *et al.*, 1993). Typical of any young field of research, the early theoretical and experimental paradigms adopted tend to be accepted, and the resultant body of literature is skewed or interpreted through a particular lens. However, as represented in a number of chapters in this text there has been a recent shift toward other frameworks or perspectives for examining questions of interest, such as ecological dynamics framework or one of its underpinning theoretical foundations of ecological psychology or dynamical systems (see Chapters 12, 19, and 24). It is paradigm shifts such as this, and hopefully others, with the concomitant different methods of tackling the same underpinning issues, that will guide the future of sport expertise research.

Better models of sport expertise will allow more systematic comparisons of expertise across different facets of the sport domain. As illustrated in this text, our understanding of sport expertise is not only informed by an exclusive focus on the performer, but can be enhanced by examination of the processes used by referees/judges and coaches (see Chapters 6, 34, and 35). Similarly, the continued accrual of evidence identifying and explaining the mediating influence of secondary factors on the development of sport expertise, such as the family, peers, and the environment, is a fertile area for greater research effort (see Chapters 27, 29, and 32), particularly if the methodological issues highlighted throughout this text are considered in future experimental work (see Chapter 14).

The development of better theory and models of sport expertise will, by extension, lead to (or be led by) the implementation of superior research designs. A critical starting point is how the sample being examined is defined. This has been a longstanding, unresolved issue within the sport expertise literature (see Abernethy et al., 1993). As illustrated by Baker and colleagues (Chapter 13), the need for a skill taxonomy on how to define expertise is long overdue. The impact of much of the extant literature is diminished when the actual expertise of the sample is considered in detail. For example, skilled youth players are not experts: they are skilled youth! While this issue is of strong theoretical significance, as illustrated in the deliberate practice literature (e.g., Ericsson, 2012), it is also particularly important in application. A coach's view on the relative efficacy of a particular research finding is tightly calibrated to the skill level of the participants examined. It is recommended that the field adopt a skill taxonomy such as that suggested here, so that the collective body of work can be more effectively mined through techniques like meta-analyses, such that the qualities of expert sport performance can be more strongly consolidated and refined.

Studies of sport expertise have also been generally limited in the statistical analyses used, typically relying on analysis of variance procedures or simple univariate models of association. On the one hand, these are necessary given the overwhelming reliance on retrospective methods of small samples of athletes. On the other hand, the way forward will involve recognition that the path to athletic greatness is likely not linear and almost certainly involves a more dynamic interaction between variables than has been examined to date. For instance, in a recent review paper on deliberate practice in sport, Baker and Young (2014) argued that more advanced statistical techniques are necessary to identify the nuances of these relationships over developmental time:

> It is possible that the relationship between deliberate practice and performance improvement is better captured through regressions using quadratic or exponential functions. Matthew effects, although not yet studied with respect to sport expertise, would posit that those who enjoy early success in sport development (e.g., because of early training) may increasingly benefit from subsequent affordances, rewards, and/or opportunities, which cause their amounts of deliberate practice to increasingly accelerate (curvilinear; e.g., Hancock, Adler, & Côté, 2013); however, other young athletes in the same cohort who were not as successful early on would not subsequently be afforded the same subsequent catalysts to deliberate practice and their skill acquisition pathway may look more linear.
>
> *(2014, p. 151)*

Researchers with the statistical know-how should also consider examining multiple independent and dependent variables in more dynamic, multilevel approaches, provided sufficient sample power can be obtained. For instance, using multilevel approaches where variables are grouped by proximity to the athlete (e.g., athlete-specific behaviors at one level, family-related variables at the

The future of sport expertise research

next, community-related variables at another, etc.) might tell us much about a) the interaction between different variables across development and, perhaps more importantly, b) the actual effect size of a variable when considered in combination with other factors.

Longitudinal investigations have been identified as a critical "next step" in the field of sport expertise for a significant period of time. Using the contributions of Bruce Abernethy (one of the field's pioneers) as an example, we see discussion and recommendations on the importance of this issue from as early as 1993 (see Abernethy *et al.*, 1993) and as recently as 2013 (see Abernethy, 2013). Yet, presumably due to the well-documented difficulty, challenges, and risks of such an approach, there remains an absence of such approaches in our literature. Currently, we all sit and watch with great interest the single deliberate practice case study of golfer-in-training Dan McLaughlin, "The Dan Plan" (thedanplan.com). Surely as a field we have to contribute more to this challenge than relying on the ambitions of motivated individuals.

While the challenges of longitudinal research are often discussed, solutions are rarely offered – other than "it will be difficult but necessary!" As suggested by Abernethy *et al.* (1993), one approach is to adopt a quasi-longitudinal design in which performers are tracked over the course of a season, or the like. While examples of this approach are apparent in the literature (e.g., Elferink-Gemser *et al.*, 2007; Raab & Farrow, in press), they are limited in number and only provide insight into a specific phase of the path to expert performance – usually an early or middle stage of talent development with skilled youth performers. A potential solution to make the shift to a longitudinal research approach somewhat easier is to establish greater collaboration with national sporting organizations or clubs. The sport expertise field has numerous examples of researchers with seemingly strong connections with their sport organizations. A good example is the University of Groningen group (see Chapter 28), which is well advanced in producing impactful, longitudinal work on talent development and related underpinning constructs such as the self-regulation of practice (e.g., Huijgen *et al.*, 2010; Toering *et al.*, 2009). Other countries such as Australia, Canada, Denmark, Germany, Belgium, and England also have produced cross-sectional work, suggesting that they too can work collaboratively and systematically with their national sport organizations or clubs (for examples, see Farrow, 2010; Moesch *et al.*, 2013; Schorer *et al.*, 2012; Vaeyens *et al.*, 2007; Williams *et al.*, 2012). A particular challenge of such partnerships is the need to design projects that provide short-term information (benefits) for key stakeholders through cross-sectional examinations while continuing to pursue the longitudinal question in a systematic fashion. It is acknowledged that changes in leadership in the partnering sport organizations are often problematic in maintaining the "momentum" of a longitudinal study.

More multidisciplinary investigations

A particular feature of this text has been the illustration of the wide variety of scientific disciplines that contribute to our understanding of sport expertise (for example, see Chapters 8, 11, 23, and 26). As stated in earlier chapters, the traditional cognitive psychology approach that was originally adopted may have in some way contributed to the field's not embracing other disciplines of (sport) science as strongly as it could have to assist in answering research questions. As the progress from description to explanation continues, it is going to be more important than ever to consider the issue of multidisciplinary investigations. In recent times we have seen the benefits of collaboration with neuroscientists who possess skills in the use of measurement approaches such as brain imaging techniques (e.g., fMRI: Functional Magnetic Resonance Imaging) (see Wright *et al.*, 2010 for an example). Similarly, the continued adoption of ecological dynamics approaches will necessitate the more principled use of disciplines such as biomechanics and motor control and the associated use of nonlinear analytical techniques. All the while, we should continue to build on the more established or traditional connection with various streams of psychology (see Chapters 10, 21, 22, and 28). While there are numerous examples of a multidisciplinary approach to sport expertise research, the focus has tended to be narrow – for instance, consideration of generic optometric qualities and sport-specific perceptual-cognitive skills (see Helsen & Starkes, 1999). The recognition that expertise is more than a physical skill proficiency test, or a perceptual-cognitive test, or a physical performance test, but is the interaction of all of the above and many other elements besides, is what is required (see Elferink-Gemser *et al.*, 2007 for a good example). It is not until more of this type of work is completed that we will gain a clearer understanding of when particular components of performance are more or less important at particular stages of development. Further, consideration of the sport specificity of such findings, or the generality across a class of sports (e.g., invasion games), is an important addendum to a larger volume of work in this area. Such information is critical to those seeking to identify and/or develop talent.

As extensively argued by Pinder, Headrick and Oudejans (Chapter 24), a key principle of future sport expertise research should be adherence to the principle of "task representativeness." While this claim is not that dissimilar to the challenge put to researchers by Abernethy *et al.* (1993) to value situation specificity and ecological validity, the theoretical shift away from a reliance on a cognitive psychology paradigm, coupled with the evolution in measurement approaches due to emergent technologies, is certainly making it harder for researchers to explain why they did not measure performance in a carefully considered representative experimental context. This mandate for task representativeness will be further explored and developed by those using environments such as virtual reality to explore sport expertise (see Craig & Cummins, Chapter 17). Additionally, ensuring that the measures selected in such work are able to sensitively determine differences in performance between levels of expertise will be critical (see Araújo and colleagues, Chapter 19).

The measurement of the underpinning processes of performance has traditionally been an element of experimental approaches where we have been disadvantaged relative to some other disciplines of sport science, such as physiology (see Chapters 11 and 23). For example, while it is easy for a physiologist to demonstrably measure heart rate or body fat and use it as a process measure of fitness or performance, this has not been, and is not always, the case in sport expertise research. A common criticism leveled at many aspects of sport expertise research is that it has always been difficult to demonstrate the underpinning mechanisms of expertise using appropriately objective and sensitive in situ measures of performance. This perhaps explains one reason for the popularity of collecting gaze behavior data, despite the commonly cited limitations (see Chapters 15 and 16). Coaches and athletes can easily identify with what is being measured and be provided feedback about their performances in real time. Although it is, and will continue to be, a difficult undertaking, researchers should continue to explore valid and reliable ways of capturing the essential elements of sport expertise and its development; moreover, they should recognize that for some measures (e.g., memories from the distant past) it may never be possible to capture them with sufficient objectivity and validity.

An eye on application

As has been consistently illustrated throughout this chapter, the applied value of our research must be significant if we are truly concerned with influencing sport policy, talent identification and development approaches not to mention coaching practice. Understanding the views of the various stakeholders representative of the above areas of application is insightful in this regard. While the construct of sport expertise is intuitively appealing to coaches, sports administrators, and the like, when the legacy of our collective work is discussed with this cohort, its translational impact is far

The future of sport expertise research

from clear. For instance, consider the following perspectives of our key stakeholders (i.e., sports administrators, coaches, etc.).

Stakeholder perspectives

What have stakeholders learned about deliberate practice over the last 20–30 years of research effort? Has it changed how their sport coaches/develops athletes? Commentary and observation of talent development programs would suggest the key recommendation adopted by the stakeholders is a focus on "hyper-specialization." In other words, parents are advised (either explicitly or implicitly) to get their children practicing the sport of choice from as young an age as possible. What is far less prevalent is a shift in consideration of the microstructure of coaching practice (see Chapter 36; Starkes, 2008) to ensure there is an evidence-based approach to each and every practice repetition. Similarly, it seems that not much weight is given to consideration of the demonstrated psychosocial ramifications of early specialization or the alternate approaches to skill development for children (see Chapters 27–31).

Coach perspective

How has sport expertise research influenced coaching practice? For example, how has the concept of quiet eye influenced golf coaching? Many golf coaches would simply answer, "I tell my players to focus on the ball for longer after they make contact." Or, "I place a marker under the ball and ask them to tell me what color it is." The practicality of the message and how easily it translates into a coaching strategy is what makes this particular research accessible to coaches. While not all sport expertise research will afford similar opportunities for translation, it is a point worthy of consideration. Further in this particular case, it is noteworthy to highlight the effort sport expertise pioneer Joan Vickers (see Chapters 3 and 16) put into ensuring the research found its way into the hands of the practitioners. This approach of validating one's work first in the scientific domain and then proactively translating the message to the practitioner should not be underestimated. Similarly, the approach highlighted by Renshaw and Gorman (Chapter 25) of involving the coach in the development of the research question is also very useful in ensuring one's work will impact practice.

Some concluding thoughts

The world of high-performance sport has evolved to the point that rapid translation of research findings is critical. Unfortunately, peer-reviewed articles and scholarly presentations are still the primary means of disseminating research results. This results in a considerable time lag between when research results appear and when they are put into practice. On the one hand, this obviously limits implementation of "cutting-edge" research into athlete training and coaching practice; on the other hand, this time lag has implications for researchers as well. More specifically, time lags between the identification of important research results and when they are put into practice results in an undervaluing of the role of the sport expertise researcher as a key member of the athlete development system. Ideally, sport development systems are integrated with the leading sport scientists so that both parties benefit through a bi-directional relationship where scientists are working on questions with the greatest practical significance, while at the same time accessing athlete samples and research funding to facilitate their research programs.

In order for this to occur, the lag between "results" and "application" needs to decrease. Some researchers have attempted to address this issue. Our text with Clare MacMahon, *Developing Sport*

Expertise (Farrow *et al.*, 2013), is focused on providing current science in a "coach friendly" way. Similarly, social media sources (e.g., @sweatscience and @Scienceofsport) provide valuable interpretations of current research. Furthermore, coaches and trainers (and athletes) are more educated in training science than ever before and increasingly seek out academic publications to inform their practice. The emergence of "open access" publications has improved coaches' access to this material. This Handbook has provided an extensive summary of current research on sport expertise and as the field continues to evolve, similar works will undoubtedly be required in the future.

References

Abernethy, B. M. (2013) 'Research: Informed practice', in D. Farrow, J. Baker, & C. MacMahon (eds) *Developing sport expertise: Researchers and coaches put theory into practice*, 2nd ed., Routledge, 249–55.

Abernethy, B. M., Thomas, K. T., & Thomas, J. R. (1993) 'Strategies of improving understanding of motor expertise', in J. L. Starkes & F. Allard (eds) *Cognitive issues in motor expertise*, Amsterdam: Elsevier, 317–56.

Baker, J., & Young, B. (2014) '20 years later: Deliberate practice and the development of expertise in sport', *International Review of Sport and Exercise Psychology*, 7: 135–57.

Elferink-Gemser, M. T., Visscher, C., Lemmink, K.A.P.M., & Mulder, T. (2007) 'Multidimensional performance characteristics and standard of performance in talented youth field hockey players: A longitudinal study', *Journal of Sports Sciences*, 25(4): 481–9.

Ericsson, K. A. (2012) 'Training history, deliberate practise and elite sports performance: An analysis in response to Tucker and Collins review – What makes champions?', *British Journal of Sports Medicine*, 47: 533–5.

Farrow, D. (2010) 'A multi-factorial examination of the development of skill expertise in high performance netball', *Talent Development and Excellence*, 2: 123–35.

Farrow, D., Baker, J., & MacMahon, C. (eds) (2013) *Developing sport expertise: Researchers and coaches put theory into practice*, 2nd ed., Oxford, UK: Routledge.

Hancock, D. J., Adler, A. L., & Côté, J. (2013) 'A proposed theoretical model to explain relative age effects in sport', *European Journal of Sport Science*, 13: 630–7.

Helsen, W. F., & Starkes, J. L. (1999) 'A multidimensional approach to skilled perception and performance in sport', *Applied Cognitive Psychology*, 13: 1–27.

Huijgen, B.C.H., Elferink-Gemser, M. T., Post, W., & Visscher, C. (2010) 'Development of dribbling in talented youth soccer players aged 12–19 years: A longitudinal study', *Journal of Sports Sciences*, 28(7): 689–98.

Moesch, K., Trier Hauge, M. L., Wikman, J. M., & Elbe, A. M. (2013) 'Making it to the top in team sports: Start later, intensify, and be determined!', *Talent Development & Excellence*, 5(2): 85–100.

Raab, M., & Farrow, D. (in press) 'Examining the stability and specificity of pattern recall in team handball', *International Journal of Sport Psychology*.

Schorer, J., Busch, D., Fischer, L., Pabst, J., Rienhoff, R., Sichelschmidt, P., & Strauss, B. (2012) 'Back to the future: A case report of the ongoing evaluation of the German handball talent selection and development system', in J. Baker, S. Cobley, & J. Schorer (eds) *Talent identification and development in sport: International perspectives*, Oxford, UK: Taylor & Francis Group, 119–29.

Starkes, J. L. (2008) 'The past and future of applied sport expertise research', in D. Farrow, J. Baker, & C. MacMahon (eds) *Developing elite sports performers: Lessons from theory and practice*, London: Routledge, 193–206.

Toering, T. T., Elferink-Gemser, M. T., Jordet, G., & Visscher, C. (2009) 'Self-regulation and performance level of elite and non-elite youth soccer players', *Journal of Sports Sciences*, 27: 14, 1509–17.

Vaeyens, R., Lenoir, M., Williams, A. M., & Philipparts, R. M. (2007) 'Mechanisms underpinning successful decision making in skilled youth soccer players: An analysis of visual search behaviors', *Journal of Motor Behavior*, 39(5): 395–408.

Williams, A. M., Ward, P., Bell-Walker, J., & Ford, P. R. (2012) 'Perceptual-cognitive expertise, practice history profiles and recall performance in soccer', *British Journal of Psychology*, 103: 393–411.

Wright, M. J., Bishop, D., Jackson, R. C., & Abernethy, B. (2010) 'Functional MRI reveals expert-novice differences during sport-related anticipation', *NeuroReport*, 21: 94–8.

INDEX

Page numbers in *italic* indicate tables and figures.

ABC Research Group 66
Abernethy, B. 3, 10, 12, 14, 68–9, *68*, 71, 121, 147, 168, 170, 172, 310, 432, 433, 441, 442
achieved identity, defined 308
achievement motivation 234–5
activation deactivation adjective checklist (AD ACL) 248
Adolphe, R. M. 29, 434
adult temperament questionnaire (ATQ) 238
"Advances in Exercise, Fitness, and Performance Genomics" (Pérusse) 295
adversarial growth 112
affect grid (AG) 248
affordances, defined 287; *see also* ecological dynamics perspective
aging *see* career length and aging
Allard, F. 3, 201
Allsop, J. 80
analogy learning, defined 420
Anderson, D. J. 420
Anderson, J. 98–9
Andrews, J. R. 88–9
Anido, R. 212
Ankersen, R. 284
Anshel, M. H. 323
anthropometric factors *see* physiological and anthropometric factors, measurement of
anticipation and pattern perception 9–18; anticipatory expertise as task specific 10–11; anticipatory skill in interceptive actions 11; and current information sources 11–15; pattern perception 16–18; and prior (contextual) information sources 15–16; sport-specific, perceptual-cognitive differences 11–16; *see also* pattern recall and recognition, measurement of

anticipatory skill, measurement of 166–73; contextual information 172; point-light display 168; progressive temporal occlusion 167; and quality of representative design 168–71; spatial occlusion 167; temporal occlusion 166; timing of response 171–2; training anticipation 172–3; visual search 167–8
Anton, M. M. 388
anxiety, coping with 114, 247
anxiety rating scale (ARS) 247
anxiety thermometer 247
Applegate, R. A. 10
Applied Sciences (ASL) Mobile Eye (ME) 179, 180–1, *180*, 182, 184
Araújo, D. 66, 99, 216
Archimedes's principle 138
arrested development, defined 350
Arutyunyan, G. A. 89
ASL Results (software) 182
associative focus 39, 40–1
attentional control 38–46; associative vs. dissociative foci 39, 40–1, *42*; external vs. internal foci 39, 42–4, *42*; learning vs. performance and time course 44–6, *44*; overt vs. covert attention 39–40
attentional control scale (ACS) 238
Australian Football League (AFL) 121–8, 378–9, 386
automaticity in sport *see* movement automaticity

Baker, A. B. 388–9
Baker, J. 71, 89, 152, 161, 312, 318, 342, 376–7, 384–5, 404, 440, 443–4
Bale, J. 377

Index

Baltes, M. M. 390
Baltes, P. B. 390
Bannister, Roger 385
Bar-Eli, M. 66
Barros, R. 212
Bartlett, R. 86–7, 90, 212
Bauer, H. U. 89
Bawden, M. 228, 229
Beane, Billy 386–7
Beckenbauer, Franz 364
Beck's depression inventory (BDI) 237
Behan, M. 31
behavioral dynamics, defined 132
behavioral inhibition/activation (BIS/BAS scales) 237
behavioral regulation in sport questionnaire (BRSQ) 234
Beilock, S. L. 41, 77, 78, 79–80, 79
Benguigui, N. 51, 288
Bereitschaftspotential (BP) 24
Bernstein, N. 132–3, 139
Berry, J. 121, 311
Bertsch, C. 312
Bicknell, K. 223–4
Bideau, B. 194
big-fish-little-pond effect (BFLPE) 376–9
Birch, J. S. 376
birthplace effects 375–9; big-fish-little-pond effect (BFLPE) 376–9; city size and trends by sport 377
Bland-Altman plots 160
Blazo, J. 335
Blondin, J. P. 246
Bloom, B. S. 3, 330
Bloom, G. A. 410
Blundell, N. 10
Bohnert, A. 308
Book, W. F. 2
Bopp, T. 386
Bortz, W. M. 387, 389
Bourbousson, J. 212
Bower, R. 87
Bradman, Donald 10
Bradshaw, E. J. 88–9
Bradshaw, Terry 284
Bray, M. S. 295
Brewer, N. 204–5
Broich, H. 212
Brown, J. 43
Bruce, L. 229–30
Brunel mood scale (BRUMS) 236
Bruner, M. 312
Brunswik, E. 66, 188
Bryan, W. L. 2
Burden, A. M. 86–7
Burke, M. 378
Busch, C. 407–8
Busemeyer, J. R. 66

Busseri, M. A. 308, 309
Button, C. 60, 89, 212, 287

calibration, defined 54
Capio, C. 312
career length and aging 383–91; and expertise retention 384–5; and expert performance in social context 385–7; managing decline of performance 387–90, 389; theories on stability of performance with advancing age 390–1
Carlson, R. C. 376
Carlton, L. G. 171
Carr, T. H. 77, 78
Carver, C. S. 246
Castagna, C. 125
Casteneda, B. 43–4, 77
Causer, J. 23–4, 29, 32, 434
CAVE (Computer Assisted Virtual Environment) systems 190
centroid, defined 211–12
Chapman, C. 433
Chappell, Greg 288
Charness, N. 389
Chase, W. A. 3, 200, 352
Cheetham, P. J. 87, 90
choking, defined 113
Chollet, D. 90
Chow, Y. J. 312
Chu, Y. 88–9
Cicero 176
Clark, S. E. 408–9
Cleary, T. J. 152
Clemente, F. 212, 213–14
coaches and coaching 394–402; effective feedback for 266–7; and emerging athletes 396–8; future research 401, 443; and high-performance athletes 399–400; individual vs. team sport 401; and performance athletes 398–9; and talent development 324; and young children 395–6; see also evidence-based practice and learning strategies
Coakley, J. 338
Cobley, S. 378
cognitive emotion regulation questionnaire (CER-Q) 250
cognitive failures questionnaire (CFQ) 238
Cognitive Issues in Motor Expertise (Starkes and Allard) 3
cognitive psychology, emergence of 3
Coleman, S. 89
collective efficacy inventory (CEI) 252
collective efficacy questionnaire for sports (CEQS) 252
Collins, M. 352
competitive orientation inventory (COI) 235
competitive state anxiety inventory-2 (CSAI-2/2R) 247

Concept of Mind, The (Ryle) 97–8
concurrent validity, defined 158–9, 163
confirmatory factor analysis (CFA) 232–3
constraints-led perspective *see* ecological dynamics
perspective; evidence-based practice and
learning strategies
construct validity, defined 233
content validity, defined 262–3
contextual interference (CI) effect 416
controlled processing mode 74, 76
convergent validity, defined 159, 163, 232–3
COPE inventory 246
coping function questionnaire (CFQ) 246
coping skills *see* psychological determinants of
expertise
coping strategies in sport competition inventory
(CICS) 246
coping styles and strategies 110–15
Corbetta, M. 23, 31
Corcos, D. M. 89
Cornus, S. 52
Correia, V. 191
Côté, J. 71, 162, 310, 311, 330, 331, 333, 339, 395,
396–7, 398, 399, 404, 412
Couceiro, M. S. 212, 213–14
covert attention 39–40
Cox, B. J. 236
criterion validity, defined 263
Crocker, P.R.E. 246
Croser, M. J. 395
Crossman, E.R.F.W. 2
CryEngine (game engine) 193
Csikszentmihalyi, M. 336
Cumming, J. 408–9, 410
Cunha, S. 212
Curtis, J. E. 376

Darwin, Charles 1, 152
Davids, K. 52–3, 60, 287, 289
Deakin, J. 69
decision-making, defined 64
decision-making, under time constraints 64–71;
content of decision-making 64–5; empirical
evidence 67; empirical findings to specific
processes 67; and expert perception 67–9, *68*;
and team sport referees 69–71, *70*; theories 65–6
declarative knowledge, defined 97–8, 99
degeneracy *see* ecological dynamics perspective
deliberate coaching 369–70
deliberate environment 358
deliberate motivation 370
deliberate play, defined 106–7
deliberate practice concept 3, 108–11
deliberate practice in sport 347–59; and deliberate
environment 358; and enjoyment tenet 354;
improvement of performance 356–7, *357*; other
types of practice 353, *354*; quality of 358; and

sampling years 355–6; studies with athletes 350–1;
10,000-hour rule, critique of 351–3; theory and
data 347–50, *348*
Delorme, N. 375
Dennett, D. C. 221
Devaney, M. C. 57
Developing Sport Expertise (Farrow, Baker and
MacMahon) 443–4
Developing Talent in Young People (Bloom) 3
developmental history of athletes questionnaire
(DHAQ) 162
developmental model of sport participation
(DMSP) 395, 396–7; *see also* family and peers,
influences of; youth sport, developmental
experiences
Dicks, M. 60, 172
Didierjean, A. 18, 203, 204
differential emotions scale (DES-IV) 247
difficulties in emotion regulation scale (DERQ) 250
Diniz, A. 216
direct-to-consumer (DTC) genetic tests 301–3
discriminant validity, defined 232–3
dispositional characteristics *see* psychological
determinants of expertise
dissociative focus 39, 40–1, *42*
Donato, A. J. 388
Doorn, H. van 50, 170
Douglas, Desmond 283
dual pathway theory of vision 170
Duarte, R. 214–15, 217
Dufek, J. S. 43
Duffy, L. 352
Dufour-Lapointe sisters 329, 331, 339, 342
Dujardin, F. H. 90
Durand-Bush, N. 330
Dutt-Mazumder, A. 212
dynamical systems theory 130–3

Eccles, D. 221–223, 226, 227, 331
ecological approach 99–100
ecological dynamics perspective 130–42; capturing
expertise in field settings 287–8; dynamical
systems theory 130–3; ecological psychology
130; on expert performance and acquisition of
expertise 130–3; exploiting system metastability
139–41, *140*; harnessing degeneracy in
neurobiological systems 138–9; perceptual
attunement to affordances 135–8, 210; on skill
acquisition 133–5, *134*
ecological psychology 130
education of attention 54
efficacy *see* psychological determinants of expertise
effortful control scale (ECS) 238
Egret, C. I. 90
Eklund, R. C. 246
Elliott, D. 184
emotional control questionnaire (ECQ) 238

Index

emotion regulation interview (ERI) 250
emotion regulation profile-revised (ERP-R) 250
emotion regulation questionnaire (ERQ) 250
emotions *see headings at* psychological
Erickson, K. 310, 406
Ericsson, A. 3, 67, 108, 110, 222, 307, 323, 347–9, 350–2, 354–5, 389–90
ESPN, statistics on youth sports 305
event-related potentials (ERP) 24
evidence-based practice and learning strategies 414–25; athletes as decision makers 414–17; game as learning tool 415–17, *415*; hands-off approach to feedback 421–2; hands-off approach to instruction 419–21; key principles of *425*; mix of demonstrations and physical practice 418–19; motivational strategies 423–4; and optimal challenges 417–18
expert-induced amnesia 78
expertise, defined 287
Expert Performance in Sports (Starkes and Ericsson) 3
explicit monitoring theories 80
exploratory factor analysis (EFA) 232–3
extrinsic motivation 234
eye movement recordings 14
eye tracking methods 176–85; calculating QE 182–4; digital x/y coding and analysis 182; eye movements 177–8; fixations 177, 179; frame-by-frame coding and analysis 182; interpretation issues 185; methodological limitations 184; physiology of eye 176–7; purpose of research on 178; pursuit tracking 177, 179; quiet eye (QE) and expertise 177–8; saccades 177, 179; and technology 180–1, 184; visual search vs. vision-in-action 179–80; *see also* quiet eye (QE) and expertise
Eys, M. A. 312
Eysenck, M. 31
Eysenck personality inventory (EPI) 235

Fairbrother, J. T. 388
Fajen, B. R. 56–7
Faloon, S. 3
family and peers, influences of 329–43; emotional climate created by parents 336; family environment 333; family informational support 335–6; family tangible support 332, 334–5; future research 340–3; investment and maintenance years 338–40; parental support through athletes' adversity 338–9; peer relations dynamics 337; personal and social development 337–8; sampling years 331–3; siblings, role of 331, 333, 339; specializing years 333–8; sport friendships 332, 333–4; teammate and peer relations 331–2, 339–40
Farrow, D. 10, 16, 169, 170, 172, 229–30, 432, 433, 443–4
Fath, F. 89

feeling scale (FS) 248
felt arousal scale (FAS) 248
field settings, capturing expertise in 282–91; collaborative approach to testing design 289–91; ecological dynamics approach 287–8; non-representative testing, challenges of 283–4; traditional approaches to measurement 284–7; whole event approach 288–9
FIFA (Fédération Internationale de Football Association) 70
Figueiredo, A. 212
Fisher, R. A. 1
Fitts, P. 75, 99
five factor model (FFM) of personality 235
fixations, defined 177
Fleisig, G. 88–9
Fonseca, S. 216
Ford, P. R. 160, 309, 323
Förster, J. 370
foundations, talent, elite, and mastery model (FTEM) 395, 398–9
four-dimension mood scale (4DMS) 236
Frank, T. D. 214
Fraser-Thomas, J. L. 330
Fredricks, J. 308
Frehlich, S. G. 178
Friedman, R. S. 370
Frost multidimensional perfectionism scale (FMPS) 235–6
Fry, A. C. 125
functions of observational learning questionnaire (FOLQ) 408–9, 410
Fusco, C. 385

Gabbett, T. J. 124, 127
Galton, F. 1, 390
Gandelman, N. 385–6
Gaudreau, P. 246
gaze behaviors *see* eye tracking methods; quiet eye (QE) and expertise
Gaze Tracker (software) 182
generalized motor ability concept 2
Genetic Studies of Genius (Terman) 1
genome-wide association studies (GWASs) 295–303; common disease-common variant hypothesis (CDCV hypothesis), 297, *298*; feasibility of identifying genetic variants by risk allele frequency 298–9, *299*; four models with SNP effects *298*; practical implications of research 301–3; single nucleotide polymorphisms (SNPs), defined 295; statistical power for GWAS 299, *300*; study cohorts *296*
German Soccer Foundation (DFB) 367
Giacobbi, P. R., Jr. 334
Gibson, J. J. 51, 54, 99–100, 131, 135, 188, 189, 287–8
Gigerenzer, G. 66

Index

Gilbert, W. 397, 404, 406
Gilgun, J. 225–6
Gimelstob, Justin 15
Gladwell, Malcolm 351–2
Glencross, D. J. 16
Glize, D. 52
global motivation scale (GMS) 234
Goldin, S. E. 200
Goodard, J. 385
Gorman, A. D. 18, 169, 204, 205, 290, 443
Gould, D. 332, 336
Graham, T. R. 246
Gray, R. 41, 43–4, 77, 79–80, *79*
Greco, P. 368
Green, C. B. 342
Greenwood, D. 289
Gréhaigne, J. F. 215
Gretzy, Wayne 16
grit, defined 110
Groot, A. D., de 3, 199, 200, 203
Groothuis, P. A. 386
group tactical behaviors 209–18; communication
  networks 216–17, *217*; division of labor 215–16;
  team center 211–12, *211*; team dispersion 212–14,
  213–14; team synchrony 214–15; theories of
  team sport expertise 209–10
Grove, R. J. 246
Guadagnoli, M. A. 417
Guilford, J. P. 364, 365–6
Gulbin, J. P. 395, 399
Gurfinkel, V. S. 89

Hackfort, D. 311
Hackl, Georg 151
Hagemann, N. 43, 432
Hall, C. 408–9
Hambrick, D. Z. 150–1
Hamilton rating scale for depression (HRSD) 237
Hancock, D. J. 375, 410–11
harmonious passion 108
Harris, A. 332
Harter, N. 2
Harvey, W. J. 410
Hasegawa, J. I. 216
Hawk Eye ball-tracking system 70
Hay, J. 339
Headrick, J. 442
Healy, A. F. 44–5
Heard, P. N. 246
Helmholtz, H. von 176
Helsen, W. F. 10, 184, 340
heritability statistic 1
Hill, J. R. 386
Hinrichs, R. N. 87
historical foundations of sports expertise 1–4;
  emergence of "expertise" as field of study 3–4;
  search for global motor ability 2–3

Hoang, H. 386
Hodges, N. J. 353
Hof, P. van 55–6
Hoffman, B. J. 283–4
Holmes, P. S. 434
Holt, N. L. 335, 338–9
Höner, O. 374–5
Hopwood, M. J. 160, 161, 162–3, 331, 333
Horn, R. R. 434
Horn, T. S. 332
Horton, S. 318, 404
Hughes, P. 10
"Human Gene Map for Performance and Health-
  Related Fitness Phenotypes, The" (Bray) 295
Human Genome Project 2
Hume, P. A. 88–9
Hurrion, P. D. 87
Hüttermann, S. 370

immersive, interactive virtual reality (i2VR)
  see perception and action coupling
implicit learning theories 76
individual affect-related performance zone models
  (IAPZ) 248
individual zones of optimal functioning
  (IZOF) 248
information-movement coupling 50–61;
  current research findings 54–9; ecological
  approach 51–4; future research 61; infants,
  development of catching in 55–6; information
  and movement control 51–3, *53*; learning
  and education of attention and calibration
  53–4; learning to avoid head-on collisions
  56–7; practical implications of research 59–60;
  preparing for action 60; required velocity
  model 57–9, *58*
injuries, coping with 113
Inkster, B. 87
internal consistency 158
International Council for Coaching Excellence
  (ICCE) 394, 395
International Tennis Federation 288
intrinsic motivation 107, 234
Irwin, G. 408–9
i2VR *see* perception and action coupling

Jack, R. 340
Jackson, R. C. 15
Jacobs, D. M. 57–9, 60
Jaitner, T. 89
James, W. 1, 176
Jiobu, R. M. 386
Johansson, G. 14
Johnson, J. 66
Jonker, L. 322–3
Jordan, Michael 11, 64
judgments, defined 64

Kamp, J. van der 50, 55, 170, 272, 312
kappa statistics 160
Kay, T. 334–5, 341–2
Kennedy, G. 212
Keogh, J. 123
Keogh, J.W.L. 88–9
Khan, L. M. 386
Kinect (Microsoft) 192
Kirk, D. 334, 337
Knievel, G. 364
knowledge, expert vs. novice 95–103; approaches to knowledge 100–2; future research 102–3; and sport expertise 95–7; types of knowledge 97–100
knowledge, measurement of 221–30; Bicknell's staircase case study 223–4; data coding 227–9; Eccles's verbal reports 221–3, 226, 227; qualitative methods 224–7; triangulating methods 229–30
Korgaokar, A. 212
Kozma, A. 387–8
Kraemer, W. J. 125
Krampe, R. T. 307, 347, 389–90
Krustrup, P. 125
Kuiken, D. 228
Kuramoto order parameter 214

Lamb, S. R. 90
Land, W. M. 78
Lauer, L. 338
Laurent, M. 52
learning strategies see evidence-based practice and learning strategies
Leavitt, J. L. 77
Lee, D. N. 52, 285–6
Lee, T. D. 417
Lees, A. 84–5
Lemyre, F. 411
Le Runigo, C. 51, 288
Lewis, M. 386–7
Lidor, R. 311
Lohse, K. R. 44–5
long-term working memory theory (LTWM) 100
Louis, Martin St. 383
Löw, Jogi 363
Lozano, L. 43
Lubart, T. I 367
Lyons, B. D. 283–4

Maçãs, V. 210
MacDonald, D. J. 161, 376–7
MacLeod, M. 89
MacMahon, C. 77, 101, 443–4
MacPhail, A. 334, 337
Magill, R. A. 420
Major League Baseball (MLB) 385, 386
Mallett, C. J. 400

Maloney, M. A. 290
Mann, D. 229–30
Mann, D. L. 170–1
Mann, D.T.Y. 10, 24, 25, 169
Marcia, J. E. 308
Marino, Dan 284
Marmèche, E. 18, 203, 204
Marnewick, M. 88–9
Marques, P. 217
Martins, L. 212, 213–14
Mason, I. S. 407–8
Mason, P. H. 138
Masters, R. 99
Masters, R.S.W. 76–7, 238, 312
Masters sports see World Masters Athletics
Maulder, P. S. 88–9
Maxwell, J. 99, 238
Maynard, I. 228, 229
McCullagh, P. 408–9, 410
McCullik, B. A. 407–8
McGarry, T. 212
McLaughlin, Dan 441
MCOPE inventory 246
McPherson, S. 99, 100–1, 103, 222
McRobert, A. P. 101–2, 222
McTeigue, M. 90
Memmert, D. 162, 312, 364, 366, 367, 368, 370
Mendes, J.F.F. 212, 213–14
mental readiness form-Likert (MRF-L) 247
mental toughness 108–9, 248
mental toughness questionnaire (MTQ) 251
Messi, Lionel 363
Mester, J. 212
metastability see ecological dynamics perspective
Michaels, C. F. 57–9, 60, 61
Michel, J. W. 283–4
Miles, H. C. 193
Milho, J. 216
Millar, S. K. 289
Mirskii, M. L. 89
modified analytic induction (MAI) 225–6
monotonic benefits assumption 348–9, 348; see also deliberate practice in sport
Montagne, G. 52, 285–6
Moore, L. J. 24
Morales, J.C.P. 368
Moran, A. 97, 98
Morgan, T. K. 334
Morley, E. J. 395
Morris, Tom 383
motivational factors see psychological determinants of expertise; specific types of motivation
motor educability 2
Mottram, R. E. 87, 90
Moura, F. 212
movement automaticity 74–82; achievement of automaticity 75–6; automaticity in sport 74–5;

and encapsulated expert performance concept 76, 78–80, 79; and expert-induced amnesia 78; impact of competitive pressure 80; research studies 76–80; and secondary tasks 77–8

Müller, S. 12, 14

multi-articular sport actions 84–91; and biochemical characteristics 84–90; inter- and intra-individual movement variability 88–9, 88; range of motion and utilization of stored elastic energy 89–90; sequencing and timing of body segment motions 85–8, 86–7

multidimensional perfectionism scale-2 (Sport-MPS-2) 236

multiple affect adjective checklist (MAACL) 236

Murphy, A. 87

muscle memory 75

naïveté, defined 148

National Basketball Association (NBA) 150, 386

National Football League (NFL) 283–4, 386

National Hockey League (NHL) 383

Neal, R. J. 87

Neumann, D. L. 43

neurobiological degeneracy *see* ecological dynamics perspective

Newell, K. M. 89, 139, 317

Newton's third law 138

Nibbeling, N. 31

Nideffer, R. M. 238

Noels, K. A. 228

Noldus Observer (software) 182

Nopp, S. 364

North, J. S. 206

Nortje, J. 88–9

novice, defined 148

Nowitzki, Dirk 146

observational method 404–12; by coaches 404–10; and expert development 405–11; by officials 404–5, 406, 408–11

obsessive passion 108

occlusion goggles 12, 13, 169

Oculus Rift HMDs 190

Oeppen, J. 383, 387

officials *see* referees

Omni treadmill (Virtuix) 192

optoelectronic methods *see* perception and action coupling

Origin of Species (Darwin) 1

Orliczek, J. 370

Orth, D. *132*

Ottawa mental skills assessment tool-3* (OMSAT-3*) 251

Oudejans, R.R.D. 170, 442

Outliers (Gladwell) 351–2, 414

overt attention 39–40

Panchuck, D. 29

passion and sports 108

Patrick, H. 337

pattern recall and recognition, measurement of 198–206; anticipatory measures 203–4; and brain imaging 206; evolution of measures 199–201; future research 205–6; innovative analysis methods 202–3; measurement of attentional focus 204–5; measurement of transfer 205; representative test stimuli and advanced scoring methods 201–2; in situ testing 205–6; in sports 201–5; *see also* anticipation and pattern perception

Paull, G. 16

Pearson correlations 159–60, 162

peer influences *see* family and peers, influences of

per cent agreement (PA) statistics 160–1

perception and action coupling 188–96; immersive, interactive virtual reality (i2VR) 189, 192, 193; interacting with virtual environments 190–1; performance analysis in VR context 193; research studies 194–6, *195*; stereoscopic head-mounted display (HMD) 190–2, *191*, *195*; study of 188–9; technological advances 193, *194*; tracking movement 191–2, *191*; virtual environment displays 190

perception of success questionnaire (POSQ) 235

perceptual-cognitive skill, training interventions for 430–6; pattern recall and recognition, training of 435; quiet eye, training of 433–5; training anticipation and decision-making 431–3

perfectionism 235–6, 246

performance-contingent switching, defined 417

Perry, N. 321

Pérusse, L. 295

Petit, J. 188

Pettigrew, C. 43

physical qualities of experts 121–8; differences between higher- and lesser-skilled players 122; discriminant analysis 122–3; interaction with skill under fatigue 127–8, *127*; intertwined with skill 128; and match physical performance in team sports 125–7; and playing performance 124–5; and skill 123–4

physiological and anthropometric factors, measurement of 259–67; anthropometric testing 259–60, 263–4; athlete monitoring 261; data analysis and interpretation 263–4; descriptive analysis 264; feedback for coaches and athletes 266–7; importance of 259–60; percentile rankings 265; quality assurance and protocol standardization 261–2; rankings of test scores 265; reference range/interval 265; reference value 264; training camps 266; validity, reliability, and experimental designs 262–3

Pinder, R. 442

Pirozzolo, F. 90

Pluijms, J. P. 290
point-light display technique 14, 168
Porter, A. 323
positive and negative affect schedule (PANAS/PANAS-X) 237, 247–8
Posner, M. I. 99
power law of practice, defined 355–6
practice, types of *354*; *see also* deliberate practice in sport; evidence-based practice and learning strategies
preserved differentiation, defined 390
procedural knowledge, defined 97–9
profile of mood states questionnaire (POMS) 236, 248, 249
proximal-to-distal sequencing of segmental motion *86*
psychological characteristics, of expert performers 106–15; ability to cope with change/adversity 111–13; adversarial growth 112; commitment to performance 108–9; coping styles and strategies 112; coping with competitive pressure 113–15; coping with injuries 113; deliberate practice concept 108–10; hardiness 112–13; intrinsic motivation 107; making sacrifices for performance 110; and passion 106–8; performance-related goals 109–10; self-regulation of learning 110–11
psychological characteristics and self-regulation 317–26; coaches and trainers, role of 324; development of effort and sport expertise 323; development of reflection and sport expertise 321–23; development of self-regulatory skills 320–21, *322*; future research 325–6; importance of 318–19; myth of sport expertise 317; practical implications of research 323–5; self-regulation and talent development 319–20, *320*; talent development model 317–18, *318*
psychological determinants of expertise 232–53; attentional style and reinvestment 237–9; dispositional anxiety 237; emotion regulation 249–50; measurement of coping skills 245–6; measurement of discrete emotional states 246–8; measurement of dispositional profiles and trait factors 235–9; measurement of motivational factors 233–5; measurement of regulation of affective experiences 248–9; mood 236; mood regulation 249–50; personality 235–6; psychological skills 250–1; selecting measurement tools 232–3; self-confidence and self-efficacy 252
psychological skills inventory for sports-R5 (PSIS-R5) 251
pursuit tracking, defined 177
Put, K. 70

Quaine, F. 52
Qualisys (motion capture) 193

quiet eye (QE) and expertise 22–35; and attention 23; and competitive pressure 29–31, *30*; defined 23; future directions 35; interceptive tasks 28–9, *28*; kinematic correlates 23–4, *24*; neural correlates 24; research evidence 25; targeting tasks 25, *26–7*; and training of 31–2, *33–4*; training of 433–5; *see also* eye tracking methods
Quiet Eye Solutions (software) 182–4, *183*

Raab, M. 66
racial discrimination in sports 386–7
Rafaelli, M. 227
Rampinini, E. 125
Randall, E. 308
Ranganathan, R. 171
rapport, defined 227
Rasher, D. 386
Raspaud, M. 375
Rathunde, K. 336
Raynor, A. 229–30
Redgrave, Steve 383
referees: decision-making of 69–71, *70*; observational method of 404–5, 406, 408–11
reflection *see* psychological characteristics and self-regulation
Reid, M. 16
reinvestment scales 238–9
relative age effects (RAEs): and elite sport 374; mechanisms of 374–5; and youth sport 373–4
Rendell, M. 169
Renshaw, I. 52–3, 289, 443
representative tasks 269–78; context, situational constraints and emotion 276–8; experimental control and representative conditions 272–5; generalizability and transfer 275–6; laboratory vs. in situ studies 269–70; representative learning design 270–1
required velocity model 57–9, *58*
Ribery, F. 363
Richardson, M. J. 214
Ricker, K. 184
Rickey, Branch 387
Ripoll, H. 188
Rivas, F. 50, 170
Road to Expertise, The (Ericsson) 3
Robben, Arjen 363–4
Robbins, M. 212
Robinson, Jackie 385, 387
Robinson, William 383
Roca, A. 18, 222
Rooney, J. F., Jr. 376
Rose, G. A. 87
Rose-Krasnor, L. 308, 309
Russell, D. G. 12
Ryle, Gilbert 97–8
Rynne, S. B. 400

Index

saccades, defined 177
Sagas, M. 386
Ste-Marie, D. M. 375, 405–11
St. Laurent, B. F. 90
Salmela, J. H. 330, 405
Salthouse, T. A. 389, 390
Sammer, Matthias 363
Sampaio, J. 210
sampling years *see* family and peers, influences of;
psychological characteristics and self-regulation;
youth sport, developmental experiences
Sanders, R. 89
Sá-Pinho, J. 217
Savelsbergh, G. J.P. 50, 55, 170, 172
Sawyer, D. T. 125
Scheier, M. F. 246
Schempp, P. G. 407–8
Schinke, R. J. 405–6
Schöllhorn, W. I. 89
Schorer, J. 89, 378, 389, 435
Schücker, L. 43
Seals, D. R. 388
Sebanz, N. 229
Seifriz, F. 212, 287
self-as-model procedure 407–8
self-assessment manikin (SAM) 248
self-control, defined 110
self-determination theory 107
self-regulating strategies of mood questionnaire (SRSMQ) 249
self-regulation *see* psychological characteristics and self-regulation
SensoMotoric Instruments (SMI) Eye Tracking Glasses (ETG) 179, *181*, 184
Sève, C. 212
Shan, G. 90
shared cognition, defined 209–10
Shaw, M. 386
Sherwood, D. E. 44–5
Shiffrar, M. 229
Shim, J. 169, 172
Shopenhauer, Arthur 22
siblings *see* family and peers, influences of
Siefert, L. 131, 138
Silva, P. 215
Simon, H. A. 3, 200, 222, 352
Simpson, D. 110
Singer, R. N. 32, 178
16 personality factor questionnaire (16PF) 235
Smeeton, N. J. 71
SMI BeGaze (software) *181*, 182
Smith, A. L. 334
Smith, J. 3
Soberlak, P. 162
Sony HMZ-T3W HMDs 196
spatial occlusion approach 12, 14, 167
Spearman's G 2

sport anxiety scale (SAS/SAS-2) 237
sport competition anxiety test (SCAT) 237
sport-confidence questionnaire (SSCQ) 252
sport expertise research, future of 439–44; and coach perspective 443; improved theory and design 439–41; multidisciplinary investigations 441–2; and stakeholders 443
sport motivation scale (SMS/SMS-6) 234
Starkes, J. 3, 10, 17, 67, 69, 77, 150, 184, 340, 353
state trait anxiety inventory (STAI) 247
stereoscopic head-mounted display (HMD) *see* perception and action coupling
Sternberg, R. J. 367
Stevenson, C. L. 331, 333, 340
Stoate, I. 42–3
Stones, M. J. 387–8
Strauss, B. 43
Syed, Matthew 283
system metastability *see* ecological dynamics perspective

tabula rasa (blank slate) 1
tactical creativity 363–71; and deliberate coaching 369–70; and deliberate motivation 370; and deliberate play 368; and deliberate practice 370; development of 366–70; and diversification 369; future research 370–1; and one-dimension games 368–9; in team and racket sports 363–4, *364*; testing of 365–6, *366*; theoretical background of 364–5, *365*
Taki, T. 216
Talent Code, The (Coyle) 414
talent development 324, 414; *see also* psychological characteristics and self-regulation; youth sport, developmental experiences
Tamminen, K. A. 338–9
Tanaka, H. 388
Tang, Y. Q. 388
task and ego orientation in sport questionnaire (TEOSQ) 234–5
Tau, defined 52
taxonomy of sport skill classification 145–54; age as confounder of skill acquisition 150; athlete development as stage-based process 150; categories *147*; early stages of skill development 148; future research 152–4, *153*; identifying expertise 145–6; non-expert, eliminating use of term 152; peak levels of skill development 149–50, *149*; proposed scheme for 147–50; purpose of 146–7; transitional stages of skill development 148–149; use of training hours to define skill levels 150–2, *151*
teams *see* group tactical behaviors
temporal occlusion approach 12, 14, 166
10,000-hour rule, critique of 351–3
Terman, Lewis 1
Tesch-Römer, C. 347

test of attentional and interpersonal style (TAIS) 238
test of performance strategies (TOPS/TOPS 2) 251
test-retest reliability 158, 163
Thomas, J. R. 99, 147
Thomas, K. T. 147
three-factor anxiety inventory (TFAI) 247
Tinning, R. 400
Todd, P. M. 66
Toering, T. T. 323
Torres, Dara 383
Toward a General Theory of Expertise (Ericsson and Smith) 3
Townsend, J. T. 66
trainers *see* coaches and coaching
training history data 156–63; future research 163; interpreting reliable and valid data 161; qualitative interviews 157; quantitative questionnaires 157–8; reliability and validity of 158–9; and retrospective recall 161–3; statistical analysis 159–60
Travassos, B. 216, 217
Triolet, C. 51, 288
Trudel, P. 397
Trussell, D. E. 333
Tucker, R. 352
Turnnidge, J. 312

Ullrich-French, S. 334
Unity 3D (game engine) 193
univariate intraclass correlation coefficient (ICC) 159–61
University of Wales Institute of Science and Technology mood adjective checklist (UWIST-MACL) 249
Unreal 4 (game engine) 193

Van Gaal, Louis 363–4
Vaupel, J. W. 383, 387
Vicente, K. J. 199
Vickers, J. N. 23, 29, 443
Vicon (motion capture) 193
video-based displays, defined 168–9
video capture *see* perception and action coupling
Vine, S. J. 32, 434
Vint, P. F. 87
virtual reality (VR) displays, defined 169; *see also* perception and action coupling
vision, dual pathway theory 170
visual information-processing model of skilled performance 68–9, *68*
Vogelbein, M. 364
Völker, K. 43
Voronoi diagrams 216
Votteler, A. 374–5

Walters, J. 10
Ward, P. 71, 101–2, 222, 430–1, 433, 435
Warren, W. H. 52, 53–4, 132, 136
Watsford, M. 87
Watson, J. 1–2
Watson, Tom 383
Weber, A. 88–9
Weber, J. 90
Weber, N. 204–5
Webster, C. 407–8
Weissensteiner, J. R. 395
Wentraub, J. K. 246
Westerhoff, P. 90
Whalen, S. 336
Whiting, H.T.A. 57, 133
Whitlock, Ed 384
Whitnauer, W. D. 385
Wierenga, S. A. 77, 78
Williams, A. M. 15, 45, 51, 71, 160, 178, 202, 203, 288, 432, 433, 434, 435
Williams, S. 80
Wilson, J. 385
Wilson, L. M. 410
Wilson, M. R. 29, 31, 32, 434
Withagen, R. 59, 61
Wohl, M.J.A. 228–9
Wolfenden, L. E. 335
Wood, G. 435
Wood, J. 10
Wooden, John 74
Woods, Tiger 385
Woolcock, G. 378
work and family orientation questionnaire (WOFQ) 235
World Masters Athletics 384, 387–8, 391
Wright, T. 407
Wrisberg, C. 110
Wulf, G. 42–3, 76

X-factor stretch 90

Young, B. 440
Young, B. W. 375, 390
Young, D. S. 52
Young, W. B. 122, 124, 125, 127–8
youth sport, developmental experiences 305–13; and deliberate play 310–13; developmental model of sport participation (DMSP) 306–9; diverse experiences 307–8; diversity before specialization 308–9; successful programs 309–10; *see also* psychological characteristics and self-regulation
Yue, Z. 212, 215–16

Zimmerman, B. J. 111, 152, 319